COLLEGE ACCESS & OPPORTUNITY GUIDE

2012 EDITION

Center *for* Student Opportunity

About Center for Student Opportunity

Center for Student Opportunity (CSO) is a 501(c)(3) nonprofit organization empowering underserved, first-generation college students to and through college by providing critical information, guidance, scholarships, and ongoing support. CSO's programs and resources connect a national network of colleges and universities with college-bound students and their supporters—parents, counselors, and mentors—to promote an understanding that the opportunity for college is within reach.

For more information or for permission to use material from this text or product, contact Center for Student Opportunity, P.O. Box 30370, Bethesda, MD 20824; or find us online at www.CSOpportunity.org.

For bulk sales to schools, organizations, colleges, and universities, please contact Center for Student Opportunity, info@csopportunity.org, (301) 363-4222

Editors: *Matt Rubinoff, Cara Martin*

Staff Contributors: *Emily Anderer, Kathryn Delaney, Alexandra Economou, Francine Gorres, Christopher Henderson, Geoffrey Henderson, Chelsea Jones, Yanique Rae, Sandra Ramos, Jenna Scafuri*

Cover Design: *Cinda Debbink*

Interior Page Design and Layout: *Cinda Debbink, Valerie Wilmot*

Special thanks to Nancy Creel, James Mayer, Bruce Poch, Lynda Ramirez-Blust, Doris Davis, Melanie Corrigan, Carolyn Stanek, Jennifer Kushlis, Joseph Tavares, Hallie Steube

Photo Credits
© Getty Images/Thinkstock *pages 1, 6, 7, 14, 21, 51, 55, 57, 62, 67, 68, 69, 77, 84, 85, 86, 87, 94, 97, 108, 109*
© JupiterImages *pages 2, 4, 5, 6, 7, 8, 9, 13, 14, 16, 21, 22, 23, 24, 30, 43, 91, 92, 103, 104, 105, 115, 116,*
© Shutterstock *pages 12, 17, 21, 26, 27, 28, 29, 31, 32, 33, 34, 47, 50, 52, 62, 66, 70, 72, 76, 80, 88, 90, 93, 95, 98, 102, 106, 107, 119, 120, 122, 124, 134, 136, 141, 142*
© IndexOpen *pages 8, 15*
© iStock *pages 47, 70, 72*

Printed in the United States of America

10 9 8 7 6 5 4 3 2 1

Contents

A Message from Center for Student Opportunity

Dear Student,

On behalf of Center for Student Opportunity, thank you for picking up this copy of the *College Access & Opportunity Guide.*

We developed the Guide to help students like you get to college and succeed. If you feel overwhelmed by the college process, don't worry! There are specific steps you need to take during the college-going process. With help from our friends at KnowHow2GO, the Guide will turn your college dreams into action-oriented goals and simplify the steps to college so you know what to do next.

It's your responsibility to find out which school is right for you. Asking the right questions and knowing what information to seek out is important. To help you get started, the Guide profiles 241 colleges and universities that are committed to helping students like you thrive in college.

Remember too that you are not alone on the college journey. In the Guide, you will read inspiring stories of students who have overcome many obstacles in their lives to become first in their family to go to college. They, along with others, share great advice on how you too can become a college student.

We wish you the best of luck on this journey to college and hope you find the *College Access & Opportunity Guide* to be valuable along the way.

The Center for Student Opportunity Team

For counselors, teachers and mentors

A free companion to the *College Access & Opportunity Guide*, our **Guide to the Guide** offers counselors, teachers and mentors a set of activities and worksheets designed to help you and the students you serve make the most of this important college guidebook.

Leading these fun and engaging activities with your students (and parents) will help set a positive climate for the college process and empower your students through it. And it's free!

Download the Guide to the Guide on our website at www.CSOpportunity.org

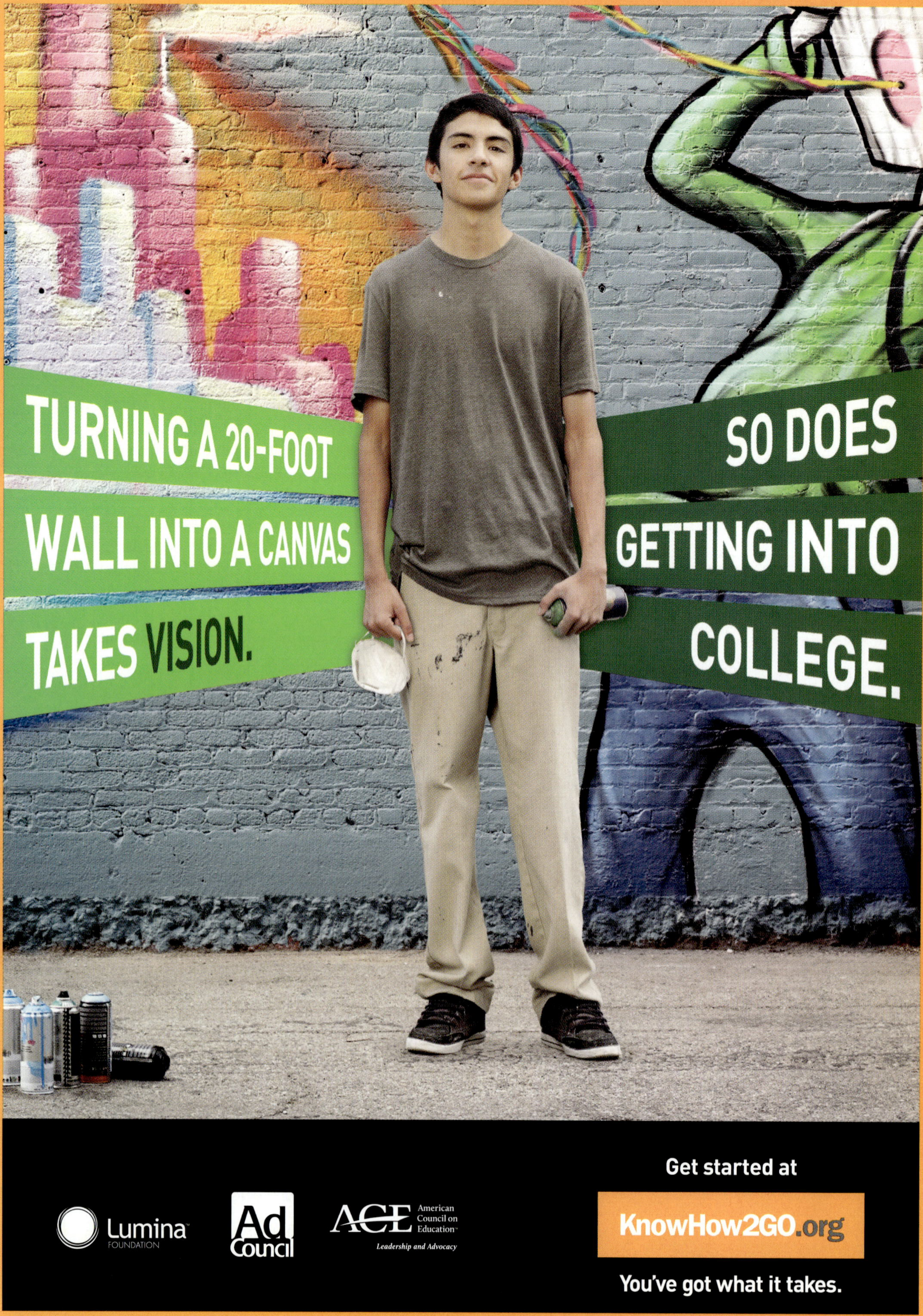
TURNING A 20-FOOT
WALL INTO A CANVAS
TAKES VISION.
SO DOES
GETTING INTO
COLLEGE.
Lumina
FOUNDATION
Ad Council
ACE American Council on Education
Leadership and Advocacy
Get started at
KnowHow2GO.org
You've got what it takes.

SPONSORED BY     IN PARTNERSHIP WITH 

The Most Costly Education Is the One Not Begun. College Doesn't Just Happen!

KnowHow2GO

You have big plans. Big dreams. You know college is where to start. But a dream is not enough. College doesn't just happen; you have to work to make it a reality. Most people know **why** to go to college. We're here to tell you **how**. There are specific steps you need to take, and remember, it's never too early—or too late—to start on the road to college.

College is the first step in pursuing a successful and fulfilling career. It's not only where you explore different career options, but also where you learn essential job skills. "But college is so far off," you may be thinking. "It's too early to start preparing now." Think again!

Planning for college takes time. There are lots of things you need to know and do. Now is exactly when you need to think about what you want to do after high school. The choices you make today will determine your life tomorrow.

THE 4 STEPS TO COLLEGE

1. Be a Pain. Let everyone know that you're going to college and need their help!

2. Push yourself. Working a little harder today will make for a smoother road to college.

3. Find the right fit. Find out what kind of school is the best match for you and your goals.

4. Put your hands on some cash. If you think you can't afford college—think again. There is lots of aid out there.

About KnowHow2GO

Young people in all socio-economic groups have college aspirations. In fact, eight out of 10 expect to attain a bachelor's degree or higher, according to the U.S. Department of Education. But despite their aspirations, low-income students and those who are the first in their families to pursue higher education are severely underrepresented on college campuses. Studies show these students often lack the guidance they need to prepare for postsecondary education.

In order to turn these students' college dreams into action-oriented goals, the **American Council on Education, Lumina Foundation for Education and the Ad Council** launched the KnowHow2GO campaign in January 2007. This multi-year, multimedia effort includes television, radio, outdoor public service advertisements (PSAs), an interactive website KnowHow2GO.org—and now collaboration with **Center for Student Opportunity's** *College Access & Opportunity Guide*—to encourage students to prepare for college using four simple steps.

1 BE A PAIN (in a good way)

Find an adult who can help you with the steps to college. Let everyone know you want to go to college. And don't stop until you find an adult who will help you.

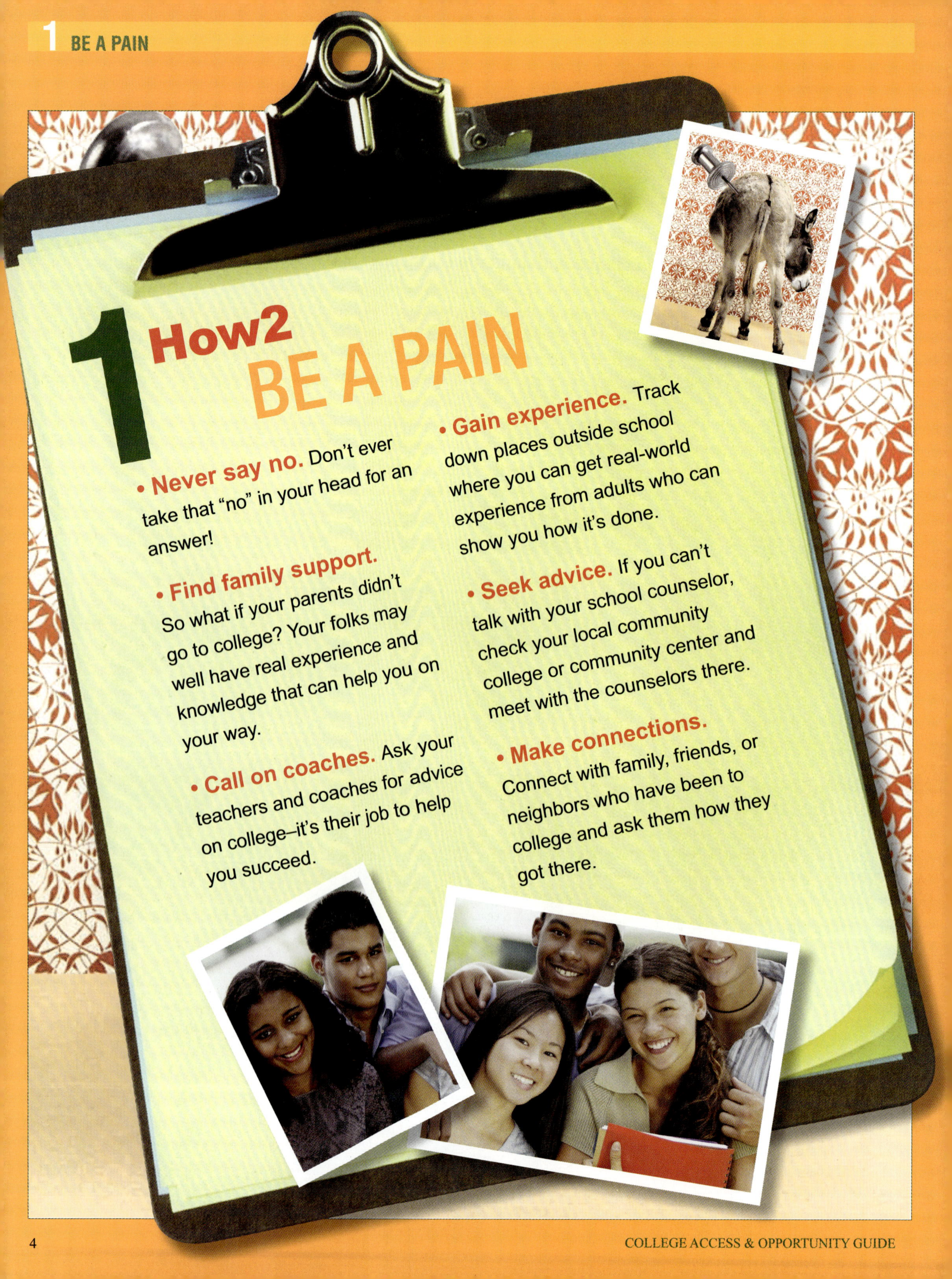

1 How2 BE A PAIN

- **Never say no.** Don't ever take that "no" in your head for an answer!
- **Find family support.** So what if your parents didn't go to college? Your folks may well have real experience and knowledge that can help you on your way.
- **Call on coaches.** Ask your teachers and coaches for advice on college–it's their job to help you succeed.
- **Gain experience.** Track down places outside school where you can get real-world experience from adults who can show you how it's done.
- **Seek advice.** If you can't talk with your school counselor, check your local community college or community center and meet with the counselors there.
- **Make connections.** Connect with family, friends, or neighbors who have been to college and ask them how they got there.

Why College

With everything you need to do to get ready for college, you may wonder if it's all worth it. Here are four quick (but very important) reasons why:

REASON # 1 Every bit of education you get after high school increases the chances you'll earn good pay. Most college graduates earn a lot more money during their working years than people who stop their education at high school.

REASON # 2 The more education you get, the more likely it is you will always have a job. According to one estimate, by the year 2028 there will be 19 million more jobs for educated workers than there are qualified people to fill them.

REASON # 3 Continuing education after high school is much more important for your generation than it was for your parents' generation. Today most good jobs require more than a high school diploma. Businesses want to hire people who know how to think and solve problems.

REASON # 4 Education beyond high school gives you a lot of other benefits, including meeting new people, taking part in new opportunities to explore your interests, and experiencing success.

Ninety percent of teens want to go to college, regardless of their income level.

TRUE FALSE

TRUE Unfortunately not all of these students have access to adult mentors who can guide them through the college preparation process.

Get the conversation started!

Planning for college isn't something you do by yourself—it's really a team effort. But it's up to you to put together your team. And that means talking to the adults in your life who can help—from your parents, guardian, or other family members to your teachers, coaches, guidance counselor, or religious leader.

YOUR PARENTS

The best way to communicate with parents, or any adult, is to keep talking to them, no matter what. Strong relationships really depend on keeping the lines of communication open. Here are some ways to approach your parents (or any adult) with a specific topic:

Plan what to say.

Think over what you want to say in advance, and write down the two or three most important points you want to make.

Be direct.

Let them know directly that there's something you'd like to discuss. Be sure you have their full attention and be direct in your language. Say, "There's something important I want to talk to you about" instead of "Hey, when you have a moment I'd like to talk."

Pick a good time to talk.

Try to approach them at a time when you know they'll be less busy and more able to focus on you. You may even want to ask if they could talk at a particular time so that you know you have their attention.

Write it down first.

Some people find it easier to put their ideas into a letter. Let the other person read it and then have your discussion.

Disagree without disrespect.

Parents are only human, and they can feel offended when their views are challenged. Using respectful language and behavior is important. Resist the temptation to use sarcasm, yell, or put down your parents and you'll have a much better chance of getting what you want.

OTHER ADULTS

No matter how good your relationship is with your parents or guardian, there will be times when you'll feel more comfortable confiding in other adults. Even if you'd rather talk to friends about certain things, an adult may have more experience, be able to contact the right person, or find the best resources to get help.

Ask for their word.

Most adults will keep your conversations confidential if you ask them to, unless they fear that your health or well-being may be in danger.

Other adults.

Other adults who may be able to help include teachers, your school guidance counselor, or other family members such as an aunt, uncle, or older sibling. Parents of a close friend may also be able to help.

Spiritual leaders.

If you're involved in a church group or belong to a synagogue or mosque, your spiritual or youth group leader may also be a good source of advice.

Extracurricular leaders.

If you're involved in an extracurricular activity, such as sports or drama, you may feel close enough to your coach or advisor to ask him or her about more personal stuff.

ARE YOU READY FOR COLLEGE Quiz

Parents are always the best people to talk to about preparing for college.

TRUE FALSE

FALSE If your parents didn't go to college, chances are there's an adult in your life who did – and would be happy to help you prepare for college.

YOUR SCHOOL COUNSELOR

Your school counselor, or guidance counselor, may be one of your best resources as you plan for college. She or he has information about admission tests, college preparation, and your education and career options. Here are some basic questions to help get you started:

Questions to ask your school counselor

- Do you have any information to help me start exploring my interests and related careers?
- What are the required and recommended courses—for graduation and for college prep?
- How should I plan my schedule so I'll complete these courses?
- Do you have any after-school or evening sessions available for college planning?
- Do you have college handbooks or other guides that I can browse or borrow?
- What activities can I do at home and over the summer to get ready for college?
- What kinds of grades do different colleges require?
- Where do other kids from this school attend college?
- What are the requirements or standards for the honor society?
- How does our school compare to others, in terms of test scores and reputation?
- Which elective courses do you recommend?
- Which AP courses are available?
- When is the PSAT/NMSQT going to be given here?
- Is this school a testing center for standardized tests, or will I need to go somewhere nearby?
- Are there any college fairs at this school or nearby?
- Can you put me in touch with recent graduates who are going to the colleges on my list?
- If my colleges need a recommendation from you, how can I help you know me better so it can be more personal?
- Are there any special scholarships or awards I should know about now so I can work toward them?
- Can I see my transcript as it stands now to see if everything is as I think it should be?
- Do you have any forms I need to apply for financial aid?

> If you find a subject hard, talk to your teacher right away about extra tutoring. If you find it boring, talk to your teacher about ways to see the subject in a different light.

YOUR TEACHERS

OK, so it may be hard to think of your teachers as real people. But they eat pizza, watch movies, and enjoy sports on the weekends just like you. And they know about more than just their subject matter. Given the chance they can offer you the kind of advice and support that might change your life forever. Here's how to build a connection:

Show some interest.

Obviously, your teachers are really interested in their subjects. Showing the teacher that you care—even if you're not a math whiz or fluent in French—sends the message that you are a dedicated student.

Schedule a conference.

Schedule a private conference during a teacher's free period to get extra help, ask questions, inquire about a career in the subject, or talk about your progress in class. You may be surprised to learn that your teacher is a bit more relaxed one-on-one than when lecturing in front of the whole class.

Be yourself.

Teachers can sense when your only motivation for trying to be a "favorite student" is to get special treatment or a good grade. Just be yourself and forget about trying to show off.

Deal with study problems.

If you find a subject hard, talk to your teacher right away about extra tutoring. If you find it boring, talk to your teacher about ways to see the subject in a different light. For example, you may hate math, but learning how to calculate averages and percentages can help you in everything from sports to leaving a tip.

Show some respect.

Just as teachers need to be fair and treat everyone equally, students have responsibilities too. You don't have to like your teacher or agree with what he or she says, but it is necessary to be polite.

2 PUSH YOURSELF

Colleges require you to take certain classes in high school. Find out which classes and sign up!

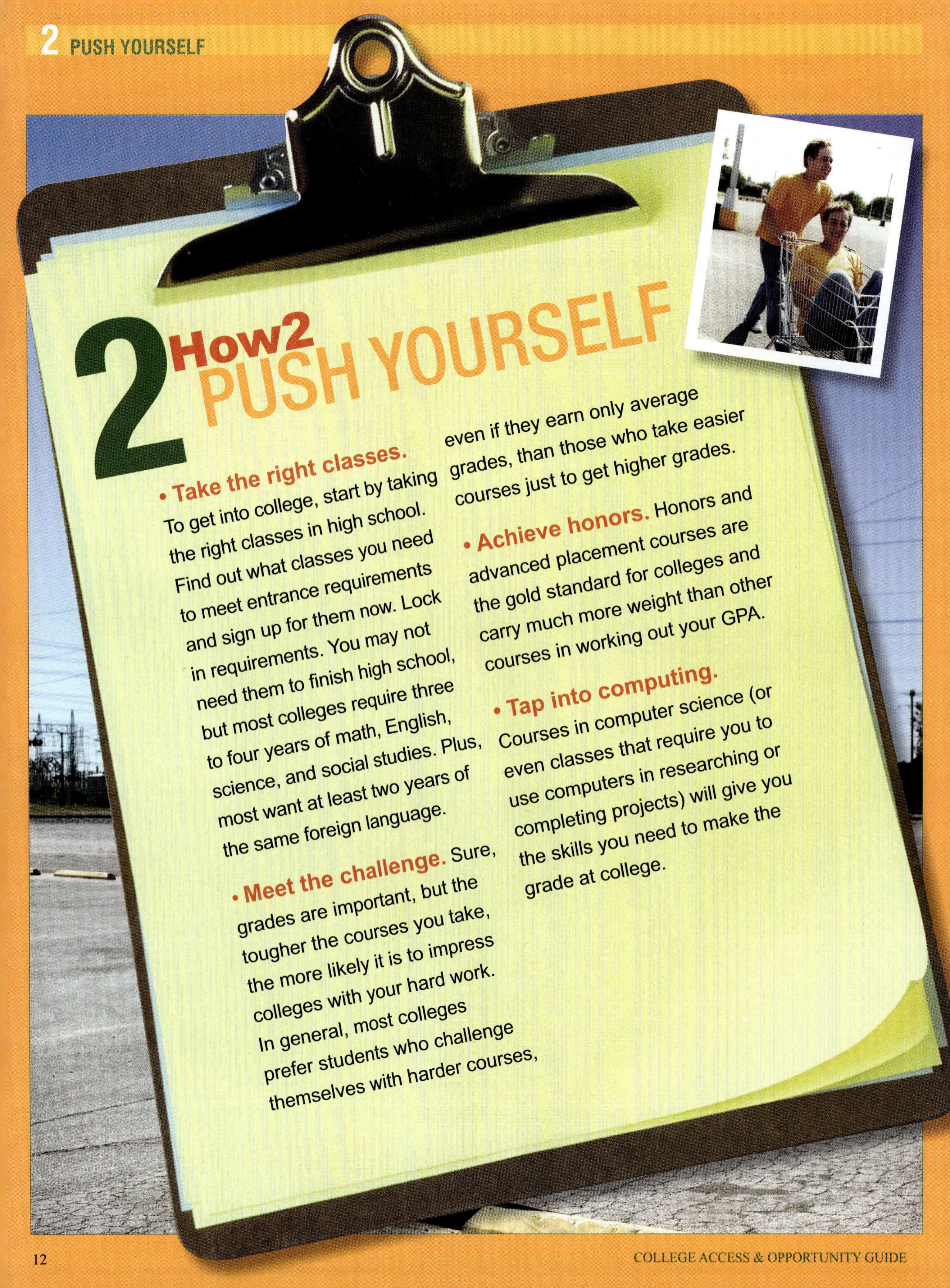

2 How2 PUSH YOURSELF

• **Take the right classes.** To get into college, start by taking the right classes in high school. Find out what classes you need to meet entrance requirements and sign up for them now. Lock in requirements. You may not need them to finish high school, but most colleges require three to four years of math, English, science, and social studies. Plus, most want at least two years of the same foreign language.

• **Meet the challenge.** Sure, grades are important, but the tougher the courses you take, the more likely it is to impress colleges with your hard work. In general, most colleges prefer students who challenge themselves with harder courses, even if they earn only average grades, than those who take easier courses just to get higher grades.

• **Achieve honors.** Honors and advanced placement courses are the gold standard for colleges and carry much more weight than other courses in working out your GPA.

• **Tap into computing.** Courses in computer science (or even classes that require you to use computers in researching or completing projects) will give you the skills you need to make the grade at college.

There's an old Chinese saying that goes, "The journey of a thousand miles begins with a single step." But no matter how unsure you feel taking that first step, every single one after that will be a little easier. Here's some helpful tips to get you started.

PLAN OUT YOUR CLASSES

Plan out a challenging program of classes.

- Colleges care about which courses you're taking in high school. Remember, you will have more options if you start planning now for college and do your best to earn good grades.
- The courses you take in high school show colleges what kind of goals you set for yourself. Are you signing up for advanced classes, honors sections, or accelerated sequences? Are you choosing electives that really stretch your mind and help you develop new abilities? Or are you doing just enough to get by?
- Colleges will be more impressed by respectable grades in challenging courses than by outstanding grades in easy ones.
- Do your high school course selections match what most colleges expect you to know? For example, many colleges require two to four years of foreign language study.
- Your schedule should consist of at least 4 college preparatory classes per year.

FILE YOUR IMPORTANT DOCUMENTS

Create a file of important documents and notes.

- Copies of report cards.
- Lists of awards and honors.
- Lists of school and community activities in which you are involved, including both paid and volunteer work, and descriptions of what you do.

FIND OUT ABOUT WHICH COLLEGES TO ATTEND

Start thinking about the colleges you want to attend.

- Create list of colleges and universities in which you are interested.
- Discuss the list with your school counselor and narrow it down to your top few.
- Start visiting the campuses.

TAKE HONOR-LEVEL CLASSES

Find out about honors-level courses at your school.

- Ask if AP or other honors courses are available.
- See if you are eligible for the honors classes you want to take.

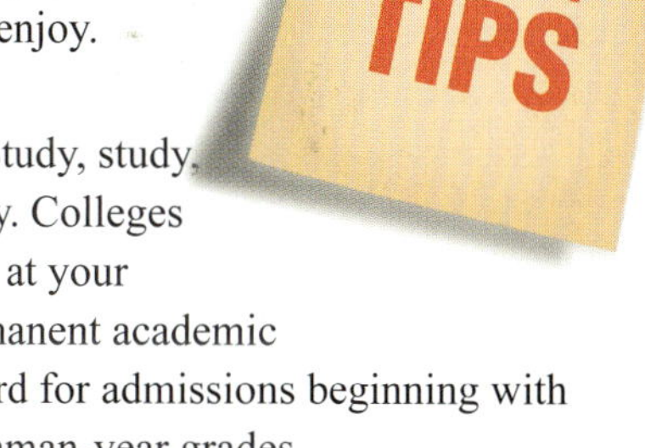

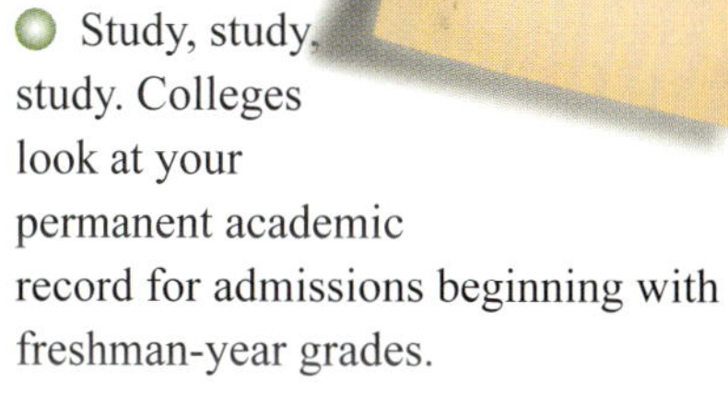

- Stay active in clubs, activities, and sports that you enjoy.
- Study, study, study. Colleges look at your permanent academic record for admissions beginning with freshman-year grades.
- Think about an after school or summer job to start saving for college.

STUDY SMARTER

Think class work and homework are a waste of your time? Well, listen up—studies show that the more math courses you take in high school, the more likely you are to graduate from college. And that's just for starters. Learning how to study smarter can give you a real edge by the time you get to college. And it's not hard if you make these habits a part of your school life:

Focus

Find a quiet, organized space—maybe a study table at the library. And turn off anything that could possibly distract you.

Plan ahead

If you have a big test or paper coming up, set aside plenty of time so that you aren't cramming. Manage your time and study your most important assignments first.

Pay attention

If you are actively contributing and listening in class, your studying will be easier and more interesting.

Check your work

Studying can tire you out—but after you've completed an assignment take a few minutes to look it over for any mistakes. You never want to turn in anything but your best effort.

Don't go it alone

Find a classmate, mentor, coach, tutor, or study buddy to help keep you going.

STAY IN SCHOOL

Over a lifetime, a high school dropout working full-time will earn $300,000 less than a high school graduate, and more than $1 million less than a college graduate. It's easy to see that if you want to do well, graduating is what you've got to do first. Here are a few more good reasons why you should stay in school:

REASON # 1 High school dropouts are four times more likely than college graduates to be unemployed.

REASON # 2 Graduating from high school will most likely determine how well you live for the rest of your life.

REASON # 3 On average, high school graduates earn $175 more per week than high school dropouts. College graduates earn $368 more per week than high school graduates.

THE BIG LESSON HERE?

You've got a lot to lose by giving up, and everything to gain by being serious about school.

Myth—A lot of extracurricular activities will make up for poor grades.

Reality—Although colleges consider extracurricular activities such as athletics, student government and the arts when they review an application, they assess academic performance first. Lots of extracurricular activities are great, but first you have to do the work.

REQUIRED COURSES

The chart below gives you a good overview on what courses you need to take in high school to meet standard college entrance requirements. Of course, every college has its own requirements—check with the ones you're interested in to see what they recommend.

SUBJECT	NUMBER OF YEARS	COURSES
English	four or more years	grammar, composition, literature, etc.
Mathematics	three or more years	algebra I and higher—does not include general math, business math, or consumer math
Natural Sciences	three or more years	earth science, biology, chemistry, physics, etc.
Social Sciences	three or more years	history, economics, geography, civics, psychology, etc.
Additional Courses (Some colleges and universities require other classes as prerequisites for admission)	two or more years one or more year	foreign language visual arts, music, theater, drama, dance, computer science, etc.

ARE YOU READY FOR COLLEGE Quiz

Colleges require you to take three years of English classes (grammar, composition, literature, etc.) during high school.

TRUE FALSE

FALSE Since reading and writing are so important to success in college, most schools require four or more years of English classes.

FACT

Studies show that the more math courses students take in high school, the more likely they are to graduate from college.[4]

4. *Clifford Adelman, "Mathematics Equals Opportunity" (U.S. Department of Education, 1997).*

STANDARDIZED TESTS

Their names can sometimes sound like alphabet soup, but the standardized tests you will take in high school are important for college. Some schools require different tests, so you want to make sure to check with each one about their requirements. Here are the four main tests you may have to take if you want to apply to most colleges:

PLAN

The PLAN is the pre-ACT test taken to help students estimate how well they will do on the ACT. This test is very important, and in some cases can have bearing or implications on scholarship opportunities and possible college placement. It is a comprehensive guidance resource that helps students measure their current academic development, explore career/training options, and make plans for the remaining years of high school and post-graduation years.

When do I take the test?

The PLAN is taken during the tenth grade.

How do I register?

The PLAN is administered in-school, so check with your high school counselor to register.

What is the test's structure?

PLAN is a four part multiple-choice test structured very similarly to the ACT with sections covering English, mathematics, reading and science.

For more information about PLAN, talk to your high school counselor or visit www.actstudent.org/plan/.

My high school grades are more important than my standardized test (ACT, PSAT, & SAT) scores.

TRUE FALSE

ACT

This standardized test is designed to assess high school students' general educational development and their ability to complete college-level work. It often is used for college admission decisions, and virtually all U.S. colleges and universities accept ACT results.

When do I take the test?

The ACT is offered usually six times during a given school year. Students generally take the test during their junior year or during the fall of their senior year.

When and how do I register?

A registration packet should be available at your high school, but you may also register online at www.actstudent.org. Be mindful of the registration deadlines for each test, as they are generally one month in advance, but it is suggested that you register at least six weeks prior to the test. Fee waivers are available for students who qualify for financial assistance, so inquire with the ACT directly.

What is the test's structure?

The ACT consists of four multiple-choice tests in English, mathematics, reading, and science, as well as an optional writing test.

How is it scored?

Each subject is scored 1-36 for a composite score, the highest being a 36 overall.

All pertinent ACT testing date information, fee information, registration information and all other questions can be answered by visiting www.actstudent.org.

Free practice tests and questions are also available online. Be sure to familiarize yourself with the test and sample questions before taking the real thing.

TRUE Colleges know that your performance in high school is a better predictor of college success than the standardized tests. That does not mean that most colleges will ignore your test scores.

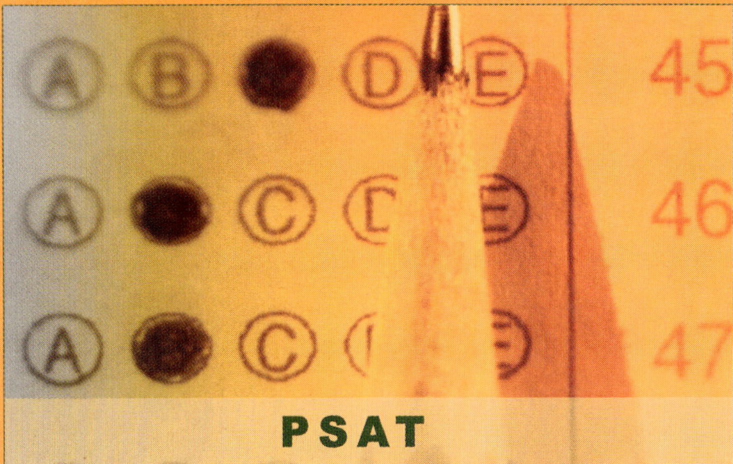

PSAT

The PSAT (Preliminary SAT) is a two-part, exam that is very similar to the SAT. Not to be taken lightly, the PSAT is generally the first indicator colleges and universities use for scholarship purposes and placement.

When do I take the test?

Most people take the PSAT in the fall of their junior year in high school. Some students choose to take it during their sophomore year, which is strongly encouraged. However, scores on the PSAT during your junior year are used to determine National Merit Scholars, students who qualify for merit-based scholarships distributed throughout the United States. Talk to your high school counselor for more information.

How do I register?

You must sign up for the PSAT at your high school. The PSAT is administered during October of every school year. There is a fee associated with taking the PSAT, but there are fee waiver opportunities for certain students. See your high school counselor for more information about fee waivers.

What is the test's structure?

The PSAT consists of two 25-minute verbal sections, two 25-minute math sections, and one 30-minute writing skills section.

For more information on the PSAT, ask your school counselor or visit www.collegeboard.com.

STANDARDIZED TESTS

SAT

The SAT is one of two standardized tests used by colleges as part of their admissions requirements. The SAT I is a three-hour exam that measures verbal, written, and math reasoning skills used for admission at most colleges. The SAT Subject Tests (formerly SAT II) consists of more than 20 subject areas, or achievement tests designed to measure subject-area knowledge. Many colleges use the Subject Tests for admissions, for course placement, and to advise students about course selection, but only some require them.

When do I take the test?

The SAT and SAT II are administered every October, November, December, February, March, May and June of each school year. Most students take the SAT during the second semester of their junior year or the first semester of the senior year.

When and how do I register?

A registration packet should be available at your high school, but you may also register online at www.collegeboard.com. Keep in mind the registration deadlines for each test, as they are generally one month in advance, but it is suggested that you register at least six weeks prior to the test. While there are costs associated with taking the test, students who require financial assistance may qualify for fee waivers. See your high school counselor for more information about fee waivers.

What's the test's structure?

The SAT is a ten-section exam consisting of critical reading, math, writing, and one experimental. The experimental section is masked to look like a regular section.

How is it scored?

Scores on each section range from 200-800 points. The scores from each section are combined, and the highest possible combined score is 2400.

All pertinent SAT testing date information, fee information, registration information and all other questions can be answered by visiting www.collegeboard.com.

Free practice tests and questions are also available online. Be sure to familiarize yourself with the test and sample questions before taking the real thing.

3 FIND THE RIGHT FIT

Think about interests and activities that you enjoy.
Explore colleges with programs that suit your interest.

3 How2 FIND THE RIGHT FIT

• **What's the right match?** The kind of college you choose to attend should reflect your goals and your personality. Whether you choose a public, private, community, technical, trade, or even online college, make sure it's the best match for you.

• **Big or small?** Do you want to attend a big university with a greater choice of studies and social activities, but also larger lecture classes? Or would you like fewer choices but more personal attention and a greater chance to stand out? You decide.

• **Home or Away?** Attending a local college versus living in a dorm—what's better? It depends. For some, residence hall life is an important part of the college experience—but commuting from home is less expensive.

• **Which major works?** Figuring out what you like doing most, plus what you're best at, can point to the careers you should consider—and what majors will help you reach your career goal.

• **Do extras matter?** Getting into extracurricular activities outside of class—band, science club, the school newspaper, or drama—or even volunteering at local organizations helps you discover what your real interests are—and where you're heading.

ARE YOU READY FOR COLLEGE Quiz

Big colleges are best if I haven't decided on a major field.

TRUE FALSE

FALSE If you are undecided, the best college is one that has core requirements or distribution requirements that ensure you will explore new areas and fields.

EXPLORE YOUR INTERESTS

What are you good at? Do you have something you love to do? Whether it's playing sports, building models, or playing an instrument, your interests today say a lot about what career you might have tomorrow. To get there, follow these ten steps. And be sure to discuss them with your school counselor and your parents or guardian:

1. **Make** a list of your skills and interests. Think hard about what you enjoy and what you are good at.
2. **Find** out more about the kinds of the jobs that interest you, along with their educational requirements, salary, working conditions, future outlook, and anything else that can help you decide what's best.

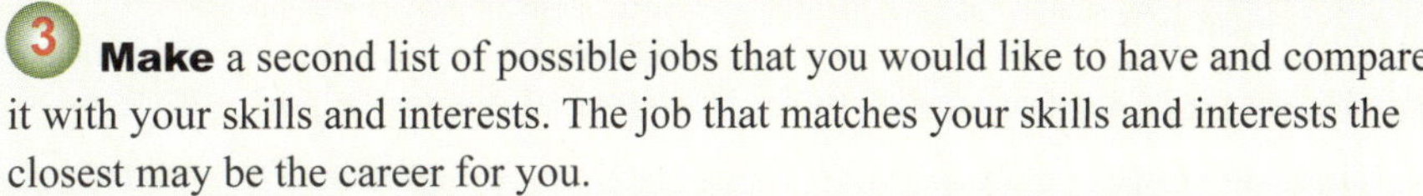

3. **Make** a second list of possible jobs that you would like to have and compare it with your skills and interests. The job that matches your skills and interests the closest may be the career for you.

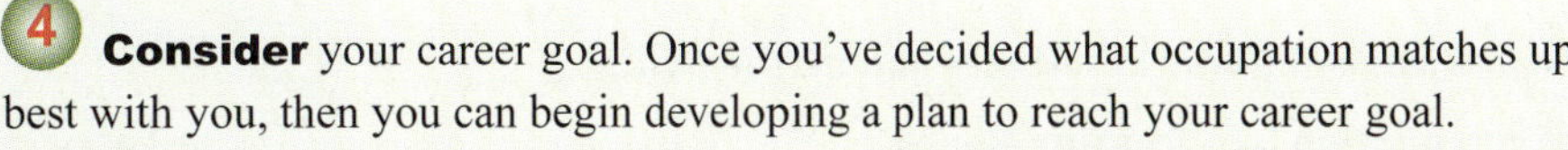

4. **Consider** your career goal. Once you've decided what occupation matches up best with you, then you can begin developing a plan to reach your career goal.
5. **Begin** a career plan. Think about what you want to do and find out more about the kind of training, education, and skills you will need to achieve your career goal.
6. **Find** schools that offer a college degree or training program that best meets your career goal and financial needs.
7. **Find** out about financial aid to help support you in obtaining your career goal.
8. **Learn** about job hunting tips as you prepare to graduate or move into the job market.

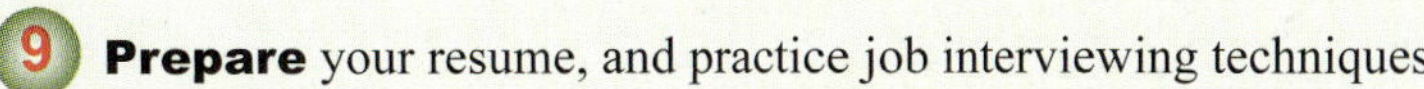

9. **Prepare** your resume, and practice job interviewing techniques.
10. **Go** to your career guidance center at school or local library for information and help on career planning.

MAKING A SAMPLE CAREER PLAN

Making a career plan is a matter of matching your skills and interests to an occupation to create a career goal, and then deciding the steps you need to take to reach that goal. Here's a sample:

My Career Plan

Career Goal:

To become a civil engineer. To design, plan, and supervise the construction of buildings, highways, and rapid transit systems.

Requirements:

- Bachelor's degree in engineering
- Ability to work as part of a team
- Creativity
- Analytical mind
- Capacity for detail
- Presentation skills
- Writing skills
- Knowledge of physical sciences and mathematics
- Accreditation by Licensing Board

Current Skills and Interests:

- Summer worker for Smith Construction Co.
- High School mathematics courses
- High School science courses
- Experience working as a team
- Attended high school writing courses
- Gave presentations in high school courses

Plan To Reach Career Goal:

- Bachelor's Degree
- Attend an accredited engineering school
- Job Experience
- Continue working for Smith Construction Co.
- Seek internships through the university career placement office
- Networking
- Join campus organizations for engineering students

Courtesy of Mapping Your Future.org / http://mapping-your-future.org/planning/careersa.htm

Myth—You need to decide on a career before you can choose a college.

Reality—College is a time to explore. Many students discover their ideal field while taking a course they didn't expect to like. If you aren't ready to decide on a major or a career, choose a college that allows you to keep your options open. Take your time.

VISIT THE CAMPUS

No matter how many brochures you read or websites you visit, nothing tells you more about a college than visiting its campus in person. Plus, you can learn a lot more just by asking questions. Here's a list to get you started:

Ask your college host:

- What activities and services are available to help students get settled (academically and socially) during their first year?
- How big are the classes?
- What is the total cost of attending the college?
- What types of financial aid does the college offer and how do I apply?
- Are all freshmen assigned to an academic advisor?
- Where do most freshmen live?
- Can I take a tour?
- What activities are available for students?
- Who teaches the courses for first-year students?
- How successful are the college's graduates in finding jobs?
- What services (such as transportation and shopping) are available locally?

Ask any students you meet:

- How easy is it to meet with faculty?
- Are you able to register for the classes you want?
- What is there to do on weekends? Do most students stay or leave campus on weekends?

Can't get to a campus? Go online:

- Visiting a college's website is an invaluable tool to learn everything you need to know about a school. You can find answers to many of the questions above and some college websites even offer a virtual tour for you to get familiar with the campus.
- KnowHow2GO-U—accessible at www.KnowHow2GO.org/campustour— is a virtual pre-college tour that replicates the experience of being on a real college campus and is designed to help you learn what to expect. By visiting various campus buildings—Admissions, Financial Aid, Academics, Career Center, Student Center, Library, Dormitories, Quad, and the Athletic Complex—you'll learn about the college environment and what it takes to get there.

KH2G KnowHow2GO University

Myth—If you haven't heard of a particular college or university, it can't be very good.

Reality—Televised athletic games are how some colleges are known, but many great colleges do not get that kind of exposure. Some of the nation's finest colleges don't field big-time sports teams. Learn about colleges by looking at college guides in the library or your counselor's office or "visit" them on the Internet.

APPLYING

Completing college applications can take a lot of time. So you want to make sure that you get it right and not make mistakes. Here are some tips to guide you through the process:

Know the guidelines.

Before you start applying to schools, find out the application deadline and fees for each school you are considering.

Plan ahead.

It takes time to get standardized test scores tabulated and mailed, and it takes time for school counselors and others providing references to gather information.

Follow the instructions and proofread.

The application is often a college admission committee's first contact with you. Make a good impression with a neat application free of spelling and grammatical errors. Ask a friend, relative, or mentor to read and provide feedback on your materials.

Work with your high school to send all records and test scores.

Go to your high school's guidance office for help getting all necessary transcripts (grade history), records, test scores, and applications sent to prospective schools. If you decide to apply to schools that have not already received your test scores, you can ask to send your scores to that college.

Make the most of personal references.

Ask people who know you well, and give the best impression of you to your school. Prepare a neat and legible reference form and give your references plenty of time to respond.

Write an outstanding essay.

Most college applications require an essay, so spend time developing a good one. While a great essay probably won't get you into college if you don't meet the other academic requirements, it could move you as a "maybe" up the list.

Be ready to interview, audition, or submit a portfolio.

Some colleges also require a personal interview or examples of work in special areas such as art or music.

Keep a copy of all your application materials. You never know when you might need them!

I will have a better chance of getting into law or medical school if I go to a university that offers those graduate programs.

TRUE FALSE

FALSE Very few universities give their students special preference for graduate study, and those that do reserve it for only the very best students.

4 PUT YOUR HANDS ON SOME CASH

There's money out there to help you pay for college. Apply for it.

4 How2 PUT YOUR HANDS ON SOME CASH

• **Who gets financial aid?** Many more students than you might think. Financial aid is awarded by need or on merit—academic achievement, athletics, or other talents. But you have to apply for aid to find out.

• **What kind of money?** Grants, scholarships, work-study, student loans—there are a lot of different types of financial aid out there and you need to find out which kind or combination works best for your needs.

• **Where do you look?** Colleges expect you and your parents to pay what you can—but schools, state and federal governments, and private businesses and organizations are also all great sources for financial aid.

• **Is it free money?** Not likely—most financial aid packages are a mixture of grants that don't need to be paid back and loans that do, but not until after you graduate from college.

• **How to apply?** Your school guidance counselor can help you, including how to file a **Free Application for Federal Student Aid (FAFSA)**, which makes you a candidate for all federal student aid. For help online, go to http://www.fafsa.ed.gov/ or http://www.collegegoalsundayusa.org/

• **Do deadlines matter?** Absolutely. College financial aid goes fast. The earlier you can get in your **FAFSA** application and all the other info that a college asks for, the sooner you'll receive your financial aid package.

COSTS AND FINANCIAL AID

Myth—Only the very best students receive financial aid from colleges.

Reality—Although high-ability students or students with special talents may receive merit-based scholarships, many scholarships are based on financial need—colleges generally want students they've admitted to be able to attend, and will help them find the resources to do so.

There's no escaping the fact that college costs are rising. According to recently released reports, most students and their families can expect to pay, on average, from $112 to $1,190 more than last year for this year's tuition and fees, depending on the type of college.

Still, there is good news. There is more financial aid available than ever before—over $135 billion. And, despite all of these college cost increases, a college education remains an affordable choice for most families.

"Sticker Price" vs. Affordability

Although some of the college price tags you hear about can be discouraging—$30,000 or more for yearly tuition and fees—most colleges are more affordable than you might think. For example, did you know that about 60 percent of students attending four-year schools pay less than $6,000 for tuition and fees? After grants are taken into consideration, the net price the average undergraduate pays for a college education is significantly lower than the published tuition and fees. And remember, financial aid will further reduce the amount your family will actually pay.

Financial Aid Makes College Affordable for You

Financial aid is intended to make up the difference between what your family can afford to pay and what college costs. Nearly two-thirds of the students currently enrolled in college receive some sort of financial aid to help pay college costs.

The financial aid system is based on the goal of equal access—that anyone should be able to attend college, regardless of financial circumstances. Here's how the system works:

Students and their families are expected to contribute to the cost of college to the extent that they're able. If a family is unable to contribute the entire cost, financial aid is available to bridge the gap.

EFC Works in Your Favor

The amount your family is able to contribute is frequently referred to as the Expected Family Contribution, or EFC. The figure is determined by whoever is awarding the aid —usually the federal government or individual colleges and universities.

The federal government and financial aid offices use "need formulas" that analyze your family's financial circumstances (things like income, assets, and family size) and compare them proportionally with other families' financial circumstances.

Most families can't just pay the EFC out of current income alone. But, not to worry—the formulas assume that families will meet their contribution through a combination of savings, current income, and borrowing.

Second, financial aid is limited. The formulas therefore measure a particular family's ability to pay against other families' ability to pay.

Don't Rule Out Colleges with Higher Costs

Say your EFC is $5,000. At a college with a total cost of $8,000, you'd be eligible for up to $3,000 in financial aid. At a college with a total cost of $25,000, you'd be eligible for up to $20,000 in aid. In other words, your family would be asked to contribute the same amount at both colleges.

Colleges want to help students get financial aid.

TRUE FALSE

TRUE The job of a college's financial aid officer is to make it possible for all admitted students to attend their college while staying within the federal guidelines.

Current Average College Costs

Average College Costs Per Year

Public, two-year: $2,361

Public, four-year: $6,185

Private, four-year: $23,712

Did you know that...

- About 60% of students attending public four-year colleges pay less than $6,000 for tuition and fees per year.
- 44% of all students attend two-year colleges. The average two-year public college student receives grant aid that reduces the average tuition to about $400.
- A record $135 billion in financial aid is available to students and their families.
- About 60% of all college students receive grant aid. Grant aid averaged $1,800 per student at two-year public colleges, $3,300 at four-year public colleges, and $9,600 at private four-year colleges.

If my parents saved for college, we can still qualify for aid.

TRUE FALSE

TRUE Saving for college is almost always a good idea. Since a lot of financial aid comes in the form of loans, the aid you are likely to receive will need to be repaid.

FINANCIAL AID: LOTS OF OPTIONS

Financial aid is any type of assistance used to pay college costs that is based on financial need. There are three main types:

Grants and Scholarships

Also called gift aid, grants don't have to be re-paid and you don't need to work to earn them. Grant aid comes from federal and state governments and from individual colleges. Scholarships are usually awarded based on merit. To search for scholarships, visit www.fastweb.com.

Work

Student employment and work-study aid helps students pay for education costs such as books, supplies, and personal expenses. Work-study is a federal program which provides students with part-time employment to help meet their financial needs and gives them work experience while serving their campuses and surrounding communities.

Loans

Most financial aid (54%) comes in the form of loans to students or parents—aid that must be re-paid. Most loans that are awarded based on financial need are low-interest loans sponsored by the federal government. These loans are subsidized by the government so no interest accrues until you begin repayment after you graduate.

MORE ABOUT LOANS

There are many different types of loans, both for students and for parents to take on behalf of their student. Read on for the basics.

Federal Student Loans

Perkins Loans

Perkins Loans are need-based loans and are awarded by the financial aid office to students with the highest need. The interest rate is very low—5 percent—and you don't make any loan payments while in school.

Subsidized Stafford or Direct Loans

Subsidized Stafford Loans are need-based loans with interest rates in the 4-6 percent range. The federal government pays the yearly interest while you're in school. This is why they're called "subsidized" loans.

Unsubsidized Stafford or Direct Loans

Unsubsidized Stafford Loans aren't based on financial need and can be used to help pay the family share of costs. You're responsible for paying interest on the loan while in school. You may choose to capitalize the interest. The advantage of doing this is that no interest payments are required. The disadvantage is that the interest is added to the loan, meaning that you will repay more money to the lender.

Grad PLUS Loans

This is a student loan for graduate students sponsored by the federal government that is unrelated to need. Generally, students can borrow Grad PLUS loans up to the total cost of education, minus any aid received. The advantage of this loan is that it allows for greater borrowing capacity. However, we recommend that students consider lower-interest loans, such as the Subsidized Stafford or Unsubsidized loans prior to taking out a Grad PLUS loan.

Parent Loans

Federal PLUS loans

The PLUS Loan program is the largest source of parent loans. Parents can borrow up to the full cost of attendance minus any aid received, and repayment starts 60 days after money is paid to college.

Private parent loans

A number of lenders and other financial institutions offer private education loans for parents. These loans usually carry a higher interest rate than PLUS Loans.

College-sponsored loans

A small number of colleges offer their own parent loans, usually at a better rate than PLUS. Check each college's aid materials to see if such loans are available.

Other Student Loan Options

Private student loans

A number of lenders and other financial institutions offer private education loans to students. These loans are not subsidized and usually carry a higher interest rate than the federal need-based loans. The College Board private loan program is an example of a private education loan for students.

College-sponsored loans

Some colleges have their own loan funds. Interest rates may be lower than federal student loans. Read the college's financial aid information.

Other loans

Besides setting up scholarships, some private organizations and foundations have loan programs as well. Borrowing terms may be quite favorable. You can use Scholarship Search to find these.

HIGH SCHOOL TIMELINES

The college planning process can be daunting for everyone. It's best to plan ahead and allow plenty of time. It also helps if you have a plan to follow from your freshman year through your senior year—and here it is.

FRESHMEN TIMELINE

START HERE FRESHMEN

FALL

- ❑ Make sure you enroll in geometry or algebra. Colleges require that you take rigorous math courses in high schools.
- ❑ Create a college information folder that you can take with you through high school.
- ❑ Start the school year off right by getting organized and practicing good study habits.
- ❑ Meet new people by signing up for extracurricular activities and trying something new!
- ❑ Explore careers on the Web on your home computer or at the library.
- ❑ Find job shadowing opportunities in the community, where you can spend a day shadowing someone at work and watching what he or she does.

SPRING

- ❑ Start to plan your sophomore year.
- ❑ Talk with your parents and counselor about summer vacation. Explore summer programs or camps to attend at local colleges and universities. Look for volunteer or service opportunities in the community. Some may be sponsored by a local church, synagogue or mosque.

SOPHOMORE TIMELINE

SOPHOMORE TIMELINE

FALL

- ❑ Polish your study skills. If you need to improve in some subjects, this is the time to do it. Colleges and future employers look at high school transcripts and are impressed with regular attendance and improving grades.
- ❑ Have you taken a career interest inventory? Ask your counselor or guidance office to give you one. These tests help assess your strengths and weaknesses and can help guide your college search and long-term career plans.
- ❑ Take the Preliminary Scholastic Aptitude test PSAT—the preliminary version of the SAT—or the PLAN, the preliminary version of the ACT. Taking the PSAT now is practice for the PSAT test in junior year which allows your student to be considered for a National Merit Scholarship. Find dates and more information about the PSAT from your high school's guidance office.
- ❑ Surf the Web to check out colleges, technical schools and apprenticeship opportunities.
- ❑ Consider job shadowing to get some work experience and test possible careers.

SPRING

- ❑ Begin exploring financial aid and scholarships options.
- ❑ Use the Internet to explore different careers.
- ❑ Select five to ten colleges to contact for brochures and applications.
- ❑ Visit your school or community Career Center.
- ❑ Plan a productive summer. The summer before 11th grade is a good time to have a part-time job to prepare for a future career.
- ❑ Choose a summer camp or find volunteer service program to jumpstart your skills.
- ❑ Remember to sign up for the most challenging classes for next year.

ARE YOU READY FOR COLLEGE

The best time to visit colleges is before I have been admitted.

TRUE FALSE

TRUE Many students find that none of the colleges to which they were admitted "felt" right when they visited. If possible, visit before you apply and again after you have been admitted.

JUNIOR YEAR TIMELINE

JUNIOR TIMELINE

August:

- ❑ Start your year off right: Talk with your guidance counselor about your options and your plans. Be sure to ask about test dates for the PSAT, ACT, and SAT. You'll need to register up to six weeks ahead of time.
- ❑ Sign up for courses with your eyes on the prize: college and money to pay for it! A tougher course load may pay off with scholarships and may get you a better chance to get admitted to the school of your choice.
- ❑ Start investigating private and public sources for financial aid. Take note of scholarship deadlines and plan accordingly.
- ❑ Sign up for activities to boost your college applications.

September:

- ❑ Find out about schools you are interested in attending. Treat your school selection process like a research paper: Make a file and gather information about schools, financial aid, and campus life to put in it. Go to college fairs and open houses and learn as much as you can from the Internet about schools.
- ❑ Begin planning college visits. Fall, winter, and spring break are good times because you can observe a campus when classes are going on.

October:

- ❑ Take the PSAT. You'll get the results by Christmas.
- ❑ Sign up for ACT or SAT prep courses.
- ❑ Do your top college picks require essays or recommendations? Now is the time to begin planning your essays and choosing whom you'd like to ask for a recommendation.

November:

- ❑ Sign up for the ACT and SAT, if you haven't already.

December:

- ❑ Begin the application process for service academies (West Point, Annapolis, etc.)
- ❑ Decide if you should take AP exams in May. Investigate the College-Level Examination Program® or CLEP, which grants college credit for achievement in exams covering many different college-level subjects.

January:

- ❑ Meet with your guidance counselor again to develop your senior schedule.
- ❑ Organize your Individual Graduation Plan.

February:

- ❑ Think about lining up a summer job, internship, or co-op.
- ❑ Plan campus visits for spring break.
- ❑ Memorize your Social Security number if you haven't already. It will be your identity on campus.

March/April:

- ❑ Get ready for AP exams next month.
- ❑ Write a résumé.

SENIOR YEAR TIMELINE

SENIOR YEAR TIMELINE

August

- ❑ Sign up for the ACT and/or SAT if you didn't take it as a junior, or if you aren't satisfied with your score.
- ❑ Review ACT and/or SAT test results and retest if necessary.

August to December

- ❑ Visit with your school counselor to make sure you are on track to graduate and fulfill college admission requirements. Consider taking courses at a local university or community college.
- ❑ Keep working hard all year; second semester grades can affect scholarship eligibility.
- ❑ Ask for personal references from teachers, school counselors, or employers early in the year or at least two weeks before application deadline.
- ❑ Follow your school's procedure for requesting recommendations.
- ❑ Visit with admissions counselors who come to your high school.
- ❑ Attend a college fair.
- ❑ Begin your college essay(s).
- ❑ Apply for admission at the colleges you've chosen.
- ❑ Avoid common college application mistakes.
- ❑ Find out if you qualify for scholarships at each college where you have applied.
- ❑ Start the financial aid application process.
- ❑ See your school counselor for help finding financial aid and scholarships.

Today Is
check timeline!

January to May

- ❑ If you need it, get help completing the FAFSA (Free Application for Federal Student Aid).
- ❑ Ask your guidance office in January to send first semester transcripts to schools where you applied. In May, they will need to send final transcripts to the college you will attend.
- ❑ Visit colleges that have invited you to enroll.
- ❑ Decide which college to attend, and notify the school of your decision.
- ❑ Keep track of and observe deadlines for sending in all required fees and paperwork.
- ❑ Notify schools you will not attend of your decision.
- ❑ Continue to look for scholarship opportunities.
- ❑ Keep track of important financial aid and scholarship deadlines.
- ❑ Watch the mail for your Student Aid Report (SAR)—it should arrive four weeks after the FAFSA is filed.
- ❑ Compare financial aid packages from different schools.
- ❑ Sign and send in a promissory note if you are borrowing money.
- ❑ Notify your college about any outside scholarships you received.

June to August

- ❑ Make sure your final transcript is sent to the school you will be attending.
- ❑ Getting a summer job can help pay some of your college expenses.
- ❑ Make a list of what you will need to take with you for your dorm room.
- ❑ If you haven't met your roommate, call, write, or e-mail to get acquainted in advance.
- ❑ Make sure housing documentation is quickly accessible when you move into the dorm.
- ❑ Learn how to get around at your new school. Review a campus map.
- ❑ Wait until after your first class meeting to buy your books and supplies.

KnowHow2GO State Partners

KnowHow2GO supports a strong grassroots network of state partners to ensure that students and adult mentors can easily find real-time, on-the-ground assistance. Whether you need information on counseling, academics or financial aid, these organizations and Web sites can help.

California

www.knowhow2gocalifornia.org

KnowHow2GOCalifornia

Partners:

Southern California College Access Network SoCal CAN, www.socalcollegeaccess.org

Campaign for College Opportunity, www.collegecampaign.org

Los Angeles Chamber of Commerce - UNITE LA, www.unitela.com

Univision (San Francisco & Los Angeles), www.univision.com

California State University, www.calstate.edu

LA Cash for College, www.lacashforcollege.org

Community College League of California, www.ccleague.org

CaliforniaColleges.edu

Campaign Highlights:

• SoCal CAN is excited for the launch of the new "You've Got What It Takes" campaign. The network's 30 member organizations will assist in implementation, taking the message into their local schools and neighborhoods.

• SoCal CAN is planning a launch event for the new campaign and hopes to have the 3 Los Angeles-based actors (skater, artist, and gamer) in attendance!

• Interested in talking with friends about college? Join the team of 100+ KnowHow2GO Ambassadors who are spreading college knowledge on middle and high schools campuses in Los Angeles County.

• The KnowHow2GoCalifornia website was upgraded to include a calendar of local college access events, including local scholarship and internship opportunities.

Connecticut

www.knowhow2goconnecticut.org

KnowHow2GOConnecticut

Partners:

CT Department of Education, www.sde.ct.gov

CT Department of Higher Education, www.ctdhe.org

CT African-American Affairs Commission, www.cga.ct.gov/aaac Unite L.A.

Campaign Highlights:

• With funding from the Lumina Foundation for Education, KnowHow2GOConnecticut awarded Education Connection (Litchfield), The Boys and Girls Clubs (Hartford), Eastern Connecticut State University (Windham), Wesleyan University - Public School Collaborative (Middletown), University of Bridgeport, (Bridgeport), Manchester Community College (Manchester), and North End Action Team (Middletown) grants for programs designed to increase access and success to post-secondary educational opportunities for traditionally underserved students.

• The KnowHow2GOConnecticut Network received a $19,000 grant from National Council for Community and Education Partnerships to promote the expansion and development of the Local college access and success networks throughout the state in collaboration with the GEAR UP Project in Bridgeport and New Haven.

• A statewide symposium on Network Building for college access and success programs was held on May 11, 2010 at the Burroughs Community Center in Bridgeport. Paul Vandeventer, the author of the book Networks that Work, facilitated and a panel included representatives from community foundations, community organizations and educators.

• KnowHow2GOConnecticut awarded the second of three rounds of re-granting to non-profit organizations in late May/early June 2010 through a grant from the Lumina Foundation for Education.

Florida

www.knowhow2goflorida.org

KnowHow2GOFlorida

Partners:

Florida College Access Network, floridacollegeaccess.org

Florida Department of Education, fldoe.org

Florida Board of Governors, flbog.org

University of South Florida, usf.edu

Florida International University, fiu.edu

Hillsborough Education Foundation, educationfoundation.com

The Brink Foundation, brinkfoundation.org

HYPE of Tampa Bay, hypehope.org

Big Brothers Big Sisters of Tampa Bay, bbbsfl.org

Big Brothers Big Sisters of Central Florida, bbbscfl.org

Big Brothers Big Sisters of Greater Miami, wementor.org

Boy's and Girl's Clubs of Tampa Bay, bgctampafl.org

Tampa Metropolitan YMCA, tampaymca.org

ASPIRA Miami-Dade Youth Leadership Development Division, aspirafl.org

enFamilia, Inc., enfamiliainc.org

Educate Tomorrow, educatetomorrow.org

Sant La Haitian Neighborhood Center, santla.org

Urban League of Greater Miami, miamiurbanleague.org

Pierre Toussaint Leadership and Learning Center, pierretoussaint.org

Advanced Pre-Collegiate Leadership Seminars, aplususa.org

Brain Expansions Scholastic Training, brainexpansions.org

Campaign Highlights:

- Florida College Access Network (Florida C.A.N.!) received approval in 2010 for a statewide expansion of KnowHow2GO from KnowHow2GOTampa Bay to KnowHow2GOFlorida. The expansion is expected to be implemented through 2012. Florida C.A.N.! has since formed a statewide collaborative network that includes state colleges, universities and youth-serving community based organizations with KnowHow2GO implementation partners in Orlando, Tampa and Miami.

- Florida C.A.N.! hosted College Goal Sunday 2011 in partnership with the Florida Association of Student Financial Aid Administrators and with the help of over 40 community-based organizations and higher ed institutions throughout the state. Together College Goal Sunday served over 2,000 students and family members.

- Florida C.A.N.! has launched several local college access networks in key areas of the state as part of a collaborative effort to build, expand, and sustain local college access services for limited-income, first generation, and underrepresented students. Key areas include communities within Tampa, Orlando, and Miami.

Idaho

www.knowhow2goidaho.org

KnowHow2GOIdaho

Partners:

J. A. & Kathryn Albertson Foundation, www.jkaf.org

Campaign Highlights:

- The J.A. and Kathryn Albertson Foundation completed a soft launch of the KnowHow2GOIdaho.org web site and has initiated work on the air campaign and ground campaign for KnowHow2GO in Idaho.

- Fifteen originating members met on March 30, 2010 to brainstorm what will become the Idaho College Access Network. Among the next steps are the creation of a steering committee and development of a mission, vision, and goals statement.

- Plans for an official launch of the KnowHow2GOIdaho.org site and special events are in the works, and many more partners are anticipated as efforts ramp up to help more Idahoans move from awareness to action through the KnowHow2GO campaign.

Illinois

www.knowhow2goillinois.org

KnowHow2GOIllinois

Partners:

Illinois Student Assistance Commission, www.collegezone.com

Illinois College Access Network, www.illinoiscan.org

Chicago Public Schools, www.postsecondary.cps.k12.il.us

Campaign Highlights:

• Since September 2009, approximately 80 College Illinois! Corps members—recent undergraduate degree recipients—have established strong relationships within their communities to promote college planning and preparation among high school students and their families utilizing KnowHow2GO as their primary outreach tool, philosophy and strategy. Their efforts have included organizing and offering outreach events, career counseling, test preparation, FAFSA completion workshops for students and parents, college selection and application assistance, and knowledge and assistance about applying for financial aid.

• College Illinois! Corps members support the work of the KnowHow2GO Illinois Vertical Access Teams throughout the state by tapping into organic and local social networks in and between area high schools and community-based organizations. They build partnerships with local schools, businesses, municipalities, and nonprofits in order to deliver free career and college planning and preparation services to students from families with no prior college-going experience.

Indiana

www.knowhow2goindiana.org

KnowHow2GOIndiana

Partners:

Learn More Indiana, www.learnmoreindiana.org

Indiana Commission for Higher Education

Indiana Department of Education

Indiana Department of Workforce Development

State Student Assistance Commission of Indiana

Indiana's colleges and universities

Indiana's College Success Coalition (composed of 500+ local organizations)

Campaign Highlights:

• KnowHow2GOIndiana launched a kickoff event and other public activities, and partnered with summer after-school programs to promote practical tips for students to KnowHow2GO back-to-school, to college and to careers.

• Held at the beginning of the academic year, College GO! Week encourages students of all ages to take specific steps to plan for college and career success. Schools and universities are provided with the tools to run a successful event, and College Success Coalitions and other partners across the state reach out in a variety of ways to help inspire and motivate students.

• The Cash for College promotion includes practical, grade-specific steps to help students pay for college, all leading up to the state's annual March 10 deadline for students to complete the Free Application for Federal Student Aid (FAFSA).

Iowa

www.knowhow2goiowa.org

KnowHow2GOIowa

Partners:

Iowa College Access Network, www.icansucceed.org

Iowa College Student Aid Commission

Iowa Department of Education

College Savings Iowa

Des Moines Public Library

GEAR UP

Iowa TRIO – Educational Talent Search

Campaign Highlights:

• Awarded $140,000 to ten Iowa education programs enabling these organizations to expand college access in their local communities.

• Partnered with GEAR UP Iowa to provide a KnowHow2GO Training Workshop for grant recipients. Attendees left the workshop armed with a KnowHow2GO toolkit and increased knowledge for expanding the campaign to their regions of the state of Iowa.

• Integrated the KnowHow2GO campaign into the ICAN High School Success presentation for eighth and ninth grade students. More than 50 programs were held throughout the state reaching just over 2,000 students.

• Featured the KnowHow2GO campaign and Algebra II at the Iowa State Fair. Algebra II posed for pictures with students of all ages and introduced fair-goers to the four steps of going to college.

Louisiana

www.knowhow2golouisiana.org

KnowHow2GOLouisiana

Partners:

Louisiana Board of Regents, www.regents.state.la.us

Louisiana GEAR UP, www.lasip.org/lagearup/rfs.asp

Louisiana Office of Student Financial Assistance, www.osfa.la.gov

Campaign Highlights:

• Louisiana officially kicked off its KnowHow2GO campaign on April 16, 2010 in coordination with a statewide meeting of the GEAR UP Explorer Club Conference. More than 500 8th to 12th grade students from across the state attended the conference, along with more than 100 parents and educators. The festivities included motivational speakers, training sessions, a "stomp the yard" celebration, formal dinner and prom style dance.

• On May 4-6, 2011 students gathered for the statewide EXPLORER Club Conference where the new KnowHow2GO media campaign was shared. Every participant took home a new KnowHow2GO t-shirt with the new media theme.

• LOSFA's residential Trailblazer Camp (open to rising Seniors) is hosted each summer and held on two college campuses. The summer program offers students an opportunity to become student ambassadors on College Access and a review of KnowHow2GO is provided.

Michigan

www.KnowHow2GOMichigan.org

KnowHow2GOMichigan

Lead State Agency:

Michigan College Access Network, www.micollegeaccess.org

Partners:

Michigan Department of Education, College Access and Outreach Unit, www.michigan.gov/mde

Michigan Campus Compact, www.micampuscompact.org

Michigan College Advising Corps and Michigan State University College Advising Corps, www.advisingcorps.org

Michigan Department of Human Services, Youth Services Unit, www.michigan.gov/dhs

Achieving the Dream, www.achievingthedream.org

EduGuide, College Goal Sunday, www.micollegegoal.org

King Chavez Parks Initiative (GEAR UP)

Promise Zones

The Imagine Fund, www.theimaginefund.org

The University of Michigan-Dearborn, www.umd.umich.edu

The Kresge Foundation, www.kresge.org/

Campaign Highlights:

• 35 Local College Access Networks have implemented the campaign in their communities. To see a complete LCAN directory visit www.micollegeaccess.org/our-network

• Michigan College Access Network has awarded more than $700,000 to help Michigan communities establish local college access networks, including incorporation of the statewide initiatives, KnowHow2GO and the Michigan College Access Portal (MichiganCAP)

• Michigan College Access Portal (MichiganCAP), a one-stop-shop web portal that helps students plan, apply and pay for college. The Portal launched during the 2010-2011 school year. It is currently being expanded to include middle school students.

• The KnowHow2GOMichigan website continues to serve as a resource and KnowHow2GOMichigan materials have been incorporated into local events across the state, such as the Muskegon Opportunity KnowHow2GO College Road Show.

Montana

www.knowhow2gomontana.org

KnowHow2GOMontana

Partners:

MT GEAR UP, www.gearup.montana.edu

Student Assistance Foundation (SAF), www.safmt.org

Campaign Highlights:

• With the assistance of a grant from Lumina Foundation for Education, SAF offers funds to Montana community organizations, colleges and other groups with education-related missions to host KnowHow2GO Week, a week of events geared to helping students get to college. Activities are based on the KnowHow2GO campaign's four steps.

• Montana College Access Network was created to provide a coordinated network of mentors, counselors, and other individuals to help students with the postsecondary process, financial aid awareness, and career development. The network facilitates educational calls/Webinars, the sharing of resources (KnowHow2GO materials) that expand services and support for Montana students, and more.

• National Training for Counselors and Mentors (NT4CM) offers counselors, educators and other professionals working with college-bound youth the opportunity to learn about current financial aid practices through free training sessions.

• At www.KnowHow2GOMontana.org, students and parents can learn the four steps to get to college, in addition to find out about Montana programs designed to help them achieve their goals.

Nebraska

www.knowhow2gonebraska.org

KnowHow2GONebraska

Partners:

EducationQuest Foundation
Office of the Governor
Nebraska P-16 Initiative
Nebraska Department of Education
University of Nebraska System
Nebraska State College System
Association of Independent Colleges and Universities of Nebraska
Nebraska Community College Association
Nebraska's Coordinating Commission for Postsecondary Education
Nebraska State Education Association
Nebraska Council of School Administrators
Nebraska Association of School Boards
Bright Futures Foundation
Foundation for Lincoln Public Schools
Latino American Commission
Nebraska Children and Families Foundation
Western Nebraska Community College
TeamMates Mentoring Program
Westfield Gateway Mall
Statewide School Districts
Statewide Community Agencies

Campaign Highlights:

• Created a new College Access Department that is devoted to college access efforts for middle school students.

• Conducted statewide Early College Awareness Training for counselors, educators and agency professionals who work with 8th, 9th and 10th grade students.

• Created a publication called KnowHow2GO Handbook – College and Career Planning for 8th, 9th and 10th Grade Students and distributed over 80,000 to Nebraska middle schools and high schools.

• Expanded the KnowHow2GONebraska Ambassador Program to more communities in Nebraska.

Ohio

www.knowhow2goohio.org

KnowHow2GOOhio

Partners:

Ohio Department of Education, www.ode.state.oh.us
Ohio College Access Network, www.ohiocan.org
Ohio Board of Regents, www.regents.ohio.gov
GEAR UP
Ohio TRiO
AmeriCorps Ohio College Guides Program
KnowledgeWorks Foundation
Business Alliance for Higher Education
The Ohio State University Economic Access Initiative
Ohio Association of Student Financial Aid Administrators
Ohio Association for College Admissions Counseling
Ohio School Counselors Association

Campaign Highlights:

• The Ohio College Access Network (OCAN) enlisted Ohio's governor in early 2007 to launch the KnowHow2GO campaign. The Campaign has staying power with its easy to follow mantra that spells out four fool-proof steps to getting to college using even easier to remember creative messaging – in print, online, on the radio, and on TV. Don't know how to go? 1) Be a pain in the behind (Find a mentor), 2) Push Yourself (Take the tough classes), 3) Find the Right Fit, and finally 4) Get your hands on some cash.

Now in its third year, KnowHow2GO has unveiled the third round of creative content, this year communicating that getting to college requires a level of determination, planning, and vision that's not all too UN-familiar for the average tween and teen. The message is: it'll take some hard work, but YOU can do it. Learn all about KnowHow2GO's four steps to college and get your hands on the latest KnowHow2GO resources.

• OCAN and KnowHow2GOOhio have awarded college access programs over $400,000. Grantees have held local launch events, created college clubs, integrated KnowHow2GO into classroom activities and much more.

• OCAN's membership includes 40 college access programs that serve nearly 200 of Ohio's school districts in 74 counties, touching nearly 100,000 students annually. High schools with OCAN member programs have an average 4.5% higher graduation rate.

Last school year, OCAN college access programs awarded nearly $3.7 Million in scholarships and grants and helped to secure over $56 Million in other outside financial aid.

Tennessee

www.CollegeforTN.org

KnowHow2GOTennessee

Partners:

TN Higher Education Commission, www.tn.gov/thec/

GEAR UP, www.CollegeforTN.org/Home/Gear_Up/_default.aspx

Campaign Highlights:

- Tennessee's public awareness campaign, "Higher Education...Put Your Mind to It," has received awards at both the national and regional level, winning three MarCom Awards and Memphis PRSA's highest honor, the Vox Grandis.
- Through a partnership with the Tennessee Association of Broadcasters, the campaign has received over $1 million in free radio and television air time.
- Over 950,000 trayliners displaying the campaign's message to "Put Your Mind to It" were distributed in McDonald's restaurants across Tennessee.
- Using social media, the campaign engages and shares important college-going messages with nearly 10,000 Tennessee students.

Washington

www.knowhow2gowashington.org

KnowHow2GOWashington

Partners:

Northwest Education Loan Association, www.nela.net

College Success Foundation, www.collegesuccessfoundation.org

Alliance for Education, www.alliance4ed.org

Campaign Highlights:

- More than 52,000 students signed up for the College Bound Scholarship! The College Bound Scholarship provides hope and incentive for low-income 7th and 8th grade students and families who otherwise might not consider college as an option because of its cost. Learn more at www.hecb.wa.gov
- College Goal Sunday and KnowHow2GOWashington partner to provide college planning information and FAFSA completion support to over 3,500 students and families. Learn more at www.collegegoalsundaywa.org
- Washington College Access Network (WCAN) launched in March 2010! This collaboration promotes and supports the use of best practices, leverages training opportunities and supports public policies to ensure all students have the opportunity and tools to succeed in higher education. Learn more at www.collegesuccessfoundation.org/wcan
- The Alliance for Education convened the Seattle College Access Network (SCAN) in March 2009 to help increase the number of students who apply for, attend, and graduate from college. This 40 member network includes public schools, two-year and four-year colleges, the Washington Higher Education Coordinating Board, education advocacy non-profits, and the funding community.

Wisconsin

www.knowhow2gowisconsin.org

KnowHow2GOWisconsin

Partners:

University of Wisconsin System, www.wisconsin.edu

Wisconsin Covenant, www.wisconsincovenant.wi.gov/

Wisconsin Department of Public Instruction, www.dpi.state.wi.us/vm-student.html

Wisconsin Association of Independent Colleges & Universities, www.waicu.org

Wisconsin Technical Colleges, www.witechcolleges.org

Wisconsin Higher Educational Aids Board, www.heab.state.wi.us

UW Help, www.uwhelp.wisconsin.edu

Campaign Highlights:

• With support from Lumina Foundation, KH2GO Wisconsin awarded over $100K in grants for the establishment of regional college access networks. Currently five lead organizations spread across Wisconsin are actively building college access networks with their regional partners and KH2GO's support. In most cases, these networks leverage existing work of college access programs and makes their collaborative efforts more formal. These regional networks are a part of what will become a state-wide college access network for Wisconsin.

• Twenty-five 25 undergraduate college students from around Wisconsin serve as KnowHow2GO Wisconsin Ambassadors. This past year they provided college-going information and support for middle and high school students through KH2GO presentations and blog postings. KH2GO Wisconsin Ambassadors are utilized by pre-college programs throughout the state.

• Our website and social media sites receive several thousand visits each month. One of the most popular areas is the free Test Prep section which offers comprehensive test prep courses for SAT, ACT, and GRE and allows parents and educators to assist students in their test preparation.

Articles | Chapter 1

I'm college bound

In the following pages you'll find insight and advice from college students and other experts to set you on the path to college.

Become a CSO Opportunity Scholar!

You're in the right place to find the help and information you need to make your college dreams a reality! In the following pages you'll find insight and advice from college students and other experts to set you on the path to college.

However, this book is just the beginning. You can continue your research and college prep on the web!

Check out www.CSOCollegeCenter.org to become a CSO Opportunity Scholar and receive FREE access to college guidance, support, and scholarships.

www.CSOcollegecenter.org

Connect with colleges recruiting students like you!

1. **Create your profile at ConnectNow to become an Opportunity Scholar.**
   - *Remember, you'll send this information to colleges and universities, so be prepared to brag! Colleges want to know everything that is great about you, and what makes you stand out as an exciting applicant.*
2. **Choose your schools.**
   - *Find even more information about the colleges featured in this book.*
   - *Save a list of schools that you think would be a "good fit."*
3. **Make the connection.**
   - *Send your profile to any of the schools that interest you. They want to hear from you and will give special consideration to Opportunity Scholars in the admissions process.*

Get College Admissions Guidance and Support!

Have a question about the college search or application process?

Just Ask the Experts on **www.CSOCollegeCenter.org**. Research our library of articles for expert advice from professionals and students and submit your questions any time of day or night.

You will also begin to receive monthly Opportunity Scholars e-newsletters, with the latest information on scholarships, To Do lists, and important information about each stage of the college search and application process!

Opportunity Scholarship

Apply for the $8,000 Opportunity Scholarship!

At the end of your senior year—when you've decided where you're going to college—apply for the **Opportunity Scholarship!**

Each year, CSO selects a group of first-generation college students attending CSO College Partner institutions to receive this $2,000 scholarship for each of their four years of college.

Not only do winners receive the scholarship, they are given the opportunity to share their college experiences and offer advice to college-bound students as bloggers on **www.CSOCollegeCenter.org**.

Our scholarship winners show that where you come from doesn't mean that you can't go to college.

Check out their inspiring posts on the Opportunity Scholars blog at **www.CSOCollegeCenter.org**.

sign up

to become an Opportunity Scholar today! www.CSOCollegeCenter.org

By Alma Powell

AMERICA'S PROMISE ALLIANCE

LITTLE RED WAGON

On behalf of the America's Promise Alliance, congratulations on being the first in your family to pursue higher education. You are right to seek a college degree; 80% of the new jobs in our 21st century economy require the higher skills and creative thinking that are hallmark of a college education. What you learn in college, about your courses and yourself, will serve you throughout your life.

Alma Powell is the chairman of the board of America's Promise Alliance, an organization founded by her husband, former Secretary of State General Colin Powell.

Finding your way across a new landscape of college will be as challenging as your first days in elementary school, or your transition to middle school and high school. But it is also an exciting experience you can shape with your energy and creativity like nothing you have encountered before. The knowledge and discipline that helped you earn a high school diploma will be compasses that enable you to successfully navigate this new world and set your course for even higher things.

I am proud to serve as chair of America's Promise Alliance, a coalition founded by my husband, Colin, on the principle that all young people need five fundamental resources to fulfill their potential. Just as surely as plants need water and sunshine, every child needs caring adults, safe places for learning and growing, a healthy start, an effective education, and, not least, the opportunity to help others and learn the critical importance of service. Experience and research confirm that, when young people receive these "promises," the odds of success swing strongly in their favor. We call them the "Five Promises" because that is what they must be: promises we keep to our children.

For our Alliance, the Little Red Wagon has always been a symbol of childhood and the hopes and dreams that propel us into adulthood. In the beginning, adults pull you along, support you, and nurture you. Soon, you will support yourselves, proudly and independently.

Think about the people who pulled your little red wagon along your way: the parents who came to this country or worked two or even three jobs so you would have a better life; the mentors, tutors and coaches who saw your potential and helped you see it, too; the teachers and guidance counselors who believed you could graduate and go on to college. These are people who kept the Promises for you, and equipped you so you could keep them for others, leading by example and pulling together to meet society's challenges.

Even as adults, we still carry our red wagons of hopes and dreams. When you feel uncertain, ill prepared, or torn between school, community and family obligations, find rapport and mutual support from your professors and peers. Be a pest if you must but keep looking for allies.

Whatever your aspirations may be, getting a higher education is the key to achieving them. You are up to the challenge. Some people may tell you differently. Don't believe them. Don't be afraid to dream big. Never give up. And just as caring adults helped pull you this far, keep the Promise for the children who need a hand in getting to their own hopes and dreams. ■

BIO *Alma Powell is the chairman of the board of America's Promise Alliance, an organization founded by her husband, former Secretary of State General Colin Powell. America's Promise Alliance serves a mission to mobilize people from every sector of American life to build the character and competence of youth.*

By Rachel Brody

Being the FIRST

First things first.

Everyone loves the first.

The first man on the moon, the first African-American president, and the first in flight. First kisses, first impressions, first place.

What is it about the first?

In many ways, it is easier for students who have siblings or parents who took on the big firsts. When it comes to college, students with parents who attended college have a better chance of attending college themselves.

So what does that mean for students who don't have a family history of higher education? These students who enroll in colleges and universities are called first-generation college students.

Yes, being the first can be lonely. Everything feels strange and different the first time. You might worry how your friends and family will see you, the first. "He thinks he is so special because he is first."

But don't hold back on being first. The great thing about being the first one is that it doesn't mean that you will be the last one. By being the first in your family to graduate from college, you open the door for younger siblings, for your children, and their children. College will not be an intimidating unknown because you went first.

OK, maybe the betterment of your imaginary grandchildren isn't the most convincing reason to take on being the first in college. So, think of yourself. College is four years that are all about you. Your discoveries, your achievements, and your firsts. People who attend college live longer, make more money, and vote more often. You will have more opportunities in your lifetime if you go to college.

Although it can be daunting, being the first is an accomplishment. It will make you a stronger and happier person. And that is what really matters. ■

BIO *Rachel Brody is a former adviser with the National College Advising Corps and past intern with Center for Student Opportunity."*

Building a Bridge

Yes, he's a Pro Bowler and Super Bowl Champion. But London Fletcher did not take your typical path to the National Football League. London admits that sports were his reason to go to college, but he wasn't an All-American destined for a career in professional sports.

to College

London was 11 when his sister was murdered and that despair led his mother to drug addiction. London found solace at the E.J. Kovacic Recreation Center, a building he and his friends call "the Rec," and a mentor in the Rec's director, Tim Isaac.

Mr. Issac taught London, a boy so strong that his family called him "Bam" after "Bamm-Bamm" on "The Flintstones," that guns and drugs would not validate him, but an education and sports could.

London's first love was basketball and after two state championships in high school, he accepted a scholarship to Saint Francis University, a small Division I school in rural Pennsylvania, becoming the first in his family to go to college. He spent one and a half years there before transferring to John Carroll University back home in Cleveland.

It was at John Carroll that London excelled in football and committed himself in the classroom.

"You don't go to John Carroll thinking you'll make it to the NFL," London said about the NCAA Division III school that doesn't offer athletic scholarships. "I focused on academics and attaining my degree to make my mother and family proud."

London's college experience is a stark contrast from most of his peers in the NFL who attended top Division I football schools. He remembers the smaller classes and one-on-one attention that helped him succeed.

"John Carroll has such a great academic reputation and I had to adjust to the academic rigor," said London, who earned a degree in sociology. "But the campus is small and I was not lost in the shuffle."

London's college experience is a stark contrast from most of his peers in the NFL who attended top Division I football schools. He remembers the smaller classes and one-on-one attention that helped him succeed.

For London, making it to the NFL was icing on the cake. Despite being the NCAA Division III defensive player of the year his senior year, the NFL passed him by in the draft. While he got his shot as a rookie free agent with the St. Louis Rams and now plays for the Washington Redskins where he earned his first Pro Bowl selection in 2010, London doesn't forget that education is the key to a better future.

Through London's Bridge Foundation, he is helping students in Cleveland, OH, Washington, DC, and Charlotte, NC with mentoring, test preparation and college scholarships.

"Often times first-generation college students don't know the route to college," London explained. "I started the foundation out of a desire to help others and to bridge that gap to college." ■

By Antoine Tate

I never expected that a young, African American male like me would enter a new environment and experience a sensational program that I would never forget. I had the privilege of participating in the College Summit workshop at Howard University in July 2007. My experience there has helped me mold my future.

The Incredible Journey of Antoine Tate

I Antoine Tate, have embarked on an incredible journey. The summer of 2007 was unquestionably a defining time in my life. I became a College Summit Peer Leader as a high school junior entering my senior year. While attending the program, I met many people with whom I continue to have strong relationships.

I was introduced to Sarah Rimer, a *New York Times* reporter who was eager to write an article about my life and experiences at the College Summit. A personal statement I wrote during the program about black stereotypes was of great interest to her.

On July 27, 2007, the article was published, and I must admit, I felt like a celebrity. Friends and family texted me, emailed me, contacted me on Myspace and Facebook, and called to congratulate me on the article. My life only got better when I received a phone call from Tom Harrison of College Summit explaining that a great man named Raymond Kurlak had offered to pay for my tuition for college. Can you say, "amazing"?

When I returned to Crossland High School in Prince George's County Maryland for my senior year, things got better. I created a relationship with the principal as well as the other staff members. I received support and feedback for the article, and to my surprise, not only was I featured in the *New York Times*, but I managed to grace the *Dallas Morning News* as well. My words went from Washington, DC, to New York and then to Texas. The article traveled all over the country!

My freshmen year at Penn State was dynamic as well! I became actively involved on my campus and am working towards a degree in Communications. I joined the Black Student Union, the Multicultural Recruitment Team, the Debate Team, the Chancellor's Special Program, and became an official member of Kappa Alpha Psi Fraternity. College is definitely the place for me.

I've always thought that I was destined for great things, but College Summit has definitely helped me BELIEVE that I am destined for great things. My experience as a Peer Leader was so rewarding while I was in high school that I decided to return as an Alumni Leader and give back to College Summit what it gave to me: knowledge and success.

So here I am, back at Penn State, waiting for a new phase in my life. Until then, I'll wait patiently, while continuing to make a difference on my campus. So far, I think I'm headed in the right direction. ■

College Summit is a national nonprofit organization that partners with schools and districts to strengthen college-going culture and increase college enrollment rates, so that all students graduate career and college-ready.

Throughout the summer, College Summit runs four-day workshops guiding 40-50 low-income high school seniors through the college transition process to:

- Complete a college common application
- Craft a personal statement
- Gain insight about the financial aid process
- Talk one-on-one with a college counselor
- Learn how to positively influence their peers outside of the workshop

Learn more at www.collegesummit.org

college summit
connect to your future

By Joyce Smith

A Day at the Fair

WITH ABOUT 4,000 COLLEGES AND UNIVERSITIES IN THE U.S., TARGETING ONE FOR YOU MAY BE CHALLENGING!

The good news is that there is a venue where you can talk directly to many colleges at once—NACAC National College Fairs.

The fairs are free to students and parents, and packed with booths that colleges have set up so they can talk to you face-to-face. The college admission representatives know almost everything about their schools—from majors, to accommodations, to scholarships. All you have to do is bring your questions!

Visit the NACAC National College Fair Website at www.nationalcollegefairs.org to investigate fair locations, which colleges will be attending, how to navigate a fair, directions, and other important details.

It's also important to bring your parents or guardians with you if you can—they will have questions too, most likely concerning things like cost of tuition, financial aid and campus safety. Where you spend the next four years of your life is ultimately your decision, but an adult perspective is helpful.

Also build in some extra time. You may need to visit the Counseling and Resource Center for questions about the admission process, and it never hurts to visit one last booth. Who knows? It may be the college of your dreams!

You may want to schedule a meeting with your school counselor before you attend a fair. They can help you narrow your search and suggest ways to research colleges, ensuring that you spend quality time at each booth, rather than rushing through the fair.

The **National Association for College Admission Counseling (NACAC)**, founded in 1937, is an organization of more than 11,000 professionals from around the world dedicated to serving students as they make choices about pursuing postsecondary education.

NACAC is committed to maintaining high standards that foster ethical and social responsibility among those involved in the transition process, as outlined in the NACAC Statement of Principles of Good Practices (SPGP).

BIO *Joyce Smith is CEO of the National Association for College Admission Counseling (NACAC).*

By John Emerson

From Foster Care to College

> **Graduating from college meant that I won.** Most of all, it meant that I would gain the knowledge to use my experience in foster care to help other people. College meant freedom from my past and the ability to choose my future.
>
> *–Maria, 2007 college graduate*

Graduating from college provides lifelong benefits such as increased earning power, health benefits, career satisfaction, and a large supportive network of friends, mentors and professors. And for students raised in foster care, college is often an essential step toward a better life. As Niki, a current college sophomore formerly raised in foster care, reflects, "College offered me the opportunity to break the negative cycle of my upbringing and make a better life for myself. I can take a negative experience and turn it into something positive with all the opportunities in front of me."

So why do so few young adults from foster care ever enroll in or graduate from college? The reasons are varied, but lack of stable guidance is all too common.

This trend seems to be changing. More and more students from foster care are now attending college and finding success. "Coming from the system is no excuse to do poorly in school," says Orlando, a college junior. "We have to break the cycle of living in poverty. Forget about the statistics against you and make something out of your lives. College is the only thing in your life that cannot be taken from you." A growing number of colleges are reaching out to this underserved population, and welcoming them into their programs.

On-campus support services that address their housing, academic, health, and career development needs are increasing. And financial aid resources from a variety of public and private sources are now making it possible for students coming from foster care to attend college without overwhelming loan obligations. Some states also offer good educational benefits for students who choose to stay in foster care until age 21.

BIO *John Emerson is the Postsecondary Education Advisor at Casey Family Programs. Casey Family Programs is the nation's largest operating foundation entirely focused on foster care.*

ADVICE FOR STUDENTS IN FOSTER CARE

What can you do to successfully prepare for college? How do you silence avoidable fears and concerns? Here are a few tips from successful college students who were formerly in foster care:

Problem: Foster care students don't dream about or plan for college, as they have experienced so much disappointment and trauma in their lives.

Solution: "When I learned that there was a section on college applications where you could write about "extenuating circumstances", it changed everything. Use this area of the application to talk about the difficulties and challenges you faced growing up in the foster care system." *Margaret*

Problem: Foster care students rarely have a stable educational advocate, mentor or "college coach" on their side to guide and encourage them to succeed.

Solution: "Sign up for college visits, financial aid events, and whatever else you can find. Become friendly with the person who runs the college office. Begin visiting colleges as soon as you can, because things really start piling up your junior and senior years, and you want to have time to fill out applications and write essays for scholarships." *Renee*

Problem: Foster care students change schools frequently; which results in lost records, credit deficiencies, repeated classes, and inconsistent high school and college advising.

Solution: "Talk to your counselor to make sure you have the classes needed for the college you want to attend." *Malcolm*

"Have a calendar or binder where you keep all of your college information in chronological order; that way everything will go smoothly." *Candice*

Problem: Colleges are usually unaware of foster care students' unique support needs and of the various issues they face.

Solution: "Use the free counseling and health center that most campuses offer. Don't be afraid to talk about any problems you may be facing." *Damon*

Problem: Foster care students don't know how or where to get enough financial aid to pay for their college careers.

Solution: "Get to know professors, financial aid advisors, counselors, and support staff throughout campus. They want to help you!" *Nicki*

Problem: Foster care students don't know who to ask for advice or who to turn to for support.

Solution: "Go and sign up for some clubs! By joining extracurricular activities you will begin building friendships and have an outlet for the pressures of college." *Renee*

"Find a study group and stick with them. They really help you get better grades." *Brigit*

Free Online Resources

Orphan Foundation of America (OFA)
www.orphan.org
OFA provides scholarships for college and post-secondary education, as well as internships, virtual mentoring, care packages, and critical resources to guide foster teens to success.

Foster Care Alumni of America (FCAA)
www.fostercarealumni.org
Founded and led by alumni of the foster care system, FCAA connects the alumni community and transforms foster care policy and practice, ensuring opportunity for people in and from foster care.

Foster Club: The National Network for Young People in Foster Care
www.fosterclub.com
Foster Club has chapters and resources available in most states that can assist you and help provide a network of support. Just click on the "State-by-State" tab.

California Youth Connection (CYC)
www.calyouthconn.org/site/cyc
Guided, focused and driven by current and former foster youth with the assistance of other committed community members, CYC promotes the participation of foster youth in policy development and legislative change to improve the foster care system. CYC has chapters in counties throughout California.

California College Pathways
www.cacollegepathways.org
The goal of the California College Pathways is to increase the number of foster youth in California who enter higher education and achieve an academic or training outcome by expanding access to campus support programs. You can find out about resources, supports and college preparation opportunities.

College Goal Sunday
www.collegegoalsundayusa.org
College Goal Sunday provides free professional assistance filling out the FAFSA (Free Application for Federal Student Aid). Check out their special section on questions about the FAFSA for Foster Youth or Wards of the Court, along with information regarding state-wide student services, financial aid resources, admission requirements, and more! ■

GROWING UP, THE IDEA OF COLLEGE WAS MORE OF A DREAM

Ashley Roberts
College: Illinois Wesleyan
Hometown: St. Peters, MO

than it was a goal. I grew up in a broken home to say the least. At the age of 11 I was put in foster care, and although I was only there for 6 months, it is something that still impacts me today.

The pressure of going through "the system" was that I was seen as a statistic. According to the officials I am supposed to be just like my mom, but my need to succeed and show that I am my own person is what keeps me going.

Neither of my parents graduated from high school, let alone went to college, and before foster care, that was the path I was on. In foster care I learned that I did not have to have the same life my parents had. I was always smart, but it was in foster care that I started putting forth the effort to do my work and make the grades.

After foster care, I was put in the care of my aunt and uncle. By this time I knew I wanted to go to college. I didn't know much else about it, but I was determined to go. I knew I wanted to help kids like me.

When it came to looking at schools I had no idea what I was doing. I had every kind of article, pamphlet, and brochure that told me how to find a school, but my biggest fear was how I was going to pay for school.

In high school I participated in a program that guaranteed I would receive two free years at a 2 year institution of my choice in my state. Although it was a blessing, I chose to attend a four-year university to increase my opportunities. I had learned that if a school wanted you, they would meet your needs. Every school I applied to gave me wonderful financial aid packages. Since I had that worry out of the way, I could focus on the other aspects I was looking for in a school to make it the school of my dreams.

I want a better life for myself and college is just a stop on the road to my goal.

ASHLEY ROBERTS is a CSO Opportunity Scholarship winner. Ashley shares her college experiences and offers advice on the Opportunity Scholars blog.

Visit www.CSOCollegeCenter.org to follow the blog, sign up to become a CSO Opportunity Scholar, and have the chance to be a future Opportunity Scholarship winner and blogger yourself!

Opportunity Scholars

advice

CSO Opportunity Scholarship winners share their college experiences and offer advice on the Opportunity Scholars blog.

oh

OH SO MANY OPTIONS

Jenny Luong
College: Amherst College
Hometown: Oakland, CA

"Just think about your options. Where are you going to be happy? Where are you going to enjoy learning? For many of us, this is the first big choice we're going to make. Choose what seems right."
– If Time is Money, I'm SO Broke

Shaun Devlin
College: Washington and Lee University
Hometown: Canton, IL

"Even though you may have your heart set on one institution, realize that you have many options. There are several schools that fit your aspirations, whether your focus is in athletics, small class sizes, diverse student organizations, or academic prestige."
– The Big Decision

Joseph Dingman
College: Occidental College
Hometown: Pueblo, CO

"When applying to schools listen to others but also think for yourself. What you want is important, and it is your education on the line here."
– Do You Feel Like Time is Running Out?

Leah Jean-Louis
College: Swarthmore College
Hometown: Cambridge, MA

"As for deciding, I can also give you this advice: do you! When trying to decide which option is best or what path to choose, think of yourself and be selfish for once in your life. It's not about what your parents want or how many of your high school friends are going to a specific college."
– Look Ma I'm Going to College

Visit www.CSOCollegeCenter.org to follow the blog, sign up to become a CSO Opportunity Scholar, and have the chance to be a future Opportunity Scholarship winner and blogger yourself!

Opportunity Scholars

By Jose Arreola

Undocumented students *can* attend college

My teachers always told me that as long as I studied hard, got good grades and challenged myself academically, I could be anything I wanted to be. What they didn't know was that my immigration status would significantly limit the options I had available to me. I knew I would find a way. Last year I graduated from a prestigious private university, and now I'm helping other undocumented students in their pursuit of college.

If you're a college-bound undocumented student, here's my advice:

Know your opportunities and limitations

If you are an undocumented student, you *can* attend college in the United States. You will have additional challenges, but these challenges should not hinder you.

For most undocumented students, the biggest obstacle is financial: we do not qualify for federal and, in most cases, state financial aid; we cannot access government loans, grants or work-study programs; we are unable to legally earn money to support ourselves; and in some states we are forced to pay higher tuition at public colleges and universities. In addition to these financial challenges, we resist asking people for help because we're afraid of being deported or putting our families at risk.

The good news is that undocumented students can apply to and attend college. Your college applications will be processed even if you don't provide your social security number, citizenship, and residency status. Remember, you don't need to worry about revealing that you're undocumented. The confidentiality of your educational records—application *and* financial aid forms—is guaranteed by the Family Educational Rights and Privacy Act (FERPA), which covers both high schools and colleges.

In terms of paying for college, you will be eligible for private scholarships that do not require social security numbers or are willing to accept ITINs (individual tax identification numbers). You should consider attending local community colleges, which are generally more affordable and may enable you to save money while living at home. You should also consider applying to private colleges and universities. While private schools are generally more exclusive, they can provide significant financial assistance to undocumented students.

Understand policies that affect you

Check to see if your state has an in-state tuition policy for undocumented students. For example, in California, undocumented students can pay in-state tuition through AB540 as long as they meet certain requirements. Keep updated about pending federal legislation, like the DREAM Act, and pending legislation in your state. You should also get a thorough review of your immigration history to see if you have any possibilities to legalize. Check out E4FC's Online Case Analysis Service, which provides free and confidential analysis, referral, and support for undocumented students nationwide.

Get advice

Don't be afraid to ask for help. No one can make it to college alone. Undocumented students, especially, need to develop comprehensive support networks in order to get the necessary academic, financial, and emotional help we require.

Connect to students who have entered or graduated from college in your area. They'll remind you that you're not alone in this struggle, and be your best source of information and inspiration.

Don't *ever* take no for an answer. Be creative. Have courage and believe in yourself. There is *always* a path to pursue your dreams—your path may just be different and more complex than the one you originally envisioned. Even after college there are many options available to undocumented students, so don't let the thought of not being able to work stop you. ■

ABOUT EDUCATORS FOR FAIR CONSIDERATION (E4FC)

The mission of Educators for Fair Consideration (E4FC) is to help immigrant students realize the American dream of college and citizenship. E4FC provides scholarships, legal services, mentoring, and professional internships to immigrant students who have grown up in the United States but face challenges due to financial need and immigration status.

For more information, please visit www.e4fc.org.

BIO *Jose Arreola is Outreach Coordinator for Educators for Fair Consideration (E4FC). Jose was born in Durango, Mexico and came to the United States when he was four years old. He attended Santa Clara University, where he received a full scholarship. As an undocumented student himself, Jose utilizes his experiences to help empower and support other undocumented students across the country.*

HOMELESSNESS and COLLEGE EDUCATION aren't often discussed in the same sentence, and it is rarely positive.

For low-income students like us, it's enough of a challenge to get through high school. Being homeless presents its own crazy challenges. Your transcript reads like the CIA's most wanted, except, instead of moving from country to country, you move from city to city, county to county, or even state to state, often within the span of weeks or days. How is education even in the cards?! You don't even have steady food or shelter.

I don't remember even participating in the first grade, or finishing the second grade, 5th grade is a blur, 6th grade was a one month stint, 7th grade was speckled with absences, tardies, and unsatisfactories for late work or no work. In middle school, teachers thought I could care less about my education, and I let them believe that. I didn't want them to know I was homeless. But I wanted to learn, I loved to learn, I needed to learn.

But there was hope. It's not as easy as going "I'm homeless, let me in your college." I had to fight feelings of insecurity and anxiety, not to mention not knowing what the college process entailed. I didn't know where and how to apply. I applied to two colleges without knowing what the heck I was doing. I didn't know what kind of recommendations I needed, or if my teachers who only knew me a couple of semesters, knew enough about me. I didn't have a computer to apply to college! Often, it was the lack of these few resources that made my college process suffer.

It can be done though. The key is to seek help. You DO NOT have to do the college application process alone. Seek programs and resources designed to help low income kids. Ask your school about college prep programs. Upward Bound is one of many great programs that you can apply to as early as 9th grade. Find people who you admire, who went to college, and ask for their help. You wouldn't believe how helpful people can be once they know you want to go to college. I got where I am today because of two things—my inner drive and the help from caring adults who I looked up to as role models. Good, caring people will want to see you succeed, and they'll go out of their way to help you if you let it be known that you will do whatever it takes to succeed.

KHADIJAH WILLIAMS is a CSO Opportunity Scholarship winner. Khadijah shares her college experiences and offers advice on the Opportunity Scholars blog.

Visit www.CSOCollegeCenter.org to follow the blog, sign up to become a CSO Opportunity Scholar, and have the chance to be a future Opportunity Scholarship winner and blogger yourself!

Opportunity Scholars

By William R. Fitzsimmons

Many colleges, including Harvard, have embarked on new efforts to meet students' aspirations and ensure that talented students from all economic backgrounds can attend.

Even though my Catholic high school was only fifteen miles from Harvard, I had never set foot on the campus. Harvard was not well regarded in our blue-collar community, as it seemed an exclusive, unapproachable place where people like us would not be welcome.

Eventually, my curiosity got the better of me and I went for an interview and an overnight visit. I had a wonderful talk with my interviewer and all of the students with whom I stayed (some of them rich but not snobs) were friendly and interesting.

When I finally decided to go to Harvard in April, one of my recommenders, a brilliant history teacher, gave me a framed copy of a Latin phrase: "Illegitimis non Carborundum" – don't let the "punks" grind you down. He exhorted me to share my background – both religious and

Colleges Value Your Experience

economic – with my Harvard classmates. "You'll learn a lot there," he said, "but you can teach them a thing or two."

Today, there has never been so much opportunity for students to pursue the college of their dreams and share their backgrounds in the process. Many colleges, including Harvard, have embarked on new efforts to meet students' aspirations and ensure that talented students from all economic backgrounds can attend.

Harvard's new financial aid program that requires no family contribution from families with under a $60,000 annual income (and a greatly reduced contribution from families with incomes up to $180,000 as well as a policy that eliminates any loan requirement) has met with great success. And many other schools are following suit, with similar financial aid programs and no debt/ no loan promises to ensure access and success for all.

Colleges recognize that students from modest income backgrounds add to a dynamic college campus. In the classroom, discussions about unemployment, welfare reform, health care for the uninsured, public housing, mass transportation, and a wide range of issues take on meaning if there are people present who have been personally affected by the topics. I'd like to think I added to my college classmates' education by giving them a reality check, especially the occasional "clueless" rich kid who had no idea that most people had to worry about making ends meet on a day-to-day basis.

It is encouraging to observe how Harvard and many other institutions have become, over the years, much more inclusive of women, minority students and those from the other side of the tracks. It has been an exciting time and the changes have been stunning – leaving America in a much better position to realize the full talents of all its citizens. ■

Adapted from "Getting to Harvard," National Association for College Admission Counseling *Journal of College Admission*, Fall 2006

BIO *One of the country's most respected and well-known experts on undergraduate education and financial aid, William R. Fitzsimmons has been the Dean of Admissions and Financial Aid at Harvard College since 1986. He grew up in the Boston area and earned his A.B. ('67), Master's ('69), and Doctorate ('71) degrees from Harvard.*

By Jay Rosner

test prep Q&A

Q: Who should do test prep?

A: Any student who is willing to commit time and energy to improving his/her test scores should considering doing test prep, which might include a test prep course or tutoring.

Q: When should a student start preparing for the SAT and/or the ACT?

A: Some students start as early as freshman year, but I generally suggest that students start planning their preparation for the SAT or ACT the summer between sophomore and junior year. Most students will pick a target SAT or ACT test date occurring in the spring of their junior year, depending on the rest of their schedule. By taking the SAT or ACT in the spring of the junior year, the student has several opportunities to retake the test in the late spring or fall, if that is desirable.

Q: How much time does it take to prepare for these tests?

A: Students should prepare most intensively in the 6-8 weeks immediately prior to their target test date. Students can begin their study of vocabulary and brush up on basic arithmetic, algebra and geometry skills prior to that intensive test prep period.

Q: Are there low cost ways to prep?

A: There are two primary low-cost options for test prep available to everyone. The first is to use two books: a book featuring methods and techniques for answering test questions (like Princeton Review's Cracking the SAT), along with a book containing lots of real test questions (the College Board's Official SAT Study Guide). Copies of these books can be found in many libraries. The second option is to use one of the several free test prep programs on the internet.

Be careful with online prep — the official SAT (and ACT) are in pencil and paper format, and the online learning and practicing format is different from the actual testing experience. Some students have access to low cost test prep programs provided by their school or in their community.

Q: Can you share a tip, hint, or strategy for success?

A: Like any important performance experience, performance on a standardized test is enhanced by sharpening the skills tested. Test skills improve through a training program of regular, high quality practice on the material to be tested, and the most effective time to sharpen these skills is in the weeks immediately before the official test being targeted. Finally, it helps to have an excellent teacher directing your test prep.

BIO *Jay Rosner is an admissions test expert. As Executive Director of the Princeton Review Foundation, he specializes in preparing and coaching underrepresented minority students for tests such as the SAT, ACT, GMAT, GRE, MCAT and LSAT.*

Articles | Chapter 2

Who can help me?

Abigail Macias
College: Dartmouth College
Hometown: Sparks, NV

PUTTING A FACE ON SUCCESS

Winter terms at Dartmouth (8-9 weeks) are said to be the worst time to be on campus and by week 6, I was drained and wanted nothing more than to leave. Many of my friends went to Miami or Cancun for two weeks, but I knew I had to see my family and surround myself with their positive, cheerful energy.

While I was home, my high school counselor and English teacher invited me to speak to their students about campus life, schoolwork, traveling, extracurricular activities, old and new friendships, my future plans, and everything in between. They told me that I would talk to a group of sophomores in the morning but oddly enough, that was not the case.

Instead of staying for an hour, I ended up staying the whole day at Sparks High. After the first group of students, one group after another came in and asked me to talk to them, and so it went on until the dismissal bell rang. Questions came at me from left and right, questions that I had never asked myself. One student asked me if I always knew that I would attend college, another student asked me what would I have done had I not enrolled at Dartmouth, and another student asked me if I believed that she or any of her classmates could one day be in my position.

It took me a few minutes to answer these questions and I figured that the students probably realized that I was not prepared with notes. But afterwards, my teacher told me that many of the students said that they loved talking to me and wondered if I could stay a bit longer to discuss their individual college plans. She told me that while I may have been nervous, the students didn't catch any of it because "success needs a face."

Some first-generation college students leave their homes with dreams to "make it big" and regularly going back to their hometown may not be part of their plan. It is a pity that those people will never realize that they could "make it big" by making a big impact on budding first-generation college students. There are an incredible number of talented students with a lot of potential in schools that are labeled as "failing" and, if you have had the opportunity to attend college, it is crucial that you go back to them and show them that a college degree is possible.

Remember your roots, remember your responsibility.

ABIGAIL MACIAS is a CSO Opportunity Scholarship winner. Abigail shares her college experiences and offers advice on the Opportunity Scholars blog.

Visit www.CSOCollegeCenter.org to follow the blog, sign up to become a CSO Opportunity Scholar, and have the chance to be a future Opportunity Scholarship winner and blogger yourself!

Opportunity Scholars

By Tomika Ferguson

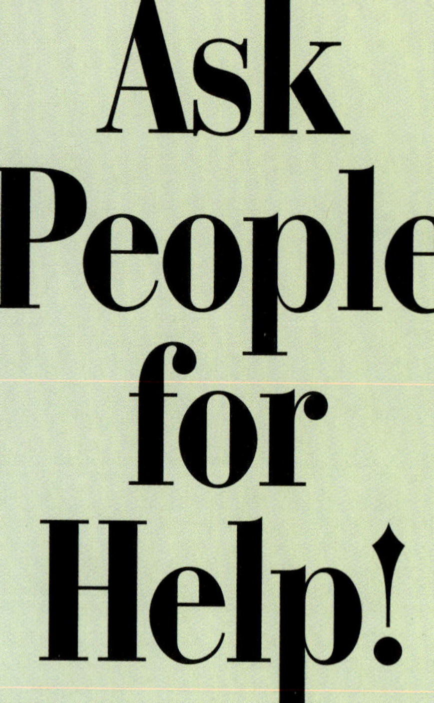

Ask People for Help!

When I was younger, I had aspirations to attend the University of Virginia. Despite not having a strong college going culture in my hometown, opportunities existed for me to accomplish my goals.

Every semester during high school, I signed up for classes that challenged me. I did not always get straight A's, but I did gain skills that prepared me for college. I was not the valedictorian of my high school class, but I was a risk taker.

My parents and I did not understand all of the specifics about applying to college since I was first in our family to do so. I took a personal risk and asked people for advice about the college application process. I didn't see asking for help as a sign of weakness, but rather getting advice was the most important step in following my dream to being accepted to the University of Virginia.

I didn't see asking for help as a sign of weakness, but rather getting advice was the most important step in following my dream.

Here are a few people who helped me throughout my college journey.

- **My English teacher** was the best writer I knew, and she helped me to organize my thoughts. I felt very confident in the essays I submitted with my college applications.

- **An older cousin** helped me craft a résumé, and it paid off big time! High school activities demonstrated my capacity for leadership and interests beyond academics.

- **My parents** didn't understand how to fill out the Free Application for Federal Student Aid (FAFSA) but with the help of my guidance counselor, we completed it well before the deadline.

As a high school student, you are surrounded by teachers, college counselors, family members and friends who want you to become successful. They will do everything they can to help you reach your goals.

It is hard to admit when you need help, but you have to be brave and take the first step and find people who have the answers you need. Without asking for help, I never would have accomplished my goal of graduating from the University of Virginia. ■

BIO *Tomika Ferguson is a doctoral candidate in the Higher Education & Student Affairs (HESA) program at Indiana University-Bloomington (IUB). Previously, she was a member of the National College Advising Corps (NCAC), a program that places recent college graduates in high schools with low college attendance in an attempt to reduce barriers to college access.*

By Johnavae Quinn

Finding a College Access Program

College Access Programs Can Help

You're not alone if you feel overwhelmed by the prospect of going to college. Fortunately, there is help for students and families through college access programs that exist in communities across the country to assist students and families in planning for their future.

These programs come in all different shapes and sizes, and most offer one-on-one college counseling, assistance filling out the necessary financial aid forms, mentorship, academic tutoring, college visits, scholarships, parental support groups and internship opportunities.

Here's a list of several web-based resources to help research programs.

When you've found a program that fits your needs, call or visit their office. These programs exist to serve students and will be happy to give you the help and information you need.

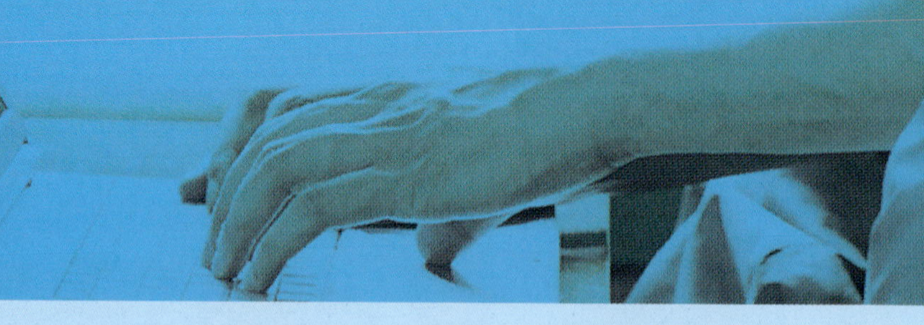

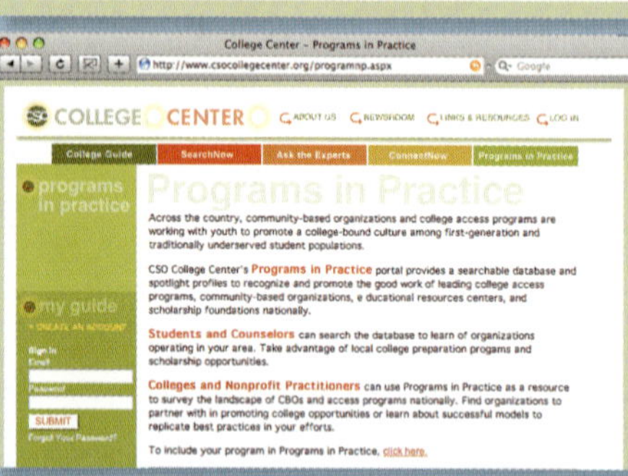

Programs in Practice on www.CSOCollegeCenter.org

www.csocollegecenter.org/programnp.aspx

www.CSOCollegeCenter.org is an online college search tool for first-generation and underserved college-bound students.The Programs in Practice portal is a searchable database with spotlight profiles promoting the good work of leading college access programs, community-based organizations, educational resources centers, and scholarship foundations from across the nation.

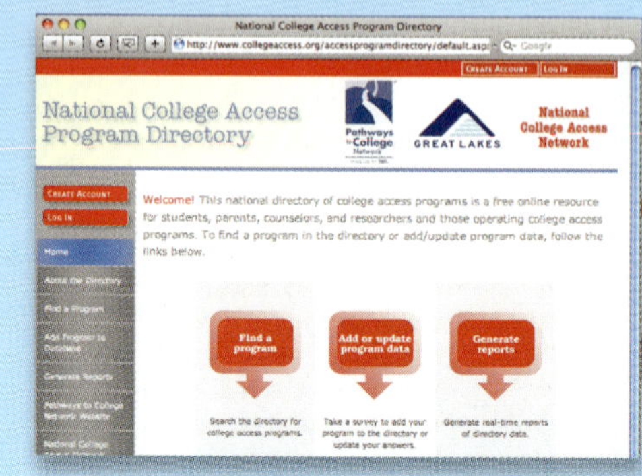

The National College Access Program Directory

www.collegeaccess.org/accessprogramdirectory/default.aspx

Developed by the National College Access Network (NCAN) and the Pathways to College Network (PCN), the National College Access Program Directory is a searchable online set of profiles of college access programs across the United States that help underserved students prepare, plan and pay for college.

National Partnership for Educational Access (NPEA)

www.educational-access.org

NPEA is a membership organization for programs working to provide underrepresented students with academic preparation, placement services and counseling, and ongoing support to ensure enrollment at and graduation from four-year colleges.Visit their website to learn about their over 180 members in 30 states.

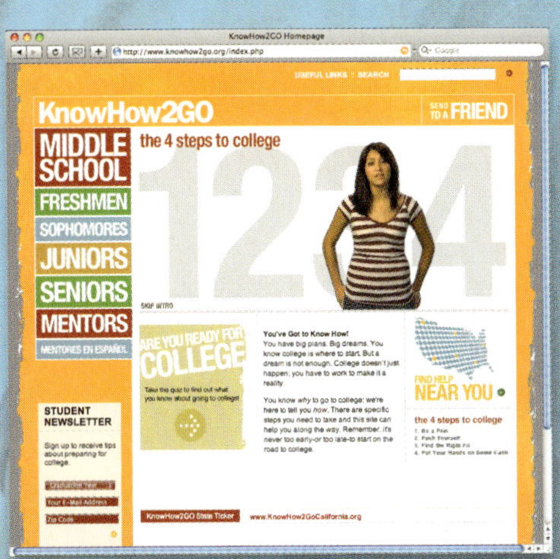

KnowHow2GO
www.knowhow2go.org

KnowHow2GO's "Find Help" page offers visitors a searchable map to help you connect with local resources.

Directory of TRIO and GEAR UP Programs
www.coenet.us

The Council for Opportunity in Education works in conjunction with colleges, universities, and agencies that host TRIO Programs to specifically help low-income students enter college and graduate and offers a directory of all TRIO and GEAR UP programs by state and institution.

BIO *Johnavae Quinn is the former Deputy Director of College Goal Sunday, a volunteer-run program that provides free expert advice about financial aid and filling out the Free Application for Federal Student Aid (FAFSA) in 37 states every January, February and March.*

REALITY CHANGERS SAVED MY LIFE.

Jesse Sanchez
College: Harvard University
Hometown: San Diego, CA

It took me away from the environment I was used to and placed me in an environment where students from all over San Diego who face the same obstacles I face were working towards the same goal—college. I didn't feel alone in the struggle anymore. I felt like I was working towards something that actually mattered. Reality Changers helped me realize the importance of working hard, the importance of determination, and the importance of a higher education.

Reality Changers also gave me hope. I can't count how many times I was told that I wasn't going to amount to anything because of where I came from, where I grew up, or how I looked. After hearing this for so long, I really began to believe it. I felt that I could never amount to anything because of my background. No one else in my family went to college, why should I? Reality Changers helped me realize that I could actually make something of myself. It gave me the tools necessary to succeed and helped me move closer to realizing my full potential. Reality Changers helped me learn to believe in myself.

Reality Changers helps you believe by giving you the chance to prove yourself. If you get a 3.5 gpa or above, you earn a scholarship to UCSD Academic Connections where you can take a college course for college credit before even graduating from high school. This is an opportunity that I would have never had if it were not for Reality Changers. Because I was able to succeed at Academic Connections, I was that much more confident in my ability to make it to college. It made me feel like I was worthy of a college education, and that it was actually possible for me to go to college.

Reality Changers puts you in an environment where the students are driven and ready to do whatever it takes to get to college. It makes you feel like you are a part of a family, and helps you stay driven. Whenever I feel like just giving up, I think back to all my friends at Reality Changers and how hard they're working and how they are counting on me to work just as hard.

We are fighting an unfair fight and Reality Changers helps us make the fight a little more even.

JESSE SANCHEZ is a CSO Opportunity Scholarship winner. Jesse shares his college experiences and offers advice on the Opportunity Scholars blog.

Visit www.CSOCollegeCenter.org to follow the blog, sign up to become a CSO Opportunity Scholar, and have the chance to be a future Opportunity Scholarship winner and blogger yourself!

Opportunity Scholars

advice

CSO Opportunity Scholarship winners share their college experiences and offer advice on the Opportunity Scholars blog.

SOS: SEEK OUT SUPPORT

Angelica Robinson
College: Dillard University
Hometown: New Orleans, LA

"Being a first-generation college student, it is imperative that I seek guidance, branch out to grasp what I need to succeed in my environment. I've realized that it is true that everyone needs someone in their corner."
– Second Semester Freshman: Through the Storm

Abigail Macias
College: Dartmouth College
Hometown: Sparks, NV

"ASK, ASK, ASK! Don't be afraid to ask questions! You may think that you'll look dumb because your classmates seem to know what they're doing or where they're headed. But, you'll only hurt yourself by not getting the information you need."
– Dumb Questions?

Jesse Sanchez
College: Harvard University
Hometown: San Diego, CA

"Not having a mentor can leave you without a sense of direction—you need someone there to go to for advice, to keep you motivated, and to help you out in times of need. It is very important to find this person in your life early on so they can help you make the right decisions from the beginning."
– Got Mentors?

DaLonn Pearson
College: So. Connecticut State
Hometown: New Haven, CT

"Ask questions even if you think it's silly. No question is too silly. Remember this is your education. Get the most out of it."
– Something Different…Life

blog

Visit www.CSOCollegeCenter.org to follow the blog, sign up to become a CSO Opportunity Scholar, and have the chance to be a future Opportunity Scholarship winner and blogger yourself!

Opportunity Scholars

By Karin Elliot

Starting Early on the Path to College

One of the best resources to help you achieve your goal of attending college is an *educational access program.* Found all across the country, these programs give you academic support after-school, academic enrichment during the summer and will start working with you during middle school.

College-Prep Programs

Do you want to take academic and elective classes, participate in leadership activities, and community service? If so you might want to learn about college-prep programs that can help you get ready for college—either after school or during the summer.

EXAMPLES:

Breakthrough Collaborative—With 35 sites across the country serving 2,700 students. Breakthrough's core belief is that it is "cool to be smart," and the program attempts to establish this belief in its student participants by setting high standards and supporting their educational goals. Students begin in Breakthrough programs as early as 5th grade and commit to involvement for a minimum of two years.

Aim High—With 12 sites in California serving more than 1,000 students, Aim High supports students starting after their 5th or 6th grade year, and students must commit to a minimum of three summers. Aim High prepares students for success in school and ensures they have an appreciation for community and an awareness of issues that affect their lives.

Placement Programs

Do you need scholarship assistance in order to attend a high-quality independent high school? If so you might want to learn about placement programs that can connect you with very generous financial aid packages and support your enrollment at competitive college-preparatory high schools.

EXAMPLES:

The Steppingstone Academy—Students in the Boston Public School system can get support from to apply to the best high schools in the city. Students who apply must demonstrate a commitment to their education and show academic promise. Steppingstone also supports students and their families as they navigate the process of choosing and applying to these rigorous schools. The Steppingstone Foundation has affiliate sites in Hartford and Philadelphia.

Daniel Murphy Scholarship Fund—This placement program in Chicago provides four-year high school scholarships and educational support, and has a number of core activities such as tutoring, mentoring, and summer opportunities.

Things to remember about educational access programs:

- No matter where you live, you can find one that will meet your needs
- They are free, but require a significant time commitment
- Programs start as early as 5th grade and will continue to support you in high school
- During the application process, you will describe your goals and share why you think accessing quality education is important for your future

How to find programs:

- Talk to your school counselor or advisor and explain what you are looking for
- Talk with your parents or guardian about the difference a program could make in your life
- Visit the National Partnership for Educational Access website at **www.educational-access.org** and search the programs that are members of this group

NATIONAL PARTNERSHIP FOR EDUCATIONAL ACCESS

BIO *Karin Elliott is director of the National Partnership for Educational Access (NPEA), a membership organization for programs working in collaboration with independent and public college preparatory schools to provide underrepresented students with academic preparation, placement services and counseling and ongoing support to ensure enrollment at four-year colleges.*

Find a TRIO program in your community

TRIO is a set of federally-funded college opportunity programs that motivate and support students from disadvantaged backgrounds in their pursuit of a college degree. Over 850,000 low-income, first-generation students and students with disabilities—from sixth grade through college graduation—are served by more than 2,800 programs nationally.

The TRIO programs have been successfully assisting students prepare for, attend and graduate from college in every state and territory in America since 1965.

TRIO programs provide:

- academic tutoring
- personal counseling
- mentoring
- financial aid and scholarship assistance
- summer programs opportunities
- cultural enrichment and educational trips
- opportunities to visit colleges
- other supports to help you enter college be successful once enrolled

TRIO students

Patrick Ewing, basketball hall of famer

Angela Bassett, Oscar nominated actress

Viola Davis, Oscar nominated actress

John Quinones, award-winning journalist

Gwendolynne Moore, U.S. Member of Congress

Shelley Berkley, U.S. Member of Congress

Ronald E. McNair, astronaut who died in the 1996 space-shuttle tragedy

TRIO Programs at a Glance

Upward Bound helps youth prepare for higher education. Participants receive instruction in literature, composition, mathematics, and science on college campuses after school, on Saturdays and during the summer. Currently, 964 projects are in operation throughout the United States.

Upward Bound Math & Science helps students from low-income families to strengthen math and science skills. In addition, students learn computer technology as well as English, foreign language and study skills. Currently, 117 projects are serving students throughout the country.

Talent Search projects serve young people in grades six through 12. In addition to counseling, participants receive information about college admissions requirements, scholarships and various student financial aid programs. More than 363,000 students from families with incomes under $33,075 (where neither parent graduated from college) are enrolled in 466 Talent Search TRIO projects to better understand their educational opportunities and options.

Student Support Services projects work to enable low-income students to stay in college until they earn their baccalaureate degrees. Participants receive tutoring, counseling and remedial instruction. Students are now being served at 947 colleges and universities nationwide.

The **Ronald E. McNair Postbaccalaureate Achievement** program, named in honor of the astronaut who died in the 1986 space-shuttle explosion, is designed to encourage low-income students and minority undergraduates to consider careers in college teaching as well as prepare for doctoral study. Students who participate in this program are provided with research opportunities and faculty mentors.

The Council for Opportunity in Education can help you find a TRIO program in your community and join the over three million who have already completed their college degree with the help of TRIO. Visit www.coenet.us *for more information and check out a directory of all TRIO programs by state and institution.*

GEAR UP Can Help Too!

GEAR UP Gaining Early Awareness and Readiness for Undergraduate Programs) is another federally funded grant program helping students from impoverished and underserved backgrounds get the assistance they need to get into college, gain access to the necessary scholarship money, and be prepared for the academic environment of college. GEAR UP starts working with students in middle school and continues throughout high school. GEAR UP's programs are in 47 states, the District of Columbia, and three territories.

Not sure if GEAR UP is in your community? Visit www.gearupdata.org *sponsored by the National Council for Community and Education Partnerships (NCCEP)*

By Mary Lee Hoganson

HOW TO Use Your High School Counselor

School counselors are one of the best sources of support for college-bound students. Whatever grade you are in, now is the time to start helping your counselor get to know you and your college dreams.

Introduce yourself and state clearly that it is your definite goal to attend college. Let your counselor know that, regardless of your test scores or grades to date, you are highly motivated.

Also, make sure to tell your counselor about yourself: your interests, activities, college and career goals and family background — including what your parents do and whether or not anyone in your family has attended college. With this initial meeting as a good starting point, your counselor can help you plot a successful course for college.

Top 10 items to cover with your counselor:

1) Plan classes that will prepare you for college.
2) Review your academic record and suggest areas that need improvement.
3) Identify the questions you should be asking, like Do I want to stay near home? Does the college have my major? How important is size?
4) Get information about specific colleges and universities.
5) Identify opportunities like college fairs, weekend or summer programs on college campuses (often free for first-generation or low-income students), internships, or community college classes open to high school students.
6) Register for college admission tests and get fee waivers if your family can't afford to pay for tests.
7) Write a letter of recommendation to colleges or universities.
8) Complete and submit college applications carefully and on time and ask colleges to waive application fees.
9) Figure out how to pay for college.
10) Compare offers of admission and financial aid from all of your colleges.

There are a few other very important things to remember about working with your school counselor:

- Most school counselors have many, many students who they want to help. So make appointments early, show up on time and submit forms that require counselor completion well in advance of due dates.
- Make backup copies of everything you mail or give to your counselor.
- Make sure that you keep your counselor "in the loop" in terms of what you are hearing from colleges. If there are any problems which arise, your counselor can act as your direct advocate with colleges.
- If you think it would be helpful, try to schedule a meeting with your counselor AND your parent(s). There are parts of the college process for which you will need a lot of help from them, such as completing the financial aid applications.
- Be sure to thank your counselor for assistance given. When you have made it successfully through the college selection and admission process, thank your counselor with a handwritten note (as well as any teachers who helped).

BIO *Mary Lee Hoganson has over 35 years experience as a high school counselor, 25 of those years focused on college counseling. She served as President of the National Association for College Admission Counseling in 2007.*

By Joni Bissell

TRANSFORM THE TRAJECTORY OF YOUR LIFE

SUMMER EXPERIENCES CAN PROPEL YOU TO COLLEGE

Every summer, seniors meet with their mentor and me, as their college advisor, to reflect on their two and a half years participating in Summer Search, a leadership development program providing students with year-round mentoring, life-changing summer experiences, college advising, and a lasting support network. Ninety-one percent of these low-income students head to college each fall and much of their courage and willingness to take this step is emboldened by the experiences of their summer trips.

During a recent meeting, one senior told me that he never thought he would go to college. He assumed he would work to provide for his siblings; a responsibility that he shouldered from a very young age. His most proud reflection, aside from his college destination, was initiating a family meeting the day before, where he talked with his siblings about their family's dynamics and history. He was, in effect, passing on responsibility in a thoughtfully mature way, which freed him to find comfort in leaving home for college soon.

We spoke about his first summer wilderness trip and the culminating hike when each student in the group was offered a choice, poetically the "hard road" or the "easy road." He took the "hard road."His second summer trip was an academic program. He fell in love with architecture and was able to experience living with a variety of peers on a college campus. Both experiences, holistically combined with Summer Search mentoring, transformed the trajectory of his life.

Summer experiential programs contribute to student success by providing an opportunity to take healthy risks and experience unfamiliar settings. Students learn to navigate social challenges as these summer experiences often consist of more wealthy, less diverse students, an experience that can be both alienating and intimidating. The courage it takes to be vulnerable in these situations is what defines their immense personal growth. Students return home with new confidence and broader options. They and their families begin to bridge the dramatic distances between college and home life.

Combined with thoughtful mentoring and best possible preparation to ensure success, summer experiences offer students practice for challenges similar to those they will face on campus. And in doing so, develop skills to be resilient leaders and voices in college, their communities and beyond. ■

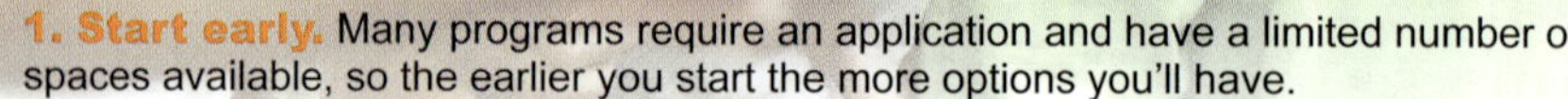

TIPS for Finding a Summer Experience

Summer Search runs offices in Boston, New York City, North San Francisco Bay, Philadelphia, San Francisco, Seattle, and Silicon Valley. If you're a student in one these cities, visit www.summersearch.org for more information.

If not, here are a few tips for researching and finding the best summer program for you:

1. Start early. Many programs require an application and have a limited number of spaces available, so the earlier you start the more options you'll have.

2. Check local colleges and universities. Many schools offer pre-college initiatives over the summer that give you a chance to preview the school while exploring your academic interests.

3. Ask your counselor or mentor. Counselors, community leaders, or mentors may be able to point you to local programs tailored specifically to high school students.

4. Search online. Tailor your search to the type of program you are interested in, and the geographic location where you are looking to spend your summer.

5. Ask for financial aid. Summer experiential programs cost money, but many will offer financial assistance and scholarships to those who need it. Just ask!

BIO *Joni Bissell is College Director Bay Area for Summer Search San Francisco.*

CHANGE YOUR LIFE IN ONE SUMMER

You've just made it through a year of high school. So, what are your plans for this summer? What about going to college? Every summer there are programs held at college campuses across the country. They range by various interests, activities, and academic areas. Some are science programs, while others enhance artistic ability or musicality, but all of them are right at your fingertips.

So, now you might be thinking, how can I afford to go to a summer program, I don't have the money? Many summer programs such as MITES (Minority Introduction to Engineering and Science) and QuestBridge affiliated summer programs offer full scholarships for all students accepted into their programs. You could attend a program the summer following your junior or even sophomore year of high school for free!

While these programs may not sound like the most exciting thing to do over your summer, let me share my experience with you.

As a high school junior, I applied to the MITES program on the campus of MIT. It is a seven week program in Science and Engineering that is aimed towards helping disadvantaged minorities and/or students from low-income backgrounds excel in the field of science. While at MIT, I was given the chance to complete research in genomics at the Broad Institute of MIT and Harvard. My research team dealt with Single Nucleotide Polymorphisms in genetic disorders such as Cystic Fibrosis and early onset Breast Cancer. Prior to the summer, I had no idea what that even meant!

Besides doing work and taking courses, I also explored the city of Boston on weekends, went to theme parks, dances, and dinners. I spent that summer at MIT living on my own and learned how to balance my time. I got a chance to experience what college might be like before actually getting into college.

Lysa Vola
College: Williams College
Hometown: Jensen Beach, FL

My point is not that all of you should apply to the MITES program, but rather, that you should consider finding out more information about summer programs like MITES. Summer programs provide you with opportunities to discover what it's like to be in a college setting prior to actually applying to or attending college. Summer programs also offer high school students an edge in the college admissions process. They are looked highly upon, because many of them are a lot of work, and prove your dedication and skill. Completing the program successfully makes you stand out from amongst thousands of high school college applicants who didn't take the opportunity to explore, learn, or take their summer seriously. Most are only a few weeks long, so you will still have time to be home and relax with friends before school starts!

So before you turn away an application to spend your summer away studying, consider how it might change your life, the new adventures you might be able to take, and the people you may meet. Never turn down an opportunity, because they are just that, something that you either take or leave, but ultimately can never be replaced!

LYSA VOLA is a CSO Opportunity Scholarship winner. Lysa shares her college experiences and offers advice on the Opportunity Scholars blog.

Visit www.CSOCollegeCenter.org to follow the blog, sign up to become a CSO Opportunity Scholar, and have the chance to be a future Opportunity Scholarship winner and blogger yourself!

Opportunity Scholars

By Bob Craves

Money and Mentors: Essentials to the College Process

If you want to be prepared for whatever may lie ahead, college is the first step and you should do all you can to get scholarship money, find a mentor and make sure you're taking the right steps to graduate.

COLLEGE SUCCESS FOUNDATION

So where do I start finding money and mentors?

Look everywhere for scholarship money

College is expensive. But you must look at it as an investment in yourself. In your search to afford college, look everywhere you can for financial aid.

There are several kinds of financial aid, scholarships being one of them. Think of scholarships (and grants) as free money – money you don't have to pay back. A person or organization has chosen to invest in you and is paying you to go to school, learn all you can, and graduate with a degree.

You don't need to be a world-class athlete or have a 4.0 grade point average. If you come from a low-income family, you could be eligible for many need-based scholarships that have very little to do with your performance in high school. You automatically qualify because of your family's financial situation. The largest of all is the Pell Grant which is a government program that could award you over $5,000 a year for every year you are in college.

Don't forget the colleges and universities to which you want to attend. Contact financial aid offices at the schools you are interested in and ask about financial aid opportunities and how to qualify/apply for them. Be sure they recognize you as a face or a voice on the phone, and not just a piece of paper in a pile of many.

Find a mentor

You've heard the expression "don't go it alone." Well, that couldn't be truer during your college search and application process. A mentor can provide you with a safety net for when the college-going process gets tough.

Find someone who knows about the college process so you have a "go to" person when you have questions. And you will have questions – many of them! If you are having trouble finding the right mentor, try asking teachers, coaches, employers, and your contacts at youth and faith-based organizations to which you belong.

My wife and I have mentored young people going to college, and have known others who have found mentoring to be very helpful. In fact, in my life, I have had the good fortune of having a mentor myself. I have learned as much from the students I've mentored, as they have learned from me.

College is a growing experience that sets the stage for the rest of your life. Enjoy it! ■

BIO *Bob Craves is the co-founder, chairman, and CEO of the College Success Foundation, an organization providing college scholarships and mentoring to low-income, high-potential students in Washington State and the District of Columbia. Prior to CSF, Bob was one of the founding officers of the Costco Wholesale Corporation.*

Articles | Chapter 3

How do I find the right fit?

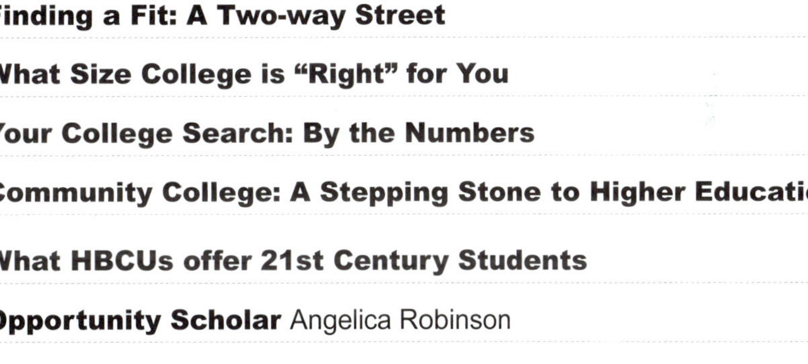

By Michelle D. Gilliard, Ph.D.

get engaged in Finding the right fit

A good college education enables students to develop the talents and skills they will use to pursue careers and explore other interests and hobbies. What you learn depends on the educational opportunities your college provides and how you take advantage of them.

So how do you find a college that will maximize your learning potential?

Don't let size fool you!

Smaller colleges, medium-sized universities and large institutions alike are capable of providing students with high-quality learning experiences in which students are required to become actively engaged in their learning. Instead of college size, think about which school environment will best develop your ability to reason, to solve complex problems, and to perform at higher levels. Finding the right fit requires you to identify the type of learning environment where you will be successful.

Review curricular offerings

A careful review of an institution's course requirements in both major concentration and general education courses is a good way to decide if the institution provides an active learning environment. See if you are required to complete a certain number of hours of community service in order to graduate, or if you are provided the opportunity to pursue internships at businesses, government entities and community agencies.

Get to know the institution

The final, and perhaps most important, step to finding a "right fit" institution is to connect with the institution directly. If visiting the campus is possible, go! Talk to students, talk to faculty, take a tour from the admissions office, sit in on a class, ask to spend the night in a residence hall, visit the library and the student union. Do anything and everything to learn about the school, its students and the academic and social environment.

If visiting the campus is not an option, go on-line and watch a video tour of the campus. Send questions and consider the answers.

Get started!

Finding an institution that provides the right fit works best when you take the time to develop a short list of institutions that (1) offer majors in your areas of interest, (2) provide you with multiple opportunities to become actively engaged in your own learning, and (3) are focused on creating an environment where students from a variety of backgrounds and experiences can be successful.

Ultimately, finding the right college fit is also about taking time to think about why you want a college education and what you hope to do with your life. A college that both challenges you and supports your educational and social development is the type of college that will lead to your success.

BIO Michelle D. Gilliard, Ph.D. is Senior Director for Workforce Development and Education at the Walmart Foundation.

By Dr. Larry D. Shinn

FINDING A FIT: A TWO-WAY STREET

"Which is the right college for me?"
"Where will I find the major I want to study?"
"What college will be the right fit?"
With colleges asking similar questions about the students who apply, you will find that your "fit" with a college is a two-way street.

What should you be looking for?

Surprisingly, more than half of college students who declare a major when they arrive as freshmen change their major one or more times before they graduate! So, selecting a college that has the major you want to study is not a sufficient reason when deciding the best college fit.

There is one consideration that all students should make in deciding the "fit" of a college: its capacity to provide an educational environment that promotes life-long learning. Even if the colleges that you are considering have programs specialized for a specific career path (e.g. fashion design, civil engineering, architecture, or teaching), every one of those professions will require continued learning beyond college.

The best fit is ultimately the college whose learning environment is diverse and where you are challenged to think and grow beyond your current interests. From internships to undergraduate research and study abroad programs, your college experience should expand your abilities and horizons in ways you cannot do yourself.

What are colleges looking for?

Again, "fit" is a two-way street. An important ingredient to your fit for a college is what that college is looking for in the students it seeks to admit.

When you are trying to decide what college best fits you, you need to ask what that college is seeking in the students it admits. Some colleges focus more on academic qualifications than others. Some colleges use standardized tests scores like the SAT or ACT as an initial screen and others don't require such scores at all. Some colleges focus more on mathematically and scientifically talented students (e.g. engineering and technical colleges) while others seek well-rounded students who want to study a discipline or major in a broader educational context (e.g., liberal arts colleges).

How do your life experiences and aspirations, previous academic studies and accomplishments, and career interests and life-long learning needs "fit" with the mission, academic programs, and learning environment of the colleges you are considering? These are the questions that both you and the colleges to which you apply will be asking to decide your mutual fit.

Conclusion

In the end, the "fit" between you and a college you are considering is about maximizing the learning you will receive. Regardless of the college or university you attend or what your major or your chosen career is, you should graduate having the ability to think, speak, and to act well—an education of your total person.

Dr. Larry D. Shinn is president of Berea College, a liberal arts college in Berea, Kentucky that provides every admitted student a four-year tuition scholarship and the opportunity to work on campus to assist with costs of room and board.

By Karen Gross

What Size College is "Right" for You

Think about what makes you most comfortable, what energizes you . . .

How can you know whether you are better suited to a larger university or a small liberal arts college? Well, instead of looking at size as the central dividing line among colleges, think instead about who you are (and who you will become)—as a person and as a learner. Think about what makes you most comfortable, what energizes you, what environment will enable you to thrive over the next four years.

Let me share with you three prominent myths about college size.

MYTH ONE: YOU MUST GO TO A COLLEGE THAT IS BIGGER THAN YOUR HIGH SCHOOL. FALSE!

The critically important differences between college and high school are NOT based on size. Colleges, whatever their size, are engaged in a different enterprise than high school. At colleges, the number and breadth of courses is vast and unlike most high school curricula. You will have lots of opportunities over your college career to select among the courses and to specialize in what most interests you.

At college, you get to focus on what most interests you, what most captures your imagination. This can happen in many academic settings, large or small.

MYTH TWO: STUDENTS GET LOST AT LARGE UNIVERSITIES AND BECOME A NUMBER NOT A NAME. FALSE!

All colleges, regardless of size, work very hard to help their students find niches within their communities. For some students, that "small" feel comes from athletics where student-athletes bond with each other and with the coaching staff. For other students, closeness comes through clubs and organizations. For some, it appears through shared academic interests where students connect with others in courses and projects.

Rather than the size of a college, the more important thing is for you to find ways to connect—to other students, to faculty members, to the community. You can do that at all colleges, large and small.

MYTH THREE: SMALL COLLEGES OFFER LIMITED OPPORTUNITIES. FALSE!

Small colleges and large universities all offer amazing opportunities—more opportunities than one student could experience fully in four years. What is important in assessing the opportunities on a college or university campus is not size but the philosophy and vision of the college and its leadership.

So, visit campuses. Walk around without an admissions guide for a while. Make sure you sit in on a class or two. Speak with students in the halls and in the dining facilities. Listen to what is happening when students interact with faculty and staff. Meet coaches. See if you can sense and feel the college's ambition and goals.

. . . what environment will enable you to thrive

Conclusion

Think about selecting the size of a college this way: If you were shopping for clothing, it is likely that there are many choices, many things that fit at many prices, with many styles, in many colors. But, some of the items selected will just feel right to you. They may not feel right to your friends or parents. But, you will find something you can see yourself wearing.

The same is true for colleges. There are many, many choices. The goal is to choose the places that feel right to you. ■

BIO *Karen Gross is the President of Southern Vermont College, a small private liberal arts college located in Bennington, Vermont.*

SIZE QUIZ 

WHAT SIZE COLLEGE IS OPTIMAL FOR YOU

Of course, some students will be happy and thrive in any academic setting. But this quiz will help you determine if you are best suited to small colleges (1,500 or fewer students) or larger universities (over 15,000 students).

There are two truisms about the choices confronting college-aged students: No one school is right for every student (even a stellar place), and there is always more than one right school for each student. So, use this quiz as a way of thinking about college size.

1. Are you one who has experienced freedom at home and in school and can handle it well, avoiding peer pressure and bad choices when confronted with limited oversight and supervision?

❒ YES ❒ NO ❒ MAYBE

2. Are you one for whom structure and personal contact will be beneficial and appealing because you thrive in a situation where you want and appreciate support from teachers, coaches, close friends, and mentors?

❒ YES ❒ NO ❒ MAYBE

3. Are you one who can make decisions easily (courses, athletics, after-school activities) and enjoys the decision making process without parental or institutional oversight and steering?

❒ YES ❒ NO ❒ MAYBE

4. Are you one for whom choosing among options takes time, requires advice or feedback from third parties to reach a decision, and for whom second-guessing or indecision is a common trait?

❒ YES ❒ NO ❒ MAYBE

5. Are you able to advocate for yourself, ask the right questions (and have experience doing this in school and in the community), identify problems and then get the right answers and solutions?

❒ YES ❒ NO ❒ MAYBE

6. Are you shy, laid-back or re-active, a person who accepts results and situations even if they are not optimal?

❒ YES ❒ NO ❒ MAYBE

7. Are you someone who can easily engage and find opportunities, friendships and adult relationships within their school and community, most particularly if you are younger than those around them?

❒ YES ❒ NO ❒ MAYBE

8. Are you one who prefers deep engagement in one activity to find your sense of place or for whom engagement (with people and opportunities) takes more time and does not come naturally?

❒ YES ❒ NO ❒ MAYBE

How to score the results:

There are no right or wrong answers to this quiz. Your preference to one environment is not a value judgment about you; instead, it is an assessment of how you function and what might optimize your college success and happiness.

QUESTIONS 1, 3, 5 and 7

"Yes" answers suggest you are likely suited to larger colleges and universities.

"No" answers suggest you may be better suited to smaller colleges and universities.

"Maybe" answers suggest you take a deeper look at whether a large college or university will be a comfortable fit for you—it probably is.

QUESTIONS 2, 4, 6 and 8

"Yes" answers suggest you will likely be well suited to smaller colleges and universities.

"No" answers suggest you may be better suited to larger colleges and universities.

"Maybe" answers suggest you take a deeper look at whether a smaller college or university will be a comfortable fit for you—it probably is.

A combination of answers suggests you think about your personality and how it might relate to different college size to determine the right fit for you.

By Emily Anderer

Your college search:
By the numbers

Eventually, I realized that to understand the strengths and weaknesses of a school I needed to look at its numbers and statistics.

I was woefully uninformed when I began my college search process. Living in Utah, I knew about most of the universities in my state but very little about schools elsewhere. I didn't know the difference between a public and a private college or what a liberal arts school was, and I don't think I was even clear on the difference between undergraduate and graduate school. The most difficult part of my college search was struggling to determine the quality of colleges I had never heard about previously.

Eventually, I realized that to understand the strengths and weaknesses of a school I needed to look at its numbers and statistics. This wasn't the most fun part of my college process, but good solid research helped me to make informed decisions.

Here are some guidelines I followed to identify and interpret college numbers and statistics:

Admissions rate - The lower a school's admission rate, the more competitive the school is considered to be to get into. For example, Harvard's admissions rate is around 7%—only one out of 14 students who apply will be admitted. It's good to aim high and apply to some schools where the odds are you may not be admitted, but also apply to some schools where the admissions rate is in your favor.

SAT and ACT range - Looking at the standardized test scores of admitted applicants is a good way to evaluate the academic ability of the student body. Compare your test scores to the school's median test scores—the 25th to 75th percentile of admitted students—to get the best idea of your admissibility.

Financial aid - Financial aid is money you get to make up the difference between the cost of attending a college and your family's ability to pay. Look for schools that have need-blind admissions, by which students are admitted regardless of their ability to pay for tuition on their own.

Merit scholarships - Schools give merit scholarships to reward academic accomplishment, particularly when a student's grades or test scores may be competitive enough for them to be admitted at a more selective institution. You may have a good chance of being offered a merit scholarship if you apply to a school where your grades or test scores are above those of their average students.

First-year retention rate - This percentage describes the number of enrolled freshmen who re-enroll as sophomores the following year. Be wary if a high percentage of the student body doesn't return for their second year. Clearly the school is not providing students something they want or need.

Six-year graduation rate - Whether students failed to graduate from a school because they transferred, dropped out, or failed to complete requirements, this is one of the most important clues to understanding the quality of a school. If this percentage is low, the school is not adequately supporting students to ensure graduation.

Don't just fall into a college because you didn't do enough research. I'm enormously thankful that I put in the time and hard work to research, identify and gain admittance to my dream school—a liberal arts college in upstate New York that none of my family or friends had ever heard of but which was perfect for me. Don't settle on a college just because you are unaware of what else is out there.

Use the numbers to help you find a college that fits your interests and needs. You won't regret it! ■

BIO *Emily Anderer is a gradute of Hamilton College in Clinton, New York and a past intern with Center for Student Opportunity.*

By Kristie Rueff, M.Ed

Community College: A Stepping Stone to Higher Education

There is more than one path to a college degree. For many students, attending a four-year college or university right out of high school is not an option. If you find yourself in this situation and you're thinking your chances of going to college are over, think again!

Depending on your personal situation, a community college can be a great option after high school. They offer the chance to save money on classes while living at home, getting a better idea of what you want to study without committing to a major, and getting some basic class credits out of the way.

Most importantly, after attending and doing well at a community college for two years, you can (and should!) transfer to a four-year college or university to pursue your bachelor's degree. Just because you attend a community college does not mean your education ends there—it should just be the beginning.

Check out Kristie's story about her successful transition from a community college to a four-year university.

BIO *Kristie Rueff is Assistant Director, Recruiting and Admissions for University of Southern California's Rossier School of Education. She holds a Bachelor's degree in English and Master's in Education, both from USC.*

Thriving in the Transfer Process.

Attending a community college was a choice I made early in life. I attended Fullerton Community College for the accessibility, affordability and diversity.

Shortly after I enrolled, my mailbox was flooded with invitations to join student organizations. The Transfer Achievement Program (TAP) flyer stood out because the program guaranteed general education courses, student-centered instruction, peer-support and transfer resources for students interested in transferring to a four-year college or university after they graduated from Fullerton. I immediately phoned the counselor to apply for TAP and was accepted.

I met regularly with my TAP faculty counselor to discuss four-year university options. My heart was set on the University of Southern California (USC). At the time, Fullerton did not provide a general education course list to transfer to USC. So, I took things into my own hands. Every semester I studied the course catalog, Associate of Arts requirements, and an antiquated USC transfer policy to build my class schedule. I highlighted, penned and notated every resource. Then, in spring 2004 I graduated with my Associates of Arts degree, and in June I was admitted to USC!

As I transitioned from Fullerton to USC, I learned that I needed to take more initiative towards getting involved and reaching my academic goals. A few weeks after classes began at USC, the university hosted an involvement fair. At the fair I signed up for Troy Camp, a local program that recruited undergraduates to mentor children in the area. Working with Troy Camp gave me an opportunity to bond with my peers and foster friendships that became imperative to my support.

I also realized that I would have to become a more active student in order to succeed in my classes. The faculty at USC encouraged students to take initiative versus Fullerton's hands-on approach. I met with faculty during their office hours and asked questions after class.

My experiences at Fullerton and USC were affected by the support systems I cultivated with students and faculty. Fullerton gave me the resources to transfer to a four-year university, and USC taught me to take charge of my future. The colleges were different, yet both positively influenced my future.

By Keisha L. Brown

What HBCUs offer 21st Century Students

Many students—African Americans and non-blacks alike—are choosing HBCUs for the unique educational experience.

Historically Black Colleges and Universities (HBCUs) have played a crucial role in America's higher education system by educating African Americans who were denied access to white institutions of higher learning in the late nineteenth and early twentieth centuries.

Today, African American students have access to a wide range of post-secondary institutions, especially since an increasing number of schools are actively recruiting minority students. But despite having more options for higher education than ever before, many students—African Americans and non-blacks alike—are choosing HBCUs for the unique educational experience they offer.

Ethnic and Racial Diversity

In the 21st century, HBCUs aren't just for black students anymore. Colleges know that in order to be competitive and train students who are prepared to succeed in the global community, they need diversity. More and more HBCUs, especially public HBCUs, are recruiting white and Hispanic students to add to their campus' rich ethnic diversity.

Even schools whose student body is totally African American exhibit remarkable diversity as students from all over the country bring a bit of their regional culture to the campus mix. Some HBCUs boast an impressive international student population too, with students hailing from Africa, the Caribbean, South America and in some cases as far away as the Middle East.

A Legacy of Academic Excellence and Success

While HBCUs represent only 3% of American institutions of higher learning, they graduate nearly 25% of all African Americans who earn Bachelor's degrees. HBCUs are leaders in training young professionals—especially in the arts, business and the sciences—who are prepared to address the unique needs of the African American community.

HBCUs also provide African American and minority students the opportunity to work with mentors who share the same cultural background as students and are successful in their respective fields. The extensive support networks available at HBCUs help students excel in academically rigorous programs. Furthermore, a substantial number of HBCU graduates go on to pursue advanced degrees, often being recruited by elite schools seeking to diversify their graduate programs.

Opportunities for Real World Experience

Every year, numerous national organizations partner with HBCUs to create programs that increase minority, particularly African American, participation in underrepresented fields such as engineering, business, and medicine among others. Businesses and corporations that are committed to increasing diversity often look first to students enrolled in HBCUs to fill internships and part-time positions that offer real world experience and develop leadership skills.

Also, many HBCUs offer students the opportunity to spend a semester or two at other leading universities through domestic exchange programs, which allow students to experience a different academic environment and network with distinguished professionals in a different region of the country.

Choosing between a HBCU or a TWI

Many students struggle with the decision to attend either a HBCU or a traditionally white institution (TWI). While both HBCUs and TWIs provide academically challenging and personally rewarding collegiate experiences, the social dynamics of HBCUs and TWIs are markedly different.

Your college experience can provide you excellent opportunities to break outside of your comfort zone and to grow and adapt in a new environment. Students who went to predominantly white high schools can benefit from the cultural exposure of an HBCU. Also, some HBCUs can be cheaper to attend than TWIs in the same region but still offer students the same solid academic instruction.

You will be spending the next four years of your life at the college you attend, so put the time, effort and research into finding the school that's right for YOU. The decision you make can result in one of the most rewarding experiences of your life.

HBCUs in the *College Access & Opportunity Guide*

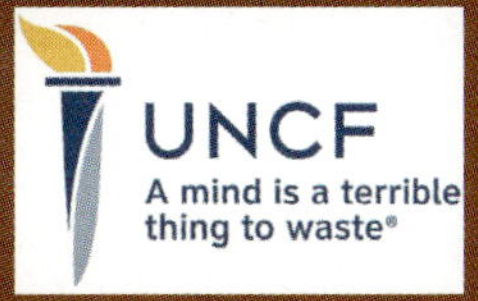

Check out the **United Negro College Fund (UNCF) at www.uncf.org** to learn about all Historically Black Colleges and Universities (HBCUs) and the many scholarships available to African American students.

BIO *Keisha L. Brown is a graduate of Howard University ('09) and a past intern with Center for Student Opportunity.*

IN ALL HONESTY MY LIFE HAS BEEN A WAR.

In all honesty, my life has been a war. Every day I have to fight. I have to fight my parents, my past, and my own insecurities and feelings of stagnation. I still struggle to make sense of things, and I carry my war wounds with me everywhere I go. From having a part-time job, traveling to two different high schools, to Hurricane Katrina, my journey to college has been full of obstacles.

Living in New Orleans during my teenage years was certainly a struggle. I've lived in the Lower Ninth Ward all my life, and after Hurricane Katrina hit, I returned to my home with no running water, no electricity, no school and no friends. Having to rebuild my home and my life at age 15 gave me the strength to crash through any barricade, leap over any hurdle.

I was taught as a youth that an individual is strengthened and defined by their struggles; an achievement isn't worth anything if it is placed into your palm. I wanted to set an example for my younger siblings by overcoming our financial obstacles and getting to college, and I wasn't going to let anything—not even a natural disaster—stand in the way of achieving my goal.

I am now attending Dillard University, a Historically Black College or University (HBCU) in New Orleans, where I am pursuing my passion for writing. Attending a HBCU has always been my dream, and I am now living it.

I've been blessed with the means to further my education and my writing career, and I am truly thankful for this opportunity. I hope my writing will inspire and give others the strength to overcome their obstacles and to find the courage to open up their world. One should never forget their struggles, but when I cross The Avenue of the Oaks to receive my diploma, I will have a smile on my face and strength in my heart.

ANGELICA ROBINSON is a CSO Opportunity Scholarship winner. Angelica shares her college experiences and offers advice on the Opportunity Scholars blog.

Visit www.CSOCollegeCenter.org to follow the blog, sign up to become a CSO Opportunity Scholar, and have the chance to be a future Opportunity Scholarship winner and blogger yourself!

Opportunity Scholars

Hispanic-Serving Institutions

Did you know that over half of all Hispanic undergraduate students in higher education are enrolled in less than 10 percent of institutions in the United States?

This concentration of Hispanic enrollment gave way to a federal program designed to support colleges and universities in the United States that assist first-generation, majority low-income Hispanic students, now known as Hispanic-Serving Institutions (HSIs).

What are HSIs?

What defines HSIs is not necessarily their mission, but their Hispanic enrollment. Unlike HBCUs and women's colleges, most HSIs were not founded with the purpose of primarily serving a specific demographic.

In 1992, the Hispanic Association of Colleges and Universities (HACU) took the lead in lobbying Congress for official recognition and federal funding for institutions of higher education with large Hispanic populations. That year HSIs were defined under federal law as accredited and degree-granting public or private nonprofit institutions of higher education with 25% or more total undergraduate Hispanic enrollment. Additionally, a minimum of 50% of the Hispanic students attending HSIs must be from low-income backgrounds.

In 1995, Congress appropriated $12 million in grants to HSIs under the Higher Education Act. Federal funding for HSIs from the Department of Education has increased sharply since then, with $117.4 million being appropriated in 2010. These grants are used for the development and improvement of academic programs, endowment funds, academic tutoring, counseling programs, student support services and more. The continual increase in government funding demonstrates a growing dedication to the advancement of higher education for Hispanic students.

Why choose an HSI?

In addition to the benefits afforded by government grants, there are many reasons why prospective college students choose to attend HSIs. Most are located in areas with large Hispanic populations such as California, Texas and New Mexico. The proximity of HSIs to these areas facilitates the transition to college life for many Hispanic students, who are able to attend an HSI close to home. HSIs also have lower tuitions, on average, than non-HSI institutions of a similar caliber.

Making a Decision

With the growing Hispanic college-age population in the United States, more and more colleges and universities are becoming HSIs by virtue of their increased Hispanic enrollment. An ever-increasing group of schools are known as "emerging HSIs," meaning that between 15 and 24 percent of their respective student populations are Hispanic. When choosing a college or university, don't write off a school for not being an HSI now; it might be in a couple of years.

Ultimately it is good to keep in mind that HSIs are, their large Hispanic populations notwithstanding, regular institutions designed to serve students from all ethnicities and walks of life. Just because you may not be Hispanic or low-income does not necessarily mean an HSI is not right for you; on the flip side, don't limit yourself to attending an HSI just because you fall within the target demographic.

Looking for scholarships, resources, and mentoring?

Check out the Hispanic Scholarship Fund at www.hsf.net and Hispanic College Fund at www.hispanicfund.org

Check out ¡Excelencia!

in Education at www.edexcelencia.org to learn about their work to accelerate higher education success for Latino students by identifying programs that positively impact Latino college enrollment and graduation.

HSIs in the *College Access & Opportunity Guide*

Barry University (FL) – Page 200

New Mexico Highlands University – Page 283

Occidental College (CA) – Page 173

Texas State University – Page 369

University of Texas at San Antonio – Page 372

Whittier College (CA) – Page 183

Because there is no official list of Hispanic-serving Institutions (HSIs), the above list reflects HSI members of the **Hispanic Association of Colleges and Universities (HACU).** Check out HACU at **www.hacu.net** to learn about all Hispanic-Serving Institutions.

EMPTY ROOMS AND CARDBOARD BOXES

Irvin Gomez
College: Dartmouth College
Hometown: Waukegan, IL

The melodies of The Killers play in the living room as I stand in the middle of my bedroom. Scattered around me lie five cardboard boxes, each hopefully holding everything I will need during my first year of college. The excitement of going to college is suddenly met with the nostalgia of packing. Who knew putting your life into cardboard boxes would be so difficult?!

As I admire the sight of what used to be my room, I can't help but feel a bit of sadness creeping in. This house has witnessed my successes in high school as well as my coming of age. I will leave all of this behind in just a few days and it will forever be a part of my past. I am sure that as you begin to pack, you will experience similar emotions. This is totally natural and expected.

Many of my friends were happy to leave home and had no second thoughts about it. I, on the other hand, had mixed emotions about leaving. Yes, I want to be at Dartmouth as much as my future classmates, but I am going to miss home. My advice to those like me is the following: enjoy every moment that you have left with your family. Hug them while you are close because you will be missing those hugs when you are miles away. Share your excitement with them since I am sure that they are as excited as you are for college.

Lastly, do not let the feelings of sadness overcome the feelings of excitement and expectation. You should be excited. I know I am. Yes, it is hard to see most of your life being placed in boxes and to hear what the future use of your room will be, but over the horizon lies a more exciting picture. Those cardboard boxes are temporary containers of your life and soon you will be standing in an empty room wondering how to make that room your home.

I will end my post with a few words from my dad from conversation about leaving home. "No matter how far away you are going, we, as a family will always be together in mind and in spirit." With these words in mind, I will embark on my journey to Dartmouth knowing that I am taking more than five cardboard boxes. I am also bringing my family along for the voyage.

IRVIN GOMEZ is a CSO Opportunity Scholarship winner. Irvin shares his college experiences and offers advice on the Opportunity Scholars blog.

Visit www.CSOCollegeCenter.org to follow the blog, sign up to become a CSO Opportunity Scholar, and have the chance to be a future Opportunity Scholarship winner and blogger yourself!

Opportunity Scholars

By Jarrid Whitney

Dancing the Circle

An Indigenous Perspective on College Admissions

As a first-generation Native American raised in upstate New York, I never really considered attending college until my senior year. Now reflecting back after working in college admissions for the last 15 years, I often make the analogy that applying to college is like a dance since it is an important form of expression for many American Indians, and most teenagers in general.

First Steps

To this day, I distinctly remember attending my first Iroquois Social Dance and feeling like I didn't belong. It seemed that everyone already knew all the right moves, which only made me feel that much more intimidated to enter the dance ring.

Similarly, many Native American and first-generation high school graduates are scared off by college. And if they do apply, they stick with what's familiar—applying only to local colleges or those that are very well known. I'm not suggesting you apply to more than 15 colleges, but it is wise to apply to a range of schools that offer varying programs and opportunities. Don't let fear hold you back.

Learning the Beat

Before I first started dancing, I needed time to listen carefully to the beat so I could coordinate my steps appropriately. Once a high school student gets over the fear of applying to a range of colleges, the next step is understanding how to interpret the beat.

Prospective applicants must research each school they are interested in and keep track of each school's application process and deadlines.

Other schools offer rolling admission or open enrollment opportunities. But if a college offers such a program, it is still best to apply as early as possible, as on-campus housing or scholarship opportunities can sometimes be limited and are often awarded on a first-come, first-serve basis.

Expressing Uniqueness

Just like most Native American dances, especially competitive powwows, there is always room for individualized self-expression.

Once a student knows which colleges they want to apply to, the next step is actually filling out the applications. Prospective students need to understand that although they have to follow the application guidelines, they should also take some liberty in expressing their identity.

The best way students can showcase their special talents, culture and heritage is through the personal essays, extracurricular lists, and even letters of recommendation. Even though ceremonial dances or making pottery are not high school functions, they can still be noted as extracurricular activities and expressed in an essay. Colleges seek to maintain a diverse student body and value those who are willing to share their life experiences with others.

Selecting Your Dance Partner

Once you have mustered up the courage to enter the dance ring, the most fun part is finding the right dance partner. But choosing a dance partner is a two-way street. To successfully dance with someone, the person you ask to dance must accept your invitation first.

Similarly, in the college admissions process, an applicant won't be able to fully control who a college will admit. But if your application and essays are representative of the best of your abilities, there will still be plenty of options.

When picking the right school to attend, it really does come down to personal fit. Each student and their family has to evaluate the academic offerings, location, size, support programs, and especially financial aid opportunities before a final "partner" can be chosen. Always try to visit before making the final decision. Often times, colleges offer specialized fly-in or open house programs for underserved populations.

Completing the Circle

Entering the dance circle of college admissions will not be easy but the outcome of a college education far outweighs any challenges. My advice to students is to enjoy the experience but never forget your roots. ■

Adapted from original article published in Winds of Change 15th Annual College Guide, 2008-09

BIO Jarrid Whitney, Six Nations Cayuga, is Director of Undergraduate Admissions at California Institute of Technology.

Charles Barry/SCU

By Carmen Lopez

College Pride, Native Pride

When selecting a college to attend, Native American, Alaska Native, and Native Hawaiian students have more choices than ever. There are over 300 colleges and universities that offer academic, social, cultural, and community services, programs, and student spaces to support and enhance the unique needs of Native students on campus.

Finding the right fit is especially important for Native students who bring a unique perspective and indigenous experience to feel comfortable in the place they will live, study, and grow in for 4 years. As a Native student you don't want to just survive college, you want to thrive—so make sure the college you attend provides the support an environment that will help you succeed as a student AND as a Native student.

Be proud of yourself for getting into college and show your Native Pride in college too!

Did you know that there are colleges out there that are excited to work with Native students and have created programs to attract them to their schools? College Horizons partners with over 50 colleges that have made a commitment to recruiting Native students and meeting their full demonstrated financial need.

Learn more at www.collegehorizons.org

Questions to Ask a College

- What is the Native student enrollment?
- What percentage of Native students graduate in 4 years and in 5 years?
- What student support services do you offer Native students?
- Are there academic programs on Native Studies or Indigenous Studies?
- How many faculty teach courses in Native Studies?
- Are there any Native faculty or Native staff at the college?
- Are Native alumni active with the college?
- What percentage of Native students go onto graduate school?

COLLEGE HORIZONS

2011 College Horizons College & University Participants

BIO *Carmen Lopez is Executive Director of College Horizons, a pre-college program for Native American high school students open to sophomores and juniors. Each summer students work with college admissions officers, college counselors, essay specialists, and other educators in a five-day "crash course" on the college application process.*

By Dreama Gentry

Pursuing College in Rural America

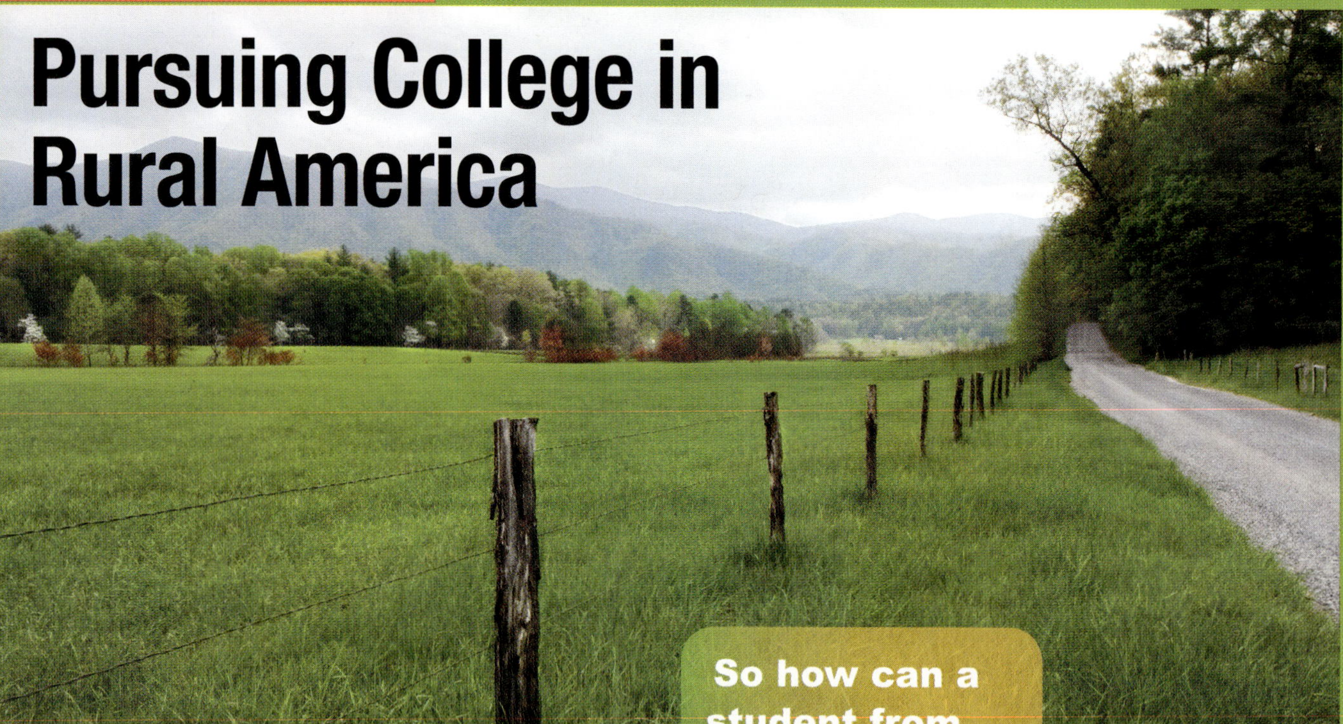

I'm lucky. I grew up in rural America. After going away to college and then to law school, I returned to make my home in rural Kentucky at the edge of the Appalachian Mountains. In this familiar setting, I work closely with students, teachers and families from rural Appalachia to ensure that more rural students build the skills and structures necessary to take advantage of postsecondary opportunities and prepare themselves for collegiate success.

While nationally, rural schools have better high school graduation rates than suburban and urban schools, rural schools have lower college-going rates. Rural America must send more young people to college.

So how can a student from a small rural area get ready for college?

You have advantages:

- The teachers and counselors in your school know you well. In some community schools, like my son's school, students spend all of their school years in a single building. Take advantage of this. Find a teacher or counselor and form a meaningful mentoring relationship with them.

- Students in small schools have more opportunities to participate in athletics, academics and extra-curricular activities. Get involved. Participate in a variety of activities and develop a breadth of skills.

- In most small towns, the businesses, county governments and civic organizations are looking for young people that want to be involved. Volunteer, find an internship, and offer your time and talents.

So how can a student from a small rural area get ready for college?

Growing up in a small town does involve limitations. Here are some ways to overcome them:

- Your school may have limited rigorous courses, such as Advanced Placement courses. Talk to your guidance counselor and do some research. Many state departments of education and community colleges offer online AP courses or first year college courses. Guidance counselors can often find funds to cover the fees for these courses if you ask.

- The closest college or university may be hours away. I was a junior in high school before I ever visited a college campus. See if there are college access programs like Upward Bound and GEAR UP that serve your school. These programs can help you prepare for college and provide you with opportunities to visit college campuses.

- The internet opens a world of possibilities to students from rural America. If you cannot visit a campus, participate in the online campus tours. You can experience the campus, hear from current students and get a feel for what the campus is like.

- Many rural areas lack diversity. Seek out opportunities to meet and interact with people from different backgrounds and cultures. Talk with your family about hosting an international student, or participate in clubs and organizations that provide opportunities to interact with diverse groups of people.

When I came to college, I found that my campus was very similar to the small town where I grew up. The skills that I developed growing up in rural America helped me find my place. The campus community became my support network, much like my family and small town had been my support system back home. ■

BIO *Dreama Gentry leads Berea College's externally funded outreach to Appalachian Kentucky. Gentry strives to improve education outcomes in rural Appalachian communities.*

By William E. Hamm

Astronomer, teacher, lawyer...person of faith

FAITH-BASED COLLEGES AIM TO SERVE THE WHOLE PERSON

Everyone knows that college is about more than earning a degree and choosing a career. Most students also use their college years to explore issues of spirituality, and faith-based institutions are good places to undertake this journey.

Faith-based colleges and universities are those related to a faith tradition. In the U.S., this usually means their heritage is Roman Catholic, Jewish or Protestant. In only rare cases are there religious requirements to gain admission, and most of these institutions have diverse student bodies. While some of these colleges are for persons of a particular faith or denominational background, most aim to support all students in their spiritual quests.

Our nation's first colleges were founded by church groups, and most have a long tradition of providing access to underrepresented groups and those with limited financial resources. Since faith-based institutions are private, it may surprise you that these institutions use financial aid to enroll some students who have little or no family financial support.

Choosing a faith-based institution is about more than just spiritual growth. These institutions offer academic and student life programs with a point of view. Their programs of general education—the part of your academic program which is common for all students—represents their faculties' views of the world. And student life programs abound with service learning opportunities. There's nothing generic about faith-based colleges, so if you consider them you'll want to ask about their general education or core program as well as student life. Your first year at a faith-based college will be a unique experience!

Because these institutions are small by comparison, students in faith-based colleges have the advantage of getting to know their professors. You'll find rich opportunities for one-on-one learning.

The faculty members who choose to teach in a faith-based college are intentional about that decision, and they bring a deep passion for teaching in this environment as well as a desire to focus on undergraduates and teaching. They are going to get to know you and they will lend a helping hand when necessary. When one thinks about it, that's what one would expect of people working in a faith-based institution.

The research is clear, too. Alumni of faith-based institutions give their education higher marks, and the experience shows in lives of service to their communities and world. ■

BIO *William E. Hamm is president of the Lutheran Educational Conference of North America (LECNA)*

By Janice Ferebee

Advice for Girls:

How to Prepare for the Female Leadership Pipeline

If you are a girl who is going to compete and succeed in the future, you need to believe you are worthy of the opportunity to attend college. Learning needs to become a lifestyle choice – beginning with realizing that college is valuable, accessible and some of the best days of your life!

Pursuing a college education will seem very discouraging at times, and you might face challenges that threaten your future and sidetrack dreams of success, including neglect or abuse; drugs, alcohol, gangs and violence; early sexual activity and teen pregnancy; or even the absence of positive role models and spiritual guidance. That said, all obstacles can be overcome with the right attitude and resources. Life is 10% what happens – 90% what you do about it.

Here are some tips for getting and staying in the Female Leadership Pipeline headed toward college:

1. Develop an "I am enough!" spirit. Don't ever be ashamed of your past. Learn to use your life experiences as a testimony to your strength and resiliency. Learn from mistakes, become aware of your strengths and weaknesses, and be proud and accepting of the wonderful girl you already are – just the way you are! No matter what life has dealt you, know that you are valuable and worthy of a college education and a great future.

2. Create a "Dream Team" of friends and women (or men) you admire. People are heavily influenced by who they choose to hang out with, so don't let just anyone in the "front row" of your life. Once you've decided that college is for you, make sure your peers have the same goals for their lives. Look for people who are doing what you want to do and invite them to be on your dream team. Their presence in your life will help guide your dream to attend college.

3. Establish "Goals and Guidelines." Use your sense of determination and your team of role models to set your sights on specific goals for your future. Become consistent, disciplined, focused and obedient to that goal. Don't let the "haters" derail your dream for a college education.

4. Build a "Bridge" to help connect your friends and family to the resources they need to pursue a college education and leadership opportunities. By sharing your experience with others, you can help them begin the same journey into the "pipeline."

With college as a natural and attainable life experience open to all girls, the *Female Leadership Pipeline* is a valuable path through which every girl has the opportunity to travel on her journey to greatness. Don't miss your chance to join the movement!

BIO *Janice Ferebee is the Director of the Bethune Program Development Center at the National Council of Negro Women, Inc. (NCNW), where she is responsible for community-based and national programs for women and girls of African descent.*

By Susan E. Lennon

A Women's College Might be for You

"Women not only see things differently from men, but they see different things."
–Ret. Lt. Gen. Claudia J. Kennedy

Why does this matter in your education and in your college search? Finding the right fit in a college is all about *you*. Why might a women's college be the right fit for you? Take a look at what matters in college—because what matters *in* college matters *after* college. And it matters in the college selection process.

Women's colleges are focused on you—your dreams and aspirations, your education, your personal and professional development for the many different roles you will assume in life, and your advancement in the ever-changing global economy.

What women's college have in common is an unequivocal commitment to your education and advancement.

Research shows that a women's college education:

- Enables students to engage with top faculty and resources.
- Creates leaders, communicators, and persuaders.
- Develops critical skills for life and career.
- Proves its value over a lifetime.

Take a look at women's colleges—they're about you!

Women's Colleges in the *College Access & Opportunity Guide*

Bay Path College (MA) – Page 243
Bryn Mawr College (PA) – Page 335
Meredith College (NC) – Page 307
Mills College (CA) – Page 172
Mount Holyoke College (MA) – Page 252
Pine Manor College (MA) – Page 254
Saint Joseph College (CT) – Page 192
Saint Mary's College (IN) – Page 223
Smith College (MA) – Page 255
Spelman College (GA) – Page 209
Trinity Washington University (DC) – Page 199
Wellesley College (MA) – Page 258

Check out the Women's College Coalition and learn more about other women's colleges at **www.womenscolleges.org**.

BIO *Susan E. Lennon is the President of the Women's College Coalition, an association of women's colleges and universities – public and private, independent and church-related, two- and four-year – in the United States and Canada whose primary mission is the education and advancement of women.*

Did you know that several colleges offer special housing and educational programs for single parents?

The **Higher Education Alliance of Residential Single Parent Programs (HEARSPP)** is a coalition of colleges and universities that offer residential degree programs for single parents. The Alliance assists single-parent families as they make decisions about higher education.

Higher Education Alliance For Residential Single Parent Programs

HEARSPP Member Institutions:

- Baldwin-Wallace College (OH)
- Berea College (KY) – Page 228
- College of Saint Mary (NE)
- Endicott College (MA)
- Misericordia University (PA)
- Saint Paul's College (VA)
- Wilson College (PA)

For more information, visit
www.singleparentcollegeprograms.org/

Wilson College also houses the **National Clearinghouse for Single Mothers in Higher Education**, a clearinghouse of information to assist single parent women in the process of becoming successful college students, as well as mothers.

For more information, visit
www.wilson.edu/nationalclearinghouse

I AM A SINGLE TEEN MOM AND I AM ENROLLED FULL-TIME AT COLLEGE WHILE WORKING FULL-TIME.

Tereza Ponce de Leon
College: Augsburg College
Hometown: Saint Paul, MN

That is a statement that you do not hear often. As most already know, when you get pregnant in high school everyone automatically assumes that you are not going to graduate high school, let alone go on to college. I am proud to say that I am still pursing my dreams and going to college.

In my opinion, getting pregnant does not prevent you from doing anything. I can take the same road as everyone else does; my road is just a little bumpier than everyone else. Is it hard? Yes, it is hard, but it is worth it.

Since my mom did not go to college and my father did not even finish high school, I came from a place where my parents struggled with money every day to raise my brother and me. I do not want that type of life for my son. I want him to be able to have a better life than I had and have more opportunities available than I had. I know that none of that can be possible if I do not go to college to get an education to better myself. Once you have a child everything you do affects your child too, and I know that bettering myself is what is best for him.

To be able to go to college full-time, work full-time, and be a mom full-time takes a lot of time management skills. Basically every minute of every day I am busy doing something. At times, it can be a bit stressful, but I just have to keep thinking about the reward at the end. To be less stressed you have to try your best to not procrastinate and keep up with your school work. If you let your school work pile up on you then it will add stress to your life that you do not need.

I hope that more teen moms realize that they can still go to college because it is not an impossible dream. It just takes hard work and determination, and in the end, it will benefit you and your child more than you know.

TEREZA PONCE DE LEON is a CSO Opportunity Scholarship winner. Tereza shares her college experiences and offers advice on the Opportunity Scholars blog.

Visit www.CSOCollegeCenter.org to follow the blog, sign up to become a CSO Opportunity Scholar, and have the chance to be a future Opportunity Scholarship winner and blogger yourself!

Opportunity Scholars

By Joe Tavares

Visiting College FOR FREE!

See about fly-in and special visit programs where schools pay for prospective students with limited financial resources to visit campus.

The biggest question you need to answer before choosing your future college home is "what would it really be like for me at this school?" No matter how much research you do, how many pictures you see, or how many people you speak with, the only way you can find out what it would be like at a school is to spend a few days there.

If you're thinking about going to school away from home, you should be familiar with fly-in and special visit programs where schools pay for prospective students with limited financial resources to visit campus. These programs can give you a unique opportunity to not only visit campus, but to spend a few days there, sit in on classes, and interact with students who may very well be your peers for the next four years.

Where do you start?

You can find out about fly-in and special visit programs by using guidebooks like this, websites like www.CSOCollegeCenter.org, and checking out schools' websites for information about visiting campus.

Does the school offer tours, on-campus interviews, and overnight stays? Do they have special events for low-income or multicultural students? If you're not sure, call up the school's Admissions Office and let them know who you are, when you want to visit and if your family has financial difficulties. They may have special programs or transportation stipends for you and your family to visit campus.

Preparing for your visit

Make sure you write down all the questions you have about a school before you go. If you're attending a special visit program, review the agenda beforehand to see if there's anything not included that you want to see or do.

Being on Campus

Make sure you speak with students and professors, look around the library, eat in a dining hall, visit a dorm, and pick up the school newspaper.

How would you fit in at the school? What would you bring to the campus community? Would you feel safe? Is this an environment you would thrive in? Are support services and professors easily accessible?

Campus visits will have a big impact on your college choice, so take advantage of special visit opportunities and fly-in programs that are available for you! ■

BIO *Joe Tavares is Director of College Counseling at Pan American School of Bahia. Previously, he worked for Center for Student Opportunity and is a past editor of the College Access & Opportunity Guide.*

Check out these programs hosted by schools featured in the *College Access & Opportunity Guide:*

Dartmouth College – Page 278
Hanover, NH
Native American Fly-In Program
Dartmouth hosts an annual Native American Fly-In Program, which is usually held during the summer and/or fall after students' junior year of high school. Other students with limited financial resources may qualify for complimentary transportation expense coverage for fly-in and other extended campus-visit programs. An application for the Fly-In program is required.

Lewis & Clark College – Page 331
Portland, OR
Lewis & Clark Fly-In Program
Each year, Lewis & Clark College invites approximately 50 newly admitted students to visit campus at the expense of the college. These selected students of color and first-generation college-goers learn about life and academics at Lewis & Clark through a series of activities. They attend classes, meet faculty and staff, spend time with current students and experience life in the residence halls.

Ohio Wesleyan University – Page 327
Delaware, OH
Campus Visit Cost Assistance
To enable multicultural and first-generation students to visit campus, Ohio Wesleyan assists with transportation arrangements and costs.

Saint Vincent College – Page 346
Latrobe, PA
Subsidized Campus Visits
In keeping with its dedication to multiculturalism and diversity, Saint Vincent College subsidizes travel expenses incurred in a visit to the college. Saint Vincent provides this assistance to low-income minority students who have been accepted to the college, thereby supporting informed matriculation decisions.

Vanderbilt University – Page 364
Nashville, TN
MOSAIC Weekend
Held in mid-March, Vanderbilt University's MOSAIC Weekend invites minority students admitted to Vanderbilt to campus for four days. The weekend features academic sessions, student activities and performances and tickets to the annual Vanderbilt Step Show. The Office of Admissions offers financial assistance for travel to students in need.

Williams College – Page 261
Williamstown, MA
Windows on Williams
Windows on Williams (WoW) is a visiting program specifically for students who are low-income or the first in their family to go to college. It is an all-expenses-paid, three-day trip that allows students to sit in on classes, meet professors and students and try Williams on for size. Applications for this program are available at the beginning of each summer.

advice

CSO Opportunity Scholarship winners share their college experiences and offer advice on the Opportunity Scholars blog.

SNEAK PEAK: THE COLLEGE VISIT

Ashley Roberts
College: Illinois Wesleyan
Hometown: St. Peters, MO

"Before your visit, contact your admissions counselor and discuss what you specifically want to see and ask about other unique features the campus offers."
– The Big V — The College Visit

Lysa Vola
College: Williams College
Hometown: Jensen Beach, FL

"There may be some schools you visit that just don't quite seem to fit your needs and that's okay. You have to find a school with a personality that fits your own."
– But it looked so nice in the brochure...

Khadijah Williams
College: Harvard University
Hometown: Los Angeles, CA

"No matter how much you read and research about a college, no matter how much you think you know about it, visiting is the best way to know. There are some things you can't measure in a college guide."
– Don't Judge a College by its Cover

Visit www.CSOCollegeCenter.org to follow the blog, sign up to become a CSO Opportunity Scholar, and have the chance to be a future Opportunity Scholarship winner and blogger yourself!

By Bob Schaeffer

TEST-OPTIONAL ADMISSIONS

Did you know that there are a growing number of "test-optional" colleges and universities that are creating more opportunities for first-generation, low-income and minority applicants seeking higher education?

There are 850 accredited, bachelor-degree granting schools that do not require all or many applicants to submit SAT or ACT results before making admissions decisions recognize that students are "more than their test scores." Instead, they want to recruit young people with skills and talents that are not measured well by filling in multiple-choice bubbles.

They recognize that teenagers who are from low-income backgrounds or are among the first in their families to consider college often have solid academic records, but not super-high exam scores. Whether the reason is test bias, lack of access to high-priced coaching courses, or simply not testing well, these schools are worth considering in your college search.

Beware of one wrinkle. Some colleges and universities, including a number that are test-optional for admission, do require test scores for some "merit" scholarships. But many make meeting your financial need their top priority.

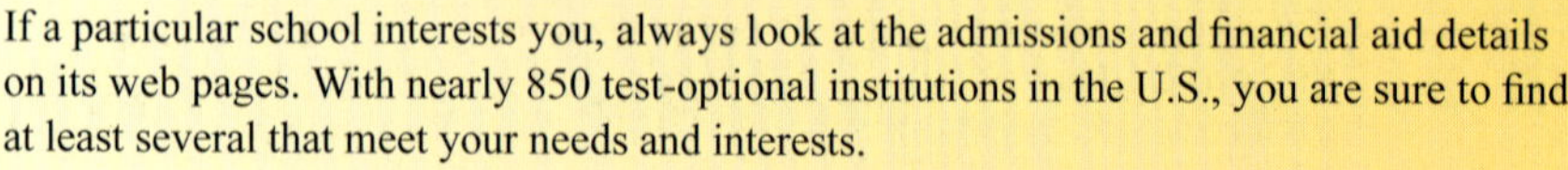

If a particular school interests you, always look at the admissions and financial aid details on its web pages. With nearly 850 test-optional institutions in the U.S., you are sure to find at least several that meet your needs and interests.

Test-optional admissions can open additional doors to college and beyond. It's up to you to take advantage of these great opportunities! ■

Schools of all sorts—from all parts of the country—now offer test-optional admission. The range of types—with a few examples from each—includes:

- National liberal arts colleges committed to diversity—Bates (ME), Mt. Holyoke (MA), Lake Forest (IL), Pitzer (CA), Agnes Scott (GA), and Lawrence (WI)
- Large public and private universities—University of Arizona (AZ), Wake Forest University (NC), and Worcester Polytechnic Institute (MA)
- Colleges whose religious traditions emphasizes access and opportunity—Holy Cross (MA), Baptist Bible (MO), Loyola (MD), Providence (RI), and Rabbinical (NY)
- Top-notch regional schools—Fairfield (CT), Rollins (FL), Baldwin-Wallace (OH), and Whitworth (WA)
- Visual and performing arts institutes—Berklee College of Music (MA), San Francisco Art Institute (CA), and Ringling College of Art and Design (FL)
- Trade or occupation-oriented institutions—Fashion Institute of Technology (NY), Johnson & Wales (RI, NC, and FL), and New School of Architecture (CA)

To see the full variety of choices available to you in the test-optional universe, check out http://www.fairtest.org/university/optional. There, you can view free lists of colleges and universities that do not need to see your SAT/ACT scores listed in alphabetical, state-by-state, and printable formats.

Be careful to follow the footnotes. Some programs require students to meet requirements, such as ranking in the top quarter of their high school class, posting "B" average grades, or submitting a graded writing project, to qualify for test-optional consideration.

BIO *Bob Schaeffer is the Public Education Director of the National Center for Fair & Open Testing (FairTest). He is coauthor of Standing Up to the SAT and Test Scores Do Not Equal Merit: Enhancing Equity & Excellence in College Admissions by Deemphasizing SAT and ACT Results.*

Articles | Chapter 4

How do I apply?

From The Education Conservancy

WE ADMIT... GUIDANCE FROM THOSE WHO DO

Applying to college does not have to be overwhelming! The following principles and guidelines can help make the college admission process more manageable and more productive.

Student Guidelines

An admission decision, test score, or GPA is not a measure of your self-worth. And, most students are admitted to colleges they want to attend. Knowing this, we encourage you to:

- **Be confident!** Take responsibility for your college admission process. The more you do for yourself, the better the results will be.
- **Be deliberate!** Applying to college involves thoughtful research to determine distinctions among colleges, as well as careful self-examination to identify your interests, learning style and other criteria. Plan to make well-considered applications to the most suitable colleges. This is often referred to as "making good matches."
- **Be realistic and trust your instincts!** Choosing a college is an important process, but not a life or death decision. Since there are limits to what you can know about colleges and about yourself, you should allow yourself to do educated guesswork.
- **Be open-minded!** Resist the notion that there is one perfect college. Great education happens in many places.
- **Use a variety of resources for gathering information.** Seek advice from those people who know you, care about you, and are willing to help.
- **Be honest; be yourself!** Do not try to game the system.
- **Resist taking** any standardized test numerous times (twice is usually sufficient).
- **Limit your applications** to a well-researched and reasonable number. No more than six should be sufficient, except in special cases.
- **Know that what you do** in college is a better predictor of future success and happiness than where you go to college.

Visit www.educationconservancy.org to learn more.

THE EDUCATION CONSERVANCY

THIS GUIDANCE IS OFFERED BY THE FOLLOWING VETERAN ADMISSION PROFESSIONALS:

Phillip Ballinger, University of Washington

Stephanie Balmer, Dickinson College

Michael Beseda, St. Mary's College of California

Jeff Brenzel, Yale University

Jennifer Delahunty, Kenyon College

J. Antonio Cabasco, Whitman College

Sean Callaway, Pace University

Sidonia Dalby, Smith College

Doris Davis, Cornell University

Melissa Ewing, The Bush School

Bill Fitzsimmons, Harvard University

Erica L. Johnson, Lewis & Clark College

Maria Laskaris, Dartmouth College

Matthew Malatesta, Union College

Brad MacGowan, Newton North High School

Bonnie Marcus, Bard College

David McDonald, Western Oregon University

Mark C. Moody, Colorado Academy

James Nondorf, University of Chicago

Marty O'Connell, Colleges That Change Lives

Bruce Poch, Pomona College

Jon Reider, San Francisco University High School

Jeff Rickey, Earlham College

Kristine Sawicki, Reed College

Stuart Schmill, Massachusetts Institute of Technology

Michael Sexton, Santa Clara University

Jim Sumner, Grinnell College

Steven Syverson, Lawrence University

BIO *After nearly twenty-eight years in the college admission and college counseling professions, Lloyd Thacker established The Education Conservancy in 2004 to help students, colleges and high schools calm the frenzy and hype that plague contemporary college admissions.*

By Tally Hart

The Importance of Your "Real Life" in Scholarships and Admissions

The days when scholarships or admissions applications relied just on grades are long past. Although grades are still important, many colleges and universities want students that bring varying backgrounds into the classroom and campus community. In fact, colleges understand that they must bring the real world into the classroom, which means recruiting students from a wide range of backgrounds so that a campus community best reflects the real world.

Since a diverse student body is so important to a college, certain aspects of your life that were once overlooked in the college application process suddenly become important indicators of future success in college. You can describe family commitments—caring for a grandparent or younger siblings, for example—on a scholarship and admission application because this dedication to the family's needs shows your efforts extend outside the classroom.

Work experience is another good example of what colleges think is important in a prospective student. You might be the primary financial support for your family, and that commitment and the time it takes to work and still stay a good student is a desirable skill set.

But here's the catch – colleges and scholarship providers need to know about these parts of your "real life" to be able to consider you in the selection process. Don't be afraid of talking about your job or even difficult situations you've solved at work when you write essays for these applications. ■

BIO *Tally Hart has served students seeking access to higher education throughout her career and presently serves as Senior Advisor for Economic Access at Ohio State University.*

I Wish Lessons Learned Through the Admissions & Financial Aid Process

By Desireé Johnson, Ohio State University, '09

The financial aid process is pretty overwhelming for a high school student, and there are a few things I would like to share with you before you begin the process.

I wish I had known the importance of applying for aid early. Coming from a family where no member had ever gone to college, I was in the dark about the college-going process until my senior year of high school. That was too late. There are many scholarships you can apply for long before then—even your freshman year.

I wish I had met priority deadlines. I barely submitted my FAFSA on time, and unfortunately, I missed certain award opportunities. For example, I did not find out about The Ohio State University's merit scholarships until after numerous deadlines had passed.

I wish I had prepared for the SAT-ACT. I had to take the ACT twice. Also, I was not aware that schools often offer full- or partial-fee waivers to cover the test costs, and that an improvement of a point or two is so crucial in opening additional doors for aid.

I wish I would have known more about loans and loan options. I made assumptions about loans, and I avoided them. Truthfully, I was intimidated by the idea of putting myself in debt, and I relied on money I saved from over-working myself in jobs during high school and my federal-work study program in college. This has been extremely stressful, not to mention a hindrance in getting involved on campus.

I wish I knew that scholarships can't always be combined. Aside from my lack of knowledge about the financial process, I had another setback in getting aid. I received a scholarship from a university program that I was not able to use since I had been awarded another university-administered scholarship. This restriction was a definite setback as I had been counting on that additional funding.

I Did

Looking back, however, there were steps I followed that I am so grateful I did, and would recommend to others.

I did approach my high school guidance counselor to ask for scholarship applications. He turned out to be very helpful in providing me with scholarships he had seen previously and contacting me when he learned of new scholarships.

I did online searches for available scholarships. Besides checking out www.scholarships.com, additionally, I researched scholarships through my community library. I checked out books that had information on available money and tips on how to go about applying for it.

I did go to financial aid events. If your school or city puts on a financial aid event, go to it and encourage your parents to attend. I can't stress enough how important it is to be informed and knowledgeable about financial aid.

I did fill out each and every application I found and met the qualifications for. The more applications you fill out, the more you increase your chances of being awarded aid. Some of my scholarships, which have shown to be among the most helpful, include those which I thought there was little-to-no-chance of me getting.

I did take the application process seriously. Think every response through thoroughly and do not get lazy or intimidated by lengthy forms or multiple essays. That extra time and effort can result in more money to fund your *future*.

By Scott Anderson

Don't ask yourself what colleges want to hear. Ask yourself what you want them to know.

Tell  your story in the application

If you are getting ready to apply to college, chances are you're about to make a mistake. It's not something that any amount of proofreading will catch, but it is something that you can avoid. At some point between now and the day you hit the submit button on your application, you are probably going to ask yourself, "What do colleges want me to tell them?" It's a good question. The problem is it's the wrong question.

It makes sense that you would try to figure out what colleges want to hear from you. After all, you are about to ask a group of people you've never met to decide whether or not you can join their community—a decision that will be based on a few pieces of paper containing a few hundred words that describe you. But believe it or not, you have more control over this process than you think.

Applying to college and asking what admission counselors want to hear is kind of like going to a restaurant and asking the chef what he feels like cooking. Think of the application as your menu. It gives you some boundaries to work within (you're not going to be able to get an egg roll at Pizza Hut), but it also gives you tremendous freedom to make the choices that feel right to you, to share your joys and your interests, your background and your obligations, your successes and your failures, your goals and your dreams—in other words, your story. And that is the key to the question—the right question. Don't ask yourself what colleges want to hear. Ask yourself what you want them to know.

Too many applicants try to package themselves as the students that they think colleges will want to admit. There are two problems with this plan. First, it's hard. It's hard to use a thesaurus when simple English would be much more effective. It's hard to strategize about which extracurricular activity sounds most impressive. It's hard to pretend that you care deeply about an issue that doesn't really interest you. Applying to college is difficult enough. Why make it tougher by pretending to be someone you're not?

That brings us to the second problem: it's inauthentic. Of all the qualities that admission counselors find appealing, authenticity tops the list. Let them know what is important to you, whether it's student government or theater or basketball or a part-time job or even taking care of your younger siblings while your parents are at work. If it matters to you, tell them about it, because in the end, the whole purpose of your college search is to find the place that will help you to be more successful that you can possibly imagine. And that success starts with a simple plan: Be yourself.

BIO Scott Anderson is Director of Outreach for The Common Application, Inc., a membership organization of nearly 400 institutions that provides a common, standardized application in both online and print for First-year and Transfer Applications.

By Jaye Fenderson

Writing a Great College Essay

Not all colleges require an essay – some require more than one, but if you're like most students, the idea of having to write an essay for the college application can be overwhelming or a complete turn-off. But before you let 500 words stand in the way of applying to the school of your dreams, here's why the essay is so important and how you can write one that will leave a great impression with the college admissions office.

Why an Essay?

Believe it or not, the colleges that ask you to write an essay are actually interested in more than just your grades and test scores. They want to get to know you - your story, how you see the world, and what you have to say - and one of the best means of getting your voice heard is by writing an essay. It should give an admissions officer a glimpse into your personality and character, and it's also a chance to discuss aspects of yourself that may not show up elsewhere in your application, like a story about your family, neighborhood or community in which you grew up or a unique experience that has had an impact on your life.

here's why the essay is so important and how you can write one that will leave a great impression

Write to Stand Out

Follow these tips to write a memorable college essay:

Start Early— Allow yourself enough time to brainstorm ideas, write a couple drafts, and proofread the final essays. That means starting the essay writing process at least one month before the application deadline, but working on your essays the summer before your senior year is a great way to get comfortable with the 500 word format and makes for one less thing you have to worry about during the fall application season.

Keep it personal— The essay is your chance to say things that test scores and grades can't communicate, so you want to give a college a sense of your personality and character. Are you funny? Caring? Serious? Courageous? Creative? Motivated? Tell stories that showcase your strengths, and let your personality shine through in your writing style. Remember that every question asked in the application is an opportunity to talk about yourself. It may feel uncomfortable at first to write so openly (especially to complete strangers!), but rest assured that colleges want to know about your background and the experiences that have shaped you.

Show, Don't Tell— It's important to not just say you're interested in a particular field but to show how your experiences have shaped your interests. That means illustrating how events, books, magazines, people, and moments have inspired you to pursue your educational and life goals. Show how you continue to cultivate your interests and talents at school, home and in your community.

Proofread— Keep in mind that the college essay is first and foremost a writing exercise to demonstrate your knowledge of the English language as well as your ability to organize your thoughts to make a statement. The biggest essay buzz-kills are spelling mistakes, grammatical errors, and typos. So don't just rely on your computer's spell-check. Have someone you trust read your essay to look for anything out of place.

Topics to Avoid

Remember that the college essay is a chance to share a part of yourself, so the cool thing about that is that there are no wrong answers! However, you'll want to steer clear of these overused and inappropriate essay topics:

Don't use an old homework assignment or report as your essay.

Don't tackle a topic that cannot be done justice in 500 words or less, like how you would achieve world peace.

Don't use the essay to make excuses for poor grades.

Don't write about other people's experiences; keep it personal!

Don't use the essay space as résumé for accomplishments and activities previously mentioned in the application.

Do write what you know, be yourself, add descriptive details, and don't forget to proofread!

An awesome essay can be the tipping point that pushes a good application into the acceptance bin, so take some time to think about what sets you apart and how you can best share your unique story in the admissions essay. ■

BIO *Jaye Fenderson is the author of Seventeen's* Guide to Getting Into College *and the producer of First Generation, a documentary about students who are first in their families to go to college.*

By Chelsea Jones

advice

CSO Opportunity Scholarship winners share their college experiences and offer advice on the Opportunity Scholars blog.

LISTEN UP!

Jesse Sanchez
College: Harvard University
Hometown: San Diego, CA

"Our stories may not seem spectacular to us but to the outside world, they have the potential to touch the hearts of the masses and inspire. For every one of us that makes it to college, that is one more person breaking the mold and beating the odds." ***– Your Story is More Amazing Than Mine, Share it***

"I doubted myself and I doubted my abilities, and the worse thing to do during the scholarship or college application process is to lower standards or expectations out of fear. Have faith in your ability to convey your intelligence, experiences and ideas in an essay or even in an interview. The first critical step is to have faith in yourself and the rest will come." ***– Take a Chance***

Lot Kwarteng
College: Miami University
Hometown: Bronx, NY

Irvin Gomez
College: Dartmouth College
Hometown: Waukegan, IL

"I love the intellectual, and at times, even physical challenge that college poses. College tests what you are really made of and I love that. I'd rather be challenged out of my comfort zone and grow than simply remain comfortable and not develop as an individual." ***– I Wouldn't Have it Any Other Way***

Duylam Nguyen-Ngo
College: Babson College
Hometown: Richmond, VA

"That is why we do what we do. Because we love our families, because they expect so much from us, because we expect so much from ourselves, as the forerunners for wealth in the future generations, this is what fuels our passion." ***– Big Bro***

Visit www.CSOCollegeCenter.org to follow the blog, sign up to become a CSO Opportunity Scholar, and have the chance to be a future Opportunity Scholarship winner and blogger yourself!

You may be an intelligent and hardworking person, but the Twitter profile picture of you smoking from a hookah will rub admissions officers the wrong way.

social media manners and etiquette 101

High schools students today are always on their cell phones texting, tweeting, Facebooking, following, and liking. We know it's fun! However, sharing too much can affect your chances of getting that job or even an acceptance letter to college. More and more, employers and colleges are using social media to scope you out. Here are a few tips to keep your online image fun, yet respectable.

Profile Pictures: Should you be in your Facebook profile picture making an inappropriate gesture or partying? Probably not. Your profile picture is the first encounter someone has with you while browsing your page, and you know that saying, "First impressions are everything"? It is absolutely true. You may be an extremely intelligent and hardworking person, but the Twitter profile picture of you smoking from a hookah will rub admissions officers the wrong way. Try posting a simple and clear headshot of yourself.

Profanity: You wouldn't use that language in front of your mother, so don't do it on social media! What you say in your Facebook status and in your tweets reflect who you are and how you feel. Potential employers and colleges want an individual who will represent their institution well. What others write on your wall also reflects the type of people you associate with. If your friend Kyle from back home drops an inappropriate comment on your Facebook wall, delete it.

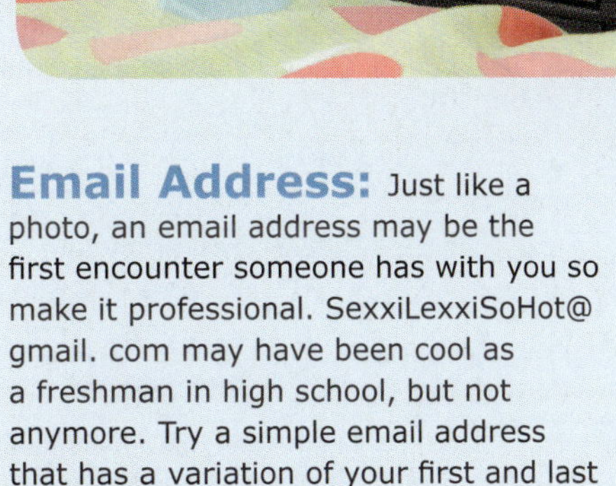

Email Address: Just like a photo, an email address may be the first encounter someone has with you so make it professional. SexxiLexxiSoHot@ gmail. com may have been cool as a freshman in high school, but not anymore. Try a simple email address that has a variation of your first and last name in it.

Voicemail: This may not be social media, but it is also very important to have an appropriate voicemail recording. No college recruiter wants to listen to an entire Lady Gaga song before they are able to leave a message on your phone. When setting up a voice message recording on your cell phone or landline, make sure there is no background noise and that you speak clearly and slowly.

Thank You Notes: Whether you've had an interview with an admissions officer or the president of a scholarship committee, mailing a personalized thank you note is always a nice gesture. This shows that you are appreciative and grateful for the opportunity given to you. Thank you emails are appropriate as well. Admissions officers speak with hundreds of students; getting a thank you may brighten up their stressful day and increase your chances of getting that acceptance letter or scholarship. ■

BIO *Chelsea Jones is Center for Student Opportunity's Outreach and Student Support Associate.*

By Dr. DeAngela Burns-Wallace

Polish Your Admissions Application

by Following Some Do's and Don'ts

Filling out applications can be a time-consuming and arduous process, but you can also make it really creative and exhilarating. It's a way for you to show an admissions office who you really are and what you are passionate about. It is also an opportunity to reflect on all that you have accomplished and experienced in high school.

Have fun with the application. Yes, I said "fun" in the same sentence as "application." Have fun, and when you click the "submit" button or seal the envelope, feel confident that the application is a true and polished reflection of who you are as a student.

To help you through the process, here are a few do's and don'ts:

Do

- DO Proofread you entire application (not just the essays) for spelling errors or grammatical mistakes.
- DO Include an e-mail address that is appropriate and professional. If your personal e-mail address is a little too casual, then you can create a new one for free using any number of popular e-mail providers. You can then use this account just for college communication.
- DO Infuse your application with your own voice, beliefs, and unique reflections.
- DO Your research on the opportunities available at a specific school before you answer at the question, "Why do you want to go to ___________ College?"
- DO Pay attention to word, character, and space limits.
- DO Write essays that will reflect your voice and your unique perspective. Write about things that interest you.
- DO Be specific when describing your activities. Remember that activities include things you do both inside and outside of school. Work, church involvement, caring for siblings, and caring for family members are all things that count as activities, and we want to hear about them.
- DO Brag about yourself. Tell us everything you have accomplished, and don't spare us the details. We want to hear it all.
- DO Write meaty essays within the word, character, or space limits.

BIO *Dr. DeAngela Burns-Wallace is Director of Access Initiatives at University of Missouri.*

Don't

- DON'T Leave words misspelled or write in texting shorthand;
- DON'T Forget to change the name of a school in an essay when you are using the same essay to apply to multiple schools.
- DON'T Use your personal e-mail address if it is inappropriate. Often time, your e-mail address in one of the first things an admissions officer will see. You might not want hotstuffxoxo@email.com to make that first impression.
- DON'T Treat you application like a Facebook profile. Your application should be a vivid portrait of you, but not a casual one.
- DON'T Copy and paste the same answer to the question, "Why do you want to go to _____College?" for every college you apply to.
- DON'T Write more than the word limit, character limit, or space will allow. Any words written beyond this limit will be lost in application outer space.
- DON'T Write essays that you think will please or impress an admissions officer.
- DON'T Assume we will know what an acronym means or will know that you were a leader in a club/group if you don't tell us. If you can't fit an appropriate explanation into the activities chart of an application, you can use the additional information section to elaborate.
- DON'T Be too humble and feel embarrassed about detailing your achievements, awards, honors, and leadership opportunities.
- DON'T Write only one or two sentences and call it an essay.

Articles | Chapter 5

How do I afford it?

Questions about the FAFSA (Free Application for Federal Student Aid) and financial aid:

What is the FAFSA?

Students use this application to apply for federal student grants, work-study money, and loans to assist them in funding their college education. They also may use this application to apply for most state and some private financial aid.

When should I complete the FAFSA?

You should apply as soon as possible after January 1. If your college has a deadline earlier than when your parents will have their taxes done, go ahead and estimate and meet the college's deadline. You can always correct the information later.

My parents are separated or divorced. Which parent fills out the FAFSA?

The parent you lived with most during the last 12 months. If you didn't live with either parent, or if you lived with each parent an equal number of days, use the parent who provided most of the support to you in the most recent calendar year.

Does my step-parent's income and assets have to be reported on the FASFA?

If the parent whose information you are reporting on the FASFA has married or remarried, you must include information about your step-parent (even if they were not married for the entire year).

What if I don't have a Social Security number or don't want to report it on the FAFSA?

You must enter your Social Security number on the FAFSA. If you don't submit your social security number, the form will be returned unprocessed and you will not be considered for federal student aid. Additionally, at least one parent has to include his/her social security number however, if neither parent has one the FAFSA instructs those parents to put 0's instead of a social security number.

The FAFSA asks about last year's income. My parent now is unemployed and our income is significantly less. What should we do?

Go ahead and fill out the FAFSA using last year's income. However, when you get your Student Aid Report (SAR) back, you need to see or write the Financial Aid Administrator at the school(s) you want to attend. Explain the situation documenting the decrease in income. Financial Aid Administrators might use professional judgment to adjust your need if it is warranted and can be documented sufficiently to meet federal guidelines.

Can my parents and I fill out the FAFSA over the internet?

Yes, you can fill out the FAFSA online. It is recommended that you and your parents get PIN codes first so you can sign the FAFSA electronically and not have to print out, sign and send in a paper signature page. Here are the web addresses:

www.pin.ed.gov

www.fafsa.ed.gov

This information furnished by College Goal Sunday, a statewide volunteer program that provides free information and assistance to students and families who are applying for financial aid for post secondary education.
Find us online at **www.collegegoalsundayusa.org**

Questions about College Goal Sunday:

COLLEGE GOAL SUNDAY

Why is College Goal Sunday important?

College Goal Sunday provides assistance in applying for financial aid to families who need it. By delivering help to families in their own communities, College Goal Sunday helps ensure that students get the help they need crossing the paper barrier to qualify for financial aid.

When and where is College Goal Sunday?

The College Goal Sunday program usually is offered on a Sunday afternoon, most often between 2 and 4 p.m. at several locations in each state. Find where you can get help at www.collegegoalsundayusa.org

Who participates in College Goal Sunday?

College Goal Sunday is open to all college-bound students regardless of age. Whether a traditional student right out of high school or an adult who is returning or pursuing higher education for the first time, College Goal Sunday will help you complete the FAFSA, accurately and on time. Dependent students (those under 24) should bring a parent or legal guardian. Independent students (24 or over) will not require a parent's income information.

By Ed Pacchetti

Don't let "sticker price" scare you

One of the most heartbreaking scenarios that unfolds all too often is one in which a low-income, first-generation student logs onto a college or university website, looks at the "sticker price" for tuition and fees, determines they and their families cannot afford it, logs off of the website and gives up on the dream of going to college.

This scenario would happen with less frequency if low-income and first-generation students and their families knew just a few things about financial aid.

1) Your family's credit history will not affect your ability to get federal student aid. The amount of financial aid that you are eligible to receive is based on many factors, such as family size and the cost of the institution that you will be attending, but it has nothing to do with credit history.

2) State aid deadlines are often earlier than federal aid deadlines. File the FAFSA as soon after January 1 of your senior year as you can. As soon as you have tax information available, you should be completing the FAFSA. Your FAFSA report will tell you what "federal aid" you qualify for, but it will not include state aid or institutional aid from the college or university you attend. The combination of federal aid, state aid and institutional aid can provide a substantial portion of your college expenses.

3) Federal aid is available to full-time and part-time students, so even if you only plan to attend college part-time, you should still fill out the FAFSA to determine what kind of federal aid you are entitled to receive.

4) Indicate on the FAFSA that you are interested in a work-study job. Answering "Yes" to this question does not obligate you to have a work-study job when you're in college. You can always turn it down later. However, if you answer "No" to that question and decide later that you need a work-study job, all of the work-study funds at your school may have been used up.

5) Don't assume that you will pay the "sticker price" that a college or university advertises. In fact, very few students pay the "full sticker price" of attending college. This price is most often discounted, and especially for students who demonstrate financial need. ■

BIO *Ed Pacchetti is Deputy Director for the U.S. Department of Education Office of Postsecondary Education (OPE). OPE formulates federal postsecondary education policy and administers programs that address critical national needs in support of increased access to quality postsecondary education. Learn more at www.ed.gov.*

By Bob Giannino-Racine

Understand Your Financial Aid Package

Congratulations, you've been accepted to college! Now comes the hard part of figuring out how much college is going to cost and how to pay for it. Below are some tips to help you understand your financial aid package and make the decision about how to pay.

Understanding Award Letters. When analyzing your award letters, consider two key categories of information—Gift Aid vs. Self-Help Aid and the Full Cost of Attendance. Gift Aid is money from the government (federal or state), the college, or other sources that do ***not*** need to be paid back. Self-Help Aid is money that either needs to be paid back or earned through work study. By comparing these two categories—on a school-by-school basis—you will find how much of the final bill you and your family will be required to foot. The second aspect of your award letter is the Full Cost of Attendance, which includes tuition, fees, room, board, books, transportation, and any miscellaneous charges.

Calculating Need. After figuring out how much school will cost and how much financial aid you'll receive, you can determine the unmet need or gap that will have to pay. To find your need, take the Full Cost of Attendance and subtract the total amount of aid offered (both Gift Aid and Self-Help Aid). All schools don't cost the same and every financial aid package is different, so it's important to follow this exercise for every one of the colleges you get in to.

Making a Decision. Finances are the number one reason cited by students for not finishing college, so it's very important that you carefully consider cost when choosing a school. Be mindful of how much debt you'll have at graduation because it can impact major life decisions like buying a home or what jobs you can accept. Once you've decided which school is the right fit academically and financially—in the short and long term—then you're ready to decide.

Final Tips.

1. Don't hesitate to call a school's financial aid office if you don't understand your award letter.

2. Remember that the offer you're considering—unless it says differently—is ***only*** for the first year, not for all four years!

3. Consider living at home if your college is close by, even for just a year or two. It can save you a lot of money!

4. Search for outside scholarships to help bring down your tuition.

5. A tuition payment plan can help break down your unmet need into small, manageable payments that are interest free! ■

BIO *Bob Giannino-Racine is the Executive Director of ACCESS (The Action Center for Educational Services and Scholarships), the leading provider of financial aid advising and scholarships for Boston Public School Students.*

By Amy Weinstein

Tips for Finding Scholarships to Help Pay for Your College Education

search and find all kinds of scholarships . . . start early and look everywhere

Did you know scholarships can help you pay for your college education? In fact, the more scholarship money you get, the less you will have to borrow to pay for tuition, room and board, books, and other expenses. Most importantly, unlike loans, scholarships do not need to be repaid and need to be an important part of your financial aid package.

You can find scholarships that are industry specific – those that have to do with science, technology, engineering, the arts or mathematics. Additionally, there are scholarships if you have overcome challenging life obstacles. There are a number of scholarships available for students who are gifted academically, artistically, athletically, or musically.

Members from the National Scholarship Providers Association (NSPA) give scholarships and are committed to access, choice and success. They offered the following tips for finding and applying for scholarships:

Start Early

"If you're a freshmen and sophomore in high school, you should be looking at scholarship applications early on, in order to see what kind of information scholarship providers request. It is overwhelming for many students who begin looking at applications late in their junior year, only to realize that they could have been a bit more proactive in their level of involvement both in their school and in their community." *Patti Ross, Coca-Cola Scholars Foundation*

Look Everywhere

"Remember to look for scholarships at your local community foundation! Other sources include high schools, libraries, employers, civic groups, community organizations, private foundations, and online searches. It's worth spending time to complete these applications. Two hours spent completing applications that can get you a $500 scholarship is like getting $250 per hour for your efforts!" *Dawn Lapierre, Community Foundation of Western Mass.*

"Applying for scholarships is like applying for college. The process is lengthy, and takes commitment on your part to find the best options available. Check with your local area merchants, guidance counselors and librarians for information on possible opportunities. Search the web. Adhere to all deadlines and information requirements. Applying late or sending incomplete information is not the message you want to send to scholarship providers." *Vanessa Evans, Ron Brown Scholar Program*

"Don't Give Up. You might be able to find scholarships your freshman year in college to fund the next year. Some scholarships are renewable each year (provided you meet certain requirements). Register on Scholarships.com while you are in high school, the earlier the better." *Kevin Ladd, Scholarships.com*

Be Thorough

"When searching for scholarships using an online matching service like FastWeb.com, try to complete the profile as thoroughly as possible. Students who answer all of the optional questions on average will match twice as many scholarships as students who answer only the required questions. If you have to pay money to get money, it's probably a scam. Never invest more than a postage stamp to obtain information about scholarships or to apply for scholarships." *Mark Kantrowitz, Publisher of FinAid.org and FastWeb.com*

"Earn it. Scholarships are free, but they require effort on your part.Write the topically specific essays first and see if you can "recycle" some of the language for the general essays. Be thorough and polite. Once you begin applying, make sure to read, understand and follow the rules. If you don't follow the rules you could be disqualified." *Kevin Ladd, Scholarships.com* ■

BIO *Amy Weinstein is Executive Director of the National Scholarship Providers Association (NSPA), the only national organization dedicated solely to supporting the needs of professionals administering scholarships in colleges and universities, non-profits and foundations.*

The following free web sites allow you to search for scholarships offering millions of dollars to help you pay for college. You'll find a range of different scholarships; find the ones that suit you best and apply. Good luck!

College Board Scholarship Search, www.collegeboard.org

The College Board Scholarship Search provides users with access to information about more than 2,300 sources of college scholarships, internships, loans and grants. Results from the site are tailored to students' educational level, talents and backgrounds; and are acquired through the College Board's Annual Survey of Financial Aid Programs.

FastWeb, www.fastweb.com

FastWeb provides students with a scholarship directory searchable by college, year of study, extracurricular activities, academic interest and race. Once you create a personal profile, you are matched with scholarships from a database of over 1.5 million scholarships. The site also offers advice on the college admission process, financial aid and student life; while providing tools such as discussion boards, checklists, and financial aid calculators.

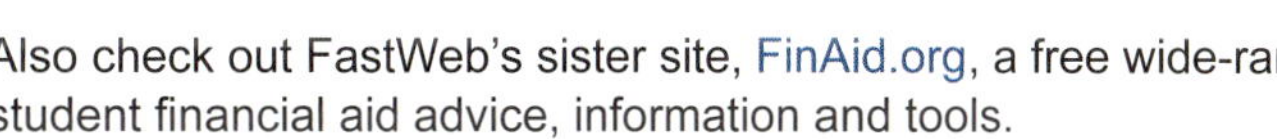

Also check out FastWeb's sister site, FinAid.org, a free wide-ranging source of student financial aid advice, information and tools.

FindTuition, www.findtuition.com

FindTuition is a free search tool through which users can research, target and manage scholarship opportunities by college, athletic interest and prospective major. Site services include a free scholarship search from a database containing over $7 billion dollars in aid, a specific loan search, an online college search and detailed information on thousands of schools.

Scholarships.com, www.scholarships.com

Scholarship.com consists of free scholarship search results, and financial aid information resources. The site contains 2.7 million frequently updated scholarships and its own scholarship awards. Many scholarship results are based on characteristics like financial need, intended field of study and community service, rather than academic achievement.

Scholarship Experts, www.scholarshipexperts.com

ScholarshipExperts.com provides students and parents with free and organized scholarship search results without comprising their privacy. These results are customized to match profiles created by student users, and are consistently updated by a team of scholarship researchers that works closely with scholarship providers. The Application Request Tool allows users to request detailed scholarship application information for specific scholarships from their search results.

Zinch, www.zinch.com

Zinch gives students access to 5,000+ school profiles and $2 billion in scholarships. Based on individual student profiles, students are matched with scholarships; and given the opportunity to learn about, interact with and get recruited by schools from around the world. Zinch also connects students to other students, and provides parents and counselors with free downloadable financial aid information guides.

Getting Free Money for College

Now is the time for you to prepare for applying to competitive scholarship programs. Consider these steps:

1 **Set goals.** Develop short- and long-term goals for your college years and beyond. Scholarship programs want you to have goals to work toward. They lay a foundation for your future.

2 **Make the grades.** It is important to do well academically. Scholarship programs are looking for students who do well in school. Strong study and note taking skills are keys to academic achievement.

3 **Be a leader.** Engage in leadership and extracurricular activities. You do not have to limit yourself to being an officer in an established organization. You can also create opportunities for leadership, such as identifying a cause that interests you and develop and implement a plan.

4 **Make a difference.** Community service can benefit those you serve and can make you competitive for scholarships. Giving back is a way to enhance your leadership skills, make a difference in the lives of others and support your community.

5 **Keep a log.** Document your leadership and community service activities. Most scholarship applications require you to provide information from 9th through 12th grade that details the date, activity and number of hours of your engagement in your activity. Include a description that measures your activities. A good example, "I coordinated a project that provided clothing for over 200 homeless people." Versus, "I participated in a clothing drive effort."

6 **Build relationships.** A teacher or other educator is often required to support your scholarship application. It is important to start developing relationships early with individuals who know your academic and/or personal achievements.

7 **Use your resources.** Family members, teachers and community organizations are all a part of your resources. Ask for their assistance in reviewing your work, reading essays for scholarships and providing tips for success.

8 **Make a commitment to succeed.** Most scholarship applications have some question(s) that determine your ability to meet challenges. Make the choice to never give up and use those experiences when you are successful to tell your story.

BIO *Mary Williams is Director of Communications & Administration for the Gates Millennium Scholars Program.*

SCHOLARSHIPS

Don't miss out on applying for these flagship scholarships for low-income, minority, and first-generation college-bound students.

CSO OPPORTUNITY SCHOLARSHIP, www.csopportunity.org

AWARD AMOUNT: $8,000 total; $2,000/year for four years
DEADLINE: May

Center for Student Opportunity's Opportunity Scholarship is awarded to graduating high school seniors who will be first in their family to attend college and are enrolling at a CSO College Partner. Scholarship winners are also given the opportunity to serve as student bloggers on CSO College Center's web blog to share their college journeys and offer advice on how to make it to college. Log on to www.CSOCollegeCenter.org and complete a ConnectNow profile to become an Opportunity Scholar for guidance through the college process before you apply for the scholarship.

GATES MILLENNIUM SCHOLARS PROGRAM, www.gmsp.org

AWARD AMOUNT: Based on financial need
DEADLINE: January

The Gates Millennium Scholars Program (GMS) is the nation's largest private scholarship program and works to eliminate financial barriers for African American, Asian/Pacific Islander, American Indian/Alaskan Native, and Hispanic American students to further their education especially in the fields of computer science, education, engineering, library science, mathematics, public health and the sciences—subjects in which these groups are severely underrepresented. Each year GMS selects 1,000 students to receive a four-year scholarship to use at any college or university of their choice, along with academic support and professional guidance throughout their collegiate career.

POSSE FOUNDATION, www.possefoundation.org

AWARD AMOUNT: Four-year, full tuition scholarship
DEADLINE: Nominations are accepted from spring of a student's junior year through the fall of their senior year.

The Posse Foundation is a college access and youth leadership development program that identifies, recruits, and selects student leaders from public high schools in Atlanta, Boston, Chicago, Los Angeles, Miami, New York or Washington, D.C., and sends them in groups called Posses to some of the top colleges and universities in the country. Each Posse is comprised of 10 Scholars who receive four-year, full-tuition leadership scholarships. Students must be nominated by their high school or community-based organization, be a high school senior, and demonstrate leadership and academic potential.

QUESTBRIDGE, www.questbridge.org

AWARD AMOUNT: Up to $200,000
DEADLINE: September

The QuestBridge National College Match Scholarship connects high-achieving low-income high school seniors with admission and full four-year scholarships to some of the nation's leading colleges. To qualify, you must be a high school senior, demonstrate academic achievement, and come from a low-income background. Historically, most awardees come from households earning under $60,000 per year.

AWARD AMOUNT: Varies
DEADLINE: March

The QuestBridge College Prep Scholarship equips high-achieving low-income students with the knowledge necessary to compete for admission to the nation's most selective colleges. To qualify, you must be a high school junior, demonstrate academic achievement, and come from a low-income background. Historically, most awardees come from households earning under $60,000 per year.

SCHOLARSHIPS

COCA-COLA SCHOLARS, www.coca-colascholars.org

AWARD AMOUNT: Up to $20,000
DEADLINE: October

Each year Coca-Cola Scholars selects 50 students as National Scholars who receive $20,000 scholarships to college, and 200 students as Regional Scholars who receive $10,000 scholarships to college. Students selected as Coca-Cola scholars commit to leadership development and community involvement for their entire collegiate career and for the rest of their lives. In addition, the Coca-Cola First-Generation Scholarship has awarded more than $19 million in scholarships to more than 1,000 students who are the first in their immediate families to go to college at approximately 400 U.S. campuses. Interested students should contact the school you plan to attend to see if the scholarship is offered.

DELL SCHOLARS PROGRAM, www.dellscholars.org

AWARD AMOUNT: $20,000 and technology
DEADLINE: January

The Dell Scholars Program provides students with $20,000 to put towards their college education over six years and support including technology, mentoring, and a network of previous Dell Scholars to assist them through their collegiate career. In order to be eligible, students must have participated in a Michael & Susan Dell Foundation approved college access or college readiness program for at least two years of high school and have demonstrated need.

UNITED NEGRO COLLEGE FUND, www.uncf.org

AWARD AMOUNT: Varies
DEADLINE: Varies

The United Negro College Fund (UNCF) works to help under-represented, low income students attend and graduate from college through scholarship opportunities, active support of HBCUs, and promotion of higher education opportunities for African Americans throughout the community. UNCF awards over 10,000 scholarships to African American students through more than 400 scholarship, internship, fellowships and grants.

HISPANIC SCHOLARSHIP FUND, www.hsf.net

AWARD AMOUNT: Varies
DEADLINE: December

The Hispanic Scholarship Fund (HSF) works to make higher education more accessible to Hispanic Americans. HSF awards scholarships to Hispanic American high school students and community college graduates with plans of attending a full-time undergraduate degree program at an accredited U.S. college or university.

THE ASIAN & PACIFIC ISLANDER AMERICAN SCHOLARSHIP FUND, www.apiasf.org

AWARD AMOUNT: Varies
DEADLINE: January

The Asian & Pacific Islander American Scholarship Fund (APIASF) awards scholarships to Asian and Pacific Islander Americans from disadvantaged backgrounds and/or with significant leadership and community service experience in high school. Once selected, scholars receive individual advising and access to support services and programs, in addition to financial assistance, to help them with the transition from high school to college and throughout their time as college students until graduation.

SHOW ME THE MONEY!

Seanna Leath
College: Pomona College
Hometown: N. Little Rock, AR

For many low-income, first-generation students, scholarships and financial aid are crucially important in the college choice process. Personally, one of my top priorities in choosing a college relied on the school's ability to provide financial aid that I could afford to repay after graduation. In my hopes of continuing on to graduate from medical school, four years of undergraduate study is only the beginning. Therefore, scholarships and financial aid were a large focus during senior year. Here are a few things that I wish I'd known beforehand, or that I learned along the way:

1. It is a process. Pursuing scholarships and financial aid does not happen overnight. Rome was not built in a day, and only on very rare occasions will a student acquire all of the funds necessary to support a college education through one source. Instead, students should plan on looking at a variety of sources for financial support, including community, school, and corporation scholarships. Many colleges have available grant money or special scholarships given annually to a select number of students. Also, just as in any process, generous amounts of time should be devoted to seeking and completing scholarship applications. Although some applications may only require demographic information, many require recommendations and essays, all of which require time, attention, and effort.

2. Just do it! Searching for scholarships is an active process of trial and error. Although there are millions of scholarship opportunities out there, many apply to a limited number of people (students born on an Indian reservation or students whose parents work at Wal-Mart). Although a great number might apply to you, there is still the process of weeding out those that don't. Using scholarship search engines can be a great way to find hundreds of opportunities that seem to fit your criteria, but you must still zone in on those that suit you best. Procrastinating is one of the worst things that can be done during this process. Start early and remain diligent.

3. Collaborate and Synthesize Although every scholarship deserves your undivided attention, the reality of being able to write new essays for every application is impractical and could potentially add extra, unnecessary stress to your senior year. Instead, determine if a certain spectacular essay can be applied to more than one scholarship. If three different applications ask about your aspirations for after college, consider writing one original and creative essay to satisfy all three. It is always beneficial to manage time wisely!

"He is able who thinks he is able" ~Gautama Siddharta

SEANNA LEATH is a CSO Opportunity Scholarship winner. Seanna shares her college experiences and offers advice on the Opportunity Scholars blog.

Visit www.CSOCollegeCenter.org to follow the blog, sign up to become a CSO Opportunity Scholar, and have the chance to be a future Opportunity Scholarship winner and blogger yourself!

By Ann Coles

Smart Borrowing for College

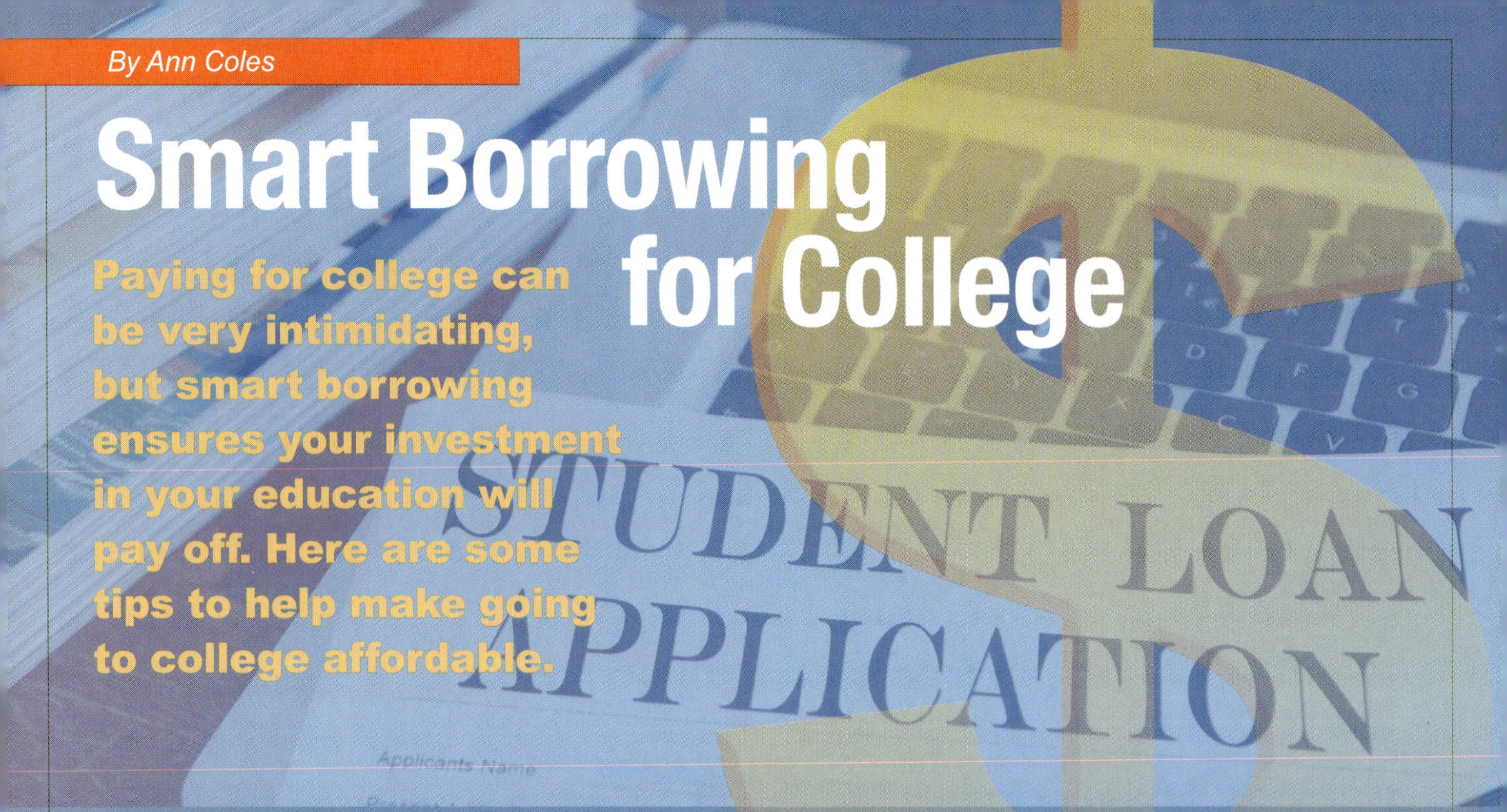

Paying for college can be very intimidating, but smart borrowing ensures your investment in your education will pay off. Here are some tips to help make going to college affordable.

STUDENT LOAN APPLICATION

1. Use scholarships, grants, savings, and work-study earnings before taking out loans

• Grants and scholarships are gift money that you never have to repay. Work-study requires you to earn the money awarded.

• Complete the FAFSA (Free Application for Federal Student Aid) before March 1 of the year you plan to go to college. Some colleges also require you to complete the CSS PROFILE. If your family has limited income, you may be eligible for a fee waiver.

• Search scholarships in online databases and talk to high school counselors, public librarians, community organization and church staff, parents' employers and college financial aid officers.

• Save as much money for college as you can from after-school and summer jobs.

• Talk to a financial aid officer at the college you want to attend if your family has special financial circumstances that make it difficult for them to help you with college costs.

2. Reduce borrowing by using other options

• Use an interest-free monthly payment plan that allows you to spread the cost of paying for college over the school year. Your college financial aid office can recommend a plan.

• Work part-time but preferably not more than 15 hours a week so that you will have enough time to do well in your studies.

• Consider going to a college that has eliminated or limited loans for most students.

3. Borrow wisely

• Borrow only what you need because loans need to be repaid—even if you don't finish college. Never use student loans to pay off other bills or buy things you may want but don't need.

• Carefully compare your financial aid award letters from different colleges. If you don't understand an award letter, call the financial aid office and ask someone to explain it to you.

• Borrow federal student loans first. Federal loans (Perkins and Stafford Loans for students, PLUS loans for parents) have low fixed interest rates and flexible repayment plans. Apply for a private student loan only if federal loans are not enough.

• Consider options for having your student loans forgiven, such as volunteer service (participating in the Peace Corps, VISTA, or AmeriCorps).

4. Never use credit cards to pay for your education

• Credit cards are the most expensive source of funds. If you must borrow, exhaust all federal loan options first and then consider private education loans to pay for expenses.

• If you have an emergency, talk to a financial aid advisor to see if your college has an emergency loan fund or can help you in some other way.

Useful Web Sites

> Federal Student Aid: www.federalstudentaid.ed.gov provides information about federal grants and loans. You also can complete the FASFA online.

> FinAid! Calculators: www.finaid.org/calculators has calculators you can use to estimate your college costs, compare your financial aid awards from different colleges, compare the cost of borrowing different types of loans, and determine how much to borrow.

> Project on Student Debt: www.projectonstudentdebt.org features advice to borrowers and a listing of colleges and universities that have decided to eliminate or limit loans from their financial aid award packages for many students.

> Simple Tuition: www.simpletuition.com allows users to compare student loans from over 90 sources. Remember, featured lenders may not necessarily be the best alternative for you.

Important Student Loan Terms

- **APR (Annual Percentage Rate):** the total cost of a loan, including the interest rate and fees, expressed as the percentage of the amount borrowed that you have to pay each year. It is a good way to compare loans from different lenders.
- **Co-borrower or co-signer:** A person who agrees to pay the loan if the primary borrower can not or does not pay. Some lenders require students to get a co-borrower with good credit before they will make a loan.
- **Cost of Attendance:** The total cost of attending a particular college for a year, including tuition and fees, housing costs, food, books and supplies, transportation, and other necessary expenses such as a personal computer and health care.
- **Credit:** Indicates a person's financial strength, which includes a history of having paid bills and the demonstrated ability to repay a future loan.
- **Discount:** A reduction in the interest rate or the fees charged on a loan.
- **Interest:** The money or price paid by the borrower to use someone else's funds. Interest is stated as a percentage of the original amount borrowed.
- **Promissory Note or Credit Agreement:** A legal contract the borrower signs with the lender that details the terms of the loan including how and when it must be repaid.

BIO *Ann Coles has been working on college readiness since the 1960s and currently serves as College Access Senior Fellow at ACCESS, an organization that works to ensure that all young people in Boston have the financial information and resources necessary to achieve their dream of a higher education.*

By Katie Delaney

Survival of the Fittest: 8 Ways to Survive College on a Budget

Look for student discounts.

Many shops, restaurants, and businesses around college campuses offer discounts to students with their student ID. Carry your student ID with you at all times, and when you need to go grocery shopping or buy anything, use coupon's, daily discounts, and compare prices at different stores to ensure you are getting the best price.

Save on college textbooks.

Textbooks have become one of the most expensive aspects of college, with book costs ranging from $500-$700 (per semester!) Rather than buying new textbooks, opt for used books at your bookstore,or buy from sites like amazon.com, half.com or chegg.com. When buying from online sellers, just be sure to search for books by ISBN number so you buy the correct edition, and place your order at least a month in advance as shipping can take longer than usual.

Make a spending plan.

Keep track of your spending habits, distinguish between needs and wants, and figure out what responsibilities you have financially (bills, food, transportation, laundry). Allot a certain amount of money for spending during each week at school to make sure you're various "needs" are accounted for, leaving wiggle room for an occasional "want" if possible.

Use public transportation.

Avoid the unnecessary cost of gas if your school offers free shuttles or inexpensive buses. And don't forget the option of walking or biking when you can; it's free and you'll also get some exercise!

Be careful with credit.

While credit cards provide students with a way to start building good credit and a safety net in case of emergency, they can also wreak havoc on a student's financial plan. Overspending, making late payments, or forgetting to make payments can do serious damage to your credit score, a number that is very important to your chances of being able to buy a car, buy a home, or even get a job later in life. If you decide to have a credit card, be sure to keep track of your spending and pay off your purchases as soon as you make them.

Get a job. Most colleges and universities offer on-campus jobs to students. Talk to your schools' business office, career center, or the department of your academic major about what's available. Jobs in your field of study, such as working as a research assistant in a science lab, serve as easy résumé builders and look great to future employers.

Check out credit unions. Credit unions offer a great alternative to big-name banks for your first credit account. Banks are trying to make money, so they may charge extra to open an account, charge fees to use other banks' ATMs, and have high penalty fees if you overdraw your account. Non-profit credit unions offer lower fees, and many colleges and universities have access to a credit union on campus or nearby in the community.

Beware identity theft. Students are particularly vulnerable to identity theft because they don't think they are likely targets since they generally do not have a lot of money. Identity theft can happen quickly and easily, by someone stealing your personal information via email/phone scams, discarded bank statements, or most commonly through information found in a stolen wallet. Make sure your personal information is protected, and avoid carrying any unnecessary information (social security card, passwords, etc.) in your wallet that you don't absolutely need.

BIO *Katie Delaney is a first-generation college student at Franklin & Marshall College and interned with Center for Student Opportunity.*

I HATE BEING BROKE

You can't do a lot of things without money. You can't go out to eat with your friends. You can't enjoy that green tea latte while relaxing at a local Starbucks. You can't buy your Chemistry textbooks (they cost A LOT). And you can't pay for the laundry because each time you use the washer or the dryer it costs you a buck and twenty-five cents (that builds up, you know.) So what are you going to do? Wear your old clothes and hope they don't smell?

Jenny Luong
College: Amherst College
Hometown: Oakland, CA

These are just some of the potential problems of a broke college student. How do I know? I have spent a Saturday night NOT going out because my student card didn't have enough money for the dryer. I ran back to my room to look for change but didn't find any. Then I realized that I couldn't ask my dorm mates for change because they were out partying. So I was just standing in the laundry room, staring stupidly at my pile of wet clothes. Not fun.

Most of us start to feel some freedom once we're in college. "Yes! Mom and Dad can't control how I spend my money anymore!" Well, don't go mad shopping; you'll regret it very soon. You're going to be broke and unhappy. There's going to be too much stuff in your already small dorm room. Besides, come summer, to those who are abroad, where are you going to store your stuff when you go home? Storage space isn't always free…

Hints: When you see piles of coupons in your post office, TAKE THEM! TAKE ALL OF THEM! (No, not really, save some for other people, too.) And do research. Ask your professors before the semester starts about which books to get. See if you can buy them earlier or if there's a secondhand book store. Amherst College has a student run program called The Option where students sell and buy used books.

Research! Save money! And then treat yourself to some wings occasionally. It's good to enjoy life, but be responsible.

JENNY LUONG is a CSO Opportunity Scholarship winner. Jenny shares her college experiences and offers advice on the Opportunity Scholars blog.

Visit www.CSOCollegeCenter.org to follow the blog, sign up to become a CSO Opportunity Scholar, and have the chance to be a future Opportunity Scholarship winner and blogger yourself!

Opportunity Scholars

Notes

Notes

Abigail Macias
College: Dartmouth College
Hometown: Sparks, NV

Darius Journigan
College: Marymount Manhattan College
Hometown: Detroit, MI

Irvin Gomez
College: Dartmouth College
Hometown: Waukegan, IL

Jenny Luong
College: Amherst College
Hometown: Oakland, CA

Jeremy Harris
College: University of Missouri
Hometown: Chicago, IL

Jordan Lillegard
College: Univ of Southern California
Hometown: Long Beach, CA

2010-2011 Opportunity Scholarship winners blog

Learn how they made it to college and get their advice on how you can too.

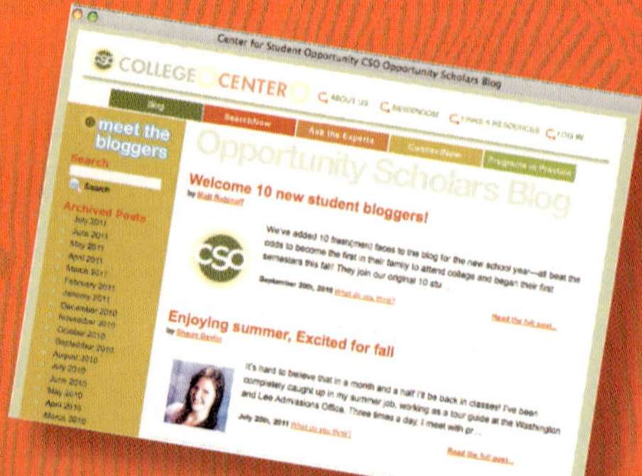

www.CSOcollegecenter.org

FREE services for students

- Connect with colleges recruiting first-generation, low-income, minority students
- Monthly newsletters, college admissions guidance and support
- Apply for CSO's $8,000 Opportunity Scholarships at the end of your senior year for your chance to become a student blogger on the Opportunity Scholars blog

Leah Jean-Louis
College: Swarthmore College
Hometown: Cambridge, MA

Lot Kwarteng
College: Miami University
Hometown: Bronx, NY

Shaun Devlin
College: Washington and Lee University
Hometown: Canton, IL

Sophia Horn
College: California State Univ, Chico
Hometown: Whittier, CA

CSO Center *for* Student Opportunity
www.CSOpportunity.org

Opportunity Scholars

Padres y Mentores en Español página 127

Parents & Mentors

Whether you're a parent, guardian, teacher, mentor, or other caring adult, chances are there's a teen in your life who wants to go to college. You can help your teen succeed by taking time to learn about college planning and financing. Together, you and the teen you care about can share this important goal and achieve it.

MENTORS: Why College?

Q

"Why should I get a college degree?" Has the teen in your life ever asked you this question? Whether you're a parent, guardian, or other caring adult, you need convincing, practical answers to share with your teen. Here they are:

A

"You'll gain greater understanding and skills to help you be successful in our complex world."

College enables you to:

- Expand your knowledge and skills.
- Express your thoughts clearly in speech and in writing.
- Grasp abstract concepts and theories.
- Increase your understanding of the world and your community.
- Gain more financial security.

"You'll find a greater range and a number of job opportunities."

In our changing world, more and more jobs require education beyond high school. College graduates have more jobs to choose from than those who don't pursue education beyond high school.

"You'll earn more money—a lot more."

A person who goes to college usually earns more than a person who doesn't. According to the U.S. Census Bureau, on average, someone with a bachelor's degree earns $51,206—almost double the $27,915 earned annually by someone with only a high school diploma.

Planning for College: Ten Steps

10

Step One

Save money as early as possible to help pay for your teen's education.

Step Two

Encourage your teen to make high school count, preparing academically for higher education.

Step Three

Discuss with your teen his or her skills and interests, career options and schools he or she is interested in attending.

Step Four

Meet with the high school guidance counselor to determine what schools match your teen's academic abilities.

Step Five

Gather information about the schools your teen is interested in attending, including information on financial aid.

Step Six

Take your teen to visit a college campus and ask the right questions.

Step Seven

Help your teen apply for admission. To apply for financial aid, help your child complete the FAFSA.

Step Eight

Consider scholarships, grants, and work-study programs. Complete any necessary applications or forms and submit them before the deadline.

Step Nine

Consider the loan programs available to you and your child.

Step Ten

Learn more about tax credits, deductions, and other considerations for education expenses.

Talking to Your Teen

It may not always be easy to talk with your teen. But it's important that you support your teen throughout their college planning—help them organize the process, meet deadlines, and talk with the right people. Here are a few tips to consider:

Listen.

Be receptive to and listen when your teen wants to discuss career and/or college plans.

Explore.

Have your teen explore career and college options and collect as much information as possible.

Encourage.

Encourage them to capture their ideas on paper. One idea is to create a scrapbook of their plans for career and college.

Be aware.

Be aware of various deadlines for applications to colleges and financial aid. Put them on a calendar that both you and your teen can look at.

Step in.

Suggest that your teen meet with a school counselor at least once a year, beginning in the 10th grade, to learn more about college and career planning.

Step out.

Give your teen the space *and* support to set some goals and take steps to reach them.

Be supportive.

Be supportive of your teen, and meet with their counselor if you sense that he or she needs additional help.

Connect to career.

Encourage your teen by helping them see the connection between college and career. Emphasize the importance of selecting a major that helps them prepare for a career.

Research.

If your teen is undecided about a career direction, do not try to fix it. Let them look into all the possibilities.

Conversation-Starters

We know that it is often difficult to break the ice with students and get them talking about the steps they need to take to go to college. Think about asking your student the following questions to encourage him or her to turn college dreams into a college plan.

Which adults in your life do you know who went to college?

What excites you about going to college?

What are the reasons you want to go?

I know you want to go to college. Who else have you told about your college plans?

Which adults do you turn to for help when you have a problem you need to solve?

STEP 1 BE A PAIN

Students know that colleges require certain courses, but they often don't know which ones or find out too late into high school to take them all. Get your student thinking about the courses required for college admission by asking some of the following questions:

What courses are you taking this year?

Which courses do you find easiest?

Which do you find the hardest?

Have you thought about which courses are required for certain majors or careers?

Does your high school offer Advanced Placement courses?

How can you sign up?

STEP 2 PUSH YOURSELF

Conversation-Starters

It is often hard for students to visualize the many postsecondary options available to them. But finding the right fit is an important factor in ensuring a student enjoys and completes college. Use the following questions to get your student thinking about the type of school that's right for him or her.

When you think about college …

Do you have thoughts on what you'd like to study?

Are you interested in going away to school or going to school close to home?

Do you like the idea of a big campus with a lot of students or a smaller campus?

Are you interested in participating in activities like sports? Music? Community service?

Would you like to be in an urban environment or somewhere more rural?

Do you want to live in a campus dorm or commute from home?

STEP 3 FIND THE RIGHT FIT

It's hard to talk about money, especially with middle or high school students who may not understand their family's financial situation. Here are some ways to start the conversation and get your student thinking about preparing financially for college.

What courses are you taking this year?

Do you know that the government provides loans to students who can't afford college?

Have you talked with your parents about how you might pay for college?

Do you have questions about how much college costs?

Where would you look first for information about loans and scholarships? Is there an adult at school who would know where to look?

STEP 4 PUT YOUR HANDS ON SOME CASH

By Jaye Fenderson

Getting Your Child To College – No Degree Required!

It all begins with knowing when to get started and how to find the information you need.

For many parents the idea of their son or daughter going to college is exciting but also overwhelming.

There's a lot to think about and plan for even if you're a parent that graduated from college. But the good news is that there is a wealth of information about how to prepare and apply for college, so even if this is your first time going through the process, rest assured that there are resources to help you and your teenager find the best college fit at an affordable price.

It all begins with knowing when to get started and how to find the information you need.

Start Early – Get a College Mindset

Many students wait until senior year before they start thinking about their college plans, but the truth is that students should actually start planning for college in middle school or junior high. Why so early, you might ask? Well, that's because colleges take into consideration all four years of high school (9th-12th) including the classes a student takes, his or her GPA, as well as any activities, leadership or awards received.

Get Organized

You'll soon receive a flood of information in the form of college brochures, scholarship and financial aid forms, and notifications from your child's guidance office. If you don't have a way to organize all this information, it can be overwhelming or worse yet, you might end up losing track of important papers.

So help your teen create a simple filing system with dividers labeled for college brochures, scholarships, financial aid, as well as one for your child's awards and accomplishments. By the time senior year rolls around, you'll easily be able to access the information you need to help your teen apply for college. You should get in the habit of keeping a calendar on the refrigerator or in your teen's bedroom that lists important college admission dates and deadlines.

Know Where to Look

Visit the high school's college and career center—this is the most important resource where you'll find information about financial aid, local scholarships, and college deadlines and requirements—and meet with your teen's counselor at the beginning of high school.

Attend a college night or college fair—most school districts will typically hold some kind of college information session where admission representatives from schools across the country will attend to share information about their programs and how to apply.

Don't Be Afraid to Ask

One of the best resources you have is the power of asking. If you're unsure about an admissions requirement, the cost of applying, or how to fill out the college or financial aid forms, talk to your teen's college counselor, call the college admissions or financial aid office, or find someone—another parent or a current college student—who has recently been through the college admissions process and may be able to answer your question.

So don't be afraid to ask for help – and once you've been through the process yourself, you'll be able to lend a hand to another family. ■

BIO *Jaye Fenderson is the author of Seventeen's* Guide to Getting Into College *and the producer of First Generation, a documentary about students who are first in their families to go to college.*

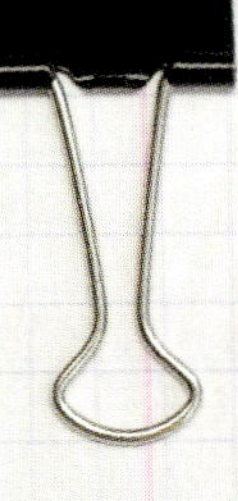

You've probably heard, and might believe, some of these common MYTHS about college. Read on for the REALITIES.

MYTH: Anyone can get into a public university, but it's hard to get into a private college.

REALITY: Some public universities are among the most competitive to get into, while other public universities are required to take nearly all applicants. It's true that some private colleges are very selective, but others take students who wouldn't even be admitted to a home state public university. Check with the colleges you are considering to learn more about the average academic credentials of its students and its admission policies.

MYTH: The college with the lowest price will be the most affordable.

REALITY: Not necessarily! Some of the colleges with a high "sticker price" have raised significant amounts of money for scholarships from their graduates and friends. As a result, they have more money to give to students in the form of scholarships, which reduces the "sticker price." After taking financial aid into consideration, a seemingly more expensive college may be more affordable than a college with a lower list price. Tip: Find out what kinds of scholarship options are available at the colleges you are considering.

MYTH: My teen can make a good living without a college education.

REALITY: There is no doubt that some people have done well without a college degree. However, a college graduate will earn on average about a million dollars more than a high school graduate in his/her lifetime. For most people, college pays.

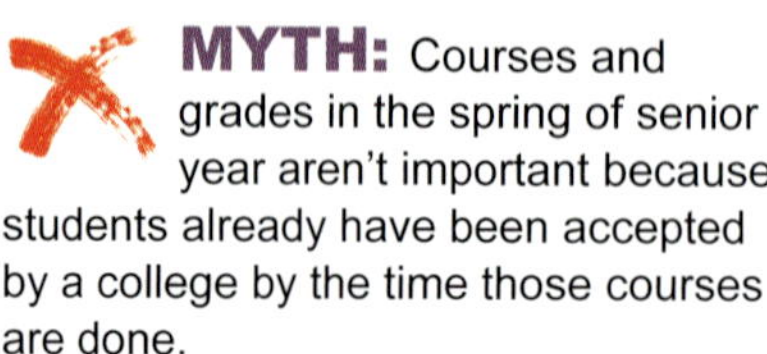

MYTH: Courses and grades in the spring of senior year aren't important because students already have been accepted by a college by the time those courses are done.

REALITY: Most colleges make statements in their admissions materials that they will look at a senior's spring grades. If the student's academic performance has dropped off substantially, colleges have been known to cancel an offer of admission.

MYTH: To make it in today's world you need a four-year college degree.

REALITY: Someone with a four-year degree may have more career options, but there are many satisfying and good-paying jobs that are possible with certain technical or two-year degrees. Your teen should start with the fields that are of interest to him and learn what kind of education is required and what the job opportunities are in those areas. Then get the degree he needs for the type of career he wants.

MYTH: I don't have the money and my teen can't afford to take out loans to pay for college, even if she wanted to go.

REALITY: Almost all students today can get low-rate education loans to help them pay for college, and education loans typically don't have to be paid back until a student is out of school. The average loan debt of undergraduate students today is roughly $20,000 – that's less than the cost of most new cars! A car lasts a few years. A college education lasts a lifetime.

MYTH: It really doesn't matter if I wait a year or two to go to college.

REALITY: Many students who don't go to college right after high school never get around to it. Others bring great experience to the college when they enroll because of what they did with the time off from school. It is wise for a student to apply to colleges of interest during senior year just like any other student. She can then ask a college to defer enrollment for a year or two, if the student needs the time away. Most colleges will hold the offer of admission, especially if the student has plans that will ultimately make the student even more interesting or valuable as a member of the campus community.

Caution: If the student works during this time away, the income of the student (if substantial) may hinder her/his need-based financial aid eligibility when s/he goes back to school. Because the student will in many cases still qualify as a dependent student, only a small amount of income will be protected under the federal formula. Amounts beyond that can hurt financial aid eligibility.

MYTH: You need to start planning for college during your junior year of high school.

REALITY: While some students may wait this late to do certain things like visiting potential colleges or taking the SAT's, there are other things that should never wait this long. For example, high school course selections and grades represent the single most important consideration in most colleges' admissions decisions. High school course decisions are made sometimes as early as the middle school years. Financial planning, saving for college, and finding out which colleges will be affordable also should be done well before the junior year.

MYTH: No one in my family has gone to college – why should my teen be the first?

REALITY: After high school, your teen may have 40 or 50 years of employment ahead. Many changes will occur in the job market during this time. A college education will certainly give him more options for the long term. Many of today's jobs which require only a high school diploma may no longer exist a few years from now. His education should prepare him for the job market of the future, not the present.

MYTH: Students today have so much loan debt that it doesn't make sense to pay a lot to go to college.

REALITY: Most students who have huge loan debt usually have either done a poor job of finding a college where their family's financial aid works well, or they made a conscious decision to take on that kind of loan debt so they can attend a particular college. (Remember, the average loan debt of undergraduate students today is roughly $20,000 – that's less than the cost of most new cars!) The goal for most families is to find in advance schools that will be financially reasonable for them, usually by using a published financial aid estimator to understand where they stand under the federal formula for financial aid.

MYTH: There isn't a lot of financial aid available, and what is available only goes to a few of the very best students.

REALITY: During the 2002-03 academic year, over $105 billion dollars in financial aid was awarded. The vast majority of this money was doled out by the federal government through grant, loan and work-study programs, while colleges' own grants and scholarships accounted for almost 20% of all financial aid. States helped too by contributing over $5.5 billion to the pot. That's a lot of money for a lot of students. In fact, over 70% of students nationally receive some kind of financial aid.

Visit the Campus

The best reason to visit a college campus is to get a personal feeling for the quality of education being offered there. While on a campus visit, you and your teen should ask questions that will reveal a school's commitment to providing the best educational environment. The questions that follow can help:

Level of academic challenge?

Challenging intellectual and creative work is central to maintaining a quality learning environment.

- To what degree is studying and spending time on academic work emphasized?
- Do faculty hold students to high standards?
- How much time do students spend on homework each week?
- How much writing is expected?
- How much reading is expected?

Active and collaborative learning?

Students learn more when they are directly involved in their education and have opportunities to collaborate with others in solving problems or mastering difficult material.

- How often do students discuss ideas in class?
- How often are topics from class discussed outside of the classroom?
- Do students work together on projects—inside and outside of class?
- How often do students make class presentations?
- How many students participate in community-based projects in regular courses?
- How many students apply their classroom learning to real life through internships or off-campus field experiences?
- Do students have opportunities to tutor or teach other students?

Student-faculty interaction?

In general, the more contact students have with their teachers, the better. Working with a professor on a research project or serving with faculty members on a college committee or community organization lets students see first-hand how experts identify and solve practical problems.

- Are faculty members accessible and supportive?
- How many students work on research projects with faculty?
- Do students receive prompt feedback on academic performance?
- How often do students talk with their teachers about what they are learning in class?

- How often do students talk with advisors or faculty members about their career plans?
- Do students and faculty members work together on committees and projects outside of course work?

Enriching educational experiences?

Educationally superior colleges offer a variety of learning opportunities inside and outside the classroom that compliment the goals of the academic program. One of the most important is exposure to students and faculty from diverse backgrounds.

- What types of honors courses, learning communities, and other distinctive programs are offered?
- In what ways do faculty use technology in their classes?
- How often do students interact with peers with different social, political, or religious views?
- How often do students interact with peers from different racial or ethnic backgrounds?
- How many students study in other countries?
- Do students participate in activities that enhance their spirituality?
- What percentage of students do community service?
- What kinds of activities are students involved in outside of the classroom?
- What kinds of events does the campus sponsor?
- Is a culminating senior year experience required?

Supportive campus environment?

Students perform better and are more satisfied at colleges that are committed to their success—and that cultivate positive working and social relationships among different groups on campus.

- How well do students get along with other students?
- Are students satisfied with their overall educational experience?
- How much time do students devote to co-curricular activities?
- How well do students get along with administrators and staff?
- To what extent does the school help students deal with their academic and social needs?

By Maria Carvalho

Be a Safety Net

How to Support Your Child During the College Application Process

Remember the feeling you had when you dropped your child off for the first day of school? I was surprised when that feeling came back years later as I helped my son and daughter navigate the college application process.

Even though they were a lot older, the experience was just as momentous. Going to college is one of the most significant transitions in a young person's life. The ultimate decision about which college is the best fit belongs to him or her, but your support as parents is critical during this complex journey.

It is important to familiarize yourself with the steps your child must take to complete the application process successfully. Serious preparation for college begins in 9th grade as students move into high school. Things really heat up in their junior and senior years. Speaking as a parent of two children who are currently in college, and as a professional in the college-readiness field, I'd like to share a few valuable tips and strategies that got me through this daunting and intense time.

THE RIGHT FIT – Be involved!

• **Get your child thinking.** The more research your child does during junior year, the more informed a decision he or she will be able to make. Ask your child questions about possible majors and career interests. What colleges would be best for those? What about college size and location?

• **Read college handbooks.** Many print resources are available to assist with the college search. Congratulations for reading one right now!

• **Do Internet research.** Websites offer many options to assist students in narrowing down their college choices. You can sort and arrange by campus type, majors, size, and setting. The CSO College Center at www.csocollegecenter.org will get you started.

• **Visit campuses.** April vacation of the junior year is a great time to tour campuses with your child. College visits allow young people to feel the energy of a school and determine if it is a good match. It's an opportunity to explore, evaluate, and get firsthand information.

• **Check academic entrance requirements.** Be sure your child is on track to meet all college/university requirements before applying: college entrance exams, GPA, required high school course load, and so on.

THE TOOLS - Be organized!

• **Get a school year planner.** Have your child record all deadlines (application and financial aid) in a planner. It's a great visual tool!

• **Use an accordion file folder.** Assign one pocket for each application.

• **Stock up on stamps and envelopes.** Your child must supply a self-addressed stamped envelope with every request for a recommendation from teachers and guidance counselors.

THE DEADLINES - Be ahead of the curve!

• **Request applications early in the senior year.** Most colleges and universities have an online application system. Your child can also receive applications by postal mail.

• **Be considerate of busy educators.** Give teachers and guidance counselors enough time to provide recommendations and transcripts. Encourage your child to request appointments with school staff as soon as possible in senior year to get the ball rolling.

• **Help your child prepare a résumé.** Colleges want to know about your child's extracurricular activities because it helps them see what kind of person he or she is. Make a list together of everything noteworthy: work experience, honors and achievements, major responsibilities (even babysitting), and hobbies.

• **Set a schedule for essay writing.** Many students find the personal essay section of the application a difficult task and are tempted to procrastinate. Don't let your child wait to get started till the day before the application is due. And remind him or her to proofread! An English teacher is often happy to help.

• **Organize your income taxes in December.** The federal financial aid form, or FAFSA, can be completed after January 1. Have your taxes prepared early, so your child won't have to file an updated FAFSA later on.

THE EMOTIONS - Be calm!

• **Be prepared for tears.** Your child may not always appreciate it when you pester him or her about deadlines. It's natural reaction. Just keep the communication open.

• **Stand back but stand by.** Remember that many decisions in this journey belong to your child. Learn how to let go. Know your role, and be a safety net. All the hard work will be worth it when those college acceptances arrive in the mail! ■

BIO *Maria Carvalho is High School Manager for The College Crusade of Rhode Island, where she oversees high school college-readiness programs and manages a team of full-time Advisors who interact daily with hundreds of students in the state's urban high schools.*

Concerns About College

For teens, going off to college represents a huge change in their lives. But this change can affect the parents and guardians just as much. While you are proud and excited about their accomplishments, there can also be a feeling of loss and separation. Dealing with these mixed emotions can be difficult, but are normal. Handling these changes can be easier if you keep these tips in mind:

Stay connected.

There can be some truth to "absence makes the heart grow fonder" but parents or guardians may worry that "out of sight means out of mind." So you and your student need to determine ways to stay involved in each other's lives and remember to say and do the little things that matter. Cards sent home, care packages sent to school, pictures of events that were missed, and email and phone calls do provide a way to stay connected and involved.

Adjust to a new relationship.

As you play a new role in your teen's life, try to adjust to the new adult-to-adult aspect of the parent-child relationship. Children always need parents, but the relationship may become more peer-like.

Expect ups and downs.

One minute college students are the models of independence, the next they call in tears. This back and forth is natural and expected, as both students and parents become more comfortable and confident in the ability of students to handle situations on their own.

Redirect your time and energy to new activities.

With your parenting time now free time, taking stock of personal interests and assets will reveal areas of your life that may have been neglected. It can be time to develop, reawaken, and pursue old and new hobbies, leisure activities, and careers.

Allow for mistakes.

You should encourage and accept the child's ability to make independent decisions. Both the college student and the parents must realize mistakes will be made along the way—it's called life. Learning from mistakes is just another type of learning.

Guide rather than pressure.

Communicating educational goals and expectations should be done in a manner respectful of your student's own style and interests. College students need to pursue their own passions. Although parental input can be useful, children should not be expected to live out their parents' dreams.

Tips from the NYU Child Study Center, www.aboutourkids.org

By Jeremy Harris

L.O.V.E. YOUR PARENTS

As I look back on my first year in college, I realize I'm at the halfway point. I'm grateful for the opportunity, but more importantly, I'm grateful for L.O.V.E. The month of February gives me a chance to express my love for those who have been in my corner. February is also a chance to thank those who have my back through whatever and whenever. That would be my parents.

We often take our parents for granted. I realize some may have grandparents or other family members who substitute as their parents. I just want to show some love to my parents because I realize how critical their assistance has been in my life up to this point.

I am pursuing higher learning because I want to achieve a level of success in life which will allow me to have my best life. The main reason I'm here today is because of the values instilled in me by my parents. My parents ensured I was in the right programs and schools in order to position myself for college. I could not have done this alone.

So, it is with love that I write this for them.

L is for the love my parents have consistently given me through the years.

O is for my continuous effort to obey their rules, advice, and guidance as they share their personal experiences with me.

V is for the value of all that love and support – it's priceless and I value them to the highest. And finally,

E is because I encourage them to continue to be a part of my life even though I'm away from home. I call my mom all the time to ask her for advice and direction. I realize that I still need them in my life – now, more than ever.

As you're preparing for college, please never forget what matters most: the L. O. V. E. you share with your parents – it's invaluable and the best thing in life!

JEREMY HARRIS is a CSO Opportunity Scholarship winner. Jeremy shares his college experiences and offers advice on the Opportunity Scholars blog.

Visit www.CSOCollegeCenter.org to follow the blog, sign up to become a CSO Opportunity Scholar, and have the chance to be a future Opportunity Scholarship winner and blogger yourself!

By Barbara Sanders

WHO ARE YOU? AND WHAT HAVE YOU DONE WITH MY SON?

I am the mother of Jeremy Harris. May he rest in peace.

No, Jeremy did not die, but the former Jeremy has been replaced by someone who is a stranger to me. I guess that goes with the territory of going off to college.

In Jeremy's junior year, we realized that he needed a game plan or a goal for his life after high school. As a parent, you're excited and proud of your child and know that the sky is the limit for them. You realize that it's going to take hard work on your part as well to ensure that your student meets all of the graduation requirements, pays all the necessary fees, narrows down their many options. It can be quite overwhelming.

I always tell new parents that being a parent is like having your heart outside of your body. On the move in date for college, my tears were fierce. I didn't want to leave my son alone to face his new world without me; but I knew that I must.

In his first year of college, Jeremy learned what he needs to do to be successful, and I learned how to be a "hands-off" mom. While they're away, you try not to be too worried about how they're coping. I'll always be there as his safety net, but sometimes we have to step back and let our children experience life for themselves. I checked in periodically with Jeremy and was relieved to know that he was doing well without me.

I couldn't wait for the breaks. Over Thanksgiving break,. Jeremy really seemed happy to be home. He missed me and familiarity of home. Then Spring break came and Jeremy appeared to have broken away from his old self and became someone foreign to me. He was more mature and calm; he had a new set of friends. It was a pleasure to see his growth after a year of college.

As the old adage goes, "No one can prepare you for what heights you will soar until you spread your wings."

Padres y Mentores

KnowHow2GO SPONSORED BY     IN PARTNERSHIP WITH 

Ya sea usted padre, tutor, maestro, mentor u otro adulto afectuoso, es probable que en su vida haya un adolescente que desea ir a la universidad. Puede ayudarlo a triunfar si toma el tiempo para aprender sobre la planificación y el financiamiento de la educación superior. Juntos, usted y el adolescente por el que se interesa pueden compartir esta importante meta y alcanzarla.

"¿Para que ir la Universidad?"

Q

¿Le ha hecho alguna vez el adolescente en su vida esta pregunta? Ya sea usted padre, tutor u otro adulto a cargo, necesita respuestas convincentes y prácticas para compartir con su adolescente. Aquí las tiene:

A

"Vas a lograr un mayor entendimiento y habilidades que te ayudarán a triunfar en este mundo complejo".

La educación superior te permite:

- Ampliar tus conocimientos y habilidades.
- Expresar claramente tus pensamientos, en forma oral y escrita.
- Captar conceptos y teorías abstractas.
- Aumentar tu comprensión del mundo y de tu comunidad.
- Obtener más seguridad financiera.

"Vas a encontrar mayor variedad y cantidad de oportunidades de trabajo".

En nuestro mundo cambiante, más y más trabajos requieren una educación posterior a la de la escuela secundaria. Los graduados de una institución de nivel superior tienen más trabajos para elegir que los que no continúan con su educación luego de la secundaria.

"Ganarás más dinero, mucho más".

La gente con educación superior generalmente gana más que la que no la tiene. Según la Oficina de Censos de los EE. UU., como promedio, la persona con un título universitario gana $51,206, casi el doble que los $27,915 que gana por año la persona que sólo tiene el título de secundaria.

Planificación para la Universidad: Diez Pasos

10

Paso Uno

Comience a ahorrar dinero lo más pronto posible para ayudar al pago de la educación de su adolescente.

Paso Dos

Aliente a su adolescente a darle importancia a la escuela secundaria, preparándose desde el punto de vista académico para la educación superior.

Paso Tres

Analice con su adolescente sus aptitudes e intereses, sus opciones de carreras e instituciones educativas a las que le interesa asistir.

Paso Quatro

Reúnase con el consejero de orientación de la escuela secundaria para determinar qué instituciones se ajustan a las capacidades académicas de su adolescente.

Paso Cinco

Recopile información sobre aquellas a las que su adolescente tiene interés en asistir, incluso información sobre asistencia financiera.

Paso Seis

Lleve a su adolescente a visitar un campus y formule las preguntas adecuadas.

Paso Siete

Ayúdelo a solicitar la admisión. Para solicitar asistencia financiera, ayude a su hijo a completar la Solicitud Gratuita de Ayuda Financiera (Free Application for Federal Student Aid, FAFSA).

Paso Ocho

Considere becas, subsidios y programas de estudio-trabajo. Complete todas las solicitudes o formularios necesarios y preséntelos antes de la fecha límite.

Paso Nueve

Considere programas de préstamos disponibles para usted y su hijo.

Paso Diez

Obtenga más información sobre créditos fiscales, deducciones y otros factores para gastos de educación.

Como hablar con su adolescente

No siempre es fácil hablar con su adolescente. Pero es importante que lo respalde a lo largo de su planificación para la universidad: ayúdelo a organizar el proceso, a cumplir con las fechas y a hablar con las personas adecuadas. Aquí presentamos algunos consejos para considerar:

- Sea receptivo y escúchelo cuando su adolescente desee analizar planes de carrera o de educación superior.
- Hágalo que explore opciones de carrera e institución educativa superior y que recopile toda la información posible.
- Anímelo a que registre sus ideas en papel. Por ejemplo, puede hacer un libro de recortes con sus planes de carrera y de educación superior.
- Esté consciente de las diversas fechas límites para presentar las solicitudes de admisión a las instituciones educativas y para asistencia financiera. Póngalas en un calendario que tanto usted como su hijo puedan mirar.
- Sugiérale que se reúna con un consejero escolar al menos una vez al año, a partir del 10mo grado, para aprender más sobre la educación superior y la planificación de su carrera.
- Bríndele su apoyo y reúnase con su consejero si le parece que su hijo necesita ayuda adicional.
- Anime a su adolescente ayudándole a ver la conexión entre la educación superior y la carrera. Enfatice la importancia de seleccionar una asignatura principal (un "major") que lo ayude a prepararse para una carrera.
- Si el joven está indeciso sobre la orientación de su carrera, no trate de decidir por él. Déjelo que explore todas las posibilidades.

Costos Ayuda Financiera

No hay forma de escapar al hecho de que los costos de la educación superior están creciendo. Según los últimos informes divulgados, la mayoría de los estudiantes y sus familias pueden esperar pagar, en promedio, de $112 a $1,190 más que el año pasado en concepto de matricula y costos este año, de acuerdo al tipo de institución educativa.

Sin embargo, hay buenas noticias. La asistencia financiera disponible es más alta que nunca: más de $135,000 millones. Y a pesar de todos los aumentos en los costos, la educación superior sigue siendo una opción accesible para la mayoría de las familias. Haga clic en los signos de "más" para ver más información:

"Precio de lista" vs. Accesibilidad

Si bien los precios de algunas de las instituciones de educación superior que se oyen pueden ser desalentadores ($30,000 anuales o más por matricula y costos), la mayoría de ellas cuesta mucho menos. Por ejemplo, ¿sabía usted que alrededor del 60 por ciento de los estudiantes que asisten a instituciones de grado de cuatro años pagan menos de $6,000 en concepto de matricula y costos? Luego de tomar en cuenta los subsidios, el precio neto que el estudiante de grado promedio paga por su educación es significativamente menor que la cifra publicada para matricula y costos. Y recuerde, la asistencia financiera puede reducir aún más el monto que su familia pagará en realidad.

La asistencia financiera hace que la universidad le resulte más accesible

La asistencia financiera pretende compensar la diferencia entre lo que su familia puede costear y el costo de la universidad. Más de la mitad de los estudiantes actualmente inscritos en instituciones de educación superior reciben algún tipo de asistencia financiera para ayudar a pagar sus costos.

El sistema de asistencia financiera se basa en la meta del acceso igualitario: que todos puedan tener educación superior, independientemente de sus circunstancias financieras. El sistema funciona así:

• Se espera que el esudiante y su familia contribuyan al costo de la educacion superior en la medida de sus posibilidades.

• Si la familia no puede aportar la totalidad del costo, hay asistencia financiera disponible para cerrar la brecha.

La contribución familiar esperada lo favorece a usted

El monto que su familia puede contribuir es comúnmente conocido como "contribución familiar esperada" (Expected Family Contribution, EFC). La cifra la determina quien quiera que otorga la asistencia; en general, el gobierno federal o cada universidad o institución de educación superior.

El gobierno federal y las oficinas de asistencia financiera utilizan "fórmulas de necesidad" para analizar las condiciones financieras de su familia (elementos como ingresos, activos y tamaño de familia) y las compara en términos de proporción con las condiciones financieras de otras familias.

La mayoría de las familias simplemente no pueden afrontar la EFC sólo con sus ingresos corrientes. Las fórmulas asumen que las familias cumplirán con su contribución a través de una combinación de ahorros, ingresos corrientes y préstamos. Verifique con las instituciones educativas para averiguar de qué modo se espera que satisfaga la EFC.

No descarte a las instituciones de educación superior de mayor costo

Por ejemplo su EFC es de $5,000. En una institución educativa con un costo total de $8,000, usted sería elegible para un máximo de $3,000 en asistencia financiera. En otra institución educativa con un costo total de $25,000, usted sería elegible para un máximo de $20,000 en asistencia financiera. En otras palabras, su familia deberá aportar la misma suma en ambas.

Conocimientos básicos de asistencia financiera

La asistencia financiera es cualquier tipo de asistencia que se utilice para pagar los costos de la educación superior y que se base en necesidad financiera. Hay tres tipos principales:

Subsidios y becas

También denominada donación para asistencia, los subsidios no deben reintegrarse y no se debe trabajar para ganarlos. Los subsidios provienen del gobierno federal y estatal y de las instituciones de educación superior individuales. Las becas en general se otorgan en función del mérito. Para buscar becas, visitewww.fastweb.com.

Trabajo

El empleo estudiantil y la asistencia de trabajo y estudio ayuda a que el estudiante pague por costos educativos como libros, insumos y gastos personales. El programa de trabajo y estudio es un programa federal que proporciona empleos de tiempo parcial a los estudiantes, de modo de ayudarlos a cubrir sus necesidades financieras, y les brinda experiencia laboral a la vez que atienden a sus campus y a las comunidades circundantes.

Préstamos

La mayor parte de la asistencia financiera (54%) se presenta en forma de préstamos a los estudiantes o padres y es una asistencia que debe reembolsarse. La mayoría de los préstamos otorgados en función de las necesidades financieras son préstamos de bajo interés, patrocinados por el gobierno federal. Estos préstamos están subsidiados por el gobierno, de modo que no se acumula interés hasta que comienzan a ser reembolsados, una vez que el estudiante se ha graduado.

Costos Promedio de La Educación Superior

Costos promedio de la educación superior para el año 2007-2008

Institución pública, dos años: $2,361

Institución pública, cuatro años: $6,185

Institución privada, cuatro años: $23,712

¿Sabía usted...?

- Alrededor del 60% de los estudiantes que asisten a instituciones públicas de educación superior de cuatro años pagan menos de $6,000 anuales por matricula y costos.

- 44% de todos los estudiantes asisten a instituciones de educación superior de dos años. El estudiante promedio en una institución de educación superior pública de dos años recibe un subsidio de asistencia financiera que reduce los costos de matricula promedio a alrededor de $400.

- Hay un monto récord de $135,000 millones en asistencia financiera disponible para los estudiantes y su familia.

- Alrededor del 60% de todos los estudiantes universitarios reciben asistencia financiera. En 2004-05 la asistencia promedio por estudiante fue de $1,800 en las instituciones públicas de dos años, de $3,300 en las públicas de cuatro años, y de $9,600 en las privadas de cuatro años.

Más información sobre préstamos

Hay distinto tipos de préstamos, para estudiantes y para padres que los toman en nombre de sus hijos. Siga leyendo para conocer la información básica.

Préstamos para padres

Préstamos federales PLUS

El programa de préstamos PLUS es la mayor fuente de préstamos para padres. Los padres pueden tomar hasta el costo total de asistencia menos cualquier asistencia recibida y el reembolso comienza a los 60 días de haber pagado el dinero a la institución educativa.

Préstamos privados para padres

Algunas instituciones financieras y de préstamos ofrecen préstamos privados para educación para padres. Estos préstamos en general tienen una tasa de interés más alta que los préstamos del programa PLUS.

Préstamos patrocinados por las instituciones educativas

Un pequeño número de instituciones de educación superior ofrecen sus propios préstamos para padres, en general con una mejor tasa de interés que el programa PLUS. Verifique los materiales sobre asistencia de cada institución educativa para ver si cuentan con ese tipo de préstamos.

Préstamos federales para estudiantes

Préstamos Perkins

Los préstamos Perkins son préstamos en función de la necesidad, que son otorgados por la oficina de asistencia financiera a aquellos estudiantes que más lo necesitan. La tasa de interés es muy baja (5%) y no se hace ningún pago durante el curso de los estudios.

Préstamos directos o Stafford subsidiados

Los préstamos Stafford subsidiados son préstamos en función de la necesidad, con tasas de interés en el orden del 4-6 por ciento. El gobierno federal paga los intereses durante el curso de los estudios. Por eso se los llama préstamos "subsidiados".

Préstamos directos o Stafford no subsidiados

Los préstamos Stafford no subsidiados no surgen de la necesidad financiera y pueden utilizarse para ayudar a pagar la porción de costos a cargo de la familia. Usted es responsable del pago de los intereses durante el curso de los estudios. Puede optar por capitalizar los intereses. La ventaja de hacerlo es que no se requiere ningún pago de intereses. La desventaja es que los intereses se suman al préstamo, lo que implica que debe reintegrarle más dinero al acreedor.

Préstamos Grad PLUS

Se trata de préstamos para estudiantes graduados, patrocinados por el gobierno federal, que no están vinculados a la necesidad. En general, los estudiantes pueden solicitar préstamos Grad PLUS por el costo total de la educación, menos cualquier asistencia recibida. La ventaja de este préstamo es que permite una mayor capacidad de endeudamiento. Sin embargo, recomendamos que los estudiantes consideren los préstamos de bajo interés, como los Stafford subsidiados o no subsidiados antes de tomar un préstamo Grad PLUS.

Otras opciones de préstamos para estudiantes

Préstamos privados para estudiantes

Algunas instituciones financieras y de préstamos ofrecen préstamos privados para educación para los estudiantes. Estos préstamos no están subsidiados y en general conllevan una mayor tasa de interés que los préstamos federales en función de las necesidades. El programa de préstamos privados del College Board es un ejemplo de préstamos educativos privados para estudiantes.

Préstamos patrocinados por las instituciones educativas

Ciertas instituciones de educación superior cuentan con sus propios fondos para préstamos. Las tasas de interés pueden ser menores que las de los préstamos federales para estudiantes. Lea la información sobre asistencia financiera de la institución.

Otros préstamos

Además de establecer becas, ciertas organizaciones y fundaciones privadas también cuentan con programas de préstamos. Los términos del endeudamiento pueden ser muy favorables. Puede utilizar Búsqueda de Becas para encontrarlos.

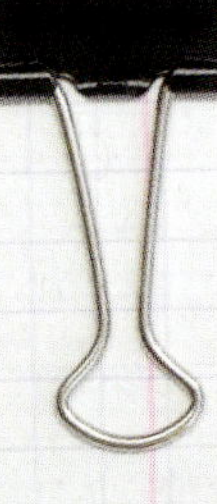

Probablemente haya oído, y tal vez crea, algunos de estos MITOS comunes sobre la educación superior. Siga leyendo para ver cuál es la REALIDAD.

MITO: cualquiera puede entrar a una universidad pública, pero entrar a una institución superior privada es muy difícil.

REALIDAD: algunas universidades públicas están entre las más competitivas en términos de admisión, mientras que otras están obligadas a aceptar prácticamente a todos los solicitantes. Es verdad que algunas instituciones educativas privadas son muy selectivas, pero otras aceptan a estudiantes que ni siquiera serían aceptados en la universidad pública de su estado. Verifique con las instituciones que esté analizando, para saber más sobre los rendimientos académicos promedio de sus estudiantes y sus políticas de admisión.

MITO: la institución educativa de menor precio será la más accesible.

REALIDAD: no necesariamente. Ciertas instituciones educativas de mayor costo han recolectado sumas de dinero significativas para becas de sus graduados y amigos. Como consecuencia, cuentan con más dinero para ofrecer a los estudiantes en la forma de becas, lo que reduce ese precio. Tras tomar en cuenta la asistencia financiera, es posible que la institución aparentemente más costosa sea más accesible que otra con un menor precio de lista. Consejo: averigüe qué tipos de opciones de becas hay disponibles en las instituciones educativas que estén analizando.

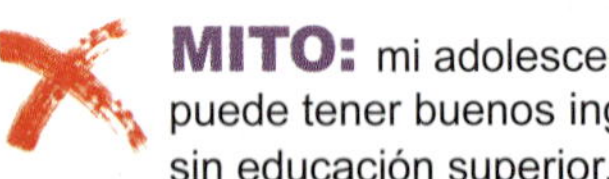

MITO: mi adolescente puede tener buenos ingresos sin educación superior.

REALIDAD: sin dudas a algunas personas les ha ido bien sin un título de grado. Sin embargo, en el curso de su vida la persona con un título de grado en promedio ganará un millón de dólares más que un graduado de secundaria. Para la mayoría de la gente, la educación superior paga.

MITO: los cursos y las notas del período de primavera del último año no son importantes porque a los estudiantes ya los han aceptado en alguna institución superior para la época en que esos cursos se llevan a cabo.

REALIDAD: la mayoría de las instituciones de educación superior incluyen notas en sus materiales de admisión donde manifiestan que tomarán en cuenta las notas de primavera del estudiante de último año. Si el rendimiento académico del estudiante muestra una caída sustancial, se sabe de instituciones que han cancelado la oferta de admisión.

MITO: para subsistir en el mundo actual se necesita un título de grado de cuatro años.

REALIDAD: la persona con un título de cuatro años puede tener más opciones de carrera, pero existen muchos trabajos satisfactorios y bien pagos que pueden obtenerse con ciertos títulos técnicos o de dos años. Su adolescente debe comenzar en las áreas que sean de su interés, y averiguar qué tipo de educación se requiere y cuáles son las oportunidades laborales en esas áreas. Y luego procurar el título que necesite para el tipo de carrera a la que aspira.

MITO: no tengo el dinero y mi adolescente no puede permitirse tomar préstamos para pagar la universidad, incluso si quisiera ir.

REALIDAD: actualmente casi todos los estudiantes pueden conseguir préstamos a tasas bajas para ayudarlos a pagar la educación superior y los préstamos para educación típicamente no deben reembolsarse hasta que el estudiante no se haya graduado. El préstamo promedio de un estudiante de grado actualmente es de alrededor de $20,000; menos que el costo de la mayoría de los autos nuevos. Un auto dura unos años. La educación superior dura toda la vida.

MITO: en realidad no importa si espero uno o dos años para ir a la universidad.

REALIDAD: muchos estudiantes que no van a la universidad inmediatamente después de la secundaria nunca se deciden a hacerlo. Otros llevan consigo una gran experiencia cuando se inscriben, gracias a lo que hicieron en el tiempo en que no estudiaron. Es sensato que el estudiante se postule a las instituciones educativas que le interesan durante el último año, como cualquier otro. Luego puede pedirle a la institución que posponga su inscripción por un año o dos, si el estudiante necesita el tiempo. La mayoría de las instituciones de educación superior acepta mantener la oferta de admisión en suspenso, en especial si el estudiante tiene planes que en definitiva lo harán más interesante o valioso como miembro de la comunidad del campus.

Precaución: si el estudiante trabaja durante ese tiempo, sus ingresos (si son grandes) pueden deteriorar su elegibilidad para asistencia financiera en función de la necesidad al retomar los estudios. Como el estudiante en muchos casos todavía calificará como estudiante dependiente, sólo un pequeño monto de ingresos estarán protegidos por la fórmula federal. Los montos que la excedan pueden afectar su elegibilidad para asistencia financiera.

MITO: se debe empezar a planificar para la universidad durante el penúltimo año de secundaria.

REALIDAD: si bien algunos estudiantes pueden esperar hasta este punto para hacer ciertas cosas como visitar las posibles instituciones educativas o tomar el SAT, hay otras que jamás deben dejarse para tan tarde. Por ejemplo, las selecciones y notas de los cursos de secundaria representan la consideración individual más importante en las decisiones de admisión de la mayoría de las instituciones de educación superior. Las decisiones de los cursos de secundaria se toman mucho antes, incluso en los años de escuela media. La planificación financiera, el ahorro para la educación superior y averiguar qué instituciones educativas se podrán costear son actividades que también deben llevarse a cabo antes del penúltimo año.

MITO: los estudiantes hoy en día tienen tanta deuda por los préstamos que no tiene sentido pagar mucho para ir a la universidad.

REALIDAD: la mayoría de los estudiantes con deudas inmensas normalmente no hicieron un buen trabajo al buscar una institución de educación superior donde la asistencia financiera de su familia funcionara bien o tomaron una decisión consciente de asumir ese tipo de deuda a fin de poder asistir a una universidad en particular. (Recuerde, la deuda promedio de los estudiantes de grado actualmente es de alrededor de $20,000; menos que el costo de la mayoría de los autos nuevos). La meta para la mayoría de las familias es encontrar por anticipado las instituciones educativas que sean razonables para ellas desde el punto de vista financiero, normalmente mediante el uso de un estimador de asistencia financiera publicado a fin de entender cuál es su posición según la fórmula federal para asistencia financiera.

MITO: la asistencia financiera disponible no es mucha, y la que hay va a unos pocos de los mejores estudiantes.

REALIDAD: durante el año académico 2002-2003, se otorgaron más de $105,000 millones de dólares en asistencia financiera. La mayor parte de este dinero fue entregado por el gobierno federal a través de subsidios, préstamos y programas de estudio y trabajo, en tanto los subsidios y becas propios de las instituciones de educación superior totalizaron casi el 20% de toda la asistencia financiera. Los estados aportaron lo suyo, contribuyendo con más de $5,500 millones al pozo. Esto es mucho dinero, para muchos estudiantes. De hecho, más del 70% de los estudiantes de todo el país reciben algún tipo de asistencia financiera.

MITO: nadie de mi familia ha ido a la universidad; ¿por qué mi hijo debería ser el primero?

REALIDAD: al terminar la secundaria, su adolescente puede tener 40 ó 50 años de trabajo por delante. Durante ese tiempo pueden ocurrir muchos cambios en el mercado laboral. Una educación superior ciertamente le dará más opciones en el largo plazo. Es posible que muchos de los trabajos actuales que sólo exigen un diploma de secundaria ya no existan en unos pocos años. Su educación lo preparará para el mercado laboral del futuro, no el actual.

Preguntas para su visita al campus

El mejor motivo para visitar el campus de una institución de educación superior es tener una impresión personal de la calidad de educación que allí se ofrece. Durante la visita al campus, usted y su adolescente deben hacer preguntas que revelen el compromiso de la institución para brindar un ambiente educativo óptimo. Las siguientes preguntas pueden ser útiles:

¿Nivel de exigencia académica?

Un trabajo creativo e intelectual exigente es fundamental para mantener un ambiente educativo de calidad.

- ¿Hasta qué punto se enfatiza el estudio y la dedicación de tiempo al trabajo académico?
- ¿El cuerpo de profesores impone parámetros elevados a los estudiantes?
- ¿Cuánto tiempo dedican los estudiantes a las tareas cada semana?
- ¿Cuánto se espera que escriban?
- ¿Cuánto se espera que lean?

¿El aprendizaje es activo y cooperativo?

Los estudiantes aprenden más cuando participan en forma directa en su educación y tienen oportunidades de colaborar con otros para resolver problemas o dominar materiales difíciles.

- ¿Con qué frecuencia los estudiantes discuten ideas en clase?
- ¿Con qué frecuencia los temas de la clase se discuten fuera de ella?
- ¿Los estudiantes trabajan en grupo en proyectos, dentro y fuera de la clase?
- ¿Con qué frecuencia los estudiantes hacen presentaciones ante la clase?
- ¿Cuántos estudiantes participan en proyectos de base comunitaria en cursos regulares?
- ¿Cuántos estudiantes aplican lo aprendido en clase a la vida real, a través de pasantías o experiencias de campo fuera del campus?
- ¿Tienen los estudiantes oportunidades de actuar como tutores o de enseñar a otros estudiantes?

¿Hay interacción entre profesores y estudiantes?

En general, mientras más contacto tienen los estudiantes con sus profesores, mejor. Trabajar con un profesor en un proyecto de investigación o trabajar junto con los miembros del cuerpo de profesores en un comité universitario u organización comunitaria permite que los estudiantes vean de forma directa cómo los expertos identifican y resuelven problemas prácticos.

- ¿Son los miembros del cuerpo de profesores accesibles y alentadores?
- ¿Cuántos estudiantes trabajan en proyectos de investigación con profesores?

- ¿Reciben los estudiantes comentarios inmediatos sobre su desempeño académico?
- ¿Con qué frecuencia hablan los estudiantes con sus profesores sobre lo que aprenden en clase?
- ¿Con qué frecuencia hablan los estudiantes con consejeros o miembros del cuerpo de profesores sobre sus planes de carrera?
- ¿Trabajan juntos los profesores y estudiantes en comités y proyectos fuera del trabajo académico?

¿Hay experiencias educativas enriquecedoras?

Las instituciones que son superiores desde el punto de vista educativo ofrecen diversas oportunidades de aprendizaje dentro y fuera del aula, que complementan las metas del programa académico. Una de las más importantes es la exposición a estudiantes y profesores de diversos orígenes.

- ¿Qué tipos de cursos honorarios, comunidades de aprendizaje y otros programas distintivos se ofrecen?
- ¿De qué forma los profesores utilizan la tecnología en clase?
- ¿Con qué frecuencia interactúan los estudiantes con pares de distintas opiniones sociales, políticas o religiosas?
- ¿Con qué frecuencia interactúan los estudiantes con pares de distintos orígenes raciales o étnicos?
- ¿Cuántos estudiantes estudian en otros países?
- ¿Participan los estudiantes en actividades que aumentan su espiritualidad?
- ¿Qué porcentaje de estudiantes prestan servicios comunitarios?
- ¿En qué tipo de actividades participan los estudiantes fuera del aula?
- ¿Qué tipo de eventos auspicia el campus?
- ¿Se requiere una experiencia de culminación del último año?

¿Hay un ambiente de apoyo en el campus?

Los estudiantes rinden más y están más satisfechos en las instituciones educativas que se comprometen con su éxito y que cultivan relaciones laborales y sociales positivas entre los distintos grupos del campus.

- ¿Qué tan bien se llevan los estudiantes unos con otros?
- ¿Están los estudiantes satisfechos con su experiencia educativa en general?
- ¿Cuánto tiempo dedican los estudiantes a actividades cocurriculares?
- ¿Qué tal se llevan los estudiantes con los administradores y el personal?
- ¿En qué medida la institución ayuda a los estudiantes a manejar sus necesidades académicas y sociales?

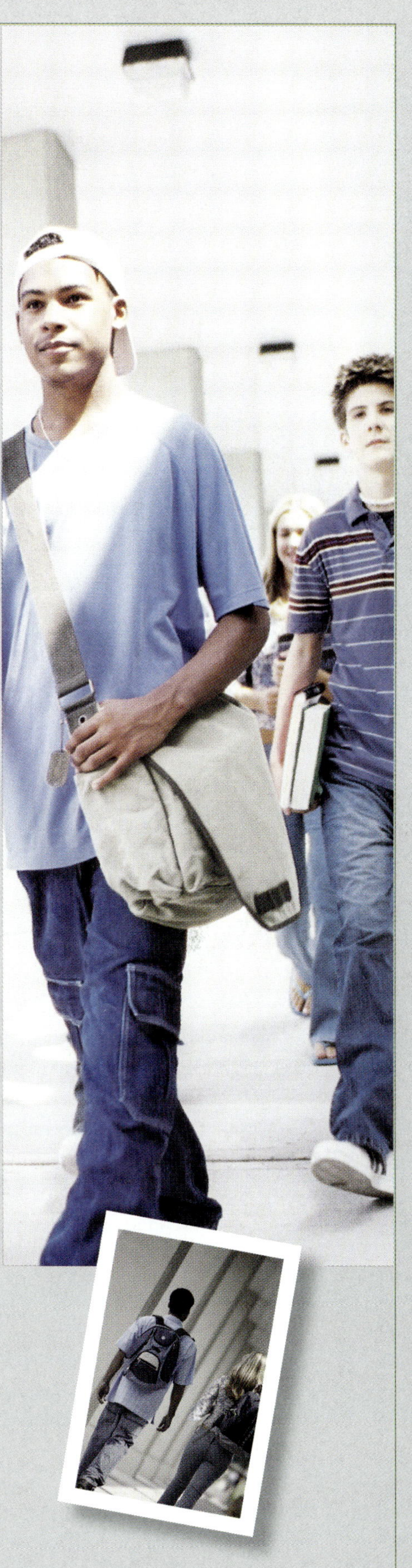

Pasos para la Universidad

El proceso de planificación para los estudios superiores puede ser atemorizante para cualquiera, de modo que es mejor planificar por adelantado y contemplar mucho tiempo. De hecho, es una buena idea comenzar las conversaciones sobre la educación superior cuando el adolescente está aun en la escuela media.

Ayude a orientar al joven a través del proceso de planificación para la educación superior. Haga clic en los signos de "más" a continuación para ver los pasos básicos en cada grado. También le recomendamos leer los consejos específicos para estudiantes haciendo clic en los niveles de grado (por ej., Primer año) en la barra de navegación principal y luego en "Pasos hacia la universidad".

CRONOGRAMA: 9NO GRADO

OTOÑO

- ❑ Consulte al consejero escolar para asegurarse que el estudiante esté asistiendo a los cursos preparatorios para la universidad, comenzando por álgebra.
- ❑ Ayude al joven a crear una carpeta de información para su educación superior.
- ❑ Comience el año escolar correctamente ayudando al joven a organizarse y a poner en práctica buenos hábitos de estudio.
- ❑ Aliente al estudiante a conocer gente nueva mediante la inscripción en actividades extracurriculares e intentando algo nuevo.
- ❑ Explore carreras por Internet, en la computadora de su casa o en la biblioteca.
- ❑ Ayude a su adolescente a encontrar oportunidades de aprendizaje por observación del trabajo en la comunidad, donde pasan el día siguiendo de cerca a una persona mientras trabaja y observan lo que la persona hace.

PRIMAVERA

- ❑ Siéntese con su estudiante para planificar el segundo año.
- ❑ Hable sobre las vacaciones de verano. Explore los programas o campamentos de verano a los que puede asistir en universidades e instituciones de educación superior locales. Busque oportunidades de servicio o voluntarias en la comunidad. Algunas pueden ser patrocinadas por una iglesia, sinagoga o mezquita local.

10MO GRADO CRONOGRAMA

CRONOGRAMA: 10MO GRADO

OTOÑO

- ❑ Apoye a su estudiante para que se prepare y tome todos los exámenes necesarios para completar los requisitos de graduación de la escuela secundaria.
- ❑ Haga que su estudiante comience el segundo año puliendo sus aptitudes de estudio. Aconseje a su hijo o hija que si necesita mejorar en ciertos temas, éste es el momento de hacerlo. Refuerce la idea de que las universidades y los futuros empleadores se fijan en certificados analíticos de la escuela secundaria y se impresionan con asistencia regular y mejoras en las calificaciones.
- ❑ Aliente al joven a hacer un inventario de intereses de carrera.
- ❑ Los estudiantes deben tomar el examen de Prueba Preliminar de Aptitud Escolar (Preliminary Scholastic Aptitude, PSTA), la versión preliminar del Examen de Aptitud Escolástica (Scholastic Aptitude Test, SAT) o el PLAN, versión preliminar del Examen Estadounidense para la Universidad (American College Test, ACT). Dar el PSAT ahora es práctica para el PSAT del penúltimo año, que permite que a su estudiante se lo considere para una beca nacional de mérito. Obtenga las fechas e información adicional sobre el PSAT en la oficina de orientación de su escuela secundaria.
- ❑ Navegue por Internet junto con el estudiante para investigar oportunidades de universidades, escuelas técnicas y aprendizajes.
- ❑ Anime al estudiante a comenzar o a seguir aprendiendo sobre carreras.

PRIMAVERA

- ❑ Comience a explorar las opciones de asistencia financiera y becas.
- ❑ Anime a su estudiante a preguntar a sus amigos, colegas y líderes de la comunidad sobre distintas carreras o use Internet para explorar distintas carreras.
- ❑ Ayude al estudiante a seleccionar de cinco a diez instituciones de educación superior a las cuales pedir folletos y solicitudes de ingreso.
- ❑ Arregle con él para visitar un centro de carreras en la zona.
- ❑ Planifique un verano productivo para su adolescente. Si todavía no tiene un trabajo en el verano anterior al 11mogrado, es un buen momento de buscar uno que lo ayude a prepararse para una futura carrera.
- ❑ Elija un campamento de verano o ayúdelo a encontrar programas de servicio voluntario para incentivar las aptitudes de su adolescente.
- ❑ Recuerde a su adolescente que se inscriba en las clases más exigentes para el próximo año.

11MO GRADO
CRONOGRAMA

CRONOGRAMA: 11MO GRADO

OTOÑO

- ❑ Verifique que su estudiante esté encaminado hacia la educación superior y tómese tiempo para analizar intereses universitarios.
- ❑ Anime a su estudiante a comenzar una carpeta de información sobre instituciones educativas de nivel superior.
- ❑ Durante el receso de otoño, visiten universidades.
- ❑ Aliente a su adolescente a tomar el examen PSAT para prepararse para el SAT y calificar para el programa de becas nacional de mérito.
- ❑ Participe en noches universitarias y ferias universitarias en la escuela o centros comunitarios locales.
- ❑ Durante el receso de invierno, sugiera reuniones con amigos que estén de regreso de la universidad y arregle visitas a campus.

PRIMAVERA

- ❑ Vuelva a verificar que su adolescente esté inscrito para dar el SAT o ACT. Busque libros para ayudarlo a prepararse. Considere qué universidades deben recibir los puntajes. Reúnase con el consejero escolar de su estudiante para saber qué universidades y becas están disponible según los resultados del examen.
- ❑ Comience una búsqueda activa de becas y asistencia financiera.
- ❑ Continúe animando a su estudiante para que mantenga el rumbo a fin de completar todos los cursos necesarios para la graduación, más cualquier otro curso requerido para la admisión a la universidad.
- ❑ Anímelo a hacer más visitas a universidades durante el verano y hable con los consejeros de admisión con respecto a lo que puede hacerse para aumentar las posibilidades de ser admitido.
- ❑ Si no puede viajar, los sitios web de las universidades e instituciones educativas de nivel superior pueden proporcionarle gran cantidad de información y recorridos en línea.
- ❑ Para adquirir una impresión de la vida universitaria y explorar posibles carreras, anímelo a participar en un programa de verano preuniversitario.

12VO GRADO CRONOGRAMA

CRONOGRAMA: 12VO GRADO

OTOÑO

- ❑ Si los hay disponibles, aliente al estudiante a inscribirse en cursos que ofrezcan créditos para la universidad, como los denominados "Advance Placement" o "AP" (equivalencia universitaria) y "Dual Enrollment" (matrícula doble).
- ❑ Ayúdelo a ir reduciendo el abanico de posibilidades de instituciones educativas y a recopilar las correspondientes solicitudes. Haga una lista de verificación con los requisitos de admisión, certificados analíticos, costos de la solicitud, puntajes de los exámenes, cartas de recomendación, ensayos y solicitudes de asistencia financiera.
- ❑ Haga que su estudiante de último año prepare una lista de todos sus servicios escolares y comunitarios junto con sus clases y premios de la secundaria. Esta lista lo ayudará al momento de comenzar a llenar las solicitudes de admisión.
- ❑ Haga que su estudiante practique el llenado del formulario y la escritura del ensayo de admisión a la universidad. Procure recomendaciones para las admisiones y becas universitarias.
- ❑ Visite las instituciones educativas que su estudiante esté considerando. Llame por anticipado para fijar citas con los funcionarios de admisión y de asistencia financiera.
- ❑ Lleve un control de las fechas límite para las solicitudes.
- ❑ Trabaje junto al estudiante a fin de completar las solicitudes aproximadamente dos semanas antes de la fecha límite. Ofrézcase a revisarlas. Verifique que la oficina de orientación escolar esté enviando los certificados analíticos y los puntajes de los exámenes a las instituciones educativas que su estudiante haya elegido.
- ❑ Si el joven no está satisfecho con los puntajes del SAT, sugiérale que tome el SAT o el ACT por segunda vez. Verifique las políticas de cada institución educativa. Muchas oficinas de admisión se concentran sólo en los mejores puntajes.
- ❑ Asista a todas las ferias universitarias y talleres de asistencia financiera que pueda.
- ❑ Ayude a su adolescente a buscar becas e información general sobre temas de asistencia financiera por Internet.

INVIERNO

- ❑ Ayude a su estudiante a llenar la Solicitud Gratuita de Asistencia Federal para Estudiantes (Free Application for Federal Student Aid, FAFSA), que se requiere a todos los solicitantes de asistencia financiera. Este formulario determinará su elegibilidad para subsidios y préstamos con miras a ayudar a cubrir los costos universitarios.

PRIMAVERA

- ❑ Verifique que se envíen las notas de mediados de año, de ser necesario, a las instituciones educativas seleccionadas. Pídale al consejero escolar del estudiante que las envíe.
- ❑ Festeje las cartas de aceptación junto a su estudiante, y empiece los planes para su primer año. Recuérdele mantener buenas notas y asistencia.
- ❑ Minimice las cartas de rechazo, y anímelo a concentrarse en la meta real: ir a la universidad.
- ❑ Repase y evalúe las ofertas de asistencia financiera. Una vez que el estudiante tome la decisión definitiva con respecto a la selección de institución educativa, verifique las fechas límites para el envío del depósito, la solicitud de alojamiento y todos los demás elementos que ésta exija. Notifique a las otras instituciones que su hijo o hija no asistirá a ellas.
- ❑ Ayude a su adolescente a empezar a buscar un trabajo para el verano.

VERANO

- ❑ Verifique que se envíen las notas finales de su estudiante a la institución educativa seleccionada.
- ❑ Ayúdelo a planificar el próximo año en la universidad, haciendo un presupuesto, un horario y una lista de números telefónicos de servicios y apoyos importantes.

Desafios

Para los adolescentes, la ida a la universidad representa un enorme cambio en sus vidas. Pero este cambio puede afectar en la misma medida a los padres y tutores.

Si bien con seguridad usted está orgulloso y entusiasmado con sus logros, también puede aparecer un sentimiento creciente de pérdida y separación. Afrontar esta mezcla de emociones puede ser difícil, pero son normales.

El manejo de estos cambios puede hacerse más fácil si tiene en cuenta estos consejos:

Manténgase en contacto.

Puede haber algo de verdad en el dicho de que la distancia aviva los sentimientos, pero los padres o tutores tal vez se preocupen de que "ojos que no ven, corazón que no siente". De modo que usted y su estudiante deben acordar las formas de seguir participando en las vidas del otro y recordar decir y hacer esas pequeñas cosas importantes. El envío de tarjetas a casa, los paquetes que se envían a la universidad, las fotos de los eventos a los que no se pudo asistir y las llamadas de teléfono y mensajes de correo electrónico son ciertamente un modo de mantenerse en contacto y participar.

Amóldese a una nueva relación.

A medida que juega un nuevo papel en la vida de su adolescente, trate de amoldarse al nuevo aspecto de adulto a adulto en la relación padre e hijo. Los hijos siempre necesitan a los padres, pero la relación puede transformarse más en una entre pares.

Espere altos y bajos.

Un día los estudiantes son un modelo de independencia y al día siguiente llaman entre llantos. Este ida y vuelta es natural y esperable, a medida que tanto estudiantes como padres se sienten más cómodos y van tomando confianza en la capacidad de los estudiantes de manejar las situaciones por sí mismos.

Reoriente su tiempo y energía hacia nuevas actividades.

Ahora que su tiempo de paternidad se ha transformado en tiempo libre, hacer un inventario de sus intereses y activos personales le revelará áreas de su vida que tal vez tenía descuidadas. Puede ser el momento de desarrollar, volver a despertar y atender viejas y nuevas aficiones, actividades placenteras y carreras.

Contemple que se cometerán errores.

Debe apoyar y aceptar la capacidad de su hijo para tomar decisiones independientes. Tanto el estudiante como los padres deben aceptar que se cometerán errores en el camino; eso es la vida. Aprender de los errores es simplemente otro tipo de aprendizaje.

Guíe sin presionar.

La comunicación de las metas y expectativas educativas debe hacerse de una manera respetuosa hacia el propio estilo e intereses de su estudiante. Los estudiantes deben perseguir sus propias pasiones. Si bien la opinión de los padres puede ser útil, no se debe esperar que los hijos hagan realidad los sueños de los padres.

Consejos del Centro de Estudios sobre los Hijos (Child Study Center) de la Universidad de Nueva York, www.aboutourkids.org

CUARTO VACÍO Y CAJAS DE CARTÓN

Las melodías de los Killers suenan en la sala mientras estoy parado en el centro de mi cuarto. Alrededor de mi están cinco cajas de cartón; espero que tengan todo lo que voy a necesitar para mi primer año de la Universidad. De repente el entusiasmo de ir a la universidad interfiere con la nostalgia de empacar. ¡¿Quien sabía que poner toda tu vida adentro de cajas de cartón seria tan difícil?!

Mientras admiro la vista de lo que solía ser mi cuarto, no puedo resistir sentir un poco de tristeza dentro de mi. Esta casa ha visto mis éxitos en la escuela secundaria y mi madurez. Voy a dejar todo esto en solo algunos días y siempre será parte de mi pasado. Estoy seguro que mientras empiezas a empacar, vas a sentir emociones parecidas. Esto es totalmente natural y anticipado.

Irvin Gomez
College: Dartmouth College
Hometown: Waukegan, IL

Muchos de mis amigos estaban felices al dejar sus casas y no tenían dudas. Yo, contrariamente, tenia emociones mixtas al dejar mi hogar. Sí, quiero ir a Dartmouth tanto como mis futuros compañeros, pero voy a extrañar mi hogar. Mi consejo para los que se encuentran en mi situación, es el siguiente: disfruta cada momento que te queda con tu familia. Abráceles cuando estas cerca porque vas a extrañar esos abrazos al estar a millas de distancia. Comparte tu entusiasmo con ellos porque estoy seguro que ellos están tan entusiasmados como tú por el ingreso a la universidad.

Finalmente, no dejes que tus sentimientos de tristeza superen los de entusiasmo y esperanza. Debes estar entusiasmado; yo se que lo estoy. Si, es difícil ver la mayoría de tu vida puesto en cajas y escuchar de que se usara tu cuarto en el futuro, pero más allá del horizonte queda una escena más excitante. Esas cajas de cartón son contenedores temporales de tu vida y pronto vas a estar parado en un cuarto vacío pensando en cómo convertir ese cuarto en tu hogar.

Voy a concluir con algunas palabras de mi padre en una conversación que sostuve con el acerca de mi viaje. "No importa que tan lejos vas a ir, nosotros como una familia siempre estaremos juntos en mente y espíritu." Con esas palabras en mi mente, voy a emprender mi viaje a Dartmouth sabiendo que estoy llevando más que cinco cajas de cartón. También estoy llevando conmigo a mi familia en este viaje.

IRVIN GOMEZ es un ganador del CSO Opportunity Scholarship. Irvin comparte sus experiencias en la universidad y ofrece consejos en el Opportunity Scholars Blog.

¡Visite www.csocollegecenter.org para seguir el blog, registrar para ser un CSO Opportunity Scholar, y tener la oportunidad de ser un futuro ganador del Opportunity Scholarship y un escritor de blog!

Opportunity Scholars

Notes

Notes

COLLEGE ACCESS & OPPORTUNITY GUIDE

2012 EDITION

College Profiles

College Profiles

In the following pages, you'll find comprehensive profiles of several hundred colleges and universities committed to serving and supporting first-generation, low-income, and minority students on their campus and in their community.

The section is organized by state, with schools presented alphabetically within each state. You are encouraged to continue your research and to connect with the colleges and universities profiled here at www.CSOCollegeCenter.org, a free online college search tool. First-generation college, low-income, and minority students can sign up on the site to become a CSO **Opportunity Scholar** and receive free college search guidance, support, and scholarships.

Criteria for Inclusion

The colleges and universities profiled here do not reflect each and every—or the only—schools that serve first-generation, low-income, and/or minority students. Still, the colleges and universities that are included exemplify the many four-year schools committed to college access and retention and are profiled in light of the programs and opportunities they present for first-generation, low-income, and minority students.

Profiled colleges and universities partner with Center for Student Opportunity to build awareness of their institution and its college access programs, recruit qualified and motivated first-generation college and other traditionally underserved college-bound students, and improve outreach, recruitment and retention efforts aimed to serve and support first-generation college, underserved students on their campuses.

Explaining the College Profile

The information and data represented in the college profiles were developed by Center for Student Opportunity staff in collaboration with and approved by the schools themselves. Because of this close editorial process, we believe the information presented in the profiles to be accurate and up-to-date. If a college did not supply a certain piece of data requested, the information either does not appear or is marked as "n/a" for "not available." We still encourage you to check with a college or university of interest to verify important information on programs, application deadlines, tuition and fees, and other necessary data.

Explaining the College Profile

Learn more about the colleges profiled in this book and send them your information at **www.CSOCollegeCenter.org**, a FREE website to research and connect with colleges.

Students who use **www.CSOCollegeCenter.org** are given the special title of **Opportunity Scholar** and receive free college search guidance, support, and scholarships.

We believe that the best way to research and select your college is not just by the numbers, but by the important programs and services that will support you academically, socially and financially through your college education and help you persist to graduation.

www.csocollegecenter.org/astate

Arkansas State University–Jonesboro
P. O. Box 1630
State University, AR 72467

ARKANSAS ...org/astate

Arkansas State University

With a population of more than 12,000 students and more than 200 degree programs, Arkansas State University provides an affordable and accessible, quality education to a diverse and dynamic array of students. The University treats each individual as an equal and important member of its community and offers more than 300 student organizations, valuing community involvement outside of the classroom as part of students' core education.

Arkansas State University–Jonesboro
P. O. Box 1630
State University, AR 72467
Ph: (870) 972-3024
admissions@astate.edu
www.astate.edu

"I decided to attend ASU after attending Senior Preview Day. I enjoyed the campus environment and felt like the campus was a home away from home. The people I met were extremely nice and made every student visiting the campus feel special and welcomed. Also, ASU was close enough to my home town, but far enough that I was able experience something different."
– Adrian E., '12
McGehee, AR
Chemistry, Education

ACCESS "Back to School" Day

"Back to School" Day provides an educational venue for students of color and first generation high school students and their parents in preparation for the start of a new academic year. Topics covered include self-esteem, importance of the ACT test, reasons to avoid the legal system, and a question and answer session for parents. The goal is to reduce the number of incidents in the schools and improve the students' motivation to succeed.

ACCESS Discover Diversity

Discover Diversity is a leadership development program designed to give students of color and first generation college students a closer look into their future by exposing them to college life through academic workshops, class lectures, financial aid presentations, and much more. Students who meet the requirements are selected by their high school counselors to participate in this event. During this program, students have the opportunity to get to know faculty, staff, alumni, and current ASU students.

OPPORUNITY Thompson Minority Scholarship

The Thompson Minority Scholarship program awards scholarships to incoming African-American freshmen and currently enrolled African-American students. This scholarship was developed to increase the enrollment of entering African-American freshmen and the retention rates of currently enrolled students by honoring academic achievement and eliminating financial barriers.

SUCCESS First Year Experience Program (FYE)

The First Year Experience Program provides incoming students with the information and skills needed to meet the expectations of college faculty, develop effective study skills, and become familiar with college policies and procedures. Topical coverage includes decision making, goal setting, planning, time management, and group team building skills.

SUCCESS Student Support Services (SSS)

Student Support Services is a comprehensive program designed to promote retention and academic success in college. It provides participants with academic and support services in a caring environment that seeks to ensure their successful completion of a baccalaureate degree at Arkansas State University. These services are offered free of charge to participants and include tutoring, academic and financial advising, counseling, mentoring, workshops, and cult... enrichment trips. Participants must demonstrate financial need, documentation of a di... be first-generation college students.

SUCCESS Summer Bridge Program

The Summer Bridge Program, supported by Student Support Services, is designed to in... incoming or nontraditional students to the resources needed for success in college. Stud... demonstrate academic or financial need, or documentation of a disability, and have been ... week prior to the start ...

F A S T   F A C T S

Fast Facts

STUDENT PROFILE

# of degree-seeking undergraduates	9,200
% male/female	41/59
% African American	18
% American Indian or Alaska Native	<1
% Asian or Pacific Islander	1
% Hispanic	
% White	
% International	
% Pell grant r...	

First-generation... Mike Beebe, governor, state of Arkansas; Maj. Gen. Elder Granger, former deputy director of the Department of Defense's TRICARE Management, former Commander, Task Force 44th Medical Command and Command Surgeon for Multinational Corps-Iraq in Baghdad, Iraq; Dr. Thomas Hill, Vice President for Student Affairs at Iowa State University, Olympic bronze medalist; The Hon. James Pardew, former U. S. ambassador to Bulgaria, former deputy assistant secretary general for NATO International; Dr. Kathy Brittain White, former chief information officer for Cardinal Health, founder and president of Rural Sourcing, Inc.

ACADEMICS

full-time faculty	461
full-time minority faculty	76
student-faculty ratio	18:1
average class size	28
% first-year retention rate	68.3
% graduation rate (6 years)	38.6

Popular majors Business, Nursing, Early Childhood Education

CAMPUS LIFE

% live on campus (% fresh.) 23 (54)

Multicultural student clubs and organizations Black Student Association, N.A.A.C.P., International Student Association, Indian Student Association, Spanish and Latino Student Association, Chinese Student Association, Nepali Student Association, Common Ground

Athletics NCAA Division I, Sunbelt Conference

ADMISSIONS

# of applicants	4,288
% accepted	82
# of first-year students enrolled	1,902
SAT Critical Reading range	460-520
SAT Math range	480-580
SAT Writing range	410-490
ACT range	18-24
average HS GPA	3.13

Deadlines

regular decision	rolling
application fee (online)	$15 ($15)
fee waiver for applicants with financial need	no

COST & AID

tuition	in-state $4,890; out-of-state $12,810
room & board	$5,056
	$9,500,000
	97
	100
	96
	28
	$18,750

...TY GUIDE

ACCESS **Discover Di...**
Discover Diversity is a leadership...
program designed to give studen...

ACCESS programs serve pre-college students beyond a college's own gates. These programs include partnerships with underserved schools and organizations and efforts that leverage administration, faculty, and student bodies to assist college-bound students with academic enrichment, mentoring, college preparation, and college guidance.

 OPPORUNITY **Thomps...**
The Thompson Minority Scholars...
freshmen and currently enrolled...

OPPORTUNITY programs serve prospective students in getting to know a college and providing financial incentives for admitted students. These programs include scholarships, financial aid initiatives, visit and open house programs, and fly-in programs that in most cases cater specifically to first-generation, low-income, and minority students.

SUCCESS **Student Sup...**
Student Support Services is a com...
academic success in college. It pro...
caring environment that seeks to e...

SUCCESS programs are academic assistance, student support services, and retention initiatives that help students persist to graduation. These programs exist both in and out of the classroom and include pre-orientation/orientation, first-year programs, academic advising, mentoring, living learning communities, and student organizations and clubs.

...I met were extremely nice an... made every student visiting t... campus feel special and welc... Also, ASU was close enough... home town, but... enough that I wa... experience som... different."
– Adrian E., '12
McGehee, AR
Chemistry, Educat...

Most profiles feature a quote from a current student about how they have benefited from an ACCESS, OPPORTUNITY, or SUCCESS program at their college.

FAST FACTS

The information and data presented here gives a snap-shot of the school's vital statistics. In addition to the program information, this data will help determine if a school is the right fit for you.

STUDENT PROFILE
How many students go here? Is it a diverse student body? Does the school serve many students from low-income backgrounds?

The data here includes number of undergraduate students, male and female percentage, the racial/ethnic breakdown of the student body, percentage of Pell grant recipients—federal grant aid given to students with the greatest financial need—and a list of distinguished alumni that happen to be first-generation college graduates or from low-income, minority backgrounds.

STUDENT PROFILE
# of degree-seeking undergraduates
% male/female
% African American
% American Indian or Alaska Native

ACADEMICS
Will you be in small or large classes? Will you know your professors? How many students drop out or do most graduate?

The data here includes number of full-time faculty, student-faculty ratio, average class size, first-year retention percentage—students returning for their sophomore year—six year graduation rate, and a short list of popular majors.

ACADEMICS
full-time faculty
full-time minority faculty
student-faculty ratio
average class size

CAMPUS LIFE
Is it a residential campus, meaning the majority of students live on campus? What opportunities exist to get involved with student organizations, clubs, or athletic programs?

The data here includes percentage of students living on campus, a list of multicultural student organizations and clubs, and an overview of the athletics program.

CAMPUS LIFE
% live on campus (% fresh.)
Multicultural student clubs and organiz
Black Student Association, N.A.A.C.P., Int
Student Association, Indian Student Ass

ADMISSIONS
How many students apply and how many get in? How do I compare to most students academically? When are the application deadlines?

The data here includes number of applicants, percentage of applicants accepted, median SAT and ACT scores of admitted students, average high school GPA of admitted students, application types, deadlines, fees, and fee waiver availability.

ADMISSIONS
# of applicants
% accepted
# of first-year students enrolled
SAT Critical Reading range

COST AND AID
What are the "sticker price" costs of attendance—similar to buying a car, it is rarely the case that a student pays the full amount? How many students receive financial aid and what kinds? Do students tend to graduate from a school with high loan debt that will need to be repaid?

The data here includes tuition and room and board, percentage of students receiving financial aid, percentage of students receiving need-based scholarship or grant aid—money you do not have to pay back—percentage of students whose need was fully met, average financial aid package in dollars, and the average student loan debt upon graduation.

COST & AID
tuition in-state $4,890; out-of-sta
room & board
total need-based institutional
scholarships/grants

Arkansas State University–Jonesboro
P. O. Box 1630
State University, AR 72467
Ph: (870) 972-3024
admissions@astate.edu
www.astate.edu

FAST FACTS

STUDENT PROFILE

# of degree-seeking undergraduates	9,200
% male/female	41/59
% African American	18
% American Indian or Alaska Native	<1
% Asian or Pacific Islander	1
% Hispanic	1
% White	71
% International	7
% Pell grant recipients	53

First-generation and minority alumni The Hon. Mike Beebe, governor, state of Arkansas; Maj. Gen. Elder Granger, former deputy director of the Department of Defense's TRICARE Management, former Commander, Task Force 44th Medical Command and Command Surgeon for Multinational Corps-Iraq in Baghdad, Iraq; Dr. Thomas Hill, Vice President for Student Affairs at Iowa State University, Olympic bronze medalist; The Hon. James Pardew, former U. S. ambassador to Bulgaria, former deputy assistant secretary general for NATO International; Dr. Kathy Brittain White, former chief information officer for Cardinal Health, founder and president of Rural Sourcing, Inc.

ACADEMICS

full-time faculty	461
full-time minority faculty	76
student-faculty ratio	18:1
average class size	28
% first-year retention rate	68.3
% graduation rate (6 years)	38.6

Popular majors Business, Nursing, Early Childhood Education

CAMPUS LIFE

% live on campus (% fresh.)	23 (54)

Multicultural student clubs and organizations
Black Student Association, N.A.A.C.P., International Student Association, Indian Student Association, Spanish and Latino Student Association, Chinese Student Association, Nepali Student Association, Common Ground
Athletics NCAA Division I, Sunbelt Conference

ADMISSIONS

# of applicants	4,288
% accepted	82
# of first-year students enrolled	1,902
SAT Critical Reading range	460-520
SAT Math range	480-580
SAT Writing range	410-490
ACT range	18-24
average HS GPA	3.13
Deadlines	
regular decision	rolling
application fee (online)	$15 ($15)
fee waiver for applicants with financial need	no

COST & AID

tuition	in-state $4,890; out-of-state $12,810
room & board	$5,056
total need-based institutional scholarships/grants	$9,500,000
% of students apply for need-based aid	97
% of students receive aid	100
% receiving need-based scholarship or grant aid	96
% receiving aid whose need was fully met	28
average student loan debt upon graduation	$18,750

College Profile List by **Name**

College Profile List by **State**

Oklahoma

Oregon

Pennsylvania

Rhode Island

South Carolina

South Dakota

Tennessee

Texas

Utah

Vermont

Virginia

Washington

West Virginia

Wisconsin

Wyoming

University of Montevallo

University of Montevallo
Station 6030
Montevallo, AL 35115-6030
Ph: (800) 292-4349 / (205) 665-6030
admissions@montevallo.edu
www.montevallo.edu

One of only 21 public liberal arts universities in the United States, the University of Montevallo offers students from Alabama (and elsewhere) an affordable, liberal arts education. Located in the town of Montevallo, 35 miles south of Birmingham, the university is spread out across a 160-acre main campus, surrounded by lawns, groves, and flower beds. The university's famed architecture and landscaping — particularly the work of the famed Olmstead Brothers — draws many to its campus. In fact, 28 campus structures and sites are listed on the National Register of Historic Places. Undergraduate programs are offered in more than 70 academic areas, and the full-time student-to-faculty ratio is roughly 17:1. Members of the faculty come from prestigious institutions from across the United States, with a large percentage holding terminal degrees in their respective academic disciplines. High achieving students can take advantage of the University of Montevallo's Honors program, which confers special benefits and recognition upon these students.

ACCESS Upward Bound

Upward Bound is a federally funded program that provides academic support, counseling, tutorial services, career mentoring, cultural exposure, and community service opportunities necessary for potential first-generation college students and/or economically disadvantaged youth to complete both high school and college. The University of Montevallo Upward Bound Program, in particular, provides academic and cultural enrichment opportunities for high school students in Shelby, Bibb and Chilton counties. Students meet about every other week from September to May to attend seminar-style academic classes that emphasize a particular skill or concept. These sessions are designed to resemble college classes as closely as possible to give the students an opportunity to experience the college setting. All services are provided at no cost to program participants and their parents.

OPPORTUNITY Minority Scholarships

Scholarships at the University of Montevallo are primarily awarded based upon ACT/SAT scores, grades, and in many cases, financial need. Minority students at Montevallo, however, are also eligible for three specific scholarship programs – the Minority Academic Recognition Scholarship, the Martin Luther King, Jr. Scholarship and the Minority Teachers Scholarship Program. The first two of these programs are open to students of all disciplines, while the latter awards scholarships to those seeking a degree that will lead to teacher certification.

SUCCESS Student Support Services (SSS)

Student Support Services (SSS) is a U.S. Department of Education TRIO program that provides free academic, career, and counseling support to eligible college students. Student Support Services can help students adjust to higher education by providing academic and personal advising/counseling, tutoring, academic success seminars, access to a computer lab equipped with Mathematics and Study Skills software, cultural enrichment activities, and study skills handouts. The program also provides referrals to appropriate university and other resources that would be beneficial for students. The goal is to deliver services and resources that will provide support for students; resulting in students having a positive experience at University of Montevallo and graduation.

FAST FACTS

STUDENT PROFILE

# of degree-seeking undergraduates	2,493
% male/female	33/67
% African American	15
% American Indian or Alaska Native	1
% Asian or Pacific Islander	<1
% Hispanic	2
% White	75
% International	2
% Pell grant recipients	29

ACADEMICS

full-time faculty	132
full-time minority faculty	17
student-faculty ratio	17:1
average class size	35
% first-year retention rate	72
% graduation rate (6 years)	41

Popular majors Art/Art Studies, Biology, Business, Elementary Education and Teaching, English Language and Literature

CAMPUS LIFE

% live on campus (% freshmen)	45 (78)

Multicultural student clubs and organizations African-American Society, Feminine Majority Leadership Alliance, German Club, International Students Association

Athletics NCAA Division II, East Division of the Gulf South Conference

ADMISSIONS

# of applicants	1,543
% accepted	69
# of first-year students enrolled	432
SAT Critical Reading (middle 50%)	n/a
SAT Math (middle 50%)	n/a
SAT Writing (middle 50%)	n/a
ACT (middle 50%)	20-26
average HS GPA	3.3
Deadlines	
regular decision	8/1
application fee (online)	$30 ($30)
fee waiver for applicants with financial need	yes

COST & AID

tuition	in-state: $8,040; out-of-state: $16,080
room & board	$5,192
total need-based institutional scholarships/grants	$2,108,374
% of students apply for need-based aid	68
% of students receive aid	57
% receiving need-based scholarship or grant aid	48
% receiving aid whose need was fully met	25
average aid package	$8,851
average student loan debt upon graduation	$19,674

University of Alaska Anchorage

University of Alaska Anchorage
3901 Old Seward Highway
Anchorage, Alaska 99503
Ph: (907) 786-1480
enroll@uaa.alaska.edu
www.uaa.alaska.edu

FAST FACTS

STUDENT PROFILE

# of degree-seeking undergraduates	12,869
% male/female	41/59
% African American	4
% American Indian or Alaska Native	8
% Asian or Pacific Islander	8
% Hispanic	3
% White	62
% International	1
% Pell grant recipients	13

ACADEMICS

full-time faculty	645
full-time minority faculty	83
student-faculty ratio	18:1
average class size	20
% first-year retention rate	71
% graduation rate (6 years)	25

Popular majors Elementary Education, Psychology, Nursing, Accounting, Business Administration

CAMPUS LIFE

% live on campus	n/a

Multicultural student clubs and organizations
AHAINA Student Programs, Native Student Services, Alaska Native/American Indian Science and Engineering Society (AISES), Chinese Language, Diversity Pre-Health Club, German Culture Club, ANIME, Hip Hop Club, International Student Association, International Youth Fellowship, Japanese Culture Club (Nihon Bunka), Polynesian College Council, Russian Club (Russki Klub), Spanish Club (La Tertulia), Students for Social Equality, The Alaska Native Oratory Society (AkNOS)

Athletics NCAA Division II, Great Northwest Athletic Conference, Hockey Division I

ADMISSIONS

# of applicants	4,250
% accepted	77
# of first-year students enrolled	1,956
SAT Critical Reading (middle 50%)	430-590
SAT Math (middle 50%)	440-570
SAT Writing (middle 50%)	n/a
ACT (middle 50%)	17-24
average HS GPA	n/a

Deadlines

regular decision	7/1
application fee (online)	$50 ($50)
fee waiver for applicants with financial need	no

COST & AID

tuition	in-state: $4,470; out-of state $15,000
room & board	$8,605
total need-based institutional scholarships/grants	$1,818,289
% of students apply for need-based aid	57
% of students receive aid	57
% receiving need-based scholarship or grant aid	43
% receiving aid whose need was fully met	73
average aid package	$10,055
average student loan debt upon graduation	$22,043

The University of Alaska Anchorage is the state's largest post-secondary institution. Located in the heart of Alaska's largest city, the campus is nestled in the middle of a greenbelt, surrounded by lakes, ponds and wildlife, and is connected to a city-wide trail system perfect for students' active lifestyles. The University offers many career pathway programs in more than 150 major study areas, including arts, sciences, business, education, human services and health sciences. Through UAA's comprehensive curriculum, students learn practical job skills and develop a strong educational foundation that prepares them for graduate or professional schools and the workplace.

ACCESS **Junior Academy**

Junior Academy is a program aimed at pre-college students who are between their junior and senior years in high school. Junior Academy students live on the UAA campus for six weeks while attending classes in biology, physics, trigonometry, chemistry and introduction to engineering. Students who successfully complete Junior Academy are awarded $2,000 scholarships toward furthering their education at any University of Alaska campus.

OPPORTUNITY **Seawolf Opportunities Scholarship**

The Seawolf Opportunities Scholarship is a four-year renewable scholarship providing financial assistance for tuition and other education expenses, including housing and licensed childcare, to degree-seeking students at the University of Alaska Anchorage who are first-generation college students and first-time freshmen.

OPPORTUNITY **Commit to Success Scholarship**

Commit to Success Scholarship is four-year renewable and provides financial assistance for tuition and other educational expenses to a full-time student from Alaska public high school, who may otherwise not likely be able to obtain a four-year college degree. Preference shall be given to first generation college students.

OPPORTUNITY **UAA First Generation Student Scholarship**

First Generation Student Scholarship provides scholarships to students who are the first in their family to complete a college education. Award amount is a minimum $2,000 per academic year.

SUCCESS **Native Early Transition (NET) Program**

NET is an exciting program which involves both rural and Native high school seniors who will be attending fall UAA classes. The program ensures their transition from rural villages to the UAA campus and the city of Anchorage be made as easy as possible.

SUCCESS **AHAINA Stars Peer Mentor Program**

This program assists freshmen and sophomore students in transitioning into the collegiate experience by providing monthly meetings that address pertinent issues and develop skills related to academic success. Peer Mentors are upperclassmen whose experiences along with specialized training provide a support network of information and resources.

SUCCESS **Native Student Services (NSS)**

Native Student Services provide quality support services to Native and rural students which promotes their scholastic achievement, student retention, and personal success. NSS foster academic excellence, career development, leadership skills, personal growth, college-transitioning, a sense of belonging, and the attainment of one's scholastic and life goals.

Arizona State University

As one of the largest public universities in the country, Arizona State University offers an unparalleled number of programs and opportunities for students. Arizona State boasts a record-high number of minority students and one of the highest numbers of Native American faculty of any national university. The nationally recognized Barrett, the honors college, offers resources supported by a $10 million endowment. When not involved in academic pursuits, Arizona State University students can cheer on the Sun Devils in PAC-12 sports or participate in one of the more than 625 clubs and student organizations.

> ACCESS Hispanic Mother Daughter Program (HMDP)

Hispanic Mother Daughter Program raises educational and career aspirations of Hispanic women by involving mothers in the education of their daughters. One-on-one mentoring opportunities and monthly on-campus workshops provide participants the opportunity to plan their academic and professional careers. The program begins when students are in eighth grade and continues through the completion of a university degree. Outstanding participants may be eligible for Arizona State scholarships.

> ACCESS African American Men of Arizona State University Program

The African American Men of Arizona State University Program is designed to positively impact the recruitment, persistence and graduation of male African-American college students. The program brings high school juniors and seniors — and their parents — to campus to prepare them for university enrollment, retention and graduation. The program provides a critical connection to Arizona State for potential and current university students. Events such as the Fall Leadership Conference, the Carter G. Woodson lecture series and various spoken-word performances serve as an invaluable complement to the academic rigor of workshops.

> ***"I am the first person in my family to attend college. I chose ASU because it has lots of opportunities and majors. I have been successful because of great professors and my personal determination to get an education. Without financial aid I would not have had this opportunity."***
>
> *– Gideon H., '12*
> *Dewey, AZ*
> *Urban Planning*

> OPPORTUNITY President Barack Obama Scholars Program

As a commitment to President Obama's challenge to enhance college accessibility, ASU expanded its most important financial aid program (ASU Advantage) and renamed it the President Barack Obama Scholars Program. Through a combination of aid sources, the program will provide funding for direct costs to all academically qualified Arizona freshmen from families that earn less than $60,000. Covered costs include tuition, fees, books, and room and board. Obama Scholars are encouraged to have a work-study job on-campus and participate in a one-on-one mentoring program. For fall 2009, 1,100 students are expected to benefit from this program.

> OPPORTUNITY ASU Advantage

ASU Advantage offers qualifying Arizona residents and low-income students a combination of financial aid resources that do not require repayment. This financial aid covers eight semesters of tuition, room, board and books for full-time enrollment. Since its inception in Fall 2005, nearly 1,000 freshmen have benefited from this program.

> SUCCESS LINK @ ASU

LINK @ ASU is a one-week, transitional summer program which introduces incoming college freshmen to the first year ASU experience. With a focus on the multicultural experience, participants meet with student leaders and become familiar with student resources and services, organizations and university traditions.

Arizona State University
P.O. Box 870112
Tempe, AZ 85287
Ph: (480) 965-7788
ugrading@asu.edu
www.asu.edu

FAST FACTS

STUDENT PROFILE

# of degree-seeking undergraduates	56,232
% male/female	49/51
% African American	5
% American Indian or Alaska Native	2
% Asian or Pacific Islander	6
% Hispanic	18
% White	62
% International	2.5
% Pell grant recipients	21

First-generation and minority alumni Christine Yaro Devine, news anchor, Fox Network (LA affiliate); Albert Hale, Arizona senator, former president, Navajo Nation; Reggie Jackson, inductee, Baseball Hall of Fame; Barry Bonds, professional baseball player; Vada Manager, director of Global Issues Management, Nike, Inc.

ACADEMICS

full-time faculty	2,530
full-time minority faculty	554
student-faculty ratio	24:1
average class size	10-19
% first-year retention rate	84
% graduation rate (6 years)	58.7

Popular majors Journalism, Business, Engineering

CAMPUS LIFE

% live on campus (% freshmen) 21 (73)

Multicultural student clubs and organizations Seventeen ethnic and multicultural fraternities and sororities, Asian/Asian Pacific American Students' Coalition, Philippine American Student Association, Aguila Leadership and Mentoring Association, Upward Bound Alumni Association, Arab Students' Association, American Indian Council, Native Americans Taking Initiative ON Success, Students Identifying Multiracial and Biracial at ASU, Hispanic Honor Society/Latino Students Union, Movimiento Estudiantil Chicana/o de Aztlan

Athletics NCAA Division I, Pacific-12 Conference

ADMISSIONS

# of applicants	29,771
% accepted	87
# of first-year students enrolled	9,544
SAT Critical Reading (middle 50%)	480-600
SAT Math (middle 50%)	490-620
SAT Writing (middle 50%)	n/a
ACT (middle 50%)	21-27
average HS GPA	3.4

Deadlines

regular decision	rolling
application fee (online)	in-state: $50 ($50); out-of-state: $65 ($65)
fee waiver for applicants with financial need	yes

COST & AID

tuition	in-state: $7,322; out-of-state: $20,257
room & board	$9,706
total need-based institutional scholarships/grants	$89,316,172
% of students apply for need-based aid	59
% of students receive aid	50
% receiving need-based scholarship or grant aid	44
% receiving aid whose need was fully met	17
average aid package	$11,482
average student loan debt upon graduation	$17,732

Northern Arizona University

Northern Arizona University
Undergraduate Admissions
P.O. Box 4084
Flagstaff, AZ 86011-4084
Ph: (888) 628-2968 / (298) 523-5511
undergraduate.admissions@nau.edu
www.nau.edu

Northern Arizona University (NAU) is a diverse, comprehensive public university that provides students with a quality, affordable education in two major cities. Founded in 1899, the university promotes a learning community where students are prepared to contribute to the social, economic, and environmental needs of a changing world. From its inception, NAU has implemented innovative and accountable teaching practices, including the effective use of technology. With nearly 22,500 undergraduate and graduate students from 50 states and 70 countries, students become active citizens, leaders, and problem solvers with an understanding of global issues.

ACCESS Nizhoni Academy

Nizhoni Academy is a pre-college program designed to encourage Native American students to seriously prepare for scholastic achievement in secondary and post-secondary education. The Academy emphasizes a rigorous academic discipline to provide students a clear understanding of the demands of college studies and the requirements of academic study skills necessary to be successful in college.

ACCESS Educational Talent Search (ETS)

Talent Search is a year round pre-college program that provides services to low income and potential first generation middle and high school students in Northern Arizona. Talent Search's goals are to increase educational and career awareness among our participants, enhance the number of students who complete high school and encourage our participants to continue and enroll in post-secondary education.

ACCESS Upward Bound

Upward Bound is a year-round program providing educational services and college preparatory assistance to Northern Arizona high school students who attend either Williams, Coconino, Hopi or Winslow high schools. There is also a 5-week summer academy held every year.

SUCCESS Successful Transition and Academic Readiness (STAR)

The STAR program offers selected new freshmen an innovating and exciting way to begin their higher education at the university. STAR assists students with making the important transition from high school to college. STAR students will earn six university credit hours, live in the STAR residence hall, develop leadership skills through Club STAR, experience campus life and connect with other new students.

SUCCESS LEADS Center

The Leadership, Engagement, Achievement, Diversity and Service (LEADS) Center encompasses three campus departments to bring the best in advising, mentoring and cultural celebrations. It encompasses the Multicultural Student Center (Peer Advisor Program, clubs and organizations, newsletter, local scholarships in addition to counseling and a resource library); Native American Support Services (culturally-sensitive support services to Native American and Alaskan Native students); and Student Support Services (a federal TRIO program designed to help low-income, first generation students adjust to campus life and the rigors of academic study).

"The STAR program was very beneficial because it not only helped me adjust to the college lifestyle, but it also taught me how to become more of an independent person and experience life on my own. During STAR, I met such a diverse group of people; many of which became some of my closest friends. I'm so happy that I was a part of the program!"

– Kristina R., '12
Gilbert, AZ
Biology Major

FAST FACTS

STUDENT PROFILE

# of degree-seeking undergraduates	20,194
% male/female	40/60
% African American	3
% American Indian or Alaska Native	5
% Asian or Pacific Islander	3
% Hispanic	15
% White	67
% International	4
% Pell grant recipients	32

First-generation and minority alumni Kevin Chase ('01), NAU Program Coordinator Sr., for Student Support Services; Claudia Clark ('08), NAU Graduate Student; Cecilia Estudillo ('09), Elementary School Teacher

ACADEMICS

full-time faculty	386
full-time minority faculty	87
student-faculty ratio	20:1
average class size	30
% first-year retention rate	71
% graduation rate (6 years)	49

Popular majors Elementary Education, Hotel and Restaurant Management, Biology, Nursing, Management

CAMPUS LIFE

% live on campus (% freshmen)	35 (88)

Multicultural student clubs and organizations Black Student Union, Hispanic Honor Society, MEChA-Native Americans United, National Society of Minorities in Hospitality, Native American Business Association, American Indian Science and Engineering Society, Club STAR

Athletics NCAA Division I, Big Sky Conference

ADMISSIONS

# of applicants	31,000
% accepted	66
# of first-year students enrolled	4,100
SAT Critical Reading (middle 50%)	470-580
SAT Math (middle 50%)	470-590
SAT Writing (middle 50%)	450-560
ACT (middle 50%)	21-25
average HS GPA	3.4

Deadlines

regular decision	rolling
priority application	3/15
application fee (online)	$25 ($25)
fee waiver for applicants with financial need	yes

COST & AID

tuition	in-state: $8,009; out-of-state: $21,184
room & board	$8,476
total need-based institutional scholarships/grants	$60,070,042
% of students apply for need-based aid	68
% of students receive aid	73
% receiving need-based scholarship or grant aid	70
% receiving aid whose need was fully met	21
average aid package	$9,713
average student loan debt upon graduation	$17,138

Arkansas State University

With a population of more than 12,000 undergraduate and graduate students and more than 200 degree programs, Arkansas State University provides an affordable and accessible, quality education to a diverse and dynamic array of students. The University treats each individual as an equal and important member of its community and offers more than 300 student organizations, valuing community involvement outside of the classroom as part of students' core education.

"I decided to attend ASU after attending Senior Preview Day. I enjoyed the campus environment and felt like the campus was a home away from home. The people I met were extremely nice and made every student visiting the campus feel special and welcomed. Also, ASU was close enough to my home town, but far enough that I was able experience something different."

– Adrian E., '12
McGehee, AR
Chemistry, Education

ACCESS "Back to School" Day

"Back to School" Day provides an educational venue for students of color and first generation high school students and their parents in preparation for the start of a new academic year. Topics covered include self-esteem, importance of the ACT test, reasons to avoid the legal system, and a question and answer session for parents. The goal is to reduce the number of incidents in the schools and improve the students' motivation to succeed.

ACCESS Discover Diversity

Discover Diversity is a leadership development program designed to give students of color and first generation college students a closer look into their future by exposing them to college life through academic workshops, class lectures, financial aid presentations, and much more. Students who meet the requirements are selected by their high school counselors to participate in this event. During this program, students have the opportunity to get to know faculty, staff, alumni, and current ASU students.

OPPORTUNITY Thompson Minority Scholarship

The Thompson Minority Scholarship program awards scholarships to incoming African-American freshmen and currently enrolled African-American students. This scholarship was developed to increase the enrollment of entering African-American freshmen and the retention rates of currently enrolled students by honoring academic achievement and eliminating financial barriers.

SUCCESS First Year Experience Program (FYE)

The First Year Experience Program provides incoming students with the information and skills needed to meet the expectations of college faculty, develop effective study skills, and become familiar with college policies and procedures. Topical coverage includes decision making, goal setting, planning, time management, and group team building skills.

SUCCESS Student Support Services (SSS)

Student Support Services is a comprehensive program designed to promote retention and academic success in college. It provides participants with academic and support services in a caring environment that seeks to ensure their successful completion of a baccalaureate degree at Arkansas State University. These services are offered free of charge to participants and include tutoring, academic and financial advising, counseling, mentoring, workshops, and cultural enrichment trips. Participants must demonstrate financial need, documentation of a disability, or be first-generation college students.

SUCCESS Summer Bridge Program

The Summer Bridge Program, supported by Student Support Services, is designed to introduce incoming or nontraditional students to the resources needed for success in college. Students must demonstrate academic or financial need, or documentation of a disability, and have been accepted into Student Support Services. The program takes place during a week prior to the start of the academic year and is offered free of charge.

Arkansas State University–Jonesboro
P. O. Box 1630
State University, AR 72467
Ph: (870) 972-3024
admissions@astate.edu
www.astate.edu

FAST FACTS

STUDENT PROFILE

# of degree-seeking undergraduates	9,489
% male/female	42/58
% African American	18
% American Indian or Alaska Native	<1
% Asian or Pacific Islander	1
% Hispanic	1
% White	69
% International	4
% Pell grant recipients	42

First-generation and minority alumni The Hon. Mike Beebe, governor, state of Arkansas; Maj. Gen. Elder Granger, former deputy director of the Department of Defense's TRICARE Management, former Commander, Task Force 44th Medical Command and Command Surgeon for Multinational Corps-Iraq in Baghdad, Iraq; Dr. Thomas Hill, Vice President for Student Affairs at Iowa State University, Olympic bronze medalist; The Hon. James Pardew, former U.S. ambassador to Bulgaria, former deputy assistant secretary general for NATO International; Dr. Kathy Brittain White, former chief information officer for Cardinal Health, founder and president of Rural Sourcing, Inc.

ACADEMICS

full-time faculty	482
full-time minority faculty	70
student-faculty ratio	19:1
average class size	28
% first-year retention rate	71
% graduation rate (6 years)	33

Popular majors Business, Nursing, Early Childhood Education

CAMPUS LIFE

% live on campus (% freshmen)	28 (60)

Multicultural student clubs and organizations Black Student Association, N.A.A.C.P., International Student Association, Indian Student Association, Spanish and Latino Student Association, Chinese Student Association, Nepali Student Association, Common Ground

Athletics NCAA Division I, Sunbelt Conference

ADMISSIONS

# of applicants	4,568
% accepted	70
# of first-year students enrolled	1,716
SAT Critical Reading (middle 50%)	450-550
SAT Math (middle 50%)	480-580
SAT Writing (middle 50%)	460-590
ACT (middle 50%)	19-25
average HS GPA	3.28

Deadlines

regular decision	rolling
application fee (online)	$15 ($15)
fee waiver for applicants with financial need	no

COST & AID

tuition	in-state $5,100; out-of-state $13,320
room & board	$6,544
total need-based institutional scholarships/grants	$13,600,000
% of students apply for need-based aid	79
% of students receive aid	61
% receiving need-based scholarship or grant aid	52
% receiving aid whose need was fully met	26
average aid apckage	$12,100
average student loan debt upon graduation	$18,750

Hendrix College

As a leader in engaged liberal arts and sciences education, Hendrix provides a demanding yet supportive environment where tomorrow's leaders learn to combine critical thought with action. A private, undergraduate institution of the liberal arts founded in 1876 and related to the United Methodist Church, Hendrix offers distinguished academic programs in a residential setting. "Your Hendrix Odyssey: Engaging in Active Learning" is an exciting and unique component of the curriculum that guarantees that each Hendrix student will participate in at least three engaging, hands-on learning experiences before graduating. In addition to the Odyssey Program, Hendrix stands apart from other colleges for its small participatory classes, close relationships between faculty and students, and its welcoming community, which is enhanced by the belief that diversity in the student body enhances the intellectual experience.

"I'm most proud to call myself a Hendrix Warrior because of how alluring Hendrix's atmosphere is. People here are open-minded, welcoming, generally relaxed, but still ambitious, goal-oriented, and fun. It feels like a small vibrant village. I hate long breaks away from Hendrix because this is easily my second home!"

– Dominique K., '11
Little Rock, AR
Art

ACCESS **Mentoring Programs**

Hendrix students take time to call high school students in order to familiarize them with the College as well as answer any questions they might have. In addition to working with the Upward Bound program, Hendrix students serve as mentors in a local "All-Stars" program that aims to help minority and low-income students with the college application process.

OPPORTUNITY **Scholarships and Financial Aid**

The availability of academic and extracurricular scholarships as well as federally funded need-based financial aid allows Hendrix to develop personalized financial aid packages, and 100 percent of enrolled students receive some form of achievement-based and/or need-based state, federal, or institutional assistance. The Robert and Ruby Priddy Scholarships are awarded to students from middle-income families who do not qualify for larger merit-based scholarships or federal grants but who show exceptional promise for leadership, service, and success.

SUCCESS **Office of Multicultural and International Student Services (MISS)**

The Office of Multicultural and International Student Services (MISS) provides students with opportunities to engage in cross-cultural reflection and promotes appreciation of diversity, service, and leadership. The services that MISS provides range in scope from student programming activities to diversity and leadership training to support. Its Cultural Connection Committee collaborates with student organizations on diversity-related issues and develops an annual outreach plan to enhance the diversity on the Hendrix campus. MISS also promotes cultural heritage immersions through programs, which include hosting speakers and organizing field trips and film screenings.

SUCCESS **Campus-Wide Retention Initiatives**

All incoming students are assigned a faculty adviser as well as an academic peer mentor who helps them adjust to academic and social life at Hendrix. The Office of Academic Support Services provides services to promote academic success, including peer tutoring in most subjects, one-on-one academic counseling and encouragement, and academic discussion and workshops in areas such as time management and test anxiety.

Hendrix College
1600 Washington Avenue
Conway, AR 72032-3080
Ph: (501) 450-1362
adm@hendrix.edu
www.hendrix.edu

FAST FACTS

STUDENT PROFILE

# of degree-seeking undergraduates	1,452
% male/female	43/57
% African American	3
% American Indian or Alaska Native	1
% Asian or Pacific Islander	3
% Hispanic	4
% White	77
% International	4
% Pell grant recipients	21

First-generation and minority alumni Theodore Bunting, Jr., senior vice president and chief accounting officer, Entergy Corporation; the Honorable Linda Pondexter Chesterfield, Arkansas state senator and former president, Arkansas Education Association; Walter Pryor, vice president of government affairs, Career Education Corporation, and former principal and general counsel, Podesta Group; T.J. Ticey, interim executive director, African American Family Services

ACADEMICS

full-time faculty	108
full-time minority faculty	12
student-faculty ratio	12:1
average class size	18
% first-year retention rate	86
% graduation rate (6 years)	60

Popular majors Biochemisty/Molecular Biology, Biology, English, Psychology, and Sociology/Anthropology

CAMPUS LIFE

% live on campus (% freshmen)	83 (99)

Multicultural student clubs and organizations Asian Culture Club, Cultural Connection Committee, International Club, Multicultural Development Committee, Students for Black Culture, Students for Latin and Iberian Culture, UNITY

Athletics NCAA Division III, Southern Collegiate Athletic Conference (SCAC)

ADMISSIONS

# of applicants	1,554
% accepted	83
# of first-year students enrolled	404
SAT Critical Reading (middle 50%)	600-700
SAT Math (middle 50%)	580-680
ACT (middle 50%)	27-32
average HS GPA	3.89
Deadlines	
early action I	11/15
early action II	2/1
regular decision	rolling after 2/1
application fee (online)	$40 ($0)
fee waived for applicants with financial need	yes

COST & AID

tuition	$33,930
room & board	$9,714
total need-based institutional scholarships/grants	$15,450,062
% of students apply for need-based aid	83
% of students receive aid	100
% receiving need-based scholarship or grant aid	64
% receiving aid whose need was fully met	42
average aid package	$24,445
average student loan debt upon graduation	$19,023

California Institute of Technology

Founded in 1891, California Institute of Technology has a long history of tackling the most challenging, fundamental problems in science and technology. With world-class scholars as their faculty mentors and access to incredible research facilities, students can prepare to become leaders in the scientific community. As part of a deliberately small undergraduate population of 900, students are surrounded by unusually talented classmates with whom they collaborate regularly. Caltech has a unique culture that combines a passion for innovation and intense intellectual curiosity with a tradition of practical jokes and pranks for which the school is widely renowned. At Caltech, it's relatively easy for one to find their niche and develop strong working relationships with both their professors and their fellow students.

ACCESS Leadership Education and Development (LEAD)

Leadership Education and Development is an intense summer program for high school students of color with outstanding academic performance and demonstrated leadership skills. The mission of LEAD is to lay the foundation through an intense curriculum for an increase in the number and quality of minority students interested in careers in engineering and computer science.

OPPORTUNITY QuestBridge Partner

QuestBridge is a non-profit program that links bright and motivated low-income students with educational and scholarship opportunities at some of the nation's most selective colleges and universities. QuestBridge is the provider of the National College Match Program and the College Prep Scholarship. Caltech partnered with QuestBridge to connect and provide access to high-achieving low-income students who are looking for an exceptional science, math, and engineering undergraduate experience.

"You have to show that you are passionate about math and science, that you want to get out there and try new things and collaborate and push the envelope."

– Teri J.,'12
El Paso, TX
Mechanical Engineering

SUCCESS Caltech Center for Diversity (CCD)

The mission of the Caltech Center for Diversity is to provide programming and support for campus activities that promote the acceptance and inclusion of underserved minority groups on campus. The CCD offers proactive academic monitoring with appropriate follow-up, advising, referrals, graduate school guidance, and activities to foster the sense of community among underrepresented groups on campus. The CCD also holds social events for students such as lunches, Midnight Study Breaks, Welcome Back BBQ, and Spring Banquet.

SUCCESS Freshman Summer Research Institute (FSRI)

Incoming freshmen may participate in this summer program designed to enhance the transition from high school to a research-based education and to assist students in developing learning behaviors that will help them excel at Caltech. Participants conduct research with mentors, write research papers, and give professional research talks.

SUCCESS Mellon Mays Undergraduate Fellowship

The Mellon Mays Undergraduate Fellowship is a prestigious national program focused on increasing the number of underrepresented students who will pursue Ph.D.s in core fields in the arts and sciences. The fellowships available to Caltech students include mentoring, research stipends, and travel support.

California Institute of Technology
383 South Hill Ave.
MC 10-90
Pasadena, CA 91125
Ph: (626) 395-6341
ugadmissions@caltech.edu
www.admissions.caltech.edu

FAST FACTS

STUDENT PROFILE

# of degree-seeking undergraduates	967
% male/female	60/40
% African American	1
% American Indian or Alaska Native	<1
% Asian or Pacific Islander	39
% Hispanic	6
% White	37
% International	12
% Pell grant recipients	10

First-generation and minority alumni Dr. Haywood Robinson '74, Physician, Brazos Medical Associates; Day S. Ivy,'06, Associate Deutsche Bank; Kamalah Chang '05, Mechanical Design Engineering, Schlumberger; Gustavo Olm '06, Nuclear Plant Operator, SoCal Edison; Michelle Giron '05, Chemical Engineer, Energent Corporation; Dr. Edray Goins '94, Associate Professor of Mathematics, Purdue University

ACADEMICS

full-time faculty	302
full-time minority faculty	47
student-faculty ratio	3:1
average class size	20
% first-year retention rate	98
% graduation rate (6 years)	89

Popular majors Engineering, Physical Sciences, Biological/Life Sciences, Mathematics, Computer Science

CAMPUS LIFE

% live on campus (% freshmen)	95 (100)

Multicultural student clubs and organizations Caltech Center for Diversity, Black Students at Caltech, Caltech Latino Association of Students in Engineering and Sciences, The Society of Hispanic Professional Engineers, The National Society of Black Engineers, The American Indian Science and Engineering Society, Mellon Mays Undergraduate Fellowship

Athletics NCAA III, Southern California Intercollegiate Athletic Conference (SCIAC)

ADMISSIONS

# of applicants	5,227
% accepted	13
# of first-year students enrolled	245
SAT Critical Reading (middle 50%)	690-760
SAT Math (middle 50%)	770-800
SAT Writing (middle 50%)	680-770
ACT (middle 50%)	30-36

*Additional testing information (required): SAT M2 (middle 50%) - 770-800; 1 SAT II Science required: SAT II BIO (middle 50%) - 740-800; SAT II CH (middle 50%) - 780-800; SAT II PH (middle 50%) - 780-800

average HS GPA	4.0

Deadlines

early decision	11/1
regular decision	1/3
application fee (online)	$65 ($65)
fee waived for applicants with financial need	yes

COST & AID

tuition	$36,387
room & board	$11,676
total need-based institutional scholarships/grants	$14,227,367
% of students apply for need-based aid	62
% receiving need-based scholarship or grant aid	53
% receiving aid whose need was fully met	100
average aid package	$34,928
average student loan debt upon graduation	$10,760

California Lutheran University

California Lutheran University
60 West Olsen Road # 1350
Thousand Oaks, CA 91360
Ph: (805) 493-3135
admissions@callutheran.edu
www.callutheran.edu

Founded in 1959, California Lutheran University is a diverse, scholarly, co-educational, private university dedicated to excellence in the liberal arts and professional studies. Rooted in the Lutheran tradition of Christian faith, the university encourages critical inquiry into matters of both faith and reason. California Lutheran University's mission is to educate leaders for a global society who are strong in character and judgment, confident in their identity and vocation and committed to service and justice.

ACCESS Upward Bound

The Upward Bound program is dedicated to providing quality academic and personal development services to high school students from low-income and/or first-generation families. Beyond increasing the rate at which high school graduates pursue post secondary education, the California Lutheran University Upward Bound program strives to increase participants' competency in English, mathematics, science, social science and foreign language. Participants receive tutoring, counseling and mentoring, as well as the opportunity to attend cultural enrichment events.

"Through SSS (Student Support Services), SOAR, and events such as the Multicultural Night you learn how much you matter and how you can change the lives of others. CLU shares opportunities in all areas of life. There is nothing you can't do!"

– Rachel M., '10
Liberal Studies

OPPORTUNITY InCLUsive Overnight Scholars Program

The InCLUsive Overnight Scholars Program was established to increase diversity within the student body and to foster a campus climate that encourages inclusive, cross-cultural interaction, respect and appreciation of diversity and global awareness. The program gives admitted high school students the opportunity to visit California Lutheran University. Participants learn what student life is like by staying in a residence hall, making connections with faculty, staff and student leaders, meeting other prospective students and interacting with current students who make California Lutheran University their home. InCLUsive participants have the opportunity to be selected for designated scholarships offered through a special InCLUsive Program essay competition.

SUCCESS FOCUS Mentoring Program

Freshmen and transfer students from traditionally underrepresented backgrounds are encouraged to sign up for a mentor. New students are assigned a faculty member or administrator to act as their personal mentor during their first year at California Lutheran University. The program provides scheduled activities, but more important are the relationships students form with their mentors.

SUCCESS Summer Orientation to Academic Resources Program

Incoming first-generation college freshmen are invited to attend this orientation program. The program gives participants an orientation to the college environment and provides them with opportunities to connect with other first-generation students. In addition, the program assists participants in the process of academic exploration by introducing them to relevant resources, challenging them to examine their values and interests and facilitating their transition to California Lutheran University. During the academic year, students participate in the Student Support Services program that offers a holistic range of services including academic counseling and personal support to assist first-generation students to successfully complete their degree.

FAST FACTS

STUDENT PROFILE

# of degree-seeking undergraduates	2,545
% male/female	57/43
% African American	4
% American Indian or Alaska Native	1
% Asian or Pacific Islander	5
% Hispanic	20
% White	57
% International	4
% Pell grant recipients	19.9

ACADEMICS

full-time faculty	154
full-time minority faculty	28
student-faculty ratio	16:1
average class size	22
% first-year retention rate	83
% graduation rate (6 years)	65

Popular majors Business Administration, Liberal Studies, Exercise Science, Psychology, Biology

CAMPUS LIFE

% live on campus (% freshmen)	63 (88)

Multicultural student clubs and organizations
Asian Club and Friends, Brothers & Sisters United, Latin American Student Organization, United Students of the World, Chinese Students Association

Athletics NCAA Division III, Southern California Intercollegiate Athletic Conference

ADMISSIONS

# of applicants	7,226
% accepted	44
# of first-year students enrolled	464
SAT Critical Reading (middle 50%)	500-590
SAT Math (middle 50%)	520-610
SAT Writing (middle 50%)	490-590
ACT (middle 50%)	20-28
average HS GPA	3.7
Deadlines	
early action	11/1
regular decision	2/1
application fee (online)	$45 ($25)
fee waiver for applicants with financial need	yes

COST & AID

tuition	$32,610
room & board	$11,190
total need-based institutional scholarships/grants	$17,763,100
% of students apply for need-based aid	88
% of students receive aid	93
% receiving need-based scholarship or grant aid	64
% receiving aid whose need was fully met	13
average aid package	$20,557
average student loan debt upon graduation	$16,000

California State University, Chico

California State University, Chico
400 West First Street
Chico, CA 95929-0722
Ph: (800) 542-4426
info@csuchico.edu
www.csuchico.edu

California State University, Chico ("Chico State"), founded in 1887, is a residential campus located in Northern California. With Little Chico Creek winding through the center of campus, CSU, Chico is known for its beauty. CSU, Chico offers more than 100 undergraduate majors and options, and maintains one of the highest graduation rates in the 23 campus CSU system. Chico is committed to its diversity, students who are the first in their family to attend college and the success of its students. CSU, Chico was recognized as a top 100 school by Hispanic Outlook in Higher Education for the number of Hispanic students who graduate. They have earned marks as high as 99 percent from graduating seniors when asked if they were satisfied with CSU, Chico as a whole.

OPPORTUNITY **MESA Schools Program**

The MESA (Mathematics, Engineering, Science Achievement) Schools Program is an academic preparation program of the University of California, working through schools and colleges throughout the state. It is designed to strengthen the academic skills needed for students to pursue mathematics and science based courses of study in college and to provide support for them to go on to careers in technology-based industries. The program seeks to motivate, support, and prepare underrepresented and disadvantaged students in order to increase their number in undergraduate programs at four-year universities with an emphasis in these fields.

OPPORTUNITY **TRIO Upward Bound**

Chico's TRIO Upward Bound programs are academic programs which assist a diverse population of motivated low-income and first-generation high school students to achieve their goals of reaching and succeeding in post-secondary education. These programs include Upward Bound Original, Upward Bound for ESL Learners, Upward Bound Math/Science, Student Support Services and Educational Talent Search.

"Chico State has everything I was looking for in a college campus. I'm glad I made the right choice and chose Chico.

– Angelica M., '10
Orland, CA
Social Science

SUCCESS **Educational Opportunity Program (EOP)**

The Educational Opportunity Program office functions as the home base for all EOP students once they have been admitted to the University. EOP students are offered support services designed to assist them in overcoming the many obstacles that a new educational and social environment may present. Services include a computer lab, supplemental instruction, Summer Bridge Program, social activities and student job opportunities.

SUCCESS **Chico Student Success Center (CSSC)**

The Chico Student Success Center is a collaborative, student development program with a decade of successful diversity recruitment and retention experiences. The CSSC serves low-income students in an effort to create and support a successful college experience while attending CSU, Chico. CSSC students use the facilities for individual and group projects, an opportunity to be around mentors and academic support, and sometimes simply to be in a comfortable environment that is focused on student achievement.

FAST FACTS

STUDENT PROFILE

# of degree-seeking undergraduates	15,989
% male/female	48/52
% African American	2
% American Indian or Alaska Native	1
% Asian or Pacific Islander	6
% Hispanic	15
% White	61
% International	5
% Pell grant recipients	34

First-generation and minority alumni Mary J. Kight, '73, adjutant general of the CA National Guard; Lily Roberts '87, Ph.D., head of evaluation, CA Dept. of Education; Nhia Vang, MD '99, family practice physician; Dean N. Williams '85, senior research computer scientist, Lawrence Livermore National Laboratory

ACADEMICS

full-time faculty	480
student-faculty ratio	24:1
average class size	32
% first-year retention rate	82
% graduation rate (6 yrs)	55

Popular majors Business, Liberal Studies (elementary education), Psychology, Construction Management, Pre-Nursing/Nursing, Kinesiology, Recreation Administration, Criminal Justice, Civil Engineering, Communication Studies

CAMPUS LIFE

% live on campus (% freshmen)	12 (64)

Multicultural student clubs and organizations American Indian club, Cross-Cultural Leadership Center, Filipino American Student Organization, Hmong Student Association, MEChA, Men of Honor, Black Leaders on Campus, Multicultural Affairs Council, Multicultural Greek Council, Pacific Islanders Connection, Southeast Asian Student Association

Athletics NCAA Division II, California Collegiate Athletic Association

ADMISSIONS

# of applicants	14,361
% accepted	62
# of first-year students enrolled	1,899
SAT Critical Reading (middle 50%)	460-560
SAT Math (middle 50%)	470-580
SAT Writing (middle 50%)	n/a
ACT (middle 50%)	20-25
average HS GPA	3.42

Deadlines

regular decision	11/30
application fee (online)	$55 ($55)
fee waiver for applicants with financial need	yes

COST & AID

tuition	in-state: $6,294; out-of-state: $17,454
room & board	$11,118
total need-based institutional scholarships/grants	$49,795,631
% of students apply for need-based aid	69
% of those requesting need-based aid who receive aid	n/a
% receiving need-based scholarship/grant aid	42
% receiving aid whose need was fully met	35
average aid package	$12,200
average student loan debt upon graduation	$24,000

Chapman University

Chapman University was the first private college or university in California to enroll students of all races and socio-economic backgrounds in the early part of the 20th century, a tradition to which the University firmly subscribes today. In addition to traditional need-based financial aid, merit, and talent-based scholarship programs, Chapman has historically offered funding for students who would be the first from their family to attend college in an effort to continue its legacy of enrolling a diverse student population.

OPPORTUNITY **Thurgood Marshall Scholarship**

The Thurgood Marshall Scholars program is designated for admitted students who are the first from their immediate family to attend college. Recipients should display strong leadership and community service orientation. Scholarship amounts vary, but average approximately $8,000 annually, and are designed to complement a financial aid/scholarship package by alleviating gaps or loans.

SUCCESS **Human Diversity**

As part of its General Education program, Chapman University requires all students to take a course focusing on human diversity and world cultures. Courses are designed to help students to address contemporary and historical issues that affect underrepresented groups, and to understand their implications and consequences.

SUCCESS **InsideTrack**

Chapman University has a partnership with InsideTrack, an organization offering life and success coaching free of charge to freshman students in an effort to motivate, inspire and help sharpen time management and organizational skills.

SUCCESS **Center for Academic Success (CAS)**

All Chapman students can take advantage of the Center for Academic Success, which oversees academic support programs including general academic advising, peer tutoring, advocacy, study strategies, and services for students with learning differences.

"I helped organize Chapman's inaugural Indian Festival. Through this, I realized the open-mindedness and willingness of Chapman students to integrate and learn about different cultures. After graduation, I plan to start my own non-profit organization helping the underprivileged in India. I hope to make a difference by helping people improve their living conditions and health. The biggest thing I take from my Chapman experience is the development of my self-confidence and realization that I can reach high for myself and also help many others along the way."

– Ria S., '10
Mumbai, India
Public Relations

Chapman University
One University Drive
Orange, CA 92866
Ph: (714) 997-6711
admit@chapman.edu
www.chapman.edu

FAST FACTS

STUDENT PROFILE

# of degree-seeking undergraduates	4,910
% male/female	42/58
% African American	2
% American Indian or Alaska Native	<1
% Asian or Pacific Islander	11
% Hispanic	11
% White	60
% International	2
% Pell grant recipients	36.7

First-generation and minority alumni Emmitt Ashford, legendary Major League Baseball Umpire; Michel Bell, Tony Award nominated star of Broadway's Showboat; John Nuzzo, internationally acclaimed tenor, star of Vienna State Opera; Hon. George L. Argyros, philanthropist and former U.S. Ambassador to Spain; Hon. Loretta Sanchez, member, U.S. House of Representatives

ACADEMICS

full-time faculty	362
full-time minority faculty	48
student-faculty ratio	14:1
average class size	23
% first-year retention rate	93
% graduation rate (6 yrs)	70

Popular majors Film and Television Production, Business and Economics, Music, Theatre, Dance

CAMPUS LIFE

% live on campus (% freshmen)	91

Multicultural student clubs and organizations Amnesty International, Black Student Union (BSU), Pua I'kena Hawai'i Club, International Culture Club, Nihongo Japanese Club, M.E.Ch.A., Native American Club, South Asian Student Organization, Students for a Free Tibet

Athletics NCAA Division III, Southern California Intercollegiate Athletic Conference (SCIAC)

ADMISSIONS

# of applicants	9,617
% accepted	45
# of first-year students enrolled	1,317
SAT Critical Reading (middle 50%)	548-666
SAT Math (middle 50%)	561-674
SAT Writing (middle 50%)	559-672
ACT (middle 50%)	25-29
average HS GPA	3.77

Deadlines

early action	11/11
regular decision	1/13
application fee (online)	$65 ($65)
fee waiver for applicants with financial need	yes

COST & AID

tuition	$40,234
room & board	$12,957
total need-based institutional scholarships/grants	$34,857,501
% of students apply for need-based aid	84
% of those requesting need-based aid who receive aid	100
% receiving need-based scholarship/grant aid	57
% receiving aid whose need was fully met	100
average aid package	$27,280
average student loan debt upon graduation	$22,955

Claremont McKenna College

Claremont McKenna College is a small, private liberal arts college located in Claremont, Calif., 35 miles east of Los Angeles. Claremont McKenna is committed to the well-being and success of all of its students, and offers specialized support services through the Asian American Resource Center, the Chicano/Latino Student Affairs Center, the Office of Black Student Affairs and its many multicultural student organizations and clubs. Claremont McKenna is dedicated to offering an affordable college education —100 percent of students receiving aid have their need fully met and the college does not package students with loans. The college's 10 research institutes provide students with graduate-level research opportunities as they work alongside distinguished faculty members and participate in joint academic programs and cross-registration in courses with the other Claremont Colleges.

ACCESS Step Up to Leadership / Kravis Mentoring Program

The Henry Kravis Leadership Institute sponsors Step Up To Leadership, a program that enables high school students to develop leadership competence and character. Participating students, nominated by their high school principals, engage in daily sessions on topics like communication skills, project planning, cultural diversity training, community service projects and outdoor leadership trips. The Henry Kravis Leadership Institute also sponsors the Kravis Mentoring Program at the college. Through a partnership with a local middle school, seventh graders and college students are brought together to form mutually meaningful relationships. These middle school students receive academic tutoring, encouragement to pursue higher education and personal mentoring from Claremont McKenna students, and partners attend group activities such as field trips and community service projects.

OPPORTUNITY Campus Visits

During the fall, Claremont McKenna College hosts two On Campus Days. During these Saturdays, students can stay overnight on campus, speak with students and professors and get a good feel for what it means to attend Claremont McKenna. Additionally, the college is committed to providing admitted students from disadvantaged backgrounds the opportunity to visit campus.

SUCCESS Student Affairs Committees of The Claremont Colleges

Students from all The Claremont Colleges come together under several joint student groups to support intercultural interests across campuses. Chicano/Latino Student Affairs maintains a strong commitment to the retention and graduation of Chicano/Latino students at The Claremont Colleges and provides support and resources to students and their families. The Office of Black Student Affairs hosts a variety of programs geared toward the success of African-American students on campus, including the Ujima Peer Mentoring Program, which provides mentoring for first year and transfer students of Pan African descent, and the Anansi Academic Advancement Program, which provides tutoring, academic programs and learning style and skills assessments that are particularly tailored for these students.

SUCCESS Summer Internship Funding

Every summer, nearly 85 percent of students complete an internship in an area of interest. Internships are often developed by students themselves, but funding is available from various college sources for international, human rights, political, community service-based and science research-oriented internships. For summer 2009, Claremont McKenna awarded more than $300,000 for internships and student-research initiatives.

Claremont McKenna College
CMC Admission and Financial Aid
890 Columbia Avenue
Claremont, CA 91711-6425
Ph: (909) 621-8088
admission@claremontmckenna.edu
www.claremontmckenna.edu

FAST FACTS

STUDENT PROFILE	
# of degree-seeking undergraduates	1,200
% male/female	54/46
% African American	7
% American Indian or Alaska Native	1
% Asian or Pacific Islander	19
% Hispanic	15
% White	51
% International	13
% Pell grant recipients	12
ACADEMICS	
full-time faculty	127
full-time minority faculty	24
student-faculty ratio	8:1
average class size	17
% first-year retention rate	97
% graduation rate (6 years)	92

Popular majors Government, Economics, History, Biology, Psychology, International Relations

CAMPUS LIFE	
% live on campus (% freshmen)	98 (100)

Multicultural Student Clubs and Organizations Asian Pacific American Mentoring Program, Black Student Affairs, Cultural Affairs Committee, Chicano-Latino Student Affairs, Civitas, Hawaiian Club, International Club, Korean Student Association
Athletics NCAA Division III, Southern California Intercollegiate Athletic Conference (SCIAC), Western Water Polo Association

ADMISSIONS	
# of applicants	4,484
% accepted	14
# of first-year students enrolled	300
SAT Critical Reading (middle 50%)	510-800
SAT Math (middle 50%)	520-800
SAT Writing (middle 50%)	n/a
ACT (middle 50%)	n/a
average HS GPA	n/a
Deadlines	
early decision	11/15
regular decision	1/2
application fee (online)	$60 ($60)
fee waiver for applicants with financial need	yes
COST & AID	
tuition	$42,240
room & board	$13,625
total need-based institutional scholarships/grants	$17,237,465
% of students apply for need-based aid	54
% of students receive aid	51
% receiving need-based scholarship or grant aid	51
% receiving aid whose need was fully met	100
average aid package	$34,900
average student loan debt upon graduation	$0

Harvey Mudd College

Harvey Mudd College
Office of Admission
301 Platt Boulevard
Claremont, CA 91711
Ph: (909) 621-8011
admission@hmc.edu
www.hmc.edu

Founded in 1955, Harvey Mudd is a private, co-educational institution and one of the premier math, science and engineering colleges in the nation. The college offers a rigorous scientific and technological education, paired with a strong emphasis on collaboration and research. Humanities and social sciences compose a third of the curriculum, as Harvey Mudd College believes that students well-versed in these fields will have a clearer understanding of the impact of their work on society. The faculty is dedicated to teaching undergraduates and mentoring student research.

ACCESS **Future Achievers in Science and Technology (FAST)**

A weekend program held annually in the fall for high school seniors from underrepresented backgrounds as part of Harvey Mudd College's On-Campus Day, Future Achievers of Science and Technology includes workshops on selective college admission and financial aid, class visits, research lab tours, academic presentations and other events. Travel expenses, meals, and accommodation on campus are provided. Participants also receive a Harvey Mudd College application fee waiver.

OPPORTUNITY **President's Scholar Program (PSP)**

This four-year, full tuition scholarship is designated for students who are first in their families to attend college or are from traditionally underrepresented gender or race backgrounds at Harvey Mudd. President's Scholars have an intellectual curiosity and a willingness to advance the college's diversity efforts and are poised to become future leaders in engineering, science, mathematics and technology. Approximately eight first-year students are accepted into the program annually. In addition to tuition assistance, students have opportunities for summer internships, research fellowships and ongoing academic and professional development support.

SUCCESS **Office of Institutional Diversity**

Harvey Mudd works to ensure the promotion of campus-wide diversity while providing support for the academic mission of the college. Staff prepare students to take responsibility for creating an environment where diversity is valued and to engage others in exploring diversity themselves. The office promotes programs and resources designed to foster the College's diversity mission by providing a forum for dialogue, as well as opportunities to celebrate the diverse individuals at Harvey Mudd College.

SUCCESS **Summer Institute (SI)**

About 25 to 30 incoming first year students are invited to participate in this program, designed to ensure their academic and personal success, each August. The program runs two and a half weeks prior to Freshman Orientation and targets students who are underrepresented in the fields of science, technology, engineering and mathematics. It includes room and board, and students get an early feel for the campus, classes, professors, workload, lingo, folklore, independence and self-responsibility of Harvey Mudd. Most importantly, program participants develop a long-lasting bond with other students and mentors prior to the commencement of the school year.

"Coming to Mudd was one of the best decisions I've ever made. Even though it's small, it's really easy to find a place to fit in, and the community starts to feel like an eccentric extended family instead of a bunch of classmates. I can't see myself being anywhere else."

– Beatrice M., '12
Dallas, TX
Computer Science

FAST FACTS

STUDENT PROFILE	
# of degree-seeking undergraduates	771
% male/female	58/42
% African American	<1
% American Indian or Alaska Native	<1
% Asian or Pacific Islander	14
% Hispanic	5
% White	46
% International	3
% Pell grant recipients	12
ACADEMICS	
full-time faculty	87
full-time minority faculty	19
student-faculty ratio	9:1
average class size	10-19
% first-year retention rate	98
% graduation rate (6 years)	87

Popular majors Engineering, Physics, Mathematics, Computer Science, Chemistry

CAMPUS LIFE	
% live on campus (% freshmen)	99 (100)

Multicultural Student Clubs and Organizations Asian Pacific Islander Support Program at Mudd (API SPAM), International Place, National Society of Black Engineers (NSBE), The Society for the Advancement of Latino Scientific Achievement (SALSA), Society of Hispanic Professional Engineers, Students for the Middle Eastern Cultural Promotion (SMECP)

Athletics NCAA Division III, Southern California Intercollegiate Athletic Conference

ADMISSIONS	
# of applicants	2,508
% accepted	25
# of first-year students enrolled	196
SAT Critical Reading (middle 50%)	670-760
SAT Math (middle 50%)	740-800
SAT Writing (middle 50%)	668-760
ACT (middle 50%)	32-35
average HS GPA	n/a
Deadlines	
early decision	11/15
regular decision	1/2
application fee (online)	$60 ($60)
fee waiver for applicants with financial need	yes
COST & AID	
tuition	$40,113
room & board	$13,198
total need-based institutional scholarships/grants	$10,382,922
% of students apply for need-based aid	62
% of students receive aid	53
% receiving need-based scholarship or grant aid	52
% receiving aid whose need was fully met	100
average aid package	$33,470
average student loan debt upon graduation	$21,018

Holy Names University

For over 140 years, Holy Names University has been educating students from throughout the California Bay Area and the world. As one of the most ethnically diverse college campuses in the country, HNU believes in the value of a varied student body, faculty and staff who come together to share ideas, challenge, and support each other. With over 40% of our student body the first in their family to go to college, the environment is one of growth and discovery through academics, leadership, and pursuit of social justice through developing an understanding of a world greater than ourselves. Four years at HNU isn't just about the time spent in the classroom with world class faculty. It's about shared ideas, development of the whole person and understanding your place in the global community.

"Being the first person in my family to go to college, the First Year Experience Program at HNU helped me with my transition to university life. My mentor in the program was also first in her family to go to college, so she was able to help me adjust from a small town to the Bay Area. She'd help us with everything from putting on events to remembering important deadlines."

– Susie R., '13
Dinuba, CA
Nursing

ACCESS The Early Admit Program

The Early Admit Program at HNU seeks to provide students from partner high schools in underserved communities with access to college by offering students admission to HNU on contract beginning their Freshman year of High School. Through this initiative, students are supported throughout their four years of high school, including mentor support each semester, to make sure each student is staying on track and meeting the necessary academic requirements.

ACCESS The New Initiative for College Access

The New Initiative for College Access at HNU is designed to provide students who are first in their family to go to college with access to resources and information to create a pathway to college success. Through the initiative, HNU provides college-readiness programming through mentoring, tutoring and workshops to help students and families in the community.

OPPORTUNITY Cal Grant A/B

Through the California Student Aid Commission, HNU accepts two types of federal grants specifically for California residents. Cal Grant A offers up to $9,708 annually to in-state students based on their financial aid and academic achievement. Cal Grant B is awarded to first year college students from disadvantaged backgrounds in California. Recipients of Cal Grant B receive $1,551 for their first year of college, then an additional $9,708 in the following years. In order to be eligible, students must submit their FAFSA and GPA verification forms by March 2nd.

SUCCESS HNU Connections Project

The HNU Connections Project, HNU's first year experience program, provides new students support to help ease the transition to college life, both academically and socially. Embedded in the program is a commitment to academic skill building, and an introduction to college culture. Upon admission, first year students are assigned to a learning community, common reading project, and student Mentor. Because so many of HNU students are first-generation college attendees, many of the program Mentors are first in their family to go to college. The Dean of Retention and Dean of Student Success focus many of their initiatives and programs on support for minority and first-generation students.

SUCCESS Student Success Center (SSC)

Open to all HNU students, the SSC provides resources and support to students from their first year to graduation. The Center provides free advising and guidance to students in a number of different ways, such as tutoring, test prep, career counseling, job skill building, and psychological counseling and support. Through the SSC, HNU demonstrates their commitment to support students during their first year, throughout college, and to provide assistance transitioning to work and life beyond.

Holy Names University
3500 Mountain Blvd.
Oakland, CA 94619
Ph: (510) 436-1351
admissions@hnu.edu
www.hnu.edu

FAST FACTS

STUDENT PROFILE

# of degree-seeking undergraduates	587
% male/female	30/70
% African American	19
% American Indian or Alaska Native	1
% Asian or Pacific Islander	9
% Hispanic	25
% White	19
% International	2
% Pell grant recipients	52

First-generation and minority alumni Miguel Bustos '93, Senior Program Manager, Levi Strauss Foundation, Commissioner, San Francisco Redevelopment Agency; Nga Do '96, Former Foreign Service Officer, U.S. Department of State; Leterria Fletcher '06, Case Manager and Supervisor, YEAH! (Youth Engagement, Advocacy and Housing); Helen Raines-Austin '04, Founder, CoCo Corner (Oakland, CA based youth education and advocacy non-profit; Jonathan Allen '10, International Relations Research Intern, International Community Corrections Association

ACADEMICS

full-time faculty	39
full-time minority faculty	4
student-faculty ratio	16:1
average class size	10
% first-year retention rate	70
% graduation rate (6 years)	35

Popular majors Business, Nursing, Biology, Psychology, Criminology

CAMPUS LIFE

% live on campus	65

Multicultural student clubs and organizations Black Student Union (BSU), International Student Club, Latinos Unidos, Pacific Islander Club, Queer Gay Straight Alliance (QGSA), Peace and Justice Club, National Society for Leadership and Success, Face A.I.D.S.

Athletics NAIA, California Pacific Conference

ADMISSIONS

# of applicants	542
% accepted	70
# of first-year students enrolled	145
SAT Critical Reading (middle 50%)	440-480
SAT Math (middle 50%)	430-470
SAT Writing (middle 50%)	430-470
ACT (middle 50%)	18-20
average HS GPA	3.18
Deadlines	
regular decision	priority 3/1
application fee (online)	$20 ($20)
fee waived for applicants with financial need	yes

COST & AID

tuition	$30,050
room & board	$10,090
total need-based institutional scholarships/grants	$8,000,000
% of students apply for need-based aid	90
% receiving need-based scholarship or grant aid	95
% receiving aid whose need was fully met	n/a
average aid package	$28,966
average student loan debt upon graduation	$19,000-$27,000

Marymount College

Marymount College
30800 Palos Verdes Drive East
Rancho Palos Verdes, CA 90275
Ph: (310) 303-7311
admission@marymountpv.edu
www.marymountpv.edu

Marymount College is a Catholic institution that welcomes students of all faiths and backgrounds into a quality, values-based education. Marymount fosters a student-centered approach to learning that promotes the development of the whole person, and in the spirit of their founders, the Religious of the Sacred Heart of Mary, they challenge their students to pursue lives of leadership and service. The college promotes an open and welcoming campus that builds skills for lifelong learning, and assists students to reach their goals in higher education. They strive to graduate students who embody the virtues of integrity, respect for human dignity, and commitment to justice.

OPPORTUNITY **Fall and Spring Preview Days**

Marymount College holds Preview Days in both the fall and the spring, giving prospective students the chance to meet with students and faculty, tour campus, have lunch with other students on campus, and talk to admissions officers about financial aid possibilities. The Preview Days are also an opportunity for students to submit their application in person and have their $40 application fee waived. This serves as an opportunity for possible students to experience firsthand the opportunities that college would offer them.

OPPORTUNITY **Walk In Application Day**

Walk In Application Day is a chance for prospective students to come to campus, meet with an Admissions counselor and apply in person. Appointments are encouraged but not necessary, but all students must bring their high school transcript to apply. It is also strongly encouraged that applicants bring in their SAT I or ACT test results. The application fee is waived for applications submitted in person.

OPPORTUNITY **Admitted Student Day**

Admitted Student Day is an opportunity for students who have already been accepted to Marymount College to come to campus and see what the college has to offer them. It gives them a chance to meet other students, talk to faculty, take a guided campus tour, sit in on classes, and attend various events hosted by the admissions office throughout the day. Admitted Student Day is a chance for possible students to see what classes at Marymount College are like and to get a sense of what to expect from their college experience.

SUCCESS **Freshmen Seminar Classes**

Marymount College offers a freshman seminar class that all students are expected to take their first semester at Marymount. The program helps students to learn how to successfully acclimate to college life. They also have a Learning Center for students that need academic assistance. Students receive two first-come, first-served academic assistance appointments each week. Each student is also assigned an academic advisor that they will meet with multiple times per semester.

FAST FACTS

STUDENT PROFILE	
# of degree-seeking undergraduates	793
% male/female	49/51
% African American	6
% American Indian or Alaska Native	0
% Asian or Pacific Islander	8
% Hispanic	22
% White	38
% International	6
% Pell grant recipients	10
ACADEMICS	
full-time faculty	32
full-time minority faculty	7
student-faculty ratio	16:1
average class size	16
% first-year retention rate	67
% graduation rate (6 years)	n/a

Popular majors Business, Media Studies, Liberal Arts, Psychology, Pre-Nursing

CAMPUS LIFE	
% live on campus (% freshmen)	53 (n/a)

Multicultural student clubs and organizations Latinos Unidos, Black Student Union, Jewish Student Union, Muslim Student Union, International Peers, Christian Outreach and Renewal (COR), Gay/Straight Alliance

Athletics NAIA soccer, club lacrosse

ADMISSIONS	
# of applicants	3,075
% accepted	90
# of first-year students enrolled	444
SAT Critical Reading (middle 50%)	450-520
SAT Math (middle 50%)	400-490
SAT Writing (middle 50%)	420-510
ACT (middle 50%)	16-19
average HS GPA	2.68
Deadlines	
regular decision	3/1
application fee (online)	$40 ($40)
fee waiver for applicants with financial need	yes
COST & AID	
tuition	$27,396
room & board	$12,074
total need-based institutional scholarships/grants	$6,441,408
% of students apply for need-based aid	6
% receiving need-based scholarship or grant aid	67
% receiving aid whose need was fully met	n/a
average aid package	$13,548
average student loan debt upon graduation	n/a

Mills College

Nestled on 135 lush acres in the heart of the San Francisco Bay Area, Mills College offers women the opportunity to study and grow in a dynamic environment that embraces diversity, supports intellectual exploration, and prepares students for excellence in their careers and graduate education. Working closely with renowned faculty members and diverse students in intimate, collaborative classes, Mills women think critically, debate intelligently, and ask questions—both inside and outside the classroom. Students can choose from more than 350 course titles and 40 undergraduate majors. Mills is committed to empowering women to overcome social barriers that have excluded them from educational and career opportunities and actively works to extend access to women from diverse backgrounds of every kind. Located in the foothills of Oakland, California, Mills provides a beautiful home with convenient access to the thriving cultural, artistic, social and professional worlds of the San Francisco Bay Area.

 ACCESS **Upward Bound**

Local high school students who come from low-income families in which neither parent holds a bachelor's degree can benefit from Mills College's Upward Bound, a pre-college program that provides students with the right tools to pursue their dreams of earning a college degree. During the academic year, students benefit from weekly tutoring, field trips and workshops at Mills.

"I was accepted by Mills and another college, but the strong Mills financial aid package won out. Without the merit and need-based scholarships and work-study aid, I couldn't have gone to college. Now I'm active in the Black Women's Collective and plan to earn my MBA at Mills too."

– Amber W., '10
Suisun, CA
Political, Legal, and Economic Analysis

ACCESS **METS Program**

The Mills Educational Talent Search Program (METS) reaches out to low-income, first-generation college-bound students aged 11–27. METS academic advisers go out into the community, visiting local schools and offering personalized academic advising and college planning, services for students who plan to re-enter high school or college, educational workshops, campus visits, access to computer labs, and referrals to additional community services.

OPPORTUNITY **Financial Aid**

Ninety-four percent of Mills students receive some portion of their aid directly from the college, with scholarship amounts ranging from $1,000 per year to full tuition. Mills strives to provide financial aid to all students who demonstrate need and offers merit and need-based scholarships specifically for first-generation and minority students.

SUCCESS **Summer Academic Workshop (SAW)**

For more than 20 years, Mills has prepared first-generation students and students of color for success in college with the Summer Academic Workshop, an intensive four-week residential program for entering first-year students from disadvantaged communities. Every summer, approximately 20 students live in the Mills residence halls with peer counselors and tutors studying English, math, sociology, and social justice. Participants also learn additional writing, study, and leadership skills. More than 90 percent of women who have completed the SAW program have gone on to graduate from college.

SUCCESS **Women of Color Resource Center (WCRC)**

The WCRC was founded by Mills students, faculty, and alumnae of color. The center is run by and for women of color and works with the Ethnic Studies Department to provide a community for women of color at Mills and in the wider community. The WCRC is dedicated to the elimination of racism, the development of leadership by young women of color, and the creation of coalitions between women of diverse ethnic origins. Activities include leadership training for young women, coalition building and networking between ethnic groups, sponsorship for academic research, and conferences.

Mills College
5000 MacArthur Blvd
Oakland, CA 94613
Ph: (510) 430-2135
admission@mills.edu
www.mills.edu

FAST FACTS

STUDENT PROFILE

# of degree-seeking undergraduates	961
% male/female	0/100
% African American	8
% American Indian or Alaska Native	1
% Asian or Pacific Islander	9
% Hispanic	19
% White	40
% International	1
% Pell grant recipients	51

First-generation and minority alumni Barbara Lee, U.S. congresswoman; Thoraya Ahmed Obaid, first Saudi Arabian woman to head a United Nations agency; Patricia Piñeda, Toyota Motor North America, Inc. group vice president, national philanthropy and the Toyota USA Foundation; Renel Brooks-Moon, voice of the San Francisco Giants, first African-American baseball announcer; Jade Snow Wong, renowned author, ceramicist

ACADEMICS

full-time faculty	102
full-time minority faculty	29
student-faculty ratio	11:1
average class size	16
% first-year retention rate	82
% graduation rate (6 years)	68

Popular majors English; Psychology; Ethnic Studies; Political, Legal, and Economic Analysis (PLEA); Studio Art

CAMPUS LIFE

% live on campus (% freshmen)	58 (92)

Multicultural student clubs and organizations Asian Pacific Islander Sisterhood Alliance, Black Women's Collective, Mills Indigenous Women's Alliance, Model Arab League, Movimiento Estudiantil Chicano de Aztlan, Mujeres Unidas, Muslim Students Association, South Asian & Middle Eastern Cultural Awareness Organization

Athletics NCAA Division III, California Pacific Conference (CAL-PAC)

ADMISSIONS

# of applicants	2,129
% accepted	57
# of first-year students enrolled	208
SAT Critical Reading (middle 50%)	520-650
SAT Math (middle 50%)	490-600
SAT Writing (middle 50%)	510-620
ACT (middle 50%)	21-27
average HS GPA	3.67

Deadlines

early action	11/15
regular decision	2/1
application fee (online)	$50 ($50)
fee waiver for applicants with financial need	yes

COST & AID

tuition	$36,428
room & board	$11,644
total need-based institutional scholarships/grants	$13,628,156
% of students apply for need-based aid	88.5
% receiving need-based scholarship or grant aid	91
% receiving aid whose need was fully met	48.6
average aid package	$35,040
average student loan debt upon graduation	$28,914

Occidental College

Founded in 1887, Occidental College (a.k.a. Oxy) is one of the oldest liberal arts colleges in the West and one of few liberal arts colleges located in an urban area. Its beautiful green campus, designed by celebrated architect Myron Hunt, is nestled 10 minutes north of downtown in the Eagle Rock neighborhood of Los Angeles. Within this scenic setting thrives a long tradition of academic rigor and community action. Over 15 percent of students are first-generation, and many choose Occidental because of its rich history, dedication to diversity, and culture of collaborative, hands-on learning.

OPPORTUNITY **Multicultural Visit Program (MVP)**

The Multicultural Visit Program (MVP) is a two-day visit to campus for high school seniors from underrepresented backgrounds. MVP is designed for students from underrepresented backgrounds to meet other prospective applicants and current Oxy students and professors while gaining an understanding of Oxy's campus and its relationship with Los Angeles. While on campus, MVP students stay overnight in a residence hall, participate in classes, interact with current students and professors, attend information sessions on admissions and financial aid, and interview with an admission officer. The fall MVP (October 23-25) is selective; this fall, Occidental's Office of Admission will select 30 outstanding high school seniors for the program. Students invited to this program will be required to submit a $50 program fee. This fee will be used as the student's Common Application fee when he or she applies to Occidental College. Interested high school seniors can access application materials online through the Office of Admission starting in August. MVP is also offered in the spring to all underrepresented students who have been admitted but have not yet had a previous opportunity to visit campus.

OPPORTUNITY **Need-Based Scholarships**

While there are no scholarships specifically geared toward minority populations and first-generation students, Occidental College is committed to meeting the full demonstrated need of all enrolled students. While a portion of need is met with loans and work programs, need-based scholarships meet the majority of need for most students. These scholarships differ from merit awards, as they are not linked to academic promise, but rather to an individual family's financial situation.

SUCCESS **The Multicultural Summer Institute (MSI)**

Occidental College chooses 50 admitted students each year to participate in a co-curricular program called the Multicultural Summer Institute. A four-week summer program taking place before students begin their first year at Occidental, the institute prepares students for their academic career by acquainting them with the campus experience. In preparing participants for college life, students participate in academic courses, community service, diversity training and other programs.

SUCCESS **Intercultural Community Center**

The Intercultural Community Center is the co-curricular resource for diversity education and social justice programming. The center fosters an inclusive, democratic community, so that socially responsible and diverse leaders can improve both leadership and communication skills. The center collaborates with student organizations, academic departments, residence halls and members of the surrounding community to sponsor programs that examine, celebrate and appreciate identity, pluralism and democracy.

"Oxy's scenery and students are what distinguish it from any other institution. Oxy has a very welcoming campus. It has so much energy and the students are passionate about what they're doing and what their classmates are doing. Everybody is really supportive of one another. It is academically challenging while, at the same time, students have time for social activities and interactions. The curriculum is less about memorization and more about understanding material and applying it to your life. Oxy nurtures well-balanced people."

– Yelka K., '12
Jackson Heights, NY
Diplomacy, World Affairs

Occidental College
1600 Campus Road
Los Angeles, CA 90041
Ph: (323) 259-2700
admission@oxy.edu
www.oxy.edu

FAST FACTS

STUDENT PROFILE

# of degree-seeking undergraduates	2,102
% male/female	43/57
% African American	6
% American Indian or Alaska Native	2
% White	57
% Asian or Pacific Islander	17
% Hispanic	14
% Pell grant recipients	19

First-generation and minority alumni Barack Obama '83, President of the United States; Roger Guenveur Smith '81, Actor, Writer, and Director; Sammy Lee '43, Doctor and 2-time Olympic Gold Medalist in Diving

ACADEMICS

full-time faculty	169
full-time minority faculty	n/a
student-faculty ratio	10:1
average class size	16
% first-year retention rate	94
% graduation rate (6 years)	85

Popular majors Economics, Diplomacy & World Affairs, English & Comparative Literary Studies, Biology, Art History & Visual Arts

CAMPUS LIFE

% live on campus (% freshmen)	80 (100)

Multicultural student clubs and organizations Asian Pacific Islander Association, Black Student Alliance, First Nations, MEChA/ALAS, Oxy PAUS (Promoting Achievement in Underrepresented Students), Pilipino United Students Organization, Queer Straight Alliance, Rebirth: Students Rebuilding New Orleans, Sista Talk, White Students Against White Supremacy

Athletics NCAA Division III, Southern California Intercollegiate Athletic Conference

ADMISSIONS

# of applicants	6,112
% accepted	39
# of first-year students enrolled	541
first-year retention rate	94
SAT Critical Reading median	650
SAT Math median	650
SAT Writing median	660
ACT median	29.5
average HS GPA	3.65

Deadlines

early decision I	11/15
early decision II	1/3
regular decision	1/10
application fee (online)	$60 ($60)
fee waiver for applicants with financial need	yes

COST & AID

tuition	$41,860
room & board	$11,990
% students receiving assistance	78
% receiving need-based institutional scholarships/grants	n/a
% of students apply for need-based aid	60
% of students receive aid	79
% receiving need-based scholarship or grant aid	50
% receiving aid whose need was fully met	100
average aid package	$31,883
average student loan debt upon graduation	$17,561

Pepperdine University

Pepperdine University
24255 Pacific Coast Hwy
Malibu, CA 90263
Ph: (310) 506-4392
admission-seaver@pepperdine.edu
www.pepperdine.edu

Pepperdine University is an independent, private Christian university enrolling more than 7,700 undergraduate and graduate students in its five colleges and schools. We draw students from every state of the union and from more than 70 countries worldwide. Pepperdine is considered to be one of the nation's finest universities, regarded for its high academic standards, its nationally acclaimed Division I athletics program, and its commitment to serving the needs of each and every Pepperdine student.

OPPORTUNITY **Posse Foundation**

Pepperdine participates in the Posse Foundation, a program that brings talented inner-city youth to campus to pursue their academics and to help promote cross-cultural communication. Posse students are nominated by their high school to the program and share a collaborative suport system with a special mentor to adjust to campus and college life. Pepperdine's Posse Scholars hail from Washington, DC.

OPPORTUNITY **Scholarships**

Pepperdine University does its best to make access for all qualified students possible. We offer four scholarships that are specific to minority students. They are the Seaver College Endowed Scholarship, Richard Eamer Endowed Scholarship, Hispanic Advisory Council Scholarship, and the Hispanic Society Endowed Scholarship. Pepperdine also works with a variety of Los Angeles schools to set up campus tours and provides information sessions for these students.

SUCCESS **Leadership Education and Development (LEAD)**

LEAD programs offer students the opportunity to enhance their self-awareness, leadership skills, and community involvement to promote impacting citizenship on campus and beyond. LEAD hosts an annual leadership training day, student leadership conference, leadership summit, Project LEAD alternative spring break trip, and more.

SUCCESS **Volunteer Center**

The Volunteer Center develops and supports student leaders who engage their peers in meaningful service and build strong partnerships with the community. The center offers 20 ongoing programs and 13 one-time volunteer opportunities that are open to the entire Pepperdine community.

SUCCESS **New Student Orientation**

Pepperdine offers an extensive new student orientation (NSO) prior to the beginning of each academic term. This will be a time for students to get acquainted with the campus and for friendships to begin developing. Highlights of NSO include, Frosh Follies, local excursions, and the President's Reception.

SUCCESS **Intercultural Affairs Office**

Intercultural Affairs serves as one of the many avenues on campus where students can gain the awareness, knowledge, and skills necessary to become culturally competent. The office facilitates and sponsors a variety of workshops, seminars, excursions, forums, debates, and convocation programs throughout the year in order to promote intercultural understanding between and amongst students.

FAST FACTS

STUDENT PROFILE	
# of degree-seeking undergraduates	3,447
% male/female	44/56
% African American	7
% American Indian or Alaska Native	1
% Asian or Pacific Islander	10
% Hispanic	12
% White	54
% International	7
% Pell grant recipients	17
ACADEMICS	
full-time faculty	372
full-time minority faculty	42
student-faculty ratio	13:1
average class size	20
% first-year retention rate	90
% graduation rate (6 years)	80

Popular majors Business, Communication, Natural Science, Social Science, Humanities

CAMPUS LIFE	
% live on campus	58

Multicultural student clubs and organizations Black Student Association, Dramatically Reconstructing Education through African-American Men, The Filipino Club, Genesis Gospel Choir, Green Team, Hawaii Club, Judaic Cultural Awareness Club, Korean Student Association, Latino Student Association, Middle Eastern Peace and Awareness, Pepperdine Asian Student Association, Pepperdine Native American Student Organization, Pepperdine International Club, Step Team, Women of Color

Athletics NCAA Division I, West Coast Conference

ADMISSIONS	
# of applicants	9,894
% accepted	30
# of first-year students enrolled	772
SAT Critical Reading (middle 50%)	540-650
SAT Math (middle 50%)	560-680
SAT Writing (middle 50%)	560-660
ACT (middle 50%)	27-31
average HS GPA	3.66
Deadlines	
regular decision	1/5 (fall term); 10/15 (spring term)
application fee (online)	$65 ($65)
fee waiver for applicants with financial need	yes
COST & AID	
tuition	$40,5000
room & board	$11,844
total need-based institutional scholarships/grants	$37,429
% of students apply for need-based aid	74
% receiving need-based scholarship or grant aid	49
% receiving aid whose need was fully met	29
average aid package	$35,954
average student loan debt upon graduation	$31,429

Pitzer College

Pitzer College
1050 North Mills Avenue
Claremont, CA 91711
Ph: (909) 621-8000
admission@pitzer.edu
www.pitzer.edu

Pitzer College, one of seven schools in the Claremont Colleges consortium, is ranked as the fifth most diverse, private, co-educational, liberal arts college in the top tier. Its graduates and alumni consistently achieve recognition for their academic accomplishments: 14 graduates of the 2006 class and four alums received Fulbright scholarships in 2006-2007 alone. Pitzer stresses an interdisciplinary approach to coursework, and, unlike in many other schools, Pitzer favors educational objectives that guide students in making registration choices rather than traditional requirements. Pitzer has the distinction of having one of the highest participation rates of study abroad programs in the nation. Indicative of the college's dedication to social responsibility, Pitzer houses the Center for California Cultural and Social Issues, which supports research and education that contributes to the understanding of critical community issues and enhances the resources of community organizations.

ACCESS **Claremont College Scholars Program (CCSP)**

First-generation and minority high school juniors from selected Los Angeles and Inland Empire schools are eligible to participate in this program. Students attend workshops designed to educate them on the unique opportunities offered by a small, liberal arts and sciences college experience, and to answer questions regarding the admission and financial aid process.

ACCESS **Targeted Admissions Partnership**

The admissions staff visits California high schools with particularly high rates of minority student enrollment. The staff also collaborates with a significant number of community agencies (such as The Fulfillment Fund, Bright Prospect, Cristo Rey Schools, Hispanic Scholarship Fund, College Match, One Voice, Young Scholars and AVID) that assist first-generation and underrepresented students who are considering applying to college.

OPPORTUNITY **Diversity Program**

In encouraging minority students to visit, apply, and enroll at the college, Pitzer invites approximately 50 high school seniors from these backgrounds for a three-day paid visit during the fall and spring semesters. The fall program is for prospective applicants and the spring program is for admitted students. During each program, students stay with an overnight host in a residence hall, attend classes and meet members of the Pitzer community, admission and financial aid staff. The fall program helps prospective applicants learn about the selection process and how to apply for financial aid. In the spring, an emphasis is placed on learning more about student life. During both programs, participants may also interview with an admissions officer or representative.

SUCCESS **Student Affairs Committee of the Claremont Colleges**

Students from all Claremont Colleges come together under several joint student groups to support inter-cultural interests across campuses. The Chicano/Latino Student Affairs Center maintains a strong commitment to the retention and graduation of Chicano/Latino students and provides support and resources to students and their families. The Office of Black Student Affairs hosts a variety of programs geared toward the success of African-American students on campus, including the Ujima Peer Mentoring Program and the Anansi Academic Advancement Program, which provide mentoring, tutoring, academic programs and learning style and skills assessments. The Center for Asian Pacific American Students (CAPAS) serves as an advocate for the Asian and Pacific Islander community and promotes an educational dialogue that embraces the unique experiences of ethnic communities, the cultural fabric of the institution.

FAST FACTS

STUDENT PROFILE

# of degree-seeking undergraduates	911
% male/female	41/59
% African American	6
% American Indian or Alaska Native	1
% Asian or Pacific Islander	8
% Hispanic	15
% White	40
% International	3
% Pell grant recipients	15

First-generation and minority alumni Fabian Nuñez, speaker, California State Assembly; Debra W. Yang, former U.S. Attorney

ACADEMICS

full-time faculty	73
full-time minority faculty	12
student-faculty ratio	12:1
average class size	13
% first-year retention rate	81
% graduation rate (6 years)	89

Popular majors Psychology, English & World Literature, Sociology

CAMPUS LIFE

% live on campus (% freshmen)	74 (100)

Multicultural student clubs and organizations Center for Asian Pacific American Students, Chicano/Latino Student Affairs Center, Office of Black Student Affairs, Black Student Union, Latino Student Union, Center for California Cultural and Social Issues, Community-Based Spanish Program, Jumpstart

Athletics NCAA Division III, Southern California Intercollegiate Athletic Conference

ADMISSIONS

# of applicants	3,812
% accepted	26
# of first-year students enrolled	1,029
SAT Critical Reading (middle 50%)	600-680
SAT Math (middle 50%)	590-670
SAT Writing (middle 50%)	n/a
ACT (middle 50%)	26-30
average HS GPA	3.8
Deadlines	
early decision	11/15
regular decision	1/1
application fee (online)	$60 ($60)
fee waiver for applicants with financial need	yes

COST & AID

tuition	$41,130
room & board	$11,950
total need-based institutional scholarships/grants	$8,892,382
% of students apply for need-based aid	44
% of students receive aid	37
% receiving need-based scholarship or grant aid	98
% receiving aid whose need was fully met	100
average aid package	$33,940
average student loan debt upon graduation	$21,044

Pomona College

Pomona College
333 N. College Way
Claremont, CA 91711
Ph: (909) 621-8134
admissions@pomona.edu
www.pomona.edu

The founding member of the seven schools in the Claremont University Consortium, Pomona College is considered among the most prestigious liberal arts colleges in the country. Pomona prides itself on its small classes and on its comprehensive liberal arts curriculum, which begins with a freshman seminar designed to help students develop critical thinking, analysis, and writing skills. The college is in close proximity to Los Angeles, as well as to famous beaches and ski resorts.

"Pomona's so multi-faceted. I can take courses in history, politics, art, philosophy, sociology, and education. The classes I've taken in both Chicana/o and Black studies also have helped me gain a stronger political consciousness, especially in terms of critical thinking and analysis."

– Rico C., '11
Berkeley, CA
Chicano/a Studies

ACCESS **Pomona Partners**

Pomona Partners is a Friday afternoon program in which Pomona College students serve as activities coordinators at Fremont Middle School in South Pomona, and at times at Garey High School. On a typical Friday, 15 Pomona students will be at Fremont leading students in college-planning activities, workshops, arts related sessions, understanding current events, fieldtrips, etc.

ACCESS **Pomona Academy for Youth Success (PAYS)**

The Pomona College Academy for Youth Success (PAYS) is an intensive 4-week academic program that serves rising sophomores through rising seniors from groups traditionally under-represented in higher education-students who are first in their family to attend college, those from low income families and those who are African American or Latina/o. The program enrolls up to 90 participants from the Los Angeles area and the Inland Valley. PAYS participants live in Pomona's residence halls from Sunday night through Friday evening.

OPPORTUNITY **Student Affairs Committees of The Claremont Colleges**

Students from all Claremont Colleges come together under several joint student groups to support intercultural interests across campuses. Chicano/Latino Student Affairs maintains a strong commitment to the retention and graduation of Chicano/Latino students at the Claremont Colleges and provides support and resources to students and their families while the Office of Black Student Affairs hosts a variety of programs geared toward the success of African-American students on campus.

SUCCESS **Asian American Resource Center (AARC)**

The Asian American Resource Center helps Asian Pacific American students develop academically and personally. Central to all programs is the value of developing leadership skills among APA students. Working in conjunction with the Intercollegiate Department of Asian American Studies, the AARC raises awareness of issues affecting Asian Americans and Pacific Islanders.

SUCCESS **Office of Black Student Affairs (OBSA)**

The Office of Black Student Affairs addresses the educational needs of students of African descent through its cultural programs and academic services. The Office seeks to create a supportive environment for students pursuing their undergraduate and graduate degrees and to help students develop emotional autonomy, a positive ethnic identity, and an education and career path. Programs and services are open to all students of The Claremont Colleges.

FAST FACTS

STUDENT PROFILE

# of degree-seeking undergraduates	1,560
% male/female	49/51
% African American	6
% American Indian or Alaska Native	<1
% Asian or Pacific Islander	11
% Hispanic	11
% White	45
% International	6
% Race/ ethnicity unknown	15

First-generation and minority alumni George Wolfe, Tony Award-winner, actor, director, producer at The Public Theater; Cruz Reynoso, former justice, California Supreme Court; Merlie Evers-Williams, civil rights leader; John Payton, president, NAACP Legal Defense Fund; Maria Luz Garcia, Ford Foundation Pre-Doctoral Fellowship for Minorities recipient; Cuc Vu, director of the national immigration program, Service Employees International Union

ACADEMICS

full-time faculty	191
full-time minority faculty	58
student-faculty ratio	7:1
average class size	15
% first-year retention rate	97
% graduation rate (6 years)	94

Popular majors Economics, Politics, Neuroscience, Molecular Biology, English

CAMPUS LIFE

% live on campus (% freshmen)	98 (100)

Multicultural student clubs and organizations Asian Pacific Islander Awareness Committee, Asian American Students Association, Chinese Student Association, Hui Laule'a, International Club, International/Intercultural Association, Korean Students Association, Movimiento Estudiantil Chicano de Aztlan (MEChA), Pan-African Students Association, Unidos, Vietnamese American Student Association, World Youth Network

Athletics NCAA Division III, Southern California Intercollegiate Athletic Conference

ADMISSIONS (FALL 2010)

# of applicants	6,764
% accepted	14.7
# of first-year students enrolled	401
SAT Critical Reading (middle 50%)	700-790
SAT Math (middle 50%)	700-790
SAT Writing (middle 50%)	700-790
ACT (middle 50%)	31-34
average HS GPA	n/a
Deadlines	
early decision	11/1, 12/28
regular decision	1/2
application fee (online)	$65($65)
fee waiver for applicants with financial need	yes

COST & AID

tuition	$39,572
room & board	$13,227
total need-based institutional scholarships/ grants	$25,155,223
% of students apply for need-based aid	59
% of students receive aid	53
% receiving need-based scholarship or grant aid	100
% receiving aid whose need was fully met	100
average aid package	$36,389
average student loan debt upon graduation	$0*

*Pomona has replaced loans with grants in their financial aid packages

Saint Mary's College of California

Rooted in the tradition of Saint John Baptist de la Salle, founder of the Christian Brothers and the patron saint of teachers, Saint Mary's College of California is a private liberal arts institution situated in the rolling hills of the Moraga Valley, 20 miles east of San Francisco. Now in its second century of providing education in the liberal arts, the sciences, business administration and economics, Saint Mary's is one of the oldest colleges in the West. At Saint Mary's, students are encouraged to embrace complexity, contemplate their place and purpose in the world and undertake a searching examination of self, spirit and society.

SUCCESS High Potential Program

The High Potential Program at Saint Mary's College has been dedicated to provide support services for first-generation, college bound students for the past 32 years. The program is geared toward students who have overcome social, economic, educational and personal factors due to racial and/or socio-economic background. The program is designed to support students who may have average high school performance as indicated by overall academic GPA, college prep course work and SAT or ACT scores, but have the potential to succeed at Saint Mary's College. The High Potential experience begins in the summer before the start of the student's freshman year at Saint Mary's College. Students in the program learn essential college success skills and are paired with a mentor for extra guidance and support.

SUCCESS The Office of Black Student Programs

Founded in 1972, the Office of Black Student Programs recognizes distinct African and African-American descended cultures and identities in the college community. The office fosters a supportive environment for academic and personal development through peer mentoring, comprehensive academic assessment and planning for field of study and post-baccalaureate degrees. Ongoing activities and services include orientation, opportunities for intercultural learning, and intellectual and social development activities.

SUCCESS The Office of Latino Student Programs

The Office of Latino Student Programs develops and implements programs and services designed to make college a culturally relevant experience for Latino students. Services include academic advising, referrals to on-campus resources and bilingual (English/Spanish) information to students and their families. In collaboration with the Latino student organizations, the office also supports celebrations for traditional Latino holidays.

SUCCESS The Foundation Generation

Students who are the first in their families to attend college in the United States are valued members of the Saint Mary's community. First-generation students make up approximately 40 percent of the incoming class of 2009 at the college. The Foundation Generation helps to support this community of students by organizing a Foundation Generation Conference, holding classes and providing avenues of communication for first generation students. Additionally, Saint Mary's created The Foundation Generation Web site, which chronicles first-generation students' challenges and success in college, as well as their family history. Each individual research project was developed and collected in an academically rigorous way and complied into a shared collection to honor the legacy of the Foundation Generation as they pave the way for future generations of college students.

"The Saint Mary's College High Potential Program offered great insight to the college and the academic expectations of the school. I was able to meet fellow classmates and faculty members during our three week academic boot camp prior to the school year starting. This was advantageous as it gave me a familiarity with the campus before the rest of the school arrived. Having this program made my transition to college easier and prepared me for all the academic work and social aspects of Saint Mary's College."

– Jacqueline G., '11
Madera, CA

Saint Mary's College of California
PO Box 4800
Moraga, CA 94575-4800
Ph: (800) 800-4762 (4SMC) / (925) 631-4224
smcadmit@stmarys-ca.edu
www.smcadmit.com

FAST FACTS

STUDENT PROFILE

# of degree-seeking undergraduates	2,621
% male/female	39/61
% African American	5
% American Indian or Alaska Native	1
% Asian or Pacific Islander	8
% Hispanic	16
% White	38
% International	2
% Pell grant recipients	25

First-generation and minority alumni Joseph Alioto, former mayor, San Francisco; Laura Garcia Cannon, news anchor, NBC-11; Shirley Griffin, executive vice president, Wells Fargo Bank; James Guyette, president and CEO, Rolls-Royce of North America, Inc; Jack Henning, California labor leader; John Henry Johnson, Pro Football Hall of Fame; Tom Lyons, activist, Catholic Relief Services; John Macken, scientist and inventor with numerous patents; Dr. Carl Wu, distinguished cancer researcher, National Institutes of Health

ACADEMICS

full-time faculty	192
full-time minority faculty	37
student-faculty ratio	12:1
average class size	20
% first-year retention rate	86.3
% graduation rate (6 years)	63.7

Popular majors Business, Communication, Liberal & Civic Studies/Integral, Psychology

CAMPUS LIFE

% live on campus (% freshmen)	59 (99)

Multicultural student clubs and organizations Asian-Pacific American Association, Black Student Union, HAPA Club, Gay-Straight Alliance, Japanese-Pop Culture Club, Latin-American Student Association, Pulses Step Team

Athletics NCAA Division I, West Coast Conference

ADMISSIONS

# of applicants	3,730
% accepted	78
# of first-year students enrolled	695
SAT Critical Reading (middle 50%)	490-600
SAT Math (middle 50%)	500-610
ACT (middle 50%)	21-26
average HS GPA	3.4

Deadlines

early action	11/15
regular decision	2/1
application fee (online)	$55 ($55)
fee waiver for applicants with financial need	yes

COST & AID

tuition	$37,000
room & board	$12,840
total need-based institutional scholarships/grants	$29,352,814
% of students apply for need-based aid	83
% of students receive aid	75
% receiving need-based scholarship or grant aid	62
% receiving aid whose need was fully met	9
average aid package	$27,959
average student loan debt upon graduation	$22,043

Santa Clara University

Santa Clara University
500 El Camino Real
Santa Clara, CA 95053
Ph: (408) 554-4000
admissions@scu.edu
www.scu.edu

As a Jesuit, Catholic university, Santa Clara seeks to provide students with both a strong academic experience, and one that underscores the importance of ethics and justice. To this end, the University offers a myriad of service opportunities for students through the Santa Clara Community Action Program, a clearinghouse for service endeavors and other student programs. The University also houses the Arrupe Center, which serves the marginalized and poor, and the Markkula Center for Applied Ethics, which is one of the most prominent forums for discussion and research on the topic of ethics nationwide. The Center for Science, Technology and Society also promotes the common good of society by providing an independent forum for public dialogue and interdisciplinary inquiry into the social and cultural dimensions of technological change in today's society.

"Santa Clara showed me a world without limitations, where minority student success is possible and necessary to create a promising future. When one minority student succeeds, the dreams and aspirations of a family, and of a community, are fulfilled."

– Claudia F., '12
San Jose, CA
Public Health, Individual Studies

OPPORTUNITY **Future Teachers Program (FTP)**

SCU's Future Teachers Program is a long-term effort designed to recruit and retain students throughout the San Francisco Bay Area who want to teach in urban and underserved communities. FTP aims to provide students with the skills needed to effectively pursue their teaching career in urban and underserved settings. Each year, six students from urban or underserved schools throughout the Bay Area are selected for the FTP Scholarship. Students receive awards for four years of undergraduate study and a fifth-year teaching credential at SCU. This scholarship must be coordinated with any other financial aid awarded, including state or federal aid. If the student demonstrates financial need, a selected student will receive an award varied in amounts. Potential candidates are generally identified by the FTP during their junior or senior years of high school.

OPPORTUNITY **Hurtado Scholars Program**

The Hurtado Scholars Program provides scholarships for Santa Clara University students who have extraordinary life circumstances and needs. The Hurtado Scholars Program enables select students to attend Santa Clara University and gain valuable study, community, and research experiences as students on campus. They may interact with the Office for Multicultural Learning and other departments, colleges, centers and community organizations. This is a very competitive scholarship and is granted on a yearly basis depending on funds donated to the pool. On average, three to four scholarships are available each year.

SUCCESS **LEAD Scholars Program / First-Generation Orientation**

The Leadership Excellence and Academic Development Scholars Program assists first-generation college students and their families in the student's journey at SCU. Participation in the program is by invitation only. Students are selected based on their being awarded a grant or scholarship by SCU and the distinction of being among the first members of their families to attend college. The LEAD Scholars Program is among those administered by the University Honors Program, and offers a variety of opportunities and services that promote success in a student's educational pursuits. The LEAD Scholars Program is a community of peers and faculty committed to scholarship, community engagement, and service. The program begins in the freshman year to ensure a student's smooth transition from high school to college, and it lasts through the senior year by connecting students with internships, graduate school preparation, and leadership opportunities.

FAST FACTS

STUDENT PROFILE

# of degree-seeking undergraduates	5,072
% male/female	49/51
% African American	4
% American Indian or Alaska Native	<1
% Asian or Pacific Islander	15
% Hispanic	18
% White	41
% International	3
% Pell grant recipients	16

First-generation and minority alumni Reza Aslan '95, writer, scholar, CBS analyst, NPR commentator; Khaled Hosseini '88, author, *The Kite Runner*, *A Thousand Splendid Suns*; Randy Winn '96, outfielder, San Francisco Giants; Noelle Lopez '09, Rhodes Scholar

ACADEMICS

full-time faculty	449
full-time minority faculty	100
student-faculty ratio	13:1
average class size	22
% first-year retention rate	93
% graduation rate (6 years)	87

Popular majors Biology, Communications and Media Studies, Engineering, Finance, Psychology

CAMPUS LIFE

% live on campus (% freshmen)	46 (92)

Multicultural student clubs and organizations Arab Cultural Society, Asian-Pacific Islander Student Union, Association of South East Asian Students, Barkada, Chicanos & Latinos in Engineering & Sciences, Chinese Student Association, Igwebuike, Intandesh, Iranian Student Organization, Japanese Student Association, Ka Mana'o O Hawaii, Latino Business Student Association, Vietnamese Student Association

Athletics NCAA Division I, West Coast Conference

ADMISSIONS

# of applicants	11,787
% accepted	58
# of first-year students enrolled	1,296
SAT Critical Reading (middle 50%)	560-660
SAT Math (middle 50%)	590-690
SAT Writing (middle 50%)	n/a
ACT (middle 50%)	26-30
average HS GPA (unweighted)	3.6
Deadlines	
early action	11/1
regular decision	1/7
application fee (online)	$55 ($55)
fee waiver for applicants with financial need	yes

COST & AID

tuition	$39,048
room & board	$11,997
total need-based institutional scholarships/grants	$22,843,727
% of students apply for need-based aid	62
% of students receive aid	43
% receiving need-based scholarship or grant aid	34
% receiving aid whose need was fully met	37
average aid package	$25,666
average student loan debt upon graduation	$23,909

Soka University of America

Soka University of America
1 University Drive
Aliso Viejo, CA 92656
Ph: (949) 480-4150
admission@soka.edu
www.soka.edu

Soka University of America provides students with an international and personalized college experience. Founded as part of the Soka schools of the Soka Gakkai International, an educational society that is among the world's largest lay Buddhist organizations, Soka which means "to create value," has established a tradition of humanistic scholarship and growth. The University offers study abroad for all students with expenses built into the tuition, and the campus serves international and U.S. students alike. A recently implemented program will waive tuition for admitted B.A. students whose family's annual income is $60,000 or less.

ACCESS **Advance Via Individual Determination (AVID) tours**

Special tours are arranged for Advance Via Individual Determination classes, which serve secondary students who will often be the first in their families to attend college and who hope to realize their academic potential. These students have opportunities to talk to college admission counselors during these tours at Soka University of America.

ACCESS **Soka Club Outreach**

Soka University of America has over 35 clubs devoted to arts, dance, music, sports and community outreach. Club members visit local elementary, middle and high schools to share international cultures and to discuss the college experience.

OPPORTUNITY **Free Tuition Policy**

Students admitted into the liberal arts program at Soka University of America do not have to pay tuition if their family's annual income is $60,000 or less and if they have neither graduated from college nor completed more than 3/4 of their required coursework towards their first undergraduate degree at the time of application to the University. Soka is one of the few private schools in California able to offer this opportunity to both American and international students.

"I will be the first in my family to graduate from a university in the United States. I chose Soka University due to its captivating mission. I always knew I wanted to create a peaceful change for the world. At Soka I have learned about the many contributions I can offer and have met students that share a common goal."

– Astrid D., '11
San Diego, CA
Liberal Arts, concentrating in International Studies

OPPORTUNITY **First-Generation and Minority Scholarships**

Various other scholarships are available to first-generation and minority students who do not qualify for free tuition. These include the Hispanic Educational Endowment Fund, which offers two scholarships of $1,500 to first-generation Latino students from Orange County, and one Makiguchi Scholarship to an international applicant who has graduated from high school in an African Nation.

SUCCESS **Opportunities for Multicultural Study**

Fifty percent of Soka University of America's students are international, hailing from more than 40 countries. All undergraduate students study a non-native language and every student participates in a semester abroad during his or her junior year. In addition to its undergraduate concentrations in environmental studies, humanities, international studies and social and behavioral sciences, Soka also offers a master's program in second and foreign language education.

FAST FACTS

STUDENT PROFILE

# of degree-seeking undergraduates	431
% male/female	36/64
% African American	4
% American Indian or Alaska Native	0
% Asian or Pacific Islander	24
% Hispanic	9.5
% White	13
% International	44
% Pell grant recipients	23

First-generation and minority alumni SUA's first undergraduate class graduated in 2005. Alumni are already working for the United Nations, World Development Bank, the Peace Corps and the education department in Venezuela.

ACADEMICS

full-time faculty	51
full-time minority faculty	15
student-faculty ratio	9:1
average class size	13
% first-year retention rate	96
% graduation rate (6 years)	87

Popular areas of study Liberal Arts, concentrating in: Environmental Studies, Humanities, Social and Behavioral Sciences, International Studies

CAMPUS LIFE

% of fresh. live on campus	99

Multicultural student clubs and organizations Chinese Club, Corea Club, Ghungroo (Indian Dance), Humanism in Action, Josho Daiko Club (Taiko drums), Kapilina Ho'olokahi (Hawaiian dance), Kendo Club, Sualseros (Salsa dance), World Bridgers, Break Dancers, Rhythmission (Hip Hop)

Athletics NAIA, California Collegiate Athletic Association (CCAA)

ADMISSIONS

# of applicants	506
% accepted	33
# of first-year students enrolled	115
SAT Critical Reading (middle 50%)	390-800
SAT Math (middle 50%)	420-800
SAT Writing (middle 50%)	430-790
ACT (middle 50%)	20-34
average HS GPA	3.85
Deadlines	
early decision	10/15
regular decision	1/15
online application fee	$30
fee waiver for applicants with financial need	no

COST & AID

tuition	$27,214
room & board	$10,628
total need-based institutional scholarships/grants	n/a
% of students apply for need-based aid	92
% of students receive aid	100
% receiving need-based scholarship or grant aid	59
% receiving aid whose need was fully met	90
average aid package	$39,416
average student loan debt upon graduation	$22,000

Stanford University

Stanford University
Undergraduate Admission, Montag Hall
Stanford, CA 94305-6106
Ph: (650)723-2091
admission@stanford.edu
www.stanford.edu

Stanford University, located on more than 8,000 acres in northern California, is one of the most selective private institutions in the world. As a respected leader in both the sciences and the humanities, Stanford brings together extraordinary faculty members and students in the pursuit of excellence. At the heart of Stanford's mission is scholarly inquiry, innovation and investigation. Opportunities for discovery begin in the classroom and extend into the rich research life of campus laboratories, libraries, studios and beyond. Stanford encourages undergraduates to join with faculty in the search for new knowledge and new artistic creation. Learning outside the classroom is supported by a vibrant residential system that emphasizes service and community. Students may choose to participate in a vast array of educational opportunities, including freshman and sophomore seminars, undergraduate research programs, 11 overseas study centers and department honors programs. Stanford has a strong commitment to diversity — more than half of the graduating class of 2015 is made up of students of color.

"Stanford put the world at my fingertips. As a student I have received funding to travel to three different countries on five different occasions, and I got to make doing what I love -- archaeology -- into a career. In just four years, I have chased my dreams, found my passions, and I am graduating with two degrees."

– Tiffany C., '11
Omaha, NE
MA Anthropology,
BA Archaeology, minor International Relations

ACCESS Youth Mentorship Programs

Through sponsored programs such as Upward Bound, which provides academic support, tutoring and college application support to high school students, and Ravenswood Reads, which provides one-to-one literacy tutoring to young elementary school students, Stanford offers a number of opportunities for its students to mentor and connect with youth in the surrounding areas. Also particularly successful is Stanford's East Palo Alto Tennis and Tutoring Program, which serves approximately 100 students who receive both tennis instruction and academic tutoring.

ACCESS Office of Undergraduate Admissions

Partnering with numerous local and regional community-based organizations, such as Foundation for a College Education, College Match, College Summit and College Track, the Office of Undergraduate Admissions provides guided campus tours, college information sessions and essay-writing workshops designed to help students think about and prepare for the transition to higher education.

SUCCESS Expanded Advising Programs (EAP) / Ethnic Centers

In addition to the faculty advisers that the Undergraduate Advising and Research (UAR) department assigns all freshmen, the Expanded Advising Programs works in conjunction with campus community and ethnic centers. Stanford's four ethnic community centers, including the Asian American Activities Center, Black Community Services Center, El Centro Chicano and the Native American Cultural Center, can help students be successful by offering them additional resources and support networks. Stanford's ethnic-themed houses — Ujamaa (the African American themed dorm), Casa Zapata (the Latino themed dorm), Muwekmah-tah-ruk (the Native themed dorm) and Okada (the Asian American themed dorm) — all serve to further these networks as well.

FAST FACTS

STUDENT PROFILE

# of degree-seeking undergraduates	6,887
% male/female	52/48
% African American	10
% American Indian or Alaska Native	3
% Asian or Pacific Islander	23
% Hispanic	14
% White	38
% International	7
% Pell grant recipients	17

First-generation and minority alumni David Henry Hwang, playwright; JuJu Chang, ABC correspondent; Maria Echaveste, White House Chief of Staff, Clinton Administration; March Kong Fong Eu, former Secretary of State, California; Cory Booker, mayor, Newark, N.J.; Valerie Jarrett – senior advisor to President Obama for Public Engagement and Intergovernmental Affairs

ACADEMICS

full-time faculty	1,002
full-time minority faculty	190
student-faculty ratio	6:1
average class size	15
% first-year retention rate	98
% graduation rate (6 years)	95

Popular majors Biology/Human Biology, Economics, International Relations, Computer Science, Engineering

CAMPUS LIFE

% live on campus (% freshman)	95 (100)

Multicultural student clubs and organizations El Centro Chicano, Black Community Services Center, Asian American Activities Center, Native American Cultural Center, Women's Community Center, LGBT Community Resources Center

Athletics NCAA Division I, Pacific 12 (PAC-12)

ADMISSIONS

# of applicants	32,400
% accepted	7
# of first-year students enrolled	1,732
Middle 50% Range:	
SAT Critical Reading (middle 50%)	650-760
SAT Math (middle 50%)	680-780
SAT Writing (middle 50%)	670-760
ACT (middle 50%)	30-34
average HS GPA	n/a
Deadlines	
restrictive early action	11/1
regular decision	1/1
application fee	$90
fee waiver for applicants with financial need	yes

COST & AID

tuition	$40,050
room & board	$12,291
total need-based institutional scholarships/grants	$115,500,000
% of students apply for need-based aid	58
% receiving need-based scholarship or grant aid	48
% receiving aid whose need was fully met	100
average aid package	$43,330
average student loan debt upon graduation	$14,058

University of San Diego

The University of San Diego is a nationally ranked Roman Catholic institution committed to advancing academic excellence, expanding liberal and professional knowledge, creating a diverse and inclusive community and preparing leaders dedicated to ethical conduct and compassionate service. The university is a co-educational, residential university serving students of diverse backgrounds from across the country and around the world. USD supports the belief that academic excellence requires inclusive engagement with diverse groups and varying perspectives, and it recognizes that the benefits of a rich, diverse learning community are most likely realized when institutions demonstrate high levels of commitment to inclusion and diversity. USD actively supports recruitment and retention of underrepresented students, staff, faculty and administrators in pursuit of the compositional diversity required to achieve excellence.

ACCESS **Upward Bound**

The University of San Diego's Upward Bound program creates an academic, diverse learning community of low-income high school students who demonstrate the desire to pursue higher education. Upward Bound works with entire communities of students, parents, teachers and staff to teach academic foundations, values building and goal-setting. In turn, this foundation encourages academic and personal success from high school to college and beyond.

SUCCESS **Center for Inclusion and Diversity (CID)**

CID's mission is to provide the resources and research necessary to recruit, retain and sustain a diverse and inclusive university. The goals of the Center are to encourage research, enhance education, create dialogue, seek resources, provide assistance, improve retention, and enhance recruitment. CID seeks to create and inclusive university where diversity, which is evident in humanity, is justly represented, respected and recognized, and where cultural capital is provided to counteract the historic and current barriers that can hinder success.

SUCCESS **Student Support Services (SSS)**

Student Support Services is a federally funded grant by the US Department of Education to serve 160 eligible undergraduates at USD. The program provides opportunities for academic development, assists students with college requirements, and serves to retain and motivate students toward successful completion of their postsecondary education at USD. Services provided include: academic counseling/advising, tutoring, career counseling, personal counseling, faculty/student mentoring, cultural activities, grant aid, FAFSA assistance, Summer Bridge Program, time management techniques, note-taking techniques, test-taking techniques, essay writing improvement, reading strategies, and graduate school application assistance.

University of San Diego
Office of Undergraduate Admissions
5998 Alcala Park
San Diego, CA 92110
Ph: (619) 260-4506
admissions@sandiego.edu
www.sandiego.edu

FAST FACTS

STUDENT PROFILE

# of degree-seeking undergraduates	5,388
% male/female	45/55
% African American	3
% American Indian or Alaska Native	3
% Asian or Pacific Islander	11
% Hispanic	14
% White	58
% International	5
% Pell grant recipients	13.7

ACADEMICS

full-time faculty	393
full-time minority faculty	72
student-faculty ratio	15:1
average class size	22
% first-year retention rate	88
% graduation rate (6 years)	74

Popular majors Business Administration, Communication Studies, Psychology, Political Science, International Relations

CAMPUS LIFE

% live on campus (% freshmen)	48 (95)

Multicultural student clubs and organizations United Front Multicultural Center, Asian Student Association, Movimiento Estudiantil Chicano de Aztlan, Association of Chicana Activists, People of the Islands, Filipino Ugnayan Student Organization, 'Aikane O Hawaii, Brothers & Sisters United, Native American Student Union, PRIDE, International Student Organization and Jewish Student Union

Athletics NCAA Division I, Pacific Coast Softball Conference, Pioneer League Football

ADMISSIONS

# of applicants	12,141
% accepted	51
# of first-year students enrolled	1,150
SAT Critical Reading (middle 50%)	550-640
SAT Math (middle 50%)	565-660
SAT Writing (middle 50%)	550-650
ACT (middle 50%)	25-29
average HS GPA	3.92

Deadlines

early action	11/15
regular decision	1/15
application fee (online)	$55
fee waiver for applicants with financial need	yes

COST & AID

tuition	$38,150
room & board	$11,602
total need-based institutional scholarships/grants	$40,918,342
% of students apply for need-based aid	60
% of students who applied that receive aid	86
% of students who applied receiving need-based scholarship or grant aid	81
% receiving aid whose need was fully met	18
average aid package	$29,415
average student loan debt upon graduation	$29,928

University of Southern California

The University of Southern California continues to be recognized as one of the most culturally diverse campuses in the United States. The Office of Admission actively recruits students from all backgrounds and socioeconomic statuses. This includes first-generation college-goers from lower income families who may need additional support as they continue on to college. The University partners with a number of organizations to ensure their students' continued academic success and that a top-tier education remains available and affordable to all students, regardless of background or ability to pay.

ACCESS Neighborhood Academic Initiative (NAI)

The USC Neighborhood Academic Initiative (NAI) offers a comprehensive college-preparation program for local middle-school students. Students also have the chance to earn a full scholarship to USC.

OPPORTUNITY QuestBridge

USC is a partner with QuestBridge, a non-profit organization that connects low-income students with educational and scholarship opportunities at 30 top colleges and universities throughout the U.S. Through the QuestBridge National College Match Program, USC has enrolled low-income students from diverse geographical areas in the U.S.

"I grew up just north of the USC campus. I was familiar with Trojan pride. Soon after starting classes, I fell into my major and built a family with my fellow students. The USC experience has enriched my life and better prepared me academically, socially and culturally for the greater world."

– Ebonee R., '10
Los Angeles, CA
USC Annenberg School for Communication & Journalism

OPPORTUNITY Posse Foundation

USC participates in the Posse Foundation, a program that brings talented inner-city youth to campus to pursue their academic goals and to help promote cross-cultural communication. Posse students are nominated by their high school to the program and share a collaborative support system with a special on-campus mentor to help in their transition to campus and college life. USC's Posse scholars hail from New York City.

OPPORTUNITY Norman Topping Student Aid Fund (NTSAF)

NTSAF offers financial support to students who demonstrate an extraordinary level of community awareness in their pursuit of higher education at USC. Primary consideration is given to applicants from neighborhoods surrounding the University Park and Health Science..

OPPORTUNITY USC Junior Day

The Office of Admission invites high school juniors from diverse populations to participate in a day of application and financial aid workshops on the USC campus.

SUCCESS Latino Alumni Association (LAA)

One of the nation's leading Latino alumni associations devoted to the academic advancement and development of Latino students attending USC. LAA is one of the few Latino alumni associations in the country with a $3 million endowment fund.

SUCCESS Black Alumni Association (BAA)

A primary alumni resource providing tuition assistance to African American students at USC, it was founded in 1976 by the late Reverend Dr. Thomas Kilgore, Jr., a peer of Martin Luther King, Jr., and special advisor to President John Hubbard. The BAA has provided over $1.7 million to 1600 USC students. BAA scholarships are awarded annually based on financial need and academic merit. BAA scholarship funds are matched 2:1 for undergraduate students.

University of Southern California
700 Childs Way
Los Angeles, CA 90089-0911
Ph: (213) 740-1111
admitusc@usc.edu
www.usc.edu

FAST FACTS

STUDENT PROFILE

# of degree-seeking undergraduates	17,500
% male/female	50/50
% African American	5
% American Indian or Alaska Native	1
% Asian or Pacific Islander	24
% Hispanic	14
% White	43
% International	11
% Pell grant recipients	18.3

First-generation and minority alumni Frank Cruz '69, USC Trustee, founder of Telemundo, chairman of Corporation for Public Broadcasting; Linda Johnson Rice '80, USC Trustee, President/ CEO of Johnson Publishing; Brenda V. Castillo '85, Director, Government & Public Affairs, Western Region, BP America, Inc.; Paul Williams '19, First African American member of AIA; John Singleton '90, Director/Producer; Karime Sanchez Bradvica '80, Vice President, External Affairs, AT&T

ACADEMICS

full-time faculty	3,300
full-time minority faculty	217
student-faculty ratio	9:1
average class size	26
% first-year retention rate	96
% graduation rate (6 years)	89

Popular majors Cinematic Arts, Business, Music, Engineering, Communications

CAMPUS LIFE

% live on campus (% freshmen)	n/a (90)

Multicultural student clubs and organizations Center for Black Cultural and Student Affairs, El Centro Chicano, Asian Pacific American Student Services, Black Student Assembly, Latino Student Assembly, M.E.Ch.A. de USC, 100 Black Men of USC, Vietnamese Student Association Athletics

Athletics NCAA Division I, Pac-10 Conference

ADMISSIONS

# of applicants	37,200
% accepted	23
# of first-year students enrolled	2,869
SAT Critical Reading (middle 50%)	640-740
SAT Math (middle 50%)	680-770
SAT Writing (middle 50%)	670-760
ACT (middle 50%)	30-34
average HS GPA	3.8
Deadlines	
for Merit Scholarship consideration	12/1
regular decision	1/10
application fee	$70
fee waiver for applicants with financial need	yes

COST & AID

tuition	$41,022
room & board	$11,580
total need-based institutional scholarships/grants	$192,300,000
% of students apply for need-based aid	n/a
% receiving need-based scholarship or grant aid	60
% receiving aid whose need was fully met	100
average aid package	n/a
average student loan debt upon graduation	n/a

Whittier College

Founded in 1887 by the Religious Society of Friends, Whittier is a private, four-year liberal-arts college within close proximity to Los Angeles. Whittier is one of the most diverse liberal arts schools in the country, with a wide range of cultural and socio-economic backgrounds. Minority and international students constitute nearly half of the student body. In 2002, Whittier was awarded a $1.5 million development grant to support students on campus in accordance with the U.S. Department of Education's recognition of Whittier as a Hispanic Serving Institution. The college offers 31 majors and minors within 23 disciplines. Located on 75 acres, Whittier has more than 60 student-run organizations and a well-respected athletic program.

ACCESS The Ortiz Programs

The Ortiz Programs, named after alumnus Martin Ortiz '48, seek to expand knowledge and awareness of Latino culture, language and history through a variety of events and activities. The Ortiz Programs provide academic and career resources, financial aid guidance, and overall emotional support, primarily to first-generation Latino students. The program serves as a liaison between Latino students, parents, alumni, community organizations and the Whittier College community.

"Being at Whittier College has allowed me to take my curriculum into my own hands and create a unique major that suits me through the Whittier Scholars Program. It has opened my mind to endless possibilities. Working with the Ortiz Programs has also allowed me to embrace my heritage more thoroughly."

– Donna O., '11
Gardena, CA
Whittier Scholars—Immigration Rights and Policy

OPPORTUNITY Latino Opportunity Scholarship (LOS)

The Latino Opportunity Scholarship is a $1,000 scholarship offered to Latino students who are slated to attend Whittier. Selected students are sent an application during the month of May.

SUCCESS Whittier Scholars Program (WSP)

The Whittier Scholars Program offers students a non-traditional curricular path. Students in the WSP design their own curriculum and can create their own interdisciplinary major. The WSP is not an honors program, but attracts those students who want to take responsibility for their education. Students work closely with faculty advisers and administrators in the WSP to ensure that each educational design has academic and intellectual integrity. Students in the WSP are also required to build an off-campus experience that complements their major, and must complete and publically present a senior project. Typically, 12 percent of a graduating class opts for the WSP.

SUCCESS Center for Advising and Academic Success

The Center for Advising and Academic Success works with students to achieve their academic goals. Students, some of whom may be under-prepared in certain areas, are given opportunities to assess their strengths and weaknesses and are then provided the tools to help them reach their potential. Professional staff members, faculty and well-trained tutors are on-hand to support and guide students to advance to the next level.

SUCCESS The Cultural Center

The Cultural Center seeks to create a campus community that appreciates and respects individuals of diverse identities and backgrounds. The center houses many programs and organizations seeking to enrich cultural interaction and dialogue throughout the Whittier campus. Heritage month celebrations, Diverse Identities Week, and diversity workshops are examples of programs, while events for underrepresented students include new student orientation receptions, graduation ceremonies and dinners. The Cultural Center collaborates with faculty to expand the understanding of cultural appreciation in the curriculum and connects underrepresented populations to academic services, career counseling and support networks.

Whittier College
13406 East Philadelphia St.
P .O. Box 634
Whittier, CA 90608-0634
Ph: (562) 907-4238
admission@whittier.edu
www.whittier.edu

FAST FACTS

STUDENT PROFILE

# of degree-seeking undergraduates	1,509
% male/female	48/52
% African American	5
% American Indian or Alaska Native	1
% Asian or Pacific Islander	10
% Hispanic	32
% White	38
% International	2
% Pell grant recipients	36

First-generation and minority alumni Martin Ortiz, educator and activist, recipient of Distinguished Service Award from the U.S. Department of Education; J. Stanley Sanders, attorney, one of the first two African-Americans in more than a half-century to be awarded a Rhodes Scholarship; Darryl Walker, vice president for business affairs, Black Entertainment Television, Rhodes Scholar; Alma Martinez, stage, screen and television actress, director, and educator, Fulbright Award recipient for study in South America; Erin Clancy, Thomas R. Pickering Foreign Affairs Fellowship recipient; Malaika (Williams) Amneus, obstetrics/gynecology, Rhodes Scholar

ACADEMICS

full-time faculty	96
full-time minority faculty	26
student-faculty ratio	13:1
average class size	18
% first-year retention rate	79
% graduation rate (6 yrs)	61

Popular majors Business Administration, English, History, Political Science, Psychology

CAMPUS LIFE

% live on campus (% freshmen)	63 (78)

Multicultural student clubs and organizations Akwaaba, Black Student Union, Hispanic Student Association, Asian Student Association, M.E.Ch.A.
Athletics NCAA Division III, Southern California Intercollegiate Athletic Conference

ADMISSIONS

# of applicants	2,885
% accepted	70
# of first-year students enrolled	453
SAT Critical Reading (middle 50%)	480-590
SAT Math (middle 50%)	480-590
SAT Writing (middle 50%)	480-590
ACT (middle 50%)	19-25
average HS GPA	3.5
Deadlines	
early action	10/15, 12/1
regular decision	2/1
application fee (online)	$50($50)
fee waiver for applicants with financial need	yes

COST & AID

tuition	$36,632
room & board	$10,428
total need-based institutional scholarships/grants	$23,383,062
% of students apply for need-based aid	82
% of students receive aid	90
% receiving need-based scholarship/grant aid	84
% receiving aid whose need was fully met	12
average aid package	$34,214
average student loan debt upon graduation	$29,399

Colorado College

Colorado College is a selective liberal arts college located in the city of Colorado Springs, at the foot of Pikes Peak. Colorado College provides rigorous and experiential learning opportunities through their unique academic schedule: The Block Plan. Dividing the year into eight three-and-a-half week blocks, during which students take one course at a time, the plan provides students with the opportunity to fully immerse themselves in their subject matter through a wide array of learning experiences.

ACCESS **NAACP College Prep Day**

Colorado College hosts the NAACP College Prep Day for high school students and their families in the Colorado Springs area. In an effort to make higher education more accessible, the day provides an opportunity for students to take the PSAT, visit a college campus with their families, and begin financial aid preparations.

ACCESS **Friends of CC Host Family Program**

Friends of CC is an outreach program which pairs minority, international, and first-generation students with friends in the community for events several times a year both on and off-campus.

OPPORTUNITY **Multicultural Open House**

The Multicultural Open House, held in November, provides an exciting opportunity for prospective students to experience life at Colorado College firsthand. Attendees will have the opportunity to take a campus tour, visit a class, stay overnight on campus with a CC student host, and participate in an admission interview and financial aid workshop. Students who are unable to attend this event are encouraged to apply for a travel grant to visit campus.

SUCCESS **Office of Minority and International Students (OMIS)**

OMIS at Colorado College supports cross-cultural inclusion and success through various advising and mentorship programs as well as campus student clubs and events. OMIS, in conjunction with Residential Life, also provides advising and support to the Glass House, a multicultural themed house located on the East Campus.

SUCCESS **Bridge Program**

The Bridge Program is a unique learning experience which is dedicated to helping incoming freshmen successfully transition academically and socially from high school to college. Students invited to participate—typically graduates of under-resourced high schools, members of historically underrepresented populations at CC, or first-generation college students—have the opportunity to improve writing, reading, and critical thinking skills while establishing a support group of invaluable relationships with CC faculty, staff, and peers.

"At Colorado College, I have come to find that the meaning of 'diversity' is relative. The unique individual characteristics and hidden talents of CC students have helped me realize that diversity encompasses more than just skin complexion. I challenge you to expand your definition of diversity."

– Johnny Reed '13
Waukegan, IL

SUCCESS **First Generation Program**

The First Generation Program provides a support system for first-generation college students who attend Colorado College and their families. The program is made up of current first-generation students as well as faculty and staff who were also first-generation students. Through a group lunch every block and social gatherings throughout the year, the program establishes a sense of community among program participants, highlighted by the program's signature pins worn by first-generation faculty and staff members and awarded to first-generation graduates at the year-end BBQ.

Colorado College
14 E. Cache La Poudre St.
Colorado Springs, CO 80903
Ph: (719) 389-6344
admission@coloradocollege.edu
www.coloradocollege.edu

FAST FACTS

STUDENT PROFILE

# of degree-seeking undergraduates	2,040
% male/female	47/53
% African American	1
% American Indian or Alaska Native	0.5
% Asian or Pacific Islander	5
% Hispanic	7
% Other Minority	4
% Total Ethnic Minorities	18
% White	76
% International	5
% Pell grant recipients	7

First-generation and minority alumni
Ryan Haygood '97, Co-Director of the Political Participation Group and Attorney at the NAACP Legal Defense & Educational Fund; Ken Salazar '77, United States Secretary of the Interior

ACADEMICS

full-time faculty	168
full-time minority faculty	28
student-faculty ratio	10:1
average class size	16
% first-year retention rate	96
% graduation rate (6 years)	85

Popular majors Biology/Biological Sciences, General Economics, General Political Science and Government

CAMPUS LIFE

% live on campus (% freshmen)	76 (99)

Multicultural student clubs and organizations
Asian American Student Union, Black Student Union, Korean-American Student Association, I Mua Lokahi/Hawaii Club, Mind, Body & Soul, Minority Association for Pre-Health Students, Multicultural Organization of Students: An International Community, The Native American Student Union, Students for the Awareness of South Asia, SOMOS "We Are"

Athletics NCAA Divison I, III, Southern Collegiate Athletic Conference

ADMISSIONS

# of applicants	4,918
% accepted	26
# of first-year students enrolled	490
SAT Critical Reading (middle 50%)	640-740
SAT Math (middle 50%)	630-720
SAT Writing (middle 50%)	640-750
ACT (middle 50%)	28-32
average HS GPA	n/a

Deadlines

early action	11/15
early decision I	11/15
early decision II	1/1
regular decision	1/15
application fee (online)	$50 ($50)
fee waiver for applicants with financial need	yes

COST & AID

tuition	$39,900
room & board	$9,416
total need-based institutional scholarships/grants	$5,799,032
% of students apply for need-based aid	51
% receiving need-based scholarship or grant aid	35
% receiving aid whose need was fully met	63*
average aid package	$33,114
average student loan debt upon graduation	$18,499

*Colorado College does meet 100% of demonstrated need for all students through a combination of scholarships, grants, loans, and work study

Colorado State University

Colorado State University, one of the nation's premier research institutions, has never lost sight of its original land-grant mission to provide access to an exceptional, affordable college education. Colorado State believes that every qualified student should have a chance to gain the knowledge and skills he or she needs for a successful future. Countless students have taken advantage of the university's outstanding research and internship opportunities, not to mention its extensive support and career counseling services. Colorado State graduates have emerged as leaders in their respective fields, using their educations to improve lives and create change on a global scale.

ACCESS **Black Issues Forum (BIF)**

BIF is a pre-collegiate leadership program that provides high school students with a vehicle to demonstrate their written and oral communication skills and to enhance their leadership. Participants meet in June after their junior year and interact with community leaders and Colorado State University faculty as they discuss and evaluate important issues that affect the black community at the local, state, national and global level. BIF participants spend significant time in the university's libraries researching pre-selected, current topics, then share their findings through presentations, debates or town meetings. In addition, BIF participants engage in social activities such as an evening of cultural expression, informal discussions and a recognition luncheon.

"I want to make sure my little brother has someone to follow, because nobody in my family has graduated from college. All my professors have worked with me—Colorado State is a really nurturing environment. If you want a great education at an affordable price, this is the place to be."

– Miguel G., '13
Fort Lupton, CO
Environmental Health

ACCESS **Lorenzo de Zavala (LDZ) Youth Legislative Session**

Hispanic/Latino high school sophomores and juniors from across the nation flock to the CSU campus each June for the Lorenzo de Zavala Youth Legislative Session (LDZ). During mock state government sessions, students debate issues of special interest to the Hispanic/Latino community. Colorado State University is the only institution of higher education in Colorado and one of only five throughout the United States and Mexico to collaborate with the National Hispanic Institute in such a program.

OPPORTUNITY **First Generation Award**

The First Generation Award was created 25 years ago to promote diversity within the University and to encourage first generation students to enroll at Colorado State. Colorado residents entering as freshmen or transfer students whose parents have not received a bachelor's degree and who demonstrate financial need are eligible to apply for these competitive awards.

OPPORTUNITY **Commitment to Colorado**

As Colorado's only land-grant university, CSU is committed to keeping higher education within the reach of the state's citizens. Colorado-resident students who are eligible for the federal Pell Grant will receive aid to cover at least the student's share of base tuition and standard fees. Colorado-resident students who are not Pell-eligible, but whose annual family adjusted gross income is $57,000 or less, will receive aid to cover at least half the student's share of base tuition. Other eligibility requirements apply.

SUCCESS **Key Communities**

Freshmen and sophomores who participate in the Key Communities expand their opportunities for success through leadership, service, civic engagement and campus involvement. They forge personal connections with faculty and other students, while learning to appreciate cultural diversity, enriching their academic experience and exploring their career options.

Colorado State University
1062 Campus Delivery
Fort Collins, CO 80523-1062
Ph: (970) 491-6909
admissions@colostate.edu
www.admissions.colostate.edu

FAST FACTS

STUDENT PROFILE

# of degree-seeking undergraduates	22,979
% male/female	49/51
% African American	3
% American Indian or Alaska Native	2
% Asian or Pacific Islander	3
% Hispanic	7
% White	84
% International	2
% Pell grant recipients	22

First-generation and minority alumni John Mosley, Tuskegee Airman; Jusef Kommunyakaa, Pulitzer Prize-winning poet; Polly Baca, CEO of Latin American Research and Service Agency (LARASA) and former presidential advisor; Stan Matsunaka, former Colorado state senator; John Amos, actor; Mark Montano, designer and co-host of "While You Were Out."

ACADEMICS

full-time faculty	920
full-time minority faculty	120
student-faculty ratio	17:1
average class size	30
% first-year retention rate	84
% graduation rate (6 years)	64

Popular majors Business, Health and Exercise Science, Psychology, Biological Sciences, Construction Management

CAMPUS LIFE

% live on campus (% freshmen)	26 (96)

Multicultural student clubs and organizations American Indian Science & Engineering Society, Black Definition, Black Student Alliance, Chinese Club, Hui 'O Hawai'i, Japan Club, La Raza, Salam, Shades of CSU, Society of Hispanic Professional Engineers/Mexican American Engineers and Scientists, Students for Holocaust and Genocide Awareness, United Men of Color, United Women of Color

Athletics NCAA Division I, Mountain West Conference (MWC)

ADMISSIONS

# of applicants	15,014
% accepted	78
# of first-year students enrolled	4,472
SAT Critical Reading (middle 50%)	510-620
SAT Math (middle 50%)	510-630
SAT Writing (middle 50%)	n/a
ACT (middle 50%)	22-27
average HS GPA	3.6

Deadlines

early action	12/1
regular decision	2/1
application fee (online)	$50 ($50)
fee waiver for applicants with financial need	yes

COST & AID

tuition	in-state $8,042; out-of-state $23,742
room & board	$8,836
total need-based institutional scholarships/grants	$1,396,436
% of students apply for need-based aid	68
% receiving need-based scholarship or grant aid	46
% receiving aid whose need was fully met	20
average aid package	$11,085
average student loan debt upon graduation	$21,224

United States Air Force Academy

United States Air Force Academy
2304 Cadet Drive, Suite 2400
USAF Academy, CO 80840-5025
Ph: (800) 443-9266
rr_webmail@usafa.edu
www.academyadmissions.com

The U.S. Air Force Academy is one of five military service academies that educates and trains young men and women in academics, leadership, character and athletics. The mission of the Academy is to educate, train and inspire men and women to become officers of character motivated to lead the United States Air Force in service to our nation. Graduates receive a Bachelor of Science degree in one of 31 majors and commission as a second lieutenant in the U.S. Air Force. The Academy has 27 NCAA Division I athletic teams. This institution offers many unique opportunities and programs, to include aviation programs, and about 50 percent of graduates are assigned an aviation career field. There are numerous other career fields the Air Force offers, ranging from engineering and acquisitions to intelligence and public affairs. The campus is located just north of Colorado Springs, Colorado, and 55 miles south of Denver.

> ***"Becoming part of the 'Long Blue Line' is a life-changing decision that will open opportunities you never thought possible. The Academy will challenge you in many ways and teach you a lot about yourself while at the same time preparing you to lead the world's greatest air and space force."***
> *– Miguel M., '12*

ACCESS The United States Air Force Academy Preparatory School

The United States Air Force Academy Prep School, better known as the "Prep School," is designed to academically, physically and militarily prepare qualified young men and women to enter the Academy. Successful completion of the Prep School improves chances for appointment as an Air Force Academy cadet, but does not guarantee one. In order to attend the tuition-free United States Air Force Prep School, students must complete the Pre-Candidate Questionnaire. The application can be completed as early as March 1 of the student's junior year, but no later than Dec. 31 of their senior year.

ACCESS Summer Seminar

The USAFA Summer seminar allows high-performing high school students to spend one week at the United States Air Force Academy at the conclusion of their junior year. In addition to living on the Air Force Academy's campus, Summer Seminar features a week filled with numerous academic workshops (of the students' choice) and some intramural sports. Moreover, this experience allows students to take a Candidate Fitness Assessment, get some brief drill and ceremony exposure, attend a few informational admissions meetings and go through the "doolie for a day" program (freshmen at the Academy are frequently referred to as "doolies"). The Summer Seminar allows high school students to gain an insight to the numerous facets of the complex freshmen year at the Academy.

SUCCESS Student Academic Affairs

The Student Academic Affairs office offers cadets self-improvement services, which include study skills, graduate school program assistance, and reading and writing assistance.

SUCCESS Major's Night

During Major's Night, the dean of the faculty brings together 20 academic departments and staff agencies to provide a one-stop opportunity for undeclared cadets to learn about the 32 disciplinary academic majors, four divisional majors and two minors available at USAFA. Professionals from varied educational backgrounds and career fields unite as one military community with a common purpose: to share with cadets their collective knowledge and inspiration collected from years of academia and military experiences.

FAST FACTS

STUDENT PROFILE

# of degree-seeking undergraduates	4,527
% male/female	80/20
% African American	8
% American Indian or Alaska Native	1
% Asian or Pacific Islander	9
% Hispanic	9
% White	73
% International	1
% Pell grant recipients	n/a

First-generation and minority alumni Heather Wilson,'82, former Congresswoman, U.S. House of Representatives; Frederick Gregory,'64, former astronaut and NASA Deputy Administrator, NASA; William T Thompson,'73, President and CEO, Association of Graduates; Nicole Malachowski,'96, first female Thunderbird pilot, USAF; Chris Howard,'91, President, Hampden-Sydney College

ACADEMICS

full-time faculty	542
full-time minority faculty	n/a
student-faculty ratio	8:1
average class size	15-20
% first-year retention rate	87
% graduation rate (6 years)	75

Popular majors Aeronautical Engineering, Systems Engineering Management, Management, Civil Engineering, Social Sciences

CAMPUS LIFE

% live on campus	100

Multicultural student clubs and organizations National Society of Black Engineers, Way of Life, Los Padrinos, Native American Heritage Club, Tuskegee Airman, Pacific Rim, Society of Women Engineers, International Club, Prior Enlisted Cadet Assembly

Athletics NCAA Division I, Mountain West Conference (MWC)

ADMISSIONS

# of applicants	9,898
% accepted	17
# of first-year students enrolled	1,368
SAT Critical Reading (middle 50%)	600-680
SAT Math (middle 50%)	630-690
SAT Writing (middle 50%)	n/a
ACT (middle 50%)	28-31
average HS GPA	3.86

Deadlines

regular decision	1/31
application fee	$0
fee waiver for applicants with financial need	yes

COST & AID

tuition	$0
room & board	$0
total need-based institutional scholarships/grants	n/a
% of students apply for need-based aid	n/a
% receiving need-based scholarship or grant aid	n/a
% receiving aid whose need was fully met	n/a
average aid package	n/a
average student loan debt upon graduation	$0

University of Denver

University of Denver
2197 South University Blvd.
Denver, CO 80208
Ph: (303) 871-2036
admission@du.edu
www.du.edu

The University of Denver offers a dynamic learning environment that prizes innovation, cross-disciplinary exploration, inclusive excellence, and adventurous learning partnerships between students and faculty. Students are groomed to excel in their life's work and to confront the great issues of the day. With a student-faculty ratio of 9:1, University of Denver students enjoy meaningful and life-changing interactions with faculty mentors. This rewarding relationship with professors continues through the undergraduate experience, with students collaborating with faculty members on research projects, fieldwork and creative endeavors. In addition, various student organizations offer leadership opportunities that give students a chance to catalyze and support positive change to campus and community. With the personal attention offered at a small liberal arts college and the resources of a large research institution, the University of Denver is the perfect choice for students looking to join other adventurous learners.

ACCESS Volunteers in Partnership

Volunteers in Partnership collaborates with students, parents, faculty and staff from Denver West High School, Abraham Lincoln High School, Pinnacle Charter School, the Denver Center for International Studies, the Denver School of Science & Technology, and Kepner Middle School. Volunteers in Partnership are committed to the promotion of self-esteem in students, to encourage students to complete high school, and to assist with transition into higher education or career training.

ACCESS Pioneer Prep Leadership Institute

A three-day summer campus experience, Pioneer Prep Leadership Institute is designed for college-focused African American high school juniors and seniors to have a dynamic learning opportunity on the University of Denver campus.

OPPORTUNITY Cherrington Global Scholars Study Abroad Program

Study and service abroad are an integral part of the University of Denver experience. About 70 percent of students study abroad. Through the Cherrington Global Scholars program, eligible juniors and seniors can study abroad at no additional charge to the cost of studying at Denver.

SUCCESS The Lamont A. Sellers Diversity & Unity Retreat

The Diversity & Unity Intergroup Relations Retreat is a two and a half day retreat that takes undergraduate and graduate students to the mountains of Colorado for self discovery and learning related to leadership and diversity.

SUCCESS The Center for Community Engagement and Service Learning (CCESL)

University of Denver students are increasingly engaged in the world and the Center for Community Engagement and Service Learning offers an array of opportunities to become involved. The Center is committed to working with community partners to involve the campus community with opportunities in the Denver community.

SUCCESS Excelling Leaders Institute

Excelling Leaders Institute students complete one week of on campus training focusing in the areas of academic preparation, interacting with faculty, learning the campus physical layout, meeting as many individuals and resources on campus as possible and most importantly, creating a tight knit community of support for themselves and other incoming students. Participants are also offered a wide range of benefits not offered to all students.

FAST FACTS

STUDENT PROFILE

# of degree-seeking undergraduates	5,054
% male/female	46/54
% African American	3
% American Indian or Alaska Native	1
% Asian or Pacific Islander	4
% Hispanic	9
% White	74
% International	8
% Pell grant recipients	16

First-generation and minority alumni
Condoleezza Rice, Former U.S. Secretary of State; Brad Anderson, former CEO, Best Buy; James Kennedy, chairman and CEO of Cox Enterprises

ACADEMICS

full-time faculty	640
full-time minority faculty	91
student-faculty ratio	9:1
average class size	21
% first-year retention rate	88
% graduation rate (6 years)	76

Popular majors Communication, Biology, Marketing, Engineering, Psychology, International Studies

CAMPUS LIFE

% live on campus (% freshmen)	45 (91)

Multicultural student clubs and organizations
AMIGOS, Black Men's Fellowship, Arab Student Association, Asian Student Alliance, Black Student Alliance, Graduate Leadership Association for Minorities & Allies, Japanese Student Association, Korean Student Association, Latino Student Alliance, Native Student Alliance, Saudi Student Club, Vietnamese Student Association

Athletics NCAA Division I, Western Athletic Conference (WAC)

ADMISSIONS

# of applicants	10,697
% accepted	70
# of first-year students enrolled	1,231
SAT Critical Reading (middle 50%)	575-650
SAT Math (middle 50%)	575-670
SAT Writing (middle 50%)	n/a
ACT (middle 50%)	25-30
average HS GPA	3.74
Deadlines	
early action	11/1
regular decision	1/15
application fee (online)	$50 ($50)
fee waiver for applicants with financial need	yes

COST & AID

tuition	$36,936
room & board	$10,440
total need-based institutional scholarships/grants	n/a
% of students apply for need-based aid	53
% of students receive aid	43
% receiving need-based scholarship or grant aid	42
% receiving aid whose need was fully met	23
average aid package	$28,195
average student loan debt upon graduation	$25,578

Central Connecticut State University

Central Connecticut State University is a leading comprehensive public university with excellent professors and a wide array of academic programs that prepare students for success in whatever field they choose. Nearly one third of our students are the first in their family to attend college. The University is committed to both access and excellence and offers a campus that warmly welcomes and supports all. CCSU's educational excellence has been nationally recognized; the Association of American Colleges & Universities chose CCSU as a "Leadership Institution"—one of only 16 institutions in the nation to be so honored for the "innovative undergraduate education" it offers. Additionally, the Princeton Review selected CCSU as one of "The Best Northeastern Colleges" and as one of "America's Best Value Colleges."

> ACCESS Pre-Collegiate and Access Services Department

The Pre-Collegiate and Access Services Department's mission is to provide a diverse population of first generation and low income students access into higher education by preparing them to meet high academic, personal, and social standards. The goals of the department include strengthening study skills and giving students the confidence and abilities to succeed in their future careers.

> ACCESS ConnCAP Program

Established in 1987 under the Connecticut Board of Governors for Higher Education, the Collegiate Awareness and Preparation Program (ConnCAP) was designed to increase the number of graduating high school students from disadvantaged backgrounds and prepare them with the necessary skills and motivation for success in college. Now, in its second decade, Central Connecticut State University's ConnCAP Program is one of the oldest and largest in the state. The program serves 120 students in grades 7 - 12, annually. Over 2,200 students have participated in CCSU's ConnCAP program, which has an average program retention rate of 90% and a college-going rate well above the national average.

"The first thing that attracted me to CCSU was the perfect size of the campus. The small classrooms allow for more accessible professors and more individualized learning experiences. In addition, the diverse student and faculty population provides an interesting group of classmates and lecturers. I've traveled abroad twice, become involved in the campus community, and I've received a high quality education."

– Kaylah S., '12
Bristol, CT
Spanish & Anthropology

> OPPORTUNITY The Educational Opportunity Program

The Educational Opportunity Program (EOP) is a five week summer program designed for students who have the potential and the desire to do college-level work, but do not meet CCSU's regular admissions standards. EOP students live on campus in CCSU residence halls during the summer with all expenses paid including books, tuition, room, and board. Graduates of the summer program are admitted to CCSU as full-time matriculated students.

> SUCCESS The Center for Advising and Career Exploration (CACE)

The Center for Advising and Career Exploration (CACE) provides academic advising services to all first-time full-time students during their first semester, and a variety of career counseling services to all students and alumni of the University. The goal of the Center is to ensure that all students are given the support that they need to achieve success in a rigorous academic setting.

> SUCCESS Connecticut College Access Success (CONNCAS)

CONNCAS is a summer access and enrichment program for African American and Latin students who plan to enroll at CCSU. This 5-week Summer Transitional program offers targeted students a safe and stimulating learning environment that enabled students to develop active learning and critical thinking skills, self-confidence, personal growth, and cultural enrichment.

Central Connecticut State University
1615 Stanley Street
New Britain, CT 06050
Ph: (860) 832-2278
admissions@ccsu.edu
www.ccsu.edu

FAST FACTS

STUDENT PROFILE

# of degree-seeking undergraduates	10,085
% male/female	52/48
% African American	9
% American Indian or Alaska Native	<1
% Asian or Pacific Islander	3
% Hispanic	8
% White	75
% International	1
% Pell grant recipients	37

First-generation and minority alumni Larry Hall BS '89, MS '96, Current Director of Recruitment and Admissions, Central Connecticut State University; Elsa Saavedra '81, Principal, Northend Elementary School; Kevin Cranford '89, Department of Children and Families, Children's Services Consultant, State of Connecticut; James Nealy, Jr, '81, Assistant Director of School Police and Security, Bridgeport Public Schools; Peter Rosa, BA '68, MS '74, Senior Program Officer, Hartford Foundation for Public Giving and Past Connecticut State University System Trustee; Curits Wiggins '93, Assistant Vice President, First Investors Corporation; Yvette Ghannam, BA '94, MS '06, Bacteriologist

ACADEMICS

full-time faculty	440
full-time minority faculty	79
student-faculty ratio	17:1
average class size	25
% first-year retention rate	81
% graduation rate (6 years)	49

Popular majors Accounting, Criminology & Criminal Justice, Education, Engineering, Graphic Design, Management, Marketing, Nursing & Psychology

CAMPUS LIFE

% live on campus (% freshmen)	26 (n/a)

Multicultural student clubs and organizations Africana Students Organization, Black Student Union, Centrals Organization for Latin American Dance Awareness, Diversity Advocates, Ebony Choral Ensemble, Habitat for Humanity, Hillel Jewish Student Organization, Latin American Student Organization, LBGT Center, Muslim Student Association, NAACP - CCSU Chapter, PPRIDE, United Caribbean Club

Athletics NCAA Division I, Northeast Conference (NEC)

ADMISSIONS

# of applicants	6,806
% accepted	60
# of first-year students enrolled	1,350
SAT Critical Reading (middle 50%)	460-540
SAT Math (middle 50%)	470-570
SAT Writing (middle 50%)	460-550
ACT (middle 50%)	19-25
average HS GPA	2.75
Deadlines	
early decision	rolling
regular decision	5/1
application fee (online)	$50 ($50)
fee waiver for applicants with financial need	yes

COST & AID

tuition	in-state: $8,055; out-of-state: $18,679
room & board	$9,814
total need-based institutional scholarships/grants	$5,408,075
% of students apply for need-based aid	87
% receiving need-based scholarship or grant aid	62
% receiving aid whose need was fully met	10
average aid package	$7,759
average student loan debt upon graduation	$19,086

Fairfield University

Founded in 1942, Fairfield University is a private, coeducational institution that seeks to create a respectful, multicultural, multiethnic, and religiously inclusive community. Grounded in the values of Jesuit learning, the University respects the personal and academic freedom of all of its students, and is known for preparing them for leadership and service. Undergraduate students receive a general education in the traditional humanities to complement their selected majors, and emphasis is placed on both theoretical and applied learning. Located just within the New York metropolitan area, Fairfield provides students with many professional development, social, and cultural opportunities.

ACCESS Cristo Rey Summer College Planning and Exploration Program

Fairfield University has partnered with the Cristo Rey Network to provide college enrollment information to students from Network high schools. This is a week-long residential program during which students partake in the annual Pre-College Workshop, including additional high school students and admission counselors from local colleges and universities. Students also visit other colleges throughout the area.

OPPORTUNITY Horizons Weekend

Admitted students of color are invited to spend a weekend exploring Fairfield University and the many academic, cultural, spiritual, and social opportunities available. Students are hosted by current students who serve as their personal guide for the weekend. They participate in class visits, lunch with faculty, staff, and administrators, and an evening social event. While visiting during Horizons Weekend, admitted students are also given the opportunity to participate in the Admitted Student Open House.

"Challenge yourself. You're entering a community of people who care about you. If you take the first step, they'll help you go further than you thought you could."

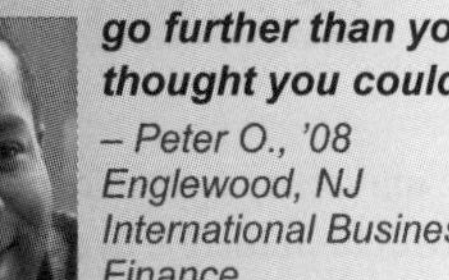

– Peter O., '08
Englewood, NJ
International Business, Finance

SUCCESS Cura Personalis Mentoring Program

This mentorship program is open to all first-year students, with a special invitation going to first generation college students and students of color. The program helps students acclimate to college. They are paired with current students and faculty and staff members who serve as their mentors. Through regular one-on-one and group meetings, students receive valuable information and useful knowledge about the many resources available to the academic, career, spiritual, and support services available on campus.

SUCCESS Academic Immersion Program

The Academic Immersion program is designed to assist admitted students from underrepresented populations with the college transition. The program focuses on the academic adjustments a student must make between high school and the first two years of college. Students are selected based on a combination of factors including first-generation to college, low-income, and race/ethnicity. It includes a four week, residential summer program during which students earn six credits completing an art history and philosophy course. Participants are provided with additional academic and personal support throughout the year.

Fairfield University
Office of Undergraduate Admission
1073 North Benson Road
Fairfield, CT 06824
Ph: (203) 254-4100
admis@fairfield.edu
www.fairfield.edu

FAST FACTS

STUDENT PROFILE

# of degree-seeking undergraduates	3,689
% male/ female	42/58
% African American	2
% American Indian or Alaska Native	<1
% Asian or Pacific Islander	1
% Hispanic	2
% White	22
% International	1
% Pell grant recipients	14.6

ACADEMICS

full-time faculty	261
full-time minority faculty	27
student-faculty ratio	12:1
average class size	23
% first-year retention rate	89
% graduation rate (6 years)	84

Popular majors Psychology, English, Finance, Nursing, Biology

CAMPUS LIFE

% live on campus (% freshmen)	76 (94)

Multicultural student clubs and organizations Asian Student Association, Spanish and Latino Student Association, Women of Color Forum, African American and Caribbean Student Association (Umoja), and Gay/Straight Alliance

Athletics NCAA Division I, Metro Atlantic Athletic Conference (MAAC)

ADMISSIONS

# of applicants	8,420
% accepted	72
# of first-year students enrolled	922
SAT Critical Reading (middle 50%)	530-620
SAT Math (middle 50%)	540-630
SAT Writing (middle 50%)	540-630
ACT (middle 50%)	23-27
average HS GPA	3.3

Deadlines

early decision	12/15
early action	11/1
regular decision	1/15
application fee (online)	$60 ($60)
fee waiver for applicants with financial need	yes

COST & AID

tuition	$39,990
room & board	$12,210
total need-based institutional scholarships/grants	$31,845,659
% of students apply for need-based aid	66
% of students receive aid	56
% receiving need-based scholarship or grant aid	49
% receiving aid whose need was fully met	21
average aid package	$28,923
average student loan debt upon graduation	$35,161

Quinnipiac University

On a scenic campus of 500 acres in southern Connecticut, just eight miles from New Haven and midway between New York and Boston, Quinnipiac University offers students a range of opportunities, including access to state-of-the-art facilities such as a financial technology center and simulated trading floor; a fully digital high-definition television broadcast and production studio, a professional-grade radiography suite and high-tech simulated patient care labs, to name a few. Founded in 1929, Quinnipiac is a private, coeducational university offering 52 undergraduate majors and 20 graduate programs and law. Quinnipiac University embodies three important values: high-quality academic programs, a student-centered environment, and a strong sense of community.

ACCESS Middle School College Awareness Program

Sponsored by the Office of Admissions, students from community middle schools are invited to the campus to spend part of a day meeting current Quinnipiac students, attending a student-led panel discussion and touring the campus. The program is designed to foster a "college-going" mindset, to demystify the college environment, and to help students view a college education as a beneficial and attainable path for their future.

OPPORTUNITY Admissions Events

The Office of Undergraduate Admissions hosts individual interviews, group information sessions, campus tours and Open House programs throughout the year for college-bound students and their families. Admissions also offers newly admitted diversity students the opportunity to participate in an overnight visit program, whereby they are paired with and "shadow" a current student and stay overnight in the residence hall to get a feel for student life at QU.

"I love the friendly environment that Quinnipiac has and the various activities on campus that make everyone feel connected in some way."

– George B., '12
Wood Ridge, NJ
Nursing

SUCCESS Quinnipiac 101

QU101, 201, and 301 are specialized courses within the university core curriculum. Beginning with the freshman year, students examine the role of the individual in the local, national, and international community. This series of 'QU' courses provides a common ground for all students, helps foster understanding and respect for differences, and assists students in the process of developing their individual role in society.

SUCCESS SHADEs/Student Diversity Board

Through the Office of Multicultural Affairs and the Multicultural Events Committee (MEC), students at Quinnipiac can have a direct role in developing the multicultural services and events on campus. Participants in SHADEs - Students Helping Advocate Diversity Education - plan multicultural programming as well as an annual diversity conference and retreat. The Student Diversity Board provides students additional opportunities for involvement by promoting diversity awareness and discussion through guest speakers, open forums, workshops and seminars.

SUCCESS ALANA Mentoring Program

To support historically underrepresented students in their transition from high school to college, the university offers the ALANA & I (African, Latino, Asian, Native American and International) Mentoring Program, which pairs new students, who wish to do so, with a Quinnipiac staff/faculty member or current student and supplies them with additional support and resources. In so doing, the program provides students with a personal, direct link to the university community, helps them navigate their college years, and strives to help students successfully complete their academic careers.

Quinnipiac University
275 Mount Carmel Ave
Hamden, CT 06518
Ph: (800) 462-1944 / (203) 582-8600
admissions@quinnipiac.edu
www.quinnipiac.edu

FAST FACTS

STUDENT PROFILE

# of degree-seeking undergraduates	5,900
% male/female	39/61
% African American	4
% American Indian or Alaska Native	0
% Asian or Pacific Islander	3
% Hispanic	6
% White	84
% Pell grant recipients	9

Distinguished first-generation and minority alums Eric Yutzy '02, sports anchor, NBC affiliate WTHR, Indianapolis

ACADEMICS

full-time faculty	308
student-faculty ratio	16:1
average class size	<25
% first-year retention rate	88
% graduation rate (6 years)	72

Popular majors Business Management, Finance Physical Therapy, Psychology, Nursing, Public Relations, Communications

CAMPUS LIFE

% live on campus (% freshmen) 75 (95)

Multicultural student clubs and organizations Latino Cultural Society, Black Student Union, Asian & Pacific Islander Student Association, Gay, Lesbian & Straight Supporters, International Club, QU Irish Club, Association to Maximize Italian Cultural Influence, Hellenic Society

Athletics NCAA Division I, Northeast Conference (NEC), Eastern College Athletic Conference – M/W Ice hockey

ADMISSIONS

# of applicants	19,535
% accepted	62
SAT Critical Reading (middle 50%)	540-610
SAT Math (middle 50%)	560-630
ACT (middle 50%)	23-27
average HS GPA	3.4

Deadlines

physical therapy, nursing, physician asst.	11/1
early decision	10/15
regular admission	2/1

COST & AID

tuition	$36,130
room & board	$13,430
% of students receiving aid	72
% receiving need-based scholarship or grant aid	68
% receiving aid whose need was fully met	14
average aid package	$21,596
average student loan debt upon graduation	$36,186

Sacred Heart University

As the first Catholic university in the nation designed to be led and staffed by laypeople, Sacred Heart University prides itself on being "ahead of the curve," providing innovative programming and resources such as its fully wireless campus - indoors and out - and one of the largest Division I athletic programs in the country, with 31 varsity sports in addition to over 25 club sports. Stressing its triumvirate of values, 'Immersion, Innovation and Integrity,' Sacred Heart provides a comprehensive academic program that is rooted in service. Students can take advantage of Sacred Heart's many volunteer and service learning programs, creating an environment characterized by active, engaged learning.

ACCESS **Young at Heart Days**

Sacred Heart University offers several programs annually which bring hundreds of local school children from underrepresented communities to campus, where they participate in educational, artistic, and physical activities. Through these programs, which have included theatre productions and a Read-Aloud, students get a chance to connect with the University community and begin imagining themselves as college-bound. Sacred Heart students, to whom the visiting students look as role models, are largely responsible for executing the event under the leadership of the University's Student Life program.

ACCESS **Upward Bound**

Local high school students who come from low-income families in which neither parent holds a bachelor's degree can benefit from Sacred Heart's Upward Bound, a pre-college program that provides a group of students with the right tools to pursue their dreams of earning a college degree. Students benefit from weekly tutoring, field trips, workshops, and a six-week summer enrichment program at the University.

"The GE (Foundation Scholars) program has been phenomenal in providing a foundation for success both in the classroom and when the time comes; the real world. I have done and seen things that I otherwise would still be ignorant of to this day and for that I am truly grateful..."

– Charles C., '12
Frederick, MD
Finance

ACCESS **College Search Assistance**

Sacred Heart University assists underrepresented students with the college search process through a variety of programs. Sacred Heart has hosted The National Hispanic College Fair for the southern Connecticut region, bringing hundreds of Hispanic high school students to campus, where they learn about the college search process, as well as about individual universities. Sacred Heart also hosts upwards of 200 students during its Gear Up Tour and Talent Search Tour programs, both of which offer tailored student programming and activities informative of the college search process.

OPPORTUNITY **Discovery Grant (Fairfield County Tuition-Free Plan for Low-Income Students)**

This plan offers full scholarships to graduating seniors who reside in Fairfield County, Connecticut, whose family income is at or below $50,000 and who have been admitted to Sacred Heart University as first-time, full-time, first-year students.

OPPORTUNITY **Foundation Scholars Program**

Founded in 1994, the GE Scholars Program, which has since accepted upwards of 150 undergraduate students, provides underrepresented students with annual scholarship assistance to help fund their Sacred Heart educations. Recipients — who must be full-time, low-income, minority students with a 3.0 GPA and show an interest in a quantitative-based field such as information technology, finance, economics, etc. — also develop a relationship with a GE executive who serves as a mentor to them, supporting their academic and career goals through a variety of workshops, professional and cultural events and individual meetings.

Sacred Heart University
5151 Park Avenue
Fairfield, CT 06825
Ph: (203) 371-7880
enroll@sacredheart.edu
www.sacredheart.edu

FAST FACTS

STUDENT PROFILE	
# of degree-seeking undergraduates	4,142
% male/female	39/61
% African American	5
% American Indian or Alaska Native	<1
% Asian or Pacific Islander	4
% Hispanic	7
% White	84
% International	1
% Pell grant recipients	18
ACADEMICS	
full-time faculty	215
full-time minority faculty	31
student-faculty ratio	13:1
average class size	22
% first-year retention rate	77
% graduation rate (6 years)	66

Popular majors Business Administration, Finance, Kinesiology and Exercise Science, Psychology, Criminal Justice

CAMPUS LIFE	
% live on campus (% freshmen)	60 (92)

Multicultural student clubs and organizations International Club, Gay/Straight Alliance, La Hispanidad, UMOJA

Athletics NCAA Division I, Northeast Conference (NEC) (football I-AA); Atlantic Hockey Association; Colonial Athletic Association; Eastern Intercollegiate Volleyball Association

ADMISSIONS	
# of applicants	7,569
% accepted	64
# of first-year students enrolled	974
SAT Critical Reading (middle 50%)	500-590
SAT Math (middle 50%)	490-560
SAT Writing (middle 50%)	n/a
ACT (middle 50%)	n/a
average HS GPA	3.3
Deadlines	
early decision	12/1
regular decision	rolling
application fee (online)	$50 ($50)
fee waiver for applicants with financial need	yes
COST & AID	
tuition	$31,224
room & board	$12,340
total need-based institutional scholarships/grants	$30,284,897
% of students apply for need-based aid	90
% of students receive aid	83
% receiving need-based scholarship or grant aid	74
% receiving aid whose need was fully met	7
average aid package	$16,366
average student loan debt upon graduation	$40,865

Saint Joseph College

Saint Joseph College is a place where students can discover their voice, live their passion, and grow in their ability to lead and succeed. Students overwhelmingly cite the College's challenging academic programs, solid career preparation, commitment to service, and investment in students' personal development as highlights of an SJC education. At SJC, students thrive in a culture of collaboration and achievement. They study alongside a community of like-minded learners—women who are passionate about their ability to make the world a better place. The students of SJC are self-aware, adventurous, confident, idealistic, and globally connected citizens.

ACCESS **CREC Summer Program**

Saint Joseph College and the Capital Region Education Council host a residential summer institute for high school students. High school juniors and seniors have the opportunity to experience college life while living on the SJC campus. Students throughout the state choose courses in the areas of biotechnology, health and medical science, intro psychology, and political psychology - and earn three college credits.

> ***"When I think of how much Saint Joseph College has changed me...Wow! I am confident and expressive. I am an independent woman and I know I can make a difference."***
>
> *– Kishana P., '09*
> *Child Study*

OPPORTUNITY **Merit Scholarships**

Scholarships for full-time, first-year students who qualify academically are awarded at the time of admission and range from $3,000 to $19,000 based on high school GPA and SAT/ACT scores. SJC also offers need-based grants in addition to state and federal grants, loans and college work study. Financial aid information sessions are part of our Open House and campus visit opportunities for freshman and transfer students.

SUCCESS **First Year Seminars**

First Year Seminars, available to all first-year students, are meant to help students make the transition between high school and college and prepare for college-level classes. The seminars cover a wide range of topics, but all help students develop college-level writing and critical thinking skills and give students information about the services and activities provided by the college. The classes are also an opportunity for students to work closely in an intimate academic setting and allow them to connect with other first-year students.

SUCCESS **Center for Academic Excellence (CAE)**

The Center for Academic Excellence at Saint Joseph College provides an award winning writing portfolio program assures that students will graduate from college with strong writing skills. Students can come to the Center to receive assistance with writing assignments from any discipline, as well as general tutoring on the subject matter of many classes. Its writing associates program hires consultants to provide assistance to both professors and students and to help facilitate the writing process for students in certain classes. The CAE also provides an online tutoring service that is used by over a thousand students every year.

Saint Joseph College
Office of Admissions
1678 Asylum Avenue
West Hartford, CT 06117
Ph: (860) 231.5216
admissions@sjc.edu
www.sjc.edu

FAST FACTS

STUDENT PROFILE

# of degree-seeking undergraduates	1,059
% male/female	1/99
% African American	8
% American Indian or Alaska Native	0
% Asian or Pacific Islander	2
% Hispanic	10
% White	44
% International	0
% Pell grant recipients	39

First-generation and minority alumni Lois Nesci '85, M'87; CEO, Cathloic Charities - Archdiocese of Hartford, Emily Carangelo Judd '85, M'88; Principal, Polk School, Jacqueline Whipp Colon '87, M'92; Assistant Principal, Bristow Middle School, Marisol Rodriquez-Colon '92; Coordinator of Volunteer Services CT Children's Medical Center, Clara Velez '85; Bilingual Math Teacher, Hartford Public Schools

ACADEMICS

full-time faculty	96
full-time minority faculty	n/a
student-faculty ratio	11:1
average class size	17
% first-year retention rate	78
% graduation rate (6 years)	41

Popular majors Special Education, Nursing, Social Work, Psychology, Child Study

CAMPUS LIFE

% live on campus (% freshmen)	41 (72)

Multicultural student clubs and organizations Diversity in Action, Global Awareness Advocates and Activists, Gay Straight Alliance, Green Team, Environmental Club, Best Buddies, Congregation of Determined Youth, Student Ambassadors, Social Work Student Alliance, Voices of Praise Gospel Choir

Athletics NCAA Division III, Great Northeast Athletic Conference (GNAC)

ADMISSIONS

# of applicants	1,292
% accepted	81
# of first-year students enrolled	232
SAT Critical Reading (middle 50%)	450-550
SAT Math (middle 50%)	440-530
SAT Writing (middle 50%)	n/a
ACT (middle 50%)	n/a
average HS GPA	3.2
Deadlines	
early decision	n/a
regular decision	rolling
application fee (online)	$50 ($0)
fee waiver for applicants for financial need	yes

COST & AID

tuition	$28,960
room & board	$13,200
total need-based institutional scholarship/grants	$12,667,457
% of students apply for need-based aid	94
% receiving need-based scholarship or grant aid	87
% receiving aid whose need was fully met	10
average aid package	$20,217
average student loan debt upon graduation	$26,000

Southern Connecticut State University

Southern Connecticut State University serves a significant number of first-generation and minority students (43 percent and 21 percent, respectively) and is positioned to meet their unique needs. The newly completed Strategic Plan has re-committed the university to core values of equity, diversity and access. The university is noted particularly for its education program, and future educators may benefit from a tuition waiver if they commit to remaining in neighboring New Haven to teach. Students also benefit from the university's metropolitan location, which provides easy access to Boston, New York and the Berkshires.

ACCESS Connecticut Collegiate Awareness and Preparation Program (ConnCAP)

Southern Connecticut State's ConnCap program provides tutoring for middle and high school students in the New Haven system. Participants take a range of college preparatory classes after-school, on Saturdays and in the summer. As with programs like Upward Bound, ConnCAP also exposes participants to the possibility of higher education.

OPPORTUNITY Summer Educational Opportunity Program (SEOP)

Southern offers SEOP, a five-week summer program which assists 50 students in refining their skills before being accepted into the university. All students live on campus, attend classes and explore campus life together. Resident advisers and peer counselors work with SEOP students and implement a variety of academic and recreational enrichment activities. SEOP participants receive a number of academic advantages, including individualized academic counseling, small classes and personal attention from faculty and staff.

> *"My experience at SCSU is characterized by challenging coursework and profound, meaningful relationships with my peers. At Southern, diversity abounds. Southern's classrooms are filled with knowledgeable professors and engaging students. As reflected in the University's strategic plan, Southern is dedicated to maintaining a diverse student body, most notably through its acclaimed summer opportunity programs."*
>
> 
>
> *– Willie G., '11*
> *Manchester, CT*
> *Recreation and Leisure*

OPPORTUNITY Future Educator Scholarships

Through a partnership with the New Haven public school system, students who intend to become teachers, particularly in underserved disciplines such as math, science and special education, can receive free tuition if they commit to teach in New Haven schools upon graduation from the university.

SUCCESS International Student Services

The International Student Services office assists international (temporary visa) and U.S. permanent resident students by handling questions pertaining to visas, employment, immigration and related matters. Students with concerns about their studies or everyday living are referred to other student services offices as appropriate.

SUCCESS Academic Advisement / Office of Study Skills Enrichment

The Academic Advisement Center assists in the advisement of all returning full-time and part-time students with undeclared majors. The Academic Advisement Center serves as the first stop center where students' questions are readily and easily answered.

Southern Connecticut State University
501 Crescent Street
New Haven, CT 06515
Ph: (888) 500-SCSU / (203) 392-5200
adminfo@southernct.edu
www.southernct.edu

FAST FACTS

STUDENT PROFILE

# of degree-seeking undergraduates	8,776
% male/female	39/61
% African American	14
% American Indian or Alaska Native	<1
% Asian or Pacific Islander	3
% Hispanic	9
% White	69
% International	1
% Pell grant recipients	27

First-generation and minority alumni Col. Adele E. Hodges '77, first woman to lead U.S. Marine Corps base Camp Lejeune; Juan Carlos Osorio '98, head coach, MLS' Red Bulls; Alexandria Earle Givan '93, won gold medal in track, 1994 Pan-American Games; Gary Highsmith '90, principal of Hamden High School, Hamden, Conn.

ACADEMICS

full-time faculty	422
full-time minority faculty	70
student-faculty ratio	15:1
average class size	10-29
% first-year retention rate	78
% graduation rate (6 years)	42

Popular majors Business Administration, Education, Exercise Science, Nursing, Psychology

CAMPUS LIFE

% live on campus (% freshmen)	32 (68)

Multicultural student clubs and organizations African American Student Association, Asian Academic Society, Baka Chan's Anime Society, Black Student Union, Chinese Student Association, CIAO Italian Club, Cultural Affairs Club, Delta Mu Delta Zeta Nu Chapter, Hispanic Cultural Society, LGBTQI Prism, Muslim Student Association, NAACP, Organization of Latin American Students, South Asian Student Association, West Indian Academic Society, Women's Center

Athletics NCAA Division II, Northeast-10 Conference (NE-10), Eastern College Athletic Conference (Division I Football) (ECAC)

ADMISSIONS

# of applicants	5,744
% accepted	70
# of first-year students enrolled	1,253
SAT Critical Reading (middle 50%)	430-530
SAT Math (middle 50%)	420-530
SAT Writing (middle 50%)	440-530
ACT (middle 50%)	18-23
average HS GPA	2.9

Deadlines

regular admission	4/1
application fee (online)	$50 ($50)
fee waiver for applicants for financial need	yes

COST & AID

tuition	in-state $4,023; out-of-state $13,020
room & board	$9,983
total need-based institutional scholarships/grants	$1,357,831
% of students apply for need-based aid	87
% of students receiving aid	59
% receiving need-based scholarship or grant aid	49
% receiving aid whose need was fully met	37
average aid package	$13,194
average student loan debt upon graduation	$17,341

Trinity College

Founded in 1823, Trinity College brings the great tradition of the liberal arts into the 21st century with its dynamic living and learning community. The college's 2,300 students work closely with faculty, broaden their education through campus activities and organizations, engage with the city of Hartford through internships and community service, and explore the wider world through study abroad and international initiatives on campus. Together, these experiences prepare Trinity graduates for fulfilling lives.

"Trinity professors work hard to help you find, create, and excel within your own niche. Our tight-knit community has allowed me to confidently challenge myself and discover new possibilities for a future career in the arts."

– Jeanika B.S., '12
East Hartford, CT
Studio Arts, Theater and Dance

ACCESS **Mentoring Programs**

Trinity students mentor middle and high school students through programs such as Rising Stars and the Vision Academic Mentoring Program (VAMP). The college subsidizes and hosts the Dream Camp for more than 300 city youth and subsidizes and staffs the Trinity/Tom Johnson Boys & Girls Club. In addition, Trinity participates in the "5th Graders and 9th Graders Go to College" program sponsored by the Hartford Consortium for Higher Education.

OPPORTUNITY **Preview Weekend**

This three-day fall program is designed to give high school seniors an opportunity to explore both the academic and social aspects of the Trinity community, with a focus on the experiences of minority students. The similar V.I.P. Days program exists in the spring for admitted students.

OPPORTUNITY **QuestBridge National College Match Program**

The QuestBridge National College Match program provides students who have achieved academic excellence in the face of economic hardship with a free application to Trinity College. The application enables these students to highlight their academic achievements in light of their low-income background and provides them the chance to receive financial aid packages covering 100% of their demonstrated need.

OPPORUNITY **Posse Foundation**

Trinity College participates in the Posse Foundation, a program that brings talented inner-city youth to campus to pursue their academics and to help promote cross-cultural communication. Posse students are nominated by their high school to the program and share a collaborative support system with a special mentor to adjust to campus and college life. Trinity's Posse Scholars hail from New York City and Chicago.

SUCCESS **Office of Multicultural Affairs**

Trinity's Office of Multicultural Affairs offers advice and support regarding personal and academic concerns, as well as advising for student groups. The office brings speakers and programs to campus and encourages interaction between Trinity's students and alumni, and students, staff and faculty from other colleges.

SUCCESS **Gateway Courses**

Trinity's efforts to raise academic performance include supplemental instruction in math and science "gateway" courses and TEAM (a small group of faculty and administrators who form a network of support for students at academic risk). The college also participates in CHAS (Consortium on High Achievement and Success), an organization initiated by Trinity with more than 30 other colleges that sponsors educational and networking workshops for faculty and staff, conducts research, and hosts several student-oriented conferences annually.

Trinity College
Admissions Office
300 Summit St.
Hartford, CT 06106
Ph: (860) 297-2180
admissions.office@trincoll.edu
www.trincoll.edu

FAST FACTS

STUDENT PROFILE

# of degree-seeking undergraduates	2,311
% male/female	50/50
% African American	7
% American Indian or Alaska Native	<1
% Asian or Pacific Islander	6
% Hispanic	7
% White	64
% International	6
% Pell grant recipients	15

First-generation and minority alumni Robert Stepto, Ph.D., literary theorist, professor of African American Studies, English and American Studies, Yale University, author, *From Behind the Veil: A Study of Afro-American Narrative, Chant of Saints — A Gathering of Afro-American Literature, Art and Scholarship, Blue as the Lake: A Personal Geography;* Francisco Borges, first black president and managing partner, Landmark Partners, Inc.; Eddie Perez, first Latino mayor, Hartford, Conn.

ACADEMICS

full-time faculty	184
full-time minority faculty	38
student-faculty ratio	10:1
average class size	20
% first-year retention rate	92
% graduation rate (6 years)	86

Popular majors Political Science, Economics, English, History, Biology, Psychology

CAMPUS LIFE

% live on campus (% freshmen)	90 (99)

Multicultural student clubs and organizations Asian-American Students Association, International Students Association, La Voz Latina, Men of Color Alliance, Caribbean Student Association, Trinity College Black Women's Organization

Athletics NCAA Division III, New England Small College Athletic Conference (NESCAC)

ADMISSIONS

# of applicants	6,967
% accepted	30
# of first-year students enrolled	600
SAT Critical Reading (middle 50%)	590-680
SAT Math (middle 50%)	610-690
SAT Writing (middle 50%)	610-700
ACT (middle 50%)	26-30
average HS GPA	3.0

Deadlines

early decision	11/15
regular decision	1/1
application fee (online)	$60($60)
fee waiver for applicants with financial need	yes

COST & AID

tuition	$41,980
room & board	$11,280
total need-based institutional scholarships/grants	$30,767,043
% of students apply for need-based aid	49
% of students receive aid	46
% receiving need-based scholarship or grant aid	44
% receiving aid whose need was fully met	100
average aid package	$38,262
average student loan debt upon graduation	$21,671

United States Coast Guard Academy

The United States Coast Guard Academy is committed to strengthening the nation's future by educating, developing, training, and inspiring leaders of character who are ethically, intellectually, professionally, and physically prepared to serve their country and humanity, and who are strong in their resolve to build on the long military and maritime heritage and proud accomplishments of the United States Coast Guard. The Coast Guard Academy is the only service Academy that brings in students based solely on merit and is open to all U.S. citizens. A full scholarship for tuition and room & board is provided for all incoming students. For those not academically prepared for the challenge, a one year prep school program is offered at no cost to the student.

ACCESS **Academy Introduction Mission (AIM) Summer Program**

AIM is a one-week summer program that provides high school students the chance to test the waters and to see if the Academy is right for them. If a student is selected, he or she will experience the rigor, discipline, and rewards of the Academy just like a cadet for a week in July following his or her junior year in high school. Students will meet faculty and staff; learn about our academic, military, and athletic programs; talk with cadets who have sailed on Eagle, flown aircrafts, and started their leadership journey. Success at AIM is a good indicator of success at the Coast Guard Academy.

OPPORTUNITY **Coast Guard Academy Scholars Program**

The Academy's Scholar Program was designed to develop the necessary foundation for success as a cadet, an officer, and most importantly, a Leader of Character. We offer one-year prep school scholarships to properly motivated students interested in demonstrating their personal potential and willingness to succeed academically, militarily and physically. Most participants who successfully complete this year of focused preparation receive a full appointment to the Academy as a member of the next entering class, where they will be recognized as leaders from the beginning of Swab Summer. CGA Scholars appointees are selected from within the general applicant pool.

SUCCESS **Cadet Sponsor Program**

The Sponsor Program pairs cadets with families who provide support, friendship and learning beyond the Academy environment as well as the comforts of a home away from home. The program exposes cadets to the local area and, when possible, to a different view of the unique military community. This helps make cadets' integration into the military easier and more effective. Families can provide a relaxed learning environment that the Academy cannot. The time commitment and contact between cadet sponsor family and cadet are individual choices.

SUCCESS **Eclipse Week**

Given the challenges and far-reaching missions of the Coast Guard, wise cadets seek to strengthen their understanding and community through cultural learning, and search for inner peace through discovery or reinforcement of personal beliefs. Members of the Coast Guard are encouraged to learn about different cultures in order to better understand themselves, those with whom they serve, as well as the public they will encounter. Each Spring, the Academy celebrates these important themes during Eclipse Week, a multi-cultural celebration of diversity.

SUCCESS **Fourth Class Academic Orientation (FCAOP)**

FCAOP creates an environment for incoming Freshman that encourages continuous academic improvement, lays the foundation for critical thinking and lifelong learning, and begins the dialogue among a community of peers about the learning process. During the Majors Information Program, early in the spring semester, cadets learn about the eight academic majors at CGA.

SUCCESS **Cadet Academic Assistance Program (CAAP)**

Staffed by faculty in science, mathematics, nautical science, and engineering, CAAP offers discipline-specific workshops for all cadets during weekday evenings.

United States Coast Guard Academy
31 Mohegan Ave
London, CT, 06320
Ph: (860) 444-8503
www.uscga.edu

FAST FACTS

STUDENT PROFILE	
# of degree-seeking undergraduates	1,000
% male/female	69/31
% African American	5
% American Indian or Alaska Native	<1
% Asian or Pacific Islander	6
% Hispanic	9
% White	77
% International	2
% Pell grant recipients	0

ACADEMICS	
full-time faculty	116
full-time minority faculty	15
student-faculty ratio	8:1
average class size	14
% first year retention rate	93
% graduation rate (6 years)	81

Popular majors Engineering, Civil Engineering (Environmental or Structural), Electrical Engineering (Computer or Systems), Mechanical Engineering, Naval Architecture and Marine Engineering, Government (International Affairs or Public Policy), Management, Marine and Environmental Sciences (Bio-Environmental, Chem-Environmental, or Physical), Operations Research, Computer Analysis

CAMPUS LIFE	
% live on campus	100

Multicultural student clubs and organizations Asian Pacific American Club (APAC), Compañeros, Genesis Club, International Council, Compass Catholic Youth Group, Fellowship of Christian Athletes (FCA), Hillel, Latter Day Saints, Officers' Christian Fellowship, St. Francis De Sales

Athletics NCAA Division III, Independent

ADMISSIONS	
# of applicants	2,344
% accepted	12
# of first year students enrolled	291
SAT Critical Reading (middle 50%)	500-790
SAT Math (middle 50%)	540-800
SAT Writing (middle 50%)	n/a
ACT (middle 50%)	23-31
average HS GPA	3.7
Deadlines	
early decision plan	yes
application closing date	11/1
early action notification date	1/17
regular decision	2/1
notification date	4/15
application fee	$0
fee waiver for applicants with financial need	n/a

COST & AID	
tuition	n/a*
room & board	n/a*

*A full scholarship for tuition and room & board is provided for all incoming students

total need-based institutional scholarships/grants	n/a
% of students apply for need based aid	n/a
% of students receive aid	100
% receiving need-based scholarship or grant aid	n/a
% receiving aid whose need was fully met	100
average aid package	$300,000
average student loan debt upon graduation	0

Wesleyan University

Wesleyan is a highly selective private liberal-arts university that attracts a diverse student body from all over the world. It is dedicated to the outreach and support of underrepresented students in Connecticut and beyond, and approximately 30 percent of undergraduates are students of color and 12 percent are first-generation college students. The University is committed to fully meeting 100 percent of undergraduates' financial need. Located in the small New England city of Middletown, Conn., Wesleyan provides students the opportunity to attend a top-notch research university with the intimate intellectual and social community of a liberal arts college.

ACCESS Wesleyan-Middletown Public Schools Collaborative

The Wesleyan-Middletown Public Schools Collaborative empowers and encourages upper-elementary and middle school students from first-generation and low-income backgrounds to achieve higher education. The program enhances students' academic performance, college preparation and career exploration through tutoring, special events and academic and cultural enrichment in the areas of math and science, art, foreign languages, college admissions and more.

ACCESS Upward Bound

Local high school students who are from low-income families can benefit from Wesleyan's Upward Bound program, a pre-college program that provides about 120 students in Middletown, Meriden and Portland with the right tools to pursue their goals of earning a college degree. Students benefit from weekly tutoring, field trips, workshops, and a summer enrichment program.

OPPORTUNITY Subsidized Visits

To encourage first-generation, low-income and other underrepresented students to enroll at Wesleyan, the university arranges and subsidizes transportation for these students to attend fall open houses and the admitted student weekend, WesFest. Wesleyan admissions officers also offer workshops throughout the country to provide outreach and college preparation programs.

"I chose Wesleyan for many different reasons. I wanted a change of scenery from my hometown of Memphis, TN. Also, Wesleyan fosters a great sense of community and provides opportunities for me to serve in a way that has contributed to my personal and academic growth. Whatever you are interested in, Wesleyan can find resources that help you to further explore and develop your talent."

– Ural G., '13 Memphis, TN

SUCCESS Mellon Mays Undergraduate Fellowship

The Mellon Mays Undergraduate Fellowship is a mentoring program that supports students from underrepresented racial and ethnic groups interested in pursuing careers in academia. The program seeks to increase the number of minorities who will pursue doctoral degrees in core arts and sciences fields through mentoring, opportunities for independent research, skills development, and introduction to the academic life. Students are typically identified in their second year.

SUCCESS The Ronald E. McNair Post-Baccalaureate Achievement Program

The Wesleyan McNair Program assists students from underrepresented backgrounds with strong academic potential, preparing them to pursue doctoral programs through involvement in research and other scholarly activities. Wesleyan provides support in and out of the classroom and financially as they complete their undergraduate and possibly graduate requirements.

Wesleyan University
70 Wyllys Ave.
Middletown, CT 06459
Ph: (860) 685-3000
admission@wesleyan.edu
www.wesleyan.edu

FAST FACTS

STUDENT PROFILE

# of degree-seeking undergraduates	2,837
% male/female	49/51
% African American	6
% American Indian or Alaska Native	<1
% Asian or Pacific Islander	7
% Hispanic	9
% White	56
% International	7
% Pell grant recipients	17

First-generation and minority alumni
Majora Carter, founder and executive Director, Sustainable South Bronx (2006 MacArthur award winner); Lin-Manuel Miranda, Tony Award-winning composer and lyricist of the musical *In the Heights*; Michael S. Roth, president, Wesleyan University; Theodore M. Shaw, Columbia Law professor and former director-counsel and president, NAACP Legal Defense Fund; Michael Yamashita, photographer, National Geographic

ACADEMICS

full-time faculty	339
full-time minority faculty	68
student-faculty ratio	9:1
average class size	18
% first year retention rate	98
% graduation rate (6 years)	94

Popular majors English, Government, Psychology

CAMPUS LIFE

% live on campus (% freshmen)	99(100)

Multicultural student clubs and organizations
African Student's Association, Alliance of Progressive South Asians, Ajua Campos, Asian American Student Coalition, Black and Latino Brotherhood, Black Women's Collective, Chinese Adopted Sibs, Chinese Students Association, Fusion, Indonesian Society, Japan Society, Kol Israel, Korean Students' Association, Lac Viet, Nosotras, PADThai Culture and Society, Pangea, PINOY, Shakti, Students of Color Coalition, Taiwanese Cultural Society, Ujamaa, WesConnection, West Indian Student Association, Women of Color Collective

Athletics NCAA Division III, New England Small College Athletic Conference (NESCAC)

ADMISSIONS

# of applicants	10,657
% accepted	21
# of first year students enrolled	748
SAT Critical Reading (middle 50%)	670-770
SAT Math (middle 50%)	670-760
ACT (middle 50%)	30-34
average HS GPA	3.77

Deadlines

early decision I, early decision II	11/15, 1/1
regular decision	1/1
application fee (online)	$55 ($55)
fee waiver for applicants with financial need	yes

COST & AID

tuition	$41,814
room & board	$11,794
total need-based institutional scholarships/grants	$40,603,860
% of students apply for need based aid	51
% of students receive aid	48
% receiving need-based scholarship or grant aid	48
% receiving aid whose need was fully met	100
average aid package	$35,548
average student loan debt upon graduation	$29,227

Yale University

As the third-oldest college in the United States, Yale University has educated a wide variety of leaders from all backgrounds. Today, Yale graduates can be found across the globe in every imaginable profession. Because the university is committed to opening up access to underrepresented minorities and students from lower socioeconomic backgrounds, financial need plays no role in the admissions process and the university meets 100 percent of admitted students' demonstrated need.

> OPPORTUNITY **Multicultural Open House / Fly-In Program**

The Multicultural Open House introduces prospective students to Yale's academic programs, campus life, admissions process and financial aid resources. Admitted students who demonstrate significant financial need are provided with a travel stipend to visit the university.

> OPPORTUNITY **QuestBridge Partner**

In 2007, Yale entered into a partnership with QuestBridge, a national organization that aims to increase the percentage of talented low-income students attending the nation's best universities.

> SUCCESS **Residential College Dean**

The primary academic adviser is a student's residential college dean. The dean is available for academic and personal advice. The college dean lives and has an office in the residential college where the students live.

> SUCCESS **Freshman Counselor Program**

Incoming students receive support from a senior counselor who lives nearby and serves as a mentor to ease the transition to college. Some freshman counselors also have special training in discussing issues of racial and ethnic identity.

> SUCCESS **Science, Technology and Research Scholars (STARS)**

STARS provides select freshmen through seniors with an integrated experience in research, course-based study and development of mentorship skills. STARS identifies and supports students from groups that are underrepresented in scientific and technological disciplines, along with students who come from disadvantaged circumstances, in any of Yale's natural sciences and engineering majors.

> SUCCESS **Peer Liaisons**

The Peer liaisons are upperclassmen who help connect freshman to the wealth of support and programming initiatives based in the residential colleges. These student leaders also help first year students adjust to life at Yale and empower each student to be an engaged, responsible, and proactive citizen on campus.

Yale University
P.O. Box 208234
New Haven, CT 06514
Ph: (203) 432-9316
student.questions@yale.edu
admissions.yale.edu

FAST FACTS

STUDENT PROFILE

# of degree-seeking undergraduates	5,279
% male/female	48/52
% African American	7
% American Indian or Alaska Native	<1
% Asian or Pacific Islander	16
% Hispanic	10
% White	52
% International	10
% Pell grant recipients	12.9

First-generation and minority alumni Clarence Thomas, Supreme Court Justice; Angela Bassett, actress; Wendell Mottley, Olympic runner; Prakazrel Samuel Michel, rapper; Michiko Kakutani, Pulitzer Prize-winning critic; Susan Choi, author; Fareed Zakaria, editor of *Newsweek International*

ACADEMICS

full-time faculty	1,100
full-time minority faculty	n/a
student-faculty ratio	6:1
average class size	10-19
% first-year retention rate	99
% graduation rate (6 years)	98

Popular majors Economics, History, Political Science, Psychology, and English

CAMPUS LIFE

% live on campus (% freshmen)	100(100)

Multicultural student clubs and organizations African Student Association, American Indian Science and Engineering Society, Asian American Students Association, Arab Students Association, Association of Native Americans at Yale, Black Student Alliance, Chinese American Students' Organization, Cuban-American Undergraduate Student Association, Chinese Undergraduate Student Association, Despierta Boricua, Dominican Student Association, Friends of Israel, International Students Organization, Japanese American Students Union, The Filipino Club, Korean American Students of Yale (KASY), Latin American Student Organization, Mexican Student Organization, Model Arab League, PorColombia, Polish Student Society, Taiwanese American Society, Vietnamese Student Association, West Indian Students' Organization

Athletics NCAA Division I, Eastern College Athletic Conference

ADMISSIONS

# of applicants	25,869
% accepted	7.9
# of first-year student enrolled	1,344
SAT Critical Reading (middle 50%)	700-800
SAT Math (middle 50%)	710-790
SAT Writing (middle 50%)	710-800
ACT (middle 50%)	32-35
average HS GPA	n/a
Deadlines	
early action	11/1
regular decision	12/31
application fee (online)	$75 ($75)
fee waiver for applicants with financial need	yes

COST & AID

tuition	$40,500
room & board	$12,200
total need-based institutional scholarships/ grants	$109,000,000
% of students apply for need-based aid	57
% of students receive aid	100
% receiving need-based scholarship or grant aid	100
% receiving aid whose need was fully met	100
average aid package	$35,400
average student loan debt upon graduation	$9,428

The George Washington University

The George Washington University
2121 Eye Street, N.W. Suite 201
Washington, D.C. 20052
Ph: (202) 994-6040
gwadm@gwu.edu
www.gwu.edu

The George Washington University attracts a multicultural, motivated, and active community, in which the leaders of today nurture the leaders of tomorrow. The University enrolls undergraduates from all 50 states, the District of Columbia, Puerto Rico, the Virgin Islands, and 125 countries worldwide. Committed to presenting multicultural points of view across the curriculum and University, it offers an array of classroom experiences, privileged access to academic resources on campus and in Washington, D.C., and a well-connected faculty. Students can create their own distinctive course of study to fit their individual needs and goals.

ACCESS **GW Pre-College Programs**

A six-week Pre-College Program offers eleventh graders the opportunity to live on campus, take classes offered by the University's renowned faculty and to earn credits, and to explore Washington, D.C. The 10-day Mini-Courses Program provides ninth, tenth and eleventh graders with an opportunity to explore various career options through lectures, famous guest speakers, and visits to important institutions and sites unique to the nation's capitol.

"The first reason that I decided to come to GW is that the school is literally in the heart of Washington D.C., where campus events can be the President of the United States giving a town hall meeting, the Speaker of the House giving a lecture or Cabinet Members using the school for diferent purposes. The second reason that I picked GW is that the student body is so diverse; everyone comes from different backgrounds, yet we all seem to balance school work with their extracurricular activities."

– Caleb R., '12

OPPORTUNITY **Need-Based Scholarship and Grant Aid**

The University has initiated a fixed tuition rate for the duration of students' undergraduate studies and has made a commitment to those eligible for need-based financial assistance by guaranteeing them a tuition grant for up to ten consecutive semesters of undergraduate enrollment. The University offers various scholarships to students who demonstrate financial need, are eligible for Federal Pell Grants, and who are academically exceptional.

SUCCESS **Colonial Inauguration and the Guide to Personal Success Program (GPS)**

The University offers Colonial Inauguration, the summer orientation program, to incoming freshman, transfer and international students. It is a two and half day event led by the Colonial Cabinet, a diverse group of student leaders who introduce students to academic advisors and current students, help them learn about academic and extra-curricular opportunities, and help them get to know their fellow classmates. Additionally, programs are provided for parents, guardians and siblings. Once students arrive on campus in the fall, they are assigned a Guide to Personal Success (GPS), a knowledgeable George Washington University staff member who helps them navigate any personal, professional, or experiential issues, and connects them with University resources.

SUCCESS **Multicultural Student Services Center (MSSC)**

The MSSC is GW's center for multicultural communication, community building and leadership. The Center offers a variety of workshops, events, and programs each semester, including the Black Men's Initiative which offers activities to advance the mission of supporting the academic, social, intellectual, and spiritual growth of Black male students; C3, a cross cultural dialogue group; and The Jackie Robinson discussion series, which consists of a number of social and cultural activities to enhance multicultural ideals.

FAST FACTS

STUDENT PROFILE

# of degree-seeking undergraduates	10,055
% male/female	44/56
% African American	7
% American Indian or Alaska Native	<1
% Asian or Pacific Islander	10
% Hispanic	7
% White	55
% International	7
% Pell grant recipients	18.3

First-generation and minority alumni Colin Powell, former U.S. Secretary of State; Kerry Washington, actress; Warren Brown, Food Network host and owner of Cake Love; Gerardo I. Lopez, CEO and President of AMC Theaters

ACADEMICS

full-time faculty	942
full-time minority faculty	194
student/faculty ratio	13:1
average class size	28
% first year retention rate	94
% graduation rate (6 years)	81

Popular majors Biology, International Affairs, Political Science, Business Administration, Biomedical Engineering, Journalism, Economics

CAMPUS LIFE

% live on campus (% freshmen)	70 (99)

Multicultural student clubs and organizations Black Student Union, George Washington Williams House, Asian Student Alliance, Organization of Latino American Students, Racially and Ethnically Mixed Student Association, Multicultural Greek Council, Organization of African Students, GW Raas, GW Bhangra

Athletics NCAA Division I, Atlantic 10 (A-10)

ADMISSIONS

# of applicants	21,548
% accepted	32.7
# of first-year students enrolled	2,300
SAT Critical Reading (middle 50%)	610-710
SAT Math (middle 50%)	630-710
SAT Writing (middle 50%)	630-720
ACT (middle 50%)	28-31
average HS GPA	n/a

Deadlines

early decision	11/10
regular decision	1/10
application fee (online)	$75 ($75)
fee waiver for applicants with financial need	yes

COST & AID

tuition	$44,103
room & board	$10,325
total need-based institutional scholarships and grants	$119,447,225
% students apply for need-based aid	68
% receiving need-based scholarship or grant aid	99
% receiving aid whose need fully met	84
average aid package	$39,578
average student loan debt upon graduation	$32,714

Trinity Washington University

Trinity Washington University
Office of Admissions
125 Michigan Avenue, NE
Washington, DC 20017
Ph: (800) 492-6882 / (202) 884-9400
admissions@trinitydc.edu
www.trinitydc.edu

Trinity Washington University, founded in 1897, is a private university in Washington, D.C. Trinity is committed to the academic success of D.C. students – nearly 50% of Trinity students are D.C. residents. Trinity is very affordable and was named "Best Value" among Washington, D.C., universities by Fox News. Trinity proudly enrolls more DC-TAG recipients than any other private institution in the region and in the nation. Trinity prepares its students to become leaders of character — passionate intellectuals excited about their future. Trinity's College of Arts and Sciences is the university's undergraduate women's college, where there is a priority on the education of women, the development of women's leadership skills, and a focus on the academic and career success of women. Trinity's prestigious graduates include Speaker of the House of Representatives Nancy Pelosi and Secretary of Health and Human Services Kathleen Sebelius.

"Trinity, in Washington, D.C., has given me fantastic opportunities. I enjoy the small classes and a personal connection with my professors. The teachers know me and I know them."

– Kamillah M., '12
Washington, DC
Chemistry

ACCESS Ensuring Smooth Transitions

Trinity works closely with the DC College Success Foundation, the DC College Access Program (DC-CAP) and other programs to ensure a smooth transition from high school to college.

OPPORTUNITY Aspiring Leader Award

Aspiring Leader awards are made to College of Arts and Sciences students who have demonstrated financial need and leadership potential.

OPPORTUNITY Trinity Scholarships and More

In 2009-10, Trinity awarded more than $2.2 million in scholarships and grants to D.C. students. Full-time Trinity students are considered for a wide range of scholarships. The average student aid package is $17,000.

SUCCESS Student Support Services

Trinity provides students with extensive academic support, including a Writing Center, tutoring services, disability support services, and workshops on transitioning to college. Trinity provides professional health care, mental health counseling and spiritual support.

SUCCESS First-Year Students Success Program

First-year students at Trinity take part in a special curriculum in which students focus on a foundation of academic skills that ensures their success as a college student. Each student takes the Critical Reading Seminar which is also the student's Learning Community and the professor is her advisor. The Learning Community also fosters an academic and social support structure for the students in that class – they support each other as they make the transition from high school to college.

SUCCESS Internships in Washington, D.C.

Internships prepare Trinity students for careers by giving them valuable work experience combined with academic training. The Washington, D.C., area offers amazing internship opportunities from Capitol Hill to the White House, Department of State, C-SPAN, *The Washington Post*, Black Entertainment Television (BET), and many corporate headquarters.

FAST FACTS

STUDENT PROFILE

# of degree-seeking undergraduates	1,561
% male/female	4/96
% African American	70
% American Indian or Alaska Native	0
% Asian or Pacific Islander	1
% Hispanic	11
% White	3
% International	6
% Pell grant recipients	74

First-generation and minority alumni Perita Carpenter '02, journalist; Michelle Mitchell '06, lawyer at Hughes, Hubbard & Reed; Philonda Johnson '05, principal of KIPP DC school

ACADEMICS

full-time faculty	75
full-time minority faculty	31
student-faculty ratio	9:1
average class size	15
% first-year retention rate	68
% graduation rate (6 years)	37

Popular majors Nursing, Criminal Justice, Psychology, Business Administration, Education, Communication

CAMPUS LIFE

% live on campus (% freshmen)	28(35)

Multicultural student clubs and organizations Latin American and Caribbean American Student Association, International Student Association, Muslim Student Association, Minority Association of Pre-Health Students, NAACP

Athletics Division III, Independent

ADMISSIONS

# of applicants	1,388
% accepted	85
# of first-year student enrolled	369
SAT Critical Reading (middle 50%)	n/a
SAT Math (middle 50%)	n/a
SAT Writing (middle 50%)	n/a
ACT (middle 50%)	n/a
average HS GPA	2.9

Deadlines

regular decision	rolling
application fee (online)	$40 ($0)
fee waiver for applicants with financial need	yes

COST & AID

tuition	$20,150
room & board	$9,210
total need-based institutional scholarships/ grants	$6,759,000
% of students apply for need-based aid	98
% receiving need-based scholarship or grant aid	96
% receiving aid whose need was fully met	46
average aid package	$17,000
average student loan debt upon graduation	$17,000

Barry University

Barry University in Miami Shores, Florida, brings the world to you, with students and faculty from nearly all 50 states and close to 120 countries. Founded in 1940, Barry is the second-largest private, Catholic university in the Southeast. *U.S. News & World Report* has ranked Barry among the top 20 schools nationwide for campus diversity. Barry offers more than 100 bachelor's, master's, and doctoral degrees in the arts and sciences, business, education, health sciences, human performance and leisure sciences, law, podiatric medicine, and social work. With small classes that offer personal attention, more than 60 student organizations, and a university commitment to service, students develop as professionals, leaders, and active citizens in a caring community. Barry's tropical main campus is just a few miles from the ocean and the dynamic, multicultural city of Miami, a hub for international business, tourism, arts and entertainment, cutting-edge medicine, and professional sports.

> OPPORTUNITY **Stamps Leadership Scholars**

Founded by South Florida philanthropists Penny and E. Roe Stamps, this full merit scholarship demonstrates Barry's commitment to attracting and cultivating outstanding students from around the nation. The Stamps Leadership Scholars Program provides full tuition and room and board over four years, plus funds for study abroad, undergraduate research, and other exceptional learning experiences. To be considered, the student must be an incoming freshman with an SAT score of 1200 or higher or an ACT score of 27 or higher, must have a high school GPA of 3.5 or higher, and must have a demonstrated and active involvement in community service and leadership.

> OPPORTUNITY **Goizueta Foundation Scholarships**

Since 2000, Barry University has been affiliated with the Goizueta Foundation for the promotion of social justice and community service. Barry has three Goizueta Foundation scholarships. The Minority Empowerment Scholarships promote and contribute to the education of minority women in the schools of Adult and Continuing Education, Arts and Sciences, Business, Education, Health Sciences, and Social Work. The Minority Science Scholarships focus on the education of successive generations of minority scientific leaders. The 2+2 Scholarships support future teachers enrolled in Barry University's Adrian Dominican School of Education.

> OPPORTUNITY **Minority Opportunities in Research**

The federally funded RISE (Research Initiative for Scientific Enhancement) and MARC (Minority Access to Research Careers) programs aim to increase the representation of minority students in the biomedical field. Select students majoring in biology, chemistry, computer science, math, or psychology can participate in on-campus research with faculty, summer research internships, and graduate school workshops. They may even have the opportunity to publish their research findings in scientific journals and attend national and international scientific meetings. Academic scholarships and funding for research and travel are also available.

> SUCCESS **Orientation and Leadership**

Barry's Division of Student Affairs sponsors both Orientation for first-year students and the Emerging Leaders Program. In Orientation, students get a head start on the academic year and the Barry experience. Here, they register for classes, meet their advisors, take part in Barry traditions and get to know their future classmates. The Emerging Leaders Program helps students develop leadership skills through training and practical experience. Students gain skills in communication, time management, networking, and ethical decision-making while interacting with campus leaders and administrators.

"The small class size at Barry is the best environment for learning. It allows you to have a more personal relationship with the professor so that they can understand you and be able to help you better. This allows professors to become mentors, not only providers of information."

– Kelsa B., '10
San Fernando, Trinidad
Photography

Barry University
11300 NE Second Avenue
Miami Shores, FL 33161-6695
Ph: (305) 899-3100
admissions@mail.barry.edu
www.barry.edu

FAST FACTS

STUDENT PROFILE	
# of degree-seeking undergraduates	5,074
% male/female	31/69
% African American	21
% American Indian or Alaska Native	1
% Asian or Pacific Islander	1
% Hispanic	26
% White	14
% International	5
% Pell grant recipients	24
ACADEMICS	
full-time faculty	341
full-time minority faculty	81
student-faculty ratio	15:1
average class size	10-19
% first-year retention rate	66
% graduation rate (6 years)	35

Popular majors Nursing, Biology, Psychology, Sport Management, Business Management

CAMPUS LIFE	
% freshmen who live on campus	63

Multicultural student clubs and organizations Bahamian Student Association, Black Student Association, Caribbean Student Association, Haitian Intercultural Association, Latin American Student Association, Kappa Alpha Psi Fraternity, Lambda Theta Phi Latino Fraternity, Omega Phi Chi Multicultural Sorority, PRIDE

Athletics NCAA Division II, Sunshine State Conference (SSC)

ADMISSIONS	
# of applicants	4,347
% accepted	62
# of first-year students enrolled	648
SAT Critical Reading (middle 50%)	420-500
SAT Math (middle 50%)	410-490
SAT Writing (middle 50%)	n/a
ACT (middle 50%)	17-21
average HS GPA	n/a
Deadlines	
regular decision	rolling
application fee (online)	$30 ($20)
fee waiver for applicants with financial need	yes
COST & AID	
tuition	$28,160
room & board	$9,300
total need-based institutional scholarships/grants	$4,365,085
% of students apply for need-based aid	81
% of students receiving aid	76
% receiving need-based scholarship or grant aid	53
% receiving aid whose need was fully met	5
average aid package	$20,365
average student loan debt upon graduation	$35,880

Lynn University

Lynn University
3601 North Military Trail
Boca Raton, Florida 33431
Ph: (800) 888-5966
admissions@lynn.edu
www.lynn.edu

Lynn University is a private, coeducational university awarding bachelor's and master's degrees in the liberal arts and sciences and professional education. Founded in 1962, Lynn offers a distinctive, innovative, and individualized approach to learning. Lynn has a remarkably international and diverse community with 2,400 students, representing forty states and eighty-four nations. Specialty programs include a Conservatory of Music, a School of Aeronautics, and the Institute for Achievement and Learning, which serves students with learning differences. Although grounded in liberal education, Lynn's programs are oriented toward emerging career opportunities, with an emphasis on real-world experience coupled with classroom study. The 16:1 student/faculty ratio provides a personalized environment with small classes and an innovative curriculum.

> ACCESS Open Houses and Campus Tours

Lynn University hosts five open houses per year; all programs are open to all interested students. Open houses give students an opportunity to meet the deans and degree program coordinators and talk to financial aid counselors. Campus tours are a great way for students to get a full taste of college life by eating lunch in the cafeteria and sitting in on a class. After the tour, admissions counselors are available to answer questions, address concerns and conduct an informational interview.

> OPPORTUNITY Lynn Scholarships and Financial Aid

Don't let cost prevent you from obtaining the college education of your dreams. Scholarships, grants, loans and other forms of financial assistance can make Lynn education more affordable than you ever imagined. In fact, for more than 62 percent of Lynn students receive some form of financial aid. Academic scholarships in the range from $6,000 to $12,000 are awarded on the basis of test scores and high school grades, in addition to need-based aid. A financial aid calculator is available on Lynn's website.

> ***"Almost every single person I've met at Lynn is on financial aid. I am paying for school myself, and it's not rare here that students depend on some sort of aid to attend the school. The value of this place is just so entirely worth it. I wouldn't have gone anywhere else."***
>
> *– Jordan A., '12*
> *Hunterdon, NJ*
> *Film Major*

> SUCCESS Institute for Achievement and Learning

The Institute for Achievement and Learning is committed to the idea that each learner has a unique set of strengths and weaknesses and is dedicated to helping those individuals achieve their academic goals by maximizing the use of their strengths and minimizing the impact of their weaknesses. The Institute strives to help students understand their learning competencies and develop them during their time at the university. The Institute's current model incorporates services such as group and/or individual tutoring, specialized learning communities and group activities. Students are not only assisted in understanding specific course content but also, in each instance, strategies for planning, organizing and implementing their studies.

FAST FACTS

STUDENT PROFILE

# of degree-seeking undergraduates	1,786
% male/female	49/51
% African American	3
% American Indian or Alaska Native	<1
% Asian or Pacific Islander	<1
% Hispanic	7
% White	47
% International	15
% Pell grant recipients	17

First-generation and minority alumni Jose Durate '98, Owner, Taranta restaurant, Boston; Tifany North '94, '97, PhD '03, education consultant; Maria Carrera '03, TV producer, Univision, San Antonio; Delsa Bush, '01, Chief of Police, West Palm Beach; Brandon Ackerman, '09, Vice President, Solar17 and Motionbrite

ACADEMICS

full-time faculty	103
full-time minority faculty	24
student-faculty ratio	15:1
average class size	17
% first-year retention rate	58
% graduation rate (6 years)	35

Popular majors Business and Management, Biology, Communications, Psychology, Hospitality

CAMPUS LIFE

% live on campus	83

Multicultural student clubs and organizations Caribbean Club, Black Student Union, Organization of Latin American Students (OLAS), International Affairs Society, Just About Kids, Students for the Poor, Interfaith Council, Gay-Straight Alliance

Athletics NCAA Division II, Sunshine State Conference (SSC)

ADMISSIONS

# of applicants	2,454
% accepted	72
# of first-year students enrolled	477
SAT Critical Reading average	200-720
SAT Math average	200-800
SAT Writing average	n/a
ACT average	13-30
average HS GPA	2.8

Deadlines

regular decision	rolling
application fee	$35
fee waiver for applicants with financial need	yes

COST & AID

tuition	$30,200
room & board	$11,950
total need-based institutional scholarships/grants	n/a
% of students apply for need-based aid	68
% receiving need-based scholarship or grant aid	36
% receiving aid whose need was fully met	61
average aid package	$20,853
average student loan debt at graduation	$34,075

Saint Leo University

Saint Leo University
PO Box 6665, MC2008
Saint Leo, FL 33574-6665
Ph: (352) 588-8342
admissions@saintleo.edu
www.saintleo.edu

Founded in 1889, Saint Leo University is Florida's oldest Catholic college and prides itself on its reputation as an internationally respected university featuring the latest advances in learning and technology. The University was founded upon the Benedictine values of excellence, community, respect, personal development, responsible stewardship and integrity. Students become a part of a community that supports their efforts, respects their heritage, nurtures their talents, and takes pride in their achievements. With an average class size of nineteen, students receive personalized attention from and develop close relationships with highly qualified professors. As a result, Saint Leo continually graduates well-rounded, active learners who understand the importance of contributing to the communities in which they live and work.

ACCESS Admission Counseling

Saint Leo offers highly personalized, individual admission counseling for first-generation college, low-income, rural and/or minority students in the community. Admission counselors evaluate individual circumstances and provide information on relevant scholarship opportunities, other financial assistance, and the application and admission process. The Student Services team helps ease the transition from home to college life, while Residence Life and Counseling Services teams assist with residential and personal counseling. Academic Student Support Services helps provide assistance and tools for success, and Career Services provides support for job searches and career planning.

"What impressed me most about Saint Leo was my admissions counselor; she took time to learn about me and most importantly, she made my parents feel very comfortable even though they both speak little English."

– Maria A., '11
Kissimmee, FL

OPPORTUNITY Scholarship Opportunities

Saint Leo is committed to offering a quality education to students of all ethnic, racial and socio-economic backgrounds. Through initiatives such as our Goizueta Scholars program, Leadership scholarships and the Center for Student Opportunity scholarships, students from all backgrounds have additional opportunities to receive assistance with meeting their educational expenses. The majority of Saint Leo University students receive financial aid in the form of grants and scholarships that they are not required to pay back. SLU considers it essential that students be able to attend their institution no matter their financial situation.

SUCCESS Academic Student Support Services (SSS)

Academic Student Support Services provides tutoring for all Saint Leo students. They offer a group of professional and student tutors who work one on one with students to assist with writing, to clarify concepts, to help with time management and other student skills. These are important areas of development for all students, but particularly for first generation students, whether they are low income, minority or rural. SLU has also begun a new mentor program for students who need coaching in executive functioning skills. The mentor is a specifically trained upper class student who meets with students one on one to help with time management, prioritizing, and other decision making skills. This can assist students to make a smoother transition from high school to college.

FAST FACTS

STUDENT PROFILE	
# of degree-seeking undergraduates	1,862
% male/female	48/52
% African American	12.8
% American Indian or Alaska Native	<1
% Asian or Pacific Islander	1.7
% Hispanic	15.9
% White	69
% International	n/a
% Pell grant recipients	31
ACADEMICS	
full-time faculty	114
full-time minority faculty	n/a
student-faculty ratio	14:1
average class size	19
% first-year retention rate	69
% graduation rate (6 years)	43

Popular majors Biology/Pre-Med, Business Administration, Criminal Justice, Education, Psychology

CAMPUS LIFE

% live on campus (% freshmen)	65 (n/a)

Multicultural student clubs and organizations Asian Culture Society, Caribbean Student Association, Goizueta Scholars, Haitian Education Project Club Intercultural Student Association, Mi Familia

Athletics NCAA Division II, Sunshine State Conference (SSC)

ADMISSIONS	
# of applicants	2,241
% accepted	73
# of first-year students enrolled	539
SAT Critical Reading (middle 50%)	400-740
SAT Math (middle 50%)	380-760
SAT Writing (middle 50%)	360-680
ACT (middle 50%)	18-32
average HS GPA	3.32
Deadlines	
regular decision	rolling
priority deadlines	3/1 (Fall); 12/1 (Spring)
application fee (online)	$35 ($0)
fee waiver for applicants with financial need	n/a
COST & AID	
tuition	$18,200
room & board	$9,120
total need-based institutional scholarships/grants	n/a
% of students apply for need-based aid	n/a
% of students receive aid	n/a
% receiving need-based scholarship or grant aid	94
% receiving aid whose need was fully met	n/a
average aid package	n/a
average student loan debt upon graduation	n/a

University of Florida

The University of Florida is a leading research institution and is ranked in the top 20 of U.S. public universities. Prestigious rankings are the result of quality education that promotes excellence and respect for diverse ideas, thoughts and perspectives. The University of Florida is committed to enrolling a community of learners, leaders and thinkers who want to leave their mark on the world. UF is the oldest and largest of Florida's 11 universities.

University of Florida
201 Criser, Box 114000
Gainesville, FL 32611-4000
Ph: (352)392-1365
freshman@ufl.edu
www.admissions.ufl.edu

ACCESS Upward Bound

Upward Bound at UF is a year-round program consisting of an intensive six week Summer Session and the Fall-Spring Academic Year. During the summer, students live on campus, enroll in college prep classes, and participate in educational, cultural, and other youth development activities. The Fall and Spring Sessions offer tutoring, workshops, counseling, and other support services. Upward Bound staff members work with each student to develop and implement an Individualized Educational Plan (IEP) according to the student's needs, potential, interests, and goals.

ACCESS UF Alliance

UF Alliance is a partnership between the University of Florida and select urban schools in the State of Florida. The program enhances college access for historically underrepresented urban youth by providing outreach/awareness activities; parental involvement strategies; cultural responsive teaching and learning; professional development of teachers and administrators, and high school reform initiatives.

"Being a Florida Opportunity Scholar in addition to serving as an FOS Mentor has allowed me to see the complexity and importance of the FOS program. I am honored to be part of a program that gives an opportunity to those individuals who are more than qualified to attend the University of Florida yet struggle to meet the financial obligations of attending the University."

– Beatriz H., '12
Miami, FL
Family Youth and Community Sciences and Political Science

ACCESS UF Shadow Days

UF's Shadow Day programs invite high-achieving high school seniors to come to UF for a day to 'shadow' a UF student and learn about educational opportunities and student life at the university. Shadow Day lets students experience for themselves what it is like to be a college student at UF. Students have the opportunity to attend UF classes and see all of what campus has to offer.

ACCESS Student Recruitment Conferences

These conferences provided the opportunity for 7th-11th Graders and their parents to learn more about admission requirements, student life at UF, leadership development opportunities, community resources and mentoring. Students participate in strategic academic preparation workshops based on grade level, financial aid and scholarship planning workshops and a University of Florida college fair.

SUCCESS Florida Opportunity Scholars Program

The Florida Opportunity Scholars Program is an initiative to ensure first-generation Florida residents students from economically disadvantaged backgrounds have the resources they need to be academically successful at the University of Florida. The goal of the program is to retain these students and have them graduate at rates equal to or greater than the undergraduate population at large.

FAST FACTS

STUDENT PROFILE

# of degree-seeking undergraduates	32,660
% male/female	45/55
% African American	9
% American Indian or Alaska Native	1
% Asian or Pacific Islander	8
% Hispanic	17
% White	59
% International	1
% Pell grant recipients	32

First-generation and minority alumni William "Willie" George Allen, '62, Law Office of W. George Allen; Hon. Stephan P. Mickle, '65 BA, '66 M. Ed., '70 JD, U.S. District Court Judge; Emmitt Smith, '96, President, SmithCypress and former Dallas Cowboy; Dr. Nils J. Diaz, '64 MS, '69 PhD, former Chairman, Nuclear Regulatory Commission; Dr. Pedro Jose "Joe" Greer, '78, Chair of Department of Humanities, Florida International University, and recipient of the Presidential Medal of Freedom

ACADEMICS

full-time faculty	3,416
full-time minority faculty	846
student-faculty ratio	20.5:1
average class size	30
% first-year retention rate	96
% graduation rate (6 years)	85

Popular majors Finance, Political Science, Psychology, Engineering, Biology

CAMPUS LIFE

% live on campus (% freshmen)	23 (87)

Multicultural student clubs and organizations Asian American Student Union, Black Student Union, Hispanic Student Organization, Islam on Campus, Jewish Student Union

Athletics NCAA Division I, Southeastern Conference (SEC)

ADMISSIONS

# of applicants	28,000
% accepted	41
# of first-year students enrolled	6,381
SAT Critical Reading (middle 50%)	590-690
SAT Math (middle 50%)	610-700
SAT Writing (middle 50%)	580-690
ACT (middle 50%)	28-32
average HS GPA	4.3

Deadlines

regular decision	11/1
application fee (online)	$30 ($30)
fee waiver for applicants with financial need	yes

COST & AID

tuition	in-state: $5,044; out-of-state: $27,321
room & board	$8,640
total need-based institutional scholarships/grants	$78,304,600
% of students apply for need-based aid	55
% receiving need-based scholarship or grant aid	31
% receiving aid whose need was fully met	14
average aid package	$13,387
average student loan debt upon graduation	$16,013

University of South Florida

University of South Florida
4202 East Fowler Avenue, SVC 1036
Tampa, FL 33620
Ph: (813) 974-3350
admissions@usf.edu
www.usf.edu/admissions

One of Florida's top three research universities, University of South Florida provides a dynamic and diverse learning environment that inspires innovation, creativity and collaboration. Academics are anchored by distinguished faculty and supported by cutting-edge facilities and technology. From biochemistry to ballet, economics to engineering, USF's extensive range of disciplines enables students to discover their passions. In 2009, Diverse Issues in Higher Education ranked USF 26th overall among the nation's leading colleges and universities for awarding bachelor's degrees to Black, Asian American, Hispanic and Native American students. USF students are engaged in their disciplines through internships, research opportunities, study abroad, work and community service experiences.

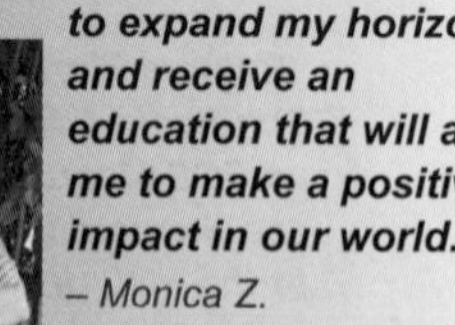

"The University of South Florida gave me a tremendous opportunity to expand my horizons and receive an education that will allow me to make a positive impact in our world."
– Monica Z.

ACCESS **Stampede to Success**

Held biannually in the fall and in the spring, Stampede to Success is an event for prospective students. Included is information specifically for those who will be the first generation in their family to graduate from college. By attending Stampede to Success students and their families will be introduced to many aspects of USF and the college selection process, including the admissions process, programs that support student success, the financial aid application process, and scholarship opportunities.

OPPORTUNITY **History of Achievement Award**

The University of South Florida's History of Achievement Award recognizes select students who have achieved above average academic records in high school while facing significant socioeconomic, educational, cultural or personal challenges. This award may be offered in combination with other university scholarships.

OPPORTUNITY **Freshman Summer Programs**

If you are in the first generation of your family to attend college, or from a family with limited income, you may be considered for placement in one of USF's Summer Success Programs: Student Support Services or Freshman Summer Institute. These residential summer programs provide college survival seminars, social and cultural enrichment programs, as well as activities designed to broaden career perspectives and promote self-confidence. Summer program students also enjoy personalized academic advising, tutorial support, mentoring opportunities, as well as enhanced financial aid assistance.

SUCCESS **Office of Student Success**

The goal of the Office of Student Success at University of South Florida is to create a learning environment in which students can gain the skills and knowledge necessary to be successful in college and in their future careers. The office recruits students, supports them with scholarships, and gives them the support and encouragement necessary for success. The office also coordinates campus-wide events through the Student Success Council to enrich the students' learning environment.

FAST FACTS

STUDENT PROFILE

# of degree-seeking undergraduates	30,285
% male/female	44/56
% African American	11.8
% American Indian	<1
% Asian	6.5
% Hispanic	15.8
% White	62.9
% International	4
% Pell grant recipients	38

First-generation and minority alumni Chucky Atkins, professional basketball player; Mark Consuelos, actor; Frank Davis, professional football player; Emilio Gonzalez, director, United States Citizenship and Immigration Services; Kenyatta Jones, professional football player; Kawika Mitchell, professional football player; Anthony Henry, professional football player; Roy Wegerle, professional soccer player

ACADEMICS

full-time faculty	1,578
student-faculty ratio	27:1
average class size	33
% first-year retention rate	88
% graduation rate (6 years)	51

Popular majors Pre-Medical Sciences, Engineering, Pre-Business Administration, Psychology, Biology

CAMPUS LIFE

% live on campus (% freshmen)	14 (64)

Multicultural student clubs and organizations Africana Students Association, American. Minority. Inspriring. Genuine. Overall. Success (AMIGOS), Black Student Union, Caribbean Cultural Exchange, Club Creole, Cuban American Student Association, Dominican American Student Association, Gospel Choir@USF, Latin American Student Association, Mexican American Student Association, Pride Alliance, Progressive Black Men, Student Support Services Club, Student Veterans Association, National Society of Black Engineers, National Association of Black Accountants, Inc., Latin American Medical Student Association, Hispanic Business Student Association

Athletics NCAA Division I, Big East Athletics (BigEast)

ADMISSIONS

# of applicants	26,366
% accepted	45
# of first-year students enrolled	4,604
SAT Critical Reading (middle 50%)	540-640
SAT Math (middle 50%)	530-630
SAT Writing (middle 50%)	490-580
ACT (middle 50%)	23-28
average HS GPA	3.81

Deadlines

application deadline	3/1
final Application deadline	4/15
application fee	$30
fee waiver for applicants with financial need	yes

COST & AID

tuition	in-state $5,800; out-of state $14,990
room & board	$9,190
total need-based institutional scholarships/grants	$5,931,218
% of students apply for need-based aid	75
% receiving need-based scholarship or grant aid	50
% receiving aid whose need was fully met	4
average aid package	$9,374
average student loan debt upon graduation	$21,679

Emory University

One of Emory University's greatest strengths lies in the diversity of students, faculty, and staff. Collectively they value difference, believing the intellectual and social energy that stems from varied voices and perspectives is one of their best assets. The richness of Emory's diversity extends beyond socio-economic background, race, ethnicity, religion, sexual orientation, gender, ableness, and national origin to include a wide range of activities, intellectual pursuits, beliefs, perspectives, political affiliations, and the like. The multiplicity of organizations, events, and programming here means that you'll be able to explore, take risks, and discover the unique identity only you possess. Whatever your interests, background, or values, at Emory you'll find a diverse group of people to share them with.

ACCESS **Éxito Emory**

Éxito Emory is a program for Latino/Hispanic high school students in the Atlanta area. Students are invited to campus to learn about the college admission process. Participants tour campus and meet with several of Emory's Latino/Hispanic student leaders, faculty, and staff members. Éxito Emory 2012 will be held on Saturday, October 1st.

"Being a QuestBridge Scholar has drastically reduced the financial burden of being a college student. I'm really grateful for the opportunity of attending such a university at such a low cost. Emory offers everything I was looking for: a well-respected institution, competitive peers, small class sizes, impressive faculty and staff, a beautiful campus and a great city."

– Ruth C., '12
Donna, TX
Neuroscience and Behavioral Biology

OPPORTUNITY **Essence of Emory**

Essence of Emory is an event specifically for Black/African American and Latino/Hispanic students who have been admitted to Emory. This program allows students to experience Emory University firsthand and to meet current students, faculty, and administrators prior to making a decision about enrolling at Emory. Students spend three nights in one of Emory's residence halls, attend classes, eat in the dining hall, explore the beautiful campus, and have the chance to meet with members of various multicultural groups.

OPPORTUNITY **QuestBridge**

Emory is a Partner College with the QuestBridge program, which helps low-income high school seniors gain admission and full four-year scholarships to colleges like Emory. Students matched with Emory through the QuestBridge program are awarded with scholarships that cover full tuition, fees, room, and board.

SUCCESS **MORE Mentoring Program**

The Multicultural Outreach and Resources at Emory (MORE) Mentoring Program assists first-year students with the social and academic transition to Emory through one-on-one mentoring relationships with upperclassmen. The organization also engages in a number of group activities including the Fall Carnival and other social and academic-related programs.

SUCCESS **Emory Crossroads Retreat**

The Emory Crossroads Retreat is held for incoming freshmen of any racial or ethnic background one week prior to their arrival on Emory's campus. Participants praise the program for easing the transition into college, creating lasting friendships, and providing a memorable experience through a ropes course, community building games, and story circles.

SUCCESS **Multicultural Council**

The Multicultural Council seeks to foster collaboration amongst and within all undergraduate student organizations on campus. By fostering interaction between diverse groups, the Council hopes that its members collaborate effectively and learn to appreciate people whose race, sexual identity, religion, ethnicity, and interests may be different from his or her own.

Emory University
Office of Undergraduate Admission - Emory College
1390 Oxford Rd NE, 3rd Floor
Atlanta, GA 30322
Ph: (800) 727-6036
admiss@emory.edu
www.emory.edu

FAST FACTS

STUDENT PROFILE

# of degree-seeking undergraduates	7,130
% male/female	45/55
% African American	10
% American Indian or Alaska Native	<1
% Asian or Pacific Islander	23
% Hispanic	4
% White	42
% International	11
% Pell grant recipients	23

First-generation and minority alumni Glenda Hatchett, Judge Hatchett television courtroom show; Michael Lomax, President and CEO of the United Negro College Fund; Patricia Lottier, co-owner and publisher, The Atlanta Tribune; James B. O'Neal, Attorney and founder, Legal Outreach (Harlem); Leah Ward Sears, former Chief Justice of the Supreme Court of the State of Georgia; Sanford D. Bishop, Jr., Current U.S. Congressman; Deborah Sawyer, Founder, President, and CEO of Environmental Design International

ACADEMICS

full-time faculty	1,271
full-time minority faculty	264
student-faculty ratio	7:1
average class size	19
% first-year retention rate	94
% graduation rate (6 years)	88

Popular majors Business/Economics, Biology, Political Science, Psychology, Neuroscience and Behavioral Biology

CAMPUS LIFE

% live on campus (% freshmen)	68 (99)

Multicultural student clubs and organizations African Student Association, All Mixed Up, Black Student Alliance, Brotherhood of Afrocentric Men, Indian Cultural Exchange, International Association, Latino Student Organization, Multicultural Council, Multicultural Yearbook, Students in Alliance for Asian American Concerns

Athletics NCAA Division III, University Athletic Association (UAA)

ADMISSIONS

# of applicants	15,550
% accepted	28
# of first-year students enrolled	1,336
SAT Critical Reading (middle 50%)	640-740
SAT Math (middle 50%)	670-760
SAT Writing (middle 50%)	650-740
ACT (middle 50%)	30-33
average HS GPA	3.84
Deadlines	
regular decision	1/15
application fee (online)	$35 ($35)
fee waiver for applicants with financial need	yes

COST & AID

tuition	$38,600
room & board	$11,198
total need-based institutional scholarships/grants	$87,488,050
% of students apply for need-based aid	52
% of students receive aid	47
% receiving need-based scholarship or grant aid	45
% receiving aid whose need was fully met	100
average aid package	$34,853
average student loan debt upon graduation	$26,311

Georgia College

As a public liberal arts university, Georgia College provides an alternative to a large, one-size-fits-all state school. At Georgia College, students benefit from smaller classes and a strong liberal arts foundation. In addition to participating in social events on campus, many students take advantage of the GIVE Center, which is the university's clearinghouse for volunteerism. Just beyond the campus, students can enjoy the small, historically significant town of Milledgeville.

ACCESS **GLIMPSE Day and GLIMPSE Shadow Day**

The GLIMPSE Day is a program for minority juniors and seniors. During GLIMPSE Day you will visit campus with your high school classmates. You'll tour campus, spend time with current students and professors and learn about the application and financial aid process. During GLIMPSE Shadow Day you'll be matched up with current students. You'll attend classes with them, grab lunch in The Max, hear insights from a panel of current students and check out Georgia College's multicultural student organizations.

OPPORTUNITY **GLIMPSE Weekend**

The GLIMPSE Weekend is a program for admitted minority seniors. You'll get the inside scoop on classes, academic advising and residence hall living. You'll also eat in The Max, have a mini seminar with a professor, take part in a team-building activity and head to the Den (our student lounge) for a social event.

"From the moment I set foot on campus, I knew this was the place for me. It is beautiful, but what really made the difference for me were the people. Both students and faculty go out of their way to be friendly – it's as though a new friend appears wherever you walk. That, plus small class sizes, more than 200 student organizations and the conscious efforts of the university to promote diversity of all kinds is why I chose Georgia College. This university has done more for me than I ever could have imagined."

– James B., '13
Augusta, GA
Political Science

OPPORTUNITY **The Goizueta Scholarship**

Georgia College and the Goizueta Foundation are pleased to announce the Goizueta Foundation Scholarship. This is a great opportunity for admitted freshmen to receive financial support with tuition, fees, books and other expenses related to the cost of education. Students must maintain a 3.0 GPA and have financial need as determined by the Georgia College Office of Financial Aid.

SUCCESS **Student Oriented Activities and Resources (SOAR)**

SOAR matches incoming minority students with student mentors to help make sure that they have a smooth transition into our university and that they are successful while they are here. We understand that mentorship is important in every phase of life, so we match student mentors with professional mentors from faculty or staff. Participants in the SOAR program get the opportunity to give back to the community through another phase of mentorship with high school students in the High Achievers Program. Students receive advising and guidance in major and career selection, and assistance in course registration.

SUCCESS **Mentoring African-Americans for Leadership and Education (MALE Connect Program)**

The MALE Connect Program aims to support the recruitment, retention and graduation of Black males at Georgia College through ongoing mentorship, academic workshops, leadership development, civic engagement, networking and positive reinforcement. This program endeavors to provide as much support as possible to offset the issues they face as an underrepresented demographic.

Georgia College
Campus Box 23
Milledgeville, GA 31061-0490
Ph: (800) 342-0471 / (478) 445-2774
info@gcsu.edu
www.gcsu.edu

FAST FACTS

STUDENT PROFILE	
# of degree-seeking undergraduates	5,715
% male/female	n/a
% African American	7.7
% American Indian or Alaska Native	0.2
% Asian or Pacific Islander	1.6
% Hispanic	4
% White	83
% International	n/a
% Pell grant recipients	16
ACADEMICS	
full-time faculty	316
full-time minority faculty	n/a
student-faculty ratio	17:1
average class size	25
% first-year retention rate	85
% graduation rate (6 years)	49
Popular majors Business Administration/ Management, Nursing, Psychology, Biology, Mass Communication	
CAMPUS LIFE	
% live on campus (% freshmen)	36 (99)
Multicultural student clubs and organizations Black Student Alliance, International Club, Pride Alliance, Art As An Agent for Change, Latino Student Association, Salsa and Latin Dance Club, Minority Association of Pre-Medical Students (MAPS), Hispanic Scholarship Scholars Network, Multicultural Fraternity and Sorority, Historically African-American Sororities and Fraternities	
Athletics NCAA Division II, Peach Belt Conference (PBC)	
ADMISSIONS	
# of applicants	4,122
% accepted	61
# of first-year students enrolled	1,159
SAT Critical Reading (middle 50%)	520-600
SAT Math (middle 50%)	510-600
SAT Writing (middle 50%)	510-590
ACT (middle 50%)	23-27
average HS GPA	3.5
Deadlines	
early admission (non-binding)	11/1
regular admission	1/1 - 4/1
application fee	$35
fee waiver for applicants with financial need	yes
COST & AID	
tuition	in-state: $6,472; out-of-state: $24,021
room & board	$9,530
total need-based institutional scholarships/grants	n/a
% of students apply for need-based aid	90
% of students receive aid	37
% receiving need-based scholarship or grant aid	41
% receiving aid whose need was fully met	<1
average aid package	$6,585
average student loan debt upon graduation	$14,312

Georgia State University

Georgia State University
PO Box 4009
Atlanta, GA 30302-4009
Ph: (404) 413-2580
admissions@gsu.edu
www.gsu.edu/admissions/apply.html

Georgia State University is one of the premiere public research institutions in the country. Located in vibrant downtown Atlanta, Georgia State has the most diverse student body in the Southeast. Georgia State students come from every state in the nation and over 160 countries. The 2010 Report of the Education Trust ranked Georgia State as top in the nation in both access and success for minority and low income students, crediting Georgia State with the fastest rising graduation rates for minority students nationwide. *Forbes* magazine ranks Georgia State #2 in Georgia and #63 in the nation for overall student satisfaction with their classes, the affordability of education, and student job placement after graduation. GSU offers over 200 different academic programs, with a student-faculty ratio of 20 to 1.

OPPORTUNITY **Hispanic Scholarship Fund Scholar Chapter at Georgia State**

The Scholar Chapter is a student group committed to promoting Latino/a student success in support of HSF's mission. The Scholar Chapter provides programming and opportunities for Latino/a students on campus to concentrate on developing the academic, pre-professional, leadership and social skills necessary for graduation and beyond.

OPPORTUNITY **The Goizueta Foundation Scholars Fund Award**

Students eligible for this award include those for whom Spanish is a first language or who demonstrate a strong interest in and familiarity with Latino/Hispanic culture through participation in Latino/Hispanic community activities. Scholarships are awarded based on academic merit, service, and financial need.

"Georgia State has offered me an excellent opportunity. I received a full ride scholarship through the Goizueta Fund at GSU, which allowed me to live on campus. With 200+ student organizations, I transitioned easily into college life and my network grew instantaneously. I've had amazing advisors and mentors throughout my time here, and I have in turn chosen to mentor Latino high school students and steer them towards the path to college and scholarship."

– Grace M., Jr, Omaha, AL Sociology

OPPORTUNITY **The Office of African-American Student Services and Programs (OAASS&P)**

OAASS&P's mission is to promote quality services and programs related to the retention, progression and graduation of African-American students at Georgia State by advocating for academic success, degree attainment, cultural awareness, civic awareness and co-curricular involvement.

SUCCESS **Freshman Learning Communities**

Freshman Learning Communities provide the opportunity for students to make a smooth transition from high school to university life and culture. Participating incoming freshmen are placed with 24 other students who take 5 classes that center around an academic theme. Freshman Learning Communities enable students to make immediate connections to other students, faculty, campus and Atlanta communities. Past participating students have had higher success rates in GPA, retention and time it takes to graduate.

FAST FACTS

STUDENT PROFILE

# of degree-seeking undergraduates	22,790
% male/female	40/60
% African American	36
% American Indian or Alaska Native	1
% Asian or Pacific Islander	11
% Hispanic	8
% White	38
% International	2
% Pell grant recipients	43

ACADEMICS

full-time faculty	1,127
full-time minority faculty	268
student-faculty ratio	20:1
average class size	23.5
% first-year retention rate	85
% graduation rate (6 years)	48

Popular majors Biological Sciences, Psychology, Accounting, Marketing, Nursing, Early Childhood Ed, Finance

CAMPUS LIFE

% live on campus	14

Multicultural student clubs and organizations African American Student Services and Programs, African Student Association, Arab Society Latin American Student Association (LASA), Latino Leadership Council, Latino Student Support and Outreach, Multicultural Greek Council, Black Student Alliance

Athletics NCAA Division I, Colonial Athletic Association (CAA)

ADMISSIONS

# of applicants	12,094
% accepted	53
# of first-year students enrolled	2,864
SAT Critical Reading (middle 50%)	510-600
SAT Math (middle 50%)	500-610
SAT Writing (middle 50%)	n/a
ACT (middle 50%)	22-27
average HS GPA	3.41

Deadlines

early decision	11/1
priority decision	2/1
regular decision	3/1
application fee (online)	$60 ($60)
fee waiver for applicants with financial need	yes

COST & AID

tuition	in-state: $7,080; out-of-state: $25,280
room & board	$11,370
total need-based institutional scholarships/grants	$160,610
% of students apply for need-based aid	71
% receiving need-based scholarship or grant aid	70
% receiving aid whose need was fully met	12
average aid package	$9,356
average student loan debt upon graduation	$18,958

Morehouse College

Founded in 1867, Morehouse College is the nation's only private, historically black, four-year liberal arts college for men. The mission of Morehouse College is to develop men with disciplined minds who lead lives of leadership and service. The college recognizes this mission by emphasizing the intellectual and character development of all of its students. Additionally, the college assumes special responsibility for teaching the history and culture of black people. As such, the college seeks students who are willing to carry the torch of excellence and who are willing to pay the price of gaining strength and confidence by confronting adversity, mastering their fears and achieving success by earning it.

ACCESS **Upward Bound Math/Science State Center**

The Morehouse College Upward Bound Math/Science State Center provides an intensive six-week summer curriculum to currently enrolled high school sophomores and juniors throughout the state of Georgia. This program assists students to develop critical thinking, scientific, analytical and language-arts skills. Students are given the opportunity to work in various laboratories and receive hands-on computer experience and exposure to a variety of science, math and engineering careers. Conducting research at various lab sites throughout southeast Georgia, students take classes in mathematics, technical writing, two sciences (including a laboratory science) and a foreign language. Applicants to the program must be first-generation and/or low-income students.

OPPORTUNITY **Prospective Student Seminar (PSS)**

Morehouse College's Prospective Student Seminar is an event designed for high school seniors to experience life at Morehouse in a unique way. During the three-day special event, prospective parents and students visit the college campus and have the opportunity to participate in panel discussions with departments such as admissions, financial aid, residential life and other student service departments. Other PSS activities include tours of the Atlanta University Center (the campuses surrounding Morehouse College), a tour of a dormitory room, class observation, academic concentration fairs for students and parents, one-on-one interaction with faculty, a historical Atlanta city tour and a visit to Atlanta's newest metropolitan center, Atlantic Station.

SUCCESS **Peer Mentoring**

To support students, Morehouse College sponsors a peer mentoring program. Upon arriving at the college, freshmen are assigned to a mentor group leader. The mentor group leader meets weekly with the mentee(s) in an individual and group setting. Upperclassmen may also participate in mentor groups to provide support and input. At the end of each semester, peer mentor group leaders host a social event for the mentor group to celebrate the end of the semester. The freshmen mentor groups are encouraged to complete community service projects together.

SUCCESS **Office of Student Support Services**

To increase the college's retention rate and promote the growth and development of an institutional climate supportive of the success of program participants, Morehouse College houses the Office of Student Support Services. Funded by the U.S. Department of Education, the program provides an interconnected series of academic support services, including study skills development, peer tutoring and counseling, both for academic and personal reasons. The office seeks to provide students with academic, cultural and career-oriented activities designed to support academic life at Morehouse College while fostering healthy intellectual, social and moral development during the student's college experience.

Morehouse College
830 Westview Drive, SW
Atlanta, GA 30314
Ph: (404) 681-2800 x2632
admissions@morehouse.edu
www.morehouse.edu

FAST FACTS

STUDENT PROFILE

# of degree-seeking undergraduates	2,796
% male/female	100/0
% African American	96
% American Indian or Alaska Native	<1
% Asian or Pacific Islander	<1
% Hispanic	<1
% White	<1
% International	2.4
% Pell grant recipients	36.4

First-generation and minority alumni Dr. Martin Luther King, Jr., Nobel Laureate and civil rights leader; Spike Lee, Academy Award nominated and acclaimed filmmaker; Mordecai Wyatt Johnson, first African American president of Howard University; Julian Bond, Executive Director of the NAACP; Calvin O. Butts, III, Pastor of Abyssinian Baptist Church; Michael Lomax, Executive Director of the UNCF; James Nabrit, U.S. Ambassador to the United Nations; Edwin Moses, Olympic champion and professional track and field athlete; Sanford Bishop, United States congressman; Samuel L. Jackson, Academy Award nominated actor

ACADEMICS

full-time faculty	164
average class size	14
student-faculty ratio	15:1
% first-year retention rate	85
% graduation rate (6 years)	67

Popular majors Business Administration/ Economics, Political Science, Biology, Engineering, Religion/Philosophy, Psychology

CAMPUS LIFE

% live on campus (% freshmen)	n/a

Multicultural student clubs and organizations National Society of Black Engineers, Morehouse College Executive Lecture Series, Black Scholars Association, NAACP, International Student Organization

Athletics NCAA Division II, Southern Intercollegiate Athletic Conference (SIAC)

ADMISSIONS

# of applicants	2,264
% accepted	64
# of first-year students enrolled	904
SAT Critical Reading (middle 50%)	470-580
SAT Math (middle 50%)	450-560
ACT (middle 50%)	19-24
average HS GPA	3.2
Deadlines	
early action	12/15
regular decision	2/15
application fee (online)	$45 ($45)
fee waiver for applicants with financial need	yes

COST & AID

tuition	$21,618
room & board	$11,494
total need-based institutional scholarships/grants	n/a
% of students apply for need-based aid	95
% of students receive aid	96.7
% receiving need-based scholarship or grant aid	42.1
% receiving aid whose need was fully met	2.2
average aid package	$11,054
average student loan debt upon graduation	$18,000

Spelman College

As a historically black college for women that dates back to the late 1800s, Spelman enjoys a world-wide reputation enhanced by its many centers of distinction, including the Women's Research and Resource Center, the first of its kind on a black campus, and the Center for Leadership Development and Civic Engagement. Spelman also benefits from its high-caliber professors, including endowed chairs and a small faculty-to-student ratio.

> ACCESS **Early College Summer Program and the College Prep Institute**

Qualified high school girls are invited to participate in these programs designed to prepare them for the college experience. Offered are math and English courses for college credit, leadership and personal development seminars and cultural activities, just to name a few.

> OPPORTUNITY **Research, Scholarships and Access**

Whether aspiring writers or future NASA engineers, Spelman has research and scholarship opportunities to support its students' interests. The college's Bonner, Women in Science and Engineering (WISE), Smith and Flanigan scholarship programs are just a few of the initiatives to support the future leaders of the world who come through Spelman. Interested high school seniors are welcome to attend our Open House program "A Day in Your Life at Spelman College" offered twice in the fall semester. "A Day in Your Life" provides prospective students and their families with a comprehensive look at the Spelman College experience.

> SUCCESS **Peer Tutoring Program / Freshman Success Program**

Students of all majors can take advantage of Spelman's peer-tutoring program, which provides College Reading and Language Association (C.R.L.A.)-certified peer tutors to help students with study techniques, content-area reading, note-taking and test strategies. Students pursuing science, technology, engineering and mathematics (STEM) majors benefit from the Freshman Success Program, which provides support and academic assistance for freshmen and a small group of sophomores whose studies are in these areas. Program support services include an orientation for incoming STEM majors, workshops in time management and textbook mastery and tutoring sessions for sophomores.

> ***"As a first-generation college student, Spelman College provides opportunities that I never thought I would have a chance to be exposed to. What I admire the most is how Spelman encourages us to become agents of change in our communities. I have been given the opportunity to really make an impact."***
>
> *– Brittaney B., '11*
> *Atlanta, GA*
> *Sociology, Public Health*

> SUCCESS **African Diaspora in the World (ADW)**

As a two-semester, interdisciplinary course, ADW provides a formal introduction to the background and culture of Spelman students. The course explores such essential issues as identity and values, and it seeks to reinforce those beliefs that are integral to the college's Statement of Purpose, especially in its institutional goals and behavioral expectations. This required, first-year course is designed to develop students' critical reflection skills as they examine contemporary political, economic, and social issues through the lens of the African Diaspora.

Spelman College
350 Spelman Lane
Atlanta, GA 30314
Ph: (800) 982-2411
admiss@spelman.edu
www.spelman.edu

FAST FACTS

STUDENT PROFILE

# of degree-seeking undergraduates	2,177
% male/female	0/100
% African American	88
% American Indian or Alaska Native	<1
% Asian or Pacific Islander	<1
% Hispanic	<1
% White	<1
% International	1
% Pell grant recipients	35.9

First-generation and minority alumni Marian Wright Edelman, founder, Children's Defense Fund; Marcelite J. Harris, first African-American female general, United States Air Force; Alberta Christine Williams King, mother of Dr. Martin Luther King, Jr.; Dr. Audrey Forbes Manley, former acting U.S. Surgeon General

ACADEMICS

full-time faculty	183
full-time minority faculty	n/a
student-faculty ratio	10:1
average class size	30
% first-year retention rate	88
% graduation rate (6 years)	73

Popular majors Biology, Psychology, Political Science, Economics, English

CAMPUS LIFE

% live on campus (% freshmen)	40 (99)

Multicultural student clubs and organizations International Student Organization, Caribbean American Student Association (CASA)

Athletics NCAA Division III, Great South Athletic Conference (GSAC)

ADMISSIONS

# of applicants	5,128
% accepted	39
# of first-year students enrolled	539
SAT Critical Reading (middle 50%)	480-560
SAT Math (middle 50%)	460-550
SAT Writing (middle 50%)	n/a
ACT (middle 50%)	20-24
average HS GPA	3.6
Deadlines	
early decision	11/1
early action	11/15
regular decision	2/1
application fee (online)	$35 ($25)
fee waiver for applicants with financial need	yes

COST & AID

tuition	$19,684
room & board	$10,986
total need-based institutional scholarships/grants	$8,490,917
% of students apply for need-based aid	95
% of students receive aid	81
% receiving need-based scholarship or grant aid	70
% receiving aid whose need was fully met	6
average aid package	$13,994
average student loan debt upon graduation	$17,500

Thomas University

Thomas University
1501 Millpond Road
Thomasville, Georgia, 31792
Ph: (800) 538-9784
admissions@thomasu.edu
www.thomasu.edu

Thomas University is a four-year co-educational university that serves the post-secondary educational needs of south Georgia and north Florida. The university is located in Thomasville, Georgia, a relatively small town of over 20,000 people in rural southwest Georgia. Thomas University provides quality education through a dynamic learning environment. Innovative models for reaching learners by our caring faculty and staff change the lives of students in our local, regional, and global communities. Offering associate's, bachelor's, and master's degrees, our highest goal is to provide an educational experience that explores and develops each student's full potential.

OPPORTUNITY Campus Visits

Prospective students are encouraged to come to campus for a guided tour and information session. Students of every ethnicity come from around the country and world. Campus tours are available from Monday through Friday.

> *"Thomas University gave me the tools and education to change my life and contribute to my community."*
> – Micky W.

OPPORTUNITY Thomas University General Endowed Scholarships

Numerous partial endowed scholarships are offered each year. Selections are made during the spring prior to the academic year in which the scholarship goes into effect. Scholarship awards are based on one or more of the following guidelines: academic performance, moral character, community or citizenship activities, financial need, and potential for benefiting from enrollment at Thomas University. Thomas University endowed scholarships can be applied to tuition, fees and books and are awarded only after all federal and state grants have been applied to a student's charges.

SUCCESS Success through Orientation Advising and Retention (SOAR)

During the pre-registration and regular registration periods, pre-professional advisors will be located in the Campus Center so that new students and those who have not completed the core curriculum can find advisors easily and receive advising efficiently. New entering freshmen will be paired with a SOAR advisor who will assist them in their transition to Thomas University and work with them to develop an academic plan tailored to fit their individual needs.

SUCCESS The Academic Resource Center (ARC)

ARC employs students who specialize in math or writing to meet with other students one-on-one in order to help them be successful in their studies. Students can set up an appointment to meet with a tutor for a one-hour session.

SUCCESS TRiO/Student Support Services (SSS)

The mission of the TRiO/Student Support Services initiative is for traditional and non-traditional, part-time and full time students, who are eligible, to achieve an undergraduate degree. It is a unique opportunity for first-generation, low-income students, and students with disabilities to complete a four-year education. The TRiO/SSS program is a student-focused center of excellence in academic advising, career exploration, disability services, mentoring, supplemental instruction, student development, and tutoring.

FAST FACTS

STUDENT PROFILE

# of degree-seeking undergraduates	835
% male/female	60/40
% African American	25
% American Indian or Alaska Native	1
% Asian or Pacific Islander	1
% Hispanic	1
% White	70
% International	5
% Pell grant recipients	52

ACADEMICS

full-time faculty	52
full-time minority faculty	1
student-faculty ratio	10:1
average class size	15
% first-year retention rate	n/a
% graduation rate (6 years)	n/a

Popular majors Business, Social Work, Criminal Justice, Film and Religious Studies

CAMPUS LIFE

% live on campus (% freshmen)	15

Multicultural student clubs and organizations Campus Activity Board(CAB). Honor Council. International Dinner Night

Athletics NAIA, Sun Conference

ADMISSIONS

# of applicants	1,320
% accepted	59
# of first-year students enrolled	n/a
Test ranges and decision dates	n/a
average HS GPA	n/a
priority processing dates	Spring semester 11/1, Summer semester 3/1, Fall semester 6/1
application fee (online)	$35 ($35)
fee waiver for applicants with financial need	n/a

COST & AID

tuition	$12,054
room & board	$4,054
total need-based institutional scholarships/grants	$1,135,942
% of students apply for need-based aid	90
% receiving need-based scholarship or grant aid	90
% receiving aid whose need was fully met	4
average aid package	$9,834
average student loan debt upon graduation	n/a

University of Georgia

University of Georgia
Office of Admissions Terrell Hall
Athens, GA 30602
Ph: (706) 542-8776
undergrad@admissions.uga.edu
www.admissions.uga.edu

The University of Georgia is America's first state chartered university. The university enrolls more than 33,000 undergraduate and graduate students from 50 states and 127 countries. UGA offers almost 170 majors and 500 student organizations. Athens is consistently rated as one of the best college towns in America. They have previously been ranked "Best Values" by *Money Magazine* and *U.S. News & World Report*. Through its programs and practices, UGA seeks to foster the understanding of and respect for cultural differences necessary for an enlightened and educated citizenry. It further provides for cultural, ethnic, gender and racial diversity in the faculty, staff and student body. The university is committed to preparing the university community to appreciate the critical importance of a quality environment to an interdependent global society.

ACCESS **Sígueme: Latino Shadow Day at UGA**

Sígueme is a one-day event hosted by the UGA student organization Students for Latino/a Empowerment that focuses on bringing Latino high school juniors and seniors from surrounding counties to the UGA campus to shadow a UGA student. Each Sígueme participant, based on their interests, is matched up with a current UGA student. Sígueme participants attend classes, eat at the dining halls, and take part in a campus tour and admissions workshop.

OPPORTUNITY **Padres e Hijos Fin de Semana**

The Parent-Student Bilingual UGA Weekend, known as Padres e Hijos, a program of the Fanning Institute, invites 25 highly academically competitive high school seniors and their parents to visit the University of Georgia. The weekend is an English/Spanish bilingual educational forum specially designed to welcome and encourage potential UGA applicants. Current Latino UGA students, parents, faculty, and alumni welcome the visitors and share their experiences. English/Spanish interpreters are available throughout the program.

"UGA is more than what you read in a pamphlet or on a website. By visiting campus and speaking with students, I was able see all that it could offer me and what I could do to make it my own."
– Jonathan J. '13
Decatur, Georgia
Biochemical Engineering

OPPORTUNITY **UGA Diversified**

This is a campus visitation program for high ability African American and Hispanic students and their families that have not gotten a chance to visit campus. The program includes campus tours, a student panel, workshops on housing, financial, and study abroad opportunities. In addition, students are given the chance to enjoy lunch in a campus dining hall as well as participate in a campus resources fair.

SUCCESS **Freshman College Experience**

Freshman College Experience is a unique summer program that streamlines a student's introduction to the collegiate environment. Students attend one of several introductory courses that fulfill core curriculum requirements, as well as in courses specifically designed to teach first-year students how to find and utilize the wealth of resources available at UGA. Enrollees are also granted early access to UGA housing. Freshman College participants are assigned rooms in Russell Hall that they will keep not only for the summer program but through the following academic year as well.

SUCCESS **Latinos Investing in the Students of Tomorrow (LISTo)**

LISTo is a peer-mentoring program that pairs upper class Latino/a students with first-year Latino/a students to provide a successful transition from high school to college and aid in the navigation of campus resources and leadership opportunities.

FAST FACTS

STUDENT PROFILE

# of degree-seeking undergraduates	25,201
% male/female	58/42
% African American	9
% American Indian or Alaska Native	1
% Asian or Pacific Islander	8.8
% Hispanic	5
% White	78
% International	3
% Pell grant recipients	9

First-generation and minority alumni Deborah Roberts, ABC news correspondent '82; Hines Ward of the NFL's Pittsburgh Steelers,'98; Natasha Trethewey, Pulitzer Prize-winning poet '89; Henry Cameron "Hadjii" Hand, creator of BET's first scripted series, *Somebodies*, '98

ACADEMICS

full-time faculty	1,751
full-time minority faculty	100
student-faculty ratio	18:1
average class size	33
% first-year retention rate	94
% graduation rate (6 years)	70

Popular majors Psychology, Public and International Affairs, Business, Biology, Pharmacy

CAMPUS LIFE

% live on campus (% freshmen)	n/a

Multicultural student clubs and organizations Pamoja Dance Ensemble, NAACP, Black Affairs Council, Indian Cultural Exchange, Latino Student Association

Athletics NCAA Division I, Southeastern Conference (SEC)

ADMISSIONS

# of applicants	18,062
% accepted	59
# of first-year students enrolled	4,800
SAT Critical Reading (middle 50%)	560-660
SAT Math (middle 50%)	570-670
SAT Writing (middle 50%)	570-660
ACT (middle 50%)	25-29
average HS GPA	3.8
Deadlines	
early decision	10/15
regular decision	1/15
application fee (online)	$60 ($60)
fee waiver for applicants with financial need	yes

COST & AID

tuition	in-state: $3,865; out-of-state: $12,970
room & board	$4,023
total need-based institutional scholarships/grants	$73,952,594
% of students apply for need-based aid	40
% receiving need-based scholarship or grant aid	34
% receiving aid whose need was fully met	30
average aid package	$9,509
average student loan debt upon graduation	$14,766

Chaminade University

Chaminade University
3140 Waialae Avenue
Honolulu, HI 96816
Ph: (800) 735-3733 / (808) 735-4711
admissions@chaminade.edu
www.chaminade.edu

Chaminade University, the only Catholic university in Hawaii, offers its students an education in a collaborative learning environment that prepares them for life, service and successful careers. Guided by its Catholic, Marianist and liberal arts educational traditions, Chaminade encourages the development of moral character, personal competencies, and a commitment to build a just and peaceful society. The University offers both the civic and church communities of the Pacific region its academic and intellectual resources in the pursuit of common aims.

> SUCCESS Summer Bridge

Summer Bridge is a mandatory program for students who have been accepted conditionally to Chaminade based on High School GPA and SAT/ACT scores. The program provides conditional students with the opportunity to take pre-college or first year level courses to prepare for their first semester in college. Students will also participate in Chaminade activities and familiarize themselves with the campus, staff, and faculty. Summer Bridge must be completed successfully with C's or better in order to enroll in the fall.

"When you are far away from home, it's good to have that wholesome feeling, to be with strangers who really make a difference in your life."

– Jenise T. '09
Saipan
Biology

> SUCCESS Academic Achievement Program (AAP)

The Academic Achievement Program is designed to assist eligible students in completing their academic goals. The AAP is a TRIO Student Support Services program, which seeks to increase retention and graduation rates for eligible students. They provide a variety of services that help students make the transition to college both academically and socially, including: tutoring, workshops, cultural events, grant aid, a laptop and media loan-out program, academic/personal advising, and preparation for graduate school exams.

> SUCCESS Multicultural Student Orientation Program

Chaminade is one of the most diverse in the U.S., and provides a model of multi-cultural interaction and understanding. The greater community of Honolulu provides another dimension of resources for cultural study and awareness. This degree program provides a background for those who would pursue specialized careers in human services, health services, planning, international relations, and education that require a knowledge of cultural diversity.

> SUCCESS Four Year Plans

The Academic Advising Office works closely with the registrar, deans, and faculty advisors to create semester schedules that work for every student. They publish four-year plans for every major so all students and advisors have a game plan.

FAST FACTS

STUDENT PROFILE	
# of degree-seeking undergraduates	1,030
% male/Female	31/69
% African American	4
% American Indian or Alaska Native	<1
% Asian American or Pacific Islander	66
% Hispanic	6
% White	18
% International	2
% Pell grant recipients	n/a
ACADEMICS	
full-time faculty	74
full-time minority faculty	n/a
student-faculty ratio	12:1
average class size	18
% first-year retention rate	75
% graduation rate	45
Popular majors Criminal Justice, Forensic Science, Business Administration	
CAMPUS LIFE	
% live on campus	29
Multicultural student clubs and organizations Diversity at Its Finest, Pacific Islander Club, Tahitian Club	
Athletics NCAA Division II, Pacific West Conference (PacWest)	
ADMISSIONS	
# of applicants	1,195
% accepted	90
# of first-year students enrolled	508
SAT Critical Reading (middle 50%)	430-510
SAT Math (middle 50%)	430-540
SAT Writing (middle 50%)	n/a
ACT (middle 50%)	18-24
average HS GPA	3.3
Deadlines	
regular decision	5/1
application fee (online)	$50 ($0)
fee waiver for applicants with financial need	no
COST & AID	
tuition	$18,300
room & board	$10,700
total need-based institutional scholarships/grants	$20,000,000
% of students apply for need-based aid	96
% receiving need-based scholarship or grant aid	74
% receiving aid whose need was fully met	14
average aid package	$12,846
average student loan debt upon graduation	$22,263

Columbia College Chicago

Columbia College Chicago
600 S. Michigan Avenue
Chicago, IL 60605
Ph: (312) 369-7130
admissions@colum.edu
www.colum.edu

The largest and most diverse private arts, media, and communication college in the nation, Columbia College Chicago has 120 academic programs and nearly 12,500 students. Columbia is an urban institution located in the heart of Chicago's Education Corridor, and its students reflect the economic, racial, cultural, and educational diversity of contemporary America. A Columbia education focuses on a strong liberal arts core and close interaction with a faculty of working artists and professionals. Columbia College allows students to begin work in their chosen fields in their freshman year and offers them extensive support in building and polishing their own portfolios. Columbia students are encouraged to treat the entire city of Chicago as an extended campus and a resource to further their academic and professional goals.

> ***"I come from kind of a diverse background growing up, so coming to Columbia was a great way to surround myself with that again. I was shy as a kid and coming here really gave me the chance to open up; I've made so many friends."***
>
> *– Branick G., '11*
> *Chicago, IL*
> *Film: Animation*

ACCESS **Community**

The Center for Community Arts Partnership, which has played an integral role at Columbia since 1998, oversees a variety of college-community partnerships in the arts. Two of its initiatives, Project AIM and Community Schools, are committed to building meaningful, sustainable partnerships by uniting the college, public schools, and the local community. It is through these unique relationships that all partners are able to create innovative arts programming that builds stronger schools and neighborhoods, and ultimately, better-educated students. Under the auspices of the Center for Community Arts Partnerships, Columbia College also offers a graduate concentration in Arts in Youth and Community Development.

OPPORTUNITY **High School Summer Institute**

Students who have completed at least their sophomore year of high school are eligible to participate in the High School Summer Institute, a five-week program geared toward students with an interest in the visual, media, performing, and communications arts. Participants not only get to work in Columbia's state-of-the-art labs, studios, concert halls, and theaters, but also receive training from the same professionals and scholars who teach at Columbia year round. Students can choose from programs in film & video production, television writing and production, radio, dance, theater, fiction and poetry writing, graphic arts, animation, fashion design, journalism, and others.

OPPORTUNITY **Scholarships**

Columbia offers a number of scholarships to both incoming and continuing students. Each of these scholarships are awarded based on their own set of criteria which may include some combination of financial need, academic achievement, and creative merit.

SUCCESS **Summer Bridge Program**

Applicants to Columbia College whose academic backgrounds have not adequately prepared them for college-level academics may be offered the chance to successfully complete the Summer Bridge Program before they are admitted to the College. During the program students have the opportunity to reinforce their academic skills through coursework, tutoring, counseling, enrichment activities, and access to all college facilities. The Bridge Program is free of charge.

FAST FACTS

STUDENT PROFILE	
# of degree-seeking undergraduates	11,400
% male/female	48/52
% African American	16
% American Indian or Alaska Native	1
% Asian or Pacific Islander	3
% Hispanic	10
% White	62
% Pell grant recipients	31
ACADEMICS	
full-time faculty	353
full-time minority faculty	n/a
student-faculty ratio	14:1
average class size	17
% first-year retention rate	66
% graduation rate (6 years)	35

Popular majors Film & Video, Art/Design, Photography, Theater

CAMPUS LIFE	
% live on campus	22

Multicultural student clubs and organizations Asian Student Organization, Black Actor's Guild, Black Student Union, Common Ground (GLBTQQIA organization), Hillel, Hispanic Journalists of Columbia, Latino Alliance, Muslim Student Association, American Sign Language Club, Association of Black Journalists

ADMISSIONS	
# of applicants	5,581
% accepted	95
# of first-year students enrolled	2,158
SAT Critical Reading (middle 50%)	n/a
SAT Math (middle 50%)	n/a
SAT Writing (middle 50%)	n/a
ACT (middle 50%)	18-25
average HS GPA	2.9
Deadlines	
priority application	n/a
regular decision	rolling
application fee (online)	$35 ($35)
fee waiver for applicants with financial need	yes
COST & AID	
tuition	$20,094
room & board	$12,360
total need-based institutional scholarships/grants	n/a
% of students apply for need-based aid	n/a
% of students receive aid	n/a
% receiving need-based scholarship or grant aid	n/a
% receiving aid whose need was fully met	n/a
average aid package	n/a
average student loan debt upon graduation	n/a

Elmhurst College

Elmhurst College
190 Prospect Avenue
Elmhurst, IL 60126
Ph: (800) 697-1871 / (630) 617-3400
admit@elmhurst.edu
www.elmhurst.edu

FAST FACTS

STUDENT PROFILE

# of degree-seeking undergraduates	2,800
% male/female	40/60
% African American	5
% American Indian or Alaska Native	<1
% Asian or Pacific Islander	5
% Hispanic	11
% White	76
% International	1
% Pell grant recipients	26

First-generation and minority alumni Hon. William J. Bauer, judge, Seventh Circuit Court of Appeals; Rev. Dr. Joseph J. Richardson, pastor and community leader; Fred Gretsch, president, Gretsch Musical Instruments; Himeo Tsumori, physician

ACADEMICS

full-time faculty	136
full-time minority faculty	14
student-faculty ratio	13:1
average class size	19
% first-year retention rate	85
% graduation rate (6 years)	71

Popular majors Business, Education, Health Sciences, Nursing

CAMPUS LIFE

% live on campus (% freshmen)	40 (70)

Multicultural student clubs and organizations Black Student Union, H.A.B.L.A.M.O.S., International Student Organization and the Coalition for Multicultural Student Empowerment

Athletics NCAA Division III, College Conference of Illinois & Wisconsin

ADMISSIONS

# of applicants	2,880
% accepted	71
# of first-year students enrolled	580
SAT Critical Reading (middle 50%)	490-630
SAT Math (middle 50%)	490-590
SAT Writing (middle 50%)	490-590
ACT (middle 50%)	22-26
average HS GPA	3.40

Deadlines

regular decision	rolling to 4/15
application fee (online)	$0 ($0)

COST & AID

tuition	$29,900
room & board	$7,864
total need-based institutional scholarships/grants	$38,000,000
% of students apply for need-based aid	97
% of students receive aid	95
% receiving need-based scholarship/grant aid	88
% receiving aid whose need was fully met	68
average aid package	$24,000
average student loan debt upon graduation	$25,500

Founded in 1871 and ranking among the top colleges in the Midwest, Elmhurst College draws from its ties with the United Church of Christ to offer a quality comprehensive education. The college's 38-acre campus rests in Elmhurst, Illinois, ranked No.1 in a *Chicago Magazine* survey of the best places to live. Recognizing that diversity is not defined only by race and ethnicity, the college offers Enrichment Scholarships to qualified students from various traditionally underrepresented groups.

ACCESS Summer Mathematics and Science Academy

The Summer Mathematics and Science Academy is a two-week program for high school students who are considering careers in mathematics, computer science, engineering, biology, chemistry, physics, medicine and nursing. In classes and seminars, students sharpen math skills, explore topics in science and master computer programs. The program is designed specifically for students from groups underrepresented in these professions. All high school students are encouraged to apply.

OPPORTUNITY The Enrichment Scholarships

The Enrichment Scholarships are offered to qualified students who are members of traditionally underrepresented groups. Elmhurst College does not limit this designation to racial or ethnic minorities, as scholarships can be given to international students or students who have overcome significant barriers to enroll at Elmhurst. The award is valued at $10,000 and recipients must be enrolled on a full-time, degree-seeking basis. The scholarship is renewable for up to four years, given the recipient maintains full-time enrollment and a cumulative GPA of at least 2.5 or above. Applicants must complete the admission application by May 1 to be considered.

SUCCESS B.R.I.D.G.E.S. Newsletter

Building Respect for Individuality and Diversity in a Globally Evolving Society (B.R.I.D.G.E.S.) is the monthly newsletter of Elmhurst's Office of Intercultural Student Affairs. The publication presents student-written stories from a variety of perspectives on diversity and other news not traditionally found in the mainstream press.

SUCCESS Office of Intercultural Education

The Office of Intercultural Education seeks to provide intercultural students with a welcoming environment and a celebration of ethnic, cultural and racial diversity. The office coordinates programs and services that bring cultural perspectives into the college's academic and social life: Off-Campus Intercultural Retreat, Hispanic Heritage Month, Native American Awareness Month, World AIDS Day, Black History Month, European Heritage Month, Women's History Month, Asian Heritage Month, documentary video series and discussion, discussion series, entertaining and educational cultural events, off-campus diversity conferences, guest speakers and lecturers, peer advising program, career mentoring program and cultural visits to Chicago.

"I plan to go into nursing so I can make a difference. In my clinical rotations, I've already experienced the impact a compassionate nurse can have on a patient. I feel fortunate to be at Elmhurst, where I'm getting the kind of education that will help me reach my goals."

*– Glen G.
Bensenville, IL
Nursing*

Illinois College

Illinois College
1101 West College Avenue
Jacksonville, IL 62650
Ph: (217) 245-3030
admissions@ic.edu
www.ic.edu

Illinois College is a small, private, residential, liberal arts institution located 30 miles from Springfield, 90 miles from St. Louis, and 250 miles from Chicago and Indianapolis. IC's student body is made up of just under 1000 students from 21 states and 14 countries. Since its founding in 1829, IC has been committed to excellence and service, both in the classroom and in the community. The campus is alive with True Blue spirit in its 80 campus organizations and 20 NCAA Division III athletic teams.

OPPORTUNITY **Illinois Monetary Award Program (MAP)**

The MAP grant program is a grant opportunity provided by the state of Illinois for students who are residents of Illinois. Eligibility is determined by a student's financial need based on the information provided in the FAFSA.

OPPORTUNITY **Federal Pell Grant and Supplemental Educational Opportunity Grant (SEOG)**

Illinois College applicants qualify for the Federal Pell Grant based on demonstrated financial need as determined by the FAFSA. In addition, IC offers Pell recipients with the highest financial need the Federal SEOG grant. The amount of the SEOG grant is based on available funding levels at IC.

SUCCESS **Yates Fellowship Program**

The Yates Fellowship Program is a yearlong learning community for first year, first-generation college students which begins with a two week on-campus program prior to the start of the academic year. During the two week program, students work closely with faculty to strengthen skills in writing and mathematics. Students will also gain practical skills in organization, study habits and how to utilize their liberal arts education to achieve their life and career goals. Throughout the year, Yates Fellows receive support from their peer mentor, an older student who is also a first-generation college student, as they work together in leadership development and community service opportunities.

> ***"Illinois College has all the resources students need to succeed. The Center for Academic Excellence offers programs that help students in a variety of ways. I was a supplemental instructor for college algebra where I presented classroom material from a peer's perspective in addition to the professor's teaching."***
>
> *– Joe G., '13*
> *High Hill, MO*
> *Mathematics Secondary Education*

SUCCESS **TRiO Program**

The TRiO program was established at Illinois College to promote the academic success, including persistence and graduation, of a select group of students who are the first in their family to attend college, low-income, or have a documented disability. The program provides social and academic support through personal counseling, career and academic guidance, study groups and workshops, and on-campus employment assistance.

SUCCESS **Center for Academic Excellence**

The Center for Academic Excellence provides academic support services for Illinois College students for all four years of their time at IC. Students can meet with the Center's Director individually or with class groups to arrange free tutoring sessions and receive guidance on study skills such as time management and tips on notetaking.

FAST FACTS

STUDENT PROFILE

# of degree-seeking undergraduates	878
% male/female	51/49
% African American	6
% Asian or Pacific Islander	<1
% Hispanic	4
% White	80
% International	3
% Pell grant recipients	36

First-generation and minority alumni Dr. Michael W. Graner, Associate Professor University of Colorado School of Medicine, Department of Neurology; Stephen J. Tharp, International Concert Organist and Recording Artist; Dalitso S. Sulamoyo, President and CEO Illinois Association of Community Action Agencies; Julie B. Macartney, Operations Manager, Academy for Educational Development; Joseph T. Calmese, Robotics Engineering Project Manager, Bastian Material Handling

ACADEMICS

full-time faculty	75
full-time minority faculty	5
student-faculty ratio	11:1
average class size	16.3
% first-year retention rate	86
% graduation rate (6 years)	61

Popular majors Biology, Business, Psychology, Education, Sociology

CAMPUS LIFE

% live on campus (% freshmen)	98 (81)

Multicultural student clubs and organizations Coalition for Ethnic Awareness, Japanese Club, Cricket Club, Model United Nations, Amnesty International

Athletics NCAA Division III, Midwest Conference

ADMISSIONS

# of applicants	1,598
% accepted	64
# of first-year students enrolled	290
SAT Critical Reading (middle 50%)	510-580
SAT Math (middle 50%)	490-640
SAT Writing (middle 50%)	460-630
ACT (middle 50%)	22-27
average HS GPA	3.32
Deadlines	
priority	12/15
early action	12/15
regular decision	3/15
application fee (online)	$0 ($0)

COST & AID

tuition	$24,030
room & board	$8,200
total need-based institutional scholarships/grants	$7,739,198
% of students apply for need-based aid	92
% receiving need-based scholarship or grant aid	83
% receiving aid whose need was fully met	26
average aid package	$20,096
average student loan debt upon graduation	$24,401

Illinois Institute of Technology

Since its founding in 1890, Illinois Institute of Technology has dedicated significant resources to enable students from a wide range of financial backgrounds to attend. A private, independent, Ph.D.-granting, co-educational research university, Illinois Institute of Technology offers students a superb education in engineering, business, architecture, the sciences, psychology and the humanities, in an environment geared toward the undergraduate student. The university is committed to providing students a distinctive and relevant experience through hands-on learning, dedicated teachers, small class sizes, and undergraduate research opportunities. Classes are taught by senior faculty, not teaching assistants, who foster a culture of innovation with their own firsthand research experience. The school's location in the world class city of Chicago gives students priceless access to the professional world through internships and employment. The university's own diverse student population mirrors the global work environment faced by all graduates.

> ACCESS Perspectives Charter Schools Partnership

Illinois Institute of Technology and Perspectives Charter Schools have partnered to create a ground-breaking, new math and science academy dedicated to improving students' achievement in these important fields. Supported through a $500,000 grant from the Motorola Foundation in partnership with the Renaissance Schools Fund, Perspectives Charter Schools/IIT Math & Science Academy is a world-class laboratory school that will provide students invaluable tools for personal and academic growth. The school's strong curriculum includes a focus on technology and engineering skills and will be the first Chicago charter school to offer a four-year Chinese language program. Perspectives Charter Schools is working in full partnership with Norman Lederman, chair, and Judith Lederman, director of teacher education, of the Mathematics and Science Education Department at Illinois Institute of Technology IT to develop a comprehensive curriculum and mentorship initiative. The new school will be based within the Benjamin W. Raymond School at 3663 S. Wabash Ave, in close proximity to the university.

> OPPORTUNITY Collens Scholarship

As a continuation of its growing relationship with Chicago Public Schools, Illinois Institute of Technology offers the Collens Scholarship. The scholarship offers eligible high school graduates the opportunity to attend with full financial support for all tuition, books and fees. In fall 2008, 34 students from 19 Chicago high schools entered Illinois Institute of Technology on the Collens Scholarship, to study 13 different majors. This need-based scholarship honors former university President Lew Collens, who served the university from 1990 to 2007, and marks his legacy of commitment to Chicago Public Schools and the city at large.

"When I looked at my award package I was so surprised at how much they were able to award me. It made me feel like my success was IIT's priority. And now that I am here, I know it is."

– Julia G., '12
Chicago, IL
Physics

> SUCCESS Exelon Summer Institute

IIT knows the transition to university life and the academic rigors of college are difficult. For over 30 years, Illinois Institute of Technology has sought to develop some of the finest and most comprehensive summer programs to help students make this transition to college. The Exelon Summer Institute for First-Year Students is a four-week, non-residential academic and community-building summer program for admitted freshmen that positions students to thrive during their academic careers. Through workshops and group learning activities, students gain subject mastery of mathematics, chemistry and physics; explore intended academic majors through reading, writing and discussion; and develop analytical thinking and communication skills. There are also extra-curricular activities, including field trips and opportunities to build social networks and faculty connections.

Illinois Institute of Technology
Office of Undergraduate Admission
Perlstein Hall 101
10 West 33rd Street
Chicago, IL 60616
Ph: (312) 567-3025
admission@iit.edu
www.admission.iit.edu

FAST FACTS

STUDENT PROFILE

# of degree-seeking undergraduates	2,602
% male/female	66/34
% African American	5
% American Indian or Alaska Native	1
% Asian or Pacific Islander	12
% Hispanic	9
% White	44
% International	20
% Pell grant recipients	25

First-generation and minority alumni Yasuhire Ishimoto, photographer; Susan Soloman, chemist, Nobel Peace Prize, recipient; Jorge Zepeda, Bell Labs engineer, designer, optical communications systems; Walter Cambell, architect, founder, National Organization of Minority Architects; Jimmy Akintonde, architect, entrepreneur and founder, Ujaama Construction

ACADEMICS

full-time faculty	386
full-time minority faculty	16
student-faculty ratio	10:1
average class size	10-19
% first-year retention rate	92.4
% graduation rate (6 years)	63.8

Popular majors Architecture, Engineering, the Sciences, Business, Psychology, Humanities

CAMPUS LIFE

% live on campus (% freshmen)	27 (70)

Multicultural student clubs and organizations African Student Organization, Iranian Students Association, Japanese Film and Animation Society, Korean Hope, Korean Student Association, Latino Fuzion, Latinos Involved in Further Education, National Organization of Minority Architecture Students, National Society of Black Engineers (NSBE), Pakistan Student Association, Arquitectos, Thai Student Association, Turkish Student Association, Vietnamese Students Association, Asian Pacific Gays, Lesbians, Allies, & More (GLAM), Black Student Union, Omega Delta, Chinese Student and Scholars Association, Indian Students Association, Indonesian Students Association, International Students Organization
Athletics NAIA Division I, Chicagoland Collegiate Athletic Conference

ADMISSIONS

# of applicants	2,295
% accepted	65
# of first-year students enrolled	403
SAT Critical Reading (middle 50%)	520-670
SAT Math (middle 50%)	610-740
SAT Writing (middle 50%)	520-650
ACT (middle 50%)	25-30.5
average HS GPA	3.92
Deadlines	
early decision	11/1
early action I	12/1
early action II	2/1
regular decision	rolling 6/11 (domestic), 4/15 (international)
application fee (online)	$0 ($0)

COST & AID

tuition	$33,800
room & board	$10,214 – $12,986
total need-based institutional scholarships/grants	$22,162,719
% of students apply for need-based aid	66
% of students receive aid	100
% receiving need-based scholarship or grant aid	99
% receiving aid whose need was fully met	16
average aid package	$25,249
average student loan debt upon graduation	$28,604

Illinois Wesleyan University

Founded in 1850, Illinois Wesleyan University is a four-year, private co-educational university. The university strives to attain the ideals of liberal education by providing students with opportunities to realize individual potential while at the same time, preparing students for life in a global society. Offering diverse curricula in liberal arts, fine arts and professional programs, as well as opportunities for interdisciplinary study and off-campus learning, Illinois Wesleyan allows students to pursue a wide variety of interests and career paths. Personal growth is cherished at Illinois Wesleyan, and the small size and dedication to student-faculty interaction imbues the university with a real sense of community, an atmosphere that is particularly conducive to both personal and intellectual development.

"Illinois Wesleyan was the most supportive academic environment that I encountered in my college search. When I began my college search, my mom and I felt lost and confused. But when I visited Illinois Wesleyan, my admissions counselor went out of her way to make me feel as though no question was too stupid or too small. Her support was also echoed by the students I met during my overnight visit and by my academic advisor."

– Bevin C., '10
Braidwood, IL
Sociology

ACCESS **College Quest**

College Quest is a summer program assisting promising Chicago public high school students in the college admission process. Successful applicants spend four days and three nights on the Illinois Wesleyan campus, where they attend seminars such as "Finding the Right College Fit," "What Colleges Are Looking For in the Application" and "Understanding the Financial Aid Process." Additionally, participants enjoy entertainment such as bowling and the local Shakespeare Festival, and they have opportunities to interact with university faculty and students on an individual and small group basis.

OPPORTUNITY **Multicultural Weekend (MCW)**

Multicultural Weekend is an all-expenses-paid opportunity for students to learn more about Illinois Wesleyan and experience campus as a real student. Held in both the fall and spring, attendees stay on campus Thursday evening through Saturday morning and have the opportunity to sit in on classes, meet with professors, and participate in clubs and activities.

OPPORTUNITY **¡TU UNIVERSIDAD!**

¡TU UNIVERSIDAD!, held in February, is designed to assist Latino/a students and families who would like to learn more about the University campus and surrounding community, receive admissions assistance, attend a Free Application for Federal Student Aid (FAFSA) completion workshop (offered in English and Spanish), and meet current students, faculty and staff. IWU arranges bus transportation.

SUCCESS **Summer Enrichment Program (SEP)**

With the goal of increasing personal and intellectual development opportunities for currently enrolled minority students, Illinois Wesleyan offers the Summer Enrichment Program. Over the course of 10 weeks, attendees go to class, work on an internship and participate in at least one volunteer project. Designed to promote academic, professional, and personal growth, the Summer Enrichment Program allows students to develop team building and leadership skills. In addition, a scholarship is awarded to all students who successfully complete the program.

SUCCESS **Giving Undergraduates Instruments to Develop and Excel (GUIDE) Mentoring Program**

Embodying Illinois Wesleyan's commitment to maintaining a close-knit, supportive university community, Illinois Wesleyan's Giving Undergraduates Instruments to Develop and Excel Program provides first-year students with student mentors to assist them through the transition from high school to college. Mentors also provide peer support, help to create a social network that models healthy behaviors and promote academic excellence and co-curricular involvement.

Illinois Wesleyan University
Admissions Office
Minor Myers, jr. Welcome Center
1211 Park Street
Bloomington, IL 61701
Ph: (309) 556-3031 or (800) 332-2498
iwuadmit@iwu.edu
www.iwu.edu

FAST FACTS

STUDENT PROFILE

# of degree-seeking undergraduates	2,088
% male/female	42/58
% African American	5
% American Indian or Alaska Native	.3
% Asian or Pacific Islander	4
% Hispanic	3
% White	75
% International	4
% Pell grant recipients	17% of first year students

First-generation and minority alumni Alfred O. Coffin, class of 1889, first African-American to receive a Ph.D. in biology in the U.S. and only the second Ph.D. awarded in any field to an African-American; Frankie Faison, actor; Akito Mizuno, CEO, Mizuno; Michael Mason, assistant director, Chief Security Officer, Verizon

ACADEMICS

full-time faculty	161 (instructional)
full-time minority faculty	19
student-faculty ratio	11:1
average class size	17
% first-year retention rate	91
% graduation rate (6 years)	81

Popular majors Business Administration/ Management, Biology, Music, English, Psychology

CAMPUS LIFE

% live on campus (% freshmen)	75 (100)

Multicultural student clubs and organizations Black Student Union, Spanish and Latino Student Association, Southeast Asian Student Association, African Student Association, International Society of IWU, Hilel, Hindu Student Association, and Sisters Actively Visualizing Vitality Through Intellect

Athletics Division III, College Conference of Illinois and Wisconsin

ADMISSIONS

# of applicants	3,547
% accepted	61
# of first-year students enrolled	617 (fall 2010)
SAT Critical Reading (middle 50%)	580-710
SAT Math (middle 50%)	580-690
SAT Writing (middle 50%)	n/a
ACT (middle 50%)	26-31
average HS GPA	3.8/4.0
Deadlines	
early action (non-binding)	11/15
regular decision	rolling after 1/15
application fee (online)	$0 ($0)

COST & AID

tuition	$36,392
room & board	$8,476
total need-based institutional scholarships/grants	$8,740,738 for new students
% of students apply for need-based aid	82
% of students receive aid	95% of first year students
% receiving need-based scholarship or grant aid	59% of first year students
% receiving aid whose need was fully met	20% of first year students
average aid package	$24,456 for first year students
average student loan debt upon graduation	$31,091

Southern Illinois University Edwardsville

Southern Illinois University Edwardsville is a premier Metropolitan University offering a rich mix of cultural opportunities and an extensive inventory of academic programs. Seven academic units include Schools of Pharmacy, Dental Medicine, Engineering, Education, Nursing, Business and a College of Arts and Sciences. As one of the best higher education values in the Midwest, SIUE has the lowest in-state tuition rate of all 12 state universities. SIUE students come from 46 states and 48 nations. 24% are first generation college students. Only 25 minutes from downtown St. Louis—with Fortune 500 companies, sports venues, cultural offerings and transportation within minutes of just about anywhere in the Metro Area—the SIUE campus is situated on 2,660 acres of beautiful, forested woodland atop the bluffs overlooking the natural beauty of the Mississippi River's rich bottom land. SIUE wants to make sure all students succeed in their academic programs, graduate and ultimately land a successful career. A variety of programs and initiatives are in place to support the recruitment, retention and academic success of underrepresented students.

SUCCESS The Summer Bridge Program

The Summer Bridge Program is an on-campus experience that allows freshman students to experience the Southern Illinois University Edwardsville environment prior to the fall term.Through structured and integrated activities, students will be prepared to meet the demands of college and bridge the gap between high school and college. In addition to classes in reading, writing, and math, students will participate in other activities designed to build academic skills and lead to a sense of community.

"Life is full of challenges but with the support system available at SIUE, success is not far out of reach."

– Jessica Johnson
Chicago, IL
Secondary Education

SUCCESS Project F.A.M.E.

Females of African-Descent Modeling Excellence (F.A.M.E.) is a peer-mentoring program designed to link incoming African-American female freshmen with experienced student mentors while guiding them through their first year of university life.

SUCCESS Project G.A.M.E.

Goal-Oriented African-American Males Excel (G.A.M.E.) is a two-semester program in which African-American males are selected to participate. Incoming freshmen are selected based on high school gpa, ACT score, leadership potential, volunteer experience and potential for success in higher education.

SUCCESS The Johnetta Haley Scholars Academy

The Johnetta Haley Scholars Academy supports undergraduate students at SIUE who choose to major in Biological Sciences, Computer Sciences, Engineering, Nursing, Physical Sciences and Teacher Education. Other majors may be considered if funds are available.

SUCCESS The SOAR Program

The SOAR Program (Student Opportunities for Academic Results) is a multicultural support system dedicated to helping students realize their greatest potential. Participation in SOAR is free and includes resources and benefits like tutoring, mentoring, academic advising and cultural events.

Southern Illinois University Edwardsville
P.O. Box 1600
Edwardsville, IL 62026
Ph: (618) 650-3705
admissions@siue.edu
www.siue.edu/prospectivestudents

FAST FACTS

STUDENT PROFILE

# of degree-seeking undergraduates	11,305
% male/female	47/53
% African American	12
% American Indian or Alaska Native	<1
% Asian or Pacific Islander	2
% Hispanic	3
% White	76
% International	2
% Pell grant recipients (2006)	32

First-generation and minority alumni Judge Milton Wharton – St. Clair County Circuit Court Judge, B.S. Business Administration '69; Dr. Ernest Jackson – Only Board Certified African American Forensic Odontologist in the World and Internationally known Certified Crime Scene Investigator, Doctor of Dental Medicine '87; Shelby Steele – Distinguished Alumnus Award – writer for *New York Times, Wall Street Journal, Harpers Magazine*. Also, an Emmy Winner, MA Sociology, '71; Reggie Thomas – International jazz pianist, instructor, recording artist, musician, teacher, Master of Music '92

ACADEMICS

full-time faculty	627
full-time minority faculty	98
student-faculty ratio	17:1
average class size	24
% first-year retention rate	72
% graduation rate (6 years)	51

Popular majors Nursing, Biology, Business Admin

CAMPUS LIFE

% live on campus (% freshmen)	30 (67)

Multicultural student clubs and organizations Hispanic Student Union, International Student Council, Black Student Union, Iranian Student Association, Turkish Student Association, Society of Chinese Students (PRC)

Athletics NCAA Division I, Ohio Valley Conference

ADMISSIONS

# of applicants	7,354
% accepted	82
# of first-year students enrolled	2,065
SAT Critical Reading (middle 50%)	n/a
SAT Math (middle 50%)	n/a
SAT Writing (middle 50%)	n/a
ACT (middle 50%)	20-25
average HS GPA	n/a
Deadlines	
regular decision	n/a
application fee	$30
fee waiver for applicants with financial need	yes

COST & AID

tuition	in-state $6,630; out-of-state $16,575
room & board	$8,051
total need-based institutional scholarships/grants	$1,868,761
% of students apply for need-based aid	86
% receiving need-based scholarship/grant aid	51
% receiving aid whose need was fully met	47
average aid package	$12,063
average student loan debt upon graduation	$21,633

The University of Chicago

Chartered in 1890, the University of Chicago quickly became a world leader in higher education and research. Over 80 Nobel laureates are associated with UChicago—the largest number affiliated with any American university. Students choose UChicago for its rigorous liberal arts curriculum, conducted in small Socratic-style seminars with a student-faculty ratio of 7:1. The residential housing system is a vital element of the College community. Modeled after the British house system, the 35 houses compete against each other in intramural sports, eat together at shared dining tables, and take trips to sporting and cultural events. UChicago's location only fifteen minutes from the city center allows the students to immerse themselves in the diversity of urban life.

ACCESS Collegiate Scholars Program

The three-year Collegiate Scholars Program offers college-level classes and enrichment seminars free of charge to high-achieving students in Chicago public high schools. Designed to prepare students for high achievement in college, the program offers summer courses in the Humanities, Social Sciences, Mathematics, Biological Sciences, Physical Sciences, Entrepreneurship and the Arts. During the school year the program provides courses and events to prepare students for college, develop the students' understanding of other cultures, and involve the students in their community.

ACCESS Small School Talent Search (SSTS)

The Small School Talent Search, established in 1960 to seek out exceptional students from America's rural communities, has expanded to include students from all small high schools that may receive less attention from selective colleges.

OPPORTUNITY QuestBridge National College Match

QuestBridge National College Match helps talented, low-income high school seniors gain admission and full four-year scholarships to some of the nation's most selective colleges and universities. These scholarships do not involve loans and meet 100% of the students' demonstrated need. The application is free of charge so economically disadvantaged students will have no trouble applying. Selection for this program is competitive and based on the applicants' academic achievement, essays and recommendations.

"Getting involved with PAECE, Performing Arts for Effective Civil Education helped me find a niche on campus, and in the greater Chicago area, because I was with other UChicago students, going to South Side high schools and working with youth. I got more comfortable with my surroundings and more knowledgeable about the city."

– Johnaé S., '11
Cleveland, OH
International Studies

SUCCESS Academic Advisers

The University of Chicago is recognized for their unique approach to advising students. When a student matriculates, he or she is assigned a full-time academic adviser from the staff of the Dean of Students who advises the student all four years. The adviser helps with academic planning, postgraduate plans, and personal, financial, or academic problems.

SUCCESS Office of Multicultural Student Affairs (OMSA)

The Office of Multicultural Student Affairs supports the academic success of students of color at the University of Chicago and works to build an inclusive campus community. OMSA's resources connect students to academic support services, information on summer internships, scholarships, and fellowships for students of color. OMSA's programs focus on enriching students' experiences and encouraging cross-cultural dialogue on campus. OMSA executes its mission in collaboration with other departments within the University of Chicago.

The University of Chicago
1101 E. 58th Street, Suite 105
Chicago, IL 60637
Ph: (773) 702-8650
collegeadmissions@uchicago.edu
www.collegeadmissions.uchicago.edu

FAST FACTS

STUDENT PROFILE

# of degree-seeking undergraduates	5,066
% male/female	51/49
% African American	6
% American Indian or Alaska Native	1
% Asian or Pacific Islander	16
% Hispanic	8
% White	43
% International	9
% Pell grant recipients	18

First-generation and minority alumni Katherine Dunham, dancer and choreographer; Carter G. Woodson, historian and founder of Negro History Week (which evolved into Black History Month); Michelle Howard-Vital, President, Cheyney University of Pennsylvania; Carol Moseley Braun, first African American woman elected to the U.S. Senate (Illinois); Myrtle Stephens Potter, CEO of Myrtle Potter & Company LLC and Myrtle Potter Media Inc., on-air business contributor and co-host for CNBC, and UChicago Trustee.

ACADEMICS

full-time faculty	1,113
full-time minority faculty	n/a
student-faculty ratio	7:1
average class size	17-19
% first-year retention rate	98
% graduation rate (6 years)	92

Popular majors Economics, Biological Sciences, Political Science, Mathematics, English Language/ Literature

CAMPUS LIFE

% live on campus (% freshmen)	65 (100)

Multicultural student clubs and organizations African and Caribbean Students Association, Asian Students Union, Movimiento Estudiantil Chicano de Aztlán, Native American Student Association, Organization of Black Students, Organization of Latin American Students (OLAS), Students Promoting Interracial Networks (SPIN)

Athletics NCAA Division III, University Athletic Association

ADMISSIONS

# of applicants	19,347
% accepted	19
# of first-year students enrolled	1,414
SAT Critical Reading (middle 50%)	700-780
SAT Math (middle 50%)	700-780
SAT Writing (middle 50%)	690-770
ACT (middle 50%)	30-34
average HS GPA	n/a

Deadlines

early action	11/1
regular decision	1/1
application fee (online)	$75 ($75)
fee waiver for applicants with financial need	yes

COST & AID

tuition	$40,188
room & board	$12,153
total need-based institutional scholarships/grants	$85,710,143
% of students apply for need-based aid	63
% receiving need-based scholarship/grant aid	46
% receiving aid whose need was fully met	100
average aid package	$38,991
average student loan debt upon graduation	$16,354

University of Illinois at Urbana-Champaign

Since its founding in 1867, the University of Illinois at Urbana-Champaign has earned a reputation as a world-class leader in research, teaching, and public engagement. Distinguished by the breadth of its programs, broad academic excellence, and internationally renowned faculty, Illinois alumni have earned Nobel and Pulitzer Prizes and Olympic medals, have orbited the earth, and lead international corporations. The campus also offers rich experiences beyond the classroom, from performing arts to Big Ten sports. Centrally located between Chicago, Indianapolis and St. Louis, students come from all 50 states and over 100 countries. Also, there are many cultural study centers at the university – which highlight regions including Africa, East Asia and the Pacific, Latin America, the Caribbean, Russia, Eastern Europe, South Asia and the Middle East. In addition to being responsive to issues of cultural diversity, *New Mobility,* a magazine, has continuously ranked the school as the No. 1 "disability-friendly college" in the country.

> ACCESS **Biotechnology Education and Outreach Program (BEOP)**

Many teachers do not have the knowledge or resources to carry out state-of-the-art science in their classrooms. The Biotechnology Education and Outreach Program is devoted to training teachers and students in biotechnology concepts and hands-on experiments. This program trains teachers in biotechnology concepts and applications and also loans biotechnology equipment and supplies to high school classrooms. To date, this outreach program has trained over 400 high school and community college teachers throughout Illinois, including both rural and urban regions. In particular, BEOP has trained Chicago Public School teachers in the areas of DNA and genomes, genetically modified organisms and DNA fingerprinting.

> OPPORTUNITY **Illinois Promise**

Economic situations often threaten the affordability of higher education, particularly for students from the lowest income levels. The University of Illinois at Urbana-Champaign, however, is committed to providing access to quality education for high achieving students from all backgrounds. University of Illinois applicants may receive funding through the Illinois Promise program, which provides grants and scholarships to Illinois residents whose families are at or below the federal poverty level. These families do not have to contribute anything toward college expenses. Recipients are expected to work 10 to 12 hours a week, however, in order to contribute to their aid package. To be considered for the Illinois Promise, students must submit the FAFSA by March 15 prior to each academic year.

"I had really high expectations for the University of Illinois, and I am not the slightest bit disappointed. In fact, the environment far exceeds my expectations. I am really excited about the diversity on campus, the school spirit, the endless opportunities for personal and professional growth, and the new people I meet everyday."

– Paula G., '11
Chicago, IL
Marketing and Management

> SUCCESS **Transition Program**

Students who demonstrate academic promise but whose academic backgrounds have not adequately prepared them for college success, may be placed in the Transition Program upon admission. Once accepted, students participate in an ongoing academic program, which supplies these students with intensive academic and career counseling, extensive academic and personal support services, plus opportunities to enroll in support-based sections of existing courses.

University of Illinois at Urbana-Champaign
601 East John St.
Champaign, Illinois 61820
Ph: (217) 333-0302
www.admissions.illinois.edu

FAST FACTS

STUDENT PROFILE

# of degree-seeking undergraduates	30,386
% male/female	53/47
% African American	6
% American Indian or Alaska Native	<1
% Asian or Pacific Islander	14
% Hispanic	7
% White	65
% International	7
% Pell grant recipients	16

First-generation and minority alumni Steve Chen, co-founder, YouTube; Sheila Crump Johnson, co-founder, Black Entertainment Television, America's first black female billionaire; Mannie Jackson, owner, Harlem Globetrotters, chairman, Basketball Hall of Fame; Ang Lee, director

ACADEMICS

full-time faculty	2,112
full-time minority faculty	457
student-faculty ratio	16:1
average class size	25
% first-year retention rate	94
% graduation rate (6 years)	82

Popular majors Business, Biology, Communications, Engineering, Architecture, Psychology

CAMPUS LIFE

% live on campus (% freshmen)	50 (100)

Multicultural student clubs and organizations African American Research and Professional Network, African Cultural Association, Asian American Association, Asian Pacific American Coalition, Baltic Club, Bangladeshi Students Association, Black Chorus at the University of Illinois, Chinese Undergraduate Student Association, Ebony Umoja Black Student Union, Indian Student Association, Japan Intercultural Network, Latino Law Students Association, MIXED, Polish Club Zagloba, PRIDE, Red Roots, Society of Signers, Women of Color and many more

Athletics NCAA Division I, Big Ten Conference

ADMISSIONS

# of applicants	27,310
% accepted	67
# of first-year students enrolled	6,924
SAT Critical Reading (middle 50%)	530-660
SAT Math (middle 50%)	680-770
SAT Writing (middle 50%)	570-670
ACT (middle 50%)	26-31
average HS GPA	n/a

Deadlines

early decision	11/1
regular admission	1/3
application fee (online)	$50
fee waiver for applicants with financial need	yes

COST & AID

tuition	in-state $13,096; out-of-state $27,238
room & board	$9,714
total need-based institutional scholarships/grants	$76,775,836
% of students apply for need-based aid	58
% of students receive aid	77
% receiving need-based scholarship or grant aid	39
% receiving aid whose need was fully met	28
average aid package	$11,029
average student loan debt upon graduation	$17,930

Western Illinois University

Western Illinois University
University Circle
115 Sherman Hall
Macomb, IL 61455-1390
Ph: (309) 298-3157
admissions@wiu.edu
www.wiu.edu

Western Illinois University is a mid-sized, public, co-educational university. Granted recognition by the Pell Institute for the Study of Opportunity as a "Best Practice Institution" for the retention of first-generation and low-income students, the University offers small class sizes and a low faculty-to-student ratio. Western Illinois students receive personal attention from their professors and mentors, and the University is comprised of two campuses that provide a wide range of academic programs, including a strong teacher education program.

ACCESS **Role Models and Success Stories**

Western Illinois University's current minority students visit high schools in the region to speak with students about college life and academics.

ACCESS **Pride and Responsibility in My Environment (PRIME)**

The University sponsors transportation to various educational programs and activities for this local minority youth program.

ACCESS **Multicultural Recruitment Advisory Board (MRAB)**

Western Illinois' Multicultural Recruitment Advisory Board (MRAB), comprised of faculty and students, hosts multicultural group visits and promotes the Western Illinois University experience to prospective minority students.

OPPORTUNITY **Western Illinois University Scholarship Program**

In 2010-11, WIU's Scholarship Programs distributed more than $3 million in support. Western Illinois scholarships include a number of offerings specifically for entering minority students, including the DuSable scholarship ($1,000 per year, renewable at $500), the Western Opportunity Grant ($1,000), the Western Opportunity Scholarship ($500 to $2,000) and the Student Services Minority Achievement Access/ Retention Grant (multiple awards ranging from $500 to $1,000).

"During my time at WIU, I've had many diverse and challenging experiences. Each has helped shape my leadership skills and self-confidence. Every professor I've had the pleasure of interacting with has been willing to answer questions and offer extra help when needed. Many of my professors have been mentors and encouraged my success."

– Tristen J.
Peoria, IL
Journalism and African American Studies

OPPORTUNITY **Cost Guarantee**

Western's Cost Guarantee is the only program in Illinois that ensures a four-year lock on total costs – tuition, fees, room and board – for undergraduate, transfer and graduate students. Transfer students earning an associate's degree and transferring to WIU the following semester receive the previous year's Cost Guarantee rates. Students from Iowa, Wisconsin and Missouri pay Illinois in-state rates for tuition and fees.

SUCCESS **Diversity and Cultural Awareness**

Western provides a wealth of resources that promote diversity and cultural awareness, including Casa Latina Cultural Center, Gwendolyn Brooks Cultural Center and the Women's Center, housed in the new Multicultural Center; Disability Support Services; the Center for International Studies; the University Diversity Council; the University Committee on Sexual Orientation, to name just a few.

FAST FACTS

STUDENT PROFILE

# of degree-seeking undergraduates	10,474
% male/female	52/48
% African American	11
% American Indian or Alaska Native	<1
% Asian or Pacific Islander	1
% Hispanic	6
% White	78
% International	1
% Pell grant recipients (2006)	32.9

ACADEMICS

full-time faculty	662
full-time minority faculty	96
student-faculty ratio	16:1
average class size	22.2
% first-year retention rate	72.9
% graduation rate (6 years)	58.1

Popular majors Law Enforcement, Biology, Elementary Education, Psychology, General Studies

CAMPUS LIFE

% live on campus (% freshmen)	36 (94)

Multicultural student clubs and organizations Black Student Association, Latin American Student Organization, NAACP, International Friendship Club, Cultural Expressions Club, Gwendolyn Brooks Cultural Center, Korean Student Association, Tradicion Hispana Dance Troupe, Unity

Athletics NCAA Division I (NCAA Football Championship Subdivision), The Summit League and Missouri Valley Football Conference

ADMISSIONS

# of applicants	8,331
% accepted	64
SAT Critical Reading (middle 50%)	n/a
SAT Math (middle 50%)	n/a
SAT Writing (middle 50%)	n/a
ACT (middle 50%)	18-23
average HS GPA	3.0
Deadlines	
regular decision	5/15
fee waiver for applicants with financial need	yes

COST & AID

tuition	in-state $7,648.50; out-of-state $10,168 (in-state provided to students from IL, MO, IA, IN, WI)
room & board	$8,460
total need-based institutional scholarships/grants	$2,600,000
% of students apply for need-based aid	78
% of students receive aid	75
% receiving need-based scholarship/grant aid	55
% receiving aid whose need was fully met	75
average aid package	$11,000
average student loan debt upon graduation	$22,007

Goshen College

Goshen College
1700 South Main Street
Goshen, IN 46526
Ph: (800) 348-7422 / (574) 535-7535
admission@goshen.edu
www.goshen.edu

Goshen was founded in 1894 with a mission to educate young people while serving the church and the world. Today it's a nationally recognized, private Christian college and the number-one destination for forward-thinking peacemakers. Approximately 1,000 peace-minded people from more than 35 states and 40 countries. 10 percent are students of color. 8 percent are international students. 100 percent have a genuine passion for building community. Goshen is home to one of the top-ranked study abroad programs in the country, and one of the few that emphasizes service and complete cultural immersion. Approximately 80 percent of students study abroad before graduating. More than half of Goshen faculty members have lived or worked abroad. Students interested in environmental stewardship and sustainable living can take avantage of Goshen's 1,189-acre Merry Lea Environmental Learning Center, which encompasses a natural sanctuary and a sustailable village.

> ***"Goshen College is a great college rich with diversity. Here at Goshen, I am not a minority; I am a student, a friend, and a worker. Here, I have the opportunity to share and express my culture, and in return, have expanded my own knowledge about others. Here, we embrace the diversity that each student has to offer."***
> *– Lizzy D.*
> *Senior*
> *Nursing Major*

ACCESS **21st Century Scholars**

Goshen College provides education workshops, both on campus and in surrounding communities, for students who have been designated as 21st Century Scholars. Students are brought onto the Goshen campus in order to help them gain a stronger understanding of how they can continue their education after completing high school. Faculty and staff from Goshen College also go into the surrounding community to talk with the 21st Century Scholars and their parents to encourage the students to think about attending college.

OPPORTUNITY **Special Visits and Scholarships**

Goshen College is a must see! We partner with high schools and community organizations to bring students to campus for both individual and group visits. In collaboration with a gospel concert with Kiki Sheard, Goshen College hosted a Christian College Fair and hosted students overnight to experience the life of a college student. In addition to academic and athletic scholarships, Goshen College offers two scholarship programs geared towards students of color.

SUCCESS **SALT (Student Academic Leadership Training)**

This program is a three-week summer program for students of color. The program is free of charge to the student as long as s/he has already been admitted into Goshen College and enrolls for the fall semester after completing Student Academic Leadership Training. Each student earns three college credits, lives in the residence halls, begins orientation to the college, and begins building and strengthening study skills.

SUCCESS **The Multicultural Affairs Office (MAO)**

The Multicultural Affairs Office (MAO) mission is to help foster intercultural understandings and promote a campus-wide environment that encourages interracial and intercultural awareness and learning. The Multicultural Affairs Office oversaw the development of the campus diversity plan. The plan's four guiding goals for advancing interracial and intercultural appreciation are to recruit and retain a diverse student body; to recruit and retain a diverse faculty and staff; to strengthen communication and partnerships with local ethnic communities; and to give increased attention to campus wide and community activities that promote racial harmony and cross cultural relationships.

FAST FACTS

STUDENT PROFILE

# of degree-seeking undergraduates	974
% male/female	40/60
% African American	3.5
% American Indian or Alaska Native	<1
% Asian or Pacific Islander	1.7
% Hispanic	6.5
% White	82.6
% International	4.3
% Pell grant recipients	19

First-generation and minority alumni Said Sheikh Samatar, African scholar

ACADEMICS

full-time faculty	69
full-time minority faculty	2
student-faculty ratio	11:1
average class size	16.5
% first-year retention rate	84.9
% graduation rate (6 years)	69.1

Popular majors Business, Education, Nursing, Music, Biology

CAMPUS LIFE

% live on campus	91.3

Multicultural student clubs and organizations Black Student Union, Latino Student Union, American Sign Language Club, AMISH (Association of Mennonites for Ice and Street Hockey), Frente Mennonita de Liberacion National, Goshen Student Women's Association (GSWA), International Student Club

Athletics NAIA, Mid-Central College Conference

ADMISSIONS

# of applicants	704
% accepted	69
# of first-year students enrolled	232
Middle 50%:	
SAT Critical Reading (middle 50%)	480-650
SAT Math (middle 50%)	600-650
SAT Writing (middle 50%)	468-620
ACT (middle 50%)	21-28
average HS GPA	3.6

Deadlines

regular admission	12/15
application fee	$25
fee waiver for applicants with financial need	yes

COST & AID

tuition	$25,700
room & board	$8,650
total need-based institutional scholarships/grants	$1,975,052
% of students apply for need-based aid	100
% of students receive aid	99.3
% receiving need-based scholarship or grant aid	68.9
% receiving aid whose need was fully met	33.8
average aid package	$19,470
average student loan debt upon graduation	$18,680

Saint Mary's College

Saint Mary's College, a private, Catholic, residential college, has been educating women in the liberal arts tradition for over 160 years. As one of the nation's oldest women's colleges, Saint Mary's is an academic community where women develop their talents and prepare to make a difference in the world. Founded by the Sisters of the Holy Cross in 1844, Saint Mary's seeks to provide academic, social and spiritual growth. Located near the city of South Bend and directly across the street from the University of Notre Dame, the Saint Mary's community includes 1,555 students from 42 states and 9 foreign countries.

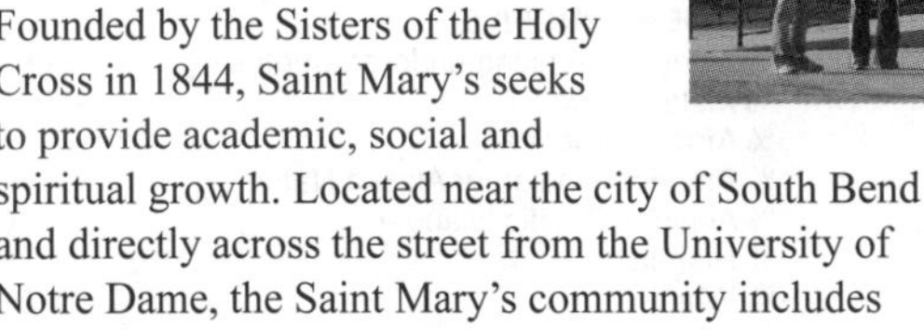

ACCESS College Academy of Tutoring Program (CAT)

The College Academy of Tutoring Program was formed in 2006 to meet the needs of at-risk students in the South Bend area. Saint Mary's students partner with Title 1 elementary schools, working as tutors, teacher's assistants, reading partners, and special program coordinators. The program also provides the partner school with physical resources (school supplies, clothing, software, and more), training, and cultural events for parents, staff, and community members.

OPPORTUNITY Holy Cross Grants

Saint Mary's offers Holy Cross grants, ranging up to $5,000/year, to Pell eligible, first-generation students.

"[The College] has impacted me in a way that I was not expecting. Saint Mary's has made me aware of what I truly believe and see as valuable in life. I got involved in diversity initiatives on campus because no one is ever the same—having the ability to learn about others can enrich a person's life in the short and long run. I have made some really great friendships—they make Saint Mary's feel very comfortable and like home."

–Danae J. '12
Double major in speech communications and theatre with a minor in women's studies

OPPORTUNITY Diverse Students' Leadership Conference (DSLC)

During this three-day conference, current and former Saint Mary's students combine energies to organize a campus-wide leadership conference that includes lectures, workshops, film presentations and panel discussions on diversity. Topics from the 2011 conference included: "Gender and Environmental Justice: Local and Global Perspectives", "Can We Talk About Race?", "Classism is "Reel" in Higher Education: A Closer Look At The Movie *Aladdin*", "Privileges We Don't Recognize: White Privilege and Heterosexism" and "Don't Ask, Don't Tell". High school students are invited to spend the day on campus and learn about diversity from a variety of perspectives – academic, social, spiritual and professional.

SUCCESS MSSP Connect

Multicultural Services and Student Programs offers MSSP Connect, a unique opportunity for incoming first year students to ease into campus life. The program introduces students to Saint Mary's before the official Welcome Week that precedes the start of classes. Participants learn how to navigate the campus, explore Saint Mary's extraordinary heritage, and are introduced to support services. As a Connect Scholar, students have an early opportunity to make friends on campus.

SUCCESS Multicultural Services and Student Programs (MSSP)

MSSP is solid evidence of Saint Mary's commitment to be a community that supports the inclusion of women of all races, ethnicities, and cultures. The MSSP Office advances the understanding of diversity at all levels by providing educational programs and services, and serving as a support network for all students. The office maintains a resource library of novels, scholarship information, art, films and literature on multicultural topics. It works with faculty and Academic Affairs to help ensure each student's successful academic and social adjustments to Saint Mary's. MSSP also provides a social and professional gathering place for meetings, small classes, study groups and social events.

Saint Mary's College
Office of Admission
Room 122, LeMans Hall
Notre Dame, IN 46556
Ph: (800) 551-7621 / (574) 284-4587
admission@saintmarys.edu
www.saintmarys.edu

FAST FACTS

STUDENT PROFILE	
# of degree-seeking undergraduates	1,555
% male/female	0/100
% African American	2
% American Indian or Alaska Native	1
% Asian or Pacific Islander	2
% Hispanic	8
% White	87
% Pell grant recipients	23.79

First-generation and minority alumni Congresswoman Donna Christensen, 1966, Congressional Delegate; Delia Garcia, 1993, President/CEO, Arizona Hispanic Chamber of Commerce; Tysus Jackson, 1999, Director of Development at Children's National Medical Center; Monica Stallworth Kolimas, 1974, Chief of Staff and Chief Medical Officer at the Western Maryland Hospital Center

ACADEMICS	
full-time faculty	134
student-faculty ratio	11:1
average class size	15
% first-year retention rate	84.8
% graduation rate (6 years)	82

Popular majors Nursing, Education, Business Administration, Communication, Biology/Pre-Med

CAMPUS LIFE	
% live on campus (% freshmen)	84 (99)

Multicultural student clubs and organizations Al Zahra, Around the World Club, Chinese Cultural Club, La Fuerza, Pacific Islanders and Asian Club (PAC), Sisters of Nefertiti, SMC Irish Club, Straight and Gay Alliance

Athletics NCAA Division III, Michigan Intercollegiate Athletic Association, 8 varsity sports including Basketball, Cross Country, Golf, Swimming, Soccer, Softball, Tennis, Volleyball,

ADMISSIONS	
# of applicants	1,446
% accepted	84
SAT Critical Reading (middle 50%)	520-630
SAT Math (middle 50%)	510-620
SAT Writing (middle 50%)	n/a
ACT (middle 50%)	23-27
HS GPA range	3.46-4.0
Deadlines	
early decision	11/15
regular decision	2/15
application fee	$0

COST & AID	
tuition	$32,000
average room & board	$9,800
% of students receiving aid	95
% receiving need-based scholarship or grant aid	86
% receiving aid whose need was fully met	14
average aid package	$23,739*
average student loan debt upon graduation	$23,215**

*Does not include PLUS or private loans.
**Federal student loans.

Grinnell College

Founded in 1846, Grinnell College is a private, co-educational, liberal arts college that seeks to educate its students in the liberal arts through free inquiry and the open exchange of ideas. Grinnell provides a lively academic community of students and teachers of high scholarly qualifications from diverse social and cultural backgrounds. The college aims to graduate women and men who can think clearly, who can speak and write persuasively and eloquently, who can evaluate critically both their own and others' ideas, who can acquire new knowledge and who are prepared to use their knowledge and abilities to serve the common good.

ACCESS **Office of Social Commitment**

Grinnell's Office of Social Commitment provides volunteer opportunities throughout the city of Grinnell for current students. Grinnell partners with local schools, after-school centers and programs, and with our local head start program, allowing students to mentor younger kids. In addition, Grinnell assists students in seeking out and completing applications for post-graduate service opportunities with organizations such as Teach for America, AmeriCorps, Grinnell Corps and the Peace Corps.

OPPORTUNITY **Grinnell Diversity Preview Program**

Before students apply to Grinnell, the college offers a fall fly-in opportunity through the Grinnell Diversity Preview Program (GDPP). Through GDPP, selected students of color and/or first-generation college students are provided a fully-funded opportunity to experience life as "Grinnellians." Grinnell also invites select students of color and first-generation college students to fly-in, free of charge, to our April Admitted Student Programs.

OPPORTUNITY **Need-Blind Admission**

Grinnell is committed to need-blind admission and accessibility for academically qualified students, and thus offers significant financial aid. Grinnell meets 100% of demonstrated need, and awards over $30 million in financial aid every year.

"I applied early decision because I had my heart set on Grinnell. Growing up in California, I knew I wanted a totally different experience for four years. Iowa IS different, but wonderful! I visited for the first time as a sophomore in high school, when I went with my best friend to see her older sister, who was a student at Grinnell. It seemed to me then that everyone knew everyone else, that at Grinnell, you would be surrounded by people you knew. That has really been true for me … the friendships I began during New Student Orientation have continued and developed. Going to college so far from home, my friends at Grinnell have really become my family."

– Michelle B., '13
Salinas, CA
Psychology

SUCCESS **Peer Connections Pre-Orientation Program**

Once students deposit they are invited to participate in the Peer Connections Pre-Orientation Program (PCPOP), operated by our Office of Diversity and Achievement. PCPOP introduces students to the variety of services available at Grinnell College, such as the Writing Lab, Reading Lab, Math Lab, Science Lab and other tutoring opportunities and pairs PCPOP participants with a currently enrolled student mentor and a faculty or staff mentor.

SUCCESS **Grinnell Science Project**

Grinnell has a program for traditionally underrepresented students in the sciences called the Grinnell Science Project (GSP). This program, developed in the early 1990s to prevent students of color and/or first-generation college students from abandoning academic goals in the sciences, brings students to campus one week before New Student Orientation to introduce them to the study of science at Grinnell College. It was recently awarded a Presidential Award for Excellence in Science, Mathematics and Engineering Mentoring.

Grinnell College
1103 Park St
Grinnell, IA 50112
Ph: (641) 269-3600
admission@grinnell.edu
www.grinnell.edu

FAST FACTS

STUDENT PROFILE

# of degree-seeking undergraduates	1,603
% male/female	45/55
% African American	5
% American Indian or Alaska Native	<1
% Asian or Pacific Islander	6
% Hispanic	7
% White	59
% International	12
% Pell grant recipients	22

First-generation and minority alumni Herbie Hancock '60, musician; Ron Gault '62, Managing Director at J.P. Morgan Securities Inc. in South Africa and former member of the Board of Higher Education of New York; Dr. Randy Morgan '65, Lifetime Trustee of Grinnell College and President of University Park Orthopedics in Sarasota, FL; Dr. Irma McLaurin '73, President of Shaw University; Dr. Eric Whitaker '87, Executive Vice President for Strategic Alliances of The University of Chicago Medical Center; David C. White '90, National Executive Director of the Screen Actors Guild

ACADEMICS

full-time faculty	161
full-time minority faculty	28 (and 17 international)
student-faculty ratio	9:1
average class size	17
% first-year retention rate	93
% graduation rate (6 years)	87

Popular majors Biology, History, English, Political Science, Economics

CAMPUS LIFE

% live on campus	88

Multicultural student clubs and organizations African Students Union, Asia and Asian American Association, Asian Media and Culture Club, Chalutzim, Concerned Black Students, International Students Organization, Queer People of Color, Student Organization of Latinas/Latinos

Athletics NCAA Division III, Midwest Conference

ADMISSIONS

# of applicants	2,845
% accepted	43
# of first-year students enrolled	415
SAT Critical Reading (middle 50%)	610-740
SAT Math (middle 50%)	610-730
SAT Writing (middle 50%)	n/a
ACT (middle 50%)	28-32
average HS GPA	n/a
Deadlines	
early decision I	11/15
early decision II	1/1
regular decision	1/15
application fee	$0 (via Common Application online)
fee waiver for applicants with financial need	yes

COST & AID

tuition	$39,250
room & board	$9,334
total need-based institutional scholarships/grants	$30,009,593
% of students apply for need-based aid	n/a
% of students receive aid	89
% receiving need-based scholarship or grant aid	72
% receiving aid whose need was fully met	100
average aid package	$29,915
average student loan debt upon graduation	$18,578

Mount Mercy University

Expect to be engaged by small classes and individualized attention from accomplished professors on our hilltop campus in the heart of historic, Cedar Rapids—a thriving city of 140,000. Hands-on, experiential learning will be a core of your education—whether handing tools to a surgeon as an intern or studying at a partner university in the Czech Republic. You'll find countless ways to get involved and hone your skills for making a difference in the world—our students give more than 12,000 hours every year to service. Experience a balance of liberal arts excellence with career preparation that will help you achieve a successful and meaningful life. More than 90 percent of our graduates are employed or in graduate and professional schools within six months of graduation.

ACCESS **Personalized Learning**

All first-year students are placed in small classes so they may benefit from individual faculty support. Portal courses introduce students to University life and learning, focusing on successful college transitions and exploring key Mercy themes like service, volunteerism, and sustainability. Faculty-student collaboration soars with the *Pathways to Scholarship* program that encourages people to form research teams and share their findings.

ACCESS **Students in Free Enterprise (SIFE)**

Mount Mercy's nationally-recognized Students in Free Enterprise (SIFE) team offers a multitude of learning experiences. SIFE challenges students to develop community outreach projects that focus on market economics, success skills, entrepreneurship, financial literacy, and business ethics. Mount Mercy's SIFE team partners with local and state organizations to enhance their business and marketing plans and to ensure their ventures remain viable in today's competitive marketplace. The SIFE program encourages and allows Mount mercy students to think creatively, to lead others within the community, and to build upon Mount Mercy's reputation as a service-oriented institution.

ACCESS **Elementary School Partnership / High School Art Day**

Education, nursing, social work, and fine arts students can take advantage of Mount Mercy's partnerships with local elementary schools to share their time and talents with students. Activities include theater lessons that encourage students to find their voice on stage and express themselves artistically. Regional high school students are also recognized at Mount Mercy during High School Art Day, where they can participate in art reviews and have their art showcased in the Janalyn Hanson White Gallery.

OPPORTUNITY **Hands-On Learning**

Mount Mercy students are engaged in a variety of hands-on service projects, both as part of the University's curriculum and through the Office of Campus Ministry and Volunteerism. Service-learning and social justice work is the backbone of the Mount Mercy experience. Students serve on the Board of Directors at several local non-profit organizations, and they are active in the Martin Luther King, Jr. Community Wide Day of Service, The Giving Tree, and Project America.

"My scholarship has opened so many doors for me. Without receiving this help there is a good chance that I could not have attended college. I feel so fortunate to have been able to enroll at Mount Mercy."

– Bryce S., '10
Prescott , IA
Outdoor Conservation

SUCCESS **Solid Outcomes**

A Mount Mercy education prepares students for the challenges of the working world and prepares them well for continued education. More than 81 percent of recent graduates reported that that their current positions were very much or somewhat like the type of job they expected after graduation. Professional networking and job planning flourish with the help of Mount Mercy's Career Services office and generous alumni connections

Mount Mercy University
1330 Elmhurst Drive NE
Cedar Rapids, IA 52402
Ph: (319) 368-6460
admission@mtmercy.edu
www.mtmercy.edu

FAST FACTS

STUDENT PROFILE

# of undergraduate enrollment	1,643
% male/female	30/70
% African American	3
% American Indian or Alaska Native	<1
% Asian or Pacific Islander	2
% Hispanic	3
% White	84
% Pell grant recipients	23

First-generation and minority alumni Nancy Penner '81, attorney, Shuttleworth & Ingersoll Law Firm; Sherrie Fletcher '79, archivist, Ronald Reagan Presidential Library; Tammy Koolbeck '86, vice president of Venue Services, VenuWorks; Jean-Paul Calabio '07, SAP & application security, Rockwell Collins; Rachel Collins '01, guidance counselor, Cedar Rapids (Iowa) Kennedy High School

ACADEMICS

full-time faculty	80
student-faculty ratio	12:1
average class size	20
% first-year retention rate	83
% graduation rate (6 years)	65

Popular majors Nursing, Biology, Business, Education, Criminal Justice, Social Work

CAMPUS LIFE

% live on campus	37

Multicultural student clubs and organizations International Club, Mount Mercy Women's Organization, College Pastoral Council, Stangs Christian Fellowship

Athletics NAIA, Midwest Collegiate Conference

ADMISSIONS

# of applicants	864
% accepted	69
SAT range	n/a
ACT (middle 50%)	20-26
average HS GPA	3.44
Deadlines	
regular admission	rolling

COST & AID

tuition	$24,360
room & board	$7,470
% of students receiving aid	92
% receiving need-based scholarship or grant aid	92

University of Northern Iowa

The University of Northern Iowa prides itself on putting "Students First" and has a reputation for providing exceptional undergraduate education. Building on its historic excellence in teacher education, the university has developed outstanding programs in business, natural sciences, humanities and fine arts, and social and behavioral sciences. The university's size — just more than 13,000 students — allows it to offer faculty, facilities, and academic choices of a large university, while retaining a friendly, small-college atmosphere on a compact, park-like campus. With more than 40 major buildings on 940 acres, the campus can still be crossed in an easy 15-minute walk.

ACCESS Multicultural Super Saturday

Multicultural Super Saturday is a comprehensive program designed for high school freshmen, sophomore, juniors, seniors and their guests. During this visit, prospective students and their parents will learn about admissions, the financial aid/scholarship process, campus housing, preparing for college and academic programs. Multicultural Super Saturday also provides the opportunity to meet with UNI students, staff and faculty, tour the campus, and have lunch in one of the dining centers.

OPPORTUNITY Financial Aid Office

Paying for college can seem like a daunting task, leaving many students and their families unsure of what to ask or where to start. The UNI Financial Aid Office prides itself on assisting families in understanding the aid process and ensuring that they can make the University of Northern Iowa accessible and affordable. Notable grants and scholarships include Iowa Minority Academic Grants for Economic Success (IMAGES), Tuition Guarantee Program for Iowans, and Tuition Guarantee Program for Multicultural Community College Iowans, Multicultural Scholar Awards, Out of State Scholar Awards, and Distinguished Scholar Awards for Iowans.

"As the first person in my family to go to college I didn't have anyone to walk me through the college-selection process. And even though I didn't know the path, I knew I wanted a quality education and I took advantage of the opportunities presented to me. UNI was a great choice!"

– Darion W., '11
Gary, Ind.
Organizational Communication

SUCCESS Jump Start Orientation Program

For over a decade, the UNI Jump Start Orientation Program has provided new students from ethnically, culturally, and socioeconomically diverse backgrounds with a "jump start" on their first year at the University. Jump Start is a special orientation program that provides students with an opportunity to make a smooth transition to the University. Students move to campus one week early to learn about campus resources, network with multicultural faculty and staff, and meet with other multicultural students on campus. Additional activities include sessions on academic success, library resources, computer lab training, on-campus job fair, and money management. Many participants are enrolled in Strategies for Academic Success, a course designed to develop effective study techniques and other skills necessary for courses at the collegiate level.

SUCCESS Gaining Panther Success (GPS) Mentor Program

This program is designed to support and encourage new students from diverse backgrounds in their academic and personal growth during their first year at UNI. The GPS program provides an excellent opportunity for students to enhance their academic and personal success in a university environment. Mentors are students who have successfully transitioned into university life at UNI. They serve as guides who meet with their new mentees in individual and group meetings. Mentees receive one-on-one encouragement, information on academic and community resources, and many opportunities to attend on- and off-campus activities with their mentors.

University of Northern Iowa
1227 West 27th Street
Cedar Falls, IA 50614
Ph: (319) 273-2281
admissions@uni.edu
www.uni.edu

FAST FACTS

STUDENT PROFILE

# of degree-seeking undergraduates	11,391
% male/female	43/57
% African American	2.7
% American Indian or Alaska Native	<1
% Asian or Pacific Islander	1
% Hispanic	2.0
% White	89.5
% International	2.9
% Pell grant recipients	29.7

First-generation and minority alumni Inta Eppright-Sanford, Assistant Principal, Nashville TN Public Schools; Clarence Lobdell, Auditor, Office of Inspector General, U.S. Government, Washington DC; Stephanie Mohorne, Assistant Principal, Waterloo (IA) Public Schools

ACADEMICS

full-time faculty	623
full-time minority faculty	81
student-faculty ratio	17:1
average class size	25-30
% first-year retention rate	82
% graduation rate (6 years)	62

Popular majors Elementary Education, Biology, Accounting, Management, Communications

CAMPUS LIFE

% live on campus (% freshmen)	37 (84)

Multicultural student clubs and organizations Asian Alliance, Black Greek Alliance, Black Male Leaders Union, Black Student Union, EXCEL, Ethnic Student Promoters, George Walker Society of Music, Hispanic/Latino Student Union, Minority Graduate Student Association, Multicultural Student Advisory Board, Multicultural Teaching Alliance

Athletics NCAA Division I, Missouri Valley Conference

ADMISSIONS

# of applicants	6,018
% accepted	81
# of first-year students enrolled	1,978
SAT Critical Reading (middle 50%)	n/a
SAT Math (middle 50%)	n/a
SAT Writing (middle 50%)	n/a
ACT (middle 50%)	21-25
average HS GPA	3.45

Deadlines

regular decision	8/15
application fee	$40
fee waiver for applicants with financial need	no

COST & AID

tuition	in-state: $7,008; out-of-state: $15,348
room & board	$7,102
total need-based institutional scholarships/grants	n/a
% of students apply for need-based aid	81
% of students receive aid	86
% receiving need-based scholarship or grant aid	42
% receiving aid whose need was fully met	19
average aid package	$7,897
average student loan debt upon graduation	$25,735

Wartburg College

Wartburg College, affiliated with the Lutheran Church (ELCA), is recognized for outstanding liberal arts and pre-professional programs, competitive athletic teams, stellar music ensembles and active, involved students. Wartburg College has been nationally classified by the Carnegie Foundation for the Advancement of Teaching as one of 62 colleges that foster community engagement in the curriculum and through community outreach and partnerships. The college's high placement rates in jobs, graduate and professional schools includes an 89 percent medical school placement rate and 100 percent placement in other medical programs. Wartburg is included on a list of best Midwestern colleges and among top 200 colleges for science. The college administers more than $37 million in financial aid, providing access to students from a wide variety of socioeconomic backgrounds. The college is named after the Wartburg Castle in Eisenach, Germany.

OPPORTUNITY The Center for Community Engagement Fellows

The Wartburg Center for Community Engagement offers a unique opportunity for students to serve the community and earn a $1,000 educational voucher as CCE Fellows. Fellows enroll as part-time AmeriCorps members and complete 300 hours of service over the course of the academic year. Service can involve internships with nonprofit organizations, completing a leadership class, participating in a service trip or service-learning project, tutoring and other volunteer opportunities. The $1,000 voucher can be used toward tuition, loans or graduate school.

OPPORTUNITY Scholarships for Underrepresented Students

The McElroy Minority Scholarship and Slife Minority Scholarship provide full-tuition scholarships for first-year underrepresented students. GPA and letters of recommendation are considered and reviewed. Preference is given to students from the Waterloo or Cedar Falls, Iowa area and scholarships are renewable based on academic performance. The "Be Orange Scholarship" is awarded to incoming first-generation students. Applicants are recommended by the Admissions Office and approved by the Financial Aid Office.

OPPORTUNITY Diversity Grant

This grant is awarded to underrepresented students with academic potential. The grant amount, up to $2,500 annually, is determined by financial need. A FAFSA must be completed for consideration.

SUCCESS The Pathways Center

The Pathways Center provides comprehensive support to students from orientation to preparing for life after college. Pathways' First Year Experience program helps students make a successful transition to college.

"Wartburg College has provided me with an incredible support system of faculty, staff, and coaches. Thanks to faculty advisers, academic support services, and financial assistance from the college, I will join my brother in becoming the first generation of our family to graduate from college. Along the way, I have made great friends from across the country and around the world, earned a national individual championship in wrestling, and participated in college service trips as a way to help others."

– Romeo D., '09
Cameroon
Religion

Wartburg College
100 Wartburg Blvd.
Waverly, IA 50677-0903
Ph: (319) 352-8200
admissions@wartburg.edu
www.wartburg.edu

FAST FACTS

STUDENT PROFILE

# of degree-seeking undergraduates	1,800
% male/female	47/53
% African American	4.8
% American Indian or Alaska Native	0.2
% Asian or Pacific Islander	1.5
% Hispanic	1.5
% White	82.2
% International	5
% Pell grant recipients	26

First-generation and minority alumni Walter Reed, Jr., director, Iowa Department of Human Rights

ACADEMICS

full-time faculty	107
full-time minority faculty	5
student faculty ratio	12:1
average class size	21
% first-year retention rate	86
% graduation rate (6 years)	69

Popular majors Business Administration, Biology, Communication Arts, Elementary Education, Music Education

CAMPUS LIFE

% live on campus (% freshmen)	81 (98)

Multicultural student clubs and organizations Mosaico, Black Student Union, International Club

Athletics NCAA Division III, IIAC

ADMISSIONS

# of applicants	2,195
% accepted	72
# of first year students enrolled	490
SAT Critical Reading (middle 50%)	410-560
SAT Math (middle 50%)	460-600
SAT Writing (middle 50%)	380-550
ACT (middle 50%)	20-26
Average HS GPA	3.5
Deadlines	
early action	12/1
regular decision	rolling
application fee	$0
fee waiver for applicants with financial need	n/a

COST & AID

tuition (09/10 Academic year)	$30,110
room & board (09/10 Academic year)	$7,975
Total need-based institutional scholarships and grants	$21,509,387
% of students apply for need-based aid	88
% of students receive aid	98
% receiving need-based scholarship or grant aid	76
% receiving aid whose need was fully met	32
average aid package	$31,063
average student loan dept upon graduation	$20,435

Berea College

Berea College offers a high quality liberal arts education to students of all races, who have great promise but limited economic resources. Every admitted student receives a four-year tuition scholarship and the opportunity to work on campus to assist with costs of room and board and to learn valuable skills. Additionally, Berea provides a laptop computer for all new students. Founded in 1855 as the first interracial and co-educational college in the South, Berea promotes understanding and kinship among all people, service to communities in Appalachia and beyond, and sustainable living practices which set an example of new ways to conserve our limited natural resources. The college's motto lays a firm foundation for this one-of-a-kind institution: "God has made of one blood all peoples of the earth."

ACCESS Women's Equality in Education Act (WEEA) Project

The Berea College Women's Equality in Education Act (WEEA) Project provides direct services to 50 Kentucky high school women interested in obtaining college degrees in math and science. Services include hands-on science academic opportunities, science professional development for high school educators, job shadowing and internship experiences, and providing STEM career planning information to students and parents. Berea College students work throughout the year and summer with the project through mentoring and tutoring the WEAA students.

ACCESS Upward Bound

Upward Bound helps young people in grades nine through twelve prepare for higher education. The program provides tutoring, instruction, counseling, career orientation, and an opportunity to experience educational development and personal growth in a college setting while still in high school. Berea College serves 85 participants in selected schools in south central Kentucky.

> ***"I never knew that I could do as well in college as I have. The professors at Berea are so helpful. I could not have done it alone. Now I will walk away with a prestigious education that will always benefit me."***
>
> *– Katie L., '12*
> *Dalton, GA*
> *Nursing*

SUCCESS Four-Year Tuition Scholarship

Berea provides all students a four-year tuition scholarship, which covers remaining tuition costs after all federal, state, institutional, and private grants have been awarded. The cost of education does not include room, board, fees, books, and supplies, but additional financial aid is available to support these costs. The average freshman pays on average only $1,500 for these costs during the first year of enrollment, but many pay nothing if their family cannot afford to contribute.

SUCCESS Work-Learning Program

Another distinctive feature of Berea College is its work-learning program. Berea requires all students to work 10-15 hours per week while carrying a full academic course load. The program provides students with valuable work experience such as teamwork, leadership, and supervising others. Students may work in any one of 130 departments — jobs range from working in food service at Berea's historic Boone Tavern to serving as a teaching assistant for an academic major to helping the local Boys & Girls Club of Madison County.

SUCCESS The Center for Excellence in Learning Through Service (CELTS)

CELTS was created in 2000 to house all of the student-led service programs and community outreach offices and to lead an initiative to integrate service into the academic curriculum.Berea College has been named to the President's Higher Education Community Service Honor Roll with Distinction for four consecutive years. This award, given annually to only a few institutions, is the highest federal recognition a college can receive in regards to innovative and effective volunteering, service-learning and civic engagement.

Berea College
CPO 2220
Berea, KY 40404
Ph: (859) 985-3500
askadmissions@berea.edu
www.berea.edu

FAST FACTS

STUDENT PROFILE

# of degree-seeking undergraduates	1,552
% male/female	41/59
% African American	18
% American Indian or Alaska Native	1
% Asian or Pacific Islander	2
% Hispanic	3
% White	68
% International	7
% Pell grant recipients	90

First-generation and minority alumni Carter G. Woodson, father of black history; John Fenn, Nobel Prize winner; Juanita M. Kreps, former U.S. Secretary of Commerce; Tharon Musser, Tony Award winner; Jack Roush, automotive engineer and designer, owner of Roush Racing

ACADEMICS

full-time faculty	119
full-time minority faculty	22
student-faculty ratio	11:1
average class size	15
% first-year retention rate	78.8
% graduation rate (6 years)	64

Popular majors Biology, Business Administration, Child/Family Studies, Psychology, Technology/ Industrial Arts

CAMPUS LIFE

% live on campus (% freshmen)	99 (99)

Multicultural student clubs and organizations African Student Association, Asian Student Union, Black Music Ensemble, Berea Middle Eastern Dance, Buddhist Student Association, Hispanic Student Association, Center for International Education

Athletics NAIA, Kentucky Intercollegiate Athletic Conference

ADMISSIONS

# of applicants	3,264
% accepted	17
# of first-year students enrolled	429
SAT Critical Reading (middle 50%)	500-620
SAT Math (middle 50%)	465-585
SAT Writing (middle 50%)	510-590
ACT (middle 50%)	21-26
average HS GPA	3.42

Deadlines

regular decision	rolling to 4/30
application fee (online)	$0 ($0)
fee waiver for applicants with financial need	n/a

COST & AID

tuition	$0
room & board	$5,574
total need-based institutional scholarships/grants	$3,592,320
% of students apply for need-based aid	100
% of students receive aid	100
% receiving need-based scholarship or grant aid	100
% receiving aid whose need was fully met	100
average aid package	$29.291
average student loan debt upon graduation	$8,049

Centre College

Centre College, a private, Presbyterian, liberal arts college founded in 1819, is known for its outstanding professors, beautiful 115-acre Greek Revival campus and remarkable alumni. By attracting and nurturing highly motivated students, the college has produced two-thirds of Kentucky's Rhodes Scholars (postgraduate study at Oxford University) in the past 50 years and more than 34 Fulbright recipients (postgraduate study and work around the world). The Centre Commitment guarantees every student an internship, study abroad and graduation within four years or the college provides up to one additional year of tuition-free study. The college's alumni include U.S. vice presidents, Supreme Court justices and the founder of Hard Rock Café.

ACCESS **Centro Latino and Spanish Program**

Centre's Spanish Program established and continues to work with Centro Latino, which serves the area Latino community with translation help and through social and educational programs. Spanish students also provide tutoring, after-school programs and reading camps for the Latino community.

ACCESS **Whitney M. Young Scholars**

Whitney M. Young Scholars spend two weeks on campus each summer through a Louisville-based program that identifies talented, low-income, predominantly African-American students in seventh grade and works with them through high school to prepare for college.

OPPORTUNITY **Posse Foundation**

Centre participates in the Posse Foundation, a program that brings talented inner-city youth to campus to pursue their academics and to help promote cross-cultural communication. Posse students are nominated by their high school to the program and share a collaborative support system with a special mentor to adjust to campus and college life. Centre's Posse Scholars hail from Boston.

OPPORTUNITY **New Horizons Scholarship**

This Centre scholarship program recognizes talented students who are likely to provide campus diversity leadership. As many as 40 students from each class are awarded a scholarship ($16,000 in 2007-08) and guaranteed priority consideration for need-based grants.

OPPORTUNITY **Bonner Scholarship**

This Centre scholarship provides access to higher education for students from underrepresented populations who demonstrate financial need and an ability to have a strong positive impact on campus and the surrounding community through their service work.

SUCCESS **Pre-Freshman Research Program**

The Pre-Freshman Research Program enables students who will be attending Centre to conduct science research during the summer before beginning their freshman year at Centre. The program is open to African-American, Hispanic, Native American and Asian and Pacific Islanders who will enroll at Centre in the fall.

SUCCESS **Academic Affairs Diversity Office**

Centre College strives for a campus community that reflects global society's racial and ethnic diversity. The Academic Affairs Diversity Office recruits and retains diverse faculty, staff and students and also promotes campus diversity by working with the Diversity Student Union, Admission Office, Student Life Office and Human Resources. Activities for the Annual Martin Luther King Celebration and other community relations are also planned through the office.

Centre College
600 W. Walnut St.
Danville, KY 40422-1394
Ph: (859) 238-5350
admissions@centre.edu
www.centre.edu

FAST FACTS

STUDENT PROFILE

# of degree-seeking undergraduates	1,214
% male/female	45/55
% African American	4
% American Indian or Alaska Native	<1
% Asian or Pacific Islander	3
% Hispanic	2
% White	88
% International	2
% Pell grant recipients	15.6

First-generation and minority alumni John Henrey Rogers, U.S. Representative; Issac Tigrett, founder of Hard Rock Café.

ACADEMICS

full-time faculty	104
full-time minority faculty	11
student-faculty ratio	11:1
average class size	18
% first-year retention rate	93
% graduation rate (6 years)	81

Popular majors Economics, English Language and Literature, History, Biology, Anthropology/Sociology

CAMPUS LIFE

% live on campus (% freshmen)	98 (99)

Multicultural student clubs and organizations Diversity Student Union, International Student Association, Hispanic Society, Muslim Student Association, Japanese Club, NAACP

Athletics NCAA Division III, Southern Collegiate Athletic Conference

ADMISSIONS

# of applicants	2,260
% accepted	74.5
# of first-year students enrolled	356
SAT Critical Reading (middle 50%)	570-690
SAT Math (middle 50%)	590-680
SAT Writing (middle 50%)	560-660
ACT (middle 50%)	26-31
average HS GPA	3.58

Deadlines

early decision	12/1
regular admission	1/15
application fee (online)	$40 ($0)
fee waiver for applicants with financial need	yes

COST & AID

tuition	$32,600
room & board	$8,150
total need-based institutional scholarships/grants	$15,610,982
% of students apply for need-based aid	71
% of students receive aid	83
% receiving need-based scholarship or grant aid	62
% receiving aid whose need was fully met	25
average aid package	$25,091
average student loan debt upon graduation	$17,190

Transylvania University

Transylvania University
300 North Broadway
Lexington, KY 40508
Ph: (800) 872-6798
admissions@transy.edu
www.transy.edu

FAST FACTS

STUDENT PROFILE

# of degree-seeking undergraduates	1,092
% male/female	41/59
% African American	5
% American Indian or Alaska Native	<1
% Asian or Pacific Islander	2
% Hispanic	1
% White	82
% International	<1
% Pell grant recipients	27

First-generation and minority alumni
Everett Bass '72, Vice President, Waste Management Inc.; Erwin Roberts '94, Attorney and Former secretary of the Kentucky Personnel Cabinet; Latarika Young '03, Software Engineer, Lexmark International; C. Shawn McGuffey '98, Assistant Professor of Sociology, Boston College

ACADEMICS

full-time faculty	90
full-time minority faculty	5
student-faculty ratio	12:1
average class size	17
% first-year retention rate	88
% graduation rate (6 years)	76

Popular majors Business, Biology, Psychology, Political Science, Spanish

CAMPUS LIFE

% live on campus (% freshmen)	80 (98)

Multicultural student clubs and organizations
Diversity Action Council, Black Student Alliance, TUnity, TERRA, International House, TUTORS (Teaching and Outreach for Refugee Children)
Athletics NCAA Division III, Heartland Collegiate Athletic Conference

ADMISSIONS

# of applicants	1,423
% accepted	79
# of first-year students enrolled	283
SAT Critical Reading (middle 50%)	550-670
SAT Math (middle 50%)	510-630
SAT Writing (middle 50%)	n/a
ACT (middle 50%)	24-30
average HS GPA	3.73

Deadlines

early decision	12/1
regular decision	2/1
application fee (online)	$30 ($0)
fee waiver for applicants with financial need	yes

COST & AID

tuition	$28,250
room & board	$8,450
total need-based institutional scholarships/grants	n/a
% of students apply for need-based aid	77
% receiving need-based scholarship or grant aid	98
% receiving aid whose need was fully met	22
average aid package	$21,914
average student loan debt upon graduation	$22,432

Founded in 1780, Transylvania is the sixteenth oldest college in the United States. Consistently ranked as one of the nation's top liberal arts colleges, it is one of only a few schools in that group located in the heart of city. Transylvania's location in vibrant Lexington, Kentucky, a city of 300,000 people, provides studens with professional, cultural, and social opportunities only available in such an environment. Over one-third of Transylvania's students are the first in their families to attend a four-year college, and they thrive in Transylvania's challenging yet supporting environment. Transylvania's faculty is among the strongest in the nation. Professors know their students well, they push students in their areas of strength, and they support students in their areas of weakness.

ACCESS Community Outreach

Transylvania students serve local children through a number of service opportunities, including Ready, Set, Study (a partnership between Transylvania University, the Carnegie Center for Literacy and Learning, and Breckinridge Elementary School), TUTORS (Transylvania University Teaching and Outreach to Refugee Children), and special tutoring programs through organizations like 3M Tutors and the Optimists Club. The Transylvania community holds an annual holiday party, Crimson Christmas, for children who participate in the local Big Brother/Big Sister Program. Transylvania partners with a variety of other organizations each year to prepare and distribute backpacks with school supplies. Transylvania also offers summer sports and academic camps for students from kindergarten through high school

> ***"What sets Transy apart is its very friendly environment. Other schools I visited seemed fake - like they were giving me the same set speech they give every prospective student who walks in the door. But here, I'm not just another name. I feel like people really want me to be here. And my financial aid package, scholarships, and campus work-study make it possible for me and my family."***
> *– Quanta T., '12*
> *Lexington, KY*
> *Cultural, Racial, and Ethnic Studies*

OPPORTUNITY Scholarships

Transylvania offers a wide range of academic scholarships and need-based awards that help bridge the cost of a Transylvania education with what students and their families can afford. Of all students, 98 percent - and 100 percent of all freshmen - receive scholarships and/or financial aid. Transylvania is well known for meeting student need, especially those with the highest level of need.

SUCCESS Diversity Action Council (DAC)

The Diversity Action Council is a student leadership organization created to promote a campus environment that respects and celebrates diversity in all dimensions. DAC works directly with the Office of Multicultural Affairs to plan diversity programs for the Transylvania community. DAC maintains a consistent working relationship with the Office of Community Service and Civic Engagement, the Office of Admissions, and the Student Activities Board while also operating as an umbrella organization for other student organizations like the Black Student Alliance and TUnity.

Dillard University

Dillard University
2601 Gentilly Boulevard
New Orleans, LA 70122
Ph: (504) 283-8822
admissions@dillard.edu
www.dillard.edu

Set on a beautiful 55-acre campus in historic New Orleans, Louisiana, Dillard University offers a high-quality, comprehensive—and affordable—education in an intimate and supportive environment that helps students reach their full potential. The faculty at Dillard not only teach, but are true mentors. Dillard's internships, rate of placements in the workplace and admissions to graduate schools are among the highest in the nation. Dillard is preparing them for world-class graduate and professional schools, and successful careers in law, medicine, science and research, education, business, and the arts and entertainment. Dillard students are being prepared for leadership roles and for giving back to their communities, their states, their nation and the world.

ACCESS Eighth Grade Initiative

The Dillard University Eighth Grade Initiative program is a cutting edge, pre-collegiate program that is designed to encourage New Orleans students from diverse backgrounds to successfully negotiate high school and to attend college. A cohort of 100 students is enrolled into the Dillard University's Eighth Grade Initiative program each year. These students remain in the Eighth Grade Initiative program until their matriculation into Dillard University. Dillard University also participates in a number of federally funded TRiO programs, including Student Support Services, Educational Talent Search, and Upward Bound.

"Dillard University allows me to be in a loving environment while receiving a quality education. Dillard is truly preparing me for graduate level programs and a very rewarding, successful life."

– Terrance M., '12
Houston ,TX
Biology

OPPORTUNITY UNCF Gates Millennium Scholars Program

Dillard University promotes the UNCF Gates Millennium Scholars Program, a scholarship sponsored by Bill Gates, as the university is a member institution with UNCF. The scholarship criteria is as follows: Students submit a nominee form (i.e. student application, nominator form, recommender form); student must be of African American, American Indian, Asian, Pacific Islander, or Hispanic American descent; be a US citizen; have a 3.3 GPA on a 4.0 scale; be a first year student attending an accredited institution; have demonstrated leadership abilities; and meet federal Pell Grant criteria.

OPPORTUNITY Emerging Scholars Program

Students whose GPA or standardized test scores fall below traditional admissions requirements may nevertheless qualify for the Emerging Scholars program, which provides sliding scores for students hailing from the metropolitan New Orleans area. Emerging Scholars receive academic, cultural and social enrichment during the summer after their senior year and, if they complete it successfully, matriculate in the fall semester.

SUCCESS Student Orientation, Advisement and Registration (S.O.A.R.)

All students are required to participate in an orientation program, during which they learn about the university resources available to them. Academic advising and class registration are major elements of the program, which is offered in a number of sessions.

FAST FACTS

STUDENT PROFILE

# of degree-seeking undergraduates	781
% male/female	29/71
% African American	97
% American Indian or Alaska Native	0
% Asian or Pacific Islander	<1
% Hispanic	<1
% White	<1
% International	n/a
% Pell grant recipients	73

First-generation and minority alumni Lisa Frazier-Page, writer, The Washington Post; Ellis Marsalis, jazz musician; Garrett Morris, comedian, actor; Ruth J. Simmons, first African-American president of an Ivy League School (Brown University)

ACADEMICS

full-time faculty	104
full-time minority faculty	94
student-faculty ratio	12:1
average class size	13
% first-year retention rate	69
% graduation rate (6 years)	28

Popular majors Biology, Nursing, Mass Communication, Business Management, Sociology

CAMPUS LIFE

% live on campus (% freshmen)	47 (100)

Multicultural student clubs and organizations International Language Club, Melton Foundation, Vision Quest

Athletics NAIA, Gulf Coast Athletic Conference

ADMISSIONS

# of applicants	1,974
% accepted	35
# of first-year students enrolled	173
SAT Critical Reading (middle 50%)	310-560
SAT Math (middle 50%)	400-560
SAT Writing (middle 50%)	310-440
ACT (middle 50%)	16-20
average HS GPA	3.2

Deadlines

regular admission	rolling
application fee (online)	$30
fee waiver for applicants with financial need	yes

COST & AID

tuition	$13,000
room & board	$8,285
total need-based institutional scholarships/grants	$5,844,681
% of students apply for need-based aid	92
% of students receive aid	98
% receiving need-based scholarship or grant aid	52
% receiving aid whose need was fully met	73
average aid package	$14,220
average student loan debt upon graduation	$23,585

Loyola University New Orleans

Loyola University New Orleans is a private, co-educational Catholic university located in the heart of the city. Loyola offers students a wide variety of academic programs, ranging from arts and sciences to business to music, all taught in the Jesuit tradition of educating the whole person. While students are challenged to seek personal excellence, they are also guided in their efforts, helped by Loyola's "person-centered" learning community. Consistent with its Jesuit and Catholic heritage, Loyola strives to develop students into a new generation of leaders who possess a love for truth, the critical intelligence to pursue it and the courage to articulate it.

ACCESS Upward Bound

Committed to providing students with a quality education, Loyola reaffirms its social responsibility by hosting an Upward Bound program open to local underserved high school students. Upward Bound consists of a six-week summer course that provides intense instruction and college credit, and a Saturday and after-school course that provides instructional and tutorial assistance to increase developmental skills in language arts, mathematics, science and foreign language. Additionally, Upward Bound students receive academic and career advisement, postsecondary orientation and preparation and participate in a variety of motivational and cultural enrichment activities.

OPPORTUNITY Jazz Brunch and President's Open House

Each fall Loyola hosts a Jazz Brunch open house for prospective students; and each spring an open house for all admitted students. The latter, the President's Open House, offers families an opportunity to gain further insight into the Loyola collegiate experience. Students and guests take part in several events held throughout the day, including a talk with the president, a meeting with the academic deans and special interest sessions.

SUCCESS Summer Bridge

In keeping with its philosophy of "person-centered" education, Loyola serves the needs of students going through the college admissions process who might need a "jump start" through the Summer Bridge program. In Summer Bridge, traditionally underserved high school seniors are conditionally admitted to Loyola with the understanding that they must attend college preparatory classes. Loyola's Summer Bridge program provides a study skills class, the opportunity to earn six college credits over the summer. With this kind of intense, individualized guidance, Summer Bridge students enter Loyola academically prepared and confident.

SUCCESS Mathematics Center

The Loyola Mathematics Center offers one-on-one tutoring for students from developmental math through calculus, differential equations, linear algebra and discrete math. In an effort to support low-income students, the Mathematics Center also offers a wide variety of mathematics tools. Interactive computer software as well as video tapes are available to those who prefer these methods of assistance.

"I was an intern at Entergy, a utility company that serves Louisiana, Texas, Mississippi, and Arkansas. Entergy is one of the largest companies in Louisiana and employees more than 14,000 people in various fields such as engineering, management, finance, and my field, accounting. Thanks go to Loyola and the College of Business for helping me to discover such a great opportunity in the city of New Orleans."

– Ryan J., '08
Missouri
Accounting

Loyola University
6363 St. Charles Avenue
Campus Box 18
New Orleans, LA 70118
Ph: (504) 865-3240
admit@loyno.edu
www.loyno.edu

FAST FACTS

STUDENT PROFILE

# of degree-seeking undergraduates	2,619
% male/female	43/57
% African American	16
% American Indian or Alaska Native	>1
% Asian or Pacific Islander	5
% Hispanic	13
% Pell grant recipients	25

First-generation and minority alumni Ellis Marsalis, jazz pianist, recording artist; Manuel A. Esquivel, former Prime Minister, Belize; Cassandra McWilliams Chandler, assistant director of the Office of Public Affairs, national spokesperson, FBI; Dr. Rose-Marie Toussaint, liver transplant surgeon, author; Michael Smith, ESPN

ACADEMICS

full-time faculty	295
full-time minority faculty	40
student-faculty ratio	10:1
average class size	19
% first-year retention rate	82
% graduation rate (6 years)	59

Popular majors Communications, Biology, Psychology, Music Industry Studies, International Business, English Writing

CAMPUS LIFE

% live on campus (% freshmen)	49 (73)

Multicultural student clubs and organizations Black Student Union, International Student Association (ISA), Loyola Asian Student Organization (LASO), Bridging the Gap

Athletics NAIA, Gulf Coast Athletic Conference

ADMISSIONS

# of applicants	5,399
% accepted	57
# of first-year students enrolled	782
SAT Critical Reading (middle 50%)	570-670
SAT Math (middle 50%)	540-650
SAT Writing (middle 50%)	550-660
ACT (middle 50%)	24-29
average HS GPA	3.8

Deadlines

priority application	12/1
regular decision	rolling
application fee (online)	$20 ($20)
fee waiver for applicants with financial need	yes

COST & AID

tuition	$32,266
room & board	$10,990
total need-based institutional scholarships/grants	$25,670,539
% of students apply for need-based aid	75
% of students receive aid	65
% receiving need-based scholarship or grant aid	65
% receiving aid whose need was fully met	18
average aid package	$23,960
average student loan debt upon graduation	$22,319

Bowdoin College

Bowdoin College
5000 College Station
Brunswick, ME 04011-8441
Ph: (207) 725-3100
admissions@bowdoin.edu
www.bowdoin.edu

Located on a 205-acre campus in coastal Brunswick, Maine, Bowdoin College has provided students with a nonsectarian liberal arts education since 1794. The college prides itself in the recruitment of first-generation and minority students, who make up approximately 40 percent of the student body. For all students, Bowdoin has a 92 percent graduation rate over six years and a 96 percent first-year retention rate. Offering more than 40 academic majors and award-winning educational facilities, Bowdoin offers an education and a residential experience focused on instilling principled leadership, lifelong learning, and service to the common good.

ACCESS Upward Bound

At Bowdoin College, Upward Bound serves first-generation, low-income students from 16 high schools in rural Maine. The program has two components — the summer program and the academic year program. Students apply to the summer program during the second semester of their sophomore year in high school. The students visit the Bowdoin College campus for two six-week summer sessions — one before the junior year and another before the senior year of high school. During the regular academic year, Upward Bound counselors visit students each month to provide academic counseling. A few Upward Bound students are accepted into the Bridge Program for the summer after high school graduation. Students earn college credit in Composition and Art History while working and living in a Bowdoin College residence.

"I am from Florida, so people always ask why I would even think of going to school in Maine. The answer is as simple as this: I fell in love with Bowdoin during my Invitational trip. With friendly students, welcoming professors, helpful staff, and gorgeous fall foliage (not to mention the delicious food), how could anyone not?"

– Carina S., '10
Coral Springs, FL
Visual Arts

OPPORTUNITY QuestBridge

Bowdoin is a partner with QuestBridge, a non-profit program that links low-income students with educational and scholarship opportunities at 26 top colleges and universities throughout the U.S. Through the QuestBridge National College Match Program, Bowdoin has enrolled low-income students from many parts of the U.S. In many cases, these are students who became interested in Bowdoin through partnership with QuestBridge.

OPPORTUNITY The Explore Bowdoin and Experience

The Explore Bowdoin and Experience programs are all–expense paid college visit programs for talented students from around the country who can contribute the college's diversity. Bowdoin knows that the most influential factor in a student's decision to attend Bowdoin is a campus visit. The programs are crucial for students who are unable to afford the trip to Maine.

SUCCESS Baldwin Program for Academic Development

The Baldwin Program offers counseling in academic skills and training in time- and stress-management techniques. The program also offers peer tutoring, study skills development, study groups for particular classes and assistance for students with different learning styles.

FAST FACTS

STUDENT PROFILE

# of degree-seeking undergraduates	1,751
% male/female	50/50
% African American	5
% American Indian or Alaska Native	1
% Asian or Pacific Islander	7
% Hispanic	12
% Two or more races	6
% White	65
% International	3
% Pell grant recipients	13

First-generation and minority alumni John Brown Russwurm, Bowdoin's first (and the nation's third) African-American graduate, teacher, writer, editor, "The Freedom's Journal," governor of Liberia; Kenneth I. Chenault, chairman and CEO, American Express; Geoffrey Canada, author, educator, president and CEO, Harlem Children's Zone

ACADEMICS

full-time faculty	181
full-time minority faculty	36
student-faculty ratio	9:1
average class size	16
% first-year retention rate	95
% graduation rate (6 years)	92

Popular majors Economics, History, Government, Biology, Environmental Studies (coordinate major), English

CAMPUS LIFE

% live on campus (% freshmen)	93 (100)

Multicultural student clubs and organizations African American Center, International Students Association, Latin American Students Association, Korean American Students Association, Asian Students Association, Southeast Asian Students Association, Caribbean Students Association

Athletics NCAA Division III, New England Small Colleges Athletic Conference

ADMISSIONS

# of applicants	6,554
% accepted	16.1
# of first-year students enrolled	484
SAT Critical Reading (middle 50%)	660-750
SAT Math (middle 50%)	660-750
SAT Writing (middle 50%)	660-750
ACT (middle 50%)	30-33

Note: Submission of standardized test is optional for admission to Bowdoin

average HS GPA	n/a
Deadlines	
early decision I	11/15
early decision II	1/1
regular decision	1/1
application fee (online)	$60 ($60)
fee waiver for applicants with financial need	yes

COST & AID

tuition	$42,386
room & board	$11,654
total need-based institutional scholarships/grants	$25,924,301
% of students apply for need-based aid	51
% of students receive aid	42
% receiving need-based scholarship or grant aid	42
% receiving aid whose need was fully met	100
% of students with loans in aid packages	0
average aid package	$39,484
average student loan debt upon graduation	$18,229

Colby College

Colby College
4800 Mayflower Hill
Waterville, ME 04901
Ph: (800) 723-3032
admissions@colby.edu
www.colby.edu

Colby College, one of the country's oldest independent liberal arts colleges, is a small, private college located in Waterville, Maine. Colby is a national leader in research and project-based undergraduate learning and has won awards for campus internationalization and environmental studies and stewardship. Colby's focus on diversity and internationalization is renowned. 70 percent of Colby students study abroad, and 66 countries are represented on campus. Colby's Oak Institute for the Study of International Human Rights supports international Oak Scholars, promotes interaction among international and American students on campus and brings a human rights practitioner to Colby for one semester every year.

OPPORTUNITY **Ralph J. Bunche Scholars Program**

The Ralph J. Bunche Scholars Program supports students of color who demonstrate leadership potential and academic strength. Each year 10 to 15 students enroll at Colby College as Bunche Scholars. Bunche Scholar weekend symposia are held each spring on the Colby campus. Additionally, as Bunche Scholars pursue internship opportunities, a stipend of $3,000 will be provided for one summer internship during the student's Colby career.

OPPORTUNITY **Posse Foundation**

Colby participates in the Posse Foundation, a program that brings talented inner-city youth to campus to pursue their academics and to help promote cross-cultural communication. Posse students are nominated by their high school to the program and share a collaborative support system with a special mentor to adjust to campus and college life. Colby's Posse Scholars hail from New York City.

OPPORTUNITY **Experience Colby and Colby Live**

Experience Colby (fall) and Colby Live (early spring) are all-expense paid college visit programs for U.S. citizens and permanent residents with African, Latino/a, Asian, and Native heritage. Colby continues to have a deep commitment to increasing campus diversity, with the ultimate goal of developing a truly multicultural community. We understand that the campus visit is an important part of any student's decision-making process, and Colby has committed resources necessary to make such visits possible.

SUCCESS **Advising Dean Program**

The Advising Dean program supports and enhances Colby's commitment to first rate individual advising of students. Designed to complement Colby's academic advising, the Advising Dean program ensures that all students have a point of contact for advice and counsel. The Advising Deans are knowledgeable about issues and problems that arise for student and are a good source of information about College resources and policies.

SUCCESS **Colby Achievement Program in the Sciences (CAPS)**

Colby Achievement Program in the Sciences is a six-week summer program designed to provide participating pre-first year students with the tools and experience to excel in their chosen science major, and to encourage career development at an early stage of their Colby education. This program, funded in large part by a grant from the Howard Hughes Medical Institute, accepts ten students per summer.

FAST FACTS

STUDENT PROFILE

degree-seeking undergraduates	1,825
% male/female	46/54
% African American	4
% American Indian or Alaska Native	<1
% Asian or Pacific Islander	7
% Hispanic	4
% White	60
% International	5
% Pell grant recipients	11

First-generation and minority alumni Ms. Hannah Beech '95 Journalist for *TIME*; Dr. Norman Fernandez Navarro '88 Obstetrician and Gynecologist; Rev. Richard L. Freeman '82 Pastor of Ocean View Baptist Church; Dr. Lynn McKinley-Grant '69, Specialized Dermatologist; Dr. Don Roland Heacock '49, Doctor of Child Psychiatry

ACADEMICS

full-time faculty	166
full-time minority faculty	20
student-faculty ratio	10:1
average class size	16
% first-year retention rate	95
% graduation rate (6 years)	90

Popular majors Biology, English, Government

CAMPUS LIFE

% live on campus (% freshmen)	94 (100)

Multicultural student clubs and organizations Anime Club, Asian-American Student Association, Asian Cultural Society, Bulgarian Club, Colby Taiko, Desi/South Asian Club, Filipino Club, Four Winds (Native American group), International Club, Irish Club, Project Ally, Society Organized Against Racism, Student Organization for Black and Hispanic Unity, The Bridge, Women's Group

Athetics NCAA Division III, New England Small College Athletic Conference

ADMISSIONS

# of applicants	5,351
% accepted	29
# of first-year students enrolled	477
SAT Critical Reading (middle 50%)	630-710
SAT Math (middle 50%)	620-710
SAT Writing (middle 50%)	610-715
ACT (middle 50%)	28-31
average HS GPA	n/a
Deadlines	
early decision I	11/15
early decision II	1/1
regular decision	1/1
online application fee	$0
fee waiver for applicants with financial need	yes

COST & AID

tuition (including room & board)	$53,800
total need-based institutional scholarships/grants	$24,784,000
% of students apply for need-based aid	49
% of students receive aid	42
% receiving need-based scholarship or grant aid	42
% receiving aid whose need was fully met	100
average aid package	$33,838
average student loan debt upon graduation	$16,050

University of Maine at Farmington

The University of Maine at Farmington is a selective, public, liberal-arts college, offering quality programs in teacher education, human services and arts and sciences. Enrollment is limited to just 2,000 students. Farmington is also one of just 20 colleges and universities across the nation featured in *Student Success in College: Creating Conditions That Matte*r, a book that identifies schools that serve as models of educational effectiveness. The university features developed individualized course "tracks" in each pre-professional area — specific courses identified as ideal for meeting the entrance requirements of medical schools, law schools and MBA programs. From Ivy League universities to prestigious research institutions, Farmington students are regularly accepted to some of the finest medical schools, law schools, MBA programs and graduate schools in the nation.

ACCESS **GEAR UP**

Farmington participates in the national GEAR UP program, which provides grants to states and organizations to provide services to high-poverty middle and high school students. In 2005, Farmington received a six-year, $2 million GEAR UP grant from the U.S. Department of Education.

OPPORTUNITY **Diversity Scholarships / Native American Waiver and Scholarship Program**

Diversity Scholarships are available each year for outstanding new first-year students whose attendance at Farmington would help create a more diverse population. Preference is given to students who have demonstrated academic achievement, who have contributed to their schools and communities, and who can contribute to diversity on campus. Farmington also offers a Native American Waiver and Scholarship Program, which covers tuition, mandatory fees and room and board charges. This program is for Native North Americans who have resided in Maine for at least one year.

OPPORTUNITY **New England Regional Student Program**

Students admitted from other New England states into a Farmington program major that is not offered by the public institutions in their home state may be eligible for reduced tuition.

SUCCESS **Summer Experience**

A week-long program where high schools students live on campus, Summer Experience is a college "test run" of sorts. Participants are enrolled in a one-credit course that gives them great insight into the liberal arts and the Farmington faculty. It is also a great opportunity for students to meet some of their classmates and get acquainted before move-in day. Summer Experience is an optional program but has proven year after year to be a great academic and social introduction to Farmington.

SUCCESS **Summer Orientation**

A four-day orientation begins students' Farmington career. On move-in day, there is an abundance of Orientation Events Staff ready to help students move in and get acquainted with their new residential community. Throughout those four days, students also participate in a number of off-campus trips, from whitewater rafting to trail riding and everything in between. The four days are designed for new students to get comfortable in their new surroundings before the upperclassmen return.

University of Maine at Farmington
246 Main St.
Farmington, ME 04938
Ph: (207) 778-7050
umfadmit@maine.edu
www.farmington.edu

FAST FACTS

STUDENT PROFILE

undergraduate enrollment	2,265
% male/female	34/66
% African American	1
% American Indian or Alaska Native	1
% Asian or Pacific Islander	1
% Hispanic	<1
% White	97
% Pell grant recipients	39

ACADEMICS

full-time faculty	130
student-faculty ratio	14:1
average class size	19
% first-year retention rate	73
% graduation rate (6 years)	59

Popular majors Elementary Education, Psychology

CAMPUS LIFE

% live on campus (% freshmen)	52 (95)

Multicultural student clubs and organizations
Otaku Club, Voices of Women on Campus

Athletics NAIA/NCAA Division III, Sunrise Conference

ADMISSIONS

# of applicants	1,902
% accepted	68
SAT Critical Reading (middle 50%)	460-580
SAT Math (middle 50%)	440-560
SAT Writing (middle 50%)	450-560
ACT (middle 50%)	n/a
average HS GPA	3.0
Deadlines	
early action	11/15
regular admission	rolling
application fee (online)	$40 ($40)
waiver for applicants with financial need	n/a

COST & AID

tuition	in-state: $9,137; out-of-state: $18,225
room & board	$8,168
total need-based institutional scholarships/grants	n/a
% of students apply for need-based aid	n/a
% of students receive aid	84
% receiving need-based scholarship or grant aid	n/a
% receiving aid whose need was fully met	13.4
average aid package	$8,433
average student loan debt upon graduation	$19,490

Bowie State University

Bowie State University
14000 Jericho Park Road
Bowie, MD 20715-9465
Ph: (301) 860-4000
ugradadmissions@bowiestate.edu
www.bowiestate.edu

Founded in 1865 and located in vibrant, affluent Prince George's County, Bowie State University is Maryland's oldest historically black institution. A comprehensive university, BSU offers exemplary bachelor's, master's, and doctoral programs with a specific focus on computer science, business, health sciences, information technology, natural sciences, education, and related disciplines that enable students to think critically, make new discoveries, value differences, and provide leadership in a highly technical, rapidly changing global society. Bowie State continues to make strides and is one of the nation's top five producers of African Americans earning master's degrees in technology, science and mathematics.

"TRIO has been an integral part of my success at Bowie State University. TRIO provided me with tutoring (Math & English), access to a computer lab, and a job. More importantly, TRIO has been a family that provided the love, support, and encouragement I needed to graduate successfully in four years."

– Anthony S., '09
Waldorf, MD
Business Administration

OPPORTUNITY **Financial Aid Survival Guide**

In addition to the Bowie State Institutional Scholarship, the Office of Financial Aid publishes an online financial aid guide that explains the basics of applying for financial aid and enumerates additional sources of financial aid for students. The guide also provides links to information about scholarships, many of which are geared toward minority students.

SUCCESS **TRIO/Student Support Services**

BSU received a $1.5 million grant from the U.S. Department of Education to enhance the TRIO/ Student Support Services program targeting low-income, first-generation or disable college students. This program allows students who have faced adversity the opportunity to be successful by providing the resources and support needed.

SUCCESS **Academic Advisement Center/ Career, Cooperative Education and International Services**

Seeking to promote academic performance and retention, the university houses the Academic Advisement Center to provide enhanced academic advisement to new freshmen and undecided majors, and to support students with low grades by helping them address outside factors, such as employment or familial concerns, that may be hindering them. Students can likewise access Career, Co-op and International Services, which provide career planning, job search assistance and programs to assist students and alumni in making meaningful career, educational and life choices.

SUCCESS **NASAP Student Leadership Institute**

The annual NASAP Student Leadership Institute provides Bowie State students with an opportunity to learn the techniques of African-centered leadership through Nguzo Saba principles. The Student Leadership Institute offers courses in conflict resolution, effective communication and ethical decision-making. The program culminates in a community service project.

SUCCESS **Counseling Services**

A component of the University Wellness Center, the center provides personal, social, career and academic counseling. To assist in the retention of freshmen and sophomore students, the center conducts freshmen and sophomore interviews to assess their psychosocial needs and provide intervention.

FAST FACTS

STUDENT PROFILE

# of degree-seeking undergraduates	4,362
% male/female	35/65
% African American	88.4
% American Indian or Alaska Native	<1
% Asian or Pacific Islander	1.8
% White	4.2
% International	1.3
% Pell grant recipients	36.4

First-generation and minority alumni Joanne Benson, Maryland State Assembly delegate; William Missouri, Maryland Circuit Court judge; Toni Braxton, R&B singer

ACADEMICS

full-time faculty	230
full-time minority faculty	n/a
student-faculty ratio	16:1
average class size	18
% first-year retention rate	74
% graduation rate (6 years)	46

Popular majors Education, Computer Science, Business, Nursing, Communications, Psychology

CAMPUS LIFE

% live on campus (% freshmen)	26 (33)

Multicultural student clubs and organizations African Student Association, Caribbean Students Association, Eyes Wide Shut, Friends of Africa Association, International Student Association, Latino/Hispanic Student Association, Muslim Student Association

Athletics NCAA Division II, Central Intercollegiate Athletic Conference

ADMISSIONS

# of applicants	4,928
% accepted	53
# of first-year students enrolled	714
SAT Critical Reading (middle 50%)	447
SAT Math (middle 50%)	434
SAT Writing (middle 50%)	n/a
ACT (middle 50%)	n/a
average HS GPA	2.77

Deadlines

regular decision	4/1 (rolling after 4/1)
application fee (online)	$40 (40)
fee waiver for applicants with financial need	no

COST & AID

tuition	in-state $4,414; out-of-state $14,938
room & board	$7,535
total need-based institutional scholarships/grants	$3,590,188
% of students apply for need-based aid	65
% of students receive aid	75
% receiving need-based scholarship or grant aid	48
% receiving aid whose need was fully met	27
average aid package	$8,016
average student loan debt upon graduation	$13,730

Johns Hopkins University

Johns Hopkins University opened in 1876 as America's first research institution. Today, Johns Hopkins remains an active, engaged community that is enhanced by perspectives from all over the world. Johns Hopkins is an institution that values diversity in all of its forms. Through the Office of Multicultural Affairs (OMA), Johns Hopkins promotes the holistic development of their students by providing direct services to underrepresented populations, including first generation students. Through OMA and other campus resources, all students have the opportunity to develop independent critical thinking, gain cultural competencies, and flourish on a socially diverse campus. Johns Hopkins is also regarded as a world leader in teaching and research, and they believe that the success of each is dependent upon the other.

"Though Hopkins' multicultural community is not the biggest, I found it to be extremely supportive. My freshman year went so smoothly because the upper class-men were always there if I needed something. Because they were so nice I feel obligated to do the same for the next class."

– Ndubisi O., '14, Baltimore, MD Public Health

ACCESS **Johns Hopkins Tutorial Project**

The Johns Hopkins Tutorial Project pairs Baltimore City elementary school children with current Johns Hopkins undergraduate tutors for one-on-one tutoring. In addition to helping children gain vital skills, this unique setting is also designed to cultivate self-esteem and confidence. The fun, supportive environment and personal attention ensures that children come away with a greater sense of their own abilities, a renewed interest in learning and doing well in school, and the knowledge that they are capable and talented and can succeed.

OPPORTUNITY **Baltimore Scholars Program**

Baltimore City public high school students that apply and are accepted to Hopkins as undergraduate students, are awarded a full-tuition, four-year scholarship by the Baltimore Scholars Program. There are specific residency requirements and award recipients must remain in good standing.

OPPORTUNITY **Hopkins Overnight Multicultural Experience (HOME)**

HOME is a fly-in, three-day, two-night program for underrepresented minority students. Prospective students experience multicultural life at Hopkins and are hosted overnight our Multicultural Student Volunteers (MSV). This program coincides with the Fall Open House program. HOME requires an application; information is available via high school counselors and an invitation from the university.

OPPORTUNITY **Discovery Days**

The Discovery Days program is for accepted underrepresented minority students. Students are hosted on campus for a three-day and two-night experience in April, during which admitted students spend the night with MSV hosts and learn about multicultural life here. The trip culminates with a sunset dinner cruise around Baltimore's Inner Harbor.

SUCCESS **Mentoring Assistance Peer Program (MAPP)**

MAPP is a freshman mentoring program that has served thousands of underrepresented Johns Hopkins students. Freshmen in the program are assigned an upperclassman who is dedicated to providing continual support. MAPP mentors are selected and trained to support students dealing with many first year experiences, including academics, career development, social connectivity, cultural exploration, and community involvement

SUCCESS **Office of Multicultural Affairs (OMA)**

OMA cultivates an environment where persons of all cultural backgrounds are understood and respected, and where civility, leadership and cultural heritage are highly regarded. OMA promotes the holistic development of Hopkins students by providing direct services to underrepresented populations.

Johns Hopkins University
3400 North Charles St. Mason Hall
Baltimore, MD 21218
Ph: (410) 516-8171
gotojhu@jhu.edu
apply.jhu.edu

FAST FACTS

STUDENT PROFILE

# of degree-seeking undergraduates	4,997
% male/female	52/48
% African American	5
% American Indian or Alaska Native	<1
% Asian or Pacific Islander	21
% Hispanic	8
% White	52
% International	8
% Pell grant recipients	11

First-generation and minority alumni Kweisi Mfume MA '84, former President/CEO of the National Association for the Advancement of Colored People (NAACP), as well as a five-term Democratic Congressman; Leslie Sanchez MBA '02, author, political analyst, founder and CEO of Impacto Group LLC; Wes Moore BA '01, youth advocate, Army combat veteran, promising business leader and author; Gil Scott-Heron MA '72, poet, singer, songwriter, author, political activist; Rafael Hernandez Colon BA '56, former Governor of Puerto Rico; Sheila Dixon Edu '85, former Mayor of Baltimore City

ACADEMICS

full-time faculty	519
full-time minority faculty	13
student-faculty ratio	12:1
average class size	16
% first-year retention rate	97
% graduation rate (6 years)	92

Popular majors Public Health, International Studies, Biology, Biomedical Engineering, The Writing Seminars

CAMPUS LIFE

% live on campus (% freshmen)	99

Multicultural student clubs and organizations Mentoring Assistance Peer Program, Students Educating and Empowering for Diversity, Black Student Union, Organizacion Latino Estudiantil, African Students Association, National Society of Black Engineers, Hopkins Organization for Minority Engineers and Scientists, Multicultural Student Volunteers, Caribbean Culture Society, Diversity Sexuality and Gender Alliance

Athletics Division I (lacrosse); Division III (all other sports), Centennial Conference

ADMISSIONS

# of applicants	19,388
% accepted	18
# of first-year students enrolled	1,245
SAT Critical Reading (middle 50%)	670-750
SAT Math (middle 50%)	690-780
SAT Writing (middle 50%)	670-770
ACT (middle 50%)	30-34
average HS GPA	3.7
Deadlines	
early decision	11/1
regular decision	1/1
application fee	$70
fee waiver for applicants with financial need	yes

COST & AID

tuition	$42,280
room & board	$12,962
total need-based institutional scholarships/grants	$61,700,000
% of students apply for need-based aid	60
% receiving need-based scholarship or grant aid	41
% receiving aid whose need was fully met	99
average aid package	$24,000
average student loan debt upon graduation	$24,307

St. Mary's College of Maryland

St. Mary's College of Maryland has a unique status in public higher education as Maryland's public honors college. This co-educational state college is committed to the ideals of afford¬ability, accessi-bility and diversity while providing an outstanding faculty, high academic standards, a challenging curriculum, small classes, a sense of community, and a spirit of intellectual inquiry. By combining the virtues of public and private education, St. Mary's provides a valuable opportunity for students and their families. The College is set in the heart of the Chesapeake Bay region, 70 miles southeast of Washington, D.C. and 95 miles south of Baltimore.

OPPORTUNITY **CollegeBound Foundation (CBF)**

The CollegeBound Foundation recognizes the hard work and dedication of the talented youth of Baltimore, many of whom face significant financial and personal challenges in their lives. The partnership between CBF and St. Mary's helps meet a common mission of encouraging and enabling Baltimore's underserved youth to go to college by motivating other youth to consider higher education. Since 2002, St. Mary's has helped Baltimore city students achieve their dream of going to college by matching dollar-for-dollar any CBF grant to an accepted student.

OPPORTUNITY **African-American Male Leadership Weekend**

The African-American Male Leadership Weekend aims to both empower and broaden the horizons of young, African-American males in today's society. The participants are high school juniors nominated by officials at their respective schools. Taking a liberal arts perspective, participants explore from all angles the issues facing young black men in our culture. We also examine the obstacles they face along their path towards obtaining higher education and achieving a successful future. By the conclusion of the weekend, the scholars develop a holistic outlook on college access and truly understand the development necessary to become the nation's next leaders.

SUCCESS **Office of Student Development**

The multicultural programs, under the Office of Student Development, serve as an advocate for students of color and provide them with support in academic, social and personal areas as they pursue their college education. The program's aim is to reach students, faculty and staff to educate the campus community about diversity and to foster awareness of and appreciation for difference. The coordinator of multicultural programs works closely with other departments and organizations on campus to meet the needs of diverse students.

"St. Mary's offers numerous opportunities for a smooth transition into college, such as The De Sousa-Brent Scholars Program. It's a great outlet for students to take full advantage of the college lifestyle; learning early about time management, workloads, and other first-year issues."

– Octavia D., '12
Baltimore, MD
English

SUCCESS **Multicultural Achievement Peer Program (MAPP)**

The Multicultural Achievement Peer Program is a retention program designed to maximize the opportunity for multicultural students to be successful at St. Mary's. The program assists multicultural students acclimate to college beyond orientation. First-year students are assigned a MAPP mentor who is responsible for guiding the students through their first year. Mentors help students around campus and discover its many resources. Mentors will also serve as liaison between Student Development and other departments at the college. Mentors are selected based on their knowledge of campus resources, proven academic proficiency, class standing, academic major and involvement in campus activities. Previous participants in the program have concurrently held major positions or moved on to hold major positions in a variety of campus organizations.

St. Mary's College of Maryland
18952 E. Fisher Road
St. Mary's City, MD 20686-3001
Ph: (240) 895-2000
admissions@smcm.edu
www.smcm.edu

FAST FACTS

STUDENT PROFILE	
# of degree-seeking undergraduates	1,978
% male/female	43/57
% African American	8
% American Indian or Alaska Native	1
% Asian or Pacific Islander	4
% Hispanic	4
% White	77
% International	1
% Pell grant recipients	11

First-generation and minority alumni W. Michael Kelley, author; Kevin Crutchfield, neurologist; Hon. Judith Guthrie, judge, Federal District Court

ACADEMICS	
full-time faculty	142
full-time minority faculty	22
student-faculty ratio	12:1
average class size	16
% first-year retention rate	91
% graduation rate (6 years)	79

Popular majors Economics, Biology, Political Science, Psychology, English

CAMPUS LIFE	
% live on campus (% freshmen)	85 (96)

Multicultural student clubs and organizations Black Student Union, Raíces Hispanas, International Student Organization, Asian Studies, Sister to Sister

Athletics NCAA Division III, ICSA (sailing)

ADMISSIONS	
# of applicants	2,411
% accepted	57
# of first-year students enrolled	488
SAT Critical Reading (middle 50%)	580-670
SAT Math (middle 50%)	550-650
SAT Writing (middle 50%)	560-670
ACT (middle 50%)	24-29
average HS GPA	3.78
Deadlines	
early decision	11/1, 12/1
regular decision	1/1
application fee	$50
fee waiver for students with financial need	yes

COST & AID	
tuition& fees	in-state $14,445; out-of-state $26,522
room & board	$10,915
total need-based institutional scholarships/ grants	$3,508,000
% of students apply for need-based aid	68
% of students receive aid	100
% receiving need-based scholarship/grant aid	33
% receiving aid whose need was fully met	n/a
average aid package	$8,500
average student loan debt upon graduation	$21,000

Washington College

Washington College
300 Washington Ave.
Chestertown, MD
Ph: (410) 778-7700
wc_admissions@washcoll.edu
www.washcoll.edu

A liberal arts school located on Maryland's Eastern Shore, Washington College is dedicated to helping students realize their potential and achieve their goals. Their combination of strong academic programs, excellent teachers, small classes, and active campus life is a good fit for students who want to be fully engaged in all aspects of their college experience. Committed to creating an inclusive environment essential for all cultural development and academic success, Washington College provides equal access to all programs and activities, and encourages students to develop skills that will help them thrive in a culturally diverse world.

"Washington College has helped me grow as a very strong individual. In my three years here so far, I've been able to accomplish so much that makes me proud. In addition to serving as an executive assistant for the Multicultural Affairs Office, helping other students succeed, I'm also a coordinator for the Alternative Dance Workshop, an organizer for the Cleopatra's sisters, and a Peer Mentor."

– Stephanie G., '13
Baltimore, MD
Sociology

ACCESS **Pre-Orientation Programs**

Washington College offers various pre-orientation programs, which allow students to come to campus early, start making connections with classmates and get a head start on the college experience. The programs include off-campus outdoor activities as well as classes on campus, and are meant to help students bond with each other and prepare them for life at college.

OPPORTUNITY **The Vincent Hynson Scholarship**

The Vincent Hynson scholarship is offered to an entering freshman who is a graduate of a secondary school in Kent County, Maryland, who meets all admissions qualifications, demonstrates financial need, and whose achievements and aspirations most closely emulate the values of Vincent Hynson. The scholarship ensures that full direct cost financial need is met after family contribution and federal and state sources are considered. The recipient must apply for and accept all federal and state need-based aid, including grants and student loans. In addition, the recipient must maintain full-time enrollment and a cumulative grade point average of 3.0 or better in order to continue the scholarship throughout all four years.

OPPORTUNITY **Overnight Visits**

Prospective students get a taste of the Washington College experience through an overnight stay during the fall and spring semesters. High school students attend programs addressing academic support services and student activities, and may attend a sporting event. As prospective students make their final decisions about college selection, this program permits students to make an honest assessment after a series of personal exchanges with faculty, staff and students. Prospective students are paired with a current student mentor for the weekend. This student mentor will be available to prospective student during the entire admissions process.

SUCCESS **Multicultural Advising Program**

The Multicultural Advising Program, run by the Office of Multicultural Affairs, is dedicated to supporting traditionally under-represented populations among the student body. Through this program, counselors work with students to encourage academic success, leadership development, social engagement, and cultural exploration.

FAST FACTS

STUDENT PROFILE

# of degree-seeking undergraduates	1,510
% male/female	40/60
% African American	5
% American Indian or Alaska Native	1
% Asian or Pacific Islander	2
% Hispanic	2
% White	85
% International	2
% Pell grant recipients	13

First-generation and minority alumni Mark Stevens '07, budget analyst, National Institute of Health; Dale Adams, '65, senior project supervisor, Alco Chemical Corporation (retired); Norris Commodore, '73, director, contracts and negotiations group, IBM Credit Corporation; Christine Lincoln '00, published author, Sap Rising

ACADEMICS

full-time faculty	94
full-time minority faculty	11
student-faculty ratio	12:1
average class size	17
% first-year retention rate	86
% graduation rate (6 years)	77

Popular majors Biology, Business Management, Economics, English, Psychology

CAMPUS LIFE

% live on campus	87

Multicultural student clubs and organizations Asian Culture Club, Black Student Union, Cleopatra's Sisters, Encouraging Respect of Sexuality (EROS) Alliance, French Club, German Club, Hillel, International Studies Club, Korean Conversation Hour, Spanish Club

Athletics NCAA Division III, Centennial Conference

ADMISSIONS

# of applicants	4,796
% accepted	57
# of first-year students enrolled	442
SAT Critical Reading (middle 50%)	550-630
SAT Math (middle 50%)	540-620
SAT Writing (middle 50%)	520-630
ACT (middle 50%)	22-27
average HS GPA	3.5
Deadlines	
early decision	11/1
regular decision	3/1
application fee (online)	$55 ($55)
fee waiver for applicants with financial need	yes

COST & AID

tuition	$36,078
room & board	$7,834
total need-based institutional scholarships/grants	$15,516,271
% of students apply for need-based aid	70
% receiving need-based scholarship or grant aid	60
% receiving aid whose need was fully met	35
average aid package	$25,895
average student loan debt upon graduation	$23,000

Amherst College

Amherst College
220 South Pleasant Street
Amherst, MA 01002
Ph: (413) 542-2328
admission@amherst.edu
www.amherst.edu

Amherst College has an educational tradition that stretches back to its founding in 1821. Since that time, the college has become one of the nation's premier liberal arts schools. Amherst's 1,795 talented and energetic students — 35 percent of whom are students of color — benefit from the personal attention afforded by an 8:1 student-to-professor ratio. Amherst, Mass., a town of 35,000 people in the western part of the state, is home to the college's scenic 1,000-acre campus. In this setting, Amherst "educates men and women of exceptional potential from all backgrounds so that they may seek, value and advance knowledge, engage the world around them and lead principled lives of consequence." Beginning in the 2008-2009 academic year, the loan component of all financial aid awards was replaced with scholarship aid.

"I never expected to attend a prestigious liberal arts college, but now Amherst is my home. I wondered about class differences, but I found that everyone was on a level field. You don't have to have money to do anything that is school-sponsored—everything is paid for by Amherst."

– Yasmin N., '10
Houston, TX
Psychology

ACCESS **Tele-mentoring Program**

Amherst College offers a tele-mentoring program in which Amherst students use e-mail and the telephone to help high school students locate and gain acceptance to colleges and universities. The Tele-mentoring Program allows nearly 30 Amherst students from socio-economic disadvantaged backgrounds to serve as mentors to talented high school students from underserved schools across the nation.

ACCESS **ABC Tutoring and Mentoring Program**

The A Better Chance (ABC) tutoring and mentoring program involves Amherst College students willing to make a difference in the lives of the young male members of the Amherst chapter. Amherst students assist participants with homework and general activities in preparation for college level work. The goals of ABC are to offer support and aid in any subjects being taken by the participants, to promote diversity by providing the opportunity for Amherst students to form meaningful relationships with students of different backgrounds, and vice versa.

OPPORTUNITY **Diversity Open House Weekends**

Amherst hosts two Diversity Open House Weekends each fall in which the college funds travel for multicultural and first-generation students. Students attend classes, cultural events and admission workshops during their three-day stay. Twelve diversity interns work for the Admission Office and help organize and coordinate the Open House weekends. The diversity interns also serve as liaisons and mentors to students with diversity questions or concerns during the event.

SUCCESS **Access to Amherst**

Matriculated students from disadvantaged backgrounds who are interested in the sciences are eligible for the Summer Science Program, while those interested in the humanities and social sciences are eligible for the Summer Humanities and Social Science Program. The two three-week courses occur before first-year orientation. Approximately 20 members of the incoming class participate in each program and gain assistance transitioning between high school and college. Participants in the science program gain further assistance in learning various approaches to math and science while those in the humanities and social science program develop writing and study skills as well as other skills aimed at achieving success.

FAST FACTS

STUDENT PROFILE

# of degree-seeking undergraduates	1,795
% male/female	49/51
% African American	12
% American Indian or Alaska Native	<1
% Asian or Pacific Islander	11
% Hispanic	12
% White	54
% International	9
% Pell grant recipients	35

First-generation and minority alumni Jide Zeitlin, Ambassador to the United Nations, Representative for U.N. Management and Reform

ACADEMICS

full-time faculty	195
full-time minority faculty	28
student-faculty ratio	8:1
average class size	17
% first-year retention rate	94
% graduation rate (6 years)	94

Popular majors Psychology, Political Science, Economics, History, English, and Biology

CAMPUS LIFE

% live on campus (% freshmen)	98 (100)

Multicultural student clubs and organizations Black Student Union, Black Men's Group, Black Women's Group, Drew House, Black Studies Department, La Causa, Chicano Caucus, La Casa, Asian Students Association, Korean Students Association, South Asian Students Association, China Awareness Organization, Asian Culture House, Amherst College Diversity Coalition, Pride Alliance, International Students Association, Marsh Art House, NOOR, African and Caribbean Students Union

Athletics NCAA Division III, New England Small College Athletic Conference

ADMISSIONS

# of applicants	8,099
% accepted	15
# of first-year students enrolled	490
SAT Critical Reading (middle 50%)	670-770
SAT Math (middle 50%)	670-770
SAT Writing (middle 50%)	680-770
ACT (middle 50%)	30-34
average HS GPA	n/a
Deadlines	
early decision	11/15
regular decision	1/1
application fee (online)	$60 ($60)
fee waiver for applicants with financial need	yes

COST & AID

tuition	$40,160
room & board	$10,660
total need-based institutional scholarships/grants	$38,997,503
% of students apply for need-based aid	63
% of students receive aid	57
% receiving need-based scholarship or grant aid	52
% receiving aid whose need was fully met	100
average aid package	$40,952
average student loan debt upon graduation	n/a

Babson College

For students who want to study business in a comprehensive, dynamic environment, Babson College may just be a dream come true. Not content to have students learn by passively sitting in their classrooms, Babson demands that students work hands-on right away; in fact, the school gives all first-year students (grouped in teams) $3,000 start-up loans to create, run and liquidate a business in their first year alone. Babson students also benefit from other professional development opportunities, such as receiving leadership coaching and participating in a management consulting program, through which they can work with real-world firms like Boston Scientific and Stacy's Pita Chips.

"I chose Babson because no other school provided such an innovative business education that placed entrepreneurial thinking and liberal arts at its core. The scholarship program provides students like myself, who have the academic skills to succeed at Babson, with an opportunity that would be unavailable to them."

– Kelvin W., '13
Dallas, TX
Finance & Law

ACCESS High School Presentations

Since the spring of 2007, Babson students have been presenting their student-designed businesses to inner-city high school students. These presentations expose at-risk populations to the various unique opportunities in higher education, as well as facilitate the notion of social responsibility for current students.

ACCESS NFTE Conference

Babson College currently hosts the northeast regional conference of the Network for Teaching Entrepreneurship (NFTE). This organization, which provides both training to students and teachers, helps young people from low-income communities build skills and unlock their entrepreneurial creativity. Thanks to the generosity of the Shelby/Cullom Davis Foundation, there is an endowed scholarship to ensure that there is always one NFTE alumnus at Babson as an undergraduate student.

OPPORTUNITY Experience Diversity / Diversity Overnight Program

Held in conjunction with the college's annual Basically Babson Day for admitted under-represented minority students, Babson's Experience Diversity campus visit program allows admitted seniors to learn about the Babson experience and the resources available to alumni of color, as students are also given the opportunity to interact with alumni. Travel scholarships are available for the program.

OPPORTUNITY Posse Foundation

Babson College participates in the Posse Foundation, a program that brings talented inner-city youth to campus to pursue their academics and to help promote cross-cultural communication. Posse students are nominated by their high school to the program and share a collaborative support system with a special mentor to adjust to campus and college life.

SUCCESS Diversity Leadership Award Support

The Diversity Leadership Awards are a set of four-year, half- or full-tuition merit scholarships awarded to students deemed to have the greatest potential for leadership in creating a richly diverse Babson community. Scholars receive student and faculty mentoring, are provided unique leadership development opportunities, and are able to participate in special academic, social and cultural activities and events.

Babson College
231 Forest Street
Babson Park, MA 02457-0310
Ph: (781) 239-5522
ugradadmission@babson.edu
www.babson.edu/ugrad

FAST FACTS

STUDENT PROFILE

# of degree-seeking undergraduates	1,956
% male/female	59/41
% African American	5
% American Indian or Alaska Native	1
% Asian or Pacific Islander	13
% Hispanic	9
% White	40
% International	27
% Pell grant recipients	17

First-generation and minority alumni Gustavo Cisneros, businessman; Rudy Crew, superintendent, Miami-Dade County Public Schools; Mir Ibrahim Rahman, television CEO; Alberto Perlman, entrepreneur

ACADEMICS

full-time faculty	167
full-time minority faculty	31
student-faculty ratio	14:1
average class size	29
% first-year retention rate	92
% graduation rate (6 years)	91

Popular majors Accounting, Entrepreneurship, Finance, Global Business Management, Marketing

CAMPUS LIFE

% live on campus (% freshmen)	84 (99)

Multicultural student clubs and organizations AMAN, Armenian Students Association, Association of Latino Professionals in Finance and Accounting, Babson African Student Organization, Babson Asian Pacific Student Association, Babson Brazilian Association, Babson Global Outreach through Entrepreneurship, Babson Korean Student Association, Babson Thai Student Association, HOLA, Japanese International Circle, ONE Tower, Open, STAND, The Global Society

Athletics NCAA Division III, ECAC East Ice Hockey League, New England Women's and Men's Athletic Conference, Pilgrim League

ADMISSIONS

# of applicants	4,061
% accepted	40
# of first-year students enrolled	490
SAT Critical Reading (middle 50%)	570-660
SAT Math (middle 50%)	630-720
SAT Writing (middle 50%)	600-680
ACT (middle 50%)	26-30
average HS GPA	3.7
Deadlines	
early action	11/1
early decision	11/1
regular decision	1/15
application fee (online)	$75 ($75)
fee waiver for applicants with financial need	yes

COST & AID

tuition	$40,400
room & board	$13,330
total need-based institutional scholarships/grants	$19,800,000
% of students apply for need-based aid	55
% of students receive aid	52
% receiving need-based scholarship or grant aid	42
% receiving aid whose need was fully met	24
average aid package	$31,375
average student loan debt upon graduation	$34,479

Bard College at Simon's Rock

Bard College at Simon's Rock is the only four-year college of the liberal arts and sciences specifically designed to provide bright, highly motivated students with the opportunity to begin college in a residential setting after 10th or 11th grade. The school's small size — approximately 400 students — allows faculty and staff to give students a great deal of individual attention both in and out of the classroom. A faculty-to-student ratio of 10:1, an average class size of 10, an intensive advising program and an active residence life team assist young students in their transition to college. All first-year students attend a week-long orientation that combines writing and thinking workshops with other programs designed to introduce students to campus life. There is a strong institutional commitment to diversity, and the W.E.B. Du Bois Scholarship supports academically talented students from underrepresented backgrounds.

ACCESS **Young Writers Workshop (YWW)**

The Young Writers Workshop at Simon's Rock selects 70 to 80 highly motivated high school students to participate in an on-campus writing workshop each summer. Participants strengthen writing, language and thinking skills while living in a college environment. Small workshop groups and intellectual autonomy prepare students for college academics. All YWW faculty are experienced teachers and writers from around the country with an interest in the needs and abilities of young writers. Some financial aid is available for students with demonstrated need, and students of color are eligible to apply for the Dorothy West Scholarship, which covers the full cost of tuition and room and board for the YWW at Simon's Rock.

OPPORTUNITY **W.E.B. Du Bois Scholarships**

Simon's Rock's W.E.B. Du Bois Scholarships meet a significant portion of financial need for eligible students from underrepresented backgrounds who enroll following 10th or 11th grade. Students must have a record of academic achievement and motivation. Du Bois Scholarships are renewable for four years with a cumulative grade point average of 2.7 and good social standing.

OPPORTUNITY **Acceleration to Excellence Program**

The Acceleration to Excellence Program awards merit scholarships that cover up to the full cost of tuition for outstanding students who enter Simon's Rock following 10th or 11th grade. Simon's Rock faculty members select recipients of this award based on academic excellence, extracurricular distinction, personal motivation and character. The most highly qualified applicants are invited to attend the Acceleration to Excellence Finalist Day, where they are introduced to the college's academic and social programs, interview with faculty and have the opportunity to receive one of the college's most substantial merit awards.

> ***"Sure we have a great time, but when it comes to education, I think we value it more than anything else in our lives...I'm always very, very astonished at just how much the class and the academics become part of us, and actually we build a lot of relationships and friendships amongst ourselves with that kind of bond."***
>
> *– R. A., '09*
> *Bronx, NY*
> *Biology, Cross-Cultural Relations*

SUCCESS **Diversity Studies**

The college's faculty offer classes and develop academic concentrations in fields that directly address issues of diversity: African American studies, Asian studies, cross-cultural relations, gender studies and Spanish and Latin American studies. Academic and personal support services are coordinated through the Win Student Resource Commons, which explores and celebrates diversity and nurtures mind, body and spirit.

Bard College at Simon's Rock
Office of Admission
84 Alford Road
Great Barrington, MA 01230-1990
Ph: (413) 538-7312
admit@simons-rock.edu
www.simons-rock.edu

FAST FACTS

STUDENT PROFILE

# of degree-seeking undergraduates	436
% male/female	40/60
% African American	7
% American Indian or Alaska Native	<1
% Asian or Pacific Islander	4
% Hispanic	5
% White	59
% International	5
% Pell grant recipients	26

First-generation and minority alumni John McWhorter, linguist; Veronica Chambers, writer

ACADEMICS

full-time faculty	68
full-time minority faculty	12
student-faculty ratio	8:1
average class size	10
% first-year retention rate	75
% graduation rate (6 years)	73

Popular majors Literary Studies, Politics/Law/Society, Psychology, Creative Writing, Engineering (in conjunction with Columbia University)

CAMPUS LIFE

% live on campus (% freshmen)	90 (96)

Multicultural student clubs and organizations Black Student Union, Multicultural Student Organization, International Students Club, Latino Student Organization

Athetics Recreational Athletic Program; basketball, climbing, fencing, racquetball, squash, swimming, soccer, tennis, volleyball, yoga

ADMISSIONS

# of applicants	322
% accepted	80
# of first-year students enrolled	140
SAT Critical Reading (middle 50%)	640-720
SAT Math (middle 50%)	560-710
SAT Writing (middle 50%)	570-700
ACT (middle 50%)	26-29
average HS GPA	n/a
Deadlines	
priority application	4/15
regular decision	5/31
application fee	$50
fee waiver for applicants with financial need	yes

COST & AID

tuition	$38,535
room & board	$11,960
total need-based institutional scholarships/grants	$3,313,882
% of students apply for need-based aid	60
% of students receive aid	86
% receiving need-based scholarship or grant aid	77
% receiving aid whose need was fully met	64
average aid package	$32,525
average student loan debt upon graduation	$44,910

Bay Path College

Founded in 1897, Bay Path College is a private college with an enrollment of more than 2,000 students at its Longmeadow campus and satellite campuses in Sturbridge/Charlton (MA) and Burlington (MA). The College offers undergraduate degrees for women; graduate degrees for men and women; and Bay Path Online, the College's distance learning center, offering graduate degrees and certificates. Bay Path is committed to women's undergraduate education that emphasizes leadership, communication, and technology, enabling women to make a difference once they graduate. A dedicated faculty enriches and supports the social and intellectual development of all students with a career-focused curriculum, which prepares students to become leaders in their fields. At Bay Path, 64 percent of undergraduates are first-generation students. The College values and promotes diversity, while fostering an environment for learning both inside and outside the classroom. The financial aid staff works with students to ensure financial barriers do not stand in their way of a college education.

ACCESS **Multi-Cultural and Spanish Presentations**

Recognizing the growing multi-cultural population and their focus on attending college, Bay Path provides Open Houses throughout the year that includes presentations and tours in Spanish. This removes the language barrier and allows families to ask the right questions and gather information that will help them in the application process. Bay Path also offers the *Lead to Succeed* program—a youth outreach for inner-city young girls that focuses on leadership development and community service.

OPPORTUNITY **Scholarships**

Bay Path offers scholarships for the support of low-income students, students from rural New England towns, students of color, and first-generation students to ensure college remains accessible and affordable to young women regardless of their level of financial need. In addition, students can qualify for merit scholarships worth up to $14,000 a year. The average total aid package for resident students with financial need for the Class of 2014 was $24,500. Bay Path also offers a three-part Education Stimulus Plan, which includes $10,000 grants toward the College's graduate programs, helping students and their families get the best value in higher education.

"From the moment I arrived on campus, Bay Path has opened the door to endless opportunities for me. By providing me with a top-rate education, Bay Path is encouraging me to make a difference in the lives of others. Bay Path is serving me well by broadening my horizons and supporting me in my future endeavors as a scientist."

– Brittany T., '13
Springfield, MA
Biology
First-generation Student

SUCCESS **The WELL Program (Women as Empowered Learners and Leaders)**

Nearly two-thirds of the students at Bay Path are the first in their families to attend college. Bay Path recognizes the significance of this step, and is committed to increasing resources to support the academic achievement of its students, as well as encouraging personal growth and engagement in their college experiences. Bay Path offers a first-year outdoor leadership course, discussion groups focusing on academic skills, peer tutoring, a mentorship program, increased funding for study abroad, and expanded community service opportunities. Students participate in the WELL Program from their first-year to their senior year. The program explores the issues and problems that are faced by women, their communities, and the world. During the four years, students develop an e-portfolio that is both a reflection of their experiences and a way to capture their life aspirations and goals—focusing them to be positive leaders in their own lives, families, communities, and ultimately their career.

Bay Path College
588 Longmeadow Street
Longmeadow MA 01106
Ph: (413) 565-1331
admiss@baypath.edu
www.baypath.edu

FAST FACTS

STUDENT PROFILE

# of degree-seeking undergraduates	over 600
% male/female	0/100
% African American	11
% American Indian or Alaska Native	<1
% Asian or Pacific Islander	2
% Hispanic	13
% White	57
% International	1
% Pell grant recipients	51

First-generation and minority alumni Jan Melnik '76, published author and president, Absolute Advantage; JoAnna Rhinehart '78, actress and producer; Ashley Uhey Carter '06, forensic scientist, Oregon State Police Crime Lab; Jennifer Fay '06, Campbell University School of Law; Sara Klimoski '08, Ross University School of Medicine

ACADEMICS

full-time faculty	42
student-faculty ratio	15:1
average class size	20
% first-year retention rate	69
% graduation rate (6 years)	56

Popular majors Forensic Science, Business, Education, Psychology, Occupational Therapy

CAMPUS LIFE

% live on campus (% freshmen)	64 (82)

Multicultural student clubs and organizations All Women Excel, Black Student Association, Essence Step Team, Hispanic American Leadership Organization, Native Cultures Club, and Women of Culture

Athletics NCAA Division III, New England Collegiate Conference (NECC)

ADMISSIONS

# of applicants	853
% accepted	66
SAT Critical Reading (middle 50%)	420-540
SAT Math (middle 50%)	420-522
SAT Writing (middle 50%)	n/a
ACT (middle 50%)	17-23
average HS GPA	3.15

Deadlines

early action	12/15
regular decision	rolling
application fee (online)	$25 ($0)
fee waiver for applicants with financial need	yes

COST & AID

tuition	$27,045
room & board	$10,950
total need-based institutional scholarships/grants	n/a
% of students apply for need-based aid	100
% of students receive aid	100
% receiving need-based scholarship or grant aid	100
% receiving aid whose need was fully met	81
average aid package	$24,499
average student loan debt upon graduation	$21,446

Bentley University

Bentley University
Office of Admission
175 Forest St.
Waltham, MA 02452-4705
Ph: (800) 523-2354
ugadmission@bentley.edu
undergraduate.bentley.edu/

Bentley University is a national leader in business education. Founded in 1917 as a school of accounting and finance, Bentley University is a private, coeducational university committed to ensuring social and cultural diversity in every dimension of institutional life. Centered on education and research in business and related professions, Bentley blends the breadth and technological strength of a university with the values and student focus of a small college. A Bentley education is an unparalleled fusion of business and the arts and sciences that allows students to truly customize their learning, including a unique Liberal Studies double major program. Bentley also stresses the benefits of hands-on learning through internships, service learning, study abroad, and corporate partnerships.

OPPORTUNITY Summer Transition Education Program (STEP)

The Summer Transition Education Program provides annual college admission support to 25 high-potential high school students, traditionally from urban areas, who do not meet all standard admission requirements. Program support includes mentoring and monitoring academic progress and academic advising and counseling. Realizing the importance of support at home, the STEP staff collaborates with students' families and guardians. Students also attend a six-week summer residential program, upon the completion of which they receive two Bentley course credits.

SUCCESS ALANA Experience

The ALANA Experience is a four-day program for all incoming Asian/Asian American, Latino/a, African American, Native American and Multiracial students. The program gives students the opportunity to network through a series of workshops, information sessions, and social events. Staff and upperclassmen help guide students in gathering the tools needed for success at Bentley University.

"Bentley supports me on all levels: academic, financial, professional and social. My professors are interested in learning about me as a person, not just a student. Professionally, Career Services has helped me to explore my options, meet corporate partners, and land a great internship. Socially, I met new friends through the ALANA Experience, a four-day orientation program through the Multicultural Center."

– Rafael J., '12
Boston, MA

SUCCESS The Multicultural Center

The Multicultural Center serves as a "home" for many ALANA students at Bentley University. The center serves to further the retention and success of the ALANA students through academic mentoring, guidance, leadership development, advocacy and personal support services. There is a committed staff that helps students with personal, academic, and career counseling. Additionally, the Multicultural Center serves as the campus-wide resource for promotion, exploration and celebration of the University's diversity mission. It organizes a full calendar of events in collaboration with all cultural organizations.

SUCCESS The ALANA Student Advancement Program (ASAP)

ASAP pairs first-year ALANA students with upperclassmen to assist them in acclimating to campus life at Bentley. ASAP Mentors play an integral role in helping first-year students gain an understanding and appreciation for the Bentley culture, introducing them to co-curricular activities and supporting them in their academic and personal growth.

FAST FACTS

STUDENT PROFILE	
# of degree-seeking undergraduates	4,292
% male/female	60/40
% African American	2
% American Indian or Alaska Native	<1
% Asian or Pacific Islander	8
% Hispanic	7
% White	67
% International	12
% Pell grant recipients	13.9
ACADEMICS	
full-time faculty	290
full-time minority faculty	37
student-faculty ratio	14:1
average class size	24
% first-year retention rate	93
% graduation rate (6 years)	88

Popular majors Finance, Accounting, Marketing, Management, International Studies

CAMPUS LIFE	
% live on campus (% freshmen)	83 (98)

Multicultural student clubs and organizations Asian Students' Association, Association of Latino Professions in Finance and Accounting, Bentley Asian Students' Christian Fellowship, Association of Chinese Students, Black United Body, International Students' Association, La Cultura Latina, National Association of Asian American Professionals, National Association of Black Accountants, National Black MBA Association, Portuguese Across Continents, PULSE Newspaper, South Asian Student Association, Vietnamese Students Association

Athletics NCAA Division II, Northeast-10 Athletic Conference, Atlantic Hockey League, Division I

ADMISSIONS	
# of applicants	6,800
% accepted	40
SAT Critical Reading (middle 50%)	540-660
SAT Math (middle 50%)	600-700
SAT Writing (middle 50%)	n/a
ACT (middle 50%)	25-29
average HS GPA	3.4/4.0 A-/B+
Deadlines	
early decision	11/1
early action	11/15
regular decision	1/15
application fee (online)	$50 ($50)
fee waiver for applicants with financial need	yes
COST & AID	
tuition	$36,840
room & board	$12,520
total need-based institutional scholarships/grants	$33,000,000
% of students apply for need-based aid	70
% students receive aid	74
% receiving need based scholarship or grant aid	50
% receiving aid whose need was fully met	75
average aid package	$35,673
average student loan debt upon graduation	$31,827

Boston University

Boston University is the alma mater of Dr. Martin Luther King, Jr., and Dr. Solomon Carter Fuller, the first African American psychiatrist in the United States. BU has been committed to diversity since its charter in 1868, when it promised to admit students of both sexes and every race and religion. It was the first university in the nation to award a Ph.D. to a woman and to award a medical degree to an American Indian student. Boston University is a world recognized, private, teaching and research university offering more than 250 programs of study in the liberal arts and professions. BU prepares students for success through rigorous academics, cutting-edge research with faculty mentors, and internships in the U.S. and abroad. At BU, students experience the city of Boston as an extension of the classroom and can explore the world through one of the nation's most extensive study abroad programs.

ACCESS COACH (College Opportunity and Career Help)

This Boston University program supports Boston public school juniors and seniors as they form post-secondary plans. Boston University student coaches work in high school classrooms, providing information on college applications, college access, and financial aid. The coaches help motivate students to make good decisions about their futures.

ACCESS Summer Pathways

Summer Pathways is a one-week residential summer program for female high school students who demonstrate promise in the fields of science and engineering. The Summer Pathways program is free of charge and seeks students from Boston public schools who would not otherwise have the opportunity to attend a summer enrichment program. Summer Pathways students learn about the wide range of academic and career opportunities in science and engineering and are connected to women working in these fields.

"When looking at BU, I thought it was important to find my home away from home. I found just that during my freshman year living in the Spanish House. I met students from Latin America, Latinos from across the U.S., and others who were interested in Latino culture and Spanish language."

– Melissa B., Senior
Lagrangeville, NY
Education

OPPORTUNITY Martin Luther King, Jr. Scholarship

Awarded in honor of Boston University's most prominent alumnus, the Dr. Martin Luther King, Jr. Scholarship provides renewable four-year, full-tuition awards to academically gifted students who have leadership abilities and a strong commitment to social justice and community involvement.

OPPORTUNITY National Hispanic Recognition Program

The National Hispanic Recognition Program offers academic recognition to Hispanic students who have received high achieving scores on the PSAT/NMSQT, taken during their junior year in high school, and who have a 3.0 GPA or higher. The program sends a list of recognized students to subscribing colleges. Boston University awards a four-year, half-tuition scholarship to National Hispanic Recognition Program finalists with exceptional high school academic records.

OPPORTUNITY The Howard Thurman Center

The Howard Thurman Center builds a sense of community for students through diverse cultural, social, and academic networks on campus. The Center provides an orientation to minority freshmen at the beginning of the year to introduce them to the resources and cultural organizations on campus. Students also work with upperclass mentors through the cultural mentorship program.

Boston University Admissions
121 Bay State Road
Boston, MA 02215
Ph: (617) 353-2300
admissions@bu.edu
www.bu.edu

FAST FACTS

STUDENT PROFILE

# of degree-seeking undergraduates	16,186
% male/female	40/60
% African American	3
% American Indian or Alaska Native	<1
% Asian or Pacific Islander	15
% Hispanic	8
% White	53
% International	9
% Pell grant recipients	18.6

First-generation and minority alums Dr. Martin Luther King, Jr., civil rights activist; Alfre Woodard, actress; Karen Holmes Ward, producer/host, ABC; Dr. Elizabeth Alexander, poet who composed and read her poem at President Obama's inauguration; Senator Edward Brooke, the first African American to be elected by popular vote to the US Senate

ACADEMICS

full-time faculty	1,632
full-time minority faculty	296
student-faculty ratio	13:1
average class size	28
% first-year retention rate	91
% graduation rate (6 years)	84

Popular majors Business Administration/ Management, Communications, International Relations, Pre-Medical Studies, Psychology, Engineering, Political Science

CAMPUS LIFE

% live on campus (% freshmen)	66 (99)

Multicultural student clubs and organizations African Students Organization, Alianza Latina, Asian Student Union, Bangladeshi Student Association, Bhangra, Brazilian Association, Chinese Student and Scholar Association, Filipino Student Association, Hong Kong Student Association, India Club, Italian Students Association, Japanese Student Association, Kalaniot, Korean Student Association, Lebanese Club, Organization of Pakistani Students, Persian Student Cultural Club, Russian American Cultural Society, Singapore Collegiate Society, Taiwanese Student Association, Thai Student Association, Turkish Student Association, UMOJA (Black Student Union), Vietnamese Student Association

Athletics NCAA Division I, American East Conference, Colonial Athletic Association, Hockey East Association

ADMISSIONS

# of applicants	41,760
% accepted	48
# of first-year students enrolled	4,000
SAT Critical Reading (middle 50%)	600-700
SAT Math (middle 50%)	630-730
SAT Writing (middle 50%)	620-710
ACT (middle 50%)	27-31
average HS GPA	3.6
Deadlines	
early decision	11/1
regular decision	1/1
application fee (online)	$75 ($75)
fee waiver for applicants with financial need	yes

COST & AID

tuition	$39,314
room & board	$12,260
total need-based institutional scholarships/grants	$158,542,872
% of students apply for need-based aid	51
% of students receive aid	91
% receiving need-based scholarship or grant aid	94
% receiving aid whose need was fully met	48
average aid package	$35,198
average student loan debt upon graduation	$31,809

Brandeis University

Located in Waltham, Mass., on 235 attractive suburban acres, Brandeis is in an ideal location just nine miles west of Boston. Characterized by academic excellence since its founding in 1948, Brandeis is one of the youngest private research universities, as well as the only nonsectarian Jewish-sponsored college or university in the country. Named for the late Justice Louis Dembitz Brandeis of the U.S. Supreme Court, Brandeis University combines the faculty and resources of a world-class research institution with the intimacy and personal attention of a small liberal arts college. For students, that means unsurpassed access — both in and out of the classroom — to a faculty renowned for groundbreaking research, scholarship and artistic output. At Brandeis, professors bring newly minted knowledge straight from the field or lab to the graduate and undergraduate classrooms.

"I chose Brandeis because of its Transitional Year Program (TYP). It is an introductory year into college fit for students who have gone to under-resourced schools, or have not had the opportunity to have a steady focus on education in high school. The Transitional Year Program allowed me the extra year to touch up and be ready to succeed at Brandeis."

– Michael S., '12
Canton, NY
Sociology, Business

OPPORTUNITY **Posse Foundation**

Brandeis Posse is a merit-based scholarship program founded by Brandeis alumna Debbie Bial, '87. Brandeis Posse Scholars are selected for their academic, leadership, and communication skills. They are expected to not only demonstrate strong academic abilities but also outstanding interpersonal and problem-solving skills. These students receive 4 year full tuition leadership scholarships. Currently, 50 Brandeis Posse Scholars are on campus.

OPPORTUNITY **MLK Scholar Program**

The MLK Scholarship has been a tradition at Brandeis since 1969, bringing over 140 Scholars to campus since its inception. This award honors those students who are committed to the principles of Dr. Martin Luther King, Jr., including community service, equality, and social justice. The scholarship includes tuition, room and board and is renewable for 4 years provided you maintain a minimum grade point average of 2.67 and participate in monthly community service programming.

SUCCESS **Transitional Year Program (TYP)**

Brandeis' Transitional Year Program (TYP), part of the Office of Academic Services, is an integral part of the University's founding and enduring commitment to social justice. Founded in 1968, the TYP is a one-year academic program for students who have not had access to the resources necessary to prepare for a rigorous 4 year undergraduate college experience. By guaranteeing small classes, rigorous academics and strong support systems this unique experience allows these students to learn about new possibilities for their lives, and to apply the focus, energy, tenacity, perseverance, and maturity previously devoted to prevailing in the face of personal challenges, to now pursuing academic success. Brandeis' TYP is the oldest continuous program of its kind in the country. Nearly 1000 students have participated in the TYP since its 1968 founding.

SUCCESS **Student Support Services Program (SSSP)**

For the past 18 years, Brandeis has been one of the few highly selective colleges chosen to have a SSSP to better serve those who are first-generation college students. SSSP is a part of a network of TRiO programs funded through grants from the U.S. Department of Education and Brandeis University. Brandeis' team of professional staff and student leaders offers many services to enhance the academic experience of all students actively involved in our program. Professional advisors work with students to create a customized academic plan tailored to their goals. Peer-tutors and graduate assistants provide one-on-one tutoring and workshops sessions in a variety of academic disciplines to promote academic achievement. SSSP helps ease the transition to college life though the peer mentoring program and cultural events that allow students to build lasting relationships.

Brandeis University
415 South Street
Waltham/MA/02453-2728
Ph: (781) 736-3500
admissions@brandeis.edu
www.brandeis.edu

FAST FACTS

STUDENT PROFILE

# of degree-seeking undergraduates	3,317
% male/female	44/56
% African American	4
% American Indian or Alaska Native	<1
% Asian or Pacific Islander	11
% Hispanic	5
% White	48
% International	11
% Pell grant recipients	15

First-generation and minority alums John Laing '90, Real Estate Developer and Social Service Consultant; Norma Sanchez '84, Attorney with a Private Practice in Family Law; Pedro Fontes '00, Second Vice President, Smith Barney; Jovenel Cherenfant '01, MD, Endocrinologist; Garnett Headley '84, MD, Anesthesiologist

ACADEMICS

full-time faculty	363
full-time minority faculty	44
student-faculty ratio	9:1
average class size	17
% first-year retention rate	92
% graduation rate (6 years)	87

Popular majors Economics, Biology, Psychology, English, Politics

CAMPUS LIFE

% live on campus (% freshmen)	88 (100)

Multicultural student clubs and organizations Black Student Organization, Arab Culture Club, Chinese Cultural Connection, Society for the Advancement of Chicanos and Native Americans in Science, Students Organized Against Racism, Muslim Student Association, African Students Organization, Diverse City, Brandeis Zionist Alliance, Asian American Students Association

Athletics NCAA Division III, University Athletic Association

ADMISSIONS

# of applicants	8,869
% accepted	39
# of first-year students enrolled	856
SAT Critical Reading (middle 50%)	630-730
SAT Math (middle 50%)	640-730
SAT Writing (middle 50%)	640-730
ACT (middle 50%)	29-33
average HS GPA	3.77
Deadlines	
early decision I	11/15
early decision II	1/1
regular decision	1/15
application fee (online)	$55 ($55)
fee waiver for applicants with financial need	yes

COST & AID

tuition	$42,060
room & board	$11,894
total need-based institutional scholarships/grants	$41,099,812
% of students apply for need-based aid	51
% receiving need-based scholarship or grant aid	56
% receiving aid whose need was fully met	24
average aid package	$32,412
average student loan debt upon graduation	$21,351

Emerson College

Emerson College is the only undergraduate institution in the United States exclusively committed to educating students in the fields of communication and performing arts. Due to efforts over the past few years to diversify the student body, nearly a quarter of the incoming class is from historically underrepresented populations. More than a year ago, President Liebergott commissioned an outside review in order to help Emerson diversify its faculty and staff, as well. The findings of that review have been incorporated into our Strategic Plan for Diversity, which was recently released online at http://www.emerson.edu/about-emerson/offices-departments/diversity/diversity-strategic-plan. Just this year, a support program for first generation students was launched with the intention of helping them acclimate to campus culture, college life, and living in Boston.

ACCESS Professional Studies

Professional Studies offers challenging one, two, and five week summer programs for high school students. The goal of the programs is to teach pre-college students competitive skills in one area of communication and the arts. High school students that participate in this program achieve basic knowledge of current industry practices, audition and portfolio materials for college applications, and skills in project presentation, debate, and research.

OPPORTUNITY Picture Yourself at Emerson

Picture Yourself at Emerson is a fly-in program for select accepted students. Emerson College will provide transportation and accommodations for a student and one parent to visit the college during the accepted student programs by invitation only. Driven by the desire to help accepted students envision attending Emerson, this spring event includes mock classes, residence hall tours, current student work, sessions geared towards parents and families, panel discussions, and a "Taste of Boston" lunch. Separate events for parents include a panel of student support services, financial aid, and overviews of specific academic departments. This program offers prospective students the chance to experience Emerson College while meeting current students, staff, and faculty members. Dates for the program are specific to the accepted student's major or department.

OPPORTUNITY Merit Based Scholarship Opportunities

Emerson has merit scholarships available for all students. The Deans Scholarship is awarded to students who possess academic distinction in their respective communities, leadership qualities, the ability to manage adversity, and other fundamental factors for success at Emerson College. This award is renewable for eight semesters, and requires no additional application or essay. The Emersonian Scholarship is awarded to students who have shown dedication to academic achievement, leadership, and high school and community involvement. There is no separate application for this scholarship, and candidates are nominated by the Admission Committee. The Trustees Scholarship is a half-tuition scholarship given to applicants who apply and are accepted to Emerson's Honors Program.

SUCCESS First Generation Program

The goals of the First Generation Program are to create a community for first generation students that includes peers and campus administrators; to keep first generation students informed on issues of college life; and to provide a safety net for first generation students during their first year of college.

> ***"Emerson is not a traditional-looking campus. Our urban environment, classrooms, and facilities stand apart from most colleges. There's a dynamic of acceptance, and an open environment that encourages creativity and originality. The diversity of our student body is a testament to that."***
>
> *– Ana G., '09*
> *Cumming, GA*
> *Political Communication*

Emerson College
120 Boylston Street
Boston, MA 02116
Ph: (617) 824-8600
admission@emerson.edu
www.emerson.edu

FAST FACTS

STUDENT PROFILE	
# of degree-seeking undergraduates	3,461
% male/female	40/60
% African American	2.8
% American Indian or Alaska Native	<1
% Asian or Pacific Islander	4
% Hispanic	9
% White	60
% International	3
% Pell grant recipients	11

First-generation and minority alumni Brent Jennings, actor; Rafael Toro, Director of Public Relations in Goya; Doug Holloway, television executive; Susan Batson, author and acting coach; Chrystee Pharris, actress

ACADEMICS	
full-time faculty	183
full-time minority faculty	36
student-faculty ratio	12:1
average class size	20-29
% first-year retention rate	87
% graduation rate (6 years)	80

Popular majors Visual and Media Arts; Performing Arts; Writing, Literature and Publishing; Communication Majors (Marketing, Journalism, Communication Studies, Political Communication, Communication Disorders)

CAMPUS LIFE	
% live on campus (% freshmen)	55 (100)

Multicultural student clubs and organizations Amigos, ASIA, EAGLE, EBONI, Speak Up, Campus Conversations on Race

Athletics NCAA (Division III), Eastern College Athletic Conference, and charter member of the Great Northeast Athletic Conference

ADMISSIONS	
# of applicants	6,866
% accepted	47
# of first-year students enrolled	825
SAT Critical Reading (middle 50%)	590-680
SAT Math (middle 50%)	560-650
SAT Writing (middle 50%)	580-680
ACT (middle 50%)	25-30
average HS GPA	3.6
Deadlines	
early action	11/1
regular decision	1/5
application fee (online)	$65 ($65)
fee waiver for applicants with financial need	yes

COST & AID	
tuition	$30,752
room & board	$12,881
total need-based institutional scholarships/grants	$19,135,884
% of students apply for need-based aid	66
% receiving need-based scholarship or grant aid	48
% receiving aid whose need was fully met	42
average aid package	$17,205
average student loan debt upon graduation	$17,459

Harvard University

Harvard University is a private, co-educational, non-denominational liberal arts college located in Cambridge, Massachusetts. Founded in 1636, Harvard is the oldest institution of higher learning in the United States, as well as the first corporation in the Americas. The College strives to open the minds of students to knowledge and to enable them to take advantage of their educational opportunities, and the support it provides is a foundation upon which self-reliance and life-long learning habits are built. Through the scholarship it fosters, Harvard seeks to promote understanding and a desire to serve society.

> ACCESS **Crimson Summer Academy**

The Crimson Summer Academy offers select high school freshmen from Boston and Cambridge the opportunity to experience college life. After a period of orientation, participants live on Harvard's campus from Sunday evenings through Friday afternoons. Over the course of three consecutive summers, Crimson Scholars engage in classes, projects, field trips and recreational activities as they prepare for success in college and beyond. Each student receives full financial support, and upon completion of the three-year program is awarded a $3,000 scholarship for use at the college or university of their choice.

> ACCESS **Campus Visits**

Throughout the year, Harvard seeks to identify organizations and schools that work with low-income, high-achieving student populations and invites those groups to visit campus. Student coordinators and admissions officers provide a customized information session stressing the importance of higher education and the availability of financial aid, give a tour of the campus, and provide an "insider's look" into the Harvard experience in a small group setting.

> ACCESS **Harvard Student Ambassadors**

In order to reach students who might not be able to travel to campus prior to applying, current undergraduates from modest backgrounds are hired to return to their hometowns and visit local middle schools as well as high schools, where they discuss Harvard and higher education in general.

> OPPORTUNITY **The Harvard Financial Aid Initiative (HFAI)**

The Financial Aid Initiative has reduced the amount families with incomes below $180,000 are expected to contribute to college costs, and parents of families with incomes below $60,000 are not expected to contribute at all. Harvard no longer considers home equity as a resource in determination of family contribution, and need-based scholarships have replaced student loans. The Initiative has reduced the cost to middle income families by one-third to one-half, making the price of education for Harvard students with financial aid comparable to the cost of in-state tuition and fees at leading public universities. The Initiative benefits all accepted students who qualify.

> SUCCESS **Harvard Financial Aid Initiative Newsletter and Initiatives**

Students are provided with a monthly electronic newsletter highlighting events and opportunities on campus of special interest to students from modest backgrounds. Each newsletter includes information on research funding, travel grants, internships and other opportunities, along with general information about understanding financial aid or ways to take advantage of the many free social and cultural campus events. Each student receives a copy of "Shoestring Strategies for Life @ Harvard," a guide to living on a budget while taking advantage of the Harvard and Cambridge community opportunities. The Financial Aid Office administers the Student Events Fund for currently enrolled undergraduates from low-income backgrounds, enabling students to receive tickets to campus events free of charge. Students receiving financial aid may also be eligible for additional funds for personal and unexpected expenses.

Harvard University
Office of Admissions and Financial Aid
86 Brattle Street
Cambridge, MA 02138
Ph: (617) 495-1551
college@fas.harvard.edu
www.admissions.college.harvard.edu

FAST FACTS

STUDENT PROFILE

# of degree-seeking undergraduates	6,678
% male/female	50/50
% African American	9
% American Indian or Alaska Native	1
% Asian or Pacific Islander	19
% Hispanic	8
% White	46
% International	10
% Pell grant recipients	12.5

First-generation and minority alumni W. E. B. Du Bois, civil rights activist; Yo Yo Ma, cellist; Fan Noli, writer, former regent, prime minister, Albania; Alan Keyes, political figure; Jose Angel Navarro, former Texas legislator; Clifton Dawson, professional football player

ACADEMICS

full-time faculty	1,712
full-time minority faculty	298
student-faculty ratio	6.8:1
average class size	10-19
% first-year retention rate	97
% graduation rate (6 years)	97

Popular majors Economics, Political Science and Government, Psychology

CAMPUS LIFE

% live on campus (% freshmen)	99 (100)

Multicultural student clubs and organizations The Harvard Foundation for Intercultural and Race Relations, Asian-American Association, Black Student Association, Society of Black Scientists and Engineers, Fuerza Latina, RAZA, Native Americans at Harvard College, Woodbridge International Student Association

Athletics NCAA Division I, Collegiate Water Polo Association, Eastern College Athletic Conference (football I-AA), Eastern Intercollegiate Volleyball Association, Eastern Intercollegiate Wrestling Association, Ivy League (football I-AA)

ADMISSIONS

# of applicants	30,489
% accepted	6.2
# of first-year students enrolled	1,666
SAT Critical Reading (middle 50%)	700-800
SAT Math (middle 50%)	700-790
SAT Writing (middle 50%)	690-790
ACT (middle 50%)	31-35
average HS GPA	n/a
Deadlines	
early action	11/1
regular decision	1/1
application fee (online)	$75 ($75)
fee waiver for applicants with financial need	yes

COST & AID

tuition	$39,849
room & board	$12,801
total need-based institutional scholarships/grants	$145,433,000
% of students apply for need-based aid	67
% of students receive aid	61
% receiving need-based scholarship or grant aid	61
% receiving aid whose need was fully met	100
average aid package	$41,650
average student loan debt upon graduation	$10,102

Lesley University

Located in Cambridge, Mass., just steps from Harvard Square and minutes from Boston, Lesley students are committed to making a difference in the lives of others. Field-based internships begin freshman year for every program and include 450 to 600 hours of professional career exposure. Classes of 16-20 students, faculty committed to teaching undergraduates, and the option to self-design your own academic program ensures that Lesley students are never just a number. Students interested in Lesley's Dual Degree Programs have the opportunity to pursue both a Bachelor's and Master's degree within an accelerated timeframe, and those interested in the visual arts can access the curriculum of the Art Institute of Boston.

"I knew that small classes meant more time with professors and more collaboration on projects and research. Add that to field-based internships that begin freshman year, and I've found that Lesley offers a dynamic learning community working to help me succeed."

– Bryant I.
Medford, MA
Business Management / Marketing Specialization

ACCESS **Admissions Office Events**

The Lesley College Admissions Office coordinates with various programs like TRIO, AVID, Kids 2 College, The Bottom Line, Stepping stone, and summer enrichment camps sponsored by the Mayor's Office. In collaboration with them, it hosts tours, information sessions, class visits, and on-campus interviews.

OPPORTUNITY **Need-Based Scholarships**

Lesley offers a guaranteed scholarship program based on prior academic performance. Merit Scholarships range from $9,000 to full tuition and are awarded annually over a student's four years of study. Additionally, in support of local communities, any student graduating from a public or charter high school in the cities of Boston, Brockton, Cambridge, Chelsea, Lawrence, Lowell, Lynn, or Somerville is automatically eligible for a $9,000 annual Urban Scholarship, assuming s/he starts at Lesley College the semester following their high school graduation. Graduates with an Associates Degree from any two-year community college in the United States are automatically eligible for a $9,000 annual Lesley University Community College Scholarship. Phi Theta Kappa Honor Society students who have graduated from a two-year institution are automatically eligible for a $13,000 annual scholarship.

SUCCESS **Advisor and Tutorial Programs**

Through the University's Advising Center, first-year students are assigned a professional advisor who will work with them through sophomore year. Freshman Transition Seminars serve to connect new students with faculty and help prepare them for their first internship/experiential learning course second semester. Tutorial assistance and help with writing or editing papers and support for learning disabilities or English as a second language may be found in the Center for Academic Achievement.

SUCCESS **Student Orientation**

Summer Orientation takes place in June and introduces new students to faculty, advisors, and the academic expectations and opportunities that await them at Lesley. An added bonus—spending the night in the residence halls, checking out Harvard Square, and experiencing student life Lesley-style. You'll meet future classmates, register for fall classes, and most importantly, have fun.

SUCCESS **Emerging Leaders Programs**

Now in its fifth year, the Emerging Leaders Program has become one of the hottest courses on campus. An eight week program designed to build and enhance student leadership skills, session topics include: Leadership Styles; Ethical Decision Making; Communication Skills; Effective Group Dynamics; Working with Diverse Populations; Community Responsibility; and How to Market your Leadership Skills.

Lesley University
29 Everett Street
Cambridge, MA 02138
Ph: (800) 999-1959 / (617) 349-8800
lcadmissions@lesley.edu
www.lesley.edu/lc/cso

FAST FACTS

STUDENT PROFILE

# of degree-seeking undergraduates	1,741
% male/ female	24/76
% African American	4
% American Indian or Alaska Native	1
% Asian or Pacific Islander	3
% Hispanic	6
% White	69
% International	2
% Two or more races	2
% Unknown	13
% Pell grant recipients	34.8

First-generation and minority alumni Lynette Correa, Founder/CEO of Career Coaching 4 Kidz, Named Top 100 Most Influential Individual in Massachusetts by *El Planeta*; Natalia Santiago, Recipient of Lesley College's Presidential Full Tuition Scholarship, English teacher; Reena Patel, Recipient of the Rotary Foundation Academic Year Ambassadorial Scholarship, studying and working with children, Mumbai; Virginia Chau, former President of LU Student Government, preparing for law school; Thomas Morgan, former President of LU Student Government, summer internship in Ghana, attending graduate school for counseling.

ACADEMICS

full-time faculty	73
full-time minority faculty	11
student-faculty ratio	10:1
average class size	16-20
% first-year retention rate	75
% graduation rate (6 yr)	62

Popular majors Counseling Psychology, Education (Early Childhood, Elementary & Secondary) Management, Creative Writing, Art Therapy

CAMPUS LIFE

% live on campus (% freshmen)	54 (85)

Multicultural student clubs and organizations ALANA Student Organization, International Student Association, Lesley UNITY Chorus

Athletics NCAA Division III, New England Collegiate Conference

ADMISSIONS

# of applicants	2,611
% accepted	67
# of first-year students enrolled	384
SAT Critical Reading (middle 50%)	470-600
SAT Math (middle 50%)	450-580
SAT Writing (middle 50%)	470-600
ACT (middle 50%)	20-26
average HS GPA	2.9
Deadlines	
early action	12/1
regular decision	rolling
application fee (online)	$50($0)
fee waiver for applicant with financial need	yes

COST & AID

tuition (2011 - 2012)	$30,170
room & board (2011 - 2012)	$13,250
total need-based institutional scholarships/ grants	$9,700,000
% of students apply for need-based aid	90
% of students receive aid	80
% receiving need-based scholarship/ grant aid	70
% receiving aid whose need was fully met	15
average aid package	$16,977
average student loan debt upon graduation	$18,000

Massachusetts College of Liberal Arts

At a cost much lower than that of private New England institutions, Massachusetts College of Liberal Arts is an attractive option for Massachusetts residents. With residents from Southern Vermont, Maine, Rhode Island and New York also qualifying for select tuition reductions, and 80 percent of students receiving some kind of financial aid and/or scholarships, it is no wonder the college ranked in *Newsweek*'s "Most for Your Money" category. Students at MCLA can take advantage of the beautiful Berkshire surroundings, which include Mt. Greylock (the highest peak in the state), access to three major ski resorts, as well as a vibrant arts community with world-renowned museums such as MASS MoCA and the Clark Art Institute. A comprehensive liberal arts and pre-professional program features small class sizes, providing programs in arts management, computer science, English/communications, business administration, physics, education and many more.

ACCESS Berkshire Compact for Education

Massachusetts College of Liberal Arts is the lead partner in the Berkshire Compact for Education. Established in February 2005, the compact is assessing the higher education and lifelong learning needs of Berkshire County residents and employers, and identifying new opportunities and strategies to better meet those needs.

"Hosting fellow students for Multicultural Overnights gives me the opportunity to inspire them to not only attend college, like MCLA, but also to help create a more diverse campus community."

– Hawa U. '12
Chelsea, MA
Interdisciplinary Studies with concentration in business and history, minor in political science

ACCESS Massachusetts Campus Compact College Access Corps

MCLA recently was selected as a host site for the Massachusetts Campus Compact College Access Corps, a collaborative program between Tufts University and the Massachusetts Campus Compact. For its part in this collaboration, MCLA will work closely with local Drury High School to support qualified students' path toward higher education. The program also will build on current projects underway at the college, including Pathways to College Success, The Write Stuff, Friends of Foster Families and other community-centered collaborations.

OPPORTUNITY Scholarships

MCLA offers and distributes more than $13 million each year in need-based and scholarship aid. This includes donor-funded scholarships to underrepresented students. The aid includes the Margaret A. Hart Scholarship, in honor of the first student of color to graduate from the college, and the Mitchell L. West Opportunity Scholarship, in honor of a college administrator who supported multicultural services.

OPPORTUNITY Multicultural Overnights

MCLA provides students from cities like New York, Boston and Springfield with an opportunity to visit the campus. Students spend a night in the residence halls, attend classes, meet faculty and tour the MCLA campus. Nearly 80 percent of these students ultimately enroll at MCLA.

SUCCESS Learning Services Center (LSC) & Summer Enrichment Program (IEP)

The Learning Services Center administers several key support services on campus, including the Individual Enrichment Program (IEP), which provides an intensive, four-week residential program to select students prior to the fall of their freshman year. Other center services include the Tutor Exchange Network and writing assistance offered through the Writing and Research Center.

SUCCESS Students Working to Assist Transitions (SWAT)

Based on their majors and co-curricular interests, all first-year students are assigned a peer adviser through SWAT, a campus peer-advising group staffed by upperclassmen. SWAT support includes peer tutoring, workshop, and seminars designed to foster student development and enhance the relationship between advisers and advisees.

Massachusetts College of Liberal Arts
375 Church Street
North Adams, MA 01247-4100
Ph: (413) 662-5410
admissions@mcla.edu
www.mcla.edu

FAST FACTS

STUDENT PROFILE

# of degree-seeking undergraduates	1,584
% male/female	41/59
% African American	5
% American Indian or Alaska Native	<1
% Asian or Pacific Islander	<1
% Hispanic	4
% White	86
% Pell grant recipients	30

First-generation and minority alumni Dr. Mary K. Grant '83, president, Massachusetts College of Liberal Arts; John Barrett III '69, former mayor, North Adams, Mass., longest-serving mayor in the state; Daniel E. Bosley '76, Massachusetts state representative; Thomas Calter '80, Massachusetts state representative; Henry Reynolds '58, former deputy director, U.S. Agency for the International Development Mission; Bob Underhill '75, executive vice president/COO, Channing Bete Company Inc.; Kevin Barbary '85, principal, Office Resources; Cynthia Borek Normandin '76, owner, Braun's Express; Paul Serino '81, president, Serino's Italian Food, Inc.; Christine Keville '85, owner, Keville Enterprises; Oscar Lanza-Galindo '01, program associate for student leadership, Amherst College; Theresa O'Bryant, '86, Associate Dean of Students, MCLA; Carla Daugherty Holness, '95, account executive, Sun Trust Bank

ACADEMICS

full-time faculty	87
full-time minority faculty	n/a
student-faculty ratio	14:1
average class size	19
% first-year retention rate	76
% graduation rate (6 years)	50

Popular majors English, Business, Education, Psychology, Sociology, Fine and Performing Arts

CAMPUS LIFE

% live on campus (% freshmen)	68 (91)

Multicultural student clubs and organizations Aikido Club, African American Studies Club, Anime Club, Asian Club, B-GLAD Bi-sexuals, Gays & Lesbians Making A Difference, Christian Fellowship, Jewish Student Union, Latin American Society, Multicultural Student Society

Athletics NCAA Division III, Massachusetts State College Athletic Conference & Eastern Conference Athletic Conference

ADMISSIONS

# of applicants	1,690
% accepted	71
# of first-year students enrolled	351
SAT Critical Reading (middle 50%)	470-590
SAT Math (middle 50%)	440-560
SAT Writing (middle 50%)	n/a
ACT (middle 50%)	20-24
average HS GPA	3.1

Deadlines

regular decision	rolling
application fee (online)	$35 ($35)
fee waiver for applicants with financial need	yes

COST & AID

tuition	in-state: $6,565; out-of-state: $15,510
room & board	$7,868
total need-based institutional scholarships/grants	$2,000,000
% of students apply for need-based aid	87
% of students receive aid	64
average student loan debt upon graduation	$19,090

Massachusetts Institute of Technology

Massachusetts Institute of Technology is widely known for both its quality of education and the exceptional alumni that it produces. The benefit of MIT, however, is not limited to those destined for careers in science. Moreover, MIT is truly accessible to qualified students from all backgrounds; and as a closer look reveals, MIT does a great deal to create an environment that is conducive to learning and growth. The Admissions Office makes its desire for student diversity transparent: women, minority and LGBT students — as well as those with unique talents and passions to bring to the table — are all especially welcomed. Despite the rigor of its academic curriculum, MIT also does not allow students to fail — freshmen cannot receive failing grades; failed courses are simply dropped from their records. Academic collaboration is also valued, and students are given the entire month of January to experience the Independent Activities Period.

ACCESS Educational Outreach Programs

Massachusetts Institute of Technology supports several major engineering outreach programs. Two such programs are Minority Introduction to Engineering and Science (MITES) and Saturday Engineering, Enrichment, and Discovery (SEED) Academy. Both of these programs target communities underrepresented in science and engineering. MITES is a rigorous six-week residential, academic enrichment summer program for promising high school juniors who are interested in studying and exploring careers in science, engineering and entrepreneurship. SEED addresses the needs of area high schoolers by helping them to increase their academic performance in math and science and builds problem solving skills for students who want to excel in technologically focused fields. There is no cost to participate in either MITES or SEED, and more information on both programs can be found on the MIT Web site.

OPPORTUNITY Need-Blind Admissions / Need-Based, Full-Need Financial Aid

One of only a few U.S. institutions with a completely need-blind admissions process and a purely need-based financial aid award system, the Massachusetts Institute of Technology makes its sterling education affordable to all U.S. citizens, permanent residents and citizens from other countries. Affirmative action also brings students from ALANA (African-American, Latino, Asian, Native American) and low-income backgrounds to campus, creating an incoming freshman class that includes 16 percent first-generation and 63 percent ALANA students.

SUCCESS Office of Minority Education (OME)

Students can benefit from a number of student support services offered by the Office of Minority Education. Of particular interest is Project Interphase, a rigorous, seven-week, residential, academic bridge program for incoming ALANA students. Interphasers have access to award-winning teachers, one-on-one tutors and intensive courses in calculus, physics and writing. During their time on campus, participants gain experience in self-reliance and time management, make new friends and become better oriented to MIT's campus. Seminar XL is another OME-sponsored program where freshmen meet weekly to learn innovative and effective small-group learning concepts. Students taking part in Seminar XL meet in small groups for up to six hours each week with a graduate student facilitator who helps develop their problem-solving abilities, analytical reasoning skills and test-taking strategies. OME also provides funding for significant research experiences for undergraduates, as well as summertime internships that help introduce freshmen to the engineering process.

Massachusetts Institute of Technology
77 Massachusetts Avenue
Cambridge, MA 02139-4307
Ph: (617) 253-3400
admissions@mit.edu
www.mit.edu

FAST FACTS

STUDENT PROFILE

# of degree-seeking undergraduates	4,241
% male/female	55/45
% African American	8
% American Indian or Alaska Native	<1
% Asian or Pacific Islander	24
% Hispanic	14
% White	37
% International	9
% Pell grant recipients	17

First-generation and minority alumni Kofi Annan, former UN Secretary General; Alex Padilla, California state senator; Luis Ferre, former governor, Puerto Rico; Virgilio Barco, former president, Columbia; Jullallan Weber, actor/dancer; Shirley Ann Jackson, president, RPI

ACADEMICS

full-time faculty	1,171
full-time minority faculty	193
student-faculty ratio	8:1
average class size	2-9
% first-year retention rate	97
% graduation rate (6 years)	91

Popular majors Electrical Engineering/Computer Science, Biology, Management, Mechanical Engineering, Biological Engineering

CAMPUS LIFE

% live on campus (% freshmen)	93 (100)

Multicultural student clubs and organizations African Student Association, American Indian Science & Engineering Society, Arab Student Organization, Armenian Student Association, Association of Puerto Rican Students, Black Students' Union, Black Christian Fellowship, Black Theater Guild, Black Women's Alliance, Caribbean Club, Chocolate City, Haitian Alliance, La Union Chicano por Aztlan, Mujeres Latinas, Mexican Student Association, National Society of Black Engineers, Native American Student Association, Society of Mexican American Engineers & Scientists, Hispanic Professional Engineers, Mes Latino, Spanish House, Vietnamese Students' Association

Athletics NCAA Division III, New England Women's and Men's Athletic Conference

ADMISSIONS

# of applicants	16,632
% accepted	10
# of first-year students enrolled	1,067
SAT Critical Reading (middle 50%)	670-760
SAT Math (middle 50%)	740-800
SAT Writing (middle 50%)	670-770
ACT (middle 50%)	32-35
average HS GPA	n/a

Deadlines

regular decision	1/1
application fee (online)	$75
fee waiver for applicants with financial need	yes

COST & AID

tuition	$40,460
room & board	$11,775
total need-based institutional scholarships/grants	$83,357,298
% of students apply for need-based aid	67
% of students receive aid	64
% receiving need-based scholarship or grant aid	62
% receiving aid whose need was fully met	100
average aid package	$37,731
average student loan debt upon graduation	$15,228

Mount Holyoke College

Mount Holyoke College
Newhall Center, 50 College Street
South Hadley, MA 01075
Ph: (413) 538-2023
admission@mtholyoke.edu
www.mtholyoke.edu

A highly selective women's liberal arts college, Mount Holyoke College has a global reputation for educating women who change the world. With 48 departmental and interdepartmental majors, including an option for students to design their own concentration of study, the college offers exceptional academic opportunities to its 2,200 talented, dynamic students. Mount Holyoke College is also a member of the Five College Consortium, a program which links its students to a collegiate community of some 30,000 students and a variety of academic opportunities at nearby Amherst, Hampshire, and Smith Colleges and the University of Massachusetts at Amherst.

OPPORTUNITY **Focus on Diversity and Experience Diversity**

Yearly, Mount Holyoke College sponsors Focus on Diversity and Experience Diversity — two programs that allow students who are particularly interested in and committed to issues of diversity — to visit Mount Holyoke, experience the college's tight-knit and dynamic student body, and dialogue about these issues. Focus on Diversity occurs in the fall for prospective students, while the Experience Diversity program takes place in the spring for accepted students and their families. Both programs have fly-in and bus-in travel arrangements for students.

OPPORTUNITY **Science Scholars Program**

The Science Scholars program is an academic honors program that provides advanced research experiences and early career development opportunities for highly talented science and math students from diverse backgrounds who enroll at Mount Holyoke College. The program takes place in the summer before first year and consists of a four-week scientific research experience, which is guided and supported by current student mentors and science faculty. Science Scholars receive transportation to and from Mount Holyoke, on-campus housing, meals, and a stipend.

SUCCESS **Pre-Orientation Program**

Promoting InterCultural Dialogue and Creating Inclusion is an optional three-day program for incoming first year students just before Orientation. Designed to further promote an inclusive campus community, this program invites all students to partake in dialogues that will meet three distinct goals: (1) deepening self-understanding of individual identity issues and cross-cultural awareness; (2) increasing sensitivity to the complexity of other racial/ethnic groups as well as your own; and (3) developing a strong set of communication and leadership skills.

"I visited Mount Holyoke College for the first time during Experience Diversity weekend in the spring of my senior year in high school. Once I got here I was in awe of the beauty of the campus and impressed with how intelligent the women were. I was immediately inspired by the stories they had to share, their dreams and aspirations. I could see myself there as a citizen of the world making a difference. It was then that I felt I had something to offer a school as much as it had to offer me."

– Saran S., '14
New York, NY
International Relations

FAST FACTS

STUDENT PROFILE

# of degree-seeking undergraduates	2,258
% male/female	0/100
% African American	5
% American Indian or Alaska Native	<1
% Asian or Pacific Islander	7
% Hispanic	7
% Multiracial (non-Hispanic)	5
% White	49
% International	21
% Pell grant recipients	21.4

First generation and minority alumni Naomi Barry-Perez, civil rights lawyer, U.S. Department of Labor; Elaine Chao, former U.S. secretary of labor; Suzan-Lori Parks, Pulitzer Prize-winning playwright; Gloria Johnson-Powell M.D., psychiatrist/author; Mona K. Sutphen, White House Deputy Chief of Staff

ACADEMICS

full-time faculty	225
full-time minority faculty	58
student-faculty ratio	9:1
average class size	20
% first-year retention rate	91
% graduation rate (6 years)	83

Popular majors Biology, English, International Relations, Psychology, Economics

CAMPUS LIFE

% live on campus (% freshmen)	94 (100)

Multicultural student clubs and organizations Arab/American and International Women's Association, Asian American Sisters in Action, Asian Students Association, Association of Pan-African Unity, South Asian Club, Bulgarian Club, Chinese Cultural Association, Hawai'i Club, Korean American Sisters Association, La Unidad, Liga Filipina, Community of Portuguese Speaking Countries, Movimiento Estudiantial Chicano de Aztlan, African and Caribbean Student Association, Native Spirit, Romanian Student Association, Vietnamese Students Association, Zim Club (Zimbabweans)

Athletics NCAA Division III, NEWMAC Conference

ADMISSIONS

# of applicants	3,359
% accepted	51
# of first-year students enrolled	540
SAT Critical Reading (middle 50%)	610-700
SAT Math (middle 50%)	580-690
SAT Writing (middle 50%)	620-710
ACT mean	29
average HS GPA	3.65
Deadlines	
early decision I	11/15
early decision II	1/1
regular decision	1/15
application fee (online)	$60($0)
fee waiver for applicants with financial need	yes

COST & AID

tuition	$41,270
room & board	$12,140
total need-based institutional scholarships/grants	$34,083,549
% of students apply for need-based aid	70
% of students receive aid	100
% receiving need-based scholarship or grant aid	70
% receiving aid whose need was fully met	100
average aid package	$35,895
average student loan debt upon graduation	$22,499

Northeastern University

Northeastern University is a leader in integrating rigorous classroom studies with experiential learning opportunities, anchored by the nation's largest, most innovative cooperative education (co-op) program. In addition to the signature co-op program, in which students alternate between classroom learning and work experience, Northeastern offers students several other experiential learning opportunities, including student research, service learning and global learning experiences. All of this takes place on a vibrant, 73-acre campus located in the heart of Boston, which offers modern academic, residential and recreational facilities.

ACCESS **Diversity Initiatives**

Northeastern is a community that is comprised of students, faculty and staff from a diversity of backgrounds and experiences. The university values the contributions of all its members and works to support its underrepresented populations through a network of active cultural centers and mentoring programs. In recruiting students, Northeastern outreaches to a wide variety of geographically distant locations nationally and internationally and works closely with a host of support programs such as Upward Bound, Gear UP and Kids to College.

"Torch has allowed me to experience a world that would have been far beyond my reach, if it weren't for the kindness and generosity of those who comprise our Torch community."

– Kathy M.. '13
Boston, MA
Human Services

OPPORTUNITY **Torch Scholars Program**

Continuing a century-old commitment to educational access, the Torch Scholars Program is a bold and innovative scholarship initiative awarded to individuals who have overcome exceptional odds and who demonstrate the potential to excel academically. Torch Scholars receive full tuition, fees, and room and board, as well as significant personal and academic support throughout their undergraduate careers.

OPPORTUNITY **$118 Million in Financial Aid**

Northeastern is committed to making college accessible and affordable for all students interested in pursuing their passions. The university offers more than $118 million in grant and scholarship assistance, participates in all federal aid programs and offers an array of alternative financing and payment plans. In addition, Northeastern offers a number of scholarships that are awarded to students who are well-prepared for success in college and demonstrate strong leadership and community values.

SUCCESS **Diverse University Community**

Reflecting the city of Boston and the world beyond, Northeastern is a rich blend of cultures, languages, religions and traditions. The university supports and celebrates these characteristics through many centers, institutes and programs including the John D. O'Bryant African-American Institute, Asian American Center, Latino/a Student Cultural Center, GLBT Community, Hillel Jewish Community, Catholic Center, Spiritual Life Center and International Student and Scholar Institute.

SUCCESS **Legacy Mentoring/Retention Program**

The Legacy Mentoring Program provides a sense of belonging, retention and academic success for the black and Latino/a community. This active program includes events such as Black and Latino New Student Orientation, a study abroad forum, financial aid and professional development workshops, community service projects and many social outings.

Northeastern University
Office of Undergraduate Admissions
360 Huntington Avenue
Boston, MA 02115
Ph: (617) 373-2200
admissions@neu.edu
www.northeastern.edu

FAST FACTS

STUDENT PROFILE

# of degree-seeking undergraduates	15,905
% male/female	49/50
% African American	5
% American Indian or Alaska Native	<1
% Asian or Pacific Islander	12
% Hispanic	7
% White	43
% International	10
% Pell grant recipients	10

First-generation and minority alumni Aisha Kahlil, singer, actor, dancer; Reggie Lewis, professional basketball player, Boston Celtics; José Juan Barea, professional basketball player, Dallas Mavericks

ACADEMICS

full-time faculty	1,033
full-time minority faculty	165
student-faculty ratio	13:1
% first-year retention rate	93
% graduation rate (6 years)	77

Popular majors Business/International Business, Engineering, Health Services/Allied Health

CAMPUS LIFE

% live on campus (% freshmen)	53 (94)

Multicultural student clubs and organizations African Student Organization, Arab Student Association, Armenian Student Association, Asian Student Association, Barkada, Black Student Association, Cape Verdean Student Association, Caribbean Students' Association, Cultural & Language Learning Society of NU, Haitian Student Unity, Hip Hop Culture Club, International Students Association, Italian Culture Society, Korean American Students Association, Latin American Students Organization (LASO), Students for Israel at Northeastern, UTSAV (South Asian Student Organization), Vietnamese Student Association

Athletics NCAA Division I, Colonial Athletic Association

ADMISSIONS

# of applicants	43,254
% accepted	35
# of first-year students enrolled	2,833
SAT Critical Reading (middle 50%)	620-700
SAT Math (middle 50%)	650-730
SAT Writing (middle 50%)	620-710
ACT (middle 50%)	29-32
average HS GPA	3.7-4.2
Deadlines	
early action	11/1
regular decision	1/15
application fee (online)	$70 ($70)
fee waiver for applicants with financial need	yes

COST & AID

tuition	$37,840
room & board	$12,824
total need-based institutional scholarships/grants	$84,772,946
% of students apply for need-based aid	65
% of students receive aid	80
% receiving need-based scholarship or grant aid	94
% receiving aid whose need was fully met	16
average aid package	$17,877
average student loan debt upon graduation	n/a

Pine Manor College

Pine Manor College
400 Heath Street
Chestnut Hill, MA 02467
Ph: (800) 762-1357
admissions@pmc.edu
www.pmc.edu

Pine Manor College is a four-year, liberal-arts college dedicated to preparing women for inclusive leadership, social responsibility and academic success. For five of the last six years, Pine Manor has been ranked No. 1 for campus diversity by *US News & World Report*. The school distinguishes itself in its Inclusive Leadership and Social Responsibility (ILSR) program with a focus on community-based leadership, and its outcomes-based Portfolio Learning Program, which assists young women in creating and achieving academic goals. With such a small student body students receive individual attention from professors and a strong feeling of community and solidarity on campus. Student groups such as ALANA (African American, Latina, Asian, Native American and All) celebrate diversity in the student body. The school is located five miles from downtown Boston, accessible by subway.

"The mentoring class brought me out of my shell. I could not remain reserved and quiet, as I usually am. I had to be proactive, able to engage everyone within the team to participate and bring forth change. I never in a million years thought that I would have the opportunity to do any kind of mentoring. I was to busy looking for one myself, that I forgot that I could impart some advice to another human-being. "

– Jeanette D., '08
Boston, MA
Business Administration

ACCESS Center for Inclusive Leadership and Social Responsibility (ILSR)

Pine Manor's Center for Inclusive Leadership and Social Responsibility builds leadership skills in high school girls from around the country. The center provides free, two-hour Leadership Workshops in local high schools, hosts an annual Summer Summit on Leadership for high school girls from around the country and supports the Susan and Jack Rudin Conference, a two-day leadership conference on campus. The aim of ILSR is to encourage leadership in girls and to prepare them for success in college. Workshops titled College 101 emphasize self-esteem, getting into college, goal setting, balancing work and family, managing relationships and working as a team. The center annually presents the Pine Manor College Award for Inclusive Leadership and Social Responsibility to women who make a positive difference in the lives of others through compassion, collaboration and inclusiveness.

OPPORTUNITY Pine Manor College Scholarships

Pine Manor College is committed to making their highly personalized, relationship-based education available and affordable to women regardless of their financial means. In addition to reducing tuition by one-third, making the college one of the least expensive private colleges in New England, Pine Manor also offers nearly $4 million in need-based scholarships to deserving students.

SUCCESS Multicultural, International and Spiritual Affairs Office (MISA)

The MISA Office provides programs to encourage the awareness of diverse cultures and spirituality for all women on campus. The MISA Office also offers ongoing guidance and support for students of color and international students on the Pine Manor campus, and MISA staff make sure that students maintain their legal status while pursuing an undergraduate degree.

FAST FACTS

STUDENT PROFILE

# of degree-seeking undergraduates	484
% male/female	0/100
% African American	42
% American Indian or Alaska Native	<1
% Asian or Pacific Islander	5
% Hispanic	22
% White	14
% International	9
% Pell grant recipients	65

First-generation and minority alumni Merle Wolin, journalist; Gloria Harrison-Hall, radio and television producer

ACADEMICS

full-time faculty	28
full-time minority faculty	n/a
student-faculty ratio	10:1
average class size	10-19
% first-year retention rate	65
% graduation rate (6 years)	40

Popular majors Business Administration/ Management, Communications and Media Studies, Psychology

CAMPUS LIFE

% live on campus (% freshmen)	74 (69)

Multicultural student clubs and organizations ALANA, Alianza Latina, Asian Student Club, BGLAD, Diversity Committee, Haitian-American Women's Alliance, International Student Organization (ISC), Ladies of Various Ebony Shades (LOVES)

Athletics NCAA Division III, Great Northeast Athletic Conference

ADMISSIONS

# of applicants	718
% accepted	53
# of first-year students enrolled	164
SAT Critical Reading (middle 50%)	360-480
SAT Math (middle 50%)	340-450
SAT Writing (middle 50%)	n/a
ACT (middle 50%)	15-19
average HS GPA	2.4

Deadlines

regular admission	rolling
application fee	$25
fee waiver for applicants with financial need	yes

COST & AID

tuition	$21,400
room & board	$12,254
total need-based institutional scholarships/grants	n/a
% of students apply for need-based aid	95
% of students receive aid	97
% receiving need-based scholarship or grant aid	n/a
% receiving aid whose need was fully met	4.9
average aid package	$15,545
average student loan debt upon graduation	$32,875

Smith College

Smith College
Office of Admission
7 College Lane
Northampton, MA 01063
Ph: (800) 383-3232
admission@smith.edu
www.smith.edu

FAST FACTS

STUDENT PROFILE

# of degree-seeking undergraduates	2,558
% male/female	0/100
% African American	7
% American Indian or Alaska Native	1
% Asian or Pacific Islander	12
% Hispanic	7
% White	43
% International	8
% Pell grant recipients	28

First-generation and minority alums Yolanda King, civil rights activist, daughter of Dr. Martin Luther King, Jr.; Maria Lopez, judge; Evelyn Boyd Granville, mathematician; Sian DeVega, model, actress; Ng'endo Mwangi, first woman physician in Kenya; Sharmeen Obaid-Chinoy, award-winning documentary filmmaker; Thelma Golden, deputy director of Studio Museum in Harlem; Martha Southgate, writer

ACADEMICS

full-time faculty	296
full-time minority faculty	48
student-faculty ratio	9:1
average class size	19
% first-year retention rate	91
% graduation rate (6 years)	88

Popular majors Psychology, Government, English Language/Literature, Biology, Economics and Art

CAMPUS LIFE

% live on campus (% freshmen)	90 (100)

Multicultural student clubs and organizations Asian Students Alliance, Black Students Alliance, Ekta, International Students Organization, Korean American Students, Multiethnic Interracial Smith College, Nosostras, Smith African and Caribbean Students Association

Athletics NCAA Division III, Eastern College Athletic Conference

ADMISSIONS

# of applicants	4,128
% accepted	45
# of first-year students enrolled	717
SAT Critical Reading (middle 50%)	600-730
SAT Math (middle 50%)	580-690
SAT Writing (middle 50%)	620-720
ACT (middle 50%)	25-31
average HS GPA	3.87

Deadlines

early decision I	11/15
early decision II	1/1
regular decision	1/15
application fee (online)	$60 ($0)
fee waiver for applicants with financial need	yes

COST & AID

tuition	$39,800
room & board	$13,390
total need-based institutional scholarships/ grants	$45,158,107
% of students apply for need-based aid	75
% of students receive aid	70
% receiving need-based scholarship/grant aid	62
% receiving aid whose need was fully met	100
average aid package	$32,713
average student loan debt upon graduation	$20,989

As the nation's largest undergraduate women's college, Smith is distinguished by a diverse student body, a culturally vibrant surrounding area, and participation in the Five College Consortium. Smith offers unique educational resources and outstanding facilities rivaling those in many universities with special programs including an engineering major, funded summer internships, and research with faculty. Smith educates women of promise to lead lives of distinction.

ACCESS **Urban Education Initiative**

The Urban Education Initiative is a service-learning program that brings Smith students to elementary, middle and high schools in New York City, Chicago and nearby Springfield, Mass. Urban Education Fellows spend three weeks in January at one of the partner schools providing one-on-one tutoring and classroom assistance.

"It's empowering to look around a lecture of 40 and realize the women surrounding you aren't built to think a certain way, but that we each have something unique to contribute. Smithies aren't just top students but amazing leaders, athletes, researchers and artists. They don't just graduate with degrees in a given topic, but leave Smith with a supreme sense of personal development, confidence and accomplishment, ready to change the world."

– Chloe W., '11
White Plains, NY
Psychology

ACCESS **Smith Summer Science and Engineering Program**

High school students from around the globe participate in a month-long summer program in science and engineering. Funding is available for low-income students.

ACCESS **Women of Distinction**

The Women of Distinction program for high school seniors highlights the opportunities at Smith for African American, Asian American, Latina and Native American students. Participants in the three-day program live in campus houses, experience academic life, and attend panels and workshops on student life and the college admission process. There is a required application and students are chosen on the basis of academic and personal qualities. All expenses are covered by Smith.

OPPORTUNITY **Springfield and Holyoke Partnership**

Through this partnership, four graduates from the Springfield and Holyoke, Mass. public schools are selected to receive a full-tuition scholarship for each of their four undergraduate years at Smith. Students are selected based on their academic record and leadership potential.

SUCCESS **Student Support Groups**

There are a number of groups for low-income students and students of color: Low-Income Students of Smith, the Minority Association of Pre-Health Students, the Union of Underrepresented Students in the Sciences and AEMES (Achieving Excellence in Mathematics, Engineering and Sciences).

SUCCESS **Bridge Pre-Orientation Program**

Through a variety of interactive student-led seminars and group activities, participants are encouraged to share their perspectives and hear the voices of their peers to better understand and appreciate their similarities and differences. The goal of the program is an examination of cultural diversity in all its forms.

Stonehill College

Boston is within easy reach of Stonehill College, a selective Catholic college located in Easton, Massachusetts. Students who study at Stonehill emerge with a comprehensive education that honors leadership, personal growth and discovery. To this end, students are required to participate in the Cornerstone Program of General Education to prepare for a life of learning and responsible citizenship by leading them to examine critically the self, society, culture and the natural world. Stonehill offers 42 major programs, the opportunity to double major and 42 minor programs.

"Stonehill has proven to me to be a place offering many resources. These resources have helped me to build a solid foundation. Now I am confident that I will attain my professional goals."

– Alexandre S., '11
Natick, MA
Psychology

ACCESS Project SEED

Project SEED provides a number of academically talented, economically disadvantaged high school students the opportunity to conduct meaningful summer research with Stonehill chemistry professors and advanced level college students.

OPPORTUNITY Minority, Low-Income and First-Generation Scholarships

Stonehill College offers several Minority, Low-Income, and First-Generation Scholarships to those who meet certain other criteria. Among the aforementioned scholarships are: the Ely Scholarship, specifically earmarked for minority males whose families are facing undue economic hardship; the William Randolph Hearst Foundation Scholars Program Scholarship, open to all minority students from low-income backgrounds; the Ron Burton Scholarship, available only to alumni from the Ron Burton Training Village summer program for disadvantaged boys; the John and Margarete McNeice Scholars Program award, open to minority students from low-income backgrounds; and, The Yawkey Scholarship, available to eligible students residing in New England or Georgetown County, South Carolina who are financially needy, academically qualified and have a life circumstance that have made study and achievement challenging.

SUCCESS The Path Program

Run by the Office of Academic Services, The Path Program is an intensive transition program designed to develop needed academic skills for first-year students. In addition to skill development in areas such as note-taking, research and text book reading, students learn about the nuts and bolts of college life such as reading a course syllabus, calculating a GPA and exploring a major area of study. This program eases the transition on campus and puts students in touch with a diverse group of upper-class students, staff and resources on campus.

SUCCESS The Summer Bridge Program

This pre-orientation program is designed for high school seniors who are accepted and plan to enroll in the science program at Stonehill. The Summer Bridge Program affords the pre-college student who may not have the most rigorous science preparation in high school the opportunity to work alongside Stonehill science faculty to gain lab experience, knowledge and added skills prior to the start of Fall classes. This program is designed to aid in the college transition process especially within a competitive science program.

Stonehill College
320 Washington Street
Easton, MA 02357
Ph: (508) 565-1373
admissions@stonehill.edu
www.stonehill.edu

FAST FACTS

STUDENT PROFILE

# of degree-seeking undergraduates	2,558
% male/female	38/62
% African American	3
% American Indian or Alaska Native	0
% Asian or Pacific Islander	1
% Hispanic	3
% White	90
% International	<1
% Pell grant recipients	11

First-generation and minority alumni Ed Cooley '94, Division I head coach, men's basketball, Fairfield University; Lois Commodore '00, Christian recording artist, founder of Soldiers of Destiny Foundation; Andrea Vandross '02, medical school, University of Chicago; Christopher Tirrell '09, law school, Stanford University

ACADEMICS

full-time faculty	157
full-time minority faculty	13
student-faculty ratio	13:1
average class size	20
% first-year retention rate	92
% graduation rate (6 years)	85

Popular majors Psychology, English, Political Science, Biology, Accounting

CAMPUS LIFE

% live on campus (% freshmen)	92 (97)

Multicultural student clubs and organizations Diversity Committee of Student Government, International Club, PRIDE, Diversity on Campus (D.O.C.), Asian American Society, La Unidad/ Spanish Club, ALANA Brothers and Sisters Leadership Program, Stonehill College chapter of Jane Doe, Raising Awareness of our Cultural Experiences (R.A.C.E.), Stonehill Alumni of Color Group

Athletics NCAA Division II, Northeast-10 Conference

ADMISSIONS

# of applicants	7,052
% accepted	64
# of first-year students enrolled	728
SAT Critical Reading (middle 50%)	550-630
SAT Math (middle 50%)	560-640
SAT Writing (middle 50%)	n/a
ACT (middle 50%)	24-28
average HS GPA	3.4
Deadlines	
early decision	11/1
regular decision	1/15
application fee (online)	$60 ($60)
fee waiver for applicants with financial need	yes

COST & AID

tuition	$33,920
room & board	$12,860
total need-based institutional scholarships/grants	$22,485,321
% of students apply for need-based aid	81
% of students recieve aid	67
% receiving need-based scholarship or grant aid	63
% receiving aid whose need was fully met	35
average aid package	$20,923
average student loan debt upon graduation	$30,435

Tufts University

Located 5 miles outside of Boston, Tufts is a highly selective university which draws a diverse student body from all over the world. The University has students from all 50 states and over 65 countries, and approximately 25 percent of undergraduates are students of color and 10 percent are first-generation students. Dedicated to preparing leaders who will address the intellectual and social challenges of the new century, Tufts values globalism, active citizenship and environmentalism in over 60 academic programs in the School of Arts & Sciences and the School of Engineering.

ACCESS **Early Awareness Initiative**

Tufts' Office of Undergraduate Admissions runs an Early Awareness Initiative, which brings Boston middle school students (with a focus on those from under-served areas) to campus weekly to expose them to college life. Current undergraduates and admissions officers explain how participants can begin preparing for the college application process, placing emphasis on the steps middle and early high school students should take to access higher education.

"The Voices Program at Tufts opened my eyes to the diverse culture that the Tufts community has to offer its students. The program highly influenced my decision to attend Tufts, and I am glad that I was able to immerse myself into a welcoming, warm, diverse community of students, faculty, and staff."

– Nicole Oliveira, '13
Stoughton, MA
Child Development

ACCESS **College Advising**

Current Tufts students volunteer with the Let's Get Ready program to help juniors at Somerville High School prepare for the SATs and admissions process. This partnership brings over 40 Tufts students to Somerville High School over the course of the year who work closely and regularly with high school juniors and seniors as they seek to access opportunities in higher education.

OPPORTUNITY **Loan Replacement Policy/Financial Aid**

Beginning with the class of 2011, Tufts will replace loans with scholarship grants for all undergraduates whose annual family income is below $40,000. The ability to provide need-blind financial aid is the top priority of the University's fundraising campaign and it is committed to meeting all demonstrated need of admitted students.

OPPORTUNITY **Voices of Tufts**

The Office of Undergraduate Admissions invites traditionally underrepresented students to visit the Tufts campus for a two-day fly-in program each fall that provides a multicultural prospective on attending the university. Bus transportation is provided from New York City and students traveling from elsewhere can apply for a travel grant.

SUCCESS **Health Careers Fellows Program (HCFP)**

The Health Careers Fellows Program seeks to support minority and disadvantaged students interested in the health professions. HCFP ensures that each student maximizes his or her academic career by providing academic tutoring, counseling and advising. Fellows have the opportunity to attend review sessions, participate in seminar series on health-related topics, and visit off-campus sites. They receive individualized support from the Program Director and Associate Director of Health Professions Advising while they are students at Tufts and go on to graduate study in health-related careers.

SUCCESS **Bridge to Engineering Success at Tufts (BEST)**

The BEST Scholars Program is a six-week summer bridge program for incoming freshmen in the School of Engineering. Invited students will have the opportunity to take math and science courses for credit and participate in workshops designed to ease the academic transition to college life. Additionally, a weekly "Exploring Engineering" lecture series introduces students to each of the engineering majors.

Tufts University
Bendetson Hall
Medford, MA 02155
Ph: (617) 627-3170
admissions.inquiry@ase.tufts.edu
www.tufts.edu

FAST FACTS

STUDENT PROFILE

# of degree-seeking undergraduates	5,224
% male/female	48/52
% African American	5
% American Indian or Alaska Native	>1
% Asian or Pacific Islander	11
% Hispanic	6
% White	57
% International	14
% Pell grant recipients	10

First-generation and minority alumni Cathy Bao Bean, author, advocate; Bill Richardson, Governor, New Mexico, former presidential candidate; Bill Thompson, comptroller, City of New York; Tracy Chapman, singer/songwriter

ACADEMICS

full-time faculty	640
full-time minority faculty	n/a
student/faculty ratio	8:1
average class size	20
% first year retention rate	96
% graduation rate (6 years)	92

Popular majors International Relations, Biology, English, Economics, Psychology

CAMPUS LIFE

% live on campus (% freshmen)	65.9 (99.9)

Multicultural student clubs and organizations African Student Organization, Arab Student Association, Asian Community at Tufts, Association of Latin American Students, Black Men's Group, Chinese Student Association, Gen-1 (First Generation College Student Organization), Multiracial Organization of Students at Tufts, Tufts Association of South Asians, Vietnamese Student Club

Athletics NCAA Division III, New England Small College Athletic Conference (NESCAC)

ADMISSIONS

# of applicants	17,130
% accepted	22
# of first-year students enrolled	1300
SAT Critical Reading (middle 50%)	680-750
SAT Math (middle 50%)	680-790
SAT Writing (middle 50%)	680-760
ACT (middle 50%)	30-33
average HS GPA	n/a
Deadlines	
early decision	11/1
regular decision	1/1
application fee (online)	$70 ($70)
fee waiver for applicants	yes

COST & AID

tuition	$41,998
room and board	$11,512
total need-based institutional scholarships and grants	$52,000,000
% students apply for need-based aid	55
% receiving need-based scholarship or grant aid	39
% receiving aid whose need fully met	100
average aid package	$32,500
average student loan debt upon graduation	$15,100

Wellesley College

Located a dozen miles from Boston, Wellesley College offers bright, motivated women a comprehensive, liberal arts education in a small college environment. Due to its need-blind admission policy for U.S. citizens and permanent residents, generous financial aid, and support of students throughout their undergraduate education, Wellesley is considered one of the most socio-economically diverse colleges or universities in the nation. Wellesley considers students for admission solely on their talents and personal qualities, not on their financial resources, and is committed to meeting 100 percent of each admitted student's demonstrated financial need. Women interested in science and technology particularly benefit from attending the College, which provides opportunities for research with faculty, and offers cross-registration with the Massachusetts Institute of Technology and Olin College of Engineering.

> ***"This is only my second semester at Wellesley and being in an environment of intellectually motivated women has made me push myself to accomplish things I never imagined."***
> *– Taylor I., '14*
> *St. Louis, MO*

OPPORTUNITY Financially Possible

Wellesley's endowment is strong. We adjust to economic trends and find ways to help if a family's needs change during the school year. We keep our packaged student loan levels low, even eliminating loans to students from families with incomes under $60,000. Financial support also exists outside the traditional financial aid model. Financial aid packages are portable to approved study abroad programs, funding is available for research and service projects, and our career office funds 300 students every year with stipends of up to $3,500 to do what would otherwise be unpaid internships - making it possible to trade your summer job for an internship.

OPPORTUNITY Campus Visit Financial Assistance

Wellesley's outreach includes recruitment efforts directed at students from a wide range of socioeconomic experiences in all areas of the country, including making connections with those from high schools with more limited resources and with students who may be the first in their families to attend college. Wellesley fully funds talented high school students from lower socioeconomic backgrounds — those who are thinking of applying and those who have been admitted — to campus at the college's expense.

OPPORTUNITY QuestBridge National College Match Program

The QuestBridge National College Match program provides students who have achieved academic excellence in the face of economic hardship with a free QuestBridge application. It enables these students to highlight their academic achievements in light of their low-income background and links them with financial aid and scholarship opportunities.

SUCCESS Supplemental Instruction Program

Wellesley's Pforzheimer Learning and Teaching Center provides academic support and advising, including peer tutoring to underrepresented students. Wellesley is also piloting a version of the nationally recognized Supplemental Instruction program, which provides additional peer-led learning opportunities in high-risk courses. In its first year, Wellesley introduced the Supplemental Instruction Program to entry-level courses in biology and chemistry, and it now offers an advanced chemistry course. A cultural advising network also provides a range of support services for students from diverse backgrounds.

Wellesley College
Admission Office
106 Central Street
Wellesley, MA 02481
Ph: (781) 283-2270
admission@wellesley.edu
www.wellesley.edu/admission

FAST FACTS

STUDENT PROFILE

# of degree-seeking undergraduates	2,284
% male/ female	0/100
% African American	6
% American Indian or Alaska Native	1
% Asian or Pacific Islander	22
% Hispanic	9
% White	45
% International	11
% Pell grant recipients	16

First-generation and minority alumni Michelle Ye, former Miss Chinese International; Regina Montoya, Latina business leader, advocate; Nayantara Sahgal, writer; Michelle Caruso-Cabrera, host, anchor, CNBC; Amalya L. Kearse, judge, U.S. Court of Appeals

ACADEMICS

full-time faculty	249
full-time minority faculty	60
student-faculty ratio	8:1
average class size	18
% first-year retention rate	94
% graduation rate (6 yrs)	90

Popular majors Economics, Political Science, English, Psychology, Biological Sciences

CAMPUS LIFE

% live on campus (% freshmen)	98 (100)

Multicultural student clubs and organizations African Students' Association, Asian Student Union, Chinese Students Association, Club Filipina, Ethos (Women of African Descent), Korean Students Association, Mezcla, Native American Student Organization, Slater International Association, Spectrum, Taiwanese Cultural Organization, United World Colleges, Association for South Asian Cultures

Athletics NCAA Division III, NEWMAC

ADMISSIONS

# of applicants	4,267
% accepted	34
# of first-year students enrolled	589
SAT Critical Reading (middle 50%)	640-740
SAT Math (middle 50%)	630-740
SAT Writing (middle 50%)	650-750
ACT (middle 50%)	29-32
average HS GPA	n/a
% in top 20% of class, if ranked	95
Deadlines	
early decision	11/1
regular decision	1/15
application fee (online)	$50($0)
fee waiver for applicants with financial need	yes

COST & AID

tuition	$40,410
room & board	$12,590
total need-based institutional scholarships/ grants	$50,000,000+
% of students apply for need-based aid	70
% of students receive aid	63
% receiving need-based scholarship/ grant aid	63
% receiving aid whose need was fully met	100
average aid package	$38,136
average student loan debt upon graduation	$12,495

Westfield State University

Founded in 1838 by Horace Mann, Westfield State is an education leader committed to providing every generation of students with a learning experience built on its founding principle as the first co-educational college in America to offer an education without barrier to race, creed or economic status. This spirit of innovative thinking and social responsibility is forged in a curriculum of liberal arts and professional studies that creates a vital community of engaged learners who become confident, capable individuals prepared for leadership and service to society.

ACCESS Urban Education Program (UEP)

Recognized across campus for its development of pre-college first-generation, low-income, and ethnically diverse student scholars, UEP is an academic support progam designed to increase the enrollment, retention, and graduation rates of these students. By way of comprehensive summer and academic year programming and services, the Urban Education Program has created and maintained a dynamic program environment that promotes intellectual, social, and emotional development, both collaboratively and individually. The Urban Education Program is comprised of five identifiable components: recruitment and participant selection, summer bridge program, academic year programming, leadership development, and career/graduate school preparation.

"The Westfield State University Summer Bridge Program experience was extraordinary! I was mentored by my peers, had the opportunity to develop myself as a leader, and I got credits for college courses that I took at the same time. By networking, I made amazing connections with people that have continued to support me throughout my time at Westfield. Thanks to the Urban Education Program here at Westfield State University, I am a year ahead in my coursework and confident about my future."

– Jaime J., '13 Criminal Justice/ Psychology

OPPORTUNITY Discover Westfield State University Day

The annual Discover Westfield State University Day is geared toward first-generation college students and students of color. Westfield provides transportation from the high schools to campus so that prospective students can meet with WSU faculty, staff, and students. The participants receive a student-guided tour of the campus and hear presentations from the Admission, Financial Aid, and Urban Education offices. Prospective students also receive an admission application with an application fee waiver.

SUCCESS TRiO Student Support Services

TRiO Student Support Services is a comprehensive federally funded TRiO Program serving matriculated students who are low performing academically and are either first-generation, low-income, or disabled (learning, physical, psychological/emotional). This program is designed to improve academic performance, retention to graduation, and assist with graduate and professional school preparation. Services such as professional tutoring, academic advisement, peer mentoring, cultural enrichment, assistance with obtaining financial aid, to name a few, are available to program students for as long as they are enrolled at the college.

Westfield State University
333 Western Avenue
Westfield, MA 01086
Ph: (413) 572-5218
admissions@westfield.ma.edu
www.westfield.ma.edu

FAST FACTS

STUDENT PROFILE

# of degree-seeking undergraduates	4,514
% male/female	47/53
% African American	4
% American Indian or Alaska Native	<1
% Asian or Pacific Islander	<1
% Hispanic	5
% White	83
% International	<1
% Pell grant recipients	26

First-generation and minority alumni Dr. Yolanda Johnson '87, Principal, Atlanta School System, GA; George Gilmer '92, Senior Vice President, Bank of New York Mellon; Eduardo C. Robreno '67, Federal Court Judge, PA; Lance Campbell '91, Urban City Planner, Boston; Tyrone Abrahamian '95, Probation Officer Supervisor, CT

ACADEMICS

full-time faculty	218
full-time minority faculty	33
student/faculty ratio	18:1
average class size	23
% first year retention rate	79
% graduation rate (6 years)	58

Popular majors Business Management, Communication, Criminal Justice, Education, Psychology

CAMPUS LIFE

% live on campus (% freshmen)	60 (90)

Multicultural student clubs and organizations Asian Appreciation Club, Latino Association for Empowerment

Athletics NCAA Division III, Massachusetts State Collegiate Athletic Conference

ADMISSIONS

# of applicants	5,586
% accepted	58
# of first-year students enrolled	1,126
SAT Critical Reading average	510
SAT Math average	530
SAT Writing (middle 50%)	n/a
ACT (middle 50%)	n/a
average HS GPA	3.04

Deadlines

regular decision	3/1
application fee (online)	$50 ($50)
fee waiver for applicants	yes

COST & AID

tuition	in-state $7,431; out-of-state $13,510
room and board	$8,525
total need-based institutional scholarships and grants	$1,380,898
% students apply for need-based aid	83
% receiving need-based scholarship or grant aid	38
% receiving aid whose need fully met	8
average aid package	$7,666
average student loan debt upon graduation	$17,965

Wheaton College

Wheaton College is a classic, selective, private, coeducational liberal arts college. The College boasts over 1600 students hailing from 42 states and almost 38 countries. Wheaton's 400 acre campus is ideally located in suburban Norton, Massachusetts, 35 miles south of Boston and 20 miles north of Providence, Rhode Island. Among its many academic opportunities include internships in every professional field, community service, and study abroad. More than 127 Wheaton students have won national academic awards since 2001, including 3 Rhodes Scholars.

ACCESS Davis United World Scholars Program

The program provides grants to Wheaton for scholars from both the United States and from overseas who have proven themselves by completing their last two years of high school at a group of international schools called United World Colleges. These UWC schools are located in the United States, Bosnia, Canada, Costa Rica, Hong Kong, India, Italy, Norway, Singapore, Swaziland, the United Kingdom, and Venezuela. By supporting scholars who are energized by building understanding in active, personal ways, the Davis UWC Scholars Program exemplifies how diversity can contribute to a much richer education and to a more internationally oriented undergraduate experience for everyone on campus.

OPPORTUNITY Posse Foundation

Wheaton College and The Posse Foundation, Inc., identify public high school students with extraordinary academic and leadership potential who may be overlooked by traditional college selection processes. Posse extends to these students the opportunity to pursue personal and academic excellence by placing them in supportive, multicultural teams. Posse Scholars receive four-year, full-tuition leadership scholarships.

OPPORTUNITY Diversity Overnight Program

Every year Wheaton invites a group of diverse and talented high school seniors to come together for an overnight visit and experience the Wheaton community. This program is designed to explore academic, extracurricular opportunities, and other important aspects of college life. Students chosen to participate are provided with housing and meals as guests of Wheaton.

OPPORTUNITY HERO Program

The Higher Education Readiness Opportunity (HERO) program partners with Brockton high school students who will be the first from their families to attend college. Students pair up with Wheaton mentors. Through the program, students get a better sense of college life and develop the abilities and confidence to acquire—and excel during—a college education.

"I came to Wheaton College through the Bottom Line College Counseling Program. I am the first of my immediate family to attend a four-year college. My mother is originally from El Salvador and came to the U.S. to give my brother and I a better life. The program gave me the resources I needed to be successful."

– Vanessa H., '11
Hyde Park, MA
Psychobiology

SUCCESS The Marshall Center for Intercultural Learning

Wheaton College recognizes that individuals have complex identities formed by biology, society, history and choice. These varied facets shape who we are, form our uniqueness, and contribute to the rich educational community that is Wheaton College. The Marshall Center exists to affirm these unique identities, to build a community that draws from them and to cultivate leaders who will introduce to the world the value of human diversity.

Wheaton College
26 East Main Street
Norton, MA 02766
Ph: (630) 752-5000
admission@wheatoncollege.edu
www.wheatoncollege.edu

FAST FACTS

STUDENT PROFILE

# of degree-seeking undergraduates	1,635
% male/female	36/64
% African American	5
% American Indian or Alaska Native	0
% Asian or Pacific Islander	2
% Hispanic	5
% White	74
% Pell grant recipients	n/a

First-generation and minority alumni Patricia A. King '63, Professor of Law, Medicine, Ethics and Public Policy at Georgetown University; Ruth Ann Stewart '63, Professor of Public Policy, New York University; Derron JR Wallace '07, Posse Scholar and Marshall, Watson, and Fulbright Scholar, Indira Henard '03, President Obama Administration

ACADEMICS

full-time faculty	142
full-time minority faculty	28
student-faculty ratio	10:1
average class size	35
% first-year retention rate	87
% graduation rate (6 years)	75

Popular majors Psychology, History, English, Economics, Biology, Sociology

CAMPUS LIFE

% live on campus (% fresh)	93 (99)

Multicultural student clubs and organizations Black Students Association, International Students Association, South Asian Students Association, Asian Student Association, Latino Students Association, Middle Eastern Students Association, Multi-Ethnic

Athletics NCAA Division III, NEWMAC

ADMISSIONS

# of applicants	3,272
% accepted	62
# of first-year students enrolled	451
SAT Critical Reading (middle 50%)	580-690
SAT Math (middle 50%)	570-660
SAT Writing (middle 50%)	n/a
ACT (middle 50%)	26-30
average HS GPA	3.42
Deadlines	
early decision	11/15
early action	11/15
regular decision	1/15
application fee (online)	$55 ($0)
fee waiver for applicants with financial need	yes

COST & AID

tuition	$41,600
room & board	$10,670
total need-based institutional scholarships/grants	$23,529,911
% of students apply for need-based aid	66
% of students receive aid	58
% receiving need-based scholarship or grant aid	55
% receiving aid whose need was fully met	52
average aid package	$33,404
average student loan debt upon graduation	$27,546

Williams College

Williams College
33 Stetson Court
Williamstown, MA 01267
Ph: (413) 597-2211
admission@williams.edu
www.williams.edu

Williams offers the best in a college education. With a committed and accomplished faculty, more than 30 majors, exciting events, and a breathtaking campus, Williams College is a highly ranked liberal arts school regarded as one of the finest in the country. When visiting in 1844, Henry David Thoreau remarked, "It would be no small advantage if every college were thus located at the base of a mountain." Williams, resting in the Berkshires in northwestern Massachusetts, at the foot of Mount Greylock, is a small college with a far-reaching name. Respected and revered by academia, this co-educational school, founded in 1793, has produced 37 Rhodes Scholars, more than any other liberal arts college in the country.

ACCESS **Counselor Visitation Program**

In select summers, Williams teams with Middlebury College to bring twenty-five counselors to the campuses. Counselors spend three days on each campus, exploring the academic, cultural, and social offerings available to students. Time is spent networking with one another and discussing college admission processes with admission counselors, seeking ways to collaborate on improving college access. To inquire about the program, please contact the Office of Admission and ask for the Diversity Recruitment Director.

"Williams offers everything a student needs to succeed. From some of the smallest class sizes, to one-on-one tutoring in most classes. Earlier on this semester my professor even pulled an all-nighter with us, helping us study for an exam. Moreover, within my first week at Williams all my professors knew my name. It was amazing to know that they cared about me."

– Maxwell R., '13
New York, NY
Undecided

OPPORTUNITY **Windows on Williams (WoW): Student Fly-In Program**

Every fall, Williams offers more than 150 low-income, first-generation, and underrepresented prospective students a three-day, all-expenses-paid trip to the college. Participants are able to attend classes, meet professors and current students, and experience life as a Williams student first-hand. To inquire about the program, please contact the Office of Admission and ask for the Diversity Recruitment Director.

SUCCESS **Summer Science / Summer Humanities and Social Sciences**

About 150 incoming first-year students participate in Summer Science and Summer Humanities and Social Sciences at Williams, special orientation programs during the month of July. Priority for admission is given to first-generation students. Participants take four courses and engage in research, allowing for an academically enriching experience that familiarizes students with campus life before the fall semester.

SUCCESS **BRIDGES**

BRIDGES is a mid-orientation diversity program that introduces new students to alumni, faculty, and staff who will guide them toward campus resources. Through workshops and discussions, an examination of the Berkshire's heritage, conversations with key college administrators, and visits to nearby towns, students are able to forge meaningful connections before classes begin.

SUCCESS **Williams Community Building Program**

The Multicultural Center at Williams College provides students a social and academic center on campus. A diverse community is supported through cultural programs, clubs and events. Including guest speakers, campus-wide forums, and other activities, over 200 multicultural events are sponsored at Williams each year.

FAST FACTS

STUDENT PROFILE

# of degree-seeking undergraduates	2,181
% male/female	49/51
% African American	11
% American Indian or Alaska Native	<1
% Asian or Pacific Islander	12
% Hispanic	10
% White	59
% International	7
% Pell grant recipients	19

First-generation and minority alumni Mayda del Valle '00, youngest-ever winner, National Poetry Slam Contest, voted one of 37 young innovators by Smithsonian magazine in 2007; Aaron Jenkins, former legislative aide for U.S. Senator John Kerry, now a director of educational access in Washington DC.

ACADEMICS

full-time faculty	267
full-time minority faculty	50
student-faculty ratio	7:1
average class size	16
median class size	13
% first-year retention rate	97
% graduation rate (6 years)	96

Popular majors Art/Art Studies, Economics, Political Science, Psychology, Research Sciences

CAMPUS LIFE

% live on campus (% freshmen)	96 (100)

Multicultural student clubs and organizations Asian American Students in Action, South Asian Student Organization, Chinese American Student Organization, Koreans of Williams, Students of Mixed Heritage, VISTA (Latino/a Student Organization), Williams Black Student Union, Minority Coalition

Athletics NCAA Division III, New England Small College Athletic Conference (NESCAC)

ADMISSIONS

# of applicants	7,030
% accepted	17
# of first-year students enrolled	548
SAT Critical Reading (middle 50%)	660-770
SAT Math (middle 50%)	650-760
SAT Writing (middle 50%)	660-770
ACT middle 50%	30-34
average HS GPA	n/a
Deadlines	
early decision	11/10
regular decision	1/1
application fee (online)	$60 ($60)
fee waiver for applicants with financial need	yes

COST & AID

tuition	$42,938
room & board	$11,370
total need-based institutional scholarships/grants	$32,372,041
% of students apply for need-based aid	57
% of students receive aid	100
% receiving need-based scholarship or grant aid	100
% receiving aid whose need was fully met	100
average aid package	$40,257
average student loan debt upon graduation	$9,214

Worcester Polytechnic Institute

Founded in 1865 with the mission of researching and teaching cutting-edge science and engineering, Worcester Polytechnic Institute has developed a reputation for innovation. WPI graduates have invented such life-altering technologies as stainless steel, the airbag safety system and the catalytic converter. The WPI Plan is hands-on and project-based and takes a humanistic view of engineering. WPI emphasizes teamwork instead of competition, fostering an environment of collaboration among students. The only test-optional techie school, WPI is half the size of Rensselaer and a third the size of MIT.

ACCESS **Camp Reach and STEM Saturdays**

Camp Reach is a summer residential program for girls in Massachusetts and Providence County, Rhode Island who have completed the 6th grade and who are interested in learning more about careers in engineering and technology. STEM Saturdays, sponsored by Intel, are four day-long workshops in the spirit of the university's popular Camp Reach. Each of the Camp Reach teachers returns to lead one day of math, science, or engineering. The participants' parents take part in sessions designed to teach them ways to encourage their daughters to excel in science, technology, engineering, and mathematics.

OPPORTUNITY **Envision Program**

The Envision Program is an annual multicultural overnight program that allows prospective students to experience life as a WPI student. Participants have to opportunity to informally "meet and greet" WPI's Coordinator of Multicultural Recruitment and Director of Diversity Programs from Student Affairs.

OPPORTUNITY **Multicultural Community Overview**

The Multicultural Community Overview is an open house that invites prospective students to learn about opportunities for students on campus and WPI's multicultural programs, meet community members, and learn about campus life.

"Although being a female of color at WPI makes me far from the majority, I have never felt like a minority. At WPI, we are all joined by a strong passion for what we do, specifically related to our major disciplines, but also through our activities and passions outside of the classroom. I plan to change the way we deal with cancer one day, and at WPI I am gaining the courage and support I need to make my plan a reality."
– Nediva A., '13
Biomedical Engineering

OPPORTUNITY **Umoja Unidad Overnight**

The Umoja Unidad Overnight is scheduled for the night prior to WPI's Closer Look open house program for admitted students and their families. This overnight program allows admitted students to experience student life at WPI, spend time with WPI's multicultural student population and meet other students admitted to WPI's latest freshman class.

SUCCESS **Excellence in Mathematics Science, & Engineering Program (EMSEP)**

The mission of the Excellence in Mathematics, Science and Engineering Program (EMSEP) is to increase the access to educational opportunities at WPI for underrepresented students of African, Latino, and American Indian descent. EMSEP is a comprehensive network of support services for students of color while enrolled at WPI. The Program empowers students by helping them establish a solid academic and personal development foundation to increase their potential for college success.

SUCCESS **ALANA Student Support Network**

The ALANA (African-American, Latino/Hispanic, Asian, and Native-American) Student Support Network is a group of administrators from several colleges and universities within the Worcester consortium whose goal is to support the recruitment and retention of ALANA students.

Worcester Polytechnic Institute
100 Institute Rd
Worcester, MA 01609
Ph: (508)-831-5286
admissions@wpi.edu
www.admissions.wpi.edu

FAST FACTS

STUDENT PROFILE	
# of degree-seeking undergraduates	3,537
% male/female	70/30
% African American	3
% American Indian or Alaska Native	<1
% Asian or Pacific Islander	6
% Hispanic	7
% White	71
% International	10
% Pell grant recipients	n/a
First-generation and minority alumni n/a	
ACADEMICS	
full-time faculty	396
full-time minority faculty	52
student-faculty ratio	14:1
average class size	20-25
% first-year retention rate	95
% graduation rate (6 years)	80
Popular majors Engineering, Natural Sciences, Mathematics, Computer Science/Interactive Media and Game Development, Business Management	
CAMPUS LIFE	
% live on campus (% fresh)	61 (95)
Multicultural student clubs and organizations Black Student Union, National Society of Black Engineers (NSBE), Society of Hispanic Professional Engineers (SHPE), Hispanic and Caribbean Student Association (HCSA)	
Athletics NCAA Division III, New England Women's and Men's Athletic Conference	
ADMISSIONS	
# of applicants	7,049
% accepted	57
# of first-year students enrolled	985
SAT Critical Reading (middle 50%)	560-650
SAT Math (middle 50%)	630-730
SAT Writing (middle 50%)	560-660
ACT (middle 50%)	26-31
average HS GPA	3.8
Deadlines	
regular decision	2/1
application fee (online)	$60 ($n/a)
fee waiver for applicants with financial need	yes
COST & AID	
tuition	$36,890
room & board	$11,160
total need-based institutional scholarships/grants	$42,212,933
% of students apply for need-based aid	75
% receiving need-based scholarship or grant aid	66
% receiving aid whose need was fully met	22
average aid package	$25,331
average student loan debt upon graduation	n/a

Albion College

Albion College will change your life. Whether you come prepared for college or are still finding yourself, ready to leave home or unsure of independence, undecided or set on a major, Albion will help you take that next step toward a successful life. Our students learn to think critically and turn thoughts into actions. They gain experiences inside and outside of the classroom. Small class sizes allow for greater interaction between faculty and students creating personal relationships and lasting connections. All of these ideas come together to create an Albion Advantage for our students. Come visit Albion to see if it is the right school for you!

"Albion wants you to be successful. My professors and coaches have definitely been there for me-whether in helping me decide on a major or deal with a personal issue. And the scholarships that alumni have set up are part of that too. I feel very fortunate to hold two of these scholarships-it's great to know that alumni who graduated many years ago are helping me out today."

– Demetrius W., '13
Albion, MI
Anthropology and Sociology

ACCESS **College Positive Volunteers**

In collaboration with the Albion Community Foundation, and with the support of a grant from the College Positive Community program, Albion College organized a new program this year to introduce elementary through high school students from the Albion community to higher education. AC invited students to attend events on campus, such as the Elkin R. Issac Student Research Symposium, where participants listened to Albion students present research findings, and the Day of Woden celebration held at the end of the semester. Giving tours of campus, talking about the college experience, and prompting students' discussion about their own academic and career goals, the College Positive Volunteers worked to eliminate common misconceptions about higher education and encourage students in the surrounding community to start thinking about college at an earlier age.

OPPORTUNITY **Albion College Diversity Award**

The Diversity Award of up to $4,000 per year is given to students who demonstrate need as well as being ethnically diverse.

SUCCESS **Intercultural Affairs Orientation**

Sponsored by the Office of Intercultural Affairs, Albion invites first year students and transfers, along with their families, to participate in the Intercultural Affairs Orientation. The Orientation features dialogue panels, information sessions, and opportunities to meet staff and upper class students to learn more about the various academic disciplines, social organizations, and campus sponsored groups offered at AC.

SUCCESS **First-Year Experience Program (FYE)**

The FYE program at Albion College provides all first year students with support and guidance throughout their first year at AC to excel in the collegiate environment both in and out of the classroom. The program includes Student Orientation, Advising, and Registration (SOAR), First Year Seminars, the Richard M. Smith Common Reading Experience, and Learning Strategy Sessions to help students adjust academically to the liberal arts coursework and socially to a new environment.

SUCCESS **Smooth Transitions Mentor Program**

Albion's Smooth Transitions Mentor Program matches first-year students from historically underrepresented racial or ethnic backgrounds with upper class student mentors. The program provides guidance and direction to participating students in order to assist them in making a successful transition to Albion, both academically and socially. As current students at AC, student mentors serve as relatable and reliable guides for first years as they explore their academic interests and passions, learn more about extracurricular and campus organizations, and adjust to college life.

Albion College
611 E Porter St.
Albion, MI 49224
Ph: (517) 629-0321
admission@albion.edu
www.albion.edu

FAST FACTS

STUDENT PROFILE

# of degree-seeking undergraduates	1,602
% male/female	48/52
% African American	3
% American Indian or Alaska Native	1
% Asian or Pacific Islander	1
% Hispanic	2.5
% White	85
% International	3
% Pell grant recipients	28.5

First-generation and minority alumni T.J. Carnegie '97 President, Full Circle Political Marketing; Marcus Gill '04, Head Men's Basketball Coach, Earlham College; Daniel Boggan '67, Independent Business Consultant, Former Senior Vice President, National Collegiate Athletic Association, Past President, National Forum for Black Public Administrators; Marty Nesbitt '85, Founder and CEO, The Parking Sport (national airport parking service), Treasurer for Barack Obama's 2008 presidential campaign; Jess Womack '65, Inspector General, Los Angeles Unified School District

ACADEMICS

full-time faculty	106
full-time minority faculty	13
student-faculty ratio	13:1
average class size	25
% first-year retention rate	85
% graduation rate (6 years)	73

Popular majors Economics & Management, Biology, Psychology, English, Political Science

CAMPUS LIFE

% live on campus (% freshmen)	96 (98)

Multicultural student clubs and organizations African-Caribbean Student Union, Asian Awareness Group, Black Student Alliance, International Student Union, Organization for Lationo/a Awareness, Umbrella

Athletics NCAA Division III, Michigan Intercollegiate Athletic Association (MIAA)

ADMISSIONS

# of applicants	2,305
% accepted	68
# of first-year students enrolled	370
SAT Critical Reading (middle 50%)	400-700
SAT Math (middle 50%)	400-700
SAT Writing (middle 50%)	n/a
ACT (middle 50%)	17-36
average HS GPA	3.5
Deadlines	
regular decision	12/1
application fee (online)	$40 ($0)
fee waiver for applicants with financial need	yes

COST & AID

tuition	$32,662
room & board	$9,260
total need-based institutional scholarships/grants	$19,010
% of students apply for need-based aid	74
% receiving need-based scholarship or grant aid	73
% receiving aid whose need was fully met	28
average aid package	$25,276
average student loan debt upon graduation	$33,310

Kalamazoo College

Kalamazoo College
1200 Academy Street
Kalamazoo, MI 49006
Ph: (269) 337-7166
admission@kzoo.edu
www.kzoo.edu

Kalamazoo College is a nationally-renowned liberal arts college with a highly individualized and experiential curriculum which combines scholarship, civic engagement and international study. "K" College is one of the 100 oldest colleges in the country, and has an established tradition of academic excellence. Their faculty are committed teachers who challenge and support students, and introduce students to global perspectives and intercultural awareness in all programs of study. Located in the city of Kalamazoo, Michigan, Kalamazoo College is an increasingly diverse institution; part of the mission of the college is to enroll talented students from diverse backgrounds who seek both academic and personal challenges in their college experience.

ACCESS Helping Youth Through Personal Empowerment (HYPE)

The HYPE program at the Kalamazoo County Juvenile Home is dedicated to promoting restorative, community-based justice by building meaningful relationships with the youth in the juvenile home and through advocacy within the Kalamazoo community on their behalf.

ACCESS Woodward Pals

Kalamazoo students staff after-school math and writing programs and in-class literacy programs. These have raised Michigan Educational Assessment Program scores, and math enrichment programs improve access for low income and minority students to academically talented programs, which lead to college

> ***"The Center for Career and Professional Development (CCPD) was useful...by helping me find an internship for the summer. Everyone in the office was so willing to give their time and the advice offered made the process that much easier. Thus, I feel more prepared to be on my own once I graduate."***
>
> *– Gabrielle W., '13, Germantown, MD, Business/Art History double major*

ACCESS Sisters in Science

Kalamazoo's female science majors partner with local middle school girls to encourage science learning and exploration through the Sisters in Science program. Sisters in Science also encourages high school girls to pursue science degrees through higher education.

OPPORTUNITY John T. Williamson Scholarship

Merit scholarship awarded to competitive applicants who are of either Hispanic or African descent. Students are automatically considered for this award by completing an application to the college.

OPPORTUNITY William Randolph Hearst Endowed Scholarship

Established by the Hearst Foundation to award scholarships annually to two first-generation students at the college. All first-generation applicants to Kalamazoo are considered for this award.

SUCCESS First Year Experience (FYE)

The award-winning First Year Experience program at Kalamazoo intertwines hands-on activity, experiential learning and mentorship within the context of rigorous undergraduate academics. First Year Experience fosters academic success, intercultural understanding and balance through First Year Seminars, First Year Forums, Academic Advising and Peer Leaders. Peer Leaders are carefully selected student-mentors that are trained to share knowledge and experiences with first-year students at the college. First Year Forums are special programs in the form of dramatic presentations, interactive learning sessions and structured conversations that focus on the goals of the First Year Experience program. They help first-year students successfully continue academic and personal growth at Kalamazoo.

FAST FACTS

STUDENT PROFILE

# of degree-seeking undergraduates	1,369
% male/female	43/57
% African American	4
% American Indian or Alaska Native	<1
% Asian or Pacific Islander	5
% Hispanic	6
% White	69
% International	7
% Pell grant recipients	13

ACADEMICS

full-time faculty	112
full-time minority faculty	27
student-faculty ratio	14:1
average class size	17
% first-year retention rate	91
% graduation rate (6 years)	75

Popular majors Economics, Biology, Chemistry, English, Polictical Science

CAMPUS LIFE

% live on campus (% freshmen)	76 (100)

Multicultural student clubs and organizations Asian Student Association, Black Student Organization, Buddhist Student Group, Jewish Student Organization, Christian Student Organization, International Student Organization, K Desi (promotes South Asian cultures), Kaleidoscope (GLBTQ), Latino Student Organization, Muslim Student Association

Athletics NCAA Division III, Michigan Intercollegiate Athletic Association (MIAA)

ADMISSIONS

# of applicants	2,223
% accepted	69
# of first-year students enrolled	390
SAT Critical Reading (middle 50%)	570-690
SAT Math (middle 50%)	560-680
SAT Writing (middle 50%)	550-680
ACT (middle 50%)	26-30
average HS GPA	3.6

Deadlines

early decision	11/10
regular decision	2/1
application fee (online)	$40 ($40)
fee waiver for applicants with financial need	yes

COST & AID

tuition	$35,820
room & board	$8,079
total need-based institutional scholarships/grants	$10,041,007
% of students apply for need-based aid	69
% receiving need-based scholarship or grant aid	58
% receiving aid whose need was fully met	39
average aid package	$27,734
average student loan debt upon graduation	n/a

Michigan State University

Students at Michigan State have a plethora of educational, social and recreational opportunities to choose from — after all, Michigan State is an internationally recognized research institution. The university's academic offerings are particularly extensive and will especially benefit those interested in studying agriculture, agribusiness or any of the many subsets of environmental studies. Michigan State further supports those interested in the farming aspect of these fields, offering certificate programs in both beef and dairy production/management.

ACCESS High School Summer Programs

Michigan State offers a number of summer programs for high school students interested in furthering their education. For example, the Broad Summer High School Scholars Program in the College of Education targets students entering 11th and 12th grades from Detroit Public Schools, providing them a four-week residential program on the university campus. Other programs, such as the Summer Business Institute and the Multicultural Apprenticeship Program (MAP), offer a more targeted experience, providing students with coursework in the business and math and science areas, respectively.

ACCESS GEAR UP / College Day Programs and Talent Search

These programs utilize a variety of strategies to educate low-income and first-generation students about the challenges and rewards of a higher education. The program begins with outreach efforts involving program representatives fostering a connection with middle school students, who then participate in campus visits. Students and parents may also take part in the social and academic workshops that are held on campus throughout the year, while other students participate in the Summer Residency Program.

OPPORTUNITY The Michigan-Louis Stokes Alliance for Minority Participation (MI-LSAMP)

MI-LSAMP is a comprehensive initiative designed to substantially increase the quantity and quality of minority students pursuing baccalaureate degrees and careers in science, technology, engineering and mathematics. This five-year, $5 million initiative is underwritten by the National Science Foundation and four institutions: The University of Michigan (lead institution), Michigan State University, Wayne State University and Western Michigan University.

OPPORTUNITY College Assistance Migrant Program (CAMP)

CAMP is an educational program designed to assist migrant and/or seasonal farm-worker students in their first-year transition to the university. The program is a collaboration of campus faculty, student services and community-based agencies meant to improve educational opportunities. Services include assistance in the admission and financial aid processes, help securing on-campus housing, assistance in developing a support system for academic success, tutorial assistance and limited supplemental financial assistance.

SUCCESS Office of Supportive Services (OSS) / College Achievement Admissions Program (CAAP)

Under the auspices of the Office of Supportive Services, Michigan State offers CAAP, which allows low-income and first generation students and students with disabilities who have the potential, but not the prerequisite background, to gain admittance to Michigan State. As a condition of their acceptance, CAAP students must enroll in particular seminars and tutorials, as well as meet with an OSS academic specialist. The OSS also provides academic advising, social counseling, personal planning, career guidance and skill enrichment seminars.

SUCCESS Office of Cultural and Academic Transitions (OCAT)

OCAT is designed to connect diverse peoples, programs and ideas to enhance student success. The office helps students to better understand themselves and others through cultural and social activities. OCAT strives to bring together individuals as well as groups of students from diverse racial, ethnic, international and domestic backgrounds for meaningful interaction. The Transition and Cultural Aide Program fosters a connection for students living in residence halls.

Michigan State University
250 Administration Building
East Lansing, MI 48824
Ph: (517) 355-8332
admis@msu.edu
www.msu.edu

FAST FACTS

STUDENT PROFILE

# of degree-seeking undergraduates	32,857
% male/female	48/52
% African American	8
% American Indian or Alaska Native	<1
% Asian or Pacific Islander	5
% Hispanic	3
% White	80
% International	9
% Pell grant recipients	19

First-generation and minority alumni Dr. Akhtar Hameed Khan, social scientist; George Ryoichi Ariyoshi, former governor, Hawaii; Adnan Badran, former prime minister, Jordan; Dee Dee Bridgewater, jazz singer; Areeya Chumsai, Miss Thailand

ACADEMICS

full-time faculty	2,538
full-time minority faculty	571
student-faculty ratio	16:1
average class size	20-29
% first-year retention rate	91
% graduation rate (6 years)	77

Popular majors Business Administration/Management, Communications Studies/Speech Communication and Rhetoric

CAMPUS LIFE

% live on campus (% freshmen)	40 (93)

Multicultural student clubs and organizations African Students Union, American Indian Science and Engineering Society (AISES), Association of Vietnamese Scholars and Students, Baha'i Association, Brazilian Community Association, Brothers of the Struggle, Caribbean Student Association, Chaldean American Student Association, Chicanos/Latinos in Health Education, Chinese Students and Scholars Association, Coalition of Indian Undergraduate Students, Delta Xi Phi Multicultural Sorority, Hausa Cultural Society, and many more

Athletics NCAA Division I, Big Ten Conference

ADMISSIONS

# of applicants	26,907
% accepted	70
# of first-year students enrolled	7,227
SAT Critical Reading (middle 50%)	450-610
SAT Math (middle 50%)	530-670
SAT Writing (middle 50%)	460-600
ACT (middle 50%)	23-28
average HS GPA	3.6
Deadlines	
priority	11/1
regular admission	rolling
application fee (online)	$50
fee waiver for applicants with financial need	yes

COST & AID

tuition	in-state: $12,187; out-of-state: $30,030
room & board	$7,770
total need-based institutional scholarships/grants	$50,084,981
% of students apply for need-based aid	66
% of students receive aid	50
% receiving need-based scholarship or grant aid	30
% receiving aid whose need was fully met	17
average aid package	$9,302
average student loan debt upon graduation	$17,347

Michigan Technological University

Michigan Technological University is a leading public research university developing new technologies and preparing students to create the future for a prosperous and sustainable world. Michigan Tech offers more than 130 degree programs in engineering; forest resources; computing; technology; business; economics; natural, physical, and environmental sciences; arts; humanities; and social sciences—all with a reputation for extraordinary hands-on learning. Michigan Tech's Enterprise program allows students to manage their own corporate-sponsored, real-world research projects and business ventures. Students can also get involved in any of over 200 organizations, campus leadership positions, multiethnic celebrations like MLK Week and the Parade of Nations, outdoor adventures like skiing, hiking, and biking, and more.

"Michigan Tech gives you the opportunity to experience new people, atmospheres, and cultures, which will help shape your experience here at Tech and your future endeavors. The staff is also welcoming and friendly—I always feel comfortable asking for help, no matter the situation."
– Chanavia S., '13, Detroit, MI, Social Sciences

ACCESS Summer Youth Programs

Each summer, Michigan Technological University hosts more than fifty weeklong career and adventure explorations for students in grades 9–11. The programs blend academics and hands-on investigation in a fun college setting, and are available in such areas as engineering, digital photography, wildlife backpacking, forensic science, and more. In addition, they offer two innovative scholarship programs for talented students—Women in Engineering and Engineering Scholars. Both offer students (many traditionally underrepresented) the opportunity to learn about different kinds of engineering through hands-on exploration, cool field trips, and time spent with industry role models. Additionally, any student who attends a Summer Youth exploration or scholarship program is qualified to apply for the Summer Youth Diversity Incentive Award—a Michigan Tech scholarship worth as much as $4,000 per year.

 OPPORTUNITY Summer Youth Diversity Incentive Award (SYDIA)

The Summer Youth Diversity Incentive Award (SYDIA) is a special scholarship opportunity available to incoming first-year students who have completed a Michigan Tech Summer Youth experience or scholarship program (including Women in Engineering and Engineering Scholars Program). Students must apply for the scholarship, which is variable and provides between $1,000 and $4,000 per year.

OPPORTUNITY University-Sponsored Campus Trips

Michigan Tech's regional admissions managers—staff who live and work in areas of downstate Michigan, Wisconsin, Illinois, and Minnesota—plan a variety of University-sponsored trips to campus. It's a great opportunity for potential students to see the area, tour campus, meet current students, and get a feel for life at Michigan Tech. Trips are planned throughout the year, including for the University's Open House weekend in October and Preview Day—an event especially for accepted students—in March.

 SUCCESS Center for Diversity and Inclusion

The Center for Diversity and Inclusion at Michigan Tech is a resource for preparing and empowering socially conscious leaders who will create the future. They encourage the intellectual, social, and professional growth of students of color; gay, lesbian, bisexual, transgender, queer, and questioning (GLBTQ) students; and women. The Center encourages cross-cultural awareness and community-building through programs, workshops, and events, including annual activities like Hispanic Heritage Month, African Night, Spirit of the Harvest Powwow, Pride Week, and Women's Week.

Michigan Technological University
1400 Townsend Drive
Houghton, MI 49931-1295
Ph: (906) 487-2335
mtu4u@mtu.edu
www.mtu.edu/admissions

FAST FACTS

STUDENT PROFILE

# of degree-seeking undergraduates	5,720
% male/female	75/25
% African American	2
% American Indian or Alaska Native	<1
% Asian or Pacific Islander	1
% Hispanic	2
% White	82
% International	7
% Pell grant recipients	21

First-generation and minority alumni LaVie Watts '97, VMP consultant, Kelly Services Inc.; Adrian Little '06, development engineer, Weatherford International Ltd.; Kahreem Hogan '04, senior design engineer, Caterpillar Inc.; Doris Strong '97, mechanical engineer, US Army RDECOM; Franklin St. John '60, owner/founder, HerbaSway

ACADEMICS

full-time faculty	456
full-time minority faculty	66
student-faculty ratio	13:1
average class size	21
% first-year retention rate	81
% graduation rate (6 years)	66

Popular majors Engineering; Natural and Physical Sciences; Computing; Forestry and Environmental Science; Technology; Business and Economics; Arts, Humanities, and Social Science

CAMPUS LIFE

% live on campus (% freshmen)	42 (90)

Multicultural student clubs and organizations Black Student Association, American Indian Science and Engineering Society (AISES), Society of Women Engineers, Society of Hispanic Professional Engineers, Society of Intellectual Sisters, African Student Organization, Keweenaw Pride, Society of African American Men, International Club, Engineers without Borders

Athletics Men's Ice Hockey: NCAA I, Western Collegiate Hockey Association (WCHA); All other sports: NCAA II, Great Lakes Intercollegiate Athletics Conference (GLIAC)

ADMISSIONS

# of applicants	4,548
% accepted	74
# of first-year students enrolled	1,115
SAT Critical Reading (middle 50%)	520-650
SAT Math (middle 50%)	560-690
SAT Writing (middle 50%)	510-620
ACT (middle 50%)	23-29
average HS GPA	3.58

Deadlines

priority consideration	1/15
regular decision	rolling
application fee (online)	$0
fee waiver for applicants with financial need	n/a

COST & AID

tuition	in-state: $12,615; out-of-state: $25,710
room & board	$8,648
total need-based institutional scholarships/grants	$16,107,762
% of students apply for need-based aid	78
% receiving need-based scholarship or grant aid	52
% receiving aid whose need was fully met	15
average aid package	$11,421
average student loan debt upon graduation	$33,310

University of Detroit Mercy

University of Detroit Mercy
4001 W McNichols Rd
Detroit MI 48221-3038
Ph: (800) 635-5020
admissions@udmercy.edu
www.udmercy.edu

University of Detroit Mercy is Michigan's largest and most comprehensive Catholic university. Sponsored by the Society of Jesus and the Religious Sisters of Mercy, UDM offers 100 academic degrees and programs through seven schools and colleges which include nationally recognized programs in architecture, engineering, digitial media studies, nursing, pre-med, and business. UDM offers the challenge, support, and hands-on experience needed to pursue a successful career. Our approach to education is to integrate the intellectual, spiritual, ethical, and social development of students, and our faculty is committed to a classroom environment that promotes educational excellence and academic exchange. UDM's education is enhanced by the culture, entertainment, and athletic events of the city of Detroit, and is consistently ranked in the top tier of Regional Universities in the Midwest.

ACCESS Detroit Area Pre-College Engineering Program (DAPCEP)

The Detroit Area Pre-College Engineering Program (DAPCEP) is a non-profit, Detroit-based organization whose mission is to increase the number of historically under-represented minority students who are interested and prepared to enter the fields of engineering and science.

ACCESS The UNITE Program

The UNITE program is a program for high school students designed to resemble a university freshman engineering curriculum. The goal is to introduce students to the subjects and skills necessary to succeed as an engineering student.

ACCESS Science Technology Engineering Preview Summer (STEPS)

STEPS (Science Technology Engineering Preview Summer camp for girls) is a summer camp program for girls in the 9th to 11th grades intended to encourage young women to consider engineering and manufacturing as a career.

OPPORTUNITY Scholarship Opportunities

University of Detroit Mercy offers multiple scholarship opportunities to help meet the need of prospective students. These include the Jessie Slaton Memorial Scholarship established in memory of a University of Detroit Mercy Law School graduate to assist talented African American students in experiencing the richness of UDM. The Hispanic Leadership Scholarship is for talented Hispanic students with an excellent academic record who will be incoming freshmen.

SUCCESS Orientation Sessions

UDM has several orientation sessions designed to ease the transition to college for incoming freshmen. Freshman Orientation is a two-day session where students become familiar with campus life by actually living on campus, touring the buildings and registering for class. Prologues Transitions & Viewpoints is a four-day fall orientation session in which students will get to know their classmates, members of the University, as well as the city of Detroit. Additionally, The First Year Experience program is designed to provide support and encouragement for new students to help ensure they succeed personally and academically.

SUCCESS Academic Advising

All students work with an Academic Advisor who helps guide each student through class selection and registration process. Discussion is centered around the student's academic and career goals, and the advisors assist students in planning out what they are going to do with their time at college.

FAST FACTS

STUDENT PROFILE

# of degree-seeking undergraduates	5,534
% male/female	40/60
% African American	11
% American Indian or Alaska Native	1
% Asian or Pacific Islander	4
% Hispanic	4
% White	n/a
% International	4
% Pell grant recipients	47

First-generation and minority alumni Allison Payne, '85, News Anchor WGN TV Channel 9; Rainy Hamilton, '78, President - Hamilton Anderson Association; Willie Green, '03, NBA Player; Daniel Roma, '84, CFO - National Coney Island; Laura Soave, '00, Head of Fiat Brant, N.A. -Chrysler Group LLC

ACADEMICS

full-time faculty	328
full-time minority faculty	n/a
student-faculty ratio	14:1
average class size	20
% first-year retention rate	81
% graduation rate (6 years)	n/a

Popular majors Nursing, Engineering, Architecture, Business, Pre-Med, Pre-Dent, Pre-PA

CAMPUS LIFE

% live on campus (% freshmen)	42 (n/a)

Multicultural student clubs and organizations National Society of Black Engineers, Society of Women Engineers, Muslim Student Association (MSA), Arab Cultural Society (ACS), Chinese Student Association, International Student Union (ISU), Chaldean American Student Association (CASA), Hispanic American Student Association (HASA), Indian Student Association, African American Student Organization

Athletics NCAA Division I, Horizon League

ADMISSIONS

# of applicants	3,324
% accepted	63
# of first-year students enrolled	564
SAT Critical Reading (middle 50%)	n/a
SAT Math (middle 50%)	n/a
SAT Writing (middle 50%)	n/a
ACT (middle 50%)	18-26
average HS GPA	3.45

Deadlines

regular admission	rolling
application fee (online)	$0 ($0)
fee waiver for applicants with financial need	yes

COST & AID

tuition	$30,662
room & board	$8,400
total need-based institutional scholarships/grants	$27,700,000
% of students apply for need-based aid	82
% receiving need-based scholarship or grant aid	74
% receiving aid whose need was fully met	23
average aid package	$24,000
average student loan debt upon graduation	$25,000

Carleton College

Carleton College
One North College Street
Northfield, MN 55057
Ph: (507) 222-4190
admissions@carleton.edu
www.carleton.edu

Founded in 1866, Carleton College is a small, co-educational, non-denominational, private liberal arts college. Best known for its academic excellence and warm, welcoming campus community, Carleton College is committed to challenging students to learn broadly and think deeply. Instead of training for one narrow career path, Carleton students develop the knowledge and skills to succeed in any walk of life. A community that fosters diversity of thought and an open exchange of ideas can only emerge from the participation of individuals with different backgrounds and worldviews. Toward this end, Carleton embraces diversity, educating talented and diverse students and acknowledging a strong commitment to underrepresented groups.

ACCESS Northfield Reads and Counts

Northfield Reads and Counts is part of Carleton College's Community Work Study. This program offers Carleton College students the opportunity to earn work-study awards off-campus performing jobs in the community's interest. Northfield Reads and Counts is a local implementation of two national educational initiatives (America Reads and America Counts) that involves community members in helping children — from kindergarten through high school — develop critical reading and mathematics skills. For two decades, Carleton has had a federally sponsored TRIO-Student Support Services program that provides assistance to both first-generation and low-income enrolled students. This student support service program serves up to 100 students and complements the support efforts of Carleton's Office of Intercultural Life.

OPPORTUNITY Carleton Access Scholarship

The Carleton Access Scholarship program is a Carleton College program of assistance targeted towards needy students. The Access Scholarship is awarded to reduce the loan debt that often becomes a financial obstacle in a student's pursuit of learning or career path. Students from families with an income level less than $40,000 are eligible for a renewable $4,000 Access Scholarship, while students from families with an income level less than $60,000 are eligible for $3,000 and students from families with an income level less than $75,000 receive $2,000. Students receiving a $4,000 Access Scholarship will likely have their total indebtedness reduced by about 70 percent when they graduate, $3,000 scholarship recipients can expect a reduction of 50 percent and $2,000 Access Scholarship recipients see a reduction of 33 percent.

OPPORTUNITY Posse Foundation

Carleton College participates in the Posse Foundation, a program that brings talented inner-city youth to campus to pursue their academics and to help promote cross-cultural communication. Posse students are nominated by their high school to the program and share a collaborative support system with a special mentor to adjust to campus and college life. Carleton's Posse Scholars hail from Chicago.

SUCCESS Intercultural Peer Leader (IPL) Program

Carleton College's Intercultural Peer Leader Program offers a variety of services to address the academic, cultural and professional development of students of color at Carleton. Intercultural Peer Leaders are sophomores, juniors and seniors who have done well academically, are active in the Carleton community and are enthusiastic about meeting and assisting new students, sharing with them their knowledge and experience. IPLs also plan programs and activities for the community as a whole. Intercultural Peer Leaders offer first-year students a personal perspective on the experience of living, growing and succeeding in a community that encourages diversity and individual differences and have often served as friends and mentors.

FAST FACTS

STUDENT PROFILE

# of degree-seeking undergraduates	1,991
% male/female	49/51
% African American	3
% American Indian or Alaska Native	<1
% Asian or Pacific Islander	6
% Hispanic	6
% White	69
% International	8
% Pell grant recipients	9

First-generation and minority alumni Walter Alvarez, geologist; Masanori Mark Christianson, musician/art director

ACADEMICS

full-time faculty	212
full-time minority faculty	49
student-faculty ratio	9:1
average class size	18
% first-year retention rate	98
% graduation rate (6 years)	93

Popular majors Biology, English, Political Science

CAMPUS LIFE

% live on campus (% freshmen)	94 (100)

Multicultural student clubs and organizations Carleton African Students Association, Coalition of Women of Color, Latin American Students Organization, Phase 2, Men of Color, Middle Eastern Society and Politics, Minority Students Prehealth Coalition, Pangea, American Native Peoples Organization, A.S.I.A, Coalition of Hmong Students, D.E.S.I., Korean Students in America, Vietnamese Student Association, Black Students Alliance, Club Caribe

Athletics NCAA Division III, Minnesota Intercollegiate Athletic Conference (MIAC)

ADMISSIONS

# of applicants	4,856
% accepted	30
# of first-year students enrolled	512
SAT Critical Reading (middle 50%)	650-750
SAT Math (middle 50%)	650-750
SAT Writing (middle 50%)	650-740
ACT (middle 50%)	29-33
average HS GPA	3.29

Deadlines

early decision application	11/15
regular admission	1/15
application fee (online)	$30 ($30)
fee waiver for applicants with financial need	yes

COST & AID

tuition	$41,076
room & board	$10,806
total need-based institutional scholarships/grants	$27,650,350
% of students apply for need-based aid	86
% of students receive aid	55
% receiving need-based scholarship or grant aid	55
% receiving aid whose need was fully met	100
average aid package	$35,456
average student loan debt upon graduation	$20,083

College of Saint Benedict and Saint John's University

The College of Saint Benedict (CSB) for women and Saint John's University (SJU) for men are two nationally-leading liberal arts colleges whose partnership offers students the educational options of a large university and the individual attention of a premier small college. Ranked among the top undergraduate colleges for the number of students who study abroad, the two colleges enroll nearly 250 international students, and offer more than 200 courses with a global focus. Students from both colleges attend classes and activities together and have access to the libraries and athletic facilities on both campuses. With 15 miles of hiking trails, a private beach, and a walking path between campuses, the College of Saint Benedict and Saint John's University are near the St. Cloud metropolitan area in central Minnesota, an hour from Minneapolis and St. Paul.

ACCESS **Upward Bound**

Local high school students who come from low-income families in which neither parent holds a bachelor's degree can benefit from the College of Saint Benedict and Saint John's University's Upward Bound, a pre-college program that provides a group of students with the right tools to pursue their goal of earning a college degree. Students benefit from weekly tutoring, field trips, workshops, and a six-week summer enrichment program at the College of Saint Benedict and Saint John's University.

"I have developed the confidence, energy, and love that I-LEAD promotes every time I talk to a staff member, lead a seminar or ask for help with questions. I will remember I-LEAD for the amount of time and knowledge that has helped me and other students succeed in college."

– Virigina O., '10
St. Paul, MN
English, Secondary Education

ACCESS **Fast Forward Youth Program**

College of Saint Benedict and Saint John's University College Mentors and staff help underrepresented high school students to prepare for college. Participants practice the ACT, visit colleges, fill out applications, navigate the financial aid process, and successfully complete high school course work.

OPPORTUNITY **Diversity Leadership Scholarships**

A four-year renewable scholarship for up to $5,000 for students who have demonstrated leadership and service in the area of cultural and ethnic diversity.

OPPORTUNITY **Twin Cities Bus Trips**

Designed for prospective students from Minnesota's Twin Cities high schools, the program arranges complimentary bus trips to the two colleges to attend special events and learn more about the campuses.

OPPORTUNITY **National Fly-Ins**

The College of Saint Benedict and Saint John's University pay up to half of the travel costs for prospective students outside of Minnesota and arranges a three-day campus experience for them along with their fellow prospective students.

SUCCESS **Intercultural Leadership, Education and Development (I-LEAD) Fellowship Program**

First-generation college students receive financial and educational support to build on the leadership skills they already demonstrate. These college student leaders attend national and international leadership conferences and promote ideals of equality, diversity and civic leadership.

SUCCESS **Retreat on Race and Ethnicity (RORE)**

This three day retreat sponsored by the Intercultural Center creates a safe atmosphere for intercultural dialogue. Participants engage in discussion and activities that highlight the realities of racism, privilege and bigotry.

College of Saint Benedict and Saint John's University
PO Box 7155
Collegeville, MN 56321
Ph: (320) 363-2196
admissions@csbsju.edu
www.csbsju.edu

FAST FACTS

STUDENT PROFILE	
# of degree-seeking undergraduates	3,938
% male/female	48/52
% African American	1
% American Indian or Alaska Native	<1
% Asian or Pacific Islander	3
% Hispanic	2
% White	88
% International	6
% Pell grant recipients	16
ACADEMICS	
full-time faculty	294
full-time minority faculty	25
student-faculty ratio	12:1
average class size	20
% first-year retention rate	90
% graduation rate (6 years)	84

Popular majors Business Management, Communication, Biology, Nursing, Psychology

CAMPUS LIFE	
% live on campus	up to 95

Multicultural student clubs and organizations Asia Club, Cultural Fusion, Archipeligo Association, Kaliente (Latino/a Student Club), International Affairs Club

Athletics NCAA Division III, Minnesota Intercollegiate Athletic Conference (MIAC)

ADMISSIONS	
# of applicants	3,233
% accepted	80
# of first-year students enrolled	1,039
SAT Critical Reading (middle 50%)	493-655
SAT Math (middle 50%)	529-658
SAT Writing (middle 50%)	n/a
ACT (middle 50%)	23-28
average HS GPA	3.67
Deadlines	
regular decision	rolling
application fee (online)	$0 ($0)
COST & AID	
tuition	$34,308
room & board	$8,956
total need-based institutional scholarships/ grants	$31,600,000
% of students apply for need-based aid	71
% receiving need-based scholarship or grant aid	61
% receiving aid whose need was fully met	42
average aid package	$22,820
average student loan debt upon graduation	n/a

Millsaps College

Founded in 1890, Millsaps College is dedicated to undergraduate teaching and is praised by the *Fiske Guide to Colleges* for "its focus on scholarly inquiry, spiritual growth, and community service." Located in Jackson, Mississippi, Millsaps is home to 1,200 students and offers undergraduate degrees in 34 subjects. Once on campus, students join a close-knit community with opportunities to become involved in more than 85 clubs, intramural sports, campus ministries, student government, and student publications. Athletes successfully compete in 18 men's and women's NCAA Division III sports. Millsaps College is one of only 40 colleges from across the country included in *Colleges That Change Lives* and is included in the 2008 edition of the Princeton Review's *America's Best Value Colleges*. Through Millsaps' aggressive scholarships program, more than 90 percent of students receive some financial aid.

ACCESS 1 Campus, 1 Community Program

The Millsaps College 1 Campus, 1 Community program enhances higher education opportunities for first-generation and underserved K-12 students in the Jackson community. Working in partnership with local public schools and nearby North Midtown, the college hosts youth for a range of events including sports camps, arts and enrichment events, and an annual block party attended by many Millsaps faculty, staff, alumni and their children, as well as North Midtown children and families. The block party includes music, food, health screenings, face painting and other games and activities, allowing students to familiarize themselves with the Millsaps campus and environment. In addition, Millsaps students work in local public schools, which are 96 percent African American and majority low income, through diverse service-learning projects in conjunction with Millsaps academic courses and through a broad array of volunteer activities such as judging book fair projects, serving as literacy mentors, staffing after-school programs, and raising money for school uniforms and supplies.

"The Multicultural Association Diversity Club is an organization that encourages and promotes multiculturalism and cultural awareness throughout Millsaps College and the Jackson community through group discussions, films, cultural displays, and special programs. The members put a lot of effort into emphasizing the importance of friendship, unity, and respect –especially needed in modern times."

– Wrijoya R., '12
Columbus, MS

OPPORTUNITY Open Door Days

Millsaps College's Open Door Days visit program provides a full day at Millsaps for prospective high school students, transfer students, and their families. Offered throughout the year, the program encourages students to explore the college's academic programs and learn about the wide range of student services and campus activities offered. Participants are invited to attend classes, tour campus, speak with faculty, enjoy lunch in the cafeteria and hear more about the scholarship and financial aid application process.

SUCCESS Millsaps College Advising and Mentoring Program (M-CAMP)

Each student is assigned a faculty adviser as part of the Millsaps College Advising and Mentoring Program. First-year students meet several times per semester with their M-CAMP adviser, who also serves as one of their first-semester classroom teachers. Students are advised individually and also in groups of five to seven peers. The M-CAMP curriculum invites students to embrace their own socio-cultural heritage as an important and valued source of identity formation and vocational wisdom.

Millsaps College
Office of Admissions
1701 North State Street
Jackson, MS 39210
Ph: (601) 974-1050
admissions@millsaps.edu
www.millsaps.edu

FAST FACTS

STUDENT PROFILE

# of degree-seeking undergraduates	999
% male/female	49/51
% African American	11
% American Indian or Alaska Native	<1
% Asian or Pacific Islander	4
% Hispanic	2
% White	80
% International	1
% Pell grant recipients	22.6

First-generation and minority alumni Randall Pinkston, news correspondent; Cassandra Wilson, jazz singer; Manisha Sethi, pediatrician; Casey Parks, journalist; James Graves, justice, Mississippi Supreme Court

ACADEMICS

full-time faculty	97
full-time minority faculty	10
student-faculty ratio	10:1
average class size	15
% first-year retention rate	79
% graduation rate (6 years)	68

Popular majors Business Administration, Psychology, English

CAMPUS LIFE

Multicultural student clubs and organizations Black Student Association, Future Black Law Students Association, International Students Association, Millsaps International Buddy System, Millsaps Multicultural Association, Mississippi Masala, Multicultural Association Diversity Group, Multicultural Culinary Club

Athletics NCAA Division III, Southern Collegiate Athletic Conference (SCAC)

ADMISSIONS

# of applicants	1,186
% accepted	77
# of first-year students enrolled	271
SAT Critical Reading (middle 50%)	520-640
SAT Math (middle 50%)	540-650
ACT (middle 50%)	24-29
average HS GPA	3.46
Deadlines	
early decision	11/15
early action	12/1
regular decision	rolling
application fee (online)	$0 ($0)

COST & AID

tuition	$27,650
room & board	$10,312
total need-based institutional scholarships/grants	$7,994,145
% of students apply for need-based aid	68
% of students receive aid	100
% receiving need-based scholarship or grant aid	99
% receiving aid whose need was fully met	35
average aid package	$22,707
average student loan debt upon graduation	$17,175

Mississippi State University

Mississippi State University is a public, land-grant, co-educational university that provides access and opportunity to students from all sectors of Mississippi's diverse population. The university offers excellent and extensive programs in teaching, research and outreach that improve the lives and opportunities of the citizens of the state, region and world. Mississippi State maintains its tradition as the "People's University" by offering integrated programs in learning, research, and service; traditional scholarship; statewide extension and outreach; and engagement with business, industry, government, communities and organizations. *Forbes* has ranked Mississippi State among the top 20 of its top 100 best college buys in America, and *Kiplinger's Personal Finance* ranked Mississippi State among the "100 Best Values in Public Colleges."

OPPORTUNITY Mississippi State Promise Program

In fulfilling Mississippi State's traditional role as the "People's University" and in keeping with the needs of Mississippi, the Mississippi State Promise Program combines access and excellence. The Promise Program helps support low-income students (either entering freshmen or community college transfer students) in their matriculation at Mississippi State University. Tuition and fees are paid with grants, scholarships and waivers. In addition, the program provides on-campus work opportunities to help offset other non-tuition costs.

OPPORTUNITY Minority Student Achievement Day/Fall Showcase Day

The Minority Student Achievement Day provides an opportunity to visit the Mississippi State University campus for minority scholars and their parents. Invitations to the annual event are sent to high school seniors who have scored well on the ACT and SAT or who have been nominated by school counselors. Activities include campus tours, a general assembly and opportunities to visit with academic advisers.

SUCCESS Summer Bridge Program

Mississippi State University uses the Summer Bridge Program to help incoming freshmen students adjust to university life. Incoming freshmen will be selected to participate from the following areas of study: Science, including Agricultural Sciences, Biological Sciences, Chemistry, and Physics; Mathematics; Engineering, Including Computer Sciences; and Technology.

"As a first-generation student from a low-income area, Mississippi State University has granted me so many opportunities. Not only was I able to obtain a degree in Political Science, I was a member of several student led organizations such as, Stennis Montgomery Association, Pre-Law Society, IMAGE, and Alpha Kappa Alpha. MSU has given so much to me that I am now giving back to it as a student recruiter informing students of my undergraduate experiences that I believe can impact the lives of others.

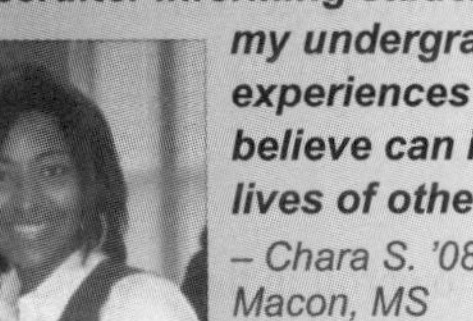

– Chara S. '08
Macon, MS
Political Science

SUCCESS Increasing Minority Access to Graduate Education (IMAGE)

Mississippi State University is home to the Increasing Minority Access to Graduate Education (IMAGE) Program. Bringing together all levels of students through financial support and mentoring, IMAGE provides partial scholarships for eligible minority students in the SME (science, mathematics, and engineering) curricula. Each participant is assigned to an upperclassman mentor before they attend the freshman orientation.

SUCCESS The Holmes Cultural Diversity Center

The Holmes Cultural Diversity Center enhances the college experience of culturally diverse students at Mississippi State University. The Center encourages the development of a climate within which all cultures are appreciated as valued members of the campus community. Specific endeavors include cultural diversity workshops, seminars, classroom lectures, problem-solving assistance, scholarship resources and employment opportunities. The Holmes Center is essential in recruiting and retaining multicultural students and in creating a college experience that is productive and successful for all.

Mississippi State University
Office of Admissions and Scholarships
P.O. Box 6334
25 Old Main, 101 Montgomery Hall
Mississippi State, MS 39762-6334
Ph: (662) 325-2224
admit@msstate.edu
www.admissions.msstate.edu

FAST FACTS

STUDENT PROFILE

# of degree-seeking undergraduates	13,456
% male/female	52/48
% African American	25
% American Indian or Alaska Native	<1
% Asian or Pacific Islander	1
% Hispanic	2
% White	81
% International	2
% Pell grant recipients	26

First-generation and minority alumni Rafael Palmeiro, professional baseball player; Eric Dampier, professional basketball player; Lawrence Roberts, professional basketball player; Jerome Keys, professional football player

ACADEMICS

full-time faculty	801
full-time minority faculty	115
student-faculty ratio	20:1
average class size	n/a
% first-year retention rate	82
% graduation rate (6 years)	58

Popular majors Biological Science, Communications, Marketing, Education, Engineering

CAMPUS LIFE

% live on campus (% freshmen)	n/a

Multicultural student clubs and organizations African Students Association, Japanese Club, Korean Student Association, NAACP, Native American Association, Pakistani Student Association, Sri Lankan Association, Taiwan Student Association, Thai Students and Scholars Association, Vietnamese Students Association, Association of Chinese Students and Scholars, Black Student Alliance, Chinese Student Association, Graduate Minority Council, Hispanic Student Association, Indian Student Association, Minorities in Agriculture, Natural Resources and Related Sciences

Athletics NCAA Division I, Southeastern Conference (SEC)

ADMISSIONS

# of applicants	9,300
% accepted	66
# of first-year students enrolled	2,701
SAT Critical Reading (middle 50%)	470-610
SAT Math (middle 50%)	490-630
SAT Writing (middle 50%)	n/a
ACT (middle 50%)	20-26
average HS GPA	3.24

Deadlines

regular decision	rolling
application fee (online)	$35 ($35)
fee waiver for applicants with financial need	yes

COST & AID

tuition	in-state: $5,461; out-of-state: $13,801
room & board	$7,729
total need-based institutional scholarships/grants	$7,135,298
% of students apply for need-based aid	68
% of students receive aid	56
% receiving need-based scholarship or grant aid	43
% receiving aid whose need was fully met	26
average aid package	$11,371
average student loan debt upon graduation	$23,413

Lincoln University

Lincoln University
Office of Admission and Recruitment
820 Chestnut St., B7 Young Hall
Jefferson City, MO 65101
Ph: (573) 681-5599
enroll@lincolnu.edu
www.lincolnu.edu

Lincoln University is a historically black, public, comprehensive institution, founded in 1866 by the soldiers of the 62nd and 65th United States Colored Infantries at the close of the Civil War, and enrolls over 3,200 students from 36 states and over 30 countries. Set upon nearly 160 acres in the state capital of Missouri, Jefferson City, it offers services to a diverse body of traditional and non-traditional students with a broad range of academic preparation and skills. Lincoln offers seven undergraduate degrees in more than 50 areas of study and graduate programs in selected disciplines that prepare students for citizenship and leadership in the global community. Alumni can be found in all corners of the globe, serving communities, regions and nations of the world.

OPPORTUNITY **Open Houses**

The Office of Admissions and Recruitment hosts Open House events for prospective students, one held in the fall and another in spring. These events allow future Lincolnites to get an up-close look at campus, as well as to meet and interact with administrators, faculty, staff, students and alumni. Each event allows the student to become an instant Blue Tiger – on-site admissions is offered to those students who come with a completed application, ACT or SAT test scores and their official high school transcript.

"The faculty and staff at Lincoln are great. I have had the privilege of getting to know many of them and each one wants to see students succeed. Each professor that I have encountered at Lincoln has a strong grasp on their specific field and a diverse background in many others."

– Alexander E., '11
Chicago, IL
Wellness

SUCCESS **Lincoln Educational Access Program (LEAP)**

LEAP is designed to strengthen the first-year experience at Lincoln University of Missouri by providing students with tools necessary to persist and succeed in college. This is a rigorous program, and is designed to assist students both academically and socially by providing access to one-on-one tutoring, academic advising and peer leaders.

SUCCESS **Learning Communities**

Learning Communities provide students with an opportunity to enroll in three common courses with peers who share similar interests. This group setting allows students the opportunity to get to know their professors and classmates better, attend out-of-class programs, learn about resources at Lincoln University and get involved with the campus community. Each Learning Community has a Peer Leader to guide the students throughout these courses.

SUCCESS **Center for Academic Enrichment (CAE)**

The Center for Academic Enrichment provides tutorial assistance in writing and mathematics and coordinates the Supplemental Instruction (SI) program, which gives students in difficult courses an opportunity to study with a group of students from the same class. Students who participate in these study sessions generally earn higher course grades.

SUCCESS **Student Support Services (SSS)**

Student Support Services provide tools and programs to help students to stay in college until they earn a degree. Tutoring, counseling, and remedial instruction are among services offered to first-generation, low-income students. Weekly workshops are held to aid students in adjusting to campus life, with the purpose of cultivating study and life skills, as well as self-sufficiency.

FAST FACTS

STUDENT PROFILE

# of degree-seeking undergraduates	2,129
% male/female	45/55
% African American	56
% American Indian or Alaska Native	<1
% Asian or Pacific Islander	1
% Hispanic	2
% White	61
% International	3
% Pell grant recipients	58

First-generation and minority alumni Wendell Oliver Pruitt, Tuskegee Airman, recipient of Congressional Gold Medal for service to his country; George Howard, Jr., first African-American to serve as a judge on the Arkansas Court of Appeals, the Arkansas Supreme Court and the Federal District Court in Arkansas; Lemar Parrish, Eight-Time NFL Pro Bowler; Dr. Edward A. Rankin, first African-American president of the American Academy of Orthopaedic Surgeons; Dr. James Frank, first African-American to serve as President of the NCAA, former President of Lincoln University

ACADEMICS

full-time faculty	142
full-time minority faculty	45
student-faculty ratio	15:1
average class size	20-29
% first-year retention rate	49
% graduation rate (6 years)	23

Popular majors Nursing Science, Criminal Justice, Business Administration, Elementary Education, Psychology

CAMPUS LIFE

% live on campus (% freshmen)	30(56)

Multicultural student clubs and organizations Community Connection of Lincoln University, International Student Association, Orientation Leader Board, Lincoln University NAACP, Impact Movement

Athletics NCAA Division II, Mid-America Intercollegiate Athletic Association (MIAA)

ADMISSIONS

# of applicants	1,578
% accepted	95
# of first-year students enrolled	561
SAT Critical Reading (middle 50%)	370-478
SAT Math (middle 50%)	355-530
SAT Writing (middle 50%)	n/a
ACT (middle 50%)	15-20
average HS GPA	2.7

Deadlines

priority application	7/15
regular decision	rolling to 8/1
application fee (online)	$20 ($20)
fee waiver for applicants with financial need	no

COST & AID

tuition	in-state $5,685; out-of-state $10,915
room & board	$5,146
total need-based institutional scholarships/grants	$1,019,272
% of students apply for need-based aid	86
% of students receive aid	77
% receiving need-based scholarship or grant aid	67
% receiving aid whose need was fully met	11
average aid package	$9,333
average student loan debt upon graduation	$21,255

Missouri University of Science & Technology

Founded Founded in 1870, Missouri University of Science and Technology is one of the nation's top technological research universities, with award-winning faculty and small classes. S&T students pursue degrees in high-demand fields like engineering, math, science, business and computing. Through co-ops and internships, design projects, research and student organizations students can build upon their interests to get the experience they need to excel in today's job market. S&T offers the career placement, student support, academic assistance and mentoring programs that one might expect from a premier university, but with a personal touch. As one of the nation's top 10 "best value" public universities and as a top 5 public university for highest starting salaries, S&T provides students with an outstanding and affordable education.

ACCESS Hit the Ground Running

Hit the Ground Running is a 3-week summer learning program that offers new students an exciting opportunity to sharpen and enhance their academic skills, work with teams on design projects, make new friends, develop leadership skills, and learn about college-level coursework expectations. This program is intended to prepare students for college life by letting them know what to expect from their college experience.

OPPORTUNITY Fly-In Weekend

The Fly-In Weekend is an overnight visit program for students to experience life on a college campus, attend a college-level class, meet current students, and meet a student mentor that will help students in their college selection process.

OPPORTUNITY Pre-College Initiative (PCI)

Pre-College Initiative prepares students for careers in math and science, especially those who may never have considered that option and need help achieving their dream career. PCI is an overnight visit program for African-American students the focuses on success in high school, tutoring, and college preparation.

OPPORTUNITY ¡Sí Se Puede!

¡Sí Se Puede! helps students to explore careers and get an inside look at college life. It is an overnight visit program for Hispanic and Latino students to explore a future career in math and science.

"Experience all that you can while you're at S&T. Take it all in, do your very best, and put yourself out there because at Missouri S&T, everyone is here to pursue excellence and be extraordinary."

*– Jared J., '12
Edmond, OK
Economics*

SUCCESS Opening Week

New students arrive on campus a week before classes start to begin the transition to college life. This allows students to get to know the campus, meet new friends, compete in a team design project (ProjectX), and learn about campus resources and attend academic workshops.

SUCCESS On-Track Academic Success Program

On-Track advising helps students that need extra help with time-management, study skills, getting involved on campus. Through group activities, networking, and study sessions, On-Track participants make important connections that will help them succeed and study more effectively.

SUCCESS Career Opportunities Center (COC)

S&T hosts the largest technological career fair in the country with over 700 employers recruiting on campus each year. The COC offers individual career advising, job negotiation, help with interviews, and guidance on internship and co-op programs.

**Missouri University of Science and Technology
106 Parker Hall, 300 W 13th Street
Rolla, Missouri 65409
Ph: (573) 341-4165
admissions@mst.edu
www.mst.edu**

FAST FACTS

STUDENT PROFILE

# of degree-seeking undergraduates	5,381
% male/female	76/24
% African American	5
% American Indian or Alaska Native	<1
% Asian or Pacific Islander	2
% Hispanic	2
% White	80
% International	5
% Pell grant recipients	20

First-generation and minority alumni: Steve Malcolm, Civil Engineering '70, former President and CEO of Williams Energy, Lt. Gen. Joe Ballard, Engineering Management '71, former Commanding General, US Army Corps of Engineers (first African-American to hold the post), Dr. Sandra Magnus, Physics '86, NASA astronaut who lived aboard the Space Station for 4 months, Steve Sullivan, Electrical Engineering '89, two-time Academy Award winner for visual effects, director of research and development at Industrial Light and Magic, Dr. Joan Woodard, Math '73, former executive VP and deputy lab director at Sandia National Laboratory

ACADEMICS

full-time faculty	445
full-time minority faculty	120
student-faculty ratio	17:1
average class size	29
% first-year retention rate	88
% graduation rate (6 years)	65

Popular majors Engineering, Biology, Business, Computer Science, Information Science

CAMPUS LIFE

% live on campus (% freshmen)	45 (95)

Multicultural student clubs and organizations Miner Mentors, Society of Hispanic Professional Engineering, American Indian Science and Engineering Society, National Society of Black Engineers, Missouri S&T Student Ambassadors, Chancellor Leadership Academy, Joe'SS Peers (student mentoring program), Adventures Abroad, Engineers Without Borders, Miner Challenge

Athletics NCAA Division II, Great Lakes Valley Conference

ADMISSIONS

# of applicants	2,756
% accepted	91
# of first-year students enrolled	1,150
SAT Critical Reading (middle 50%)	550-680
SAT Math (middle 50%)	600-710
ACT (middle 50%)	25-31
average HS GPA	3.56

Deadlines

regular decision	12/1
application fee (online)	$45
fee waiver for applicants with financial need	yes

COST & AID

tuition	in-state: $10,354; out-of-state: $23,148
room & board	$8,342
total need-based institutional scholarships/grants	$17,234,757
% of students apply for need-based aid	92
% receiving need-based scholarship or grant aid	42
% receiving aid whose need was fully met	49
average aid package	$13,362
average student loan debt upon graduation	$21,700

Southeast Missouri State University

Southeast Missouri State University is the University of First Choice for students, in a geographical area that includes eastern Missouri and surrounding states. The University is nationally recognized as a leader in serving the agriculture, arts, business, education, health, human service, science, and technology needs of the region. For underserved, first-generation college students, multiple programs and services are available to promote educational access and academic progress; provide assistance in overcoming barriers; engage in leadership and development opportunities and academic and educational mentoring.

> *"Southeast has been the perfect fit for me. There have been some ups and downs, more ups than downs; and I have enjoyed every minute of it. There are a plethora of activities and on campus involvement opportunities that keep me busy and focused on my academics and my future."*
>
> *– Reggie W., '12*
> *St. Louis, MO*
> *Mass Communications and Sports Management*

ACCESS **GEAR UP**

The Gaining Early Awareness and Readiness for Undergraduate Program (GEAR UP) accelerates the academic achievement of middle school students to increase enrollment in and completion of college by first generation students. At Southeast, this program works with different districts to have a larger impact covering what is known as the "Bootheel".

OPPORTUNITY **Southeast Showcase**

The Southeast Showcase is a multicultural recruitment program for students and their families. If you are within our service region, we provide you with transportation from designated locations to and from Cape Girardeau for the event. During Southeast Showcase, you will tour campus with a current Southeast student, meet with professors in your areas of interest, eat in the campus dining halls, and learn more about living on campus and becoming an involved student.

OPPORTUNITY **College Access Partnership Award (CAP-A)**

CAP-A is available to first year students who meet the required cumulative high school GPA, have successfully completed a designated College Access Partnership Program or Scholarship Organization/Foundation and have a letter of recommendation from the Partner Program, Foundation or Organization. Southeast dedicates over $125,000 of grants annually to this award.

SUCCESS **The Academic Enhancement Program (AEP)**

AEP provides first-year students with additional support in an effort to help them reach their academic goals. Students in AEP work closely with an academic coach to discuss and address acclimation to the campus and academic goals and focus.

SUCCESS **The Minority Mentor Program (MMP)**

MMP offers students demonstrating academic potential the opportunity to earn a foundation for college success through a mentoring relationship. A faculty or staff member serves as a mentor and supervisor to the student in a campus work environment.

SUCCESS **Educational Access Programs (EAP) and Learning Assistance Programs (LAP)**

EAP provides leadership in administration of academic intervention, mentoring and financial aid programs for U.S. ethnic minorities. LAP provides services that enhance academics and personal enrichment skills. The office provides direct services and resources through in-person and online programming for students to assist in the development of critical thinking skills and to support their educational goals and attainment.

Southeast Missouri State University
#1 University Plaza, Mailstop 3550
Cape Girardeau, MO 63701
Ph: (573) 651-2590
admissions@semo.edu
www.semo.edu

FAST FACTS

STUDENT PROFILE

# of degree-seeking undergraduates	10,035
% male/female	42/58
% African American	7.8
% American Indian or Alaska Native	0.5
% Asian or Pacific Islander	0.8
% Hispanic	1.3
% White	79.7
% International	4.6
% Pell grant recipients	n/a

First-generation and minority alumni Wendy Timmon-Ducasse', '02, Social Worker, Brentwood High School; D'Ante Ducasse', '01, Webmaster, Ladue Schools; Brian Hendricks, '04, Recruiter, Edward Jones; Tameka Herrion, '02, Director, Student Support Services Ranken Techincal College; Reyna Spencer-Gurly, '00, Assistant City Manager, Berkely, MO

ACADEMICS

full-time faculty	423
full-time minority faculty	55
student-faculty ratio	24:1
average class size	22
% first-year retention rate	74
% graduation rate (6 years)	46

Popular majors Nursing, Elementary Education, Psychology, Accounting, Early Childhood Education, Criminal Justice: Law Enforcement

CAMPUS LIFE

% live on campus (% freshmen)	25 (75)

Multicultural student clubs and organizations Association of Black Collegians, Bangladeshi Student Association, Chinese Student and Scholar Association, Diversity Peer Educators, International Student Association, Men Encouraging New Ways, Muslim Students' Association (MSA), Nepalese Students Association (NSA), Sanskriti Cultural Club (SCC), SELF (Sisterhood, Empowerment, Leadership and Femininity)

Athletics NCAA Division I, Ohio Valley Conference (OVC)

ADMISSIONS

# of applicants	4,144
% accepted	97
# of first-year students enrolled	1,928
SAT Critical Reading (middle 50%)	400-570
SAT Math (middle 50%)	430-610
SAT Writing (middle 50%)	n/a
ACT (middle 50%)	20-25
average HS GPA	3.33

Deadlines

regular decision priority	12/15; fall 7/1
application fee (online)	$30 ($30)
fee waiver for applicants with financial need	yes

COST & AID

tuition	in-state: $5,634; out-of-state: $10,674
room & board	$6,370
total need-based institutional scholarships/grants	$4,932,060
% of students apply for need-based aid	78
% receiving need-based scholarship or grant aid	52
% receiving aid whose need was fully met	14
average aid package	$8,527
average student loan debt upon graduation	$22,400

Truman State University

Truman State University is Missouri's premier liberal arts and sciences university and the only highly selective public institution in the state. Truman has established an impeccable reputation in the Midwest and throughout the nation for the high-quality undergraduate programs offered. In fact, for the fourteenth consecutive year, *U.S. News & World Report* has ranked Truman State University as the number one master's level public institution in the Midwest. It is in the University's mission to provide an affordable education and to maintain a student-centered living and learning environment that will attract, nurture, and challenge diverse, outstanding students.

ACCESS **Upward Bound**

Truman was among the first five institutions in the country to sponsor Upward Bound, a program that assists high school students in building skills and motivation necessary for college success. Upward Bound provides students with academic skill development, tutoring, and college career assistance.

SUCCESS **Truman Week**

During Truman Week, an orientation period for new students, underrepresented students participate in Directions, a special orientation program designed to help them become acclimated to campus.

"I was attracted to Truman by the potential for individual attention. Many of the other universities I considered had huge class sizes that would not provide the opportunity to get to know and build relationships with professors. Truman definitely has given me the chance to do so."

– Hazar K., '12
Jefferson City, MO
Biology

SUCCESS **Peer Mentor Program**

The Peer Mentor Program is a program that pairs underrepresented students with upperclassmen mentors. These mentors advise students on picking classes, joining organizations, and becoming ingrained in the campus community.

SUCCESS **Student Success Center**

The Student Success Center is a multi-faceted academic support program that provides a range of services to enhance both a student's individual learning and in-class performance. The center provides tutoring services, collaborative group study for specific courses, peer mentoring, and learning and study skills workshops.

SUCCESS **SEE Scholars Program**

The SEE Scholars Program is a two-week summer program for incoming, underrepresented college freshman that takes place on the campus of Truman State University. Through SEE Scholars, students are introduced to college life, resources, and support systems in ways that will help them succeed at the university level.

SUCCESS **McNair Program**

The McNair program was designed to provide disadvantaged college students with effective preparation for doctoral studies. McNair Scholars are matched with faculty mentors who supervise research and assist students in achieving their individual post-baccalaureate educational goals. Students participate in pre-research internships during their sophomore year and summer research internships during their junior year. During their senior year, the focus is on graduate school placement.

Truman State University
100 E Normal Ave
Kirksville, MO 63501
Ph: (660) 785-4114
admissions@truman.edu
www.truman.edu

FAST FACTS

STUDENT PROFILE

# of degree-seeking undergraduates	5,501
% male/female	41/59
% African American	4
% American Indian or Alaska Native	<1
% Asian or Pacific Islander	2
% Hispanic	3
% White	80
% International	5
% Pell grant recipients	20

First-generation and minority alumni Lenvil Elliot, professional football player; Ken Norton, professional boxer; Byron (Bol) Crawford, Hip Hop critic and blogger; Scott Piper, professional opera singer; Dr. Kia (Hartfield) Johnson, Assistant Professor of Communication Sciences and Disorders and the Director of the Developmental Stuttering Research Laboratory at James Madison University

ACADEMICS

full-time faculty	338
full-time minority faculty	37
student-faculty ratio	16:1
average class size	26
% first-year retention rate	87
% graduation rate (6 years)	70

Popular majors Business, Biology, English, Psychology

CAMPUS LIFE

% live on campus (% freshmen)	49 (99)

Multicultural student clubs and organizations African Students Organization, Association of Black Collegians, Hispanic American Leadership Organization (HALO), International Club, GlobeMed, Hablantes Unidos/United Speakers, Namaste Nepal, Sigma Lambda Beta (formerly Hermanos Unidos), Society for Sino-American Studies

Athletics NCAA Division II, Mid-America Intercollegiate Athletic Association (MIAA)

ADMISSIONS

# of applicants	4,546
% accepted	73
# of first-year students enrolled	1,417
SAT Critical Reading (middle 50%)	540-660
SAT Math (middle 50%)	560-660
SAT Writing (middle 50%)	n/a
ACT (middle 50%)	25-30
average HS GPA	3.76

Deadlines

early decision	Priority scholarship deadline, December 1
regular decision	rolling
application fee (online)	$0 ($0)
fee waiver for applicants with financial need	yes

COST & AID

tuition	in-state: $6,772; out-of-state: $12,316
room & board	$7,254 (average rate)
total need-based institutional scholarships/grants	n/a
% of students apply for need-based aid	70
% receiving need-based scholarship or grant aid	47
% receiving aid whose need was fully met	82
average aid package	$6,299
average student loan debt upon graduation	$19,118

University of Missouri

University of Missouri
230 Jesse Hall
Columbia, MO 65211
Ph: (573) 882-7786
MU4U@missouri.edu
www.missouri.edu

Located in Columbia, Missouri, Mizzou is an exceptional place, a university where students will find more majors, more talented and dedicated teachers and more top-notch facilities—all of which add up to more opportunities to explore, grow and succeed. The University of Missouri works with students to develop a personalized academic plan for the first semester. Students may join a Freshman Interest Group (FIG), a Learning Community, or consider joining a student organization. At the start of the semester, students participate in Fall and Spring Welcome activities to get better connected with the campus and their department. Mizzou wants students to have a successful start to their college career. The Learning Center, Academic Advising, Academic Retention Services and other programs are available to help develop learning strategies to enhance success. Positive freshman retention rates indicate Mizzou students are well served by these programs by helping them define, clarify and achieve their academic, personal and professional goals throughout their program of study.

> ACCESS MU Engineering Scholars Camp

MU offers a wide variety of academic enrichment and leadership summer opportunities that provide exposure and engagement to college for 6th-12th grade students. MU Engineering Scholars Camp provides an opportunity to learn what engineers really do and the tools they use, introducing students to engineering's various disciplines through hands-on activities and team design competitions.

> ACCESS High School Mini Medical School

This is a one-week experience designed to give students a preview of medical school. The program includes: participation in a medical school style curriculum; hospital tours; hands-on experience in anatomy, microbiology, and clinical skills; meaningful interactions with current medical students, faculty, and staff of the School of Medicine and seminars on college and medical school entrance and medical school life.

> OPPORTUNITY Mizzou Days and Black and Gold Days

Throughout the year Mizzou Days and Black and Gold Days are designed to help prospective students and their families learn everything they'd ever want to know about Mizzou, from the award-winning residential dining halls to a campus rich in tradition. Students visit with admissions staff, explore the campus during a student led tour, interact with faculty in the academic areas that they have the most interest in and visit student facilities.

> SUCCESS Academic Retention Services (ARS)

Academic Retention Services provides services designed to support the academic/intellectual, social, personal and cultural development of students. From the time of admittance to Mizzou and up until graduation, students are offered a wide array of programs and services to enhance their overall campus experience. ARS is committed to the development of students by creating opportunities that foster campus involvement, leadership development and academic excellence. ARS also serves as a resource office to parents, students, faculty and staff by providing culturally related information.

> SUCCESS Exposure to Research for Science Students (EXPRESS)

The EXPRESS program is specially designed for freshmen and sophomores to receive an opportunity to work in a faculty research lab as underclassmen. Students acquire a faculty mentor, learn valuable laboratory skills, become involved in cutting-edge research, and participate in a variety of supplemental activities.

FAST FACTS

STUDENT PROFILE

# of degree-seeking undergraduates	24,603
% male/female	48/52
% African American	7
% American Indian or Alaska Native	1
% Asian or Pacific Islander	2
% Hispanic	3
% White	82
% International	2
% Pell grant recipients	16

ACADEMICS

full-time faculty	1,289
full-time minority faculty	229
student-faculty ratio	20:1
average class size	n/a
% first-year retention rate	84
% graduation rate (6 years)	69

Popular majors Business, Journalism and Communication, Health professions

CAMPUS LIFE

% live on campus (% freshmen)	28 (86)

Multicultural student clubs and organizations
Legion of Black Collegians, Hispanic American Leadership Organization (HALO), From the Four Directions (Native American Student Group) Asian American Association, National Society of Black Engineers (NSBE), Hispanic Professional Engineers (SHPE), Minorities in Agriculture, Natural Resources and Related Sciences, Minority Association of Pre-Health professionals, National Society of Minorities in Hospitality, 9 National Pan-Hellenic Greek Organizations

Athletics NCAA Division I, Big 12 Conference

ADMISSIONS

# of applicants	17,465
% accepted	84
# of first-year students enrolled	6,089
SAT Critical Reading (middle 50%)	540-650
SAT Math (middle 50%)	530-650
SAT Writing (middle 50%)	n/a
ACT (middle 50%)	23-28
average HS GPA	n/a
Deadlines	
regular decision	5/1
application fee (online)	$50 ($50)
fee waiver for applicants with financial need	yes

COST & AID

tuition	in-state: $7,848; out-of-state: $20,643
room & board	$8,643
total need-based institutional scholarships/grants	$25,315,524
% of students apply for need-based aid	69
% receiving need-based scholarship or grant aid	41
% receiving aid whose need was fully met	11
average aid package	$12,797
average student loan debt upon graduation	$22,145

The University of Montana

The University of Montana offers students academic excellence in addition to outstanding outdoor recreational opportunities and quality of life. Students receive a high-quality, well-rounded education through the university's five colleges — arts and sciences, education and human sciences, forestry and conservation, health professions and biomedical sciences, and technology — and four professional schools — journalism, law, business and fine arts. The University of Montana was founded in 1893 in the pioneer town of Missoula, fewer than 90 years after Lewis and Clark and their Corps of Discovery explored the area. Today, the university dedicates a considerable amount of time, energy and resources to working with first-generation, minority and low-income students. Located in the midst of western Montana's stunning natural landscape, The University of Montana's campus has been deemed the most scenic in America by *Rolling Stone*.

ACCESS **Minority Admissions Counselor**

The University of Montana Minority Admissions Counselor travels around Montana, the U.S. and Canada speaking with groups about the possibility of college and about The University of Montana. The Minority Admissions Counselor also plans tours, admissions visits, mock orientations, student panels, program presentations, scavenger hunts and hands-on learning experiences for TRIO whose programs also include Upward Bound, Talent Search and GEAR UP.

OPPORTUNITY **Tribal Colleges**

The state of Montana is home to seven Tribal Colleges, one on each of the seven reservations. In Dual Admissions Agreements with all of the Tribal Colleges, The University of Montana offers dual enrollment to students enrolled in Tribal Colleges, allowing students to get the benefits of being a UM student, complete with advising, an early registration period and an application fee waiver. Approximately 25 percent of The University of Montana's Native American students are transfer students from Tribal Colleges. Many of the Tribal Colleges bring students, faculty and staff to the university to learn about specific programs, to interact with students, to participate in specific campus activities, or to become more acquainted with the campus in general. Transfer Transition provides Tribal College transfer students with an enhanced orientation where students come on campus for one day and register for courses.

"I chose The University of Montana because there were a lot of American Indian Students going there and a lot of support for them. At first it was really awkward because I didn't know anyone but right away I got involved in a lot of activities and clubs on campus. Now I love it!"

– Meryl B. '08
Bishop Paiute Reservation (CA)

OPPORTUNITY **Native American Scholarships**

The University of Montana's Native American Studies Department provides Native American students with over $130,000 in scholarships each year. The Davidson Honors College awards $1,500 per year to an American Indian student who has been admitted into the Honors College.

SUCCESS **The University of Montana Diversity Committee**

The Diversity Committee is formed by students who create working partnerships with other student groups, staff and faculty to create learning and leadership opportunities, explore common interests, identify common problems and possible solutions, engage students in social activities and overall, improve campus life.

The University of Montana
Enrollment Services
Lommasson Center
32 Campus Drive
Missoula, MT 59812
Ph: (800) 462-8636 / (406) 243-6266
admiss@umontana.edu
www.umt.edu

FAST FACTS

STUDENT PROFILE

# of degree-seeking undergraduates	11,468
% male/female	55/45
% African American	<1
% American Indian or Alaska Native	2
% Asian or Pacific Islander	1
% Hispanic	3
% White	87
% International	3
% Pell grant recipients	28

First-generation and minority alumni Mike Mansfield; Joe McDonald; Bonnie HeavyRunner; Henrietta Mann Morton; Judy Blunt; Dorothy M. Johnson; George M. Dennison; Gary Niles Kimble; Kenneth Ryan

ACADEMICS

full-time faculty	592
full-time minority faculty	14
student-faculty ratio	17:1
average class size	29
% first-year retention rate	74
% graduation rate (6 years)	48

Popular majors Business Administration, English, Education, Natural Resources/Conservation

CAMPUS LIFE

% live on campus (% freshmen)	25 (83)

Multicultural student clubs and organizations American Indians in Science and Engineering, American Indian Business Leaders, Coalition on Bias and Discrimination, Indian Hall of Fame, Kyi-Yo Native American Student Association, Le Gente Unida, Native American Journalist Association Student Chapter, Native American Law Student Association, ROSNA/PACE, Traditional American Indian Games Association, WA YA WA American Indian Education Association

Athletics NCAA Division I, Big Sky Conference

ADMISSIONS

# of applicants	9,417
% accepted	61
SAT Critical Reading (middle 50%)	490-620
SAT Math (middle 50%)	500-620
SAT Writing (middle 50%)	480-600
ACT (middle 50%)	21-28
average HS GPA	3.3

Deadlines

regular admission	rolling
application fee (online)	$30($30)
fee waiver for applicants with financial need	no

COST & AID

tuition	in-state: $6,168; out-of-state: $18,291
room & board	$7,900
total need-based institutional scholarships/grants	$1,687,225.70
% of students apply for need-based aid	67
% of students receive aid	50
% receiving need-based scholarship or grant aid	36
% receiving aid whose need was fully met	6
average aid package	$11,285
average student loan debt upon graduation	$21,000

Dartmouth College

A member of the Ivy League, Dartmouth is distinctive for being a vibrant and yet highly-accessible and student-centered residential liberal arts college with world-class resources and research opportunities. Aspiring to provide the best undergraduate education in the country, Dartmouth enables students to individualize their experience through its unique academic calendar (the D-Plan) and extensive study abroad programs. Its intellectual and social community is built on the diverse backgrounds, perspectives and interests of its student body and faculty. Dartmouth is committed to the success of all of its students, particularly its high percentage of historically underrepresented and first generation students through its Office of Pluralism and Leadership, First Generation Student Network, students of color advising groups and community-building cultural programming such as the Martin Luther King, Jr. Celebration, annual PRIDE celebration, Dartmouth Asian Organization culture nights, and the largest Pow-Wow in New England.

"I came to Dartmouth because of the sense of community. Dartmouth's manageable size paired with our unique academic calendar, provides the campus with a tight-knit community that remains fresh as people regularly cycle through and share their wonderful experiences from around the world. Matriculating at Dartmouth is much more than the opportunity to study at a great four-year institution of higher education, it's the chance to join a lifelong Dartmouth family."

– Clark M., '13
Atlanta, GA
History

ACCESS Dartmouth Bound

Every year Dartmouth's Admissions Office invites a small, promising group of college-bound rising seniors for an extended campus visit through the Dartmouth Bound programs. Participants are provided with roundtrip airfare and overnight accommodations in residence halls, and are given the opportunity to visit classes and interact freely with Dartmouth faculty, administrators and students. Participating students are selected on the basis of their academic achievement, personal character, and potential for college success.

OPPORTUNITY Need Blind Admissions

Dartmouth practices need-blind admissions for all applicants, which means students' financial need has no bearing on their admission to Dartmouth. Furthermore, Dartmouth guarantees to meet 100 percent of the demonstrated financial need for all admitted students, including free tuition for students who come from families with total annual incomes below $75,000 with typical assets. Student financial aid packages provide a combination of scholarships and grants, with small loans and employment eligibility.

SUCCESS Office of Pluralism and Leadership (OPAL)

Dartmouth's Office of Pluralism and Leadership is a critical resource in the College's effort to support historically underrepresented populations and to encourage the building of cultural bridges within the Dartmouth community. In addition to facilitating programs and advising networks designed to support students' academic success, the program also provides opportunities for leadership development, cultural enrichment, and community engagement. Through its collaboration with students and over 50 campus offices, OPAL works to enhance Dartmouth's institutional commitment to diversity.

SUCCESS Affinity Programs

Dartmouth's affinity programs provide residential learning opportunities for students based on either a self-defined academic or special interest focus. Through Dartmouth's affinity programs, undergraduates have the opportunity to live with other students who share a common interest or background. These programs include the Chinese Language House, the Inter-faith Living and Learning Center (IFLLC), La Casa, the Latin American, Latino & Caribbean Studies House (LALACS), the Cutter-Shabazz African American Center for Intellectual Inquiry, and the Native American House.

Dartmouth College
6016 McNutt Hall
Hanover, NH 03755
Ph: (603) 646-2875
admissions.office@dartmouth.edu
www.dartmouth.edu

FAST FACTS

STUDENT PROFILE

# of degree-seeking undergraduates	4,196
% male/female	51/49
% African American	8
% American Indian or Alaska Native	4
% Asian or Pacific Islander	14
% Hispanic	7
% White	53
% International	7
% Unknown	6
% Pell grant recipients	14.5

First-generation and minority alumni Aisha Tyler, actress, "Friends" and "CSI", former host of "Talk Soup"; Shonda Rhimes, creator, head writer, and executive producer of "Grey's Anatomy"; Keith Boykin, editor of "The Daily Voice", CNBC contributor, co-host of BET's "My Two Cents"; Leah Daughtry, CEO of 2008 Democratic National Convention, Howard Dean's chief of staff; Louise Erdrich, Native American author, 2009 finalist for the Pulitzer Prize in Fiction; Jose W. Fernandez, Assistant Secretary of State

ACADEMICS

total faculty	1,044
total minority faculty	132
student-faculty ratio	8:1
average class size	10-19
% first-year retention rate	98
% graduation rate (6 years)	95

Popular majors Economics, Government, Psychological & Brain Sciences, History, Biology, English

CAMPUS LIFE

% live on campus (% freshmen)	90 (100)

Multicultural student clubs and organizations AfriCaSO, Afro-American Society, Dartmouth Asian Organization, Dartmouth Chinese Culture Society, Dartmouth Japan Society, Dartmouth Taiwanese Association, Hokupa'a, International Students Association, Korean American Students Association, La Alianza Latina, M.E.Ch.A. (Movimiento Estudiantil Chicano/a de Aztlan), Milan, MOSAIC, Native Americans at Dartmouth, Vietnamese Student Association.

Athletics NCAA Division I, Eastern College Athletic Conference, Ivy League (ECAC)

ADMISSIONS

# of applicants	18,778
% accepted	11.7
# of first-year students enrolled	1,138
SAT Critical Reading (middle 50%)	670-780
SAT Math (middle 50%)	690-790
SAT Writing (middle 50%)	680-790
ACT (middle 50%)	29-34
Deadlines	
early decision	11/1
regular decision	1/1
application fee (online)	$75 ($75)
fee waiver for applicants with financial need	yes

COST & AID

tuition	$39,978
room & board	$11,838
total need-based institutional scholarships/grants	$91,600,000
% of students apply for need-based aid	64.9
% of students receive aid	59.1
% receiving need-based scholarship or grant aid	55.1
% receiving aid whose need was fully met	100
average aid package	$35,855
average student loan debt of scholarship recipients upon graduation	$12,522

Felician College

Felician College is a co-educational institute of higher learning with 1,300 traditional undergraduate students. It is a Catholic college in the Franciscan tradition, committed to putting STUDENTS FIRST. Felician offers 55 academic and professional programs in the liberal arts tradition to help prepare today's college student to assume their roles as members of an increasingly global community. Felician College has been named one of the top (#5) Best Colleges for racial diversity for Baccalaureate Colleges in the North by the *U.S. News & World Report* ranking. You will find that Felician is small and personable, and students state positively that Felician is a place where students can sit and talk with professors and feel their individual talents are nurtured.

ACCESS Jumpstart

Jumpstart runs for 5 weeks and is designed to help students strengthen their skills in Math and English. At the end of the program, Jumpstart students take a placement exam in order to test out of one or more of the developmental courses in which they were originally placed, allowing them to take college-level courses sooner.

ACCESS The Educational Opportunity Fund Program (EOF)

The Educational Opportunity Fund (EOF) program, is designed to provide an opportunity for higher education for New Jersey residents, who are found to be economically and academically disadvantaged. EOF offers great advantages such as: an extra grant towards tuition, additional tutoring for classes, a summer program to prepare students for the first college level English and Math courses and an opportunity to get to know future classmates before the semester begins.

"Initially, I was not sure if I was college material. But, I met Dinela Huertas, EOF Associate Director during my college search process; she believed in me and thought I had what it took to be a college student. Now, I have close to a 3.0 GPA and I am on the road to complete my degree in Education."

– Daniel R.
Newark, NJ
Education

OPPORTUNITY Scholarships

Felician College aims to make college more affordable by keeping the cost low and offering generous scholarships. Scholarships are designed to reward students for academic achievement and help pay for college. Please visit www.felician.edu to view merit based scholarships.

SUCCESS Freshman Year Experience (FYE)

This program entails a one-credit course which meets weekly in both the fall and spring semesters of your freshman year. It is taught by a Felician faculty member, usually from the participating student's academic discipline and, in most cases, this faculty member will also serve as their academic advisor during their first year.

SUCCESS Academic Support Services

The Academic Support Services at Felician are in a collaborative and cooperative learning environment where students from all disciplines can discover the tools, strategies and resources necessary to become life-long learners. The Center for Learning is staffed by professors, professional tutors, and peer tutors who provide free consultations to students in areas such as English, math, science, and other selected academic disciplines.

Felician College
262 South Main Street
Lodi, NJ 07644
Ph: (201) 559-6131
admissions@felician.edu
www.felician.edu

FAST FACTS

STUDENT PROFILE	
# of degree-seeking undergraduates	1,761
% male/female	22/78
% African American	13
% American Indian or Alaska Native	<1
% Asian or Pacific Islander	9
% Hispanic	15
% White	45
% International	<1
% Pell grant recipients	49
ACADEMICS	
full-time faculty	114
full-time minority faculty	9
student-faculty ratio	9:1
average class size	15
% first-year retention rate	68
% graduation rate (6 years)	34
Popular majors Business, Education, Nursing and Criminal Justice	
CAMPUS LIFE	
% live on campus	25
Multicultural student clubs and organizations International Cultural Club, United Latino Club, and many other professional organizations	
Athletics NCAA Division II, Central Atlantic Collegiate Conference (CAAC)	
ADMISSIONS	
# of applicants	1,479
% accepted	63.6
# of first-year students enrolled	255
SAT Critical Reading (middle 50%)	380-480
SAT Math (middle 50%)	400-500
SAT Writing (middle 50%)	390-490
ACT (middle 50%)	17-24
average HS GPA	3.0
Deadlines	
regular decision	rolling
application fee (online)	$30 ($30)
fee waiver for applicants with financial need	yes
COST & AID	
tuition	$18,900
room & board	$7,432
total need-based institutional scholarships/grants	$1,181,136
% of students apply for need-based aid	86
% receiving need-based scholarship or grant aid	73
% receiving aid whose need was fully met	77
average aid package	$14,340
average student loan debt upon graduation	$19,500

Montclair State University

Montclair State offers the advantages of a large university – a comprehensive undergraduate curriculum with a global focus, a broad variety of superior graduate programs through the doctoral level, and a diverse faculty and student body – combined with a small college's attention to students. For over 100 years, ambitious people from all walks of life have come to Montclair State to fulfill their potential and reach for their dreams. In February 2010, Montclair State University was named a "Top Gainer" and a "Top Gap Closer," and listed among the top 25 public four-year colleges and universities in the nation for its improvements in minority graduation rates by The Education Trust, a Washington DC-based, non-profit advocacy group. Among the Carnegie classification's 186 public master's institutions included in the study, Montclair State was the only New Jersey institution to be listed in the top 25.

ACCESS Upward Bound Program

The Upward Bound Program at Montclair State University assists low-income and first generation students with academic support services to increase their opportunity to graduate from high school. The main thrust of the project is to increase the skills and motivation needed to successfully complete an undergraduate course of studies. Participants are recruited from the federally approved target areas of Newark, Passaic, and Paterson.

OPPORTUNITY Educational Opportunity Fund Program

The Educational Opportunity Fund (EOF) Program provides special admission, financial aid, and academic support services for highly motivated low-income students who do not meet Montclair State University's regular admission criteria. Students admitted to the program must be members of economically disadvantaged families, have a background of academic under-preparedness, but demonstrate potential to be successful in college. Eligible students who are admitted to the program receive a maximum amount of financial aid based on their individual need. Also students are provided with a broad range of academic support services including counseling, tutoring, leadership development, and workshops. Counselors interact with students in individual and small group settings, which cover academics, course advising, careers, personal and financial aid issues. For more information, visit: http://www.montclair.edu/eop/

"Montclair State University and the EOF Program means having a family where you are given a chance to express yourself, to communicate with your counselor, to set goals for yourself, and knowing that there are people who believe in you. It's a community where your opinion and education matters."

– Dianne F.
Newark, NJ
Psychology

OPPORTUNITY The Health Careers Program (HCP)

The Health Careers Program (HCP), funded jointly by Montclair State University and the New Jersey Educational Opportunity Fund, is an undergraduate program that provides highly motivated and academically capable students from financially and educationally disadvantaged backgrounds an opportunity for admission to health professions schools and careers in the sciences.

Montclair State University
1 Normal Avenue
Montclair, NJ 07043
Ph: (973) 655-4444
undergraduate.admission@montclair.edu
www.montclair.edu

FAST FACTS

STUDENT PROFILE

# of degree-seeking undergraduates	14,383
% male/female	40/60
% African American	10
% American Indian or Alaska Native	<1
% Asian or Pacific Islander	6
% Hispanic	23
% White	56
% International	5
% Pell grant recipients	27

First-generation and minority alumni Alread Bundy, Producer and Public Relations Specialist, Bundy Productions, BA 1975, MA 1980; Christopher C. Catching, ED.D Dean/Director, Multicultural Engagement, Rutgers, The State University of New Jersey, Office of Undergraduate Education, New Brunswick, NJ, 1999; Dr. Antoinete "Toni" Clay, Assistant Vice President, Instructional Student Support Services, Montclair State University BA in Psychology, 1980; Lynette N. Harris, Director of Judicial Affairs, The College of New Jersey, Bachelor of Arts in Sociology (1990) and a Masters of Arts in Counseling in Higher Education (1995)

ACADEMICS

full-time faculty	569
full-time minority faculty	149
student-faculty ratio	17:1
average class size	23
% first-year retention rate	81
% graduation rate (6 years)	62

Popular majors Business Administration, Family & Child Services, Psychology, English, Biology

CAMPUS LIFE

% live on campus (% freshmen)	38 (55)

Multicultural student clubs and organizations Active Students Serving in Society Together (ASSIST), Caribbean Student Organization (CaribSO), Haitian Student Association (HSA) Helping Each Other and Redefining Tomorrow (HEART), International Student Organization (ISO), Latin American Student Organization (LASO), Minority Association of Pre-Health Students (MAPS), Multicultural Inclusive Teacher Candidates Organization (MINTCO), National Association for the Advancement of Colored People (NAACP), Native African Student Organization (NASO), Organization of Students for African Unity (OSAU)

Athletics NCAA Division III, New Jersey Athletic Conference (NJAC)

ADMISSIONS

# of applicants	13,133
% accepted	50
# of first-year students enrolled	2,232
SAT Critical Reading (middle 50%)	440-540
SAT Math (middle 50%)	460-550
SAT Writing (middle 50%)	450-550
ACT (middle 50%)	n/a
average HS GPA	3.23

Deadlines

early action	11/15
priority decision	12/15
regular decision	3/1
application fee (online)	$65 ($65)
fee waiver for applicants with financial need	yes

COST & AID

tuition	in-state $9,771; out-of-state $17,783
room & board	$10,208
total need-based institutional scholarships/grants	$200,000
% of students apply for need-based aid	71
% receiving need-based scholarship or grant aid	32
% receiving aid whose need was fully met	15
average aid package	$9,217
average student loan debt upon graduation	$18,307

Princeton University

Princeton University
Undergraduate Admissions Office
P.O. Box 430
Princeton, NJ 08542
Ph: (609) 258-3060
uaoffice@princeton.edu
www.princeton.edu

Princeton University is a private, four-year, research university located in Princeton, NJ. The University's commitment to undergraduate education is distinctive among leading research universities. Princeton is recognized globally for its academic excellence; the University embraces open-mindedness, critical thinking, and the core principles of responsibility, integrity, and courage in its students. Although admission to Princeton is highly selective, the institution is committed to building a diverse campus community to ensure that students explore their interests, discover new academic and extracurricular pursuits, and learn from each other. More than ever, through initiatives such as its generous financial aid program, Princeton is making its distinctive education accessible to students from a broad range of cultural, ethnic, and economic backgrounds. Princeton's no-loan financial aid program assists all qualified applicants with generous need-based grants, rather than loans, making the University affordable to low- and middle-income families. About 60 percent of Princeton's student body receives aid each year. The University supports minority students on campus through college preparatory programs, one-on-one mentoring, tutoring, and other programs and resources.

"Princeton lives up to its name and beyond. I'm really happy to be here every day. And I didn't have to take out loans. That's a blessing in itself. Not having to worry about being in debt is priceless."

– Esther C.,'12
East Orange, NJ
Sociology

ACCESS Princeton University Preparatory Program

The Princeton University Preparatory Program (PUPP) is a rigorous academic and cultural enrichment program that supports high-achieving, low-income high school students from local districts. The program helps students from ninth grade through high school graduation to build the academic skills, confidence, and leadership abilities necessary to both gain access to — and guarantee success in — higher education. Each summer, participants attend an intensive program on the Princeton campus. Participants are also provided year-round academic and cultural enrichment opportunities. Program staff members assist students and their families with the college application process and encourage students through every step, from SAT tutoring to extracurricular involvement.

OPPORTUNITY Need-Based Financial Aid

Princeton University has one of the strongest need-based financial aid programs in the country, reflecting our core value of equality of opportunity and our desire to attract the most talented students. In 2011-12, Princeton expects to provide $110 million in grants to more than 3,100 undergraduates. Princeton's no-loan policy means that the University provides grants, not loans, to students who demonstrate financial need. The policy makes it possible for students to graduate debt-free. The average financial aid grant covers nearly 100 percent of tuition. Grants for lower-income students also typically cover room and board costs.

SUCCESS Black Student Union Leadership and Mentoring Program

Through the Black Student Union Leadership and Mentoring Program, Princeton upperclassmen offer one-on-one mentoring for incoming students. The program provides a support network that encourages academic and social exploration and success.

FAST FACTS

STUDENT PROFILE

# of degree-seeking undergraduates	5,044
% male/female	51/49
% African American	8
% American Indian or Alaska Native	1
% Asian or Pacific Islander	16
% Hispanic	9
% White	49
% Pell grant recipients	9

First-generation and minority alumni Sonia Sotomayor, Supreme Court Justice; Mohsin Hamid, novelist; Stanley Jordan, jazz guitarist; Michelle Obama, lawyer, first lady; Angela Ramirez, executive director, Congressional Hispanic Caucus; Anthony Romero, executive director, ACLU; John Thompson III, men's basketball coach, Georgetown University

ACADEMICS

full-time faculty	843
student-faculty ratio	6:1
% first-year retention rate	98
% graduation rate (6 years)	96

Popular majors History, Economics, Politics, Public and International Affairs, Molecular Biology

CAMPUS LIFE

% live on campus (% freshmen)	98 (100)

Multicultural student clubs and organizations Acción Latina, AKWAABA: African Students Association, Arab Society of Princeton, Asian American Students Association, Asian Pacific American Heritage Council, Black History Month Planning Committee, Black Student Union, Bulgarian Undergraduate Society, Chicano Caucus, Chinese Students Association, Cuban American Undergraduate Student Association, Hillel (Center for Jewish Life), Hong Kong Students Association, International Students Association of Princeton, Japanese Student Association, Korean American Students Association, Latin American Studies Student Organization, Latino Heritage Month Committee, Minority Business Association, National Society of Black Engineers, Native Americans at Princeton, Pehchaan (Pakistanis at Princeton), Persian Society of Princeton, Princeton Association of Black Women, Princeton Caribbean Connection, Singapore Society, South Asian Students Association, Taiwanese American Students Association, Ukrainian Alliance

Athletics NCAA Division I, Ivy League

ADMISSIONS

# of applicants	27,189
% accepted	8.5
SAT Critical Reading (middle 50%)	700-790
SAT Math (middle 50%)	710-800
SAT Writing (middle 50%)	700-790
ACT (middle 50%)	31-34
Deadlines	
Single-Choice Early Action	10/1
regular admission	1/1
application fee (online)	$65 ($65)

COST & AID

tuition	$37,000
room & board	$12,069
% of students receiving aid	60
% receiving need-based scholarship or grant aid	60
% receiving aid whose need was fully met	100
average aid package	$38,000
average student loan debt upon graduation	$2,800

Rutgers University

One of the original colonial colleges in the U.S., Rutgers is ranked among the nation's top five universities for commitment to diversity by *DiversityInc.* magazine. New Jersey is one of the most diverse states in the nation, and Rutgers follows suit with students from every U.S. state and more than 167 countries. *U.S. News and World Report* has named Rutgers-Newark the most diverse national university for 14 straight years. With three regional campuses in Camden, New Brunswick, and Newark, Rutgers is a major state university, offering all of the advantages of a public institution: reasonable tuition, big-time athletics, and some of the best research and academic resources, as well as a contemporary liberal arts education in a traditional northeastern college setting.

ACCESS **Upward Bound**

Local high school students who come from low-income families in which neither parent holds a bachelor's degree can benefit from Rutgers' Upward Bound, a pre-college program that provides students with the right tools to pursue their goal of earning a college degree. Students benefit from weekly tutoring, field trips, workshops, and a six-week summer enrichment program on campus.

> ***"With the extensive program support available to help me, I never felt alone or lost at Rutgers. I found the strength and courage that I needed to excel."***
>
> *– Jackasha-Janaee W., '10*
> *Plainfield, NJ*
> *History, Women & Gender Studies*

OPPORTUNITY **Rutgers Educational Opportunity Fund**

The Rutgers Educational Opportunity Fund (EOF) program provides access to higher education for highly motivated New Jersey residents whose economic and educational circumstances have placed them at a disadvantage. The EOF program's comprehensive services and highly dedicated staff guide students in all areas of university life: academic, financial, personal, career and social. The program includes a Summer Institute to help ease the transition from high school to the university and sharpen students' math, writing, and other skills.

SUCCESS **The Office for Diversity and Academic Success in the Sciences (ODASIS)**

The Office for Diversity and Academic Success in the Sciences (ODASIS) has a threefold mission to increase the numbers of Hispanic, African-American, Native American, and New Jersey Educational Opportunity Fund students majoring in the sciences. ODASIS does this by providing a supportive environment, improving retention rates, enhancing students' levels of academic achievement, and increasing students' entry rates into graduate or professional schools, or in their chosen fields in the workforce.

SUCCESS **Student Support Services**

Student Support Services (SSS) is a federally funded program maintained by Rutgers to increase retention and graduate rates by helping first-generation and low-income students make the transition from one level of higher education to the next. Student Support Services (SSS) include one-on-one tutoring, mentoring, career and academic counseling, and assistance in pursuing higher level education. SSS participants who are receiving Federal Pell Grants are also eligible to receive grant aid.

SUCCESS **The TRIO Ronald E. McNair Post-Baccalaureate Achievement Program**

The Rutgers Ronald E. McNair Program assists students from underrepresented backgrounds with strong academic potential and prepares them to pursue doctoral programs through involvement in research and other scholarly activities. Rutgers works closely with students, providing them with academic and financial support as they complete their undergraduate requirements. Participating students are encouraged to enroll in graduate programs, and their progress is tracked through the successful completion of advanced degrees.

Rutgers University
Office of Undergraduate Admissions
65 Davidson Road - Room 202
Piscataway, NJ 08854-8097
Ph: (732) 445-INFO (4636)
admissions@ugadm.rutgers.edu
www.admissions.rutgers.edu

FAST FACTS

STUDENT PROFILE

# of degree-seeking undergraduates	38,308
% male/ female	50/50
% African American	11
% American Indian or Alaska Native	<1
% Asian or Pacific Islander	24
% Hispanic	14
% White	52
% International	2

First-generation and minority alums Avery F. Brooks, Actor and Educator, Livingston College 1973, Mason Gross School of the Arts 1976; James Dickson Carr, Attorney and First African-American Graduate of Rutgers, Rutgers College 1892; Clement A. Price, Historian and Professor, Graduate School – New Brunswick 1975; Paul Robeson, Athlete, Singer, Actor, Political Activist, Rutgers College 1919; Joseph H. Rodriquez, Federal Judge, School of Law-Camden 1958; Junot Diaz, Pulitzer Prize winning author, Rutgers College 1992

ACADEMICS

full-time faculty	2,409
full-time minority faculty	423
student-faculty ratio	14:1
average class size	<30
% first-year retention rate	91
% graduation rate (6 yrs)	74

Popular majors Biology/Health Sciences, Business, Communication, Engineering, Fine and Performing Arts

CAMPUS LIFE

% live on campus (% freshmen)	36 (83)

Multicultural student clubs and organizations Fusion: The Rutgers Union of Mixed People; Diversity WORKS; Global Thought Society of Rutgers; Black Student Union; Indian Student Association; Douglas Asian Women Association; Latino Student Council; National Hispanic Business Association (NHBA) - Rutgers NB Chapter; Rutgers Union of Cuban American Students; Association of Philippine Students (Rutgers); Haitian Association; Latin American Student Organization and West Indian Student Organization

Athletics Rutgers-New Brunswick: NCAA Division I, Big East conference; Rutgers-Camden: NCAA Division III, New Jersey Athletic Conference (NJAC); Rutgers- Newark: NCAA Division III, New Jersey Athletic Conference (NJAC)

ADMISSIONS

# of applicants	47,731
% accepted	57
# of first-year students enrolled	7,476
SAT Critical Reading (middle 50%)	510-620
SAT Math (middle 50%)	550-670
SAT Writing (middle 50%)	530-640
ACT (middle 50%)	n/a
average HS GPA	n/a

Deadlines

regular decision	12/1
application fee (online)	$65 ($65)
fee waiver for applicants with financial need	yes

COST & AID

tuition	in-state $10,104; out-of-state $22,766
room & board	$11,262
total need-based institutional scholarships/ grants	$45,883,915
% of students apply for need-based aid	75
% of students receive aid	86
% receiving need-based scholarship/ grant aid	n/a
% receiving aid whose need was fully met	n/a
average aid package	$13,778
average student loan debt upon graduation	$17,359

New Mexico Highlands University

New Mexico Highlands University
Office of Admissions
Box 9000
Las Vegas, NM 87701-9000
Ph: (505) 454-3439
admissions@nmhu.edu
www.nmhu.edu

New Mexico Highlands University is a co-educational, non-denominational, comprehensive public university serving the global community by integrating education, research, public service and economic development while celebrating its distinctive northern New Mexico cultures and traditions. Founded in 1893, New Mexico Highlands University is committed to programs that focus on its multi-ethnic student body with special emphasis on the rich heritage of Hispanic and Native American cultures that are distinctive to the state of New Mexico. The university perceives that its success depends upon an appreciation of the region's cultural and linguistic identities. By reinforcing cultural identity and encouraging the use of these assets, the university empowers students and the region's ethnic populations to achieve full involvement in the activities of society.

"New Mexico Highlands University has a 'can do' environment that has helped me accomplish everything."

– Tiffany N., '11 Business Management and Music

ACCESS University College Student for a Day

The New Mexico Highlands University's College Student for a Day program is a central part of the university's GEAR UP program. Serving approximately 1,250 seventh graders from 22 northern New Mexico school districts, GEAR UP increases the number of low-income students who will be prepared to enter and succeed in college. Following the New Mexico Regional and State Science Fair competition, GEAR UP students are bused to New Mexico Highlands University for the College Student for a Day program. Students proceed to mini lectures in groups of 20 conducted by university professors in various disciplines, including biology, chemistry, human performance and physics. Hands-on activities are incorporated into the classroom experience. Additionally, university researchers conduct tours of the laboratories and other science facilities.

ACCESS Student Ambassadors

The New Mexico Highlands University Student Ambassadors are volunteer students who help the recruitment office with outreach into the local community. Ambassadors help recruit underserved students, mentor and encourage local high school students to continue with their education. Ambassador activities include facilitating the University Honors banquet for high school students, organizing career day participants for the local elementary, middle and high school events as well as organizing a "cowboy lunch" for all local high schools. The New Mexico Highlands cosponsored event is held every year and encourages students to attend "College Night," an event allowing prospective students to gather information about the university.

SUCCESS Early and Mid-Term Alert Program

The Early and Mid-Term Alert Program is an early intervention program that aids in identifying students (dual-enrolled, freshmen and sophomores) who are experiencing poor academic performance and excessive absenteeism in any of their introductory level courses. Academic advisers contact the at-risk students via e-mail or telephone, or personally visit their classrooms or residential halls. Advisers discuss their concerns regarding the student's academic performance and work with the students to identify the various services that are available to assist them to be more academically successful.

FAST FACTS

STUDENT PROFILE

# of degree-seeking undergraduates	1,514
% male/female	38/62
% African American	5.1
% American Indian or Alaska Native	6.4
% Asian or Pacific Islander	2.1
% Hispanic	57.6
% White	23.4
% Pell grant recipients	63.5

First-generation and minority alumni Anthony Edwards, professional football player; Reggie Garrett, professional football player; Lionel Taylor, professional football player

ACADEMICS

full-time faculty	76
student-faculty ratio	25:1
average class size	n/a
% first-year retention rate	58
% graduation rate (6 years)	20

Popular majors Business Administration, Social Work, Education

CAMPUS LIFE

% live on campus	n/a

Multicultural student clubs and organizations Bilingual Education Student Organization, Hispanic Cultural and Language Club, International Club, Los Rumberos, Native American Club, NMHU Mariachi, Pre-Law Association del Norte, Sendero, Servicios Especiales, Society of Hispanic Professional Engineers, Umoja

Athletics NCAA Division III, Rocky Mountain Athletic Conference (RMAC)

ADMISSIONS

# of applicants	1,146
% accepted	71
SAT Critical Reading (middle 50%)	n/a
SAT Math (middle 50%)	n/a
SAT Writing (middle 50%)	400-500
ACT (middle 50%)	15-19
average HS GPA	3.6
Deadlines	
early decision	1/1
regular decision	8/1
application fee (online)	$15 ($15)

COST & AID

tuition	$3,198
room & board	$5,590
% of students receiving aid	97
% receiving need-based scholarship or grant aid	78
% receiving aid whose need was fully met	19
average aid package	$6,415
average student loan debt upon graduation	$12,147

Barnard College

Barnard is a small, selective liberal arts college for women, located in New York City. Our students are taught by leading scholars who serve as dedicated, accessible mentors and teachers. Barnard also enjoys a unique partnership with Columbia University, situated directly across the street, providing students with additional course offerings, extracurricular activities, NCAA Division I Ivy League athletic competition, and a fully coed social life.

Our location In NYC grants students access to thousands of internship opportunities in addition to unparelellled cultural, intellectual, and social resources. Barnard's diverse student body includes residents from nearly every state and 40 countries worldwide. The incoming class is almost 40% students of color and one-quarter of the class comes from non-college/4 year degree backgrounds.

> ***"Barnard has given me more than I can express. Never have I felt this welcomed in any institution. Not only has financial aid been extremely helpful in getting me through college, but the advisors and professors have always been there when I needed them. If you ask questions, you will always get an answer."***
>
> *– Maisha R., '10*

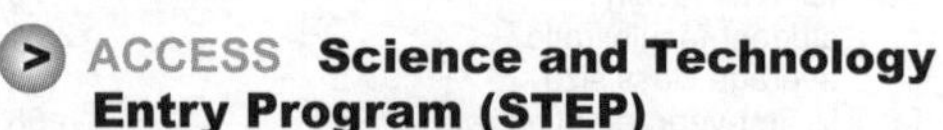

ACCESS Science and Technology Entry Program (STEP)

The Science and Technology Entry Program (STEP) is designed to give students an opportunity to pursue their love and talent in Mathematics, the Sciences, Technology and the Health related fields. The STEP program is funded by New York State and is structured for students that have been historically under represented and/or economically disadvantaged. The program at Barnard College is specifically geared toward students in grades 9 thru 12.

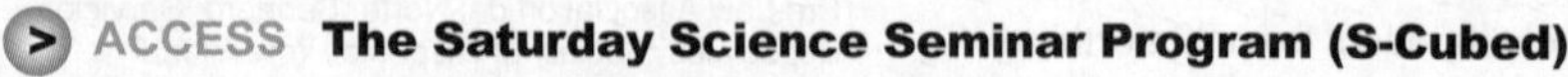

ACCESS The Saturday Science Seminar Program (S-Cubed)

The Saturday Science Seminars (The S-Cubed program) brings young women in the 11th grade with strong academic ability and interest in science and mathematics to Barnard over the course of five Saturdays in January, February, and March. Capable young women are nominated for the program by science teachers in New York City high schools. Admission to the program is highly selective and limited so that students truly gain from the interactive experience of a small class. There is no fee to participate.

OPPORTUNITY Barnard Bound

Barnard Bound is a fall recruitment program for rising seniors who otherwise cannot afford to visit. Barnard College is 100% need-blind admissions and 100% need-based aid; this policy has been adopted so that the admissions and financial aid process does not discriminiate against any kind of student regardless of circumstance.

OPPORTUNITY The Arthur O. Eve Higher Educational Opportunity Program (HEOP) and the Barnard Opportunity Program (BOP)

The Arthur O. Eve Higher Education Opportunity Program (HEOP) gives high-achieving New York State residents from disadvantaged financial backgrounds the support they need to succeed at Barnard and beyond. Additionally, a small number of students who are not New York State residents are identified by the office of admissions as Barnard Opportunity Program (BOP) Scholars. Both HEOP and BOP scholars benefit from resources such as full financial aid packages, a fully funded five-week summer program, and free tutoring and counseling.

SUCCESS First-Year Focus (FYF)

First-Year Focus (FYF) is an extension of Barnard's pre-orientation program. It assists first-year students in adjusting to college life, Barnard, and New York City. Students are hand-matched for an advisor for the first two years, and the First Year Dean helps each student individually select their first semester courses. Tutoring is always available as are other academic and personal resources thoroughout the academic year.

Barnard College
3009 Broadway
New York, NY 10027
Ph: (212) 854-2014
admissions@barnard.edu
www.barnard.edu

FAST FACTS

STUDENT PROFILE

# of degree-seeking undergraduates	2,456
% male/female	0/100
% African American	4
% American Indian or Alaska Native	<1
% Asian or Pacific Islander	16
% Hispanic	9
% White	66
% International	7
% Pell grant recipients	53

First-generation and minority alumni Edwidge Danticat, HEOP alumna, winner of Pushcart Author for "Breathe, Eyes, Memory," 2009 MacArthur Fellows Genius Grant winner; Jhumpa Lahiri , 2000 Pulitzer Prize for Fiction for "Interpreter of Maladies;" Zora Neale Hurston, American folklorist, anthropologist, author of the novel "Their Eyes Were Watching God;" Sheila Abdus-Salaam, New York Supreme Court Justice; Margaret Mead, anthropologist

ACADEMICS

full-time faculty	208
full-time minority faculty	36
student-faculty ratio	9:1
average class size	15
% first-year retention rate	94
% graduation rate (6 years)	90

Popular majors English, Economics, Psychology, Biology, Anthropology

CAMPUS LIFE

% live on campus (% freshmen)	96 (98)

Multicultural student clubs and organizations Asian American Alliance (AAA), Barnard Organization of Soul Sisters (BOSS), Caribbean Students Association (CSA), Chinese Students Club (CSC), Grupo Quisqueyano (Dominican students organization), Haitian Students Association, Liga Flipina, Malama Hawaii, Organization of Pakistani Students (OPS), Club Zamana (South Asian organization), etc.

Athletics NCAA Division I, Ivy League

ADMISSIONS

# of applicants	4,618
% accepted	28
# of first-year students enrolled	45
SAT Critical Reading (middle 50%)	630-730
SAT Math (middle 50%)	620-710
SAT Writing (middle 50%)	650-750
ACT (middle 50%)	28-32
average HS GPA	3.8
Deadlines	
early decision	11/15
regular decision	1/1
application fee (online)	$55 ($55)
fee waiver for applicants with financial need	yes

COST & AID

tuition	$40,542
room & board	$12,950
total need-based institutional scholarships/grants	$26,884,466
% of students apply for need-based aid	50
% receiving need-based scholarship or grant aid	40
% receiving aid whose need was fully met	100
average aid package	$26,654
average student loan debt upon graduation	$14,142

Columbia University

One of the oldest universities in the country, Columbia University offers students the benefits of an Ivy League education as well as access to one of the world's most vibrant, dynamic cities. The university is also proud to be among the schools that have recently revamped their financial aid policies in order to make attending the university possible for low- and middle-income families. Columbia continues to have the highest percentage of Pell grant recipients among any Ivy League school and one of the most socio-economically, racially, ethnically, and religiously diverse student bodies in the country.

"I ultimately decided that for me, Columbia was just the total package. I wanted an education and degree that were globally recognized and I wanted to experience culture, food, internships, life in an incredible city for the next four years. It also didn't hurt that my financial aid here was more generous than that of so many other schools."

– Daniel B.
El Paso, TX
Chemical Engineering

ACCESS Double Discovery Center

A department of Columbia College, the Double Discovery Center began in the 1960s and today serves over 1,000 low-income and first generation college-bound New York City youth each year through its Talent Search and Upward Bound programs. Students learn about colleges and careers, improve their academic work, and participate in personal development activities.

ACCESS College Access Outreach

The Office of Undergraduate Admissions collaborates with more than 500 non-profit/community-based organizations nationwide, such as QuestBridge and College Horizons, to improve college access and opportunity. The Multicultural Recruitment Committee (MRC), a student volunteer group, assists Admissions to recruit a vibrant and dynamic first-year class.

ACCESS Multicultural Fly-In Program

The Columbia Engineering Experience (CE^2) invites applications from under-represented students nationwide to attend a funded, 3-day overnight program exposing them to The Fu Foundation School of Engineering and Applied Science.

OPPORTUNITY Columbia is Affordable

Columbia meets 100% of the demonstrated financial need for all students, for all four years of study. Columbia has eliminated loans for all students receiving financial aid, whatever their family income, and replaced them with university grants. Students whose parents' calculated incomes are below $60,000 (with typical assets) are not expected to contribute any of their income or assets to tuition, room, board or mandatory fees, while families with calculated incomes between $60,000 and $100,000 and typical assets have a significantly reduced parent contribution. Students may also apply for additional funding to support study abroad, research, internship and community service opportunities.

SUCCESS Academic Success Programs (ASP)

Through a network of comprehensive programs and services, ASP provides transitional programming, tutoring, skill-building seminars, educational and personal advising and mentoring to students. Academic Success Programs include Opportunity Programs, The Higher Education Opportunity Program (HEOP), National Opportunity Program (NOP) and the Ronald E. McNair Post-Baccalaureate Achievement Program (McNair Fellows Program), among others.

SUCCESS Office of Multicultural Affairs (OMA)

Responding to the needs of its diverse undergraduate student body, OMA oversees programming in the areas of critical intellectual inquiry, mentoring, advocacy, social justice and intercultural programming, leadership development and training, diversity education and training and cultural and identity-based student organization advising. Of particular note are the heritage months that this office helps to run, which provide awareness campaigns focused on the Latino, African-American, Native American and Asian Pacific communities.

Columbia University
212 Hamilton Hall, MC 2807
1120 Amsterdam Avenue
New York, NY 10027
Ph: (212) 854-2522
ugrad-ask@columbia.edu
www.columbia.edu

FAST FACTS

STUDENT PROFILE

# of degree-seeking undergraduates	5,888
% male/female	52/48
% African American	12
% American Indian or Alaska Native	2
% Asian or Pacific Islander	19
% Hispanic	15
% White	33
% International	12
% Pell grant recipients	15.7

First-generation and minority alumni Barack Obama, President of the United States; Constance Bake Motley, first African-American woman elected to New York State Senate; David Paterson, governor, New York; Kiran Desai, Booker Prize winning author; Langston Hughes, poet; Ben Jealous, youngest President and CEO of the National Association for the Advancement of Colored People (NAACP)

ACADEMICS

full-time faculty	1,444
full-time minority faculty	n/a
student-faculty ratio	6:1
average class size	10-19
% first-year retention rate	99
% graduation rate (6 years)	96

Popular majors Political Science, Economics, Engineering, English, History, Biology

CAMPUS LIFE

% live on campus (% freshmen)	95 (99)

Multicultural student clubs and organizations Accion Boricua, African Students Association, Arab Students' Organization (Turath), Black Students Organization, Caribbean Students Association, Chicano Caucus, Chinese Students and Scholars Association, Korean Students Association, Native American Council, Organization of Pakistani Students, Taiwanese American Students Association, United Students of Color Council, Vietnamese Student Association

Athletics NCAA Division I, Eastern College Athletic Conference (ECAC), Ivy League

ADMISSIONS

# of applicants	34,929
% accepted	7
# of first-year students enrolled	1,391
SAT Critical Reading (middle 50%)	690-780
SAT Math (middle 50%)	700-790
SAT Writing (middle 50%)	690-780
ACT (middle 50%)	31-34
average HS GPA	n/a
Deadlines	
early decision	11/1
regular decision	1/1
application fee (online)	$80 ($80)
fee waiver for applicants with financial need	yes

COST & AID

tuition	$43,088
room & board	$11,020
total need-based institutional scholarships/grants	$92,000,000
% of students apply for need-based aid	73
% of students receive aid	60
% receiving need-based scholarship or grant aid	50
% receiving aid whose need was fully met	100
average aid package	$38,356
average student loan debt upon graduation	n/a

The Cooper Union for the Advancement of Science and Art

The Cooper Union for the Advancement of Science and Art is an all honors private college that occupies a singular place in America's educational and social landscape. Established in 1859, Cooper Union has a long tradition of giving all of their students full tuition scholarships to ensure that they are able to afford their education. It is located in a vibrant urban setting and boasts a low student to faculty ratio and small class sizes, which facilitate strong working relationships between students and their professors. The Cooper Union's graduates, with a rigorous education in architecture, art or engineering, become the visionary thinkers, creators and innovators who change the world in the service of humankind.

ACCESS The Saturday Program

Each year over 200 New York City public high school students enroll in Saturday Program for classes in Drawing, Graphic Design, Painting, Sculpture, Sound Composition, Architecture and Portfolio Preparation. All classes combine 'hands on' studio work, with free classroom supplies included. The program also offers creative writing workshops and field trips to cultural sites. The Saturday Program accepts students from New York City Public High Schools, grades 9-12.

ACCESS The Outreach Program

The Outreach Program is a full scholarship, year-round program for New York City area high school students, grades 10-12, and is ideal preparation for students interested in pursuing a degree in art. Studio classes include: introduction to drawing, printmaking, photography, two-dimensional design, three-dimensional design, as well as courses that investigate creative writing and contemporary art issues.

ACCESS Summer Research Internship Program

The School of Engineering's Research Internship Program provides a great opportunity for high school students to tackle research problems in a college setting. Interns work in teams comprising of both high school sophomores and juniors on applied research projects under the constant guidance of Cooper Union undergraduate teaching assistants. The program is for New York City high school students only. There is an application process, but the program is free for those who are admitted.

OPPORTUNITY Full Tuition Scholarship

While the published tuition at Cooper Union is $37,500 per year, dating back to the school's founding 150 years ago, every admitted student receives a full tuition scholarship and is not responsible for tuition-related costs. Cooper Union students are still responsible for living and miscellaneous expenses, yet financial aid is available based on need.

OPPORTUNITY Art Portfolio Review Days

Four Art Portfolio Review Days are offered in November and early December where students can show their portfolio. This allows students to learn more about the school, meet the professors, go on a guided tour of the campus, and have a personal meeting with an alum or faculty member to look over their art portfolio.

OPPORTUNITY Engineering Open House Program

In mid-November students can visit campus to tour, meet with faculty members and current students to learn more about engineering. This allows students to get a feel for what would be expected from them in a college engineering program.

SUCCESS Center for Writing at Cooper Union

The Center for Writing at Cooper Union is a resource for all students, staff and faculty at the Cooper Union, offering many different kinds of programming and support in the areas of written and spoken communication.

The Cooper Union for the Advancement of Science and Art
30 Cooper Square, 3rd Floor
New York, NY 10003
Ph: (212) 353-4120
admissions@cooper.edu
cooper.edu

FAST FACTS

STUDENT PROFILE

# of degree-seeking undergraduates	910
% male/female	63/37
% African American	7
% American Indian or Alaska Native	1
% Asian or Pacific Islander	25
% Hispanic	10
% White	41
% International	18
% Pell grant recipients	19

First-generation and minority alumni Daniel Libeskind R,'70, International Architect and designer; Whitfield Lovell Art '81, Painter/Installation Artist, 2007 MacArthur Fellow, winner of The Augustus Saint-Gaudens Award at Cooper Union; Roy DeCarava Art '40, American Photographer, Winner of the Guggenheim Fellowship, Awarded National Medal of Arts in 2006; Simon Lok, '97, founder, chief scientist of Lok Technology, Inc

ACADEMICS

full-time faculty	55
full-time minority faculty	8
student-faculty ratio	8:1
average class size	20
% first-year retention rate	94
% graduation rate (6 years)	85

Popular majors Architecture, Art and Engineering are our fields of study

CAMPUS LIFE

% live on campus (% freshmen)	25 (85)

Multicultural student clubs and organizations National Society of Black Engineers (NSBE), Society of Hispanic Engineers (SHPE), Society of Women Engineers (SWE), Black Student Union, Chinese Students Association, Enclave , Korean Association, South Asia Society, Hillel, Muslim Students Association

Athletics NCAA Division III, Hudson Valley Athletic Conference (HVAC)

ADMISSIONS

# of applicants	3,354
% accepted	8
# of first-year students enrolled	214
SAT Critical Reading (middle 50%)	610-730
SAT Math (middle 50%)	610-780
SAT Writing (middle 50%)	620-740
ACT (middle 50%)	29-33
average HS GPA	3.6
Deadlines	
early decision	12/1
regular decision	1/6-Art, 1/9-Architecture, 2/1-Engineering
application fee (online)	$65 ($65)
fee waiver for applicants with financial need	yes

COST & AID

tuition	$37,500
room & board	$13,700
total need-based institutional scholarships/grants	$5,000
% of students apply for need-based aid	45
% receiving need-based scholarship or grant aid	31
% receiving aid whose need was fully met	47
average aid package	$42,500
average student loan debt upon graduation	$11,037

Cornell University

Founded in 1865 as both a private, co-educational university and the land-grant institution of New York State, Cornell University has a history of egalitarian excellence and diversity. Cornell educates leaders of tomorrow and extends the frontiers of knowledge in order to serve society. The university community fosters personal discovery, growth, scholarship and creativity, and engages men and women from every segment of society. Valuing enrichment of the mind, Cornell pursues understanding and knowledge beyond the barriers of ideology and disciplinary structure.

ACCESS Encourage Young Engineers and Scientists (EYES)

Encourage Young Engineers & Scientists is a community-service organization committed to promoting engineering and the sciences as career fields and to increasing the math and science skills of elementary, middle and high school students. Each year, teams of Cornell students create exciting, project-based math and science lessons and experiments that are taught at local schools and after-school programs. These programs encourage local youth to pursue academic success.

ACCESS Let's Get Ready!

Cornell's "Let's Get Ready!" program mobilizes those who live and work around disadvantaged students to actively support education. It provides free SAT preparation courses and college/financial aid advising to underserved high school students, and it involves families, schools, churches and businesses in offering these services. College students from surrounding communities run the programs and serve as instructors, role models and mentors to the students, helping them to navigate the college admissions process.

OPPORTUNITY Diversity Hosting

To encourage multicultural students to matriculate to Cornell, the University sponsors Diversity Hosting. This admitted student program occurs throughout April to offer students the chance to "get to know" Cornell. Diversity Hosting provides limited transportation to participants and families are welcome.

OPPORTUNITY Higher Education Opportunity Program (HEOP)

Cornell offers both a Higher Education Opportunity Program and an Education Opportunity Program. Both are programs for New York State residents who possess neither the traditional academic profile nor the financial means to afford college, but who do have the potential for success in a competitive academic environment. Students accepted under the EOP/HEOP programs receive academic counseling, assistance completing the financial aid application, and a financial aid package to make a Cornell education affordable.

SUCCESS Office of Academic Diversity Initiatives (OADI)

Cornell's Office of Academic Diversity Initiatives facilitates academic and personal adjustment to Cornell for the minority community. It encourages institutional change, when necessary, to ensure that the University embraces its diverse student population. The Office also offers referrals to campus-wide services, announcements of events and scholarships, and a student-produced yearbook.

SUCCESS The Learning Strategies Center

Providing tutoring and supplemental courses in biology, chemistry, economics, mathematics and physics, the Learning Strategies Center is the central academic support unit for Cornell students. Semester long courses, workshops, individual consultations and website resources offer assistance in improving general study skills. From time management to exam preparation, the center is a vital resource in helping students to develop effective learning strategies.

Cornell University
Undergraduate Admissions Office
410 Thurston Ave.
Ithaca, NY 14850-2488
Ph: (607) 255-5241
admissions@cornell.edu
www.cornell.edu

FAST FACTS

STUDENT PROFILE

# of degree-seeking undergraduates	13,935
% male/female	50/50
% African American	5
% American Indian or Alaska Native	1
% Asian or Pacific Islander	16
% Hispanic	8
% White	46
% International	9
% Pell grant recipients	16

First-generation and minority alumni
Toni Morrison, winner, Nobel Prize for Literature; Jimmy Smits, actor; Mae Jamisen M.D., astronaut; Ed Lu, astronaut; Derrick Harmon, professional football player

ACADEMICS

full-time faculty	1,638
full-time minority faculty	284
student-faculty ratio	9:1
average class size	n/a
% first-year retention rate	96
% graduation rate (6 years)	93

Popular majors Biological Sciences, Economics, Business, English, Engineering

CAMPUS LIFE

% live on campus (% freshmen)	57 (100)

Multicultural student clubs and organizations
African, Latino, Asian, Native American Programming Board (ALANA), Alpha Kappa Alpha, Asian & Asian-American Forum, Asian Pacific Americans for Action, Association of Students of Color, Baraka Kwa Wimbo Gospel Ensemble, The Black Cornellian Woman, Black Students United Caribbean Students Association, Chinese Student Association, Delta Sigma Theta, Filipino Association, Ghanaians at Cornell, Haitian Students Association, Kappa Alpha Psi, Lambda Pi Chi, Lambda Theta Alpha, Lambda Theta Phi, Men of Color Council, Mexican Students Association at Cornell, Minorities in Agriculture, Minority Business Students Association, Minority Industrial and Labor Relations Student Organization

Athletics NCAA Division I, Ivy League, Eastern College Athletic Conference (football I-AA), Eastern Intercollegiate Wrestling Association

ADMISSIONS

# of applicants	36,338
% accepted	18
# of first-year students enrolled	3,178
SAT Critical Reading (middle 50%)	640-730
SAT Math (middle 50%)	670-770
SAT Writing (middle 50%)	n/a
ACT (middle 50%)	29-33

Deadlines

early decision	11/1
regular decision	1/2
application fee (online)	$75 ($75)
fee waiver for applicants with financial need	yes

COST & AID

tuition	in-state $25,401; out-of-state $41,541
room & board	$13,154
total need-based institutional scholarships/grants	$192,281,189
% of students apply for need-based aid	56
% of students receive aid	49
% receiving need-based scholarship or grant aid	49
% receiving aid whose need was fully met	100
average aid package	$37,425
average student loan debt upon graduation	$20,648

Daemen College

Daemen is a private, nonsectarian, co-educational, comprehensive college. Its attractive suburban location offers convenient access to metropolitan Buffalo, Niagara Falls, and nearby Canada. Daemen has achieved a creative balance between providing career preparation and education in the liberal arts. Programs in the major and the competency-based core curriculum encourage students to expand their horizons beyond the classroom through internships, service-learning, clinical and field experiences, collaborative research with faculty, and global education opportunities. The Core Curriculum is designed to develop students' skills and competencies in seven areas that will benefit them personally and professionally throughout their lives. Daemen College seeks students from diverse backgrounds, experiences and socio-economic circumstances that exemplify the following qualities: academic achievement, vision for self and society, enthusiasm and inspiration, academic and personal discipline and leadership ability.

"I chose Daemen because of the scholarship opportunities and the Business Administration program. The best part of being a student at Daemen is the accessibility and availability of my advisor, the professors and faculty. They have had a tremendous impact on my academic success."

– Roberto S., '12
Manhattan, NY
Business Administration: Human Resource Management

ACCESS The Arthur O. Eve Higher Education Opportunity Program (HEOP)

The Arthur O. Eve (HEOP) summer program is an intensive five-week program that provides students from New York State information on orientation and life at Daemen, testing and evaluation and a rigorous educational experience designed to promote sound study skills and reinforce basic skills for success in college and their future careers.

ACCESS College Summit

Daemen hosts College Summit workshops to help students overcome significant obstacles to college, including low income and lack of home support. Students have the potential for college achievement, but each lacks the support and know-how to allow them to successfully navigate the higher education admissions process.

OPPORTUNITY Vision

Vision students must apply for State and Federal financial aid including student loans. Daemen College then contributes a special grant to assist in tuition payment. Vision students receive a voucher each semester to use towards books.

SUCCESS The Learning Center

The office employs a staff of professional coaches, supplemented by successful student coaches, who assist students in mastering required course work.

SUCCESS Academic Support Services

The Academic Advisement office provides assistance to all Daemen students regarding academic planning and college success skills.

SUCCESS The Peer Mentor Program

The Peer Mentor program at Daemen College places an experienced student in each section of the freshmen seminar Critical Relationships (IND 101), the College's first-year experience course. Peer Mentors are available to freshmen students both in and out of class for support during their transition to college.

SUCCESS Early Alert

Students are monitored closely on their progress particularly within the first and second semesters of college. Daemen's early alert system allows intervention by faculty and academic support staff to prevent what could become a problem in the future.

Daemen College
4280 Main Street
Amherst, New York 14226
Ph: (716) 839-8225
admissions@daemen.edu
www.daemen.edu

FAST FACTS

STUDENT PROFILE

# of degree-seeking undergraduates	2,095
% male/female	26/74
% African American	13
% American Indian or Alaska Native	<1
% Asian or Pacific Islander	2
% Hispanic	3
% White	74
% International	2
% Pell grant recipients	41

First-generation and minority alumni Dr. Nedra Harrison, General Surgeon, Scottsdale Healthcare-Shea; Luis A. Santiago, Owner/Agent, State Farm Insurance, Brenda J. Stitt, Owner/Agent, Allstate Insurance; Christopher O'Neal, Site Coordinator for The Leadership Program in NY, NY; Elida Alvarez, Case Manager of TASA (Teenage Services Program)

ACADEMICS

full-time faculty	111
full-time minority faculty	9
student-faculty ratio	15:1
average class size	18
% first-year retention rate	77
% graduation rate (6 years)	39

Popular majors Business Administration, Education, Nursing, Physical Therapy, Physician Assistant, Psychology, Social Work

CAMPUS LIFE

% live on campus (% freshmen)	37 (60)

Multicultural student clubs and organizations Brother-to-Brother, Sister-to-Sister, Multi-Cultural Association, Step Team, Greek Life, Cynergy
Athletics NAIA, American Mid-East Conference

ADMISSIONS

# of applicants	2,316
% accepted	61
# of first-year students enrolled	443
SAT Critical Reading (middle 50%)	444-560
SAT Math (middle 50%)	470-580
SAT Writing (middle 50%)	430-550
ACT (middle 50%)	21-25
average HS GPA	3.6
Deadlines	
early decision	n/a
regular decision	rolling
application fee (online)	$0 ($0)
fee waiver for applicants with financial need	yes

COST & AID

tuition	$21,800
room & board	$10,300
total need-based institutional scholarships/grants	$3,279,170
% of students apply for need-based aid	93
% receiving need-based scholarship or grant aid	92
% receiving aid whose need was fully met	32
average aid package	$20,400
average student loan debt upon graduation	$27,444

Dowling College

Dowling College
150 Idle Hour Blvd.
Oakdale, NY 11769
Ph: (800) DOWLING (369-5464)
admissions@dowling.edu
www.dowling.edu

Dowling College is an independent comprehensive educational institution in the liberal arts tradition whose mission is to provide students with a well-rounded education based upon innovative teaching, informed and engaging research, and a commitment to democratic citizenship with a community service component. Dowling's Schools of Arts and Sciences, Aviation, Business, and Education emphasize excellence in teaching. They offer a challenging curriculum where students and teachers actively engage one another in developing ideas and bringing them to fruition. Dowling's campus promotes individualism and celebrates diversity with a wealth of international students.

OPPORTUNITY Higher Education Opportunity Program (HEOP)

The HEOP has a thirty year longevity and has as its goal the provision of educational opportunity for students who are New York State residents and do not meet the traditional academic profile nor have the economic ability to meet educational expenses. This support services program that offers tutoring, financial literacy, and personal counseling coupled with the student's desire to excel is the perfect combination for potential success.

"The one-on-one interaction with faculty and staff truly helped me navigate my way to success!"

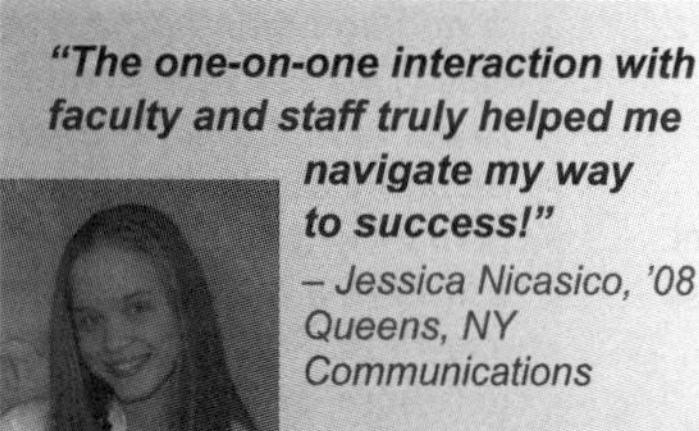

*– Jessica Nicasico, '08
Queens, NY
Communications*

SUCCESS Academic Support Service Center (ASSC)

The mission of the ASSC is to provide a network of academic resources and programs that assist the student through the rigors of academic coursework, thereby maximizing success. This office has oversight of several retention strategies designed to give students accurate and frequent feedback regarding academic progress. Coupled with the Office of Student Services, students are mentored and guided by the liaison between staff and faculty.

SUCCESS Student Support Services (SSS)

Student Support Services (SSS) is a federally funded support services program designed to offer educational opportunity to first generation students. SSS offers an array of services including academic counseling, career counseling, academic advising, financial aid services, and cultural enrichment in an environment that is confidential, professional, supportive, friendly and caring.

SUCCESS Center for Minority Teacher Development and Training (CMTDT)

The CMTDT is a preparation program for high school and college students desiring a career in the teaching profession. Specifically, the Center seeks to identify minority students who are interested in teaching, increase the number of minority teachers locally, regionally and nationally and enhance the quality and effectiveness of instruction for diverse student populations.

FAST FACTS

STUDENT PROFILE

# of degree-seeking undergraduates	3,351
% male/female	45/55
% African American	9
% American Indian or Alaska Native	<1
% Asian or Pacific Islander	4
% Hispanic	8
% White	56
% International	6
% Pell grant recipients	n/a

First-generation and minority alumni Sandra J. Brewster-Walker '72, President, L & P International and CEO, Caretakers; Dr. Kevin Bedell '71, Vice Provost for Research and John H. Rourke Professor of Physics, Boston College; Kevin R. Bland '03, Special Agent, Air Force Office of Special Investigations; Gerald J. Curtin '71, CEO, Statewide Roofing, Inc.; Rosalind O'Neal '06, Founder and CEO, African-American/Caribbean Education Associates, Inc.

ACADEMICS

full-time faculty	121
full-time minority faculty	14
student-faculty ratio	17:1
average class size	15
% first-year retention rate	67
% graduation rate (6 years)	36

Popular majors Education, Aviation, Business, Psychology

CAMPUS LIFE

% live on campus (% freshmen)	7 (11)

Multicultural student clubs and organizations International Club, Students Taking a New Direction, La Familia, Overdrive Dance Project, Humanitarian Club

Athletics NCAA Division II, East Coast Conference (EAC)

ADMISSIONS

# of applicants	2,164
% accepted	86
# of first-year students enrolled	544
SAT Critical Reading (middle 50%)	390-510
SAT Math (middle 50%)	400-530
SAT Writing (middle 50%)	n/a
ACT (middle 50%)	n/a
average HS GPA	2.67

Deadlines

regular decision	rolling
application fee (online)	$35 ($35)
fee waiver for applicants with financial need	yes

COST & AID

tuition	$24,118
room & board	$10,200
total need-based institutional scholarships/grants	n/a
% of students apply for need-based aid	73
% receiving need-based scholarship or grant aid	88
% receiving aid whose need was fully met	n/a
average aid package	$15,077
average student loan debt upon graduation	n/a

Fordham University

Fordham University
441 East Fordham Road
Bronx, NY 10458
Ph: (718) 817-4000
enroll@fordham.edu
www.fordham.edu

Founded in 1841, Fordham University is an independent university in the Jesuit tradition. Fordham's undergraduate student body reflects the diversity of the metropolitan area in which the university is located. Students from around the world are attracted to New York's cosmopolitan culture. Whether educated at the Rose Hill campus in the Bronx or the Lincoln Center campus in Manhattan, Fordham students benefit from close contact with a distinguished faculty who teach at the undergraduate, graduate and professional levels. At Fordham, students will acquire the knowledge, skills, confidence and experience to succeed in their chosen fields. Fordham offers a firm foundation and a competitive advantage that makes Fordham students leaders at work and successful in life.

ACCESS **Federal TRiO programs**

Fordham participates in three federally funded TRiO programs—Upward Bound, Talent Search and Student Support Services—that are designed to increase access and success for low-income, first-generation and underserved college students.

"I'm glad I didn't go anywhere else. This is exactly where I want to be. I think that Fordham can help any student achieve their goals—whether you want to be a lawyer, a doctor, a director, anything, Fordham can help you get there, and I think that's unique for a school."

– Joseph Carnevale, FCLC '11

OPPORTUNITY **Merit Scholarships**

The UPS Foundation/Lafarge Endowed Fellowships assist resident students from underrepresented populations who show leadership and academic competence as well as financial need. Candidates are selected by an admissions review committee and receive an average annual award of $7,000 for four years. The Metro Grant is a $6,000 grant awarded to incoming freshmen commuting to Fordham from their permanent residence in New York City or the surrounding areas. It is renewable up to four years for eligible students who continue to commute and maintain satisfactory progress toward their degree. National Merit, Achievement and Hispanic Recognition finalists and semi-finalists who are also in the top 10 percent of their high school classes are considered for a full-tuition award for all four years.

OPPORTUNITY **The Higher Education Opportunity Program (HEOP)**

The Higher Education Opportunity Program (HEOP) provides economically and educationally disadvantaged students from New York state with the possibility of a Fordham education. The HEOP programs at Rose Hill and Lincoln Center provide support services for all incoming, pre-freshmen and continuing students enrolled in the program, including a pre-freshman summer program; tutorial services; academic advisement; career, personal, and financial aid counseling; developmental reading; and selected workshops in various academic and non-academic areas.

SUCCESS **Internship Program and Diversity Networking Career Fair**

The professional achievements of Fordham's graduates arise, in part, from the University's extensive internship program. This highly successful program offers students the opportunity to intern with more than 2,600 of New York's most prestigious employers. More than 600 students participate in internships each year. The Office of Career Services hosts the Diversity Networking Banquet each fall for graduating seniors to connect with employers seeking greater diversity in their workplace. Career Services also supports all undergraduate students and alumni with individual counseling, mock interviews, resume-writing workshops, and advice on graduate school preparation, dining etiquette and other useful skills.

FAST FACTS

STUDENT PROFILE

# of degree-seeking undergraduates	8,106
% male/female	45/55
% African American	5.2
% American Indian or Alaska Native	<1
% Asian or Pacific Islander	8
% Hispanic	14
% Pell grant recipients	25.4

First-generation and minority alumni Denzel Washington, Academy Award-winning actor; Vince Lombardi, NFL Hall of Fame coach; Mary Higgins Clark, bestselling author

ACADEMICS

full-time faculty	699
full-time minority faculty	104
student-faculty ratio	13:1
average class size	22
% first-year retention rate	90.3
% graduation rate (6 years)	79

Popular majors Business, Communications, Psychology, Political Science, Biology, Pre-Professional Programs

CAMPUS LIFE

% live on campus (% freshmen)	55 (76)

Multicultural Student Clubs and Organizations Office of Multicultural Affairs, African Diaspora, Asian Cultural Exchange, International Students Association, Academia Hispana, *El Grito de Lares*

Athletics NCAA Division I, Atlantic 10 Conference, Patriot League (A-10)

ADMISSIONS

# of applicants	27,676
% accepted	51
# of first-year students enrolled	1,895
SAT Critical Reading (middle 50%)	580-670
SAT Math (middle 50%)	580-670
SAT Writing (middle 50%)	570-680
ACT (middle 50%)	26-30
average HS GPA	3.54
Deadlines	
early action	11/1
regular decision	1/15
application fee (online)	$50 ($50)
fee waiver for applicants with financial need	yes

COST & AID

tuition	$39,235
room & board	$14,926
total need-based institutional scholarships/grants	$59,034,963
% of students apply for need-based aid	85
% of students receive aid	74
% receiving need-based scholarship or grant aid	73
% receiving aid whose need was fully met	20
average aid package	$26,057
average student loan debt upon graduation	$33,365

Hamilton College

Originally founded in 1793 as the Hamilton-Oneida Academy, Hamilton has grown to become one of the nation's most highly regarded colleges. The open curriculum gives students the freedom to shape their own liberal arts education within a research and writing-intensive framework. Hamilton believes that its community will confront and engage most rewardingly with the issue of diversity when it is pursued not just as a social issue, but also as an intellectual one. Diversity thereby expands the breadth and augments the rigor of the intellectual life of the college. Woven throughout Hamilton's curriculum is the study of the world's races, cultures, religions and ideologies. Ultimately, the college wants to continue fostering an intellectual atmosphere that reflects its commitment to exploring and acknowledging the significance of different ideas and perspectives. For more information regarding diversity opportunities or resources, please visit www.hamilton.edu/diversity.

ACCESS The Days-Massolo Center

The Days-Massolo Center enhances the academic, intellectual, social, cultural and leadership dimensions of the Hamilton community. Through forums, panels, lectures and other programming, the Days-Massolo Center serves as a central resource for exploring intersections between gender, race, culture, religion, sexuality, socioeconomic class and other facets of human difference.

OPPORTUNITY HEOP and Hamilton College Scholars Program

The Arthur O. Eve Higher Education Opportunity Program, established by the New York State Legislature in 1969, provides access to independent colleges and universities for economically and educationally disadvantaged students. Students enrolled in this program do not meet the institution's traditional admissions profile, but are the top performers from the high schools and academies they may attend. The Hamilton Scholars Program assists students who are ineligible for HEOP due to economic or residential factors but have similar profiles. Students attend summer classes before freshman year and receive support services throughout their time at Hamilton.

"My first year at Hamilton challenged me and taught me a lot about myself in preparation for the future. I had an insightful freshman year."
– Victoria M., '14
Hazel Crest, IL
Geoscience

OPPORTUNITY Posse Foundation

Hamilton participates in the Posse Foundation, a program that brings talented inner-city youth to campus to pursue their academics and to help promote cross-cultural communication. Posse students are nominated by their high school to the program and share a collaborative support system with a special mentor to adjust to campus and college life. Hamilton's Posse Scholars hail from Boston and Miami.

SUCCESS Residential Engagement in Academic Life (REAL)

Residential Engagement in Academic Life is a special housing option open to four groups of 16 freshmen every year. Students live together in South Residence Hall and take one of their four courses in a South seminar room with Hamilton's best teachers. The faculty members who teach in the hall are also academic advisors for the program, so there are increased opportunities for interaction with professors and classmates on a regular basis, which strengthens the connection between students' intellectual and social pursuits during their first year of college.

Hamilton College
Office of Admission
198 College Hill Road
Clinton, NY 13323
Ph: (800) 843-2655
admission@hamilton.edu
www.hamilton.edu

FAST FACTS

STUDENT PROFILE (FOR 2008-2009)

# of degree-seeking undergraduates	1,861
% male/female	47/53
% African American	4
% American Indian or Alaska Native	1
% Asian or Pacific Islander	8
% Hispanic	5
% White	67
% International	5
% Pell grant recipients	14.6

First-generation and minority alumni Mason Ashe, President, Ashe Sports and Entertainment Consulting; Drew S. Days III, Professor of Law, Yale University, and former Solicitor General of the United States; Fabio Freyre, Group Vice President, Corporate Sales and Marketing, Time Inc., former Publisher, *Sports Illustrated*; Robert P. Moses, Leader, Civil Rights Movement, and founder of The Algebra Project, Kamila N. Shamsie, award-winning author

ACADEMICS

full-time faculty	221
full-time minority faculty	38
student-faculty ratio	9:1
average class size	75% have less than 20
% first-year retention rate	95
% graduation rate (6 years)	88

Popular majors Economics, Government, Mathematics, Psychology, Biology and English

CAMPUS LIFE

% live on campus	97

Multicultural student clubs and organizations Asian Culture Society, Black and Latino Student Union, Brothers Organization, International Students Association, Sistah Girls, West Indian and African Alliance

Athletics NCAA Division III, New England Small College Athletic Conference (NESCAC)

ADMISSIONS (BASED ON FALL 2011 APPLICATIONS)

# of applicants	5,265
% accepted	27
# of first-year students enrolled	487
SAT Critical Reading (middle 50%)	640-740
SAT Math (middle 50%)	650-730
SAT Writing (middle 50%)	640-730
ACT (middle 50%)	n/a
average HS GPA	n/a
Deadlines	
early decision	11/15
regular decision	1/1
application fee (online)	$60
fee waiver for applicants with financial need	yes

COST & AID (FOR 2010-2011)

tuition	$41,280
room & board	$10,480
total need-based institutional scholarships/grants	$25,649,043
% of students apply for need-based aid	n/a
% of students receive aid	50
% receiving need-based scholarship or grant aid	50
% receiving aid whose need was fully met	100
average aid package	$33,381
average student loan debt upon graduation	$17,000

Hobart and William Smith Colleges

Hobart and William Smith Colleges
629 S. Main St.
Geneva, NY 14456
Ph: (315) 781-3622
admissions@hws.edu
www.hws.edu

Hobart and William Smith Colleges are a student-centered learning environment, globally focused, grounded in the values of equity and service, developing citizens who will lead in the 21st century. Located at the shore of Seneca Lake in the heart of the Finger Lakes Region, the campus and surrounding community provide an ideal setting for exploring ideas and establishing close and lasting friendships with students, faculty and staff.

> OPPORTUNITY **Academic Opportunity Programs**

The Academic Opportunity Programs, including HEOP and HWS AOP, helps students who are capable but do not have adequate academic background due to limited financial resources. The Academic Opportunity Programs provide students counseling and advising support in academic, financial, social and career. Students admitted through the Academic Opportunity Programs will be required to attend a five-week intensive summer program prior to their freshman year. The program includes courses in English/writing, grammar lab, mathematics and reading/study skills and a social equities class to ensure the student are prepared for college work-load. During their freshman year, students are required to meet their Academic Opportunity Programs advisor at least once a week where all academic works are reviewed and discuss any issues.

> SUCCESS **CTL Programs**

The Center for Teaching and Learning provides a variety of programs available to all Hobart and William Smith students. These programs are designed to enhance the academic experience and assist students in achieving their academic goals. Students who need content-area skills, meet with peer Teaching Fellows in anthropology, biology, chemistry, economics, geoscience, philosophy, physics, psychology, sociology, and Spanish and Hispanic studies. Students who need help with papers can meet by appointment with peer Writing Colleagues or professional writing specialists for individualized support in the writing process. Semester-long Peer Tutoring is also available, individually and in groups, for those students wishing to improve their performance in their coursework.

> SUCCESS **Office of Intercultural Affairs**

Promoting racial and ethnic pluralism by fostering interaction among people of many cultures, ICA provides opportunities for all HWS community members to celebrate their cultural heritage by regularly hosting a variety of cultural events, like Kwanzaa, Ramadan, Hispanic Heritage Month and Women's History Month.

FAST FACTS

STUDENT PROFILE

# of degree seeking undergraduates	2,901
% male/female	42/58
% African American	4
% American Indian or Alaska Native	<1
% Asian or Pacific Islander	3
% Hispanic	3.5
% White	77
% International	2
% Pell grant recipients	15

First-generation and minority alumni Diane-Louise K. Wormley '70, Director of Neighborhood Rehabilitate Initiatives for the University City District in Philadelphia, Penn.; William T. Whitaker, Jr. '73, Emmy Award Winning Correspondent for CBS News; Dr. Sandra A. Rivera '85, Assistant Director for the U.S. International Trade Commission; Horace D. Allen '85, Co-founder, Chief Executive Officer of TeamPact

ACADEMICS

full time faculty	168
full-time minority faculty	n/a
student-faculty ratio	11:1
average class size	17
first-year retention rate	86
% graduation rate (6 yr)	79

Popular majors Economics, Psychology, English Language and Literature, Political Science and Government, Environmental Science

CAMPUS LIFE

% live on campus (% freshmen) 90 (100)

Multicultural student clubs and organizations Asian Student Union, Caribbean Student Association, Chinese Culture Club, Latin American Organization, Native American Student Association, Russian Society, Sankofa: Black Student Union, South Asian Culture Club

Athletics NCAA Division III, Eastern College Athletic Conference (ECAC)

ADMISSIONS

# of applicants	Hobart 2,402; William Smith 2,805
% accepted	Hobart 51; William Smith 60
# of first-year students enrolled	Hobart 233; William Smith 316
SAT Critical Reading (middle 50%)	560-650
SAT Math (middle 50%)	560-650
SAT Writing (middle 50%)	n/a
ACT (middle 50%)	25-28
avg. H.S. GPA	3.49

Deadlines

early decision I	11/15
early decision II	1/1
regular decision	2/1
application fee (online)	$40 ($0)
fee waiver for applicants with financial need	yes

COST & AID

tuition	$39,114
room & board	$10,024
total need-based institutional scholarships/grants	$8,631,058
% of students apply for need-based aid	91
% receiving need-based scholarship or grant aid	79
% receiving aid whose need was fully met	85
average aid package	$34,400
average student loan debt upon graduation	$30,970

Iona College

Iona College
715 North Ave.
New Rochelle, NY 10801
Ph: (914) 633-2502
admissions@iona.edu
www.iona.edu

FAST FACTS

STUDENT PROFILE	
# of degree seeking undergraduates	3,249
% male/female	46/54
% African American	6
% American Indian or Alaska Native	<1
% Asian or Pacific Islander	2
% Hispanic	11
% White	68
% Pell grant recipients	19
ACADEMICS	
full time faculty	183
full time minority faculty	n/a
student-faculty ratio	13:1
average class size	18
first-year retention rate	85
% graduation rate (6 yr)	62

Popular majors Mass Communication, Accounting, Psychology, Finance, Education, Marketing

CAMPUS LIFE	
% live on campus	64

Multicultural student clubs and organizations Council of Multicultural Leaders, Hispanic Organization for Latin Awareness (HOLA), Students of Caribbean Ancestry, Iona College Diversity Collaborative

Athletics NCAA Division I, Metro Atlantic Athletic Conference (MAAC)

ADMISSIONS	
# of applicants	7,313
% accepted	58
# of first-year students enrolled	792
SAT Reading range	540-640
SAT Math (middle 50%)	550-660
SAT Writing (middle 50%)	n/a
ACT (middle 50%)	17-21
avg. H.S. GPA	3.5
Deadlines	
early action	12/1
regular decision	2/15
application fee (online)	$50 ($50)
fee waiver for applicants with financial need	yes
COST & AID	
tuition	$28,192
room & board	$12,154
total need-based institutional scholarships/grants	$4,227,251
% of students apply for need-based aid	97
% of students receive aid	75
% receiving need-based scholarship or grant aid	49
% receiving aid whose need was fully met	29
average aid package	$18,067
average student loan debt upon graduation	$24,213

Dedicated to academic excellence in the tradition of the Christian Brothers, Iona College is a private, Catholic, liberal-arts college located in suburban Westchester County, just minutes north of New York City. At Iona, differences and diversity are viewed as valuable resources. The College is home to various multicultural groups and hosts annual events such as Hispanic Heritage Month Festivities, Black History Month Festivities and Heritage Week. In the rich heritage of the Christian Brothers, Iona College fosters intellectual inquiry and the values of justice, peace and service.

"College is important to me because it affords me opportunities to succeed in what I love to do and shine in an increasingly competitive world. The intellectual growth I have experienced at college has not only prepared me for the working world post-graduation, but has enriched my life as a whole. I chose to earn my degree at Iona College because of its intimate size and opportunity for hands-on assistance, its close proximity to New York City, and its ACEJMC-accredited journalism program."

– Alana R., '10, Warwick, NY Mass Communications/ Journalism

ACCESS Gaining Early Awareness and Readiness for Undergraduate Programs (GEAR UP)

This program aims to significantly increase the number of pre-collegiate low-income students who are prepared to enter and succeed in post-secondary education through academic enhancement, cultural enrichment, social awareness, and parental involvement.

ACCESS The Success Center

Iona students serve as college mentors to elementary and middle school students in this after-school homework help program. The Success Center provides a positive atmosphere that encourages achievement.

ACCESS Science and Technology Entry Program (STEP)

The Science and Technology Entry Program enhances the math, science and technology skills of minority and low-income regional high school students. Its goal is to encourage participating students to continue their education after graduation in the fields of mathematics, science, technology and/or the licensed professions where minorities are traditionally underrepresented.

OPPORTUNITY Today's Students Tomorrow's Teachers (TSTT)

Iona College, in cooperation with Today's Students Tomorrow's Teachers, seeks to attract students from heavily diverse populations in the tri-state area into the teaching profession. Iona offers a half-tuition scholarship to any students who fulfill program requirements during their four years of high school and who gain admission to Iona as education majors.

SUCCESS The Rudin Center

The Rudin Center is an academic support center that provides students at Iona College with a wide array of support services to enable them to become independent self-learners. Working one-on-one or in small groups, the professional staff, graduate assistants and undergraduate tutors help students acquire, improve, review and strengthen skills. The center stresses academic support in areas related to the college core: reading, composition, mathematics, and computer science.

Ithaca College

Located in a small city that boasts an impressive range of cultural activities against a stunning backdrop of waterfalls and gorges, Ithaca is a private, residential college that unites tradition with a dynamic living and learning environment. Resting on the south hill of Ithaca, N.Y., this former music conservatory offers a compelling blend of a liberal arts and professional degree programs. Students may select from among more than 100 degree programs within the college's five schools and its Division of Interdisciplinary and International Studies. From classes taught by expert faculty to exciting internships, co-curricular activities and study abroad, students will find all the opportunities and facilities of a large university on Ithaca's vibrant campus of 6,400 students.

ACCESS Ithaca College – Frederick Douglass Academy Partnership

Through an ambitious access program, Ithaca College and Frederick Douglass Academy, a public middle and high school located in Harlem, N.Y., have forged a productive partnership that focuses on cross-cultural communication and understanding of the educational challenges facing inner-city youth. This partnership provides Ithaca's teacher education students with hands-on teaching experience and encourages them to pursue future careers in urban settings. In turn, the college provides practical support for students with college-bound goals.

OPPORTUNITY Martin Luther King Jr. Scholar Program

Exceptional minority students may apply to Ithaca College's Martin Luther King Jr. Scholar program. Much more than a financial award, this dynamic learning community develops future leaders who are committed to promoting King's legacy of social justice and equality in their personal and professional lives. Scholars engage in an array of seminars, interact with distinguished guests and lecturers and take part in funded international and domestic travel and research. Selected participants receive up to full tuition in aid, with a minimum merit-based scholarship of $18,000.

OPPORTUNITY African, Latino, and Native American (ALANA) Merit Scholarships

These scholarships recognize superior academic achievement and are presented to select entering undergraduate students who are members of an underrepresented group, regardless of their financial need. Scholarships range from $2,000 to $7,000 and may be renewed annually so long as the recipient maintains full-time enrollment, a minimum GPA of 3.0 and satisfactory progress toward a degree. ALANA scholarships are reserved for undergraduate students.

SUCCESS Ithaca Achievement Program (IAP)

Participants in this program are committed to personal and academic success. Underrepresented students who elect to join the Ithaca Achievement Program receive support in both academic and career development. Students may join the program in their first, second, or third year; participants are involved in a broad range of activities to help support their academic goals. Those students in the first year of the program attend the summer institute sponsored by Academic Enrichment Services.

SUCCESS Housing Offering a Multicultural Experience (HOME)

This residential program presents an opportunity for new and returning students to live in a culturally diverse environment. The program offers an excellent residential option for students preparing to study abroad as well as for international students who are living in the United States for the first time.

Ithaca College
953 Danby Road
Ithaca, NY 14850-7000
Ph: (607) 274-3124
admisssions@ithaca.edu
www.ithaca.edu

FAST FACTS

STUDENT PROFILE

# of degree-seeking undergraduates	6,321
% male/female	44/56
% African American	3
% American Indian or Alaska Native	<1
% Asian or Pacific Islander	3
% Hispanic	6
% White	74
% International	2
% Pell grant recipients	16

First-generation and minority alumni Sandra Pinckney, host of Food Finds, Food Network; CCH Pounder, Emmy-nominated actress, star of The Shield; Erica Reynolds, president/CEO of Moka Marketing, LLC; Edgardo Rivera, investment advisor at Gold State Capital LLC and former vice president of marketing, J Records

ACADEMICS

full-time faculty	473
full-time minority faculty	47
student-faculty ratio	12:1
average class size	17
% first-year retention rate	86
% graduation rate (6 years)	77

Popular majors Business Administration, Communications, Health Sciences and Human Performance, Music, Theater Arts

CAMPUS LIFE

% live on campus (% freshmen)	70 (99)

Multicultural student clubs and organizations African-Latino Society, Amani Gospel Singers, Asian Culture Club, Brothers For Brothers, Ithaca Achievement Program, KUUMBA Repertory Theater, Martin Luther King Scholars, Native American Cultural Club, Sister 2 Sister

Athletics NCAA Division III, Eastern College Athletic Conference (ECAC)

ADMISSIONS

# of applicants	13,191
% accepted	69
# of first-year students enrolled	1,617
SAT Critical Reading (middle 50%)	530-640
SAT Math (middle 50%)	530-630
SAT Writing (middle 50%)	530-630
ACT (middle 50%)	n/a
average HS GPA	n/a

Deadlines

early decision	11/1
regular decision	2/1
application fee (online)	$60 ($60)
fee waiver for applicants with financial need	yes

COST & AID

tuition	$35,278
room & board	$12,854
total need-based institutional scholarships/grants	$68,638,883
% of students apply for need-based aid	78
% of students receive aid	69
% receiving need-based scholarship or grant aid	67
% receiving aid whose need was fully met	49
average aid package	$28,737
average student loan debt upon graduation	n/a

Long Island University – Brooklyn Campus

Expressed in its still-relevant motto "Urbi et Orbi," the mission of Long Island University since 1926 has been to open the doors of the city and the world to men and women of all ethnic and socioeconomic backgrounds. The institution's mission is to awaken, enlighten and expand the minds of its students. As the original unit of Long Island University, the Brooklyn Campus has enrolled and educated generation after generation of students from varied, yet primarily urban backgrounds. Like their predecessors, many of today's students are new to America and new to the English language and often are the first in their families to seek a college education. At the Brooklyn Campus, students find an academic community where cultural, ethnic, religious, racial, sexual and individual differences are respected and where commonalities are affirmed.

ACCESS **Gaining Early Awareness and Readiness for Undergraduate Programs (GEAR UP)**

Through GEAR UP, the Brooklyn Campus helps hundreds of students annually to develop the skills necessary to gain acceptance into the colleges of their choice, while engaging families in their student's educational progress. Participants have the opportunity to develop academically, prepare for the SAT, visit colleges, attend financial aid workshops, go on cultural outings and plan for future careers.

"Long Island University's Brooklyn Campus is like none other. Through the office of Career Services I landed an internship that allowed me to work on a music video set with Wyclef Jean. Being with a student every step of the way isn't just a motto for LIU's Brooklyn Campus; it's a pledge."

– Rich T., '12, The Bronx, NY Psychology

ACCESS **Summer Bridge Program**

The Summer Bridge Program is an intensive learning experience for high school students between their junior and senior years, allowing participants to earn three college credits while developing five critical skills: writing, speaking, critical thinking, research and creativity. After completion, students are eligible to enroll in two tuition-free college courses during the regular academic year.

ACCESS **Liberty Partnership Program**

The aim of the Liberty Partnership College Readiness dropout prevention program is to motivate students and prepare them to finish high school, attend college and find employment. Through this program the Brooklyn Campus annually provides nearly 200 students and their families with services such as high school and college prep counseling, tutoring and workshops.

OPPORTUNITY **Arthur O. Eve Higher Education Opportunity Program (HEOP)**

The Arthur O. Eve Higher Education Opportunity Program (HEOP) provides a wide range of services for New York State students who have a strong desire to earn a college degree but would not otherwise be able to attend college due to economic or academic circumstances. The HEOP office provides personalized attention to students throughout their college careers along with tutoring, financial assistance and course counseling.

SUCCESS **Office of First Year Programs**

The Office of First Year Programs, part of the Office of Student Development and Retention (OSDR), provides all new students with a supportive community through specialized advising, exploration communities and orientation programs. Welcome Week and the Orientation Seminar help students begin college with a strong foundation for success.

SUCCESS **Plan for Academic Success (PAS)**

The Plan for Academic Success (PAS) is a program dedicated to providing students with personalized attention and one-on-one academic counseling by a professional adviser. Throughout the academic year, PAS students receive workshops, advisement sessions and mentorship opportunities for academic achievement.

Long Island University - Brooklyn Campus
1 University Plaza
Brooklyn, NY 11201
Ph: (718) 488-1011
admissions@brooklyn.liu.edu
www.liu.edu/brooklyn

FAST FACTS

STUDENT PROFILE

# of degree seeking undergraduates	5,103
% male/female	29/71
% African American	38
% American Indian or Alaska Native	n/a
% Asian or Pacific Islander	22
% Hispanic	13
% White	27
% International	8
% Pell grant recipients	58

First-generation and minority alumni Ray Ramirez '86, Head Athletic Trainer, New York Mets; Velma Scantlebury-White '77, first African-American female transplant surgeon; Daniel "Danny" Simmons '85, Founder, Def Poetry Jam on HBO

ACADEMICS

full time faculty	309
full-time minority faculty	34
student-faculty ratio	14:1
average class size	20
first-year retention rate	64
% graduation rate (6 yr)	18

Popular majors Pharmacy, Nursing, Psychology, Business Management, Biology

CAMPUS LIFE

% live on campus (% freshmen)	15 (28)

Multicultural student clubs and organizations Model UN Club, Skittles Entente (GLBTQ), Students for Humanity Society, Women in Power, Helping Hands, International Students Organization

Athletics NCAA Division I, Northeast Conference

ADMISSIONS

# of applicants	9,535
% accepted	43
# of first-year students enrolled	899
SAT Critical Reading (middle 50%)	380-490
SAT Math (middle 50%)	390-520
SAT Writing (middle 50%)	n/a
ACT (middle 50%)	17-21
average H.S. GPA	75

Deadlines

early decision	2/1
regular decision	rolling
application fee (online)	$40 ($0)
fee waiver for applicants with financial need	yes

COST & AID

tuition	$938/credit
room & board	$12,200
total need-based institutional scholarships/grants	$4,386,079
% of students apply for need-based aid	93
% receiving need-based scholarship or grant aid	94
% receiving aid whose need was fully met	46
average aid package	$15,300
average student loan debt upon graduation	$41,000

Manhattan College

Manhattan College, overlooking Van Cortlandt Park in Riverdale, is an independent Catholic college which embraces qualified men and women of all faiths, races and ethnic backgrounds. Established in 1853, the College is founded upon the Lasallian tradition of excellence in teaching, respect for individual dignity, and commitment to social justice. Today Manhattan College maintains that tradition by providing scholarships and financial aid to many students who are the first in their family to attend college and by keeping tuition reasonably priced for all. Add to that exceptional academic programs and values-based Catholic education that nurture the whole student—some of the significant differences that make a Manhattan education one-of-a-kind—and you have a standard of excellence in education.

ACCESS CollegeBound Initiative (CBI)

The CollegeBound Initiative is a school-based college guidance program that helps students in inner-city public schools reach their potential and attend college. Manhattan's partnership with CBI, beginning in fall 2011, represents the College's commitment to educating first-generation college students rooted in Manhattan's Lasallian Catholic traditions. The CollegeBound Initiative collaborates with public high schools by placing full-time college counselors in the schools to interact with students and make them more aware of the various college options available including financial aid assistance and scholarships. In the next school year, CBI will serve nearly 800 seniors in 13 schools in New York City and Philadelphia. As a university partner with CBI, Manhattan will gain assistance in further diversifying the College's student body, allowing students to receive a first-rate education that they may not have had access to without the program's resources.

"I was the first member of my family to go to college.... The "caring" community which is part of the LaSallian tradition at Manhattan immediately attracted me....One of the wonderful things about our College is that if you want to do something, Manhattan will help you as much as possible."

– Ana A. '11
Chemical Engineering

OPPORTUNITY Scholarship Opportunities for First-Generation and Minority Students

Manhattan College has a variety of scholarships available for first generation and minority students. Among them are the Horan Family Scholarship, established by the late John Horan '40, former CEO and Chairman of Merck and Co., and his wife Julie; and the James Patterson Minority Scholarship, established by famous author James Patterson '69. Admissions and financial counselors are always available to help prospective students with this process.

SUCCESS The Arches

The Arches is a living-learning community within the college that houses roughly one hundred students in East Hill Hall and facilitates these students' transition to college life. Students have access to a classroom and an academic office within their dorm for a close relationship with their faculty. The program involves two courses, English and Religious Studies. This program also provides community service and cultural learning opportunities in New York City to allow the students to give back to and learn more about the New York City community.

Manhattan College
4513 Manhattan College Parkway
Riverdale, NY 10471
Ph: (800) MC2-XCEL (622-9235)
admit@manhattan.edu
www.manhattan.edu

FAST FACTS

STUDENT PROFILE

# of degree seeking undergraduates	2,913
% male/female	53/47
% African American	3
% American Indian or Alaska Native	<1
% Asian or Pacific Islander	3
% Hispanic	12
% White	68
% International	2
% Pell grant recipients	22

First-generation and minority alumni John H. Banks III '85, VP Government Relations/Con Edison; Ronald Ellis '72, Judge in US Federal court; Charles Ntamere '96, Director, Global Customer Experience at American Express; Aliann Pompey '99, Olympic track runner (still running internationally); Jose Serrano, Jr. '95, NYS senator

ACADEMICS

full time faculty	201
full-time minority faculty	27
student-faculty ratio	12:1
average class size	22
first-year retention rate	83
% graduation rate (6 yr)	76

Popular majors Accounting, Chemical Engineering, Communication Studies, Psychology, Secondary Education

CAMPUS LIFE

% live on campus (% freshmen)	60 (81)

Multicultural student clubs and organizations Asian Culture Club, Association for Black Culture, International Student Association, Multi-cultural Student Union, Just Peace, L.O.V.E (Lasallian Outreach Volunteer Experience), National Society of Black Engineers, Society of Hispanic Professional Engineers

Athletics NCAA Division I, Metro Atlantic Athletic Conference (MAAC)

ADMISSIONS

# of applicants	5,766
% accepted	63
# of first-year students enrolled	658
SAT Critical Reading (middle 50%)	490-580
SAT Math (middle 50%)	510-610
SAT Writing (middle 50%)	490-590
ACT (middle 50%)	22-26
average H.S. GPA	3.3
Deadlines	
early decision	11/15
regular decision	rolling
application fee (online)	$60 ($60)
fee waiver for applicants with financial need	yes

COST & AID

tuition	$27,600
room & board	$11,420
total need-based institutional scholarships/grants	$26,153,676
% of students apply for need-based aid	81
% receiving need-based scholarship or grant aid	62
% receiving aid whose need was fully met	13
average aid package	$17,995
average student loan debt upon graduation	$18,911

Marymount Manhattan College

Marymount Manhattan College is an urban, independent, liberal arts college. The mission of the college is to educate a socially and economically diverse student body by fostering intellectual achievement and personal growth and by providing opportunities for career development. Inherent in this mission is the intent to develop an awareness of social, political, cultural and ethnic issues, in the belief that this awareness will lead to concern for, participation in, and improvement of society. To accomplish this mission, the College offers a strong program in the arts and sciences for students of all ages, as well as substantial pre-professional preparation. Central to these efforts is the particular attention given to the individual student. Marymount Manhattan College seeks to be a resource and learning center for the metropolitan community.

OPPORTUNITY **Arthur O. Eve Higher Education Opportunity Program (HEOP)**

Provides supportive services and supplementary financial assistance to students who demonstrate potential for academic success. The Program has been a part of Marymount Manhattan College since 1969.

OPPORTUNITY **Freshman Academic Excellence Awards**

These awards are offered to students with a 3.0 or higher GPA and an SAT of 1150 or higher (Critical Reading and Math). There are also various need based programs to assist students who demonstrate financial need.

SUCCESS **Jump Start**

Jump Start helps students transition smoothly into the college community of Marymount Manhattan College and New York City. Students gain an advantage by experiencing the campus, becoming familiar with academic support services and engaging in a credit-earning course and many cultural activities. In a three-week intensive program of college course work, first-year students earn credit, meet friends, explore cultural offerings of New York City and connect with the Marymount Manhattan College Community.

"When I think of what Marymount has to offer, a quote from Vince Lombardi comes to mind: 'The quality of a person's life is in direct proportion to their commitment to excellence, regardless of their chosen field of endeavor.' This quote is the basic embodiment of what Marymount Manhattan College stands for. Simply put, this school gives us the tools, the help, and the chance to make our lives better no matter what career path we choose."

– Julio R.

Marymount Manhattan College
221 East 71 Street
New York, NY 10021
Ph: (212) 517-0430
admissions@mmm.edu
www.mmm.edu

FAST FACTS

STUDENT PROFILE	
# of degree-seeking undergraduates	2,000
% male/female	25/75
% African American	9
% American Indian or Alaska Native	<1
% Asian or Pacific Islander	4
% Hispanic	14
% White	72
% International	4
% Pell grant recipients	22
ACADEMICS	
full-time faculty	92
full-time minority faculty	11
student-faculty ratio	12:1
average class size	18
% first-year retention rate	68
% graduation rate (6 years)	46
Popular majors Communication Arts, Theatre, Dance, Psychology, Business Management	
CAMPUS LIFE	
% live on campus (% freshmen)	50 (87)
Multicultural student clubs and organizations Bedford Hills College Program Club, Black & Latino Student Association, Global Citizens' Society, Gay-Straight National Alliance Project	
Athletics NCAA Division I, Metro Atlantic Athletic Conference (MAAC)	
ADMISSIONS	
# of applicants	4,000
% accepted	69
# of first-year students enrolled	470
SAT Critical Reading (middle 50%)	430-750
SAT Math (middle 50%)	400-680
SAT Writing (middle 50%)	450-650
ACT (middle 50%)	20-31
average HS GPA	3.2
Deadlines	
regular decision	rolling
application fee (online)	$60($60)
fee waiver for applicants with financial need	yes
COST & AID	
tuition	$24,708
room & board	$14,030
total need-based institutional scholarships/grants	$5,595,877
% of students apply for need-based aid	85
% of students receive aid	85
% receiving need-based scholarship/grant aid	75
% receiving aid whose need was fully met	12
average aid package	$12,334
average student loan debt upon graduation	$16,903

Molloy College

Molloy College, an independent, comprehensive institution, offers a rich and multidimensional educational experience and encourages critical thinking and creative exploration from within a personalized community setting. Moreover, Molloy combines academic excellence and leadership with personal, compassionate mentoring to bring out the best in every student. Molloy College rests on a 30-acre campus in Rockville Centre, Long Island. Established as a women's college in 1955, the institution became co-educational in 1982. Today, Molloy College welcomes men and women diverse in age, race, religious belief and cultural background. In particular, the undergraduate student body, which has grown to nearly 3,000, consists of 58 percent first-generation students and 35 percent minority students.

ACCESS **TRiO Program**

This federally funded program highlights Molloy College's commitment to a quality education for all students regardless of race, ethnic background or economic circumstance. The TRiO Program is open to incoming freshmen or transfer students who are first-generation, low-income, physically challenged, or who have learning disabilities. Services offered by the TRiO Program include academic assessments in reading, writing and mathematics, academic and career advisement, academic support and assistance with admission, financial aid and other applicable Molloy College services. Students benefit from professional mentoring and resources regarding grants, scholarships, volunteer placement, internships and other opportunities.

ACCESS **Mentoring Latinas**

The Mentoring Latinas Program at Molloy College is a project originally designed for Latina students at Mineola High School but now also includes Uniondale's middle schools. Molloy Latina undergraduates mentor high school young women and provide support, friendship and positive role models. Some of the planned activities include visits to the nursing and language labs, art and music departments, and meeting the dance and athletic teams. This program is jointly administered by Molloy's departments of Social Work, Modern Languages, Service-Learning and Advancement. Molloy students also provide mentoring and guidance to children in the Uniondale school district through another program, Molloy Mentors.

SUCCESS **Academic Enrichment (AcE) Program**

AcE helps students achieve their academic potential in mathematics, science and modern languages. The program develops self-confidence and self-esteem, thereby producing rewarding results for the participants, and provides remediation for students with a "C" average in their major course of study. Supplemental help is also provided if a student is passing a course but still needs assistance. Each of the diverse group of professional coaches is either an active or semi-retired teacher certified in the field in which they coach.

SUCCESS **Success Through Expanded Education Program (STEEP)**

STEEP provides the academic assistance needed for those with learning disabilities to reach their full potential. Participants find the learning methods that best help them achieve academic success. Learning disability specialists address particular study habits, help prepare for tests, improve class participation and assist with schedule preparation and course selection. Students develop life skills in time management, their most appropriate learning style, critical-thinking skills, goal setting and stress management.

Molloy College
PO Box 5002
Rockville Centre, NY 11571
Ph: (516) 678-5000
admissions@molloy.edu
www.molloy.edu

FAST FACTS

STUDENT PROFILE

# of degree-seeking undergraduates	3,175
% male/female	23/77
% African American	15
% American Indian or Alaska Native	<1
% Asian or Pacific Islander	7
% Hispanic	11
% White	65
% International	<1
% Pell Grant Recipients	27

ACADEMICS

full-time faculty	169
full-time minority faculty	14
student-faculty ratio	10:1
average class size	15
% first-year retention rate	89
% graduation rate (6 years)	62

Popular majors Nursing, Education, Business Management, Music Therapy, Criminal Justice, Social Work

CAMPUS LIFE

% live on campus	0

Multicultural student clubs and organizations African-American Caribbean Organization, Union Hispana de Molloy, Global Learning Office, Asian Cultural Exchange

Athletics NCAA Division II, East Coast Conference (ECC)

ADMISSIONS

# of applicants	1,803
% accepted	59
# of first-year students enrolled	420
SAT Critical Reading (middle 50%)	390-720
SAT Math (middle 50%)	400-730
SAT Writing (middle 50%)	380-760
ACT (middle 50%)	n/a
average H.S. GPA	3.35

Deadlines

early action	12/1
regular decision	rolling
application fee (online)	$30 ($30)
fee waiver for applicants with financial need	yes

COST & AID

tuition	$22,290
room & board	n/a
total needs-based institutional scholarships/grants	$11,161,094
% of students apply for need-based aid	97
% of students receive aid	80
% receiving need-based scholarships or grant aid	72
% receiving aid whose need was fully met	14
average aid package	$12,007
average student loan debt upon graduation	$22,754

New York University

Founded in 1831, New York University is a large, private, coeducational research university in urban New York City. NYU is known for its dedication to equal access and opportunity, having been one of the first institutions to accept immigrants and women. Located in downtown New York, NYU is the opposite of a typical "bubble" campus: with no walls or gates separating them from the city, NYU students—while living on campus—are truly members of the New York City community.

ACCESS NYU College Access Leadership Institute (NYU-CALI)

NYU College Access Leadership Insitute (NYU-CALI) is a pre-college program offered to rising juniors and seniors in the New York Metro area who come from underrepresented communities or low income families or are the first in their family to attend a 4 year institution. This 4-day residential program is designed to demystify the college application process at no cost to the student. The curriculum includes workshops and small group sessions on college admissions, college-entrance test preparation, essay and resume writing, interviewing and presentation skills, and financial aid literacy. Graduates are expected to act as advocates and ambassadors for higher education and mentors to their peers.

ACCESS NYU Pre-College Summer Program

NYU Pre-College Summer Program offers rising high school juniors and seniors the opportunity to experience academic and student life at NYU by taking college-level courses for academic credit which may be applied to a future degree. Participants take their credit-bearing courses with college students. Additionally students have the opportunity to participate in a free college writing workshop taught by NYU's distinguished writing experts. Limited scholarships are available.

OPPORTUNITY Diversity Open House

Hosted each Fall, Diversity Open House is an on-campus event for prospective students and their families with a focus on promoting and increasing campus diversity. Throughout the day, students engage with faculty, administrators, current students and alumni as they learn more about the resources and opportunities offered at NYU.

OPPORTUNITY Opportunity Programs

NYU has two programs for qualified NYU undergraduates: the Arthur O. Eve Higher Education Opportunity Program (Arthur O. Eve HEOP) and the Collegiate Science Technology Entry Program (CSTEP), which provide a means for traditionally underserved, low-income students from New York State to obtain admission as well as academic and financial support.

SUCCESS Academic Achievement Program (AAP)

AAP is a multi-faceted program designed to develop and enhance the academic and leadership potential of Black, Latino and Native American students. AAP events include discussion sessions and a games day in which students can express their opinions and meet other AAP students. AAP has its own student lounge that serves as a study space and a hangout spot for AAP students. As part of the Big Brothers and Big Sisters Program the AAP freshmen are mentored by upperclassmen to help acclimate them to college life. AAP students also give back to the community by serving as mentors for students at a high school in the South Bronx.

SUCCESS Center for Multicultural Education and Programs (CMEP)

The Center produces intentional and sustained educational initiatives and campus-wide programs in the area of diversity and social justice. Through collaborations with a broad range of students, faculty, administrators and community partners, the Center's efforts are designed to make an institutional impact in enhancing intercultural awareness and offer compelling ways to explore the complex intersection of race, gender, religion, socio-economic class, ethnicity, sexual orientation, national origin and many other aspects of identity in our daily lives.

New York University
Admissions Office
665 Broadway
New York, NY 10012
Ph: (212) 998-4550
admissions.ops@nyu.edu
www.admissions.nyu.edu

FAST FACTS

STUDENT PROFILE	
undergraduate enrollment	21,269
% male/female	38.5/61.5
% African American	4
% American Indian or Alaska Native	<1
% Asian or Pacific Islander	19
% Hispanic	8
% White	48
% International	6
% Pell grant recipients	n/a
ACADEMICS	
full-time faculty	3,949
full-time minority faculty	851
student-faculty ratio	1:12
average class size	Under 30
% first-year retention rate	92
% graduation rate (6 years)	86
CAMPUS LIFE	
% live on campus (% freshmen)	94% first year students living on campus
Athletics NCAA Division III, University Athletic Association (UAA)	
ADMISSIONS	
# of applicants	37,073
% accepted	30
# of first-year students enrolled	4,998
SAT Critical Reading (middle 50%)	650-740
SAT Math (middle 50%)	660-760
SAT Writing (middle 50%)	660-750
ACT (middle 50%)	28-31
average HS GPA	3.7
Deadlines	
early decision	11/1
early decision II	1/1
regular decision	1/1
application fee (online)	$70 ($70)
fee waiver for applicants with financial need	yes
COST & AID	
tuition ($42,075 for Stern School of Business, $45,683 for Tisch School of the Arts)	$41,614
room & board	$15,181
total need-based institutional scholarships/grants	$127,606,900
% of students apply for need-based aid	n/a
% of students receive aid	70
% receiving need-based scholarship/grant aid	70
% receiving aid whose need was fully met	71
average aid package	$27,701
average student loan debt upon graduation	$41,000

Rochester Institute of Technology

Rochester Institute of Technology is one of the world's leading career-oriented, technological institutions. Students are from all 50 states and over 100 countries and have equally as diverse academic interests. Typically, more than one-fifth of entering freshmen come from minority or international student groups. Rochester Institute of Technology's National Technical Institute for the Deaf supports over 1,400 deaf and hard-of-hearing students, adding a social and educational dynamic not found at any other university. The Institute's eight colleges offer more than 90 undergraduate programs in engineering, computing, information technology, engineering technology, photography, business, science, art, design and the liberal arts.

ACCESS National Action Council for Minorities in Engineering (NACME)

RIT is a NACME block grant recipient which provides support for scholarships and academic support services for underrepresented students in the areas of science, technology, engineering and mathematics. In addition, RIT supports collegiate chapters of the National Society of Black Engineers (NSBE), Society of Hispanic Professional Engineers (SHPE) and the American Indian Science and Engineering Society (AISES), as well as many other organizations committed to student success.

OPPORTUNITY Hillside Work-Scholarship Connection (HWSC)

Hillside Work-Scholarship Connection links urban adolescents to a support network of youth advocates and employers. Rochester Institute of Technology commits up to five, $10,000 per year renewable scholarships to students who successfully complete the program and enter the Institute as full-time freshmen, and up to five, $10,000 per year renewable scholarships for students who enter as full-time transfer students from Monroe Community College.

SUCCESS The Upstate Louis Stokes Alliance for Minority Participation

The Upstate Louis Stokes Alliance for Minority Participation (ULSAMP) was formed to attract and maximize the potential of students from underrepresented populations, specifically African-American, Latino American and Native American (AALANA) attending college in Upstate New York who are enrolled in STEM fields. Supported by a grant from the National Science Foundation, the ULSAMP program will work across the alliance of 7 Upstate colleges and universities to increase recruitment and the subsequent graduation rate of both first-time freshmen and transfer students, by enhancing academic experiences and opportunities.

SUCCESS Multicultural Center for Academic Success (MCAS)

Established in 2000 as part of a RIT wide initiative to increase student retention and graduation, MCAS serves all students but primarily exist to retain and graduate African American, Latin American, and Native American (AALANA) students. In addition to being an academic support unit, MCAS emphasizes and supports student development through personal advising, advocacy, leadership development opportunities, cultural diversity education, cultural programming and a connection to campus and community resources. The MCAS Summer Bridge Program is a four-week summer academic enrichment, confidence, and community-building program available to first-year students that consists of credit-bearing courses, enrichment education, exposure to research, and community service programs.

"The Higher Education Opportunity Program (HEOP) program was a critical key to my success at RIT. The program provided me with the academic, social and financial support that enabled me to reach my full potential. It certainly was a cornerstone of my undergraduate career and I am grateful to have been given the opportunity to take advantage of all that RIT has to offer."

– Alvin R., '09
Buffalo, NY
Hospitality and Service Management

Rochester Institute of Technology
60 Lomb Memorial Drive
Rochester, NY 14623-5604
Ph: (585) 475-7424
admissions@rit.edu
www.rit.edu

FAST FACTS

STUDENT PROFILE

# of degree-seeking undergraduates	13,511
% male/female	67/33
% African American	5
% American Indian or Alaska Native	<1
% Asian or Pacific Islander	5
% Hispanic	4
% White	69
% International	10
% Pell grant recipients	25

First-generation and minority alums Dan Loh, Pulitzer Prize winner, photojournalism

ACADEMICS

full-time faculty	961
% full-time minority faculty	16
student-faculty ratio	14:1
average class size	25
% first-year retention rate	92
% graduation rate (6 years)	69

Popular majors Engineering, Computing, Engineering Technology, Business Administration/ Management, Information Technology

CAMPUS LIFE

% live on campus (% freshmen)	68 (95)

Multicultural student clubs and organizations Asian Culture Society, Korean Student Association, Latin American Student Association, Organization of African Students, Organization of the Alliance of Students from the Indian Subcontinent, Taiwanese Student Association, Vietnamese Student Association, Chinese Student Scholar Association

Athletics NCAA Division III, Atlantic Hockey Association (NCAA Division I, m ice hockey only); ECAC West Ice Hockey League (w ice hockey); Liberty League; New York State Women's Collegiate Athletic Association

ADMISSIONS

# of applicants	14,423
% accepted	59
# of first-year students enrolled	2,710
SAT Critical Reading (middle 50%)	540-630
SAT Math (middle 50%)	560-670
SAT Writing (middle 50%)	520-620
ACT (middle 50%)	25-30
average HS GPA	3.5

Deadlines

early decision	12/1
regular decision	rolling
application fee (online)	$50 ($50)
fee waiver for applicants with financial need	yes

COST & AID

tuition	$31,584
room & board	$10,413
total need-based institutional scholarships/grants	$89,346,000
% of students apply for need-based aid	77
% of students receive aid	88
% receiving need-based scholarship or grant aid	83
% receiving aid whose need was fully met	78
average aid package	$17,500
average student loan debt upon graduation	$23,800

St. John's University

For over 140 years, St. John's University has provided access and opportunity for students of diverse economic backgrounds. A Catholic university in the Vincentian tradition of excellence and service, St. John's values the talents of every student. With its New York City location, St. John's also reflects the harmonious diversity of immigrants and minority groups that add to the city's energy. St. John's has three residential New York City campuses; a campus in Oakdale, NY; and campuses in the center of Paris, France and Rome, Italy. More than 95 percent of St. John's students receive in excess of $430 million in financial aid through scholarships, loans, grants and work-study. All new students receive their own wireless laptop computer and benefit from St. John's focus on quality academics, service, global learning, high-tech resources and an outstanding residence life program.

ACCESS **Scholars Program**

St. John's prepares qualified high school students for college. To apply, juniors submit to the Admissions Committee their high school transcripts and recommendations from their principal or counselor. Accepted students take two courses during the summer after their junior year. As seniors, they enroll for one fall and spring college-level course.

"Everyone at St. John's is so encouraging and supportive, I've received all the support I've needed to help me achieve my academic, personal and career goals."

–Audree M, '09
Brooklyn, NY
Criminal Justice and English

ACCESS **GEAR-UP Program**

With the U.S. Department of Education and Higher Education Services Corporation, St. John's offers academic services for lower-income, first-generation students from local middle and high schools, including college tours, tutoring, mentoring, residential summer camp, parent workshops, SAT/PSAT preparation and summer youth employment through the city's Department of Youth and Community Development.

ACCESS **College Bound: Liberty Partnerships Program**

Coordinated with the New York State Department of Education, the program provides support services to middle and senior high school students who demonstrate college potential but need assistance to graduate. Services include counseling, tutoring and enrichment activities.

OPPORTUNITY **Options Program**

St. John's provides academic and financial assistance to eligible students at its Staten Island campus. Qualified students are from out-of-state and demonstrate circumstances that would hinder their attending college. Offered through the Division of Special and Opportunity Programs, the program includes tutoring, mentoring and other services.

SUCCESS **College Science and Technology Entry Program (CSTEP)**

This program prepares New York State residents from underrepresented backgrounds for careers in science, technology, health-related and licensed professions including pharmacy. Selected as freshmen and sophomores, students enjoy career and academic counseling, tutoring and workshops.

SUCCESS **Ronald E. McNair Scholars Program**

Named for the African-American astronaut who perished in the Challenger accident, this Queens-campus program prepares first-generation, low-income students from underrepresented groups for post-baccalaureate and graduate study.

SUCCESS **Mentoring Programs**

All students benefit from mentoring. Count On Alumni for Career Help (C.O.A.C.H.) provides alumni mentors. The Alpha Mentoring Program assigns on-campus peer mentors. Through the University Freshman Center, professional counselors guide freshmen to success.

St. John's University
8000 Utopia Parkway
Queens, NY 11439
Ph: (888) 661-1334
admissions@stjohns.edu
www.stjohns.edu/learnmore/01757.stj

FAST FACTS

STUDENT PROFILE

# of degree-seeking undergraduates	12,211
% male/female	42/58
% African American	13
% American Indian or Alaska Native	<1
% Asian or Pacific Islander	15
% Hispanic	14
% White	44
% International	6
% Pell grant recipients (freshman)	48

First-generation and minority alumni Haron A. Amin, '99C, '05G, ambassador to Japan, Afghanistan Embassy; Louis Carnesecca, '05C, '60GEd, '00HON, former head men's basketball coach, St. John's University; Hon. Charles B. Rangel '60L, '83HON, congressman, New York's 15th District, U.S. House of Representatives; Hon. Reinaldo E. Rivera '76L, associate justice, appellate division, Second Judicial Department, New York State Unified Court System

ACADEMICS

full-time faculty	648
full-time minority faculty	145
student-faculty ratio	19:1
average class size	28
% first-year retention rate	78
% graduation rate (6 years)	58

Popular majors Pharmacy, Liberal Studies, Finance, Psychology, Accounting

CAMPUS LIFE

% live on campus (% freshmen)	30 (48)

Multicultural student clubs and organizations African Students Association, Albanian American College Club, Arab Students United, Asian Students Association, Caribbean Students Association, Chinese Cultural Association, Guyanese Students Association, Indian Sub-Continent Student Organization, Japanese Cultural Association, Korean Students Association, LASO, Organization of Pakistani Students, Polish Students Association, Taiwanese Students Association, Vietnamese Cultural Organization

Athletics NCAA Division I, Big East Conference (BigEast)

ADMISSIONS

# of applicants	54,871
% accepted	45
# of first-year students enrolled	3,117
SAT Critical Reading (middle 50%)	480-590
SAT Math (middle 50%)	490-620
SAT Writing (middle 50%)	n/a
ACT (middle 50%)	n/a
average HS GPA	3.2
Deadlines	
regular decision	rolling
application fee (online)	$50 ($0)
fee waiver for applicants with financial need	yes

COST & AID

tuition	$31,980
room & board	$14,025 avg.
total need-based institutional scholarships/grants	$50,682,149
% of students apply for need-based aid	87
% of students receive aid	79
% receiving need-based scholarship or grant aid	68
% receiving aid whose need was fully met	8
average aid package	$20,524
average student loan debt upon graduation	$21,793

Union College

Founded in 1795, Union College offers programs in the liberal arts and engineering. Union enjoys a rich history, yet keeps an eye to the future. Converging Technologies — interdisciplinary programs which link engineering and the liberal arts — offer students opportunities for courses, programs and research in an increasing number of fields such as nanotechnology, digital art and entrepreneurship. Union also utilizes Minerva, a unique housing system that allows students to interact with each other and with faculty, and affords them space to work, play and even host parties. International study and community service are other strong tenets of a Union education, prompting students to remain engaged with the outside world.

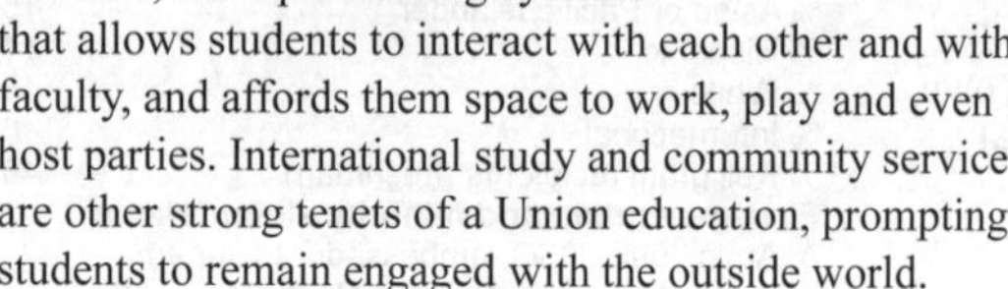

"Union is a welcoming place. It feels like I'm living in a small village. What I like best are the small classes. I can focus. I'm getting to know my professors, and they know my name."

– Gina C., '11
Brighton, MA
Biochemistry, Spanish

ACCESS **Science and Technology Entry Program (STEP)**

Co-sponsored by the New York State Department of Education, STEP helps students in grades seven through 12 from underrepresented and low-income backgrounds to prepare for academic programs in scientific, technical, health-related and licensed professions. Participants receive high-quality instruction in math, science and technology, including academic tutoring, college-level courses for enrichment and opportunities to work on research projects. STEP takes place through workshops offered during the school year, as well as through a summer camp program.

OPPORTUNITY **Multicultural Weekends: Getting to Know "U" (fall) and Represent "U" (spring)**

Prospective students from diverse cultural backgrounds are invited to stay overnight on campus and experience what Union has to offer. The weekends are planned to be informational and to provide hands-on experience with the college process. The programs include cultural and academic-life panel discussions, workshops on applying to college, as well as information on what type of supportive services are offered and should be sought in college.

OPPORTUNITY **Posse Foundation**

Union College participates in the Posse Foundation, a program that brings talented inner-city youth to campus to pursue their academics and to help promote cross-cultural communication. Posse students are nominated by their high school to the program and share a collaborative support system with a special mentor to adjust to campus and college life. Union's Posse Scholars hail from Boston.

OPPORTUNITY **AOP/HEOP Program**

The Academic Opportunity Program, an extension of the New York State Higher Education Opportunity Program, brings approximately 20-25 students to the college who are from academically and financially disadvantaged backgrounds. Participants are talented students who benefit from the financial and academic support services offered through the program such as individual advising, tutoring and full-need financial aid packaging.

SUCCESS **Office of Multicultural Affairs**

In support of the college's strategic plan objectives and institutional goals, the Office of Multicultural Affairs develops and implements diversity leadership programs for the community. Serving as a location for the development and awareness of all campus-wide multicultural programs, the office provides programming assistance for cultural events, LGBTQ programs, religious and multi-faith programs, interdisciplinary studies and other special events.

Union College
Grant Hall, Union College
Schenectady, NY 12308
Ph: (518) 388-6112
admissions@union.edu
www.union.edu

FAST FACTS

STUDENT PROFILE

# of degree-seeking undergraduates	2,150
% male/female	51/49
% African American	5
% American Indian or Alaska Native	<1
% Asian or Pacific Islander	6
% Hispanic	5
% White	78
% International	4
% Pell grant recipients	12

First-generation and minority alumni Allen Sessoms, president, University of the District of Columbia; Robert F. Murray, Jr., chief, Division of Medical Genetics, Dept. of Pediatrics and Child Health, professor of medicine and genetics, Howard University School of Medicine; Jennifer Smith Turner, author, poet

ACADEMICS

full-time faculty	196
full-time minority faculty	21
student-faculty ratio	10:1
average class size	19
% first-year retention rate	93
% graduation rate (6 years)	83

Popular majors Political Science and Government, Psychology, Economics, Mechanical Engineering, History

CAMPUS LIFE

% live on campus (% freshmen)	85 (100)

Multicultural student clubs and organizations African and Latino Alliance of Students, Asian Student Union, Black Student Union, Circulo Estudiantil Latino Americano, Middle Eastern Civilization and Culture Association

Athletics NCAA Division III, Liberty League

ADMISSIONS

# of applicants	4,946
% accepted	42
# of first-year students enrolled	554
SAT Critical Reading (middle 50%)	580-670
SAT Math (middle 50%)	610-700
SAT Writing (middle 50%)	580-680
ACT (middle 50%)	27-30
average HS GPA	3.50

Deadlines

early decision	11/15
regular decision	1/15
application fee (online)	$50 ($0)
fee waiver for applicants with financial need	yes

COST & AID

tuition	$52,329
room & board	$1,136
total need-based institutional scholarships/grants	$30,923,182
% of students apply for need-based aid	61
% of students receive aid	51
% receiving need-based scholarship or grant aid	49
% receiving aid whose need was fully met	97
average aid package	$34,600
average student loan debt upon graduation	$14,652

University of Rochester

The University of Rochester, founded in 1850, is one of the nation's leading private, co-educational, nonsectarian universities. Located near downtown Rochester, the campus offers a balance between urban access and spacious comfort, thus creating a comfortable and unique learning environment. This environment no doubt contributes in part to the academic reputation of the institution: In 2007, the University of Rochester was named one of 25 'New Ivies.' The university's 5,400 undergraduate students enjoy a well-rounded college experience and 96 percent of freshmen return for their sophomore year. In maximizing retention and success among all community members, the University of Rochester offers a breadth of services targeted to the specific needs of minority and first-generation students.

ACCESS National Hispanic Institute (NHI) Lorenzo de Zavala Youth Legislative Session

The Lorenzo de Zavala Youth Legislative Session is designed for students with college and leadership potential. Students learn to see themselves as leaders, and then learn how to become leaders within the context of electoral politics. Participants create their own government, write and pass legislation and collaborate to support community prosperity.

ACCESS Science and Technology Entry Program

The Science and Technology Entry Program serves students enrolled in high school grades eight through 12. In particular, participants come either from economically disadvantaged backgrounds or from groups that are historically underrepresented in scientific, technical, health-related, and licensed professions. The program works to raise participants' interest in the aforementioned fields, thereby encouraging them to join the professional workforce in medicine and the health care professions.

OPPORTUNITY Higher Education Opportunity Program (HEOP) & Early Connection Opportunity (ECO)

The University of Rochester's HEOP and ECO programs are designed to serve students of diverse racial, ethnic and cultural backgrounds. HEOP addresses the specific needs of students who have had economic or educational challenges in high school. For eligible students, the program provides a strong support network, academic advising, personal counseling, and substantial financial assistance. Meanwhile, ECO is designed to help students positively and appropriately establish themselves within the academic setting. The program prepares students for classes, informs them about services and introduces them to social life on campus.

SUCCESS McNair Program

The objective of the McNair Program is to increase the numbers of low-income, first-generation and underrepresented undergraduates who pursue doctoral degrees and go on to careers in research and teaching at the university level. The program prepares students for the rigors of graduate study by providing the opportunity to conduct research under the guidance of faculty mentors. Students accepted to the program attend a series of colloquia, receive training for the Graduate Record Exam and are trained to present the results of their research at university-sponsored and national academic conferences.

"My time at the University of Rochester has been incredible! Through a liberal arts education I have maximized my academic experience to earn a B.A. in Financial Economics, a minor in German, a Management Studies Certificate in conjunction with the Simon School of Business, and an International Relations Certificate. Personally, I have made many great friends through my undergraduate journey; they are people who have influenced me on many aspects. Additionally, I have complemented my academic experience with three challenging internship opportunities in the banking field: Miami, the Middle East, and Wall Street. Following graduation, I plan to earn an MBA in Finance."

– Edgard D., '09
Pembroke Pines, FL
Financial Economics

University of Rochester
300 Wilson Boulevard
Box 270251
Rochester, NY 14627-0251
Ph: (585) 275-3221
admit@admissions.rochester.edu
www.rochester.edu

FAST FACTS

STUDENT PROFILE

# of degree-seeking undergraduates	5,416
% male/female	49/51
% African American	4
% American Indian or Alaska Native	<1
% Asian or Pacific Islander	11
% Hispanic	6
% White	63
% International	9
% Pell grant recipients	20

First-generation and minority alumni Dr. Steven Chu, Nobel Prize winner, physics, and current Secretary of Energy; David Satcher, former U.S. Surgeon General; Kathy Waller, VP and chief of internal audit, Coca-Cola; Brian Roseboro, former Under Secretary of the Treasury; Awista Ayub, founder, the Afghan Youth Sports Exchange, winner, 2006 ESPY Arthur Ashe Courage Award

ACADEMICS

full-time faculty	530
full-time minority faculty	73
student-faculty ratio	9:1
average class size	25
% first-year retention rate	96
% graduation rate (6 years)	84

Popular majors Psychology, Political Science, Economics, Biological Sciences, Engineering

CAMPUS LIFE

% live on campus (% freshmen)	86 (100)

Multicultural student clubs and organizations National Society of Black Engineers, Society of Hispanic Professional Engineers, Black Students' Union, Chinese Students' Association, Filipino American Students' Association, Korean American Students' Association, Spanish and Latino Students' Association, Student Assoc for the Dev. of Arab Cultural Awareness

Athletics NCAA Division III, Liberty League; University Athletic Association (UAA)

ADMISSIONS

# of applicants	12,805
% accepted	38
# of first-year students enrolled	1,177
SAT Critical Reading (middle 50%)	600-690
SAT Math (middle 50%)	630-730
SAT Writing (middle 50%)	600-700
ACT (middle 50%)	29-32
average HS GPA	3.8
Deadlines	
early decision	11/1
regular decision	1/1
application fee (online)	$60 ($30)
fee waiver for applicants with financial need	yes

COST & AID

tuition	$40,040
room & board	$12,120
total need-based institutional scholarships/grants	$57,384,010
% of students apply for need-based aid	63
% of students receive aid	88
% receiving need-based scholarship or grant aid	87
% receiving aid whose need was fully met	96
average aid package	$33,607
average student loan debt upon graduation	$28,100

Appalachian State University

Appalachian State University
A.S.U. Box 32004
Boone, NC 28608
Ph: (828) 262-2000
admissions@appstate.edu
www.appstate.edu

Located in the Blue Ridge Mountains of North Carolina, Appalachian State University combines the best attributes of a small liberal arts college with those of a large research institution. This dynamic university features high-quality academics at an affordable price, and an energetic campus life with incredible opportunities for leadership, service-learning and study abroad. The beautiful mountains surrounding campus provide unique opportunities academically, culturally and recreationally. Small classes and close interactions between faculty and students create a strong sense of community, which is an Appalachian hallmark.

> ACCESS GEAR UP

Appalachian encourages young people to have high expectations, stay in school, study hard, and take the right courses to go to college. The main objectives of the GEAR UP program are to ensure that all students have access to rigorous college courses, provide early information about college admission process and offer information to families about the costs of college and the availability of student financial assistance The mission of the GEAR UP initiative is to accelerate the academic achievement of middle and secondary school students, so that increasing numbers will graduate from high school and enroll and succeed in college.

"Through Appalachian's ACCESS program I've been given the opportunity to attend a four year university and have educational opportunities that I didn't think were attainable coming from a low income family. Appalachian has allowed me the gift of education."

– Ivan P., '11
Durham, NC
Biology

> ACCESS Western NC Network for Access & Success (WNCNAS)

As a clearinghouse of information and data related to higher education access improvement activities in the state, serving the entire Appalachian region of North Carolina, WNCNAS provides opportunities for high schools to apply for mini-grants to improve high school graduation and post-secondary enrollment.

> ACCESS Upward Bound

At Appalachian, rising seniors who participate in the Upward Bound program take part in the Senior Adventure Group Experience (SAGE), which has been nationally recognized as a model program. Based on the concept of experiential education, the program brings students to sites like the Appalachian Trail, the Biltmore Estate and the Nantahala River in order to experience these environments first-hand. SAGE students also visit colleges, learn about leadership and prepare for college-entrance exams.

> OPPORTUNITY Diversity Scholarships

As part of the university's effort to create a more diverse student body, diversity scholarships are awarded to students who demonstrate and value academic achievement, exhibit strong leadership potential, and eagerly identify ways to implement positive change. Although priority is given to students from underrepresented groups, students from all ethnic backgrounds who can contribute to campus diversity are considered for this award.

FAST FACTS

STUDENT PROFILE

# of undergraduate enrollment	14,219
% male/female	48/52
% African American	3
% American Indian or Alaska Native	<1
% Asian or Pacific Islander	1
% Hispanic	3
% White	92
% International	<1
% Pell grant recipients	14

First-generation and minority alumni Dr. Harry Williams, president, Delaware State University

ACADEMICS

full-time faculty	862
full-time minority faculty	63
student-faculty ratio	16:1
average class size	25
% first-year retention rate	87
% graduation rate (6 years)	66

Popular majors Business Administration/ Management, Communication, Elementary Education, Psychology

CAMPUS LIFE

% live on campus (% freshmen)	34 (99)

Multicultural student clubs and organizations African Student Association, AIESEC, Asian Student Association, ASU Anime Club, Hip Hop Oasis, Hispanic Student Association, International Friendship Association, NOW, Sexuality and Gender Alliance, TransAction

Athletics NCAA Division I, Southern Conference (SoCon), Northern Pacific Field Hockey Conference (NorPac)

ADMISSIONS

# of applicants	12,434
% accepted	69
# of first-year students enrolled	2,823
SAT Critical Reading (middle 50%)	510-610
SAT Math (middle 50%)	530-610
SAT Writing (middle 50%)	490-590
ACT (middle 50%)	22-26
average HS GPA	3.9

Deadlines

regular admission	rolling
application fee (online)	$50 ($50)
fee waiver for applicants with financial need	yes

COST & AID

tuition	in-state $2,961; out-of-state $14,273
room & board	$6,600
total need-based institutional scholarships/grants	$6,229,162
% of students apply for need-based aid	49
% of students receiving aid	46
% receiving need-based scholarship or grant aid	41
% receiving aid whose need was fully met	42
average aid package	$9,127
average student loan debt upon graduation	$15,529

Davidson College

Davidson College
Box 7156
Davidson, NC 28035-7156
Ph: (800) 768-0380
admission@davidson.edu
www.davidson.edu

Davidson is a highly selective independent liberal arts college of approximately 1,900 students located 20 minutes north of Charlotte in Davidson, N.C. Since its establishment in 1837, the college has been consistently regarded as one of the top liberal arts colleges in the country. Through The Davidson Trust, the college became the first liberal arts institution in the nation to replace loans with grants in all financial aid packages, giving all students the opportunity to graduate debt-free. The college values diversity in all forms and the role it plays in creating a rich and meaningful experience for all students. Davidson competes in NCAA athletics at the Division I level, and a student-managed Honor Code is central to student life at the college.

OPPORTUNITY **The Davidson Trust**

Through The Davidson Trust, the college meets 100 percent of demonstrated financial need through grants and students employment. Financial aid counselors are available to help families navigate the financial aid process.

OPPORTUNITY **Need Blind Admission**

Davidson practices a need-blind admission policy, which means an applicant's character, academic achievement, potential and talents are the factor's considered for admission, not the family's bank balance.

> ***"Davidson College immediately welcomes you with open arms. It is an all around pleasant place that offers many opportunities to expand ones horizons. This can be done in class and by becoming a part of various organizations and clubs on campus."***
>
> *– Claudia R., '11*
> *Chicago, IL*
> *Sociology*

SUCCESS **Leadership Development**

Through the office of leadership development, Center for Civic Engagement, mentoring and other programs, Davidson prepares students for the challenges and opportunities that come with a first class education

SUCCESS **Exchange Programs**

Davidson College has cooperative arrangements with Howard University and Morehouse College which provide students opportunities for study at campuses with significant African- American student, faculty and staff populations. Study may be arranged for a year or a semester.

SUCCESS **Students Together Reaching for Individual Development & Education (STRIDE)**

STRIDE is a support program purposed to assist first year ethnic minority students with their adjustment to Davidson College. A series of designed experiences offer academic, cultural, and social support as well as vital information to aid students in understanding and working effectively within the college community.

SUCCESS **The Emerging Professionals Group (EPG)**

The EPG works to prepare black students for the challenges of people of color in corporate America through education, exposure, and empowerment in career and professional development. The group meets monthly and focuses on resume writing, corporate culture, business etiquette, and interviews.

FAST FACTS

STUDENT PROFILE

# of degree-seeking undergraduates	1,742
% male/female	49/51
% African American	6.5
% American Indian or Alaska Native	1
% Asian or Pacific Islander	5
% Hispanic	5
% White	72
% Other/Not Reported	6.5
% International	4
% Pell grant recipients	6.8

First-generation and minority alumni Ketan Bulsara, professor of neurosurgery, Yale University School of Medicine; Anthony Foxx, attorney, Mayor of Charlotte; Jana Mashonee, recording artist; Rosie Molinary, writer, author

ACADEMICS

full-time faculty	167
full-time minority faculty	23
student-faculty ratio	10:1
average class size	12-15
% first-year retention rate	96
% graduation rate (6 years)	91

Popular majors Biology, Chemistry, Political Science, History, Economics

CAMPUS LIFE

% live on campus (% freshmen)	94 (100)

Multicultural student clubs and organizations Black Student Coalition, Davidson International Association, Organization of Latin American Students, Asian Cultural Awareness Association, Davidson African Students Association, Middle Eastern Cross-Cultural Association, Muslim Students Association, Sistahs of Essence, United Community Action, MultiCultural House

Athletics NCAA Division I, Southern Conference (SoCon), Pioneer League

ADMISSIONS

# of applicants	4,759
% accepted	25.8
# of first-year student enrolled	490
SAT Critical Reading (middle 50%)	640-740
SAT Math (middle 50%)	650-740
SAT Writing (middle 50%)	640-730
ACT (middle 50%)	29-33

Deadlines

early decision	11/15
regular decision	1/2
application fee (online)	$50 ($50)
fee waiver for applicants with financial need	yes

COST & AID

tuition	$38,886
room & board	$10,857
total need-based institutional scholarships/grants	$16,402,058
% of students apply for need-based aid	49
% of students receive aid	85
% receiving aid whose need was fully met	100
average aid package	$27,251
average student loan debt upon graduation	$13,410

Duke University

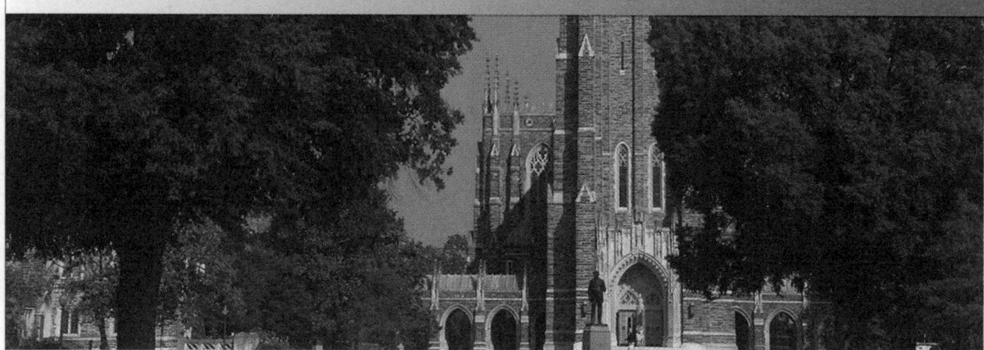

Duke University
2138 Campus Drive
Durham, NC, 27708
Ph: (919) 684-3214
undergrad-admissions@duke.edu
www.duke.edu

Duke University is among the most community-oriented of the nation's major universities. Duke offers students a rigorous academic program combined with exceptional flexibility in course selection and degree programs. Duke strongly believes that a student's financial resources should not be a barrier to enrollment. For U.S. citizens and permanent residents, a family's ability to pay is not considered in the admission decision, and nearly half of Duke's undergraduates receive financial assistance. From orientation forward, a sense of belonging and school spirit permeate the Duke campus. This is evident in the collaboration between faculty and students, and between campus and the local Durham community. Located between Atlanta and Washington, D.C., Durham is a city of 240,000 with vibrant research, medical, and cultural communities.

ACCESS The Talent Identification Program

Duke offers a number of summer academic programs ranging from sciences to the arts. Financial aid is available for all of these programs, which take place on the Duke campus. These programs give high school students (and younger) the opportunity to familiarize themselves with a college environment while broadening their academic and life experiences. The Talent Identification Program offers advanced summer studies courses through eight different institutes, including creative writing, psychology, pre-law studies and leadership.

ACCESS Duke Continuing Studies Youth Programs

Duke Continuing Studies Youth Programs offer courses in Constructing Your College Experience, and drama and journalism, among others.

OPPORTUNITY Need Based-Financial Aid

Duke's commitment to need-based financial aid is among the strongest in the country. Nearly half of our students receive financial aid, and whether or not a student applies for financial aid does not figure into the admissions decision, a rarity in higher education.

OPPORTUNITY Blue Devil Days, Black Student Alliance Invitational Weekend, and Latino Student Recruitment Weekend

As students who have been admitted to Duke University make their final college choices, Duke provides three major spring opportunities to visit the campus: Blue Devil Days, Black Student Alliance Invitational Weekend, and Latino Student Recruitment Weekend. These provide time for students to spend the night in a residence hall as the guest of a current student, to attend classes, to meet other prospective students, and to see for themselves that Duke is the right match for them

SUCCESS The Student Access Office

The Student Access Office provides support to those with learning differences. Comprehensive tutoring is available as needed.

SUCCESS Student Support

Duke provides extensive support for first-year students, from Welcome Week, where Maya Angelou is the perennial featured speaker to academic advising and student mentoring. Support from resident advisors and faculty in residence is augmented by peer mentoring through the Black Student Leadership Summit, Sister-to-Sister Retreat, the Protégé Program and the Brothers' Advance Workshop. The Office of Multicultural Affairs and the Mary Lou Williams Center for Black Culture, among other Student Affairs offices, are welcoming centers for student support.

FAST FACTS

STUDENT PROFILE

# of degree-seeking undergraduates	6,504
% male/female	41/59
% African American	10
% American Indian or Alaska Native	0.4
% Asian or Pacific Islander	22
% Hispanic	7
% White	47
% International	7
% Pell grant recipients	9

First-generation and minority alumni Daniel Blue, Jr., North Carolina House of Representatives, Chair of Duke University Board of Trustees; Cleon Thompson, Chancellor of Winston-Salem State University 1985-1995; Grant Hill, NBA All-Star; Wilhelmina Reuben-Cooke, former Provost and Vice President for Academic Affairs at the University of the District of Columbia, currently Professor of Law at David Clarke School of Law

ACADEMICS

full-time faculty	1,113
% of faculty self-identified as minority	20
student-faculty ratio	8:1
average class size	20
% first-year retention rate	97
% graduation rate (6 years)	95

Popular majors Economics, Psychology, Biology, Public Policy, Biomedical Engineering

CAMPUS LIFE

% live on campus (% freshmen)	83 (100)

Multicultural student clubs and organizations Black Student Alliance, Mi Gente, Students of the Caribbean Association, Center for Race Relations, Minority Association for Pre-Medical Students

Athletics NCAA Division I, Atlantic Coast Conference (ACC)

ADMISSIONS

# of applicants	29,800
% accepted	12.8
# of first-year students enrolled	1,726
SAT Critical Reading (middle 50%)	680-770
SAT Math (middle 50%)	690-780
SAT Writing (middle 50%)	690-780
ACT (middle 50%)	30-34
average HS GPA	n/a
Deadlines	
early decision	11/1
regular decision	1/2
application fee (online)	$75 ($75)
fee waiver for applicants with financial need	yes

COST & AID

tuition	$40,665
room & board	$13,240
total need-based institutional scholarships/grants	$5,723,876
% of students apply for need-based aid	42.3
% receiving need-based scholarship or grant aid	41
% receiving aid whose need was fully met	100
average aid package	$42,280
average student loan debt upon graduation	$22,000

Meredith College

Meredith College
3800 Hillsborough Street
Raleigh, NC 27607
Ph: (919) 760-8581
admissions@meredith.edu
www.meredith.edu/admissions

Meredith College has grown to become one of the largest independent private women's colleges in the U.S. They offer a comprehensive liberal arts undergraduate education, with a focus on leadership, experiential learning and individual attention. In addition to welcoming students and faculty from 31 states and 46 countries, Meredith College enjoys a strong population of first generation college students. Meredith College is also a partner with the Zawadi Africa Education Fund and the Initiative to Educate Afghan Women.

"I never imagined that I would attend one of the best women's colleges in the nation. I am the first member of my family to go to college. I am well prepared because Meredith College, my family, my professors and friends have given me the tools I needed."
– Nayely Perez-Huerta, '09
Community Organizer
El Pueblo, Inc.

ACCESS **¡Levántate, North Carolina! College Fair**

This college fair, which highlights colleges and scholarship organizations, is hosted by Meredith College for the Hispanic population of Central and Eastern North Carolina. The fair is set up to assist Latino high school students and their families in understanding the importance of going to college. Students have the opportunity to meet representatives from more than 40 colleges and scholarship organizations.

ACCESS **Meredith Hues Program**

The Meredith Hues Program is a student group run through the Office of Admissions that allows multicultural freshmen the opportunity to assist in the recruitment of new multicultural students.

OPPORTUNITY **Meredith Promise Scholarships**

In recognition of academic ability, intellectual promise and leadership skills, Meredith College has established the Meredith Promise Scholarship for students from underrepresented groups. The scholarship is renewable up to a total of four years, provided the recipient remains in good standing, is a full-time student, and maintains a 2.5 quality point ratio on all courses taken at Meredith.

SUCCESS **The First Year Experience Class**

The FYE Class is a one-hour credit class taught by a variety of faculty and staff across campus. This class is designed to help students make a successful transition into college. Topics covered include: effective study skills for college, time management, communicating with professors and academic dialogue, critical thinking skills, diversity, learning about Raleigh and dealing with homesickness. Because the class is small and interactive, it also provides a support group for new students, as well as the chance to develop a strong relationship with a faculty/staff member.

SUCCESS **The Learning Center**

The Learning Center is a free academic support program for all Meredith College students staffed by students who are trained to assist their peers. The Learning Center offers subject specific tutoring in 100 and 200 level courses, including English, writing, grammar, mathematics and other subjects that vary by semester. Writing tutors work with students writing papers for any course, regardless of level.

SUCCESS **Summer Symposium**

Meredith College's Summer Syposium is a two-day educational and transitional experience to foster a sense of community among incoming first-year and transfer multicultural students.

FAST FACTS

STUDENT PROFILE

# of degree-seeking undergraduates	1,774
% male/female	0/100
% African American	11
% American Indian or Alaska Native	<1
% Asian or Pacific Islander	3
% Hispanic	3
% White	75
% International	3
% Pell grant recipients	n/a

First-generation and minority alumni
C.C. Wiggins, '76, first woman and first African American officer in command and support roles in the Chaplain Corps

ACADEMICS

full-time faculty	124
full-time minority faculty	12
student-faculty ratio	11:1
average class size	17
% first-year retention rate	79
% graduation rate (6 years)	60

Popular majors Psychology, Biology, Interior Design, Business

CAMPUS LIFE

% live on campus (% freshmen)	57 (92)

Multicultural student clubs and organizations
Association of Cultural Awareness, Meredith International Association, Meredith "N" Harmony, SGA Unity Council, Diversity Council, Meredith Hues

Athletics NCAA Division III, USA South Conference (USASouth)

ADMISSIONS

# of applicants	1,586
% accepted	65
# of first-year student enrolled	366
SAT Critical Reading (middle 50%)	450-570
SAT Math (middle 50%)	450-570
SAT Writing (middle 50%)	n/a
ACT (middle 50%)	19-24
average HS GPA	3.3

Deadlines

regular decision	2/15
application fee (online)	$40 ($40)
fee waiver for applicants with financial need	yes

COST & AID

tuition	$27,770
room & board	$7,950
total need-based institutional scholarships/grants	$9,716,075
% of students apply for need-based aid	81.6
% receiving need-based scholarship or grant aid	72.5
% receiving aid whose need was fully met	10.4
average aid package	$19,325
average student loan debt upon graduation	$22,518

North Carolina Agricultural and Technical State University

North Carolina Agricultural and Technical State University
1601 East Market Street, Webb Hall
Greensboro, NC 27410
Ph: (336) 334-7946
uadmit@ncat.edu
www.ncat.edu

North Carolina Agricultural and Technical State University is a public, doctoral research, land-grant university committed to exemplary teaching and learning, scholarly and creative research, and effective engagement and public service. The University offers degrees at the baccalaureate, master's and doctoral levels and has a commitment to excellence in a comprehensive range of academic disciplines. Our unique legacy and educational philosophy provide students with a broad range of experiences that foster transformation and leadership for a dynamic and global society.

"NC A&T SU is an HBCU that has allowed me to understand more about my culture and history. I have learned more about myself as well as my field of study. NC A&T SU believes in starting you with your core curriculum courses early. This gives you true understanding about your major and allots for adjustments if needed. My mind has been opened and enhanced since my enrollment at NC A&T SU."

– Rayelle G., '13
Civil Engineering

OPPORTUNITY Diversity Scholarships

North Carolina A&T makes an effort to recruit and retain students from underrepresented minority groups. To be considered for a scholarship, a student must be an incoming student in good academic standing, and be a resident of North Carolina. Students may apply throughout the year in advance of enrolling, and awards are based on available funding.

SUCCESS Office of New Student Orientation

The Office of New Student Orientation offers programs that help students make a successful transition from high school to college life. Through their summer orientation sessions, students meet with their new academic advisors, register for classes, and attend information sessions to learn more about the academic environment at college. It is also an opportunity for students to meet and connect with their future classmates and to get an idea of what to expect from life at college.

SUCCESS Center for Academic Excellence

The University offers several academic, student support and retention initiatives for our students. The Center for Academic Excellence offers centralized academic advising, tutorial services in a wide variety of disciplines, and supplemental instruction programs. Through the Center there are two programs for first-year minority students, Male Aggies Resolved to Change History (M.A.R.C.H) and Sisters Inspiring Success through Education Reform and Service (S.I.S.T.E.R.S).

SUCCESS The M.A.R.C.H. and S.I.S.T.E.R.S. Programs

Male Aggies Resolved to Change History (M.A.R.C.H.) and Sisters Inspiring Success through Education Reform and Service (S.I.S.T.E.R.S.) are programs that offer mentoring, advising and cultural development programs. The goal of these programs is to encourage retention of minority students by providing them with the necessary knowledge and skills to be successful in a competitive academic environment.

FAST FACTS

STUDENT PROFILE

# of degree-seeking undergraduates	10,196
% male/female	48/52
% African American	85
% American Indian or Alaska Native	.3
% Asian or Pacific Islander	1
% Hispanic	1.5
% White	7
% Pell grant recipients	83

First-generation and minority alumni David Richmond; Franklin McCain, '63; Jibreel Khazan/ Ezell Blair Jr. '63; Dr. Joseph McNeil, '63 Greensboro Four, Student Sit In Pioneers; Dr. Ronald McNair '71 NASA Astronaut; Reverend Jesse Jackson, Sr, '64, Civil Rights Activist, Baptist Minister, Founder of 'Rainbow/ PUSH; Joe L. Dudley '62, Founder, Dudley Hair Care

ACADEMICS

full-time faculty	519
full-time minority faculty	390
student-faculty ratio	18:1
average class size	29
% first-year retention rate	72
% graduation rate (6 years)	37

Popular majors Engineering, Biology, Animal Science, Criminal Justice, Business and Economics

CAMPUS LIFE

% live on campus (% freshmen)	89 (n/a)

Multicultural student clubs and organizations Student Government Association, Student University Activities Board, Pan-Hellenic Council, Residence Hall Association, Council of Presidents, Blue and Gold Marching Machine (Band), Cheerleading, Gospel Choir, Modeling Troupes, National Association of Black Engineers, Honor Societies

Athletics NCAA Division I, Mid-Eastern Athletics Conference (MEAC)

ADMISSIONS

# of applicants	8,300
% accepted	54
# of first-year students enrolled	2,053
SAT Critical Reading (middle 50%)	400-480
SAT Math (middle 50%)	410-500
SAT Writing (middle 50%)	n/a
ACT (middle 50%)	17-21
average HS GPA	3.04

Deadlines

priority deadline	2/15
regular admission	rolling
application fee (online)	$45 ($45)
fee waiver for applicants with financial need	no

COST & AID

tuition	in-state: $4,667.50; out-of-state: $14,301.50
room & board	$6,029
total need-based institutional scholarships/grants	$4,826,042
% of students apply for need-based aid	94
% receiving need-based scholarship or grant aid	63
% receiving aid whose need was fully met	86
average aid package	$12,853
average student loan debt upon graduation	$21,644

North Carolina State University

Founded in 1887, North Carolina State University is a comprehensive public university with a multi-cultural and diverse student body. NC State is widely renowned for its pioneering research in science and technology. Located in Raleigh, which has been ranked as one of the best places to live in the United States, NC State has also been ranked by the Princeton Review as one of the best value colleges in the country. Students can choose between more than 300 different undergraduate and graduate programs in 65 departments, and can begin taking classes in their major as soon as they come to campus.

> ***"NC State has everything I was looking for - student organizations, outstanding faculty and the culture of Raleigh."***
> *– Marycobb R.*
> *Business Administration, Finance*

ACCESS **The Saturday Program for Academic and Cultural Education (SPACE)**

SPACE is named after Lt. Colonel Guion (Guy) Stewart Bluford, Jr., the first African American astronaut in space. An academic program designed for 6th through 8th grade students from Wake County and surrounding school districts, the program provides interactive learning and cultural activities in writing, math, science, social studies and technology throughout the academic year.

ACCESS **North Carolina Mathematics and Science Education Network Pre-College Program (NC-MSEN)**

The mission of NC-MSEN is to prepare underserved students at the middle and high school levels (grades 6-12) for careers in education and science, technology, engineering and mathematics (STEM).

OPPORTUNITY **Multicultural Visitation Day**

For students who were admitted to NC State, this event is invitation-only and features representatives from student organizations, faculty from several academic departments, and admissions staff to answer questions specifically for students of various cultural and ethnic backgrounds.

OPPORTUNITY **University Open House**

The University Open House offers all prospective students an opportunity to visit campus to collect more information on the various academic and develomental programs available at NC State

SUCCESS **Peer Mentor Program**

The Peer Mentor Program targets first-year African American, Native American and Hispanic students. The primary objective of the program is to contribute to the advancement of first-year students by aiding in their academic, emotional and social adjustments to college.

SUCCESS **Cultural Symposiums**

NC State holds several symposiums, including the African American Symposium, the Native American Symposium, and the Hispanic/Latino Symposium, in order to maximize the academic success of incoming first-year students of underrepresented minorities. This is achieved by providing information about campus resources, support personnel, cultural heritage, networking and other strategies for success.

SUCCESS **Student Support Services**

The Student Support Services (SSS) program is one of three TRIO programs originally funded under the Higher Education Act of 1965, whose objective is to help students overcome class, social, and cultural barriers to complete their college education. Funded by the U.S. Department of Education, SSS is committed to helping low-income, first generation college students, and students with disabilities achieve a bachelor's degree.

North Carolina State University
203 Peele Hall Campus Box 7103
Raleigh, NC 27695
Ph: (919) 515-2434
undergrad_admissions@ncsu.edu
admissions.ncsu.edu

FAST FACTS

STUDENT PROFILE

# of degree-seeking undergraduates	25,246
% male/female	55/45
% African American	8
% American Indian or Alaska Native	<1
% Asian or Pacific Islander	5
% Hispanic	3
% White	76
% International	2
% Pell grant recipients	16

ACADEMICS

full-time faculty	1,750
full-time minority faculty	364
student-faculty ratio	17:1
average class size	35
% first-year retention rate	90
% graduation rate (6 years)	73

Popular majors Engineering, Business Administration, Biological Sciences, Textiles, Design

CAMPUS LIFE

% live on campus (% freshmen)	32 (77)

Multicultural student clubs and organizations Native American Student Association, African-American Student Affairs, Union Activities Board, Mi Familia, Student Mentor Association, Peer Mentor Program, Multicultural Student Affairs, African-American Student Advisory Council,Hispanic Student Affairs

Athletics NCAA Division I, Atlantic Coast Conference (ACC)

ADMISSIONS

# of applicants	19,514
% accepted	54
# of first-year students enrolled	4,558
SAT Critical Reading (middle 50%)	530-620
SAT Math (middle 50%)	560-660
SAT Writing (middle 50%)	510-610
ACT (middle 50%)	23-28
average HS GPA	4.24

Deadlines

early decision	no
regular admission	2/1; 11/1-College of Design
application fee (online)	$70 ($70)
fee waiver for applicants with financial need	no

COST & AID

tuition	in-state: $7,018; out-of-state: $19,852
room & board	$8,536
total need-based institutional scholarships/grants	$37,789,499
% of students apply for need-based aid	65
% receiving need-based scholarship or grant aid	46
% receiving aid whose need was fully met	28
average aid package	$11,879
average student loan debt upon graduation	$19,988

University of North Carolina at Asheville

University of North Carolina at Asheville
One University Heights
Asheville, NC 28804-8502
www.unca.edu/admissions
Ph: (828) 251-6481
admissions@unca.edu
www.unca.edu

The University of North Carolina at Asheville is a co-educational, public liberal arts university. Since 1927, the University of North Carolina at Asheville has offered a superior liberal arts education for well-prepared students who are committed to learning and personal growth. Its education is liberating, promoting the free and rigorous pursuit of truth, respect for differing points of view and heritage and an understanding that values play a role in thought and action. Through this education, the university aims to develop students of broad perspective who think critically and creatively, communicate effectively and participate actively in their communities.

"I wanted a small private school experience at a reasonable public school price. UNC Asheville offered me a unique community where I could thrive as both a student and a leader. Part of what I enjoy as an upper classman is taking part in mentoring and advising students who are thinking about college through our campus's access opportunities like AVID and GEAR UP. It's great to be a role model!"

– Ashley P., '09
Literature and Language, 9-12 English Licensure

ACCESS **Advancement Via Individual Determination (AVID) Program**

The University of North Carolina at Asheville partners with Asheville City Schools to provide tutors for the AVID program. Through AVID, college students work with 250 students in sixth to 12th grade from Asheville Middle, Asheville High School and SILSA (School of Inquiry and Life Sciences Asheville). AVID targets students with a GPA between 2.0 and 3.5 and considers first-generation college, low-income, historically underserved and special-circumstance students.

OPPORTUNITY **Minority Presence Grant Program**

The University of North Carolina funds the Minority Presence Grant Program, allocating money to historically white and historically black institutions to aid them in recruiting financially needy North Carolina students who would be minority presence students at the respective institutions by enabling the institutions to offer relatively more aid for minority presence students in the form of grants rather than loans.

SUCCESS **Summer Opportunity for Academic Success (SOAR)**

This intensive six-week program invites a hand-selected group of recent high school graduates to campus to ensure a smoother transition to college. During SOAR, students are exposed to UNC Asheville's academic expectations through Math and Liberal Studies writing courses, which are taught by dedicated faculty with a commitment to the development of each student. Additional support from SOAR Mentors and math and writing tutors provide assistance in and out of the classroom and they become familiar with the cultures of our campus and the greater Asheville community through a variety of on and off-campus programs and trips. In the fall semester, SOAR students continue to interact with each other and SOAR faculty and staff and since they are well-established on campus, they become campus leaders and role models for their peers.

SUCCESS **The Center for Diversity Education**

The Center for Diversity Education at UNC Asheville celebrates and teaches diversity in order to foster conversation and respect among cultures. Each year the Center works with over 15,000 students and teachers in school districts throughout Western North Carolina with Road Shows, Exhibits, Staff Development and a lending library. Students at UNC Asheville are integral to those programs as interns, volunteers and researchers. To learn more about the Center visit www.diversityed.org.

FAST FACTS

STUDENT PROFILE	
# of degree-seeking undergraduates	3,107
% male/female	43/57
% African American	3
% American Indian or Alaska Native	<1
% Asian or Pacific Islander	2
% Hispanic	4
% White	96
% International	<1
% Pell grant recipients	20

First-generation and minority alumni Ty Wigginton, Second/Third Baseman, Baltimore Orioles; Ann B. Ross ('84),10-time *NY Times* Best Selling Author; Michael Cogdill ('84), Emmy Award-Winning News Anchor; Wilma Dykeman ('38), Author, Environmental Activist; Roy A. Taylor ('29), Member of Congress, 1959-1976; Michael Gugino ('01), Musician, Steep Canyon Rangers

ACADEMICS	
full-time faculty	216
full-time minority faculty	28
student-faculty ratio	14:1
average class size	19
% first-year retention rate	82
% graduation rate (6 years)	55

Popular majors Psychology, Management, Environmental Studies, Biology, Art, Literature

CAMPUS LIFE	
% live on campus (% freshmen)	33 (95)

Multicultural student clubs and organizations Africana Club, Alliance, Asian Students in Asheville (ASIA), Black Student Association (BSA), EPEC (Hispanic), Hispanic Outreach for Learning Awareness (HOLA), Hillel, International Students Association, Student Diversity Association, N.U.E. Noize Step Team

Athletics NCAA Division I, Big South Conference (BigSouth)

ADMISSIONS	
# of applicants	2,362
% accepted	77
# of first-year students enrolled	593
SAT Critical Reading (middle 50%)	540-650
SAT Math (middle 50%)	520-620
SAT Writing (middle 50%)	510-620
ACT (middle 50%)	22-27
average HS GPA	3.9
Deadlines	
early action	11/15
regular admission	2/15
application fee (online)	$50 ($50)
fee waiver for applicants with financial need	yes

COST & AID	
tuition	in-state: $2,626; out-of-state: $15,398
room & board	$7,040
total need-based institutional scholarships/grants	$1,329,522
% of students apply for need-based aid	73
% of students receive aid	47
% receiving need-based scholarship or grant aid	46
% receiving aid whose need was fully met	50
average aid package	$10,775
average student loan debt upon graduation	$15,972

University of North Carolina at Chapel Hill

Founded in 1795, the University of North Carolina at Chapel Hill is a public, co-educational, research university, and the oldest institution in the University of North Carolina System — in fact, it was the only public university in the United States to graduate students in the 18th century. The university seeks to serve all as a center for scholarship and creative endeavor. Teaching students at all levels in an environment of research, free inquiry and personal responsibility, the University of North Carolina at Chapel Hill strives to expand the body of knowledge, improve the condition of human life through service and publication and to enrich culture.

ACCESS Camp Carolina Scholars

The University of North Carolina at Chapel Hill's Camp Carolina Scholars brings talented high school freshmen and sophomores, with a special emphasis on first-generation, minority, low-income, rural and disadvantaged students, to campus to experience residential college life. Students spend three days on campus living in a residence hall, learning about academic and extra-curricular preparation for selective admissions and scholarship opportunities. Sessions include information on admissions, financial aid and scholarship, time management, study habits, test preparation and other important skills needed for high school and college success.

ACCESS National College Advising Corps (NCAC)

Headquartered at the Office of Undergraduate Admissions at Chapel Hill, the National College Advising Corps (NCAC) places college advisers in high schools with low college-going rates to assist existing guidance efforts. NCAC recruits dynamic recent college graduates to serve in a one- to two-year commitment, similar to programs such as the Peace Corps and Teach for America. Advisers spend two to three days per week in each of two assigned high schools. Their work supplements, not competes with, the work of guidance counselors already present in member-schools. Not only does NCAC increase college recruitment and retention rates for traditionally underserved students, but it also creates a generation of young public servants who will remain informed and committed to these issues over a lifetime.

OPPORTUNITY Carolina Covenant

The Carolina Covenant is a college financing commitment between the University of North Carolina at Chapel Hill and historically low-income youth throughout the nation. The covenant pledges that the university will meet 100 percent of an admitted, eligible student's financial need with a combination of grants, scholarships and a reasonable amount of federal work-study. This combination of financial aid, together with the amount the family is expected to pay, gives students who qualify and who work 10 to 12 hours per week in a work-study job, the opportunity to earn a baccalaureate degree at Chapel Hill without having to borrow to meet their financial need.

SUCCESS The Learning Center

The Learning Center at the University of North Carolina at Chapel Hill aims to help students become self-confident, self-directed learners. While the immediate goal of the Learning Center is improving students' abilities to learn, remember and solve problems, the center's ultimate goal is increasing student achievement, retention and graduation from the university. The center's programs include one-on-one academic counseling, laboratories that teach effective reading and learning strategies, guided study groups and peer tutoring.

University of North Carolina at Chapel Hill
CB# 2200, Jackson Hall
Chapel Hill, NC 27599-2200
Ph: (919) 966-3621
unchelp@admissions.unc.edu
www.unc.edu

FAST FACTS

STUDENT PROFILE

# of degree-seeking undergraduates	17,475
% male/female	40/59
% African American	9
% American Indian or Alaska Native	<1
% Asian or Pacific Islander	7
% Hispanic	11
% White	68
% Pell grant recipients	13

First-generation and minority alumni Stuart Scott, anchor, ESPN; Karen Leslie Stevenson '79, first black female Rhodes Scholar; Rachel Mazyck '05, Rhodes Scholars; Randall Kenan, writer; Ken Jeong, actor

ACADEMICS

full-time faculty	1,656
full-time minority faculty	373
student-faculty ratio	14:1
average class size	10-19
% first-year retention rate	97
% graduation rate (6 years)	90

Popular majors Biology, Chemistry, Mass Communications/Media Studies, Psychology

CAMPUS LIFE

% live on campus (% freshmen)	42 (82)

Multicultural student clubs and organizations Black Student Movement, Carolina Hispanic Association, Hellenic Student Association, Carolina Indian Circle, Korean-American Student Association, South Asian Awareness Organization, Association of International Students, African Student Association, Asian Student Association

Athletics NCAA Division I, Atlantic Coast Conference (ACC)

ADMISSIONS

# of applicants	23,272
% accepted	32
# of first-year students enrolled	3,946
SAT Critical Reading (middle 50%)	590-700
SAT Math (middle 50%)	610-710
SAT Writing (middle 50%)	590-690
ACT (middle 50%)	27-31
average HS GPA	4.4
Deadlines	
early action	11/2
regular decision	1/15
application fee (online)	$70 ($70)
fee waiver for applicants with financial need	yes

COST & AID

tuition	in-state $4,815; out-of-state $23,430
room & board	$9,306
total need-based institutional scholarships/grants	$35,131,506
% of students apply for need-based aid	67
% of students receive aid	36
% receiving need-based scholarship or grant aid	36
% receiving aid whose need was fully met	98
average aid package	$13,509
average student loan debt upon graduation	$14,936

University of North Carolina Wilmington

Founded in 1946, the University of North Carolina Wilmington is a co-educational, non-denominational, comprehensive public university. The College of Arts and Sciences, the professional schools and the graduate school seek to stimulate intellectual curiosity, imagination, critical thinking and thoughtful expression in a broad range of disciplines and professional fields. Encouraging public access to its educational programs, the university is committed to diversity, international perspectives and regional service. The Wilmington campus community strives to create a safe, supportive and technologically progressive environment in which students, faculty and staff work together to develop their interests, skills and talents to the fullest extent. The university seeks to celebrate and study the heritage and environment of the coastal region, and to enrich its quality of life, economy and education.

ACCESS **GEAR UP SUMMER INSTITUTE**

The GEAR UP Summer Institute is a 5-day, 4-night residential program for 9th grade students, who reside on campus and experience college life first-hand during the summer months. The program includes sessions led by UNCW faculty, staff and students. There are opportunities for exploratory, hands-on, and themed-based experiences that connect students with academic disciplines, and encourage them to pursue post secondary education. Enrichment experiences are also built into the residential program and allow for teamwork, social interaction and problem solving. Students also participate in sessions for college exploration and admissions.

ACCESS **NEED 2 LEAD**

Need 2 Lead is a 4-day, 3-night residential program designed for action-oriented, rising high school juniors who want to make a difference in their communities. This intense leadership weekend consists of dynamic workshops and programs designed to enhance leadership skills. The hallmark of the program is helping students create and organize a service project. UNCW student mentors inspire vision and provide direction and accountability for students implementing their project in their communities.

OPPORTUNITY **Success Opportunities Aid and Responsibilities (SOAR)**

The SOAR program is a financial assistance program that facilitates continued academic success and graduation for low-income students while limiting their accrual of student loan debt. A minimum GPA of 2.5 enables participation in the program, but increased financial awards are awarded at the start of each academic year to recipients that achieve higher GPAs. Students utilize a host of campus resources that lead to individual success and gains for the university community. To qualify, a student must be a North Carolina resident, enrolled full-time, have a combined family income of less than 200% of the federal poverty level and provide the required documentation to demonstrate they meet criteria.

SUCCESS **SAND**

SAND members work with the UNCW admission staff in recruiting students. By leading campus tours, accompanying admission representatives on high school visits and attending other recruitment events, students are trained to use their leadership skills to encourage minority students to pursue a college education. SAND members attend regular training sessions to build skills in public speaking, business etiquette, networking and more. These leadership skills make SAND students appealing to prospective employers.

"I was impressed that UNCW is one of the top three film schools in the nation, and EUE Screen Gems Studios is right in its backyard. UNCW is an invitation to embark on a journey that will help shape the course of your life with faculty and staff who are determined to invest in your future."

– T. Nelson, '12
Hampton, VA
Communication Studies/
SAND President

University of North Carolina Wilmington
Office of Admissions
601 S. College Rd.
Wilmington, NC 28403
Ph: (910) 962-3000
admissions@uncw.edu
www.uncw.edu

FAST FACTS

STUDENT PROFILE

# of degree-seeking undergraduates	10,660
% male/female	40/60
% African American	5
% American Indian or Alaska Native	1
% Asian or Pacific Islander	2
% Hispanic	5
% White	83
% International	1.3
% Pell grant recipients	33

First-generation and minority alumni Ernest Fullwood, Senior Resident Superior Court Judge

ACADEMICS

full-time faculty	588
full-time minority faculty	89
student-faculty ratio	17:1
average class size	21
% first-year retention rate	85
% graduation rate (6 years)	65

Popular majors Business, Marine Biology, Film, Psychology, Creative Writing, Education, Nursing

CAMPUS LIFE

% live on campus (% freshmen)	36 (93)

Multicultural student clubs and organizations Black Student Union, NAACP, Mi Gente, International Student Organization

Athletics NCAA Division I, Colonial Athletic Association (CAA)

ADMISSIONS

# of applicants	11,410
% accepted	48
# of first-year students enrolled	2,030
SAT Critical Reading (middle 50%)	550-630
SAT Math (middle 50%)	560-640
SAT Writing (middle 50%)	530-620
ACT (middle 50%)	23-28
average HS GPA	3.98
Deadlines	
early action	11/1
regular decision	2/1
application fee (online)	$60($60)
fee waiver for applicants with financial need	yes

COST & AID

tuition	in-state $3,226; out-of-state $15,046
room & board	$7,900
total need-based institutional scholarships/grants	n/a
% of students apply for need-based aid	68
% of students receive aid	47
% receiving need-based scholarship or grant aid	40
% receiving aid whose need was fully met	45
average aid package	$9,275
average student loan debt upon graduation	$16,980

Western Carolina University

Western Carolina University is a co-educational public university associated with the University of North Carolina System. Founded in 1889, the University offers an environment in which students, faculty and staff jointly assume responsibility for learning and in which high standards of scholarship prevail. Valuing critical thinking, effective communication, problem solving, the responsible use of information and technology, as well as the creative and performing arts, Western Carolina University is committed to personal growth and life-long learning.

"Western Carolina University and the Office for Teacher Education Recruitment provide for college access through the Teachers of Tomorrow Program. I am currently a Birth-Kindergarten major and enjoy participating in the Teachers of Tomorrow conference. Teacher recruitment and college access are critical to students in North Carolina."

– Brynn J., '10
Bryson City, NC
Birth to Kindergarten

ACCESS **Legislators' School for Youth Leadership Development (LSYLD)**

This is a summer residential leadership program for rising 8th through 11th graders. Legislators' School helps these students to develop their skills in thinking, communication and leadership while participating in community service. They also attend informational sessions focused on choosing a college, admissions processes, and scholarship initiatives.

ACCESS **Pre-College Program (PCP)**

The Western Carolina University-sponsored North Carolina Mathematics and Science Education Network Pre-College Program seeks to broaden the pool of students graduating from high school with sufficient preparation to pursue mathematics and science programs at the university level and to move into careers in those fields. To achieve these goals, the program offers enrichment classes and activities in science and mathematics to traditionally underserved middle and high school students. Saturday Academies and Summer Scholars programs comprise the core curriculum and include career awareness, leadership training, academic advising and tutoring, academic competitions and hands-on laboratory experiences.

ACCESS **Teachers of Tomorrow (TOT) Programs**

Teachers of Tomorrow is a program held on the Western Carolina University campus for middle and high school students who are interested in exploring teaching as a career. Regional high school students attend an on-campus program each October; regional middle school students attend each February. Professional educators and speakers lead breakout sessions presenting information on topics related to college access, scholarships and financial aid, teaching in a diverse world, admissions processes, campus tours, and how to choose a college or university.

OPPORTUNITY **Experience Western**

Experience Western is a program designed to introduce prospective minority students to Western Carolina University resources and to promote a supportive and educational experience at the University. Students who attend Experience Western get a preview of life on campus over the course of two days, and arrive in Cullowhee for their freshman year already connected to the University. Participants tour the campus and interact with current Western students and staff during panel discussions, information sessions, and social activities, and they also have the chance to stay in the residence halls.

SUCCESS **Project C.A.R.E. (Committed to African-American Retention in Education)**

Project C.A.R.E. is a combination of programs that seek to improve the academic performance and retention of Western Carolina University's African-American student population. A fall retreat for African-American first-year and transfer students takes place the first weekend after classes begin. The retreat is designed as an extension of the orientation process. The primary focus is to address specific questions and concerns about life as an African-American student at Western Carolina University. Students meet peer counselors, other entering freshmen and African-American faculty and staff, and develop friendships that help them through their undergraduate years and beyond.

Western Carolina University
Office of Admissions
102 Camp Building
Cullowhee, NC 28723
Ph: (822-928-4968) / (828) 227-7211
admiss@email.wcu.edu
www.wcu.edu

FAST FACTS

STUDENT PROFILE

# of degree-seeking undergraduates	6,269
% male/female	48/52
% African American	7
% American Indian or Alaska Native	<1
% Asian or Pacific Islander	<1
% Hispanic	2
% White	84
% International	<1
% Pell grant recipients	28

First-generation and minority alumni Kevin Martin, professional basketball player; Joyce Dugan, first woman chief, Eastern Band – Cherokee Indians

ACADEMICS

full-time faculty	451
full-time minority faculty	42
student-faculty ratio	13:1
average class-size	19
% first-year retention rate	67
% graduation rate (6 yr)	47

Popular majors Elementary Education, Marketing, Nursing

CAMPUS LIFE

% live on campus (% freshmen)	45 (95)

Multicultural student clubs and organizations Organization of Ebony Students, Cultures in Asia, Black Theater Ensemble, International Club, La Voz Latina, National Pan-Hellenic Council (Historical African American Fraternities & Sororities), Native American Student Awareness Society, Di Ga Li I, Western's B.E.S.T. (Black Educational Support Team), Black Student Fellowship

Athletics NCAA Division I, Southern Conference (SoCon)

ADMISSIONS

# of applicants	4,792
% accepted	68
# of first-year students enrolled	1,259
SAT Critical Reading (middle 50%)	450-550
SAT Math (middle 50%)	470-560
SAT Writing range	430-530
ACT (middle 50%)	18-23
average HS GPA	3.35
Deadlines	
early action	11/15
priority deadline	2/1
regular decision	4/1
application fee (online)	$40 ($0)
fee waiver for applicants with financial need	yes

COST & AID

tuition	in-state $2,816; out-of-state $12,413
room & board	$6,370
total need-based institutional scholarships/ grants	$1,927,126
% of students apply for need-based aid	69
% of students receive aid	97
% receiving need-based scholarship/grant aid	96
% receiving aid whose need was fully met	58
average aid package	$8,114
average student loan debt upon graduation	$11,285

Winston-Salem State University

Winston-Salem State University offers a quality baccalaureate program in a traditional, residential setting as well as flexible weekend, evening, and online courses to accommodate students in the workforce. As a comprehensive, historically black constituent of the University of North Carolina, Winston-Salem State University contributes to the social, cultural, intellectual and economic vitality of the Triad region and the state. Students find easy access to their professors, who have a long history of working closely with their students to ensure their success. Campus life pulses with the energy of student organizations, a full roster of men's and women's athletics, and a wealth of internship and volunteer options are available to enrich students' experiences and give them a leg up in the knowledge-based economy.

> OPPORTUNITY **Financial Aid Office**

WSSU offers scholarships to admitted students who have at least a 3.5 GPA and a total SAT score of 1100 or an ACT composite score of 24. In addition, the Financial Aid Office works with students to ensure they have taken all necessary steps to secure financial assistance. Approximately 89% of students receive some type of financial assistance.

> OPPORTUNITY **Open House**

WSSU hosts an Open House each Fall and Spring to showcase academics, organizations, campus life, students and faculty. Prospective students and their families are encouraged to schedule a campus visit.

> SUCCESS **The STEM Scholars Program**

The Science, Technology, Engineering and Mathematics (STEM) Scholars Program offers an academically and culturally enriched undergraduate experience that will prepare historically underrepresented students interested in STEM fields to earn a Ph.D. degree. There is a Summer Bridge Program component that is designed to assist with making the transition from high school to college and provides students with a foundation for a successful undergraduate experience. It includes course work, educational seminars, career exploration, and assessment. To be considered for the program, students must have a GPA of 3.5 or higher, SAT score of 1100 or higher or ACT score of 24 or higher, submit an essay about career aspirations and reasons for interests in the program, and participate in an interview with WSSU faculty and administrators.

> SUCCESS **University College**

University College (UC) is the academic home of all new students at Winston-Salem State University until they complete the requirements necessary to declare a major. Services include academic advising (including registration, major selection advice, and all other academic concerns), learning support, supplemental instruction, tutoring, and more. UC advisors, instructors, and tutors effectively and accurately communicate university-wide regulations, procedures, and expectations, provide services designed to promote student achievement, and work to ensure that all freshmen meet their common core requirements and successfully prepare for their intended majors. They help students help themselves, through computerized and individual academic support.

"From the time I was a toddler, my mother instilled in me the importance of academics. But I knew she wouldn't be able to afford my tuition as a single parent. I am so appreciative of my scholarship, and the opportunity I've had to combine athletics with helping people."

– Shaun T., '10
Exercise Science major, School of Education and Human Performance, Chancellor's Scholar

Winston-Salem State University
601 S. Martin Luther King Jr. Drive
Winston-Salem, NC 27110
Ph: (336) 750-2070
admissions@wssu.edu
www.wssu.edu

FAST FACTS

STUDENT PROFILE

# of degree-seeking undergraduates	5,975
% male/female	30/70
% African American	83
% American Indian or Alaska Native	<1
% Asian or Pacific Islander	1
% Hispanic	1
% White	12
% Pell grant recipients	60

First-generation and minority alumni Lorraine Hairston '38, Mayor of Evanston, Ill.; Elias Gilbert '60, World Class Olympic Hurdler; Earl "The Pearl" Monroe '68, selected one of NBA's Top 50 greatest players in league history; Joseph Johnson '73, listed as one of the top African-American attorneys in the U.S. by *Black Enterprise Magazine*; Stephen A. Smith, '92, sports writer, talk show host, and NBA commentator

ACADEMICS

full-time faculty	400
full-time minority faculty	269
student-faculty ratio	16:1
average class size	n/a
% first-year retention rate	73
% graduation rate (6 years)	43

Popular majors Nursing, Education, Mass Communications, Business, Computer Science

CAMPUS LIFE

% live on campus	37.8

Multicultural student clubs and organizations Black Men for Change, Black Women for Change, Club Latino, Gay-Straight Student Alliance, Justice Studies Club, NAACP, National Black MBA Association, Nontraditional Adult Student Organization

Athletics NCAA Division II, Central Intercollegiate Athletics Association (CIAA)

ADMISSIONS

# of applicants	4,069
% accepted	53
# of first-year students enrolled	1,357
SAT Critical Reading (middle 50%)	432
SAT Math (middle 50%)	442
SAT Writing (middle 50%)	n/a
ACT (middle 50%)	17
average HS GPA	2.93

Deadlines

early action	11/15
regular decision	3/15
application fee (online)	$50 ($50)
fee waiver for applicants with financial need	yes

COST & AID

tuition	in-state $2,379; out-of-state $6,952
room & board	$3,181
total need-based institutional scholarships/grants	n/a
% of students apply for need-based aid	76
% of students receive aid	86
% receiving need-based scholarship or grant aid	64
% receiving aid whose need was fully met	77
average aid package	$6,522
average student loan debt upon graduation	$10,500

Case Western Reserve University

Case Western Reserve University is a private, four-year, comprehensive university located in the heart of Cleveland, Ohio's cultural and intellectual district. The campus offers an intimate collegiate setting within a city bustling with activity in health care, law and business. The university is home to four colleges offering undergraduate and graduate programs (arts and sciences, engineering, management and nursing) as well as six professional schools (medicine, dentistry, law, management, nursing and applied social sciences). As a major research university, there are many opportunities for students to get involved with a faculty member's research, and faculty members are deeply involved with students and their scholarship. A Case education pairs classroom learning with hands-on experience throughout all four years. Case is dedicated to the support, retention and success of all students, with additional offices, programs and resources dedicated to addressing the needs of students from underrepresented groups.

"As a student who is attending college without any financial assistance from my family, I have found the financial aid office at Case Western Reserve University to be especially sensitive to the unique barriers that many minority students encounter in their pursuit of higher education."

– Sean H., '11 Cleveland, OH Philosophy and Biochemistry

ACCESS **Upward Bound**

Local high school students who come from low-income families in which neither parent holds a bachelor's degree can benefit from Case Western Reserve University's Upward Bound, a pre-college program that provides a group of students with the right tools to pursue their dreams of earning a college degree. Students benefit from weekly tutoring, field trips, workshops, and a six-week summer enrichment program at Case.

ACCESS **Pre-College Scholars Program**

Case's Pre-College Scholars Program allows highly motivated and able high school students to enroll in college courses at Case during either the summer or the academic year. Pre-College Scholars attend classes with Case undergraduates for a first-hand college experience.

OPPORTUNITY **Diversity Scholarships**

Provost's Special Scholarships are partial tuition awards granted to promising applicants who will add to the diversity and the value of the education offered by Case. Congressional Black Caucus (CBC) Foundation Scholarships are full-tuition scholarships awarded to students nominated by members of the Congressional Black Caucus. High school curriculum and academic performance, extracurricular involvement, standardized test results and leadership are factors considered for both scholarships. For the CBC Foundation Scholarship, preference is given to competitive students who are economically and/or educationally disadvantaged.

SUCCESS **The Office of Multicultural Affairs (OMA)**

The Office of Multicultural Affairs encourages, supports and facilitates the success of students by providing opportunities for diverse interactions and cultural education that occur outside of the classroom. While the primary goal of the OMA is to assist students in being academically successful during their college career at Case, it also provides students with professional networking and mentoring opportunities, skill-building workshops and job and internship opportunities, in collaboration with the Career Center. Additional programming and resources include book vouchers, a freshman retreat, and 3.0 and Up Club, which recognizes academic achievement.

SUCCESS **Case/Cleveland Scholarship Program (CSP) Partnership**

The Case/CSP Partnership supports underrepresented, low-income and first-generation students through programs that prepare students to transition from high school to college, acclimate to university life and develop academic skills and habits that will ensure academic success. Participants are further supported with academic advising, tutoring, mentoring, career coaching and additional financial aid.

Case Western Reserve University
10900 Euclid Avenue
Cleveland, OH 44106-7055
Ph: (216) 368-4450
admission.case.edu
www.case.edu

FAST FACTS

STUDENT PROFILE

# of degree-seeking undergraduates	4,071
% male/female	58/42
% African American	5
% American Indian or Alaska Native	<1
% Asian or Pacific Islander	16
% Hispanic	3
% White	56
% International	6
% Pell grant recipients	19

First-generation and minority alumni Dr. David Satcher, 16th U.S. Surgeon General; Hon. Louis Stokes, first African American member of Congress, Ohio; Stephanie Tubbs-Jones, first Ohio African-American woman elected to the House of Representatives; Fred Gray, attorney, friend of Dr. Martin Luther King Jr., defended Rosa Parks

ACADEMICS

full-time faculty	749
full-time minority faculty	138
student-faculty ratio	9:1
average class size	10-19
% first-year retention rate	92
% graduation rate (6 years)	82

Popular majors Biology, Management, Psychology, Engineering, Nursing

CAMPUS LIFE

% live on campus (% freshmen)	78 (96)

Multicultural student clubs and organizations African Students Association, Asian American Alliance, Black Greek Council, Black Women's Society, Undergraduate Indian Student Association, Intercultural Dialogue Group, Korean Student Association, La Alianza, Middle Eastern Club, Muslim Student Association, National Association of Black Accountants, National Society of Black Engineers, Society of Hispanic Professional Engineers

Athletics NCAA Division III, University Athletic Association (UAA)

ADMISSIONS

# of applicants	9,472
% accepted	67
# of first-year students enrolled	1,021
SAT Critical Reading (middle 50%)	600-700
SAT Math (middle 50%)	650-750
SAT Writing (middle 50%)	590-700
ACT (middle 50%)	28-32
average H.S. GPA	n/a

Deadlines

early action	11/1
regular decision	1/15
application fee (online)	$0 ($0)

COST & AID

tuition	$38,760
room & board	$11,938
total need-based institutional scholarships/grants	$53,528,375
% of students apply for need-based aid	71
% of students receive aid	64
% receiving need-based scholarship or grant aid	62
% receiving aid whose need was fully met	86
average aid package	$33,130
average student loan debt upon graduation	$37,892

College of Mount St. Joseph

The College of Mount St. Joseph is a Catholic, four-year college that provides more than 2,400 students with a liberal arts and professional education. The Mount's goals are to assist students in becoming leaders in their professions and in their communities, and to prepare them for their life journey equipped with values, integrity and a sense of social responsibility. Smaller class sizes, individual attention, career preparation, and service learning opportunities support students' development and success. In addition to nearly 40 undergraduate degree programs, the Mount offers graduate and associate degrees as well a certificates and licensure programs. The College is a close-knit campus community that includes a newly renovated residence hall, athletic facilities, theatre, daycare center, state-of-the-art computer centers, and WI-FI access.

> ACCESS Summer Collegiate Orientation Program and Enrichment (Project SCOPE)

Through this program African-American high school sophomores from the Greater Cincinnati area reside on the Mount's campus and attend classes for one to two weeks. Classes improve skills in sciences, computer literacy, psychology and spoken word. Students attend workshops about the college admission process, library research, financial aid and study skills. The program is offered for three consecutive years, culminating in college preparedness and six transferable college credits for high school seniors.

> ACCESS Upward Bound

Local high school students who come from low-income families in which neither parent holds a bachelor's degree can benefit from the College of Mount St. Joseph's Upward Bound, a pre-college program that provides a group of students with the right tools to pursue their dreams of earning a college degree. Students benefit from weekly tutoring, field trips, workshops, and a six-week summer enrichment program at the Mount.

"My advice to other first-generation students is to join any club or organization or sports team, take charge and put energy into it. It will only benefit you because when you're involved, you're connected. Us at the Mount, we're a big family and that's how it should be."

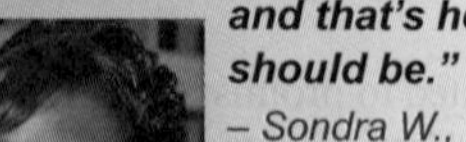

– Sondra W., '10
Cincinnati, OH
Communications Studies

> OPPORTUNITY Discovery Days/Get Acquainted Days (GAD)

Discovery Days and Get Acquainted Days allow potential Mount students the opportunity to explore academic programs and tour the campus as well as learn about financial aid and other support services at the college. Students enjoy lunch with faculty and current Mount students. Representatives from all academic majors and support services are on-hand to provide additional information.

> SUCCESS Office of Multicultural Affairs

The Office of Multicultural Affairs at the College is committed to an on-campus environment that values and respects all of its students, faculty and staff, regardless of gender, age, race, sexual preference, cultural background, religion, nationality, or beliefs. Through diversity awareness and multicultural education, a safe environment is supported on campus and in the Greater Cincinnati area. The office also oversees on-campus cultural events, the Black Student Union, and the International Student Association among other services and organizations.

College of Mount St. Joseph
5701 Delhi Road
Cincinnati, OH 45233-1670
Ph: (513) 244-4531
admission@mail.msj.edu
www.msj.edu

FAST FACTS

STUDENT PROFILE

# of degree-seeking undergraduates	2,055
% male/female	46/54
% African American	4.8
% American Indian or Alaska Native	<1
% Asian or Pacific Islander	<1
% Hispanic	1
% White	83
% International	<1
% Pell grant recipients	44

First-generation and minority alumni Bernadette Coutain Plair, life-long wildlife conservationist

ACADEMICS

full-time faculty	120
full-time minority faculty	4
student-faculty ratio	11:1
average class size	n/a
% first-year retention rate	71
% graduation rate (6 years)	56

Popular majors Nursing, Business Administration, Sport Management, Biology, Athletic Training, Psychology

CAMPUS LIFE

% live on campus	39

Multicultural student clubs and organizations Office of Multicultural Affairs, Black Student Union, International Student Association

Athletics NCAA Division III, Heartland Collegiate Athletic Conference (HCAC)

ADMISSIONS

# of applicants	1,610
% accepted	65
# of first-year students enrolled	382
SAT Critical Reading (middle 50%)	n/a
SAT Math (middle 50%)	440-540
SAT Writing (middle 50%)	n/a
ACT (middle 50%)	19-23
average HS GPA	3.24

Deadlines

regular decision	rolling to 8/15
application fee (online)	$25 ($25)
fee waiver for applicants with financial need	yes

COST & AID

tuition	$23,500
room & board	$7,432
total need-based institutional scholarships/grants	$1,626,297
% of students apply for need-based aid	94
% of students receive aid	99
% receiving need-based scholarship or grant aid	75
% receiving aid whose need was fully met	99
average aid package	$20,522
average student loan debt upon graduation	$35,569

The College of Wooster

College of Wooster
847 College Avenue
Wooster, OH 44691-2363
Ph: (330) 263-2322
admissions@wooster.edu
www.wooster.edu

The College of Wooster is nationally recognized for its emphasis on mentored independent research. Each Wooster senior creates an original research project, written work, performance or exhibit of artwork on a topic of his or her choosing, supported one-on-one by a faculty adviser. If the project requires travel or special equipment, to study the lives of West African immigrants in Paris or produce a documentary on survivors of Hiroshima, for example, significant grant funding is available. This independent study project, combined with a strong liberal arts curriculum, fosters creativity, resourcefulness, critical thinking, and communication skills in every Wooster student. Generations can attest to the life-changing quality of a Wooster education.

"Coming to college is a big step and can be very scary, but the Emerging Wooster Scholars program helped to ease some of my butterflies and concerns. During the program we had an opportunity to meet professors, deans, and other faculty members who showed us the various resources that are offered here at The College of Wooster. The Writing Center, Math Center and Learning Center all help students individually to improve a particular skill and assist in becoming a better students and critical thinker"

– Carmen G., '12
Oakwood Village, OH

ACCESS Youngstown Early Intervention Program

Select students from Youngstown, Ohio can participate in the Youngstown Early Intervention Program, which brings students to campus for two-week summer programs. During the summer sessions, students take math and English courses, as well as enrichment offerings in theater, science, college advising and other areas.

ACCESS Emerging Wooster Scholars Program

The Emerging Scholars program consists of a select group of students who represent an array of backgrounds who will benefit from the opportunity to enhance their foundation of academic skills. Students stay in a campus residence hall for three weeks and attend a tuition-free class, sessions on important college success skills, and earn money through an on-campus job.

OPPORTUNITY Multicultural and Underrepresented Scholarships

The College of Wooster awards several merit-based scholarships to deserving multicultural and underrepresented students. These include the Clarence Beecher Allen Scholarship, named for the first African-American student at The College of Wooster, and Making a Difference Scholarships, awarded to students committed to promoting diversity awareness. Awards range from $2,000 to two-thirds tuition and are renewable each year for four years.

OPPORTUNITY Posse Foundation

Wooster participates in the Posse Foundation, a program that brings talented inner-city youth to campus to pursue their academics and to help promote cross-cultural communication. Posse students are nominated by their high school to the program and share a collaborative support system with a special mentor to adjust to campus and college life. Wooster's Posse Scholars hail from Atlanta.

SUCCESS Summer Early Engage Research

The Summer Early Engaged Research (SEER) program will provide fellowships to underrepresented graduating high school seniors interested in the sciences to participate in a four week summer research experience, under the guidance of a faculty member and an upper class student mentor.

FAST FACTS

STUDENT PROFILE

# of degree-seeking undergraduates	1,815
% male/female	46/54
% African American	6
% American Indian or Alaska Native	<1
% Asian or Pacific Islander	2
% Hispanic	3
% White	70
% International	5
% Pell grant recipients	20

First-generation and minority alumni Solomon Oliver, U.S. District Court judge; Lance Mason, Ohio state senator; Dr. April Sorrell-Taylor, pediatric oncologist; June Millikan, sculptor, artist

ACADEMICS

full-time faculty	132
full-time minority faculty	17
student-faculty ratio	11:1
average class size	17
% first-year retention rate	89
% graduation rate (6 years)	77

Popular majors English, History, Psychology, Philosophy, Biology, Political Science

CAMPUS LIFE

% live on campus (% freshmen)	97 (96)

Multicultural student clubs and organizations Babcock International Hall, Black Students' Association, Chinese Culture Club, Dene House, DREAM Program, Women of IMAGES, International Student Association, Men of Harambee, Proyecto Latino, Pueblo de Esperanza, South East Asia Committee, UJAMAA

Athletics NCAA Division III, North Coast Athletic Conference (NCAC)

ADMISSIONS

# of applicants	4,635
% accepted	67
# of first-year students enrolled	482
SAT Critical Reading (middle 50%)	560-670
SAT Math (middle 50%)	550-670
SAT Writing (middle 50%)	550-650
ACT (middle 50%)	24-29
average HS GPA	3.51
Deadlines	
early decision	11/15
early action	11/15
regular decision	2/15
application fee (online)	$40 ($0)
fee waiver for applicants with financial need	yes

COST & AID

tuition	$38,290
room & board	$9,310
total need-based institutional scholarships/grants	n/a
% of students apply for need-based aid	80
% of students receive aid	95
% receiving need-based scholarship or grant aid	97
% receiving aid whose need was fully met	46
average aid package	$24,820
average student loan debt upon graduation	$25,140

Denison University

Denison University
100 West College Street
Granville, OH 43023
Ph: (800) DENISON (336-4766)
admissions@denison.edu
www.denison.edu

With its multicultural student enrollment over 22 percent, Denison University maintains a deep-rooted commitment to diversity, defining itself as an "intercultural university that values each member for his or her uniqueness while building on common strengths." The university provides numerous unique opportunities for its students, such as an innovative summer research program that gives selected students a stipend and free housing while they pursue collaborative research projects with professors. Denison also offers substantial service opportunities for its students.

ACCESS **Denison Community Association/Service Learning**

The Denison Community Association oversees 32 volunteer service programs such as the After School Mentoring and Tutoring program through which Denison students work with elementary and middle school students from nearby Newark to provide tutoring, literacy-related activities, and educational games. Denison also has a comprehensive service-learning program. One program of note is "Hispanic Culture Service," which brings students into local Hispanic communities.

OPPORTUNITY **Merit Scholarships**

Denison has a number of merit scholarships available, including the Bob and Nancy Good, Tyree/Parajon and Hla/Fisher Scholarships, all of which are awarded to students who can help diversify the university community. Underrepresented students can also benefit from the Upward Bound Scholarship, which is awarded to outstanding participants in the Upward Bound program.

"Sustained Dialogue at Denison is unlike any organization I've ever been in. It makes people open their minds and talk about issues in a meaningful way. SD has shown me that after college I want to do something that will make an impact on people and change lives."
– LaForce B., '10
Chicago, IL
Communication

OPPORTUNITY **Posse Foundation**

Denison University participates in the Posse Foundation, a program that brings talented inner-city youths to campus to pursue their academics and to help promote cross-cultural communication. Posse students are nominated by their high school to the program and share a collaborative support system with a special mentor to adjust to campus and college life. Denison's Posse Scholars hail from Chicago and Boston.

SUCCESS **Sustained Dialogue**

An outgrowth of a program started at Princeton University, Denison University houses one of approximately 15 to 20 college-based Sustained Dialogue programs, which facilitate discussions about issues of race and diversity on campus. Students must apply to be a part of the group, which meets bi-monthly and is led by two moderators.

FAST FACTS

STUDENT PROFILE	
# of degree-seeking undergraduates	2,257
% male/female	44/56
% African American	6.2
% American Indian or Alaska Native	5
% Asian or Pacific Islander	2.5
% Hispanic	4.3
% White	71
% International	5.5
% Pell grant recipients	15

First-generation and minority alumni Jose Rivera '77, first Puerto Rican screenwriter nominated for an Oscar; Alberto J. Verme '79, Chief Executive Officer of Europe, Middle East and Africa, Citigroup Global Markets Inc.; Kelly Brown Douglas '79, Episcopal priest, professor of theology, Howard University

ACADEMICS	
full-time faculty	205
full-time minority faculty	35
student-faculty ratio	10:1
average class size	19
% first-year retention rate	89.3
% graduation rate (6 years)	83

Popular majors Economics, Biology, Communication, Psychology, History, English-Literature

CAMPUS LIFE	
% live on campus (% freshmen)	100 (100)

Multicultural student clubs and organizations Asian Culture Club, Black Student Union, Denison International Student Association, Denison Muslim Student Association, La Fuerza Latina, Asian-American Student Union, Outlook, Sustained Dialogue

Athletics NCAA Division III, North Coast Athletic Conference (NCAC)

ADMISSIONS	
# of applicants	4,758
% accepted	48
# of first-year students enrolled	635
SAT Critical Reading (middle 50%)	600-700
SAT Math (middle 50%)	590-680
SAT Writing (middle 50%)	n/a
ACT (middle 50%)	27-30
average HS GPA	3.5
Deadlines	
early decision I	11/5
early decision II	1/15
regular decision	1/15
application fee (online)	$40 (0)
fee waiver for applicants with financial need	yes

COST & AID	
tuition	$39,330
room & board	$9,960
total Denison gift money (merit and aid)	$40,858,897
% of students apply for need-based aid	55.6
% of students receive aid	93
% receiving need-based scholarship or grant aid	53
% receiving aid whose need was fully met	26
average aid package	$20,131
average student loan debt upon graduation	$16,258

John Carroll University

John Carroll University is a Jesuit Catholic university founded in 1886. Known for its rigorous and highly regarded undergraduate curriculum, John Carroll offers degree programs in more than 30 major fields of the natural sciences, education, arts, the social sciences and business. The 60-acre suburban campus consists of 26 buildings located in University Heights, just 10 miles east of downtown Cleveland. The region is a cultural mecca boasting the country's second largest performing arts complex (Playhouse Square), the world-renowned Cleveland Symphony Orchestra and a metro-park system with a combined 52,000 acres and over 275 biking trails across Northeast Ohio.

ACCESS Early Awareness

John Carroll helps families start planning for the goal of a college degree early. Annually, middle and high school students spend a day on the university campus. Participants come from public and parochial schools in Greater Cleveland, Lorain, Akron and Canton. They experience a true day in the life, meet with admission and financial aid staff, the Office of Multicultural Affairs staff and John Carroll students of color, tour the campus, eat lunch and have a recreation period. Students are informed of the importance of a college education and how to prepare for success in college.

> ***"I chose John Carroll specifically for the Ohio Access Initiative. The financial support in exchange for a commitment to service is such a unique program. To be honest, I never thought I would be at such a great school. The people here are helpful and caring. I don't know where I'd be without the OAI Program."***
>
> *– Jennylee G., '12*
> *Cleveland, OH*
> *Biology*

OPPORTUNITY Ohio Access Initiative

The commitment to keeping private education affordable is quite visible at John Carroll. The Ohio Access Initiative is the newest financial aid program at the school, making it possible for qualified Ohio families with annual incomes below $40,000 to enroll their incoming freshmen tuition-free. Students are expected to participate in 30 hours of service through the university's Center for Service and Social Action.

OPPORTUNITY Pathways to Success Scholarship Program

Pathways to Success focuses on providing support tools to help students explore majors and career options, obtain internships, and prepare for the work world. In addition to a $1,000 award, Pathways to Success provides an orientation session, resume writing workshop, resume and cover letter review, interview training and attendance at a career fair. The scholarship is renewable for up to four years.

SUCCESS Pathways to Success

In an effort to help students of color successfully transition from high school to college, John Carroll University offers a distinct first year program focused on the first year adjustment to John Carroll, designed to prepare students academically and socially for their college experience. It is an excellent opportunity for incoming students to become acquainted with the campus and university services and establish bonds with other incoming students. Some benefits to participating in the Pathways to Success Program include free participation, up to $500 for textbooks in both the fall and spring semesters, valuable information from JCU faculty and administrators about effective study and time management skills. The Pathways program enables students to develop relationships with other incoming students of color. These relationships often serve as important support systems for students during the academic year.

John Carroll University
20700 N. Park Boulevard
University Heights, OH 44118
Ph: (215) 397-4294
admission@jcu.edu
www.jcu.edu

FAST FACTS

STUDENT PROFILE

# of degree-seeking undergraduates	2,868
% male/female	49/51
% African American	5
% American Indian or Alaska Native	<1
% Asian or Pacific Islander	2
% Hispanic	4
% White	85
% International	0
% Pell grant recipients	28

First-generation and minority alumni Dr. Evelyn Jenkins Gunn, Carnegie Scholar & Fellow (NBCT), National Academy (Carnegie Academy for the Advancement of Teaching & Learning); Annette L. Haile, vice president, IBM; Ric Harris, executive vice president and general manager, Digital Media & Strategic Marketing, NBC Universal; London Fletcher, NFL linebacker, Washington Redskins; Dr. Monique Ogletree, Ph.D., cardiovascular researcher, Baylor College of Medicine and Texas Children's Hospital; Tim Russert, moderator, Meet the Press, senior vice president and Washington bureau chief, NBC News

ACADEMICS

full-time faculty	199
full-time minority faculty	26
student-faculty ratio	13:1
average class size	17
% first-year retention rate	90
% graduation rate (6 years)	74

Popular majors Communications, Biology, Education, Business, Psychology, Political Science

CAMPUS LIFE

% live on campus (% freshmen)	58 (93)

Multicultural student clubs and organizations Black Student Union, International Student Union, African American Alliance, Asian Cultural Organization, Hip Hop Dance Club, Japan Society, Latin American Student Association (LASA), Middle Eastern Student Association

Athletics NCAA Division III, Ohio Athletic Conference (OAC)

ADMISSIONS

# of applicants	3,216
% accepted	81
# of first-year students enrolled	703
SAT Critical Reading (middle 50%)	490-600
SAT Math (middle 50%)	490-600
SAT Writing (middle 50%)	490-580
ACT (middle 50%)	22-26
average HS GPA	3.38

Deadlines

regular decision	2/1
application fee (online)	$0 ($0)
fee waiver for applicants with financial need	n/a

COST & AID

tuition	$29,250
room & board	$8,750
total need-based institutional scholarships/grants	$18,812,536
% of students apply for need-based aid	85
% of students receive aid	76
% receiving need-based scholarship or grant aid	75
% receiving aid whose need was fully met	18
average aid package	$24,519
average student loan debt upon graduation	$19,079

Kent State University

Located in Kent, Ohio, Kent State University features nearly 900 acres and 24 residence halls and enrolls more than 41,000 students across eight campuses. Kent State offers over 280 academic programs at the undergraduate level and engages students in diverse learning environments that expand their intellectual horizons and encourage them to become responsible citizens. The University provides a supportive community devoted to teaching excellence, first-tier scholarship, and academic freedom.

SUCCESS Student Multicultural Center

The Student Multicultural Center seeks to ensure the successful enrollment, retention and graduation of underrepresented students. The Center develops and implements holistic retention programs and encourages mutual respect through cultural, educational and social programming.

SUCCESS Department of Pan-African Studies

The Department of Pan-African Studies encompasses the Center for Pan-African Culture and the Institute for African-American affairs. Its mission is to offer an Afrocentric academic curriculum grounded in the cultural traditions and experiences of people of African descent. Providing a major and minor that span the humanities, fine arts, and social sciences, the Department fosters tolerance for cultural diversity on campus and throughout the surrounding community. This is implemented through its African Community Theatre and Outreach Programs.

SUCCESS Academic STARS (Students Achieving and Reaching for Success)

Academic STARS is a retention program for African American, Latino and Native American freshmen who want to enhance their opportunity for academic success, to develop leadership, and to enrich their college experience. The program kicks off with a five-week program during which participants participants will earn six credit hours to be applied toward graduation. Students also learn success strategies and skills through advising and workshops throughout the school year.

"Kent State has made me a well-rounded person. My favorite class, honors writing, was basically a roundtable discussion on books and novels. There were only 20 of us, and Professor Cutti encouraged us to think critically about storytelling, so our conversations were always interesting."

– Miranda M., '10
Columbus, OH
Nursing

SUCCESS Kupita/Transiciones

Kupita/Transiciones is a four-day holistic enrollment management, orientation and retention program for newly admitted African American, Latino, American Indian freshmen and transfer students. It includes academic success workshops a week before the start the start of the semester.

SUCCESS The University Mentoring Program

This program is a transition and retention support program designed to enhance the college and life-management skills of under-represented students by building a community of support around the freshman student.

Kent State University- Kent Campus
161 Schwartz Center
Kent, OH 44242
Ph: (800) 988-5368 / (330) 672-2444
admissions@kent.edu
www.kent.edu

FAST FACTS

STUDENT PROFILE

# of degree-seeking undergraduates	20,557
% male/female	42/58
% African American	9
% American Indian or Alaska Native	<1
% Asian or Pacific Islander	2
% Hispanic	2
% White	83
% International	1
% Pell grant recipients	43

First-generation and minority alumni Bertice B. Berry, Ph D., Comedian, Speaker and Writer; Robert L. Billingslea, Corporate Director of Urban Affairs, Disney Worldwide Services; Edmund D. Cooke, Jr., Attorney, Partner Drinker Biddle & Reath LLP; Albert "Al" Fitzpatrick, Retired executive and editor, Knight Ridder; Arsenio Hall, Entertainer

ACADEMICS

full-time faculty	886
full-time minority faculty	50
student-faculty ratio	20:1
average class size	32
% first-year retention rate	78
% graduation rate (6 years)	49.9

Popular majors Architecture, Business, Education, Journalism, Nursing

CAMPUS LIFE

% live on campus (% freshmen)	36 (84)

Multicultural student clubs and organizations Association of International Students, Black Greek Council, Black United Studies, Harambee, Indian Student Association, Native American Student Association, Spanish and Latino Student Association

Athletics NCAA Division I, Mid-American Athletic Conference (MAAC)

ADMISSIONS

# of applicants	15,637
% accepted	70
# of first-year students enrolled	4,009
SAT Critical Reading (middle 50%)	460-570
SAT Math (middle 50%)	460-580
SAT Writing (middle 50%)	450-550
ACT (middle 50%)	20-25
average HS GPA	3.21

Deadlines

regular decision	rolling to 8/1
application fee (online)	$40 ($40)
fee waiver for applicants with financial need	yes

COST & AID

tuition	in-state: $9,326; out-of-state: $17,306
room & board	$8,830
total need-based institutional scholarships/grants	$13,718,897
% of students apply for need-based aid	70
% of students receive aid	100
% receiving need-based scholarship or grant aid	69
% receiving aid whose need was fully met	53
average aid package	$7,895
average student loan debt upon graduation	$23,957

Kenyon College

Kenyon College is a nationally prominent co-ed liberal arts college where academic challenge goes hand in hand with a strong sense of community. Small classes, close relationships with professors, and a beautiful campus provide a supportive environment where students thrive. Professors serve as advisors and mentors, getting to know their students personally and often involving them in collaborative research. Kenyon also puts a high value on diversity. American students of color represent 14 percent of the student population, which also includes students from 43 foreign countries. About 65 percent of students receive financial aid, and the College guarantees a loan-free education to selected students with the greatest need.

"I feel like I'll walk away from Kenyon a better person. Because of the support and the education here, I'll have the strength to face whatever life throws at me. And I'll have taken classes with cool professors who make this place what it is."

– Gabrielle T., '13
Newark, NJ
Political Science

ACCESS **College Horizons**

Kenyon College proudly partners with College Horizons, a nonprofit organization offering pre-college workshops for Native American, Alaskan Native, and Native Hawaiian high school students. Students spend five and a half days on a college campus with admissions officers and college counselors who help them prepare for the college admission and financial aid process.

OPPORTUNITY **Trustee Opportunity Travel Grants**

Trustee Opportunity Travel Grants help cover the cost of campus visits to Kenyon College for first-generation, African-American, Asian-American, Latino/Hispanic-American, and Native American students. The grants cover up to 90 percent of airfares or up to $50 to offset driving costs.

OPPORTUNITY **Cultural Connections Visit Weekends**

Every year, Kenyon College hosts two Cultural Connections Visit Weekends, designed for prospective students who are interested in multiculturalism at Kenyon. Participants have a unique opportunity to experience life on campus firsthand, while exploring Kenyon's dedication to cultural diversity. First-generation and minority students are eligible to use the Trustee Opportunity Travel Grants to attend these visit weekends.

OPPORTUNITY **Trustee Opportunity and Newman's Own Foundation Scholarships**

The most competitive and valued merit scholarships offered at Kenyon, Trustee Opportunity Scholarships are awarded to top students who come from underrepresented backgrounds, including first-generation students. Newman's Own Foundation Scholarships are awarded to socioeconomically disadvantaged students, with priority given to those from underrepresented backgrounds, including first-generation students. Both scholarships eliminate loans from students' financial aid packages.

SUCCESS **Kenyon Educational Enrichment Program (KEEP)**

KEEP is a selective program providing academic and social support to twelve students in each Kenyon class who come from diverse ethnic, racial, and socioeconomic backgrounds. The experience begins with a six-week pre-college intensive summer academic program and continues with four years of enrichment and support.

SUCCESS **Recognizing Each Other's Ability to Conquer the Hill (REACH)**

REACH is a peer mentoring and tutoring program that helps first- and second-year minority and first-generation students adjust to college life. Divided into 3 components—the Mentoring Program and Tutorial Program during freshman year and the Sophomore Experience Program—REACH caters to students' various needs throughout their collegiate career.

Kenyon College
Office of Admissions, Ransom Hall
Gambier, OH 43022
Ph: (740) 427-5776
admissions@kenyon.edu
www.kenyon.edu

FAST FACTS

STUDENT PROFILE

# of degree-seeking undergraduates	1,632
% male/female	46/54
% African American	4
% American Indian or Alaska Native	1
% Asian or Pacific Islander	6
% Hispanic	4
% White	79
% International	5
% Pell grant recipients	8

First-generation and minority alumni James Wright '52, Pulitzer Prize-winning poet; Richard L. Thomas '53, retired chairman, First Chicago Corporation; William E. Lowry Jr. '56, retired executive, John D. and Catherine T. MacArthur Foundation and civic leader, Chicago; Ulysses B. Hammond '73, Vice President for Administration, Connecticut College and former chief executive officer, District of Columbia Courts; Allison Joseph '88, Associate Professor of English, Southern Illinois University and award-winning poet; Shaka Smart '99, head basketball coach, Virginia Commonwealth University

ACADEMICS

full-time faculty	157
full-time minority faculty	22
student-faculty ratio	10:1
average class size	15
% first-year retention rate	93
% graduation rate (6 yr.)	89

Popular majors English, Political Science, History, Psychology, International Studies

CAMPUS LIFE

% live on campus (% freshmen)	99 (100)

Multicultural student clubs and organizations ADELANTE, Asian Awareness, Chinese Culture Club, Black Student Union, German Club, International Students at Kenyon, Japan Club, La Tertulia, Middle East Students Association, SAMOSA

Athletics NCAA Division III, North Coast Athletic Conference (NCAC)

ADMISSIONS

# of applicants	4,272
% accepted	33
# of first-year students enrolled	472
SAT Critical Reading (middle 50%)	640-740
SAT Math (middle 50%)	610-690
SAT Writing (middle 50%)	640-730
ACT (middle 50%)	28-32
average HS GPA	3.84

Deadlines

early decision	11/15, 1/15
regular decision	1/15
application fee (online)	$50 ($0)
fee waiver for applicants with financial need	yes

COST & AID

tuition	$41,090
room & board	$10,020
total need-based institutional scholarships & grants	$22,385,820
% of students apply for need-based aid	55
% receiving need-based scholarship or grant aid	82
% receiving aid whose need was fully met	48
average aid package	$36,652
average student loan debt upon graduation	$17,536

Marietta College

Since receiving its charter in 1835, Marietta College has provided a strong liberal arts foundation to generations of students, empowering them to be lifelong learners, critical thinkers and agents of change. The college focuses on preparing students to thrive in diverse surroundings, to positively affect their chosen professions and to stand out as leaders in their communities. Through programs such as Study Abroad, the Charles Sumner Harrison Organization, community service projects and a far-reaching goal to foster and celebrate diversity and multiculturalism, Marietta's 1,400 students have a wealth of opportunities to share their unique backgrounds and forge relationships with others striving to do the same.

ACCESS Inner City Visit Day

The office of Minority Affairs has hosted a bus load of students from various schools in the Cleveland area for the past few years in an effort to reach out to first-generation, low income and minority students near the inner city of Cleveland, OH. The bridge program called S.I.T.E. (Student Initiatives Towards Excelling) helps students with their transition from high school to college.

"I am the first in my family of 10—seven children and my mother and father—to receive a bachelor's degree. Ultimately I want to work in the ministry and with at-risk children and families."

–Courtney M., '11
Cleveland, OH
Psychology

OPPORTUNITY Summer Enrollment Days

Over the summer Marietta College holds several Summer Enrollment Days on which incoming freshmen are encouraged to visit the school. Students are given their identification card, mailroom key or combination, college e-mail address and a schedule for the fall semester. This is the first part of the orientation process, and allows students to begin making connections with their classmates and get a feeling for what life at college will be like.

OPPORTUNITY Charles Sumner Harrison Award

The Charles Sumner Harrison Award is available to diverse students and those with clearly demonstrated involvement and leadership in multiculturalism. The award is for $5,000 and is renewable for up to four years provided the student remains in good academic standing. No application is required to receive the grant.

SUCCESS Minority Student Orientation

Minority Student Orientation is generally two days long and takes place the two days directly before the General Freshman Orientation. "Making the Grade" Mentoring Program. This program helps students get accustomed to the campus community through peer guidance, various information sessions and workshops.

SUCCESS First Year Program

In the student's first year, freshmen are enrolled in First Year Seminar and the College Life and Leadership Laboratory. Both of these are courses that are designed to help students make the transition from high school to college. In addition, all students are required to complete (or otherwise earn credit for) English 101, an introductory writing course, and Communication 101, a public speaking course.

Marietta College
215 Fifth St.
Marietta, OH 45750
Ph: (740) 376-4600
admit@marietta.edu
www.marietta.edu

FAST FACTS

STUDENT PROFILE

# of degree-seeking undergraduates	1,463
% male/female	51/49
% African American	5
% American Indian or Alaska Native	0
% Asian or Pacific Islander	1
% Hispanic	1
% White	72
% International	12
% Pell grant recipients	29

First-generation and minority alumni Major General Randy Randolph M.D. '65, Major General in the US Air Force; Major General Christopher Cortez '71, 1st Hispanic General in the Marine Corps, Commanding General US Marine Corps Recruiting Command, Linda Robinson Doughty '75, Director of The California Student Opportunity and Access Program (Cal-SOAP)

ACADEMICS

full-time faculty	108
full-time minority faculty	7
student-faculty ratio	12:1
average class size	20
% first-year retention rate	78
% graduation rate (6 yr.)	59

Popular majors Petroleum Engineering, Advertising, Finance, Marketing, Psychology

CAMPUS LIFE

% live on campus (% freshmen)	82 (94)

Multicultural student clubs and organizations Charles Sumer Harrison Organization, which is a diversity organization that sponsors activities and community events for campus; the Marietta College Dance Team, Diverse Dancers Rising (DDR) and the newly created Step Team, MC Essence Steppers, which perform during athletic, campus and community events in Marietta; The American International Association (AIA); The MC Model United Nations Club; The Quidditch Team

Athletics NCAA Division III, Ohio Athletic Conference (OAC)

ADMISSIONS

# of applicants	3,523
% accepted	69
# of first-year students enrolled	390
SAT Critical Reading (middle 50%)	490-630
SAT Math (middle 50%)	510-630
SAT Writing (middle 50%)	490-610
ACT (middle 50%)	21-27
average HS GPA	3.45

Deadlines

regular decision	rolling
application fee (online)	$25 ($0)
fee waiver for applicants with financial need	yes

COST & AID

tuition	$28,950
room & board	$9,090
total need-based institutional scholarships & grants	$17,341,850
% of students apply for need-based aid	93
% receiving need-based scholarship or grant aid	74
% receiving aid whose need was fully met	32
average aid package	$25,310
average student loan debt upon graduation	$34,152

Miami University

Miami University encourages students to become citizen leaders, infused with the desire to learn and think critically. Dedicated to grounding students in a liberal arts education, Miami consistently places among the top public universities in national college guides and is specifically cited by *U.S. News and World Report* for academic programs that lead to student success. Miami students graduate at a rate above the national average, due largely to the personal attention and support they receive from their professors.

OPPORTUNITY **BRIDGES: A Plan for Excellence**

The BRIDGES Program serves outstanding underrepresented students who are interested in studying at Miami University. BRIDGES recruits high-school seniors who maintain at least a 3.0 cumulative GPA in a college preparatory curriculum, who are active in extracurricular activities, and who demonstrate leadership. The program offers an all-expenses-paid overnight visit to the Oxford campus. Students participate in activities that prepare them for college, the admission process, and offer financial aid information. Students completing this program receive a four year renewable scholarship upon enrollment at Miami.

SUCCESS **Miami Advising Resource Center (MARC)**

The goal of Miami Advising Resource Center (MARC) is to enhance and support the Miami University campus-wide academic advising system by serving as a one-stop source of information for general advising questions. We assist undergraduate students with navigating the MU advising system and provide direction when students are wondering who to ask and where to go with a specific advising question that will ultimately lead to student satisfaction and retention. MARC works to enhance student support programming for some special populations of students including Foster Youth Alumni, Veterans, Prospective Transfer and Relocating Students. Also, MARC can approve short-term loans to any qualified student who is in need of financial assistance for school-related or book expenses.

SUCCESS **MADE@Miami**

MADE@Miami, MU's Pre-First Year Institute, comprises qualities valued by the University community – Mentoring, Achievement, Diversity, and Excellence. This program provides a diverse group of academically ambitious first- year students the opportunity to engage in workshops to ease their transition to the University community, contribute to their academic success, and stimulate thinking related to their common experience.

"Ever since I was young, I wanted to be an inventor. I'm in the Scholastic Enhancement Program, and I'm paired with an engineering professor to learn how to do research. We built a robot, and it's been a great experience. I also received a Miami Access Initiative scholarship, which helps."

–Justinn E., '11
Cleveland, OH
Mechanical Engineering

SUCCESS **Rinella Learning Center**

The Rinella Learning Center offers individual and group tutoring, a learning disabilities program, and help with study skills. The mission of the Bernard B. Rinella, Jr. Learning Center is to help students reach their individual academic goals by empowering them with skills needed to be independent and successful learners and to provide academic support through various programs and services with the help of the center's staff.

SUCCESS **Connection Coaches Peer Mentor Program**

The Office of Diversity Affairs (ODA) Connection Coaches Peer Mentor Program is designed to pair first-year students with a trained peer coach, or mentor, who can help new students feel more connected and comfortable at the university by helping with transition difficulties often faced in the first year. Whether helping students navigate the university community by referring them to resources, acting as a sounding board, or introducing students to athletic and cultural events, these mentors will offer assistance, motivation and support to achieve success.

Miami University
301 S. Campus Avenue
Oxford, OH 45056
Ph: (513) 529-2531
admission@muohio.edu
www.muohio.edu

FAST FACTS

STUDENT PROFILE

# of degree-seeking undergraduates	14,699
% male/female	46/54
% African American	5
% American Indian or Alaska Native	1
% Asian or Pacific Islander	3
% Hispanic	2
% White	84
% International	3
% Pell grant recipients	14

First-generation and minority alumni Rita Dove '73, former U.S. poet laureate (first African American and youngest); Wil Haygood '76, journalist, *The Washington Post*; Marilyn Gaston '60, former assistant surgeon general

ACADEMICS

full-time faculty	867
full-time minority faculty	135
student-faculty ratio	17:1
average class size	31
% first-year retention rate	90
% graduation rate (6 yr.)	82

Popular majors Zoology, Psychology, Marketing, Finance, Education

CAMPUS LIFE

% live on campus (% freshmen)	46 (98)

Multicultural student clubs and organizations Historically Black and Latino-interest Greek Fraternities and Sororities, Hillel, Spectrum, Miami Ambassadors Advocating for Diversity, Indian Student Association, International Club, Japanese Culture and Language Club, Muslim Student Association, Love you Like a Sister, Miami University Gospel Singers, Minority Health Association, Association of Latino and American Students, Chinese Student and Scholars Friendship Association, Asian American Association, Diwali, National Association for the Advancement of Colored People, Minority Business Association, Black Student Action Association, GLTBQ Alliance

Athletics NCAA Division I, Mid-America Conference (MAC)

ADMISSIONS

# of applicants	16,950
% accepted	75
# of first-year students enrolled	3,595
SAT Critical Reading (middle 50%)	520-630
SAT Math (middle 50%)	550-650
SAT Writing (middle 50%)	n/a
ACT (middle 50%)	24-29
average HS GPA	3.66

Deadlines

early decision	11/1
early action	12/1
regular decision	2/1
application fee (online)	$50 ($50)
fee waiver for applicants with financial need	yes

COST & AID

tuition	in-state: $12,728; out-of-state $27,516
room & board	$9,458
total need-based institutional scholarships & grants	$8,533,340
% of students apply for need-based aid	57
% of students receive aid	98
% receiving need-based scholarship or grant aid	40
% receiving aid whose need was fully met	17
average aid package	$10,940
average student loan debt upon graduation	$27,315

Oberlin College

Oberlin College, founded in 1833, is a four-year, highly selective liberal arts college and home to America's oldest continuously operating music conservatory. From its founding, Oberlin has been a community of thinkers, scholars, scientists, musicians, athletes, activists and artists. Students are united by a commitment to social justice and a willingness to confront social issues that many would prefer to ignore. Oberlin invented coeducation in 1837 and made interracial education central to its mission in 1835. Oberlin offers 47 majors and 42 minors and areas of concentration. Students pursue studies in the College of Arts and Sciences, the Conservatory of Music or both divisions through a distinctive five-year double-degree program. More Oberlin graduates have gone on to earn a Ph.D. than those at any other American college.

"When I started researching Oberlin I fell in love with its history of change and progressive activism... Students here are just as active and committed as they have ever been. Their continued commitment to changing the world, social justice, and environmental sustainability were all things that drew me to Oberlin."

– Justin B., '09
Cincinnati, OH
Politics, Psychology

ACCESS **Ninde Scholars Program**

An outgrowth of Oberlin College's community-based Writing Program, the Ninde Scholars Program pairs Oberlin rhetoric and composition students with Oberlin High School students who are low-income, first-generation and/or from underrepresented minority groups in post-secondary education. Ninde Scholars receive support in navigating the college process while building writing and research skills as necessary tools for college success.

OPPORTUNITY **Multicultural Visit Program**

Six times each year, Oberlin's Office of Admissions sponsors a Multicultural Visit Program, an all-expenses-paid campus visit for minority students interested in a liberal arts education.

OPPORTUNITY **Oberlin Access Initiative**

The Oberlin Access Initiative allows Oberlin to maintain its historic leadership in providing access to a diversity of individuals. It ensures that any qualified student who wishes to attend Oberlin College will be able to do so, regardless of his or her ability to pay. Students who are eligible to receive the federally funded Pell Grant will receive loan-free financial aid packages.

OPPORTUNITY **Posse Foundation**

Oberlin participates in the Posse Foundation, a program that brings talented public school youth to campus to pursue their academics and to help promote cross-cultural communication. Posse students are nominated by their high school to the program and share a collaborative support system with a special mentor to adjust to campus and college life. Oberlin's Posse Scholars hail from Chicago.

OPPORTUNITY **QuestBridge**

Oberlin partners with QuestBridge, a national program that links bright, motivated, low-income students to some of the nation's best colleges. The target is to "match," a process similar to early decision, approximately five students with Oberlin annually. Approximately 70 percent of QuestBridge scholars are minority students and come from households with annual incomes under $29,000.

OPPORTUNITY **Office of Undergraduate Research**

Each year the Office of Undergraduate Research selects ten Oberlin College Research Fellows and five Mellon Mays Undergraduate Fellows from low-income families, first-generation students, and students underrepresented in graduate studies to encourage them to pursue Ph.D.s. Fellows are mentored by faculty during the academic year and participate in intensive research projects for two summers.

Oberlin College
101 North Professor St
Oberlin, OH 44074
Ph: (440) 775-8411
college.admissions@oberlin.edu
www.oberlin.edu

FAST FACTS

STUDENT PROFILE

# of degree-seeking undergraduates	2,901
% male/female	45/55
% African American	6
% American Indian or Alaska Native	<1
% Asian or Pacific Islander	4
% Hispanic	7
% White	73
% International	6
% Pell grant recipients	9

First-generation and minority alumni Ishmael Beah, author, *A Long Way Gone: Memoirs of a Boy Soldier*; Johnnetta Betsch Cole, first African-American to serve as chair of the Board of the United Way of America, first African-American woman to serve as president of Spelman College; Chris Broussard, NBA reporter, ESPN's SportsCenter, columnist, *ESPN the Magazine*; Adrian Fenty, mayor of Washington, D.C.; James McBride, author, *The Color of Water*; Eduardo Mondlane, the father of modern Mozambique; Carl Rowan, prominent African-American journalist; Anthony Stallion, chairman, Diversity Councils for Cleveland Clinic hospitals; Moses Fleetwood Walker, first African-American to play major league baseball, member of Toledo Blue Stockings

ACADEMICS

full-time faculty	285
full-time minority faculty	31
student-faculty ratio	11:1
average class size	19
% first-year retention rate	94
% graduation rate (6 years)	87

Popular majors Biology/Biological Science, English Language and Literature, History, Environmental Studies, Music, East Asian Studies

CAMPUS LIFE

% live on campus (% freshmen)	89 (100)

Multicultural student clubs and organizations Asian American Alliance, African Student Association, Chinese Student Association, Filipino American Student Association, La Alianza Latina, Middle Eastern Students Association, Oberlin Korean Students Association

Athletics NCAA Division III, North Coast Athletic Conference (NCAC)

ADMISSIONS

# of applicants	7,222
% accepted	31
# of first-year students enrolled	784
SAT Critical Reading (middle 50%)	650-740
SAT Math (middle 50%)	630-710
SAT Writing (middle 50%)	650-740
ACT (middle 50%)	28-32
average HS GPA	3.6

Deadlines

early decision	11/15
regular decision	1/15
application fee (online)	$35 ($35)
fee waiver for applicants with financial need	yes

COST & AID

tuition	$41,234
room & board	$11,010
total need-based institutional scholarships/grants	$41,048,711
% of students apply for need-based aid	64
% of students receive aid	57
% receiving need-based scholarship or grant aid	42
% receiving aid whose need was fully met	100
average aid package	$32,845
average student loan debt upon graduation	$17,579

Ohio Northern University

Ohio Northern University
525 South Main Street
Ada, OH 45810
Ph: (888) 408-4ONU (4668)
admissions-ug@onu.edu
www.onu.edu

When many colleges were debating whether to admit women, Ohio Northern University had been doing it since its inception in 1871. A private, independent school located in the rural community of Ada, Ohio and affiliated with the United Methodist Church, this former teaching institution was built from the ground up by local educator Henry Solomon Lehr. Today, Ohio Northern boasts five colleges, including a law school, a robust curriculum, and a range of organizations and activities, including 21 varsity sports for men and women.

ACCESS Multicultural Overnight Visit Experience (MOVE)

The Multicultural Overnight Visit Experience or M.O.V.E. is an alternative to traditional visit program. It will be an opportunity for students to not just observe the intellectual process but to engage in meaningful dialogue, creative problem solving, and experience life as an ONU student for a day. Students will be paired with current ONU students and will enjoy complimentary meals and entertainment.

"As a student of color, Ohio Northern has provided me with opportunities to learn and grow with the resources I need to be successful. Being here has allowed me to interact with and learn from students from different cultural backgrounds, which will prepare me to pursue a career in the field of business."

*– Terryn T., '12
Lima, OH
Business
Management*

OPPORTUNITY Dimension Award

The Dimension Award financially assists accepted students from underrepresented ethnic backgrounds. Award amounts start at $5,000 in gift aid. Accepted students who apply for the Dimension Award are encouraged to file the FAFSA to ensure maximum assistance. The award is coordinated with other financial aid programs and awards. The Dimension Award is available to new full-time undergraduate students (four years for pharmacy) and transfer students.

SUCCESS Office of Multicultural Development

The Office of Multicultural Development offers a seven-step series as a part of an aggressive initiative to acknowledge, retain, and embrace its multicultural student population. The office opened in 1991 and has sponsored a wealth of programs and events to celebrate diversity. The components include activities and programs that serve both academic and social objectives that educate the entire campus community.

FAST FACTS

STUDENT PROFILE

# of degree-seeking undergraduates	2,312
% male/female	52/48
% African American	3
% American Indian or Alaska Native	<1
% Asian or Pacific Islander	1
% Hispanic	1.5
% White	89
% International	2.5
% Pell grant recipients	28

First-generation and minority alumni Floyd A. Keith '70, Executive Director, Black Coaches and Administrators; Judge Benjamin H. Logan B.A. '68, J.D. '72, Judge in the 61st District Court of the State of Michigan

ACADEMICS

full-time faculty	243
full-time minority faculty	24
student-faculty ratio	11:1
average class size	23
% first-year retention rate	83
% graduation rate (6 yr)	66

Popular majors Business, Education, Engineering, Pharmacy, Biology

CAMPUS LIFE

% live on campus (% freshmen)	68 (96)

Multicultural student clubs and organizations Black Student Union, Asian American Student Union, Indian Student Association, Open Doors, Latino Student Union, Men of Distinction, Sister Circle, World Student Organization

Athletics NCAA Division III, Ohio Athletic Conference (OAC)

ADMISSIONS

# of applicants	3,147
% accepted	81
# first-year students enrolled	608
SAT Critical Reading (middle 50%)	520-630
SAT Math (middle 50%)	560-670
SAT Writing (middle 50%)	510-620
ACT (middle 50%)	24-29
Average HS GPA	3.7

Deadlines

early action (Pharmacy only)	11/1
early action II (Arts & Sciences; Business Administration; and Engineering)	12/1
regular decision (Arts & Sciences; Business Administration; and Engineering)	2/1
application fee (online)	$30 ($0)
fee waiver for applicants with financial need	yes

COST & AID

tuition	$34,380
room & board	$9,844
total need-based institutional scholarships/grants	$31,353,685
% of students apply for need-based aid	98
% of students receive aid	84
% receiving need-based scholarship or grant aid	84
% receiving aid whose need was fully met	18
average aid package	$27,281
average student loan debt upon graduation	$48,886

The Ohio State University

The Ohio State University is a co-educational, non-denominational, public research university. The university was founded in 1870 as a land-grant university and is currently among the largest universities in the United States. With an overarching goal of advancing the well-being of the people of Ohio and the global community through the creation and dissemination of knowledge, Ohio State strives to pursue knowledge for its own sake, ignite in its students a lifelong love of learning, produce discoveries that make the world a better place, celebrate and learn from its diversity and "open the world" to its students.

ACCESS **Blueprint: College**

The Ohio State University's free series of college planning workshops is designed especially for the parents of children enrolled in local elementary schools. The program has two main goals: to provide first-generation, low-income and/or minority parents with tips on how to prepare their children for college and to relay the importance of college to their children. The program begins with a kick-off dinner in the spring and is then held weekly for five weeks. Two Saturday campus visits also occur. Dinner, transportation and childcare are provided by the university.

"Growing up, I realized how hard it was for my mother to support me and my two brothers. Though she always pushed for me to go to college, we both knew our family could not afford it. But I was determined to go! When I applied to Ohio State, I filled out the FAFSA and OSU gave me many scholarships and grants. Keeping my grades up so that I can continue to go to school for free is the least I can do."

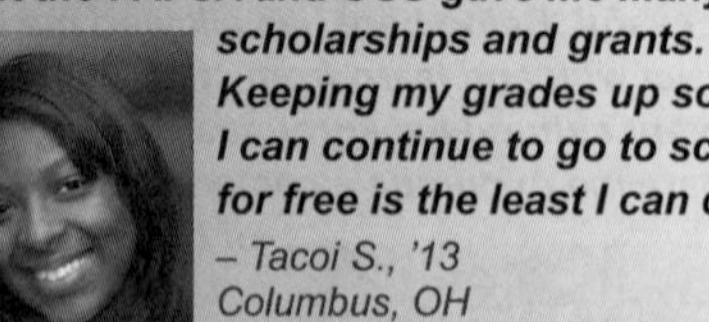

– Tacoi S., '13
Columbus, OH
Math

ACCESS **Economic Access Initiative**

The Economic Access Initiative ensures that qualified students who lack financial resources and information about the college process are not denied the opportunity to attend Ohio State. The university has developed initiatives throughout the state for educating low-income students and their parents about available financial aid resources and programs.

OPPORTUNITY **Land Grant Opportunity Scholarship**

The Land Grant Opportunity Scholarship program was established to help high-ability, low-income students enroll at Ohio State. Through the program, the full in-state cost of education at Ohio State is covered via a combination of scholarships, grants, and work-study opportunities for one or more qualified students from each of Ohio's 88 counties.

OPPORTUNITY **Morrill Scholars Program (MSP)**

This is a merit scholarship program for students who contribute to diversity at Ohio State. The Office of Minority Affairs offers this program to promote diversity, multiculturalism and leadership and to enrich the educational experiences of all Ohio State students so they will be prepared for optimum success in the world community. Eligible students include racial and ethnic minorities, Ohio Appalachian, first-generation and low-income students. Nearly 600 students were offered an MSP scholarship for fall 2008, with the minimum award being full in-state tuition.

SUCCESS **First-Year Success Series**

The First-Year Success Series helps to promote success by offering short courses on the common concerns and questions first-year students have during their transition to university life. The very first week of sessions focuses on issues related to financial literacy and understanding financial aid, covering topics including managing a checking account, credit card debt and "Financial Aid 101." Additional topics include study skills, procrastination, leadership, health and wellness, sexual health, drugs and alcohol awareness and diversity issues. First-year students are required by their academic adviser to attend two to four of these sessions.

The Ohio State University
Undergraduate Admissions and First Year Experience
110 Enarson Hall, 154 W. 12th Ave.
Columbus, OH 43210
Ph: (614) 292-3980
askabuckeye@osu.edu
www.osu.edu

FAST FACTS

STUDENT PROFILE

# of degree-seeking undergraduates	38,300
% male/female	53/47
% African American	7
% American Indian or Alaska Native	<1
% Asian or Pacific Islander	6
% Hispanic	3
% White	83
% International	6
% Pell grant recipients	30.6

First-generation and minority alumni Samella Lewis, artist; Chester Himes, writer; Aimee Nezhukumatathil, poet; Manu Mehta, CEO, Matabyte Networks, Inc.; Phuthuma Nhleko, CEO, MTN Group; Yang Huiyan, China's wealthiest person in 2007; Ruby Elzy, opera singer; Ljubica Acevska, diplomat of the Republic of Macedonia to the United States; Amodou Ba, Diplomat Senegal Ambassador; Chester Crocker, former undersecretary of state for African Affairs; Jayaprakash Narayan, Indian freedom fighter; Ken Nnamani, senate president, Nigeria; Roberto Sanchez Vilella, former governor of Puerto Rico; Jesse Brown, first African-American Navy pilot; P. Chungmoo Auh, president, Korean Institute of Energy Research; Robert Henry Lawrence, Jr., first African-American NASA astronaut; Esther Takeuchi, inventor; Michael White, former mayor, Cleveland

ACADEMICS

full-time faculty	3,360
full-time minority faculty	709
student-faculty ratio	19:1
average class size	26
% first-year retention rate	93
% graduation rate (6 years)	78

Popular majors Biology, Finance, Political Science, English, Accounting, Marketing, Communication, Psychology

CAMPUS LIFE

% live on campus (% freshmen)	25 (92)

Multicultural student clubs and organizations African-American Media Organization, Afrikan Student Union, American Indian Council, Asian-American Association, Black Law Student Association, Hispanic groups, Indian-American Student Association, NAACP; African, Asian, Chinese, Egyptian, Indian, Indonesian, Japanese, Korean, Laotian, Malaysian, Pakistani, Singaporean, Taiwanese, Thai, Turkish and International student associations

Athletics NCAA Division I, Big Ten Conference (Big10) (football I-A), Central Collegiate Hockey Association (CCHA), Great Western Lacrosse League (GWLL), Midwestern Intercollegiate Volleyball Association (MIVA), Western Collegiate Hockey Association (WCHA)

ADMISSIONS

# of applicants	24,302
% accepted	68
# of first-year students enrolled	6,654
SAT Critical Reading (middle 50%)	540-650
SAT Math (middle 50%)	590-700
SAT Writing (middle 50%)	540-640
ACT (middle 50%)	26-30
average HS GPA	n/a
Deadlines	
regular decision	2/1
application fee (online)	$40 ($40)
fee waiver for applicants with financial need	yes

COST & AID

tuition	in-state: $9,309; out-of-state: $24,204
room & board	$9,180
total need-based institutional scholarships/grants	$62,208,188
% of students apply for need-based aid	69
% of students receive aid	55
% receiving need-based scholarship or grant aid	40
% receiving aid whose need was fully met	15
average aid package	$10,575
average student loan debt upon graduation	$18,425

Ohio Wesleyan University

In 1842, Ohio residents Adam Poe and Charles Elliott decided to establish a university "of the highest order" in central Ohio. Today, with several support programs at Ohio Wesleyan University for pre-college, first-generation, underserved students, the university continues to be a leader in cultural diversity and international education in all its forms. For example, the President's Commission on Racial and Cultural Diversity issues an annual report with recommendations and concerns about the state of racial and cultural diversity at Ohio Wesleyan. Also, the school offers on-campus housing options focusing on multicultural issues, including the House of Black Culture as one of the University's small living units.

"OWU does a great job of incorporating all students. I've been to El Salvador and New Orleans on mission trips and have studied in Spain. I also have had a great relationship with a successful alumnus through the Black Alumni Network. He was very helpful."

– Alfonso T. '11, Oakland, CA International Business and Spanish

ACCESS **Upward Bound**

Upward Bound is one of six national federally funded TRIO Programs. The mission is to provide high school students (low-income and potential-first-generation college students) with the skills and motivation needed to enter and complete a college or university of their choice. Over the past 40 years, the program has served hundreds of Columbus-area families. OWU Upward Bound has a 100 percent college-placement rate and a 64 percent college graduation rate.

OPPORTUNITY **Campus Visit Cost Assistance**

To enable multicultural and first-generation students to visit campus, Ohio Wesleyan assists with transportation arrangements and costs.

OPPORTUNITY **Branch Rickey Scholarships**

In recognition of the importance of cultural diversity in its student body, these awards are made in the amount of $14,000. This award can be renewed at the same value for up to three years of full-time enrollment if students attain the required level of academic performance and maintain it each year.

SUCCESS **Multicultural and First-Generation Pre-Orientation**

Multicultural and first-generation students arrive for orientation two days prior to other first-year students. This pre-orientation program provides an opportunity for students to connect individually with their advisers and administrators. In addition, they familiarize themselves with the campus, the facilities and the community. Most importantly, these students begin relationships with others who have the same feelings and fears that they have.

SUCCESS **Student Advising Registration and Testing (StART)**

First-year students (and parents) are invited to connect to Ohio Wesleyan academically by attending one of several sessions to register for the fall semester, learning about distribution requirements and taking language placement exams. Individual advising regarding course selections and other support services is available.

SUCCESS **Office of Multicultural Affairs**

The Office of Multicultural Student Affairs at Ohio Wesleyan provides extensive programming and support for multicultural students from academic, social, personal and cultural perspectives. Some of the events sponsored by the office include Hispanic Awareness Week, Cultural Minifest, Asian Heritage Month, Kushinda, Rafiki Wa Afrika African Festival, Black History Month, Kwanzaa celebration, SUBA Step Show, and Women of Color Month.

Ohio Wesleyan University
75 South Sandusky Street
Delaware, OH 43015-2398
Ph: (740) 368-3020
owuadmit@owu.edu
www.owu.edu

FAST FACTS

STUDENT PROFILE

# of degree-seeking undergraduates	1,850
% male/female	47/53
% African American	5
% American Indian or Alaska Native	1
% Asian or Pacific Islander	2
% Hispanic	2
% White	78
% International	9
% Pell grant recipients	20.7

First-generation and minority alumni Byron Pitts, chief national correspondent, CBS News, Contributor, *60 Minutes*; Greg Moore, managing editor, *Boston Globe*, editor, *Denver Post*; Barbranda Lumpkins Walls, former travel editor at *USA Today*, features editor at *AARP Bulletin*, author, *Soul Sanctuary: Images of the African American Worship Experience*

ACADEMICS

full-time faculty	137
full-time minority faculty	9
student-faculty ratio	12:1
average class size	16.4
% first-year retention rate	87
% graduation rate (6 years)	63

Popular majors Psychology, Economics, Education, Pre-Med, Zoology

CAMPUS LIFE

% live on campus (% freshmen)	81 (97)

Multicultural student clubs and organizations SUBA (Student Union on Black Awareness), Black Men of the Future, Sisters United, VIVA (recognizes Latin American cultures), Rafiki Wa Afrika, Black Presidents Council, S.T.R.I.D.E. (Standing Together to Reduce Intolerance and Develop Equality), Muslim Students Association, SANGAM (recognizes East Asian cultures), Chinese Culture Club

Athletics NCAA Division III, North Coast Athletic Conference (NCAC)

ADMISSIONS

# of applicants	4,139
% accepted	71
# of first-year students enrolled	555
SAT Critical Reading (middle 50%)	520-650
SAT Math (middle 50%)	520-650
SAT Writing (middle 50%)	510-640
ACT (middle 50%)	23-29
average HS GPA	3.46
Deadlines	
early action I	11/30
early action II	1/15
regular decision	3/1
application fee (online)	$35 ($0)
fee waiver for applicants with financial need	yes

COST & AID

tuition	$37,580
room & board	$9,964
total need-based institutional scholarships/grants	$7,000,000
% of students apply for need-based aid	67
% of students receive aid	97
% receiving need-based scholarship or grant aid	95
% receiving aid whose need was fully met	26
average aid package	$30,400
average student loan debt upon graduation	$26,500

Youngstown State University

Youngstown State University is a public university located in Northeast Ohio. As one of the top three of the most cost effective state universities in Ohio, YSU is well known as a university of opportunity, providing comprehensive financial aid coupled with affordable tuition, a wide range of academic and personal support services, and faculty and staff who want to see students succeed. With over 100 undergraduate majors and a wide variety of extracurriculars, campus groups, clubs, and organizations for students to choose from, YSU values a diverse experience for its students. The first-year retention rate for minority students who use available support resources is significantly higher than the national average for 4-year open-admissions institutions, demonstrating YSU's dedication to providing the support its students need.

ACCESS Upward Bound and Academic Achievers

Youngstown State supports a number of programs to aid in college preparation for high school students in the area. Upward Bound is a federally funded TRIO program that provides free tutoring, a Saturday enrichment program, summer residential program, academic counseling, and ACT prep to first generation students in Youngstown City. YSU also sponsors Academic Achievers, a privately funded college-preparation program for academically average high school students from Warren Harding High School. The program also provides free tutoring, ACT prep, a Saturday enrichment program, and an annual summer camp as an initiative to help inner city students prepare for college.

ACCESS Early College

In 2008 and 2009, Youngstown State University was recognized by the Ohio Department of Education as a School of Excellence for their Early College program, an initiative that provides YSU college credit to Youngstown City high school students. The program gives local high school students the opportunity to graduate with both a high school degree and an associate's degree for free, along with career guidance and community service experience.

"The Summer Bridge program was phenomenal! We got coaching, advice, referrals—and that's helped me all along the way. I tell my friends, 'College is hard by yourself. At YSU, you're not doing it by yourself."

– Mark J., '13 Social Work

OPPORTUNITY CSP Summer Bridge Program

Sponsored by the Center for Student Progress Multicultural Student Services, the Summer Bridge Program is a one week free residential program for entering first-year multicultural students. In order to help ease the transition from high school to college, students participate in college prep courses during the summer and take courses together as a learning community in the fall.

OPPORTUNITY Martin Luther King Inner City Acheivement Award

The Martin Luther King Inner City Achievement Award, funded by the YSU Foundation, provides up to $1,500 in scholarship awards to graduates of Youngstown/Warren inner city schools. Students must have at least a 2.5 gpa and must complete their FAFSA by February 15th in order to be considered.

SUCCESS The Center for Student Progress

Youngstown State University's Center for Student Progress sponsors a variety of programs dedicated to providing students with the resources they need to succeed, including weekly peer mentoring for all first-year students beginning at Orientation, individualized academic coaching, student tutoring, supplemental instruction, multicultural student services, and disability services. The Center was nationally recognized by the Educational Policy Institute and awarded its 2007 EPI Student Retention Award, which is presesnted annually to institutions that serve students who are historically underserved at the postsecondary level.

Youngstown State University
1 University Plaza
Youngstown, OH 44555
Ph: (330) 941-1657
enroll@ysu.edu
www.ysu.edu

FAST FACTS

STUDENT PROFILE

# of degree-seeking undergraduates	13,890
% male/female	47/53
% African American	18
% American Indian or Alaska Native	<1
% Asian or Pacific Islander	1
% Hispanic	2
% White	71
% International	<1
% Pell grant recipients	44

First-generation and minority alumni Linda Gooden, Executive Vice President of Lockheed Martin's Information Systems and Global Solutions; Nathaniel Jones, former judge U.S. Court of Appeals Sixth Circuit: Riyad Mansour, Permanent Observer of Palestine to the United Nations

ACADEMICS

full-time faculty	456
full-time minority faculty	74
student-faculty ratio	20:1
average class size	23
% first-year retention rate	69
% graduation rate (6 years)	35

Popular majors Nursing,Criminal Justice, Early Childhood Education, Business Management, Psychology

CAMPUS LIFE

% live on campus (% freshmen)	10 (18)

Multicultural student clubs and organizations African Student Union, Latino Organization, Los Buenos Vincinos, Muslim Students Association, National Society of Black Engineers, Speak Out Loud, Student Chapter of African American Brotherhood, Student Chapter of African American Sisterhood, Students for Social Justice, Bridges Out Of Poverty Student Union

Athletics NCAA Division I, Horizon Conference

ADMISSIONS

# of applicants	7,181
% accepted	87
# of first-year students enrolled	2,668
SAT Critical Reading (middle 50%)	400-530
SAT Math (middle 50%)	420-540
SAT Writing (middle 50%)	380-510
ACT (middle 50%)	17-23
average HS GPA	2.8
Deadlines	
early registration priority	2/15
regular decision	8/1
application fee (online)	$30 ($30)
fee waiver for applicants with financial need	yes

COST & AID

tuition	in-state $7,452; out-of-state $13,408
room & board	$7,900
total need-based institutional scholarship/grants	$808,522
% of students apply for need-based aid	86
% receiving need-based scholarship or grant aid	60
% receiving aid whose need was fully met	5
average aid package	$8,438
average student loan debt upon graduation	$20,463

Oklahoma Baptist University

As a Christian liberal arts university, Oklahoma Baptist University's mission is to transform lives by equipping students to pursue academic excellence, integrate faith with all areas of knowledge, engage a diverse world, and live worthy of the high calling of God in Christ. Toward that goal, the university offers ten bachelor's degrees in 84 areas of study. Driven by Christian values, OBU intends to provide the knowledge, skills, and preparation to prepare students for whichever career path they are called to, while maintaining their dedication to truly make a difference. OBU also embraces a diverse environment for their students, with 1,777 students coming to OBU from 39 states and 20 other countries in the fall of 2010.

ACCESS **Intensive English Program**

OBU offers the Intensive English Program for students who would like to improve their English language proficiency in a variety of contexts. With a focus on English comprehension through practice in reading, writing, conversation, and listening, the program enables students to succeed at English speaking colleges, universities, or professional environments and meet the English qualifications required for admission to OBU. Students must be at least 16 years of age, have completed secondary school, and qualify as non-native speakers of English in order to apply.

OPPORTUNITY **OBU Bison Grants and OBU Endowed Scholarships**

For students whose need is not met by federal student aid, scholarships, grants, or loans, OBU offers the OBU Bison Grants and OBU Endowed Scholarships. Amounts of these scholarships vary based on students' demonstrated need and financial aid packages.

OPPORTUNITY **Oklahoma Tuition Equalization Grant (OTEG) and Allen Scholarships**

OBU offers a variety of scholarships to students who live in-state. For Oklahoma residents with family incomes of $50,000 or less, OBU offers the $2,000 OTEG scholarship. Students from Western Oklahoma with unmet demonstrated need qualify for the Allen Scholarship, ranging from $1,000 to $5,000.

> *"The OBU Honors Program has been helpful to me in preparing me for a successful academic career at OBU and beyond. The program offers a diverse, stimulating curriculum that enhances the standard liberal arts curriculum by challenging students to reach their full potential and experience the best of what OBU has to offer."*
>
> *– Kelsey P., '12 Biology*

SUCCESS **Learning Communities (LCs)**

Every fall, OBU provides 190 freshmen with the opportunity to join LCs, groups created to enhance students' learning experience, help them transition from high school to college, and establish a support group of peers, faculty, and staff. Each community is made up of 15-20 students taking 3-4 of the same courses, which gives students a chance to bond over similar interests and passions. With 10 communities organized by different themes or majors, LCs cater to a wide range of interests.

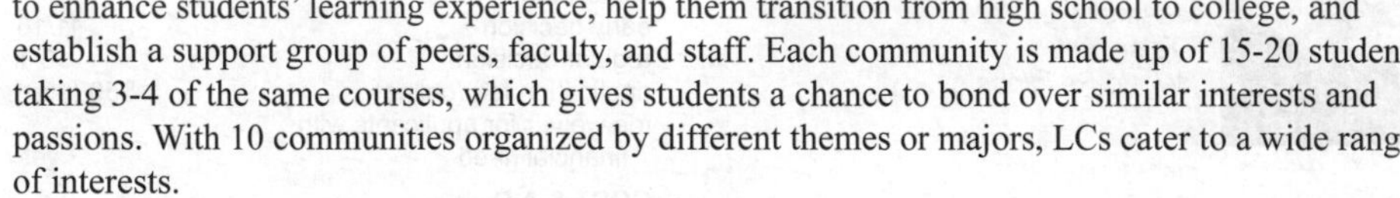

SUCCESS **Student Success Initiatives**

OBU's Student Success initiatives provide academic and writing support across the curriculum for students of all classifications, majors, and academic needs. One initiative, academic orientation, begins during the enrollment process for new students and is also supported by a robust and integrated new student orientation program. Two courses, Success 101 and 102, are designed to transition students into the university community as well as provide them with tools for academic improvement. In addition, the Student Success Center is open more than 25 hours per week and is staffed by 35 upper-class students to provide students with the tools they need to succeed in college. The Center offers help with writing assignments, tutoring in a variety of subjects, assistance in research, and help with organizing study groups and receiving academic feedback.

Oklahoma Baptist University
500 W. University
Shawnee, OK 74804
Ph: (800) 634-3285
admissions@okbu.edu
www.okbu.edu

FAST FACTS

STUDENT PROFILE	
# of degree-seeking undergraduates	1,717
% male/female	40/60
% African American	6
% American Indian or Alaska Native	7
% Asian American	<1
% Hispanic	4
% White	68
% International	5
Pell grant recipients	23
ACADEMICS	
full-time faculty	112
full-time minority faculty	5
student-faculty ratio	15:1
Average class size	18
% first-year retention rate	75
% graduation rate	54
Popular majors Bible/Bible Studies, Elementary Education and Teaching, Nursing/Registered Nurse (RN, ASN, BSN, MSN)	
CAMPUS LIFE	
% live on campus (% freshmen)	68 (94)
Multicultural student clubs and organizations Philos (campus ministry club) for International Students learning English, International Student Organization, United Students of Color, Native American Heritage Association, Black Student Fellowship	
Athletics NAIA, Sooner Athletic Conference	
ADMISSIONS	
# of applicants	3,778
% accepted	67
# of first-year students enrolled	414
SAT Critical Reading (middle 50%)	410-740
SAT Math (middle 50%)	370-760
SAT Writing (middle 50%)	n/a
ACT (middle 50%)	17-35
average HS GPA	3.7
Deadlines	
regular decision	8/1
application fee (online)	$0 ($0)
fee waiver for applicants with financial need	no
COST & AID	
tuition	$17,994
room & board	$6,000
total need-based institutional scholarships/grants	$7,225,924
% of students apply for need-based aid	77.6
% receiving need-based scholarship or grant aid	100
% receiving aid whose need was fully met	93
average aid package	$21,291
average student loan debt upon graduation	$18,331

Oklahoma City University

Founded in partnership with the United Methodist church in 1904, Oklahoma City University offers academic rigor and unique access to a vibrant metropolitan community. Beyond its location in Oklahoma City, the university offers an educational experience unique in both priority and population. Oklahoma City University prides itself in providing personal attention to each of the undergraduate students, of which nearly half are minority or international students. The university prepares students to become effective community leaders by offering a rigorous curriculum focused on intellectual, moral and spiritual development.

OPPORTUNITY Clara Luper Scholarship Program

The Clara Luper Scholarship Program helps recipients from underserved populations to realize the dream of a private college education. Each year, five recipients of the Clara Luper Scholarship are also chosen to be Devon Energy scholars and could receive career opportunities. After all available state aid, federal aid, tribal aid and/or external scholarships received have been applied, the Clara Luper Scholarship could pay the remaining balance for tuition and provides a $200 per-semester book allowance. Applicants must be first-time, entering freshmen and complete a separate application in addition to the regular undergraduate application for admission.

OPPORTUNITY American Indian Scholarship Program

Oklahoma City University is committed to investing in the future of American Indians. The American Indian Scholarship Program helps to provide a private college education to well-deserving American Indian students who may not otherwise have the opportunity. Each year, the university awards scholarships to incoming American Indian students. After all available state aid, federal aid, tribal aid and/or other external scholarships have been applied, the American Indian Scholarship could pay the remaining balance for tuition and provides a $200 per semester book allowance. Additionally, the American Indian Scholarship Program provides support services dedicated to the growth, welfare and success of each student. Scholarship candidates must be admitted to Oklahoma City University, complete a separate application in addition to the regular undergraduate application for admission, provide an essay and provide a copy of their Certificate of Degree of Indian Blood (CDIB) card.

OPPORTUNITY OCU V.I.P.

Oklahoma City University aspires to provide prospective students personal attention and make them feel like they are already a part of the OCU community. Being an OCU V.I.P. will allow you to learn more about campus life, programs of study, financial aid and the admissions process. You will receive e-mails from professors, invitations to events, financial aid announcements, scholarship awards and campus events. Visit www.okcu.edu/vip to sign up.

"The Honors Program experience has been a breath of fresh air. Not only do my fellow students have the same drive and motivation as I do, but the 'Pizza with a Professor' Thursdays are always fun and a learning experience."

– Ainsley L., '12
Tulsa, OK
World Religions

SUCCESS Department of Multicultural Student Affairs

The Department of Multicultural Student Affairs promotes cultural diversity, fosters positive human relations, and addresses the needs of those who are historically underrepresented or underserved in the campus setting. The department provides vision, leadership, coordination and long-range planning for the university's comprehensive diversity program. The department actively supports diversity workshops, student leadership development, student career development, the Clara Luper Scholarship program, the American Indian Scholarship Program, the Multicultural Student Association and other cultural campus organizations.

Oklahoma City University
2501 North Blackwelder
Oklahoma City, OK 73106
Ph: (405) 208-5050
admissions@okcu.edu
www.okcu.edu

FAST FACTS

STUDENT PROFILE

# of degree-seeking undergraduates	2,314
% male/female	39/61
% African American	8
% American Indian or Alaska Native	4
% Asian or Pacific Islander	2
% Hispanic	6
% White	57
% International	17
% Other/Unknown	2
Pell grant recipients	28.4

First-generation and minority alumni Jacqueline Miller '85, '91, '92, Judge, Oklahoma Corporation Commission; Rana Husseini '90, '93, Human Rights Activist, Middle East; Freddy Sanchez '00, Second Base, San Francisco Giants; Marquita Lister '85, Opera Singer, Various Companies

ACADEMICS

full-time faculty	201
full-time minority faculty	14
student-faculty ratio	11:1
Average class size	17
# first-year retention rate	77
# graduation rate	52

Popular majors Nursing, Acting, Dance, Business Administration, Music Theatre

CAMPUS LIFE

% live on campus (% freshmen)	69 (94)

Multicultural student clubs and organizations President's Advisory Council on Diversity, Black Student Association, Hispanic Student Association, Indian Student Association, Multicultural Student Association, Thai Student Association, S.A.A.S. (Sisterhood of African American Students), Amnesty International, Korean Student Association, Black History Month, Latino Youth Leadership Conference, FACES Program

Athletics NAIA, Sooner Athletic Conference

ADMISSIONS

# of applicants	1,253
% accepted	76
# of first-year students enrolled	416
SAT Critical Reading (middle 50%)	520-630
SAT Math (middle 50%)	520-640
SAT Writing (middle 50%)	490-600
ACT (middle 50%)	22-28
average HS GPA	3.5
Deadlines	
early decision	11/15
regular decision	3/1
application fee (online)	$50 ($50)
fee waiver for applicants with financial need	yes

COST & AID

tuition	$24,740
room & board	$9,170
total need-based institutional scholarships/grants	$13,599,826
% of students apply for need-based aid	79
% of students receive aid	89.3
% receiving need-based scholarship or grant aid	83.8
% receiving aid whose need was fully met	77
average aid package	$17,823
average student loan debt upon graduation	$19,470

Lewis & Clark College

Lewis & Clark College rests on a 137-acre campus in the southwest hills of Portland. This private institution is known for its academic rigor and a focus on community involvement, having earned recognition as "A Best Western College" and "A College with a Conscience" by the *Princeton Review*. The student body — more than a third of which consists of first-generation students — can choose from among 27 academic majors and study abroad options in nearly two dozen countries to build their academic experience.

ACCESS Oregon Independent Colleges Foundation

As a member of the Oregon Independent Colleges Foundation, Lewis & Clark partners with local community-based organizations to give local students insight into life at the college. Each year the program brings to Lewis & Clark more than 100 middle and high school students from Self-Enhancement, Inc. and the Native American Youth Association.

OPPORTUNITY Lewis & Clark Fly-in Program

Each year, Lewis & Clark College invites approximately 50 newly admitted students to visit campus at the expense of the college. These selected students of color and first-generation college-goers learn about life and academics at Lewis & Clark through a series of activities. They attend classes, meet faculty and staff, spend time with current students and experience life in the residence halls.

SUCCESS Lewis & Clark Intercultural Network for Connecting Students (LINCS)

LINCS is a peer-mentorship program that focuses on diversity and retention. The program helps incoming students of diverse ethnic and cultural backgrounds adjust to college, and all entering students are invited to participate in the program. Successful returning students connect new students to resources on campus and help them as they develop relationships with Lewis & Clark faculty, staff and peers.

SUCCESS Ray Warren Multicultural Symposium

The Ray Warren Multicultural Symposium is a three-day annual event to increase the college's awareness of cultural history, ethnic identity and knowledge of social issues that impact minority communities, both locally and nationally. Named for the late Ray Warren, it is one of four student-planned academic symposia held each year on campus. All events are free and open to the public.

SUCCESS Multicultural Residence Hall

Students from diverse backgrounds come to Akin Hall to live with and learn from one another. Here the residents educate themselves through the celebration and exploration of diverse cultural identities. They promote understanding of ethnic and racial diversity and contribute to Lewis & Clark's awareness of international and multicultural issues. Toward this end, the residence hall sponsors diversity-focused programs such as the annual Cultural and International Fairs.

Lewis & Clark College
0615 SW Palatine Hill Road
Portland, OR 97219-7899
Ph: (503) 768-7040
admissions@lclark.edu
www.lclark.edu

FAST FACTS

STUDENT PROFILE

# of degree-seeking undergraduates	1,904
% male/female	39/61
% African American	2
% American Indian or Alaska Native	1
% Asian or Pacific Islander	6
% Hispanic	6
% White	58
% International	6
% Pell grant recipients	11

First-generation and minority alumni Serena Cruz Walsh '89, former commissioner, Multnomah County; Sandra Osawa '64, Native American independent filmmaker; Adam Bradley '96, assistant professor; Sagala Ratnayaka '93, member, Sri Lankan Parliament; Linda Castaneda '98, Cat Ambassador Program, Cincinnati Zoo; Randy Massengale '78, president, Spinoza Technologies; Shahzeb Jillani '94, radio editor, BBC Urdu

ACADEMICS

full-time faculty	230
full-time minority faculty	25
student-faculty ratio	12:1
average class size	19
% first-year retention rate	83
% graduation rate (6 years)	76

Popular majors Psychology, English, Biology, International Affairs, Studio Art

CAMPUS LIFE

% live on campus (% freshmen)	65 (97)

Multicultural student clubs and organizations Office of Multicultural Affairs, Lewis & Clark Intercultural Network for Connecting Students (LINCS), Multicultural Themed Residence Hall (Akin), Interdisciplinary minor in Ethnic Studies offered, Asian Student Union, Black Student Union, Gente Latina Unida, Hawai'i Club, Native Student Union, International Students of Lewis & Clark, Interfaith Council, Jewish Student Union, United Sexualities, Music Ensembles (African Marimba, African Rhythm & Dance, Gamelan, and West African Rhythms)

Athletics NCAA Division III, Northwest Conference

ADMISSIONS

# of applicants	5,281
% accepted	68
# of first-year students enrolled	493
SAT Critical Reading (middle 50%)	600-700
SAT Math (middle 50%)	580-675
SAT Writing (middle 50%)	580-680
ACT (middle 50%)	26-30
average HS GPA	3.69

Deadlines

early action	11/1
regular decision	2/1
application fee (online)	$50 ($0)
fee waiver for applicants with financial need	yes

COST & AID

tuition	$38,140
room & board	$10,014
total need-based institutional scholarships/grants	$20,298,917
% of students apply for need-based aid	67
% of students receive aid	55
% receiving need-based scholarship or grant aid	53
% receiving aid whose need was fully met	27
average aid package	$27,829
average student loan debt upon graduation	$20,611

Linfield College

Linfield College, a private, comprehensive, undergraduate institution located in the Pacific Northwest, connects learning, life and community through collaborative and experiential education opportunities. Recognizing the importance of diversity in its student body, Linfield College offers both financial and academic support to attract and retain minority students. With Linfield's challenging and exciting academic program, featuring a broad liberal arts core, it is nationally recognized for its strong faculty, outstanding academic programs and distinctive international emphasis. Over half of Linfield students study internationally and approximately 90 percent are in a job or graduate school within one year of graduation.

ACCESS **Upward Bound**

Linfield College is home to one of Oregon's Upward Bound programs. Funded through the U.S. Department of Education, Upward Bound is a college preparatory program designed to assist high school students with building the skills and motivation necessary for success in post-secondary education. Linfield's program serves over 60 area high school students throughout the academic year.

"When I talk to my friends at larger institutions, they have never even talked to their professors, and that's kind of strange to me because I always make it a priority to meet with my professors outside of class. Everyone here is willing to help. That has really helped me reach my academic goals."

– Graciela G., '09
McMinnville, OR
Elementary Education

ACCESS **College Information Nights**

Linfield hosts an annual College Night for Yamhill County high school juniors and seniors along with their parents. Information about Linfield's academic programs, international study, and student life is presented, along with an overview of the application and financial aid process. There are Spanish-speaking faculty members present to better serve local families.

OPPORTUNITY **Linfield Diversity Grant**

Students of color who are likely to make a significant contribution to the Linfield community are eligible for an award of $1,000 to $6,000, determined by financial need and other factors. Recommendations for the grant are made to the Director of Multicultural Programs in consultation with the Director of Financial Aid and the Director of Admission.

SUCCESS **Colloquium**

Groups of 20 incoming students are each assigned a faculty advisor and peer advisor. Advisors stay in contact with new students over the summer; groups meet daily during new student Orientation and weekly for 10 weeks in the fall semester. Topics such as academic advising, academic resources, academic expectations and time management are discussed.

SUCCESS **Office of Learning Support Services**

The Office of Learning Support Services coordinates the peer tutoring program and academic department study sessions. The office offers a Learning Skills course every semester, dealing with topics like time management, test-taking, and memory enhancement. The office also works individually with students who have documented learning differences.

Linfield College
900 SE Baker Street
McMinnville, OR 97128-6894
Ph: (503) 883-2213
admission@linfield.edu
www.linfield.edu

FAST FACTS

STUDENT PROFILE

# of degree-seeking undergraduates	1,697
% male/female	41/59
% African American	2
% American Indian or Alaska Native	2
% Asian or Pacific Islander	8
% Hispanic	5
% White	66
% International	6
% Pell grant recipients	27

First-generation and minority alumni Baruti Artharee, Director of Diversity Program, Providence Health System; Gale Castillo, Executive Director, Hispanic Chamber of Commerce; Leroy Fails, Vice President, The College Board; Jose Gaitan, Owner, Gaitan Group; Sandra Thompson, Judge, Los Angeles Superior Court

ACADEMICS

full-time faculty	118
full-time minority faculty	8
student-faculty ratio	12:1
average class size	17
% first-year retention rate	80
% graduation rate (6 years)	68

Popular majors Business Administration, Elementary Education, Mass Communications, Nursing

CAMPUS LIFE

% live on campus (% freshmen)	75 (100)

Multicultural student clubs and organizations Office of Multicultural Programs, Hawaiian Club, Multicultural Student Club, Asian Culture Club, International Club

Athletics NCAA Division III, Northwest Conference

ADMISSIONS

# of applicants	2,179
% accepted	76
# of first-year students enrolled	530
SAT Critical Reading (middle 50%)	490-610
SAT Math (middle 50%)	500-610
SAT Writing (middle 50%)	480-590
ACT (middle 50%)	21-26
HS GPA range	3.32-3.83

Deadlines

early action	11/15
regular decision (priority)	2/15
application fee (online)	$0 ($0)
fee waiver for applicants with financial need	n/a

COST & AID

tuition	$32,100
room & board	$9,000
total need-based institutional scholarships/grants	$19,389,566
% of students apply for need-based aid	73
% of students receive aid	93
% receiving need-based scholarship or grant aid	64
% of need met for students receiving aid	85
average aid package	$27,165
average student loan debt upon graduation	$31,135

Willamette University

Willamette University was founded in 1842 as a forward-thinking, co-educational institution — its first graduate was a woman. The 81-acre campus is located in the center of Salem, across the street from the Oregon State Capitol building. This proximity has given generations of Willamette students the opportunity to participate in the important social and political issues of their day through internships and other direct action. The university motto, "Not Unto Ourselves Alone Are We Born," provides the underpinnings for a campus culture that is committed to service and making a difference in the world. Among the campus organizations that reflect this commitment are the Council for Diversity and Social Justice and the Council for Sustainability.

ACCESS **Willamette Academy**

Willamette University sponsors the Willamette Academy, an experiential, academic enrichment program for underrepresented and ethnically diverse seventh graders from the local community. The five-year commitment of the participants and their families helps them prepare for higher education by enhancing critical thinking skills, developing leadership skills and inspiring their love of learning.

OPPORTUNITY **Financial Aid Programs**

Approximately 20 percent of Willamette undergraduates receive federal Pell grants. The university's comprehensive, need-based financial aid program is supplemented by a generous, merit-based scholarship program. More than 90 percent of the student body is receiving some financial assistance to put a Willamette education within reach.

OPPORTUNITY **Black United Fund Partnership Scholarship / Scholarship for Oregon Latinos (SOL)**

The Black United Fund Partnership Scholarship provides $15,000 for two African-American students from Oregon who demonstrate academic strength and community and school leadership. The Scholarship for Oregon Latinos provides up to $15,000 for Latin-American students from Oregon who demonstrate school and community leadership and an excellent academic record.

SUCCESS **Ohana Pre-Orientation Program**

Ohana, the Hawaiian word for "family," is the theme of a four-day retreat for new students of color at Willamette. Student leaders of campus multicultural organizations welcome new students and help orient them through outdoor activities, service projects and a "Cultural Food and Shop Tour" of Salem and Portland, ensuring that new students begin their first day of class already familiarized with their new home.

SUCCESS **Committee for Academic Success**

This is a standing faculty committee that monitors student progress and offers direct support and intervention to students who are struggling academically.

SUCCESS **Office of Multicultural Affairs**

The Office of Multicultural Affairs promotes diversity throughout the campus community through education, enrichment and support. It also serves the campus community as a clearinghouse for the various multicultural resources that Salem has to offer.

Willamette University
900 State Street
Salem, OR 97301-3931
Ph: (503) 370-6303
libarts@willamette.edu
www.willamette.edu

FAST FACTS

STUDENT PROFILE

# of degree-seeking undergraduates	1,786
% male/female	44/56
% African American	2
% American Indian or Alaska Native	<1
% Asian or Pacific Islander	8
% Hispanic	6
% White	54
% Pell grant recipients	18

First-generation and minority alumni Lin Sue Glass Cooley, evening news anchor, KPNX-TV; Ricardo Baez, vice president for marketing and sales, partner, Puentes Brothers Inc. / Don Pancho Authentic Mexican Foods; Harold Sublett, Jr., commercial banker, Wells Fargo Bank; Danny Santos, labor policy adviser to the governor, Oregon; Carmen Bendixon-Noe, former fellow and staffer, Congressional Hispanic Caucus Institute, Sen. Barbara Boxer (D-Calif.)

ACADEMICS

full-time faculty	229
full-time minority faculty	39
student-faculty ratio	10:1
average class size	14
% first-year retention rate	90
% graduation rate (6 years)	78

Popular majors Biology, Economics, English

CAMPUS LIFE

% live on campus	70 (98)

Multicultural student clubs and organizations Alianza, Hawaii Club, Native American Enlightenment Association, Black Student Organization, Unidos por Fin

Athletics NCAA Division III, Northwest Conference

ADMISSIONS

# of applicants	7,785
% accepted	42
# of first-year students enrolled	427
SAT Critical Reading (middle 50%)	570-680
SAT Math (middle 50%)	570-660
SAT Writing (middle 50%)	570-670
ACT (middle 50%)	27-30
average HS GPA	3.7

Deadlines

early action	11/1, 12/1
regular decision	2/1
application fee (online)	$50 ($50)
fee waiver for applicants with financial need	yes

COST & AID

tuition	$38,800
room & board	$9,350
total need-based institutional scholarships/grants	$26,395,801
% of students apply for need-based aid	73
% of students receive aid	64
% receiving need-based scholarship or grant aid	63
% receiving aid whose need was fully met	40
average aid package	$31,308
average student loan debt upon graduation	$24,465

Arcadia University

The Arcadia Promise affirms that students will have a distinctively global, integrative and personal learning experience that prepares them to contribute and prosper in a diverse and dynamic world. The Arcadia Promise sums up the collective experiences of generations of alumni and the collective efforts of the faculty and staff who create Arcadia's distinguished learning environment. Arcadia students are challenged to achieve their full potential and recognize their ability and responsibility to make choices that affect the future of their world. Whether they pursue an undergraduate, graduate or continuing education path, they are part of a mutually supportive community. Through interactions with faculty, staff and peers representing a diversity of cultural backgrounds, they gain self-confidence and respect for others, learn by using the latest technologies, and acquire essential skills and knowledge that prepare them for a rich and meaningful life.

ACCESS Gateway to Success Program

Through the Gateway to Success Program, the Office of Enrollment Management identifies and offers admission to certain students who they deem as having the potential to succeed at Arcadia University despite some modest elements in their credentials.

ACCESS Meet the MAC

Meet the MAC is a series of programs sponsored by a consortium of Pennsylvania colleges and universities that share common bonds in providing academic excellence. The members of this consortium will sponsor programs which give students, who have historically been underrepresented in higher education, the opportunity to interact with admissions professionals dedicated to increasing awareness of the opportunities available at small liberal arts institutions.

"Since entering Arcadia, I have had so many opportunities to live out my dreams, I believe in myself more, and I have this University to thank."

– Julia S., '11
Bethlehem, PA
International Studies

OPPORTUNITY ENON Tabernacle Baptist Church Scholarships

Beginning in Fall 2011, Arcadia will offer two annual scholarships to members of our community partner, ENON Tabernacle Baptist Church. Although these scholarships, which will cover the amount of full tuition minus federal and student grant aid for up to four years for each of the two recipients, are not expressly "for minorities or dubbed diversity scholarships" the majority of the ENON membership is of African descent.

SUCCESS Office of Institutional Diversity

The Office of Institutional Diversity provides outreach, supplemental academic advisory support services, and direct mentoring and advocacy for students identifying as being of African American, Latino, Asian or Native American descent (ALANA), and/or Lesbian, Gay, Bi-sexual, Transgender or Queer.

SUCCESS ACT 101

The ACT 101 Program is intended for economically and educationally disadvantaged first generation college students who are residents of Pennsylvania. The program offers tutoring, mentoring, counseling, curricular innovation, and cultural enrichment activities to support these students.

SUCCESS Gateway to Success Program

The Gateway to Success Program, for educationally and/or economically disadvantaged first generation college students, serves as an intensive academic and counseling support program. The program provides a variety of services designed to help develop the levels of academic proficiency and social and leadership skills necessary for achieving academic success.

Arcadia University
450 S Easton Road
Glenside, PA 19038
Ph: (877) 272-2342
admiss@arcadia.edu
www.arcadia.edu

FAST FACTS

STUDENT PROFILE

# of degree-seeking undergraduates	2,229
% male/female	27/73
% African American	8
% American Indian or Alaska Native	<1
% Asian or Pacific Islander	4
% Hispanic	5
% White	80
% International	1
% Pell grant recipients	27

First-generation and minority alumni Teressa Moore Griffin, Founder and CEO, Spirit of Purpose; Rosemarie McNeil-Sampson, Principal and CEO, Widner Partnership Charter School; Anna Deavere Smith, Actress, Playwright, Professor, New York University

ACADEMICS

full-time faculty	125
full-time minority faculty	20
student-faculty ratio	14:1
average class size	16
% first-year retention rate	76
% graduation rate (6 years)	62

Popular majors Biology, Education, Business, Fine Arts, Communications and Psychology

CAMPUS LIFE

% live on campus (% freshmen)	76 (80)

Multicultural student clubs and organizations Arcadia Hindu Cultural Society, AU Muslim Student Association (AUMSA), Asian Students in American (ASIA), Black Awareness Society, Hillel (Jewish Student Organization), International Club, Latino Association, Puro Ritmo

Athletics NCAA Division III, Mid Atlantic Conference, Commonwealth Conference

ADMISSIONS

# of applicants	5,938
% accepted	65
# of first-year students enrolled	552
SAT Critical Reading (middle 50%)	510-620
SAT Math (middle 50%)	500-610
SAT Writing (middle 50%)	500-610
ACT (middle 50%)	22-27
average HS GPA	3.6

Deadlines

priority deadline	1/15
regular decision	3/1
application fee (online)	$30 ($0)
fee waiver for applicants with financial need	yes

COST & AID

tuition	$34,150
room & board	$11,640
total need-based institutional scholarships/grants	$25,406,923
% of students apply for need-based aid	94
% receiving need-based scholarship or grant aid	87
% receiving aid whose need was fully met	13
average aid package	$23,005
average student loan debt upon graduation	$33,765

Bryn Mawr College

Bryn Mawr College is a private, women's liberal arts college located just outside of Philadelphia and only two hours by train from New York City and Washington, D.C. Because of its unique academic history, Bryn Mawr students may take classes at nearby Haverford and Swarthmore Colleges, as well as the University of Pennsylvania. Providing a rigorous education and encouraging the pursuit of knowledge in preparation for life and work, Bryn Mawr College has taught and valued critical, creative and independent habits of thought and expression since 1885. Bryn Mawr's dedication to sustaining a community diverse in nature and democratic in practice is guided by an overarching belief — it is only through considering many perspectives that individuals can gain a deeper understanding of each other and the world. Bryn Mawr women share an intense intellectual commitment, a purposeful vision of their lives and a desire to make a meaningful contribution to the world.

OPPORTUNITY Travel Scholar Information

Bryn Mawr College is dedicated to cultivating young women as leaders, intellectuals and barrier breakers and will award travel scholarships to deserving high school seniors. Students must be U.S. citizens living in the U.S. or in U.S.territories who want to visit and experience the College first-hand. Because the scholarship is competitive, students are asked to submit both a high school transcript and standardized test scores in addition to the travel scholar application.

OPPORTUNITY Standardized Testing

Bryn Mawr College has adopted a new testing policy that will give students greater flexibility in applying to the college and is more in line with current research regarding the role standardized tests should play in the admissions process. The policy sets a new precedent for the use of Advanced Placement (AP) tests in the admissions process and allows for an option that focuses exclusively on subject mastery.

> ***"Bryn Mawr is a place where you will be challenged, both academically and socially. Your professors will challenge your mind and ways of thinking while Mawrters will challenge your values and beliefs. At Bryn Mawr, I have come to acknowledge the power of my voice and the strength of my actions."***
>
> *– Arielle H., '11*

SUCCESS Customs Week

The College and the Bryn Mawr-Haverford Customs Week Committee provide orientation for first-year and transfer students, who take residence before the College is opened to upperclass students. Faculty members are available for consultation, and all incoming students have appointments with a dean or other adviser to plan their academic programs for the fall semester. Undergraduate organizations at Bryn Mawr and Haverford Colleges acquaint new students with other aspects of college life.

SUCCESS The Emily Balch Seminar

The Balch Seminars introduce all first-year students at Bryn Mawr to a critical, probing, thoughtful approach to the world and our roles in it. These challenging seminars are taught by scholar/teachers of distinction within their fields and across academic disciplines. They facilitate the seminars as active discussions among students, not lectures. Through intensive reading and writing, the thought-provoking Balch Seminars challenge students to think about complex, wide-ranging issues from a variety of perspectives.

SUCCESS The Undergraduate Deans

The Undergraduate Dean's Office promotes the academic and personal growth of undergraduates at the College. They work with students through their educational and personal Bryn Mawr journey. Bryn Mawr help students learn about available opportunities and resources and make decisions about when and how to take advantage of them.

Bryn Mawr College
Office of Admissions
101 North Merion Avenue
Bryn Mawr, PA 19010
Ph: (610) 526-5152
admissions@brynmawr.edu
www.brynmawr.edu

FAST FACTS

STUDENT PROFILE

# of degree-seeking undergraduates	1,281
% male/female	0/100
% African American	6
% American Indian or Alaska Native	1
% Asian or Pacific Islander	13
% Hispanic	10
% White	39
% International	12
% Pell grant recipients	13

First-generation and minority alumni Maya Ajmera, founder, The Global Fund for Children; Sarmila Bose, journalist; Ana Patrica Botin, CEO, Banesto; Salima Ikram, Egyptologist; Frederica de Laguna, anthropologist; Rosemarie Said Zahlan, historian, writer; Kaity Tong, journalist; Neda Ulaby, NPR reporter; Betty Peh T'i Wei, historian; Mai Yamani, anthropologist, activist

ACADEMICS

full-time faculty	156
full-time minority faculty	24
student-faculty ratio	8:1
average class size	17
% first-year retention rate	93
% graduation rate (6 years)	80

Popular majors Growth and Structure of Cities, Political Science, Biology, Math, Psychology

CAMPUS LIFE

% live on campus (% freshmen)	95 (99)

Multicultural student clubs and organizations Asian Students Association, Association of International Students, Bryn Mawr Caribbean and African Student Organization, Bahai Club Barkada, Coming to Racial Understanding Through Community Involvement, Action and Learning, Ethnic Studies Committee, Mujeres, Muslim Students Association, Rainbow Alliance, Sisterhood, South Asian Society, Vietnamese Culture Club, Women's Center, Zami

Athletics NCAA Division III, Centennial Conference

ADMISSIONS

# of applicants	2,271
% accepted	48
# of first-year students enrolled	369
SAT Critical Reading (middle 50%)	590-720
SAT Math (middle 50%)	580-700
SAT Writing (middle 50%)	600-700
ACT (middle 50%)	26-30
average HS GPA	n/a
Deadlines	
early decision I	11/15
early decision II	1/1
regular admission	1/15
application fee (online)	$50 ($0)
fee waiver for applicants with financial need	yes

COST & AID

tuition	$39,860
room & board	$12,890
total need-based institutional scholarships/grants	$21,990,628
% of students apply for need-based aid	64
% of students receiving aid	59
% receiving need-based scholarship or grant aid	59
% receiving aid whose need was fully met	100
average aid package	$36,789
average student loan debt upon graduation	$19,049

Bucknell University

Bucknell University is home to exceptionally talented students from across the U.S. and around the world. With academic programs in the arts, engineering, humanities, management, and social and natural sciences, and broad learning opportunities outside of class, the University prepares students for success in an increasingly complex and interconnected global society. Its 3,500 undergraduates can choose from more than 50 majors and 65 minors. Students can build robots, write and perform in their own plays or debate solutions to the crisis in Sudan. Engineers can make art, artists can analyze DNA and philosophers can make music. Each student chooses his or her own pathway, but what unites everyone is a shared passion for learning and a desire to achieve deeper levels of understanding about life and the world.

OPPORTUNITY **Scholarships and Recruitment**

Bucknell seeks students who value diversity and inclusiveness and who want to explore the sometimes difficult – and often rewarding – terrain of differences among cultures, mindsets and backgrounds. To attract the most academically engaged and globally focused students, the University will offer more than $44 million in need-based financial aid in 2011-12, plus a limited number of merit awards. Additionally, Bucknell builds diversity among students through targeted recruitment programs in Baltimore (through the Bauer Scholars Program); in Washington D.C., Boston and Los Angeles (through a partnership with the Posse Foundation); and in Texas (through a partnership with YES Prep). The University offers scholarships to talented students in music, the fine arts, creative writing and theatre and dance through a competitive Arts Merit Scholars program. The Bucknell Community College Scholars Program provides mentorship and full-tuition scholarships to select transfer students from five partner community colleges.

SUCCESS **Mentorship and Community**

In addition to close faculty-student interaction, Bucknell offers several programs of support and mentorship to its students. These include 1) the Engineering Success Alliance, which provides targeted tutoring to engineering students who did not have access to a strong education in mathematics before enrolling at Bucknell, 2) the Together Everyone Achieves More (TEAM) mentoring program, which connects minority first-year students with minority mentors in their sophomore, junior or senior year; these mentors connect first-year students to campus resources and student communities and 3) the Bucknell Student Government Peer Mentoring Program, through which students in upper class years mentor first-year students. Additionally, first-year students who participate in the Residential Colleges, which are themed living-learning communities, benefit from being part of an extremely close-knit, academically focused group of students living in the same hall. They interact closely with faculty advisers and students who previously participated in the program.

"When you get to campus, you really realize how much is available at Bucknell. It has all the resources I need to learn — academically, and in every part of my life. There is a community here that has allowed me to grow as a student and as a person."

– Kopano Majara '12, accounting major in the School of Management at Bucknell

SUCCESS **High Career Placement and Salary Potential**

Bucknell graduates succeed in their careers because they offer the combination of skills, knowledge, and flexibility of mind that employers seek. To prepare students, the University offers a number of services through the Career Development Center, including advising, networking, mock interviews, internship and externship connections and employer fairs. These services are available to all students and alumni, beginning with the first-year. Bucknell's job placement rate is consistently high: 88 percent of the Class of 2010 was employed or in graduate school within nine months of graduation. For the Class of 2010, the mean salary was $50,172, and mid-career salary potential is among the highest nationally.

Bucknell University
Freas Hall
Lewisburg, PA 17837
Ph: (570) 577-1101
admissions@bucknell.edu
www.bucknell.edu

FAST FACTS

STUDENT PROFILE

# of degree-seeking undergraduates	3,500
% male/female	49/51
% African American	3
% American Indian or Alaska Native	<1
% Asian or Pacific Islander	6
% Hispanic	4
% White	81
% International	3
% Pell grant recipients	11.7

First-generation and minority alumni Gbenga Akinnagbe, actor; Michael E. Flowers, first African American selected chair of the Business Law Section, American Bar Association; Edward McKinley Robinson, former member of the senior staff and vice president for development, Colin Powell's America's Promise Alliance; Gerald Purnell, judge; Maria Lopez, human resources manager, Morgan Stanley in Hong Kong

ACADEMICS

full-time faculty	354
full-time minority faculty	47
student-faculty ratio	10:1
average class size	20
% first-year retention rate	94
% graduation rate (6 years)	91.3

Popular majors Engineering, BSBA/Management, Economics, Psychology, Biology

CAMPUS LIFE

% live on campus (% freshmen)	86 (99)

Multicultural student clubs and organizations Black Student Union, Bucknell African Students Association, Common Ground (student-led diversity immersion retreat program), Greeks for the Advancement of Multicultural Education, Jelani (African American Cultural Dance Group), Multicultural Council of Presidents (leadership council for promoting diversity), National Society of Black Engineers, OHLAS (Latino/Hispanic club)

Athletics NCAA Division I, Patriot League

ADMISSIONS

# of applicants	7,939
% accepted	27.6
# of first-year students enrolled	921
SAT Critical Reading (middle 50%)	620-720
SAT Math (middle 50%)	660-750
ACT (middle 50%)	29-32
average HS GPA	3.63
Deadlines	
early decision	11/15
regular decision	1/15
application fee (online)	$60 ($60)
fee waiver for applicants with financial need	yes

COST & AID

tuition	$43,628
room & board	$10,374
total need-based institutional scholarships/grants	$44,000,000
% of students apply for need-based aid	57.8
% of students receive aid	62
% receiving need-based scholarship or grant aid	50
% receiving aid whose need was fully met	95
average aid package	$27,000
average student loan debt upon graduation	$20,000

Dickinson College

Dickinson College, founded in 1783, is a highly selective, private, liberal arts college known for its innovative curriculum. Its mission is to offer students a useful education in the arts and sciences that will prepare them for lives as engaged citizens and leaders. Dickinson fosters a community that thrives on the collegial exchange of differing opinions. It promotes individual expression and encourages the celebration of disparate backgrounds and experiences. Dickinson is committed to bringing the world to campus. But it's the students — their beliefs, ideals and passions — who bring the greatest enlightenment to campus diversity.

OPPORTUNITY Posse Foundation and Other Foundations

Dickinson participates in the Posse Foundation, a program that brings talented inner-city youth to campus to pursue their academics and to help promote cross-cultural communication. Posse students are nominated by their high school to the program and share a collaborative support system with a special mentor to adjust to campus and college life. Dickinson's Posse Scholars hail from New York City and Los Angeles. Other foundations also help to select and prepare talented inner-city students for college. In addition to Posse, Dickinson partners with Philadelphia Futures, the Wight Foundation (Newark, N.J.), CollegeBound (Baltimore) and DC-CAP (Washington, D.C.).

SUCCESS Office of Diversity Initiatives

The Office of Diversity Initiatives (ODI) at Dickinson College is a resource center charged with advancing Dickinson's commitment to broadening the understanding of and building a pluralistic society that promotes equality and integrity on the campus, within the community and in the world. The office provides individuals with the opportunity to enrich their cultural experiences through participation in diversity programs and training workshops. The office encourages and facilitates activities that allow students to voice their opinions, serve the community and advocate for making Dickinson a place that welcomes difference and individuality.

SUCCESS Office of Academic Resource Services

The Office of Academic Resource Services offers individual and group programming which supports the intellectual development of Dickinson students. Programming includes evening workshops to assist students in developing skills in time management, note-taking and exam preparation, library research skills and stress management.

SUCCESS Mosaic: Learning by Living

The Community Studies Center encourages joint student and faculty fieldwork and community-oriented research through the American and Global Mosaic programs. During a semester of fieldwork immersion, Mosaic students interview a community's residents, listen to their histories and learn from their experiences. Through this cross-cultural program, students make connections between theory and practice, among people and ideas, across academic disciplines and around the world. They also set off on a journey of personal discovery — learning much about their own lives as they listen to the lives of others.

SUCCESS Crossing Borders

The Crossing Borders program allows students to study in several locations in one year. Recently, the program has been conducted as a joint venture with Dillard and Xavier universities, two historically black institutions in New Orleans. In the summer, students from Dickinson, Dillard and Xavier travel to Dickinson's study center in Cameroon, West Africa, where they are immersed in local culture — learning first-hand about the traditions, beliefs and culture of West Africa. The next planned Crossing Borders is a Comparative Black Liberation Mosaic. Students go to South Africa in the summer, spend the fall at Dickinson with a trip to the Mississippi Delta, and then go either to Dillard or Morehouse University in the spring.

Dickinson College
P.O. Box 1773
Carlisle, PA 17013-2896
Ph: (800) 644-1773 / (717) 245-1231
admit@dickinson.edu
www.dickinson.edu

FAST FACTS

STUDENT PROFILE	
# of degree-seeking undergraduates	2,357
% male/female	45/55
% African American	4
% American Indian or Alaska Native	<1
% Asian or Pacific Islander	4
% Hispanic	6
% White	77
% International	7
% Pell grant recipients	9
ACADEMICS	
full-time faculty	200
full-time minority faculty	20
student-faculty ratio	10:1
average class size	17
% first-year retention rate	90
% graduation rate (6 years)	83
Popular majors Biology, English, History, International Business & Management, Political Science, Psychology	
CAMPUS LIFE	
% live on campus (% freshmen)	94 (100)
Multicultural Student Clubs and Organizations African-American Society, ABOLISH, Active Minds, Amnesty International, Asian Social Interest Association, Club Afrique, Delta Sigma Theta, Dickinson Christian Fellowship, Dickinson Desi Association, Hillel, Latin American Club, Middle Eastern Club, Muslim Student Association, Newman Club, Spectrum, Students for Social Action, Sustained Dialogue, Third Degree Steppers, Umoja, Zatae Longsdorff Center for Women	
Athletics NCAA Division III, Eastern College Athletic Conference (ECAC)	
ADMISSIONS	
# of applicants	5,033
% accepted	48
# of first-year students enrolled	657
SAT Critical Reading (middle 50%)	600-680
SAT Math (middle 50%)	600-688
SAT Writing (middle 50%)	590-690
ACT (middle 50%)	27-30
average HS GPA	n/a
Deadlines	
early decision I	11/15
early decision II	1/15
regular application	2/1
application fee (online)	$65 ($65)
fee waiver for applicants with financial need	yes
COST & AID	
tuition	$42,610
room & board	$10,800
total need-based institutional scholarships/grants	$32,880,718
% of students apply for need-based aid	60
% of students receive aid	54
% receiving need-based scholarship or grant aid	52
% receiving aid whose need was fully met	73
average aid package	$34,687
average student loan debt upon graduation	$21,924

Franklin and Marshall College

Located in historic Lancaster, Pennsylvania, Franklin & Marshall College is a private, residential liberal arts college dedicated to academic excellence and hands-on learning. With a student-to-faculty ratio of 10:1 and a culture of close faculty-student collaboration, F&M students are challenged by their professors in small classes to investigate real-world problems and to learn by doing, not by listening and watching. Through F&M's distinctive College Houses, each F&M student becomes part of a tight-knit student community.

"The faith F&M has in me is overwhelming. Whether it is the opportunity to be Black Student Union president, or to volunteer in Ghana this summer for free, F&M has given me opportunities that I may otherwise have never received. In my heart, I know I'm in the right place."

– Jessica D., '13
Philadelphia, PA
Sociology Major, Film & Media Studies Minor

ACCESS Collegiate Leadership Summit

Each fall and spring, F&M invites high school students from diverse backgrounds with a strong history of leadership to campus for the Collegiate Leadership Summit to explore their leadership abilities as they transition to a college environment. At the Summit, students participate in group work, admission interviews, and meet with current students, faculty, and staff. The cost of attendance is covered by the College, and each year, six participants are offered full-tuition scholarships to F&M.

ACCESS National College Advising Corps - Keystone Region

Based at F&M, this organization provides underserved, rural high schools in Pennsylvania with trained college advisers to help low-income, first-generation students make the transition from high school to college. Advisers assist students with the college search and application process through both individual and group meetings.

OPPORTUNITY The William H. Gray Scholarship Program

Approximately 90 Gray Scholars from traditionally underrepresented backgrounds are chosen each year on the basis of academic strength, leadership ability and commitment to service. Scholarship recipients meet regularly with campus mentors to network with one another and form a peer support system.

OPPORTUNITY Posse Foundation

F&M is proud to be a partner college with Posse New York and Posse STEM in Miami, offering Posse students four-year, full-tuition scholarships and special opportunities and support throughout their time at F&M. Posse provides full tuition scholarships to students with strong academic backgrounds and leadership experience who may not have received the same opportunities as others in the college admission process. Coming into F&M with an established peer support group and a campus mentor that meets with the group every other week, Posse helps students transition to life at F&M and continue to strive for excellence in the collegiate setting.

OPPORTUNITY Multicultural Overnight Diplomat Experience (MODE)

Every spring, F&M hosts MODE for admitted multicultural and first-generation students from across the country to get a closer look at life at F&M first hand. For three days and two nights, MODE participants stay overnight with a current F&M student, meet with current students, faculty and alumni who share their background and experiences, and experience what life would be like on F&M's campus as a student. The cost of attendance and transportation is covered by the College.

SUCCESS The Office of Multicultural Affairs (OMCA)

F&M's OMCA provides comprehensive support and advising services for students from diverse backgrounds. The department funds student groups and activities that promote cultural awareness, and offers academic support, such as peer mentoring and student tutoring in science, math and English writing.

Franklin and Marshall College
P.O. Box 3003
Lancaster, PA 17603
Ph: (877) 678-9111
admission@fandm.edu
www.fandm.edu

FAST FACTS

STUDENT PROFILE

# of degree-seeking undergraduates	2,279
% male/female	47/53
% African American	3
% American Indian or Alaska Native	<1
% Asian or Pacific Islander	3
% Hispanic	6
% White	75
% Two or more races	2
% International	9
% Pell grant recipients	13

First-generation and minority alumni Wanda Pompey Austin, Ph.D., '75, President, Aerospace Corporation; William H. Gray III '63, Former President and CEO, United Negro College Fund and former Majority Whip, U.S. House of Representatives; Anthony Ross '91, President, United Way of Pennsylvania; LeRoy Pernell '71, Dean, College of Law, Florida A&M University; Modia Butler '95, Chief of Staff, City of Newark, N.J.

ACADEMICS

full-time faculty	211
full-time minority faculty	26
student-faculty ratio	10:1
average class size	25
% first-year retention rate	94
% graduation rate (6 years)	87

Popular majors Business, Government, Economics, History, Psychology

CAMPUS LIFE

% live on campus (fresh.)	99 (100)

Multicultural student clubs and organizations AfroCaribe Club, Asian Cultural Society, Black Student Union, IMPACT, International Club, LGBTA, Mi Gente Latina, SANGAM (South Asian Culture and Heritage Club), S.I.S.T.E.R.S, THRI, The Human Rights Initiative

Athletics NCAA Division III, Centennial Conference

ADMISSIONS

# of applicants	5,105
% accepted	38.39
# of first-year students enrolled	607
SAT Critical Reading (middle 50%)	610-680
SAT Math (middle 50%)	630-710
SAT Writing (middle 50%)	n/a
ACT (middle 50%)	28-31
Deadlines	
early decision I	11/15
early decision II	1/15
regular decision	1/31
application fee (online)	$60 ($60)
fee waiver for applicants with financial need	yes

COST & AID

tuition	$42,410
room and board	$11,500
total need-based institutional scholarships/grants	$24,949,453
% of students who applied for need-based aid	54
% receiving need-based scholarship or grant aid	44
% receiving aid whose need was fully met	95
average aid package	$32,018
average student loan debt upon graduation	$28,451

Gettysburg College

Gettysburg College
300 N. Washington St.
Gettysburg, PA 17325
Ph: (800) 431-0803
admiss@gettysburg.edu
www.gettysburg.edu

Gettysburg College, a historic institution with a reputation for academic excellence, provides students with a liberal arts education characterized by academic intensity and learning by getting involved. Founded in 1832 by anti-slavery theologian Samuel Simon Schmucker, Gettysburg College prides itself on a 10:1 student-faculty ratio that fosters close relationships and spirited class discussions. A champion for independent thinking and public action, Gettysburg students graduate with a love of learning, knowledge and skills they need for success and new insight into the world, their place in it, and their obligations to it. Gettysburg College engages highly motivated students in a comprehensive educational experience that prepares them for lives of personal fulfillment, career success, and responsible, engaged citizenship.

"Whether it's faculty or alumni, if you're willing to put in the effort, somebody at Gettysburg will help you accomplish your goal. At Gettysburg, if you can dream it up, you get there."

– Lawrese B., '10
East Orange, NJ
Interdisciplinary Major—Writing for Public Policy

OPPORTUNITY Making College Affordable for All Students

Gettysburg College is committed to working with students and their families to ensure that one's ability to pay not become an obstacle to a Gettysburg education. Approximately 70 percent of all students receive some form of financial aid, and the average aid package exceeds $30,000 a year. Most aid is awarded based on financial need, but academic merit and music scholarships are also available. Gettysburg College awarded $38 million in scholarships and grants for the 2010-2011 academic year. Merit-based scholarships range from $7,000 to $25,000 per year.

SUCCESS Intercultural Resource Center

The Intercultural Resource Center celebrates Gettysburg's diversity by providing a warm and affirming home on campus for students from all backgrounds and by sponsoring activities that build mutual respect and understanding. The IRC brings speakers to campus who address topics related to diversity, provides services such as tutoring and mentoring, runs discussion groups to foster open conversation on important issues, hosts meals with ethnic themes, and offers a variety of other services to create a welcoming atmosphere on campus. The IRC encourages involvement in its activities from all students at Gettysburg. It has a particular commitment to the academic and personal development of African American, Asian American, Latino and American Indian students on campus.

SUCCESS First-Year Residential College Program

First year students' residence hall assignments are linked to First-Year Seminar and College Writing courses, which helps extend class discussions into the less-formal arena of the living environment and promotes the open exchange of ideas. The program benefits new students by easing their transition to the college life, introducing them to the kind of thoughtful conversation that is characteristic of a good liberal arts education, enriching their learning and serving as a kind of academic ice-breaker, helping them to build relationships with hallmates. The First-Year Residential College also offers opportunities for peer tutoring, faculty counseling and mentoring with upper-class students.

FAST FACTS

STUDENT PROFILE

# of degree-seeking undergraduates	2,472
% male/female	47/53
% African American	4
% American Indian or Alaska Native	0
% Asian or Pacific Islander	2
% Hispanic	4
% White	81
% International	2
% Pell grant recipients	14

First-generation and minority alumni Bruce Gordon '68, former NAACP president and CEO

ACADEMICS

full-time faculty	209
full-time minority faculty	36
student-faculty ratio	10:1
average class size	18
% first-year retention rate	90
% graduation rate (6 years)	85

Popular majors Management, History, English, Psychology, Political Science, Biology

CAMPUS LIFE

% live on campus (fresh.)	94 (100)

Multicultural student clubs and organizations Black Student Union, Diaspora House, Intercultural Resource Center, Muslim Student Association, NAACP, Office of Intercultural Advancement, SALSA (Spanish and Latino Students' Association)

Athletics NCAA Division III, Centennial Conference

ADMISSIONS

# of applicants	5,662
% accepted	40
# of first-year students enrolled	730
SAT Critical Reading (middle 50%)	610-690
SAT Math (middle 50%)	620-680
SAT Writing (middle 50%)	n/a
ACT (middle 50%)	n/a
average HS GPA	n/a

Deadlines

early decision I	11/15
early decision II	1/15
regular decision	2/1
application fee (online)	$55 ($55)
fee waiver for applicants with financial need	yes

COST & AID

tuition	$42,610
room and board	$10,180
total need-based institutional scholarships/grants	$39,841,300
% of students who applied for need-based aid	54
% of students receive aid	70
% receiving need-based scholarship or grant aid	70
% receiving aid whose need was fully met	96
average aid package	$33,937
average student loan debt upon graduation	$23,258

Haverford College

Haverford College
370 Lancaster Avenue
Haverford, PA, 19041
Ph: (610) 896-1350
admission@haverford.edu
www.haverford.edu

Haverford is a coeducational, residential liberal arts college located 8 miles west of center city Philadelphia. Haverford's 1,200 students represent an exceptional diversity of interests, backgrounds, and talents, with individuals hailing from nearly all 50 states, DC, Puerto Rico, and more than 40 countries around the world. The Haverford experience revolves around opportunities for students to be directly engaged with their education – through strong personal relationships with faculty and peers, through small, seminar-based classes, and through tremendous opportunities for research and independent scholarship. The Haverford Honor Code, affirmed by the student body each year, embodies the community values and philosophy of conduct within the College: students are expected to maintain a strong sense of individual responsibility as well as intellectual integrity, honesty, and genuine concern for others.

OPPORTUNITY **Commitment to Financial Aid**

Haverford has a long-standing commitment to making college affordable, meeting 100 percent of the demonstrated need of all students for the full four years of undergraduate study. Beginning with the Haverford Class of 2012 financial aid awards are loan-free, with this portion of the award replaced by additional scholarship funds.

OPPORTUNITY **QuestBridge**

Haverford partners with QuestBridge, a non-profit program that links bright, motivated low-income students with educational and scholarship opportunities at some of the nation's best colleges. Through QuestBridge, Haverford has been able to reach out to and enroll many students who may not have otherwise considered Haverford, providing greater opportunities for these students and enriching the Haverford student body.

OPPORTUNITY **Haverford Summer Science Institute**

The Summer Science Institute is an intensive, residential, five-week introduction to college-level science study for incoming first-year students who come from groups traditionally underrepresented in the sciences or who come from families with little or no college experience. With the help of more than 15 Haverford professors, administrators, and staff members, HSSI students participate in seminar-like courses and lab modules in Chemistry, Biology, Mathematics, Physics, Psychology, and Writing.

SUCCESS **Multicultural Scholars Program**

The Multicultural Scholars Program offers a series of workshops to enhance students' academic success, peer tutoring and mentoring, and opportunities for research during the summer and academic year. The program provides guidance, support, and a variety of opportunities to Haverford students from historically underrepresented groups, helping students to succeed academically in their four years at Haverford and fostering future success in graduate school and career plans.

SUCCESS **The Office of Multicultural Affairs (OMA)**

The OMA provides a comprehensive program to ensure that historically under-represented groups in particular, and all Haverford students in general, will have rich learning experiences in and outside the classroom. The OMA provides opportunities for cultural exploration, dialogue, personal reflection, and leadership development, and supports student cultural organizations such as the Black Student's League, the Alliance of Latin American Students, and the Asian Students Association.

FAST FACTS

STUDENT PROFILE

# of degree-seeking undergraduates	1,177
% male/female	47/53
% African American	7.6
% American Indian or Alaska Native	0.2
% Asian or Pacific Islander	9.6
% Hispanic	8.5
% White	69.1
% International	5.3
% Pell grant recipients	10.2

ACADEMICS

full-time faculty	119
full-time minority faculty	31
student-faculty ratio	8:1
average class size	14.4
% first-year retention rate	96
% graduation rate (6 years)	92.7

Popular majors Biology, Economics, English, History, Political Science, Psychology

CAMPUS LIFE

% live on campus (% freshmen)	99 (100)

Multicultural student clubs and organizations Alliance of Latin American Students, Asian Students Association, Japanese Culture Club, Korean Students Association, Black Students League, Committee on International Initiatives, International Students Association, Queer Discussion Group, Re-Mix Multiracial Students Organization, Simurgh, Sons of Africa, South Asian Society, Women of Color

Athletics NCAA Division III, Centennial Conference

ADMISSIONS

# of applicants	3,476
% accepted	25
# of first-year students enrolled	330
SAT Critical Reading (middle 50%)	670-770
SAT Math (middle 50%)	660-770
SAT Writing (middle 50%)	670-770
ACT (middle 50%)	n/a
average HS GPA	n/a

Deadlines

early action	11/15
regular decision	1/15
application fee (online)	$60 ($60)
fee waiver for applicants with financial need	yes

COST & AID

tuition	$41,830
room & board	$12,842
total need-based institutional scholarships/grants	$19,100,895
% of students apply for need-based aid	57
% of students receive aid	52
% receiving need-based scholarship or grant aid	49
% receiving aid whose need was fully met	100
average aid package	$37,509
average student loan debt upon graduation	$16,238

*Starting with the Class of 2012, Haverford eliminated loans from all need-based aid packages.

King's College

King's College is a Catholic liberal arts college founded in 1946 by the Congregation of Holy Cross from the University of Notre Dame. The college is located on a small urban campus in Wilkes-Barre, Pa. King's aims for its students to be success-oriented, and provides them with top-notch faculty, technology and facilities. The college has a nationally recognized CORE curriculum and career placement program that prides itself on helping all King's students and graduates find meaningful employment. The campus is service-oriented, with faculty, staff and students coming together for volunteer projects on and off campus. The Office of College Diversity assists in making the campus inclusive and tolerant. King's students describe the campus as friendly and warm, with a strong sense of community.

"If I had it to do again, I would certainly choose King's. I have built some of the best friendships of my life. I have grown in ways that are impossible to put into words. I am confident in the education and training I have received while here and would not trade it. I am proud to be a member of the King's College Community."

– Candice R., '11
Elementary Education

ACCESS College Discovery Program

Gifted local high school students may take introductory college courses during the academic year and summer at King's College. The purpose of these course offerings is to challenge talented high school students, to orient them to the college environment, and to encourage a local college-bound culture.

ACCESS McGowan Hispanic Outreach Program

King's College is dedicated to its McGowan Hispanic Outreach Program, which consists of outreach programs to the local Hispanic population, a mentorship program for Hispanic King's students, and hosting Hispanic cultural events and conferences on campus.

OPPORTUNITY Diversity Award and Presidential Scholarships

The Diversity Award is a need-based award granted to multicultural first-year applicants to the college who are enrolled in a college preparatory curriculum. The award amount varies. Eight to 12 full-tuition Presidential Scholarships are given to students demonstrating the highest level of academic achievement. Students must be in the top 5 percent of their high school class, have a minimum SAT score of 1870 (ACT 28), a minimum GPA of 3.5, and a campus interview.

SUCCESS College Entry Program

The College Entry Program is a pre-orientation summer program that prepares students for the challenges of college life at King's. The program allows students to earn up to six college credits in King's CORE curriculum with the advantage of smaller class sizes and academic support staff on hand. Career planning professionals meet with students to assist with career planning strategies. College Entry Program students also receive priority advisement, may plan their fall schedule ahead of time and consistently achieve grades equal to or surpassing classmates in later semesters at King's.

King's College
Office of Admission
133 North River Street
Wilkes-Barre, PA 18711
Ph: (570) 208-5858
admissions@kings.edu
www.kings.edu

FAST FACTS

STUDENT PROFILE

# of degree-seeking undergraduates	1,999
% male/female	51/49
% African American	3
% American Indian or Alaska Native	<1
% Asian or Pacific Islander	1
% Hispanic	5
%White	82
% Pell grant recipients	30

First-generation and minority alumni William G. McGowan, founder, MCI; Santo Loquasto, Academy Award winner, Tony Award winner; Patrick J. Murphy, former U.S. Congressman

ACADEMICS

full-time faculty	130
full-time minority faculty	6
student-faculty ratio	13:1
average class size	18
% first-year retention rate	78
% graduation rate (6 years)	70

Popular majors Business Administration, Physician Assistant, Biology, Education, Accounting

CAMPUS LIFE

% live on campus (% freshmen)	52 (72)

Multicultural student clubs and organizations Multicultural/International Club

Athletics NCAA Division III, Freedom Conference, Middle Atlantic States Collegiate Athletic Conference

ADMISSIONS

# of applicants	2,420
% accepted	74
# of first-year students enrolled	528
SAT Critical Reading (middle 50%)	460-560
SAT Math (middle 50%)	460-570
SAT Writing (middle 50%)	460-560
ACT (middle 50%)	19-24
average HS GPA	3.3

Deadlines

regular decision	rolling
application fee (online)	$30 ($0)
fee waiver for applicants with financial need	yes

COST & AID

tuition	$27,860
room & board	$10,670
total need-based institutional scholarships/grants	$19,571,123
% of students apply for need-based aid	91
% of students receive aid	97
% receiving need-based scholarship or grant aid	82
% receiving aid whose need was fully met	16
average aid package	$19,426
average student loan debt upon graduation	$31,113

Lafayette College

Lafayette College is committed to maintaining and supports diversity through the understanding that awareness, a deeper sense of cultural knowledge, and the ability to operate in a pluralistic community are essential to an undergraduate education. Lafayette is uniquely positioned among America's leading colleges for its strictly undergraduate focus that offers the best in liberal arts and engineering programs. Through active learning experiences in small-group seminars, student-centered team projects, independent study, student-faculty research, study abroad, and internships, students have the opportunity to cross academic boundaries in the arts, sciences, and engineering. An independent, coeducational, residential, undergraduate institution, Lafayette maintains a growing faculty of distinction.

OPPORTUNITY **Multicultural Student Visit Opportunities**

Each November, prospective students of color experience campus life on Multicultural Visit Day. In April Lafayette hosts admitted students from multicultural backgrounds for Prologue, a day-long campus program. The college flies a number of these students to campus and hosts many students of color who visit through the activities of community-based organizations, including TORCH, Prep for Prep, and the Princeton University Pre-Collegiate Program.

OPPORTUNITY **Posse Foundation**

Lafayette participates in the Posse Foundation, a program that brings talented inner-city youth to campus to pursue their academics and to help promote cross-cultural communication. Posse students are nominated to the program by their high school and share a collaborative support system with a special mentor to adjust to campus and college life. Lafayette's Posse Scholars hail from New York City and Washington DC.

"I have really started to love this school. Lafayette is a purely undergraduate school, and you are getting introductory courses by senior professors. We are really lucky as undergraduates to be able to do research with these professors and to really feel like you're the number one on campus."
– Fairouz F., '11
Washington, DC
Music, Africana Studies

SUCCESS **Office of Intercultural Development (OID)**

The Office of Intercultural Development affirms that the presence of diversity and cultural richness is an essential component of student learning and enhancing students' cultural experience. It provides the community with intercultural programming and cross-cultural dialogue, as well as information, advice, and services to African, Latino/a, Asian and Native American (ALANA) students and the wider Lafayette community.

SUCCESS **Portlock Black Cultural Center**

An integral part of the College's effort to provide multicultural education to the campus community, the Portlock Center provides a way to assess the educational and social experiences of ALANA students and to initiate and improve programs. It features an art gallery, seminar and meeting room, social spaces, and a library on issues of cultural diversity and social justice. Activities include exhibits, workshops, alumni events, guest lectures, classes, receptions and film showings. The center works with community organizations to increase cultural awareness, support community-wide programs, and provide a forum for networking.

SUCCESS **Lafayette Intercultural Networking Council (LINC)**

The Lafayette Intercultural Networking Council promotes intercultural exchange with dialogue and collaborative efforts among student groups and organizations, administration offices, and faculty/academic departments.

Lafayette College
118 Markle Hall
Easton, PA 18042
Ph: (610) 330-5100
admissions@lafayette.edu
www.lafayette.edu

FAST FACTS

STUDENT PROFILE

# of degree-seeking undergraduates	2,360
% male/female	53/47
% African American	5
% American Indian or Alaska Native	0
% Asian or Pacific Islander	4
% Hispanic	5
% White	67
% International	6
% Pell grant recipients	6

First-generation and minority alumni David Kearney McDonogh, Lafayette's first African American graduate and perhaps the first person with legal status as a slave to receive a college degree, physician (Harlem's first hospital named for him); Riley K. Temple, founder, Temple Strategies, Washington, D.C.; Darlyne Bailey, assistant to the president, University of Minnesota; Marcia Bloom Bernicat, U.S. Ambassador to Senegal and Guinea-Bissau; Winston Thompson, physician, Department of Obstetrics and Gynecology, Morehouse School of Medicine, Atlanta, Ga.

ACADEMICS

full-time faculty	213
full-time minority faculty	26
student-faculty ratio	10:1
average class size	18
% first-year retention rate	94
% graduation rate (6 years)	89

Popular majors Economics, English, Engineering, Government and Law, Biology, Art, Psychology

CAMPUS LIFE

% live on campus (% freshmen)	94 (100)

Multicultural student clubs and organizations African and Caribbean Students Association, Asian Culture Association, Association of Black Collegians, Brothers of Lafayette, Heritage of Latin America, Hispanic Society, International Students Association, NIA (multicultural women's group)
Athletics NCAA Division I, Patriot League

ADMISSIONS

# of applicants	5,822
% accepted	42
# of first-year students enrolled	648
SAT Critical Reading (middle 50%)	570-670
SAT Math (middle 50%)	610-700
SAT Writing (middle 50%)	590-680
ACT (middle 50%)	26-30
average HS GPA	3.41
Deadlines	
early decision	1/1
regular decision	1/1
application fee (online)	$65 ($65)
fee waiver for applicants with financial need	yes

COST & AID

tuition	$40,340
room & board	$12,362
total need-based institutional scholarships/grants	$27,921,687
% of students apply for need-based aid	60
% of students receive aid	44
% receiving need-based scholarship or grant aid	43
% receiving aid whose need was fully met	88
average aid package	$35,451
average student loan debt upon graduation	$18,747

Lehigh University

Lehigh University
27 Memorial Drive West
Bethlehem, PA 18015
Ph: (610) 758-3100
admissions@lehigh.edu
www.lehigh.edu

A selective private school in Bethlehem, Pa., Lehigh University is noted for both its strong academic programs and picturesque campus, located within 100 miles of both New York City and Philadelphia. While Lehigh offers many broad academic programs, the university prides itself on the personal connection that professors have with their students. Lehigh's 4,800+ undergraduate students and 2,100 graduate students can experience interesting, independent research and work closely with faculty who offer their time and attention to projects, internships, and innovative studies. With more than 90 majors in the liberal arts, business, education, engineering and the sciences, students are able to customize their college experience. Academic support, career services, and other departments work closely with faculty to ensure that students, and their families have access to an open door that allows students to take advantage of all resources designed for their success both in the classroom and after graduation.

"Choosing to attend Lehigh was one of the best decisions I have ever made and I believe the rewards of a Lehigh University education will never cease. I am still discovering more and more opportunities that Lehigh has to offer. If you are looking for an institution that will work just as hard for you as you work for it, then Lehigh University is your best choice."

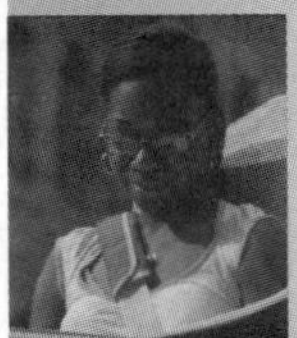

– Adrienne L., '11
Bucks County, PA
Molecular Biology

ACCESS **Students That Are Ready (STAR) Academies**

A partnership between Lehigh University and local schools, businesses, and parents, the Students That Are Ready Academies provide local middle and high school aged students with access to two unique programs: a year-long academic success and mentoring program for students in sixth through twelfth grades, and a three-week summer program in math, science and technology for students entering sixth through ninth grades. STAR also offers a Summer Eighth Grade Experience (SEE) that helps current academy students transition into high school. The fundamental mission of the academy is to enable students to develop intellectually, socially, spiritually and emotionally so that they will become productive citizens.

ACCESS **March for Education**

Founded by the National Society of Black Engineers, the March for Education brings Lehigh students, faculty and staff, along with local community college members and members from the community at large into the homes of local families to talk about the importance of higher education. Information is presented regarding SAT preparation and local testing centers, as well as information about local colleges and universities in the area.

OPPORTUNITY **Diversity Recruitment and Accepted Student Programs**

Throughout the year, any student interested in visiting Lehigh can meet with the Director or Assistant Director of Diversity Recruitment to discuss any specific questions and concerns they may have about applying to Lehigh. Personalized attention, follow through, and support are what makes the Diversity Recruitment aspect of Lehigh's admissions process so special. Accepted students have the opportunity to visit at Lehigh's cost for the April Diversity Life Weekend, where students attend classes, stay with current Lehigh students, and experience the range of academic and social opportunities available.

FAST FACTS

STUDENT PROFILE

# of degree-seeking undergraduates	4,766
% male/female	59/41
% African American	3.6
% American Indian or Alaska Native	<1
% Asian or Pacific Islander	6.2
% Hispanic	7
% White	71
% International	4.5
% Pell grant recipients	13

First-generation and minority alumni Pongpol Adireksarn, Thai politician; Ali Al-Naimi, oil minister, Saudi Arabia; Dr. Ron Williams, vice president, College Board in Washington, D.C.; Dr. Frank Douglas, MD, Ph.D., executive director, Center for Biomedical Innovation at MIT

ACADEMICS

full-time faculty	473
full-time minority faculty	78
student-faculty ratio	10:1
average class size	25-30
% first-year retention rate	93
% graduation rate (6 years)	88

Popular majors Accounting, Civil Engineering, Finance, Mechanical Engineering, Psychology

CAMPUS LIFE

% live on campus (% freshmen)	69 (99)

Multicultural student clubs and organizations African-Caribbean Cultural, Anime Eki Animation, Asian Cultural Society, Association of International Students, Bhangra, Black Students Union, Chinese Cultural, Hispanic Union of Business Students, Indian Students Association, Korean Students, Mariachi, National Society of Black Engineers, Society of Hispanic Engineers, South American and Latino Students Alliance, Thai Students at Lehigh

Athletics NCAA Division I (football – championship subdivision), Eastern Intercollegiate Wrestling Association, Patriot League

ADMISSIONS (BASED ON FALL 2010)

# of applicants	10,328
% accepted	38
# of first-year students enrolled	1,212
SAT Critical Reading (middle 50%)	580-670
SAT Math (middle 50%)	640-720
SAT Writing (middle 50%)	n/a
ACT (middle 50%)	27-31
average HS GPA	n/a

Deadlines

early decision	11/15
regular decision	1/1
application fee (online)	$70 ($70)
fee waiver for applicants with financial need	yes

COST & AID (BASED ON FALL 2010)

tuition	$40,660
room & board	$10,840
total need-based institutional scholarships/grants	$49,152,403
% of students apply for need-based aid	57
% of students receive aid	77
% receiving need-based scholarship or grant aid	94
% receiving aid whose need was fully met	89
average aid package	$30,528
average student loan debt upon graduation	$31,922

Rosemont College

Rosemont College
1400 Montgomery Avenue
Rosemont, PA 19010
Ph: (610) 527-0200
admissions@rosemont.edu
www.rosemont.edu

At Rosemont College you will gain knowledge, develop critical skills, and grow as a person of character. Located in suburban Philadelphia, Rosemont College offers students an exceptional and comprehensive coeducational learning experience. With 23 undergraduate majors; seven graduate programs; 10 pre-professional, certification, and dual-degrees programs; 13 varsity sport teams; and numerous clubs, Rosemont develops your unique talents emphasizing what you're best at and remains connected to what you want to do.

OPPORTUNITY **Rosemont Scholarship**

Rosemont College seeks to provide an affordable college education to all students, regardless of family income, who demonstrate the potential for academic success. In order to promote academic excellence while providing opportunities to students of all backgrounds the College offers both merit based awards, Rosemont Scholarships, and need based awards, Rosemont Grants.

"The responsibility to succeed is on me, but I feel as though the faculty and my friends are constantly encouraging me to do my best, and to achieve my dreams and goals."
– Chris P., Philadelphia, PA Sociology

SUCCESS **Bridge to Success Program**

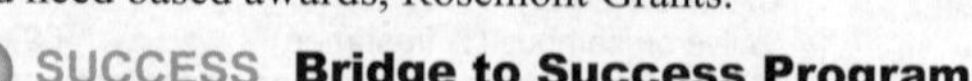

Rosemont conducts the Bridge to Success Program each August for incoming students. Bridge is a pre-orientation program which offers: academic support emphasizing writing and reading, college readiness, and study skills, individual mentoring, and team-building to a selected group of students. Under the guidance of a Bridge Coordinator, and with the instructional expertise of two Rosemont professors, students attend four days of classes prior to the start of the academic year. During the course of the year both the Coordinator and the staff of Student Academic Support will "touch base" with each student regularly, as well as with the student mentors.

SUCCESS **Mission Plan**

Within the first few days at Rosemont, students take a number of surveys that identify their personal and academic strengths, career interest, and learning styles. This information helps them work more efficiently and helps others be better teachers and mentors. Students will also work closely with professors and advisors to draft their personalized Mission Plan, a four year road map for their Rosemont experience. The Mission Plan guides students' intellectual and extracurricular lives, helps them develop leadership skills and strength of character and ensure that all the things they do in college work together to prepare for their future.

FAST FACTS

STUDENT PROFILE

# of degree-seeking undergraduates	422
% male/female	18/82
% African American	49
% American Indian or Alaska Native	0
% Asian or Pacific Islander	n/a
% Hispanic	8
% White	31
% International	1
% Pell grant recipients	52

First-generation and minority alumni Mari Carmen Aponte, executive director, Puerto Rico Federal Affairs Administration; Yvonne Chism-Peace, educator, award-winning author; Gwen Owens, multiple Emmy Award-nominated news veteran and news anchor; Varsovia Fernandez, executive director, Greater Philadelphia Hispanic Chamber of Commerce.

ACADEMICS

full-time faculty	27
full-time minority faculty	0
student-faculty ratio	10:1
average class size	12
% first-year retention rate	64
% graduation rate (6 years)	62

Popular majors English, Psychology, Business

CAMPUS LIFE

% live on campus (% freshmen)	60 (60)

Multicultural student clubs and organizations Association of Latin American Students, French Club, International Club, Irish Heritage Society, Italian Club, Muslim Student Association, Organization of African American Students

Athletics NCAA Division III, Colonial States Athletic Association (CSAC)

ADMISSIONS

# of applicants	1,090
% accepted	51
# of first-year students enrolled	100
SAT Critical Reading (middle 50%)	450-540
SAT Math (middle 50%)	420-540
SAT Writing (middle 50%)	380-500
ACT (middle 50%)	18-23
average HS GPA	3.05

Deadlines

regular decision	rolling
application fee (online)	$35 ($0)
fee waiver for applicants with financial need	yes

COST & AID

tuition	$27,730
room & board	$11,440
total need-based institutional scholarships/grants	n/a
% of students apply for need-based aid	93
% of students receive aid	80
% receiving need-based scholarship or grant aid	84
% receiving aid whose need was fully met	15
average aid package	$25,237
average student loan debt upon graduation	$22,619

Saint Francis University

Saint Francis University
P.O. Box 600
117 Evergreen Drive
Loretto, PA 15940
Ph: (814) 472-3100
admissions@francis.edu
www.francis.edu

As a Franciscan institution located in rural Pennsylvania, Saint Francis University strives to imbue its students with "a mind for excellence, a spirit for peace and justice [and] a mind for service." To this end, the university has opened the state-of-the-art DiSepio Institute for Rural Health and Wellness, an education and research center featuring physical training, conference, clinical, human performance laboratory and meditation spaces. It is used both to foster the science and health programs at the university and to help the school serve those suffering from illnesses common to rural areas. The oldest Franciscan institution of higher learning in the United States, Saint Francis University offers 25 undergraduate majors to nearly 2,000 students, and is an inclusive community that welcomes all people. By emphasizing values, skills and knowledge, each of its academic programs provides an understanding of Franciscan heritage, values and traditions.

ACCESS Upward Bound

Saint Francis University participates in the federally funded Upward Bound program, a federal TRIO program funded through the U.S. Department of Education, which has prepared over 1,500 disadvantaged high school students for the rigors of postsecondary education since 1966. Provided at no cost to participants, the program offers a wide variety of academic, career, cultural, and social development activities for high school students from Blair and Cambria counties. Each participant must come from a low-income family and/or be a potential first-generation college student. From September through May, the students participate in follow-ups held on campus and tutorials held after-school in their communities. Additional academic year activities include college visits, SAT sessions, and college fairs. During a six-week residential summer program, students attend academic classes each day and participate in a wide variety of cultural and recreational activities. Each summer Upward Bound Bridge students take Saint Francis University courses for credit.

OPPORTUNITY Scholarship Opportunities

Saint Francis University believes every person who desires higher education has the right to pursue it. The university offers a variety of awards to supplement families' funds whenever possible, and aggressively seeks financial aid for those demonstrating need. The university offers a comprehensive program of merit-based scholarships, institutional grants, loans, part-time employment and federal and state financial assistance.

SUCCESS Opportunities for Academic Success in Studies Program

Students are expected to meet with their counselor on a monthly basis through the Opportunities for Academic Success in Studies program, which is designed to assist first-year students who have not yet fully developed their academic potential. The program provides academic assistance and support services to enhance student growth, success, and persistence towards attaining a college degree. Although the support programming and services are important factors for success, the motivation to take advantage of these workshops and tutorials comes from within the student.

FAST FACTS

STUDENT PROFILE

# of degree-seeking undergraduates	1,832
% male/female	41/59
% African American	5
% American Indian or Alaska Native	<1
% Asian or Pacific Islander	<1
% Hispanic	1
% Pell grant recipients	36

First-generation and minority alumni Maurice Stokes, Norm van Lier, Kevin Porter Former, former basketball players

ACADEMICS

full-time faculty	114
full-time minority faculty	4
student-faculty ratio	14:1
average class size	22
% first-year retention rate	83
% graduation rate (6 years)	69

Popular majors Business Administration/ Management, Biology, Chemistry, Occupational Therapy, Physical Therapy and Physician Assistant Science, Education

CAMPUS LIFE

% live on campus (% freshmen)	76 (82)

Multicultural student clubs and organizations Office of Multicultural Affairs, Multicultural Awareness Society, Center for International Education and Outreach, Student Government Association, Student Activities Organization

Athletics NCAA Division I, Eastern Intercollegiate Volleyball Association, Northeast Conference

ADMISSIONS

# of applicants	1,584
% accepted	71
# of first-year students enrolled	432
SAT Critical Reading (middle 50%)	470-570
SAT Math (middle 50%)	470-590
SAT Writing (middle 50%)	n/a
ACT (middle 50%)	21-27
average HS GPA	3.46

Deadlines

regular decision	rolling
PT, PA, OT application deadline	1/15
application fee (online)	$30 ($30)
fee waiver for applicants with financial need	yes

COST & AID

tuition	$26,758
room & board	$9,520
total need-based institutional scholarships/grants	$17,901,577
% of students apply for need-based aid	94
% of students receive aid	86
% receiving need-based scholarship or grant aid	68
% receiving aid whose need was fully met	33
average aid package	$19,963
average student loan debt upon graduation	$21,000

Saint Vincent College

Saint Vincent College
300 Fraser Purchase Road
Latrobe, PA 15650-2690
Ph: (742) 805-2500
admission@stvincent.edu
www.stvincent.edu

Saint Vincent College is a private, co-educational, liberal arts college with an educational tradition that dates back to 1846. Rooted in the tradition of the Catholic faith, the heritage of Benedictine monasticism, and a liberal approach to life and learning, Saint Vincent encourages students to pursue their intellectual gifts, professional aptitudes, and personal aspirations. With a welcoming hospitality—nearly 15% of the incoming freshman class is comprised of students of color—and an attention to individual needs, Saint Vincent teaches students to integrate their professional aims with the broader purposes of human life.

"I chose Saint Vincent College because I was looking for a college close to home that provided a good education. The faculty and staff here are friendly, intelligent and always willing to help students. They are very approachable."
– Nettisha H., '09
Gibsonia, PA
Communications

ACCESS The Challenge Program

The Challenge Program at Saint Vincent College is designed for gifted, creative, or talented students, grades six through 12. The school offers exciting daytime courses in subjects like computers, history, and the humanities for highly motivated youth who seek opportunities to explore new interests and develop their creativity and talents. In addition to the classroom experience, Challenge also includes evening recreation and social interaction.

ACCESS Pathways to Success

Pathways to Success empowers underserved local middle school and high school students. Saint Vincent students act as mentors during the year-round program and provide participants with support structures and on-going educational opportunities. With special attention to academic development, cultural awareness, community service, and personal development, the program tailors educational content and methods to complement both the goals of cooperating schools and Pennsylvania's academic standards. Thus, learning experiences adapt to changing needs as students progress from middle school through high school.

OPPORTUNITY Special Admission Policy

The Opportunity SVC/ACT 101 Program is a statewide academic support system funded, in part, by the Commonwealth of Pennsylvania through Act 101. Placement in the program is determined after the Admission Committee evaluates the applicant's grades, test scores, and recommendations. Although each candidate is evaluated according to individual merits and potential, academic and financial eligibility requirements may be taken into consideration in accordance with Act 101 state guidelines. The Opportunity staff provides ongoing academic support and counseling to the student throughout his or her college years. In addition, a fall transitional semester is an added benefit of the program.

SUCCESS Office of Multicultural and International Student Life

The Office of Multicultural and International Student Life is the "connective tissue" for the many national, ethnic and cultural groups of the Saint Vincent College community. The office not only seeks to ensure a diverse environment at both the curricular and co-curricular levels, but also works to ensure everyone at Saint Vincent feels comfortable, valued, and connected. The office offers special programming, activities, on-campus employment opportunities, and a special multicultural orientation.

FAST FACTS

STUDENT PROFILE

# of degree-seeking undergraduates	1,680
% male/female	49/51
% African American	7
% American Indian or Alaska Native	<1
% Asian or Pacific Islander	3
% Hispanic	4
% White	90
% International	1
% Pell grant recipients	28.4

First-generation and minority alums Ramon Martin, M.D., Ph.D., Physician, Brigham and Women's Hospital, Harvard Medical School, Boston; Warner Johnson, Director of Alumni, Robert Morris University; James Overton, Chief Financial Officer, United Way of Allegheny County; Dr. Willette Stinson, Ph.D.; Bryan K. Ulishney, Vice President Finance and Operations, A Second Chance Inc.; Christina Domasky, Bridal Consultant, Nemacolin Woodlands Resort and Spa; Antoine D. Terrar, Program Manager, Pearson Peacekeeping Centre

ACADEMICS

full-time faculty	208
full-time minority faculty	5
student-faculty ratio	14:1
average class size	20
% first-year retention rate	82
% graduation rate (6 years)	72

Popular majors Business Administration, Biology, Communication, Environmental Studies, Psychology/Education

CAMPUS LIFE

% live on campus (% freshmen)	83 (90)

Multicultural student clubs and organizations Minority Student Coalition, Italian Club, International Student Union

Athletics NCAA Division III, Presidents' Athletic Conference

ADMISSIONS

# of applicants	1,843
% accepted	65
# of first-year students enrolled	447
SAT Critical Reading (middle 50%)	470-570
SAT Math (middle 50%)	480-590
SAT Writing (middle 50%)	460-570
ACT (middle 50%)	19-24
average HS GPA	3.57

Deadlines

regular decision	4/1
application fee (online)	$25 ($0)
fee waiver for applicants with financial need	yes

COST & AID

tuition	$28,854
room & board	$9,138
total need-based institutional scholarships/grants	$14,528,589
% of students apply for need-based aid	97
% of students receive aid	100
% receiving need-based scholarship or grant aid	100
% receiving aid whose need was fully met	28
average aid package	$20,563
average student loan debt upon graduation	$17,500

Swarthmore College

Swarthmore College
500 College Avenue
Swarthmore, PA 19081
Ph: (800) 667-3110 / (610) 328-8300
admissions@swarthmore.edu
www.swarthmore.edu

Swarthmore, founded by Quakers in 1864, is a nonsectarian, liberal arts college and a forward-thinking school that encourages students to discuss and embrace their passion, whether it's ending genocide, singing in a gospel choir or building a robot. The lush campus facility, with its outstanding resources and distinguished faculty, promises students a memorable and rewarding college life. One of the many compelling features of Swarthmore is its size. As a highly-regarded private Pennsylvania college with about 1,500 students, the college basks in the positives of being small, yet consistently competitive. Located on a 425-acre campus, Swarthmore boasts an 8:1 student-to-faculty ratio, allowing rich academic relationships to develop between students and faculty.

ACCESS **Chester Children's Chorus**

Children living in the Chester-Upland School District are given the opportunity to expand their intellectual and cultural horizons through the Chester Children's Chorus. The rigorous musical training includes school year and summer rehearsals, a full day Summer Learning Program with two to three hours of music daily plus reading, science, art and African Dance and Drumming, all taking place at Swarthmore College in the state-of-the-art Lang Music Building.

ACCESS **Science for Kids (SFK)**

The Science for Kids program, held on campus during the summer, exposes elementary school children from Chester, PA to a variety of experiences in science and math. The SFK program is one of several innovations in science education supported by a $1.6 million grant from the Howard Hughes Medical Institute (HHMI) designed to foster diversity and interdisciplinary thinking and teaching. Since 2004, the five-week summer program has had students participating in science workshops taught by Swarthmore faculty, instructors and undergraduate SFK counselors.

OPPORTUNITY **Discover Swarthmore!**

Discover Swarthmore! is a weekend overnight program for prospective students of color. High school seniors accepted to the program will receive an all-expenses-paid trip to campus to experience a lot of what Swarthmore has to offer. Discover Swarthmore! events include student hosted social events, financial aid workshops, panel discussions on the value of a liberal arts education, lunch and dinner with faculty, deans and students, the opportunity to attend classes, campus tours, and an overnight in the dorms hosted by a current Swarthmore student.

SUCCESS **Swarthmore Summer Institute**

The Swarthmore Summer Institute Program is a week-long orientation sponsored by Swarthmore for first-year students who are interested in exploring issues of multicultural identity and leadership, especially relating to race, class, and gender. The program consists of a series of interactive workshops and seminars led by Swarthmore administrators and Student Resource Persons (SRPs).

SUCCESS **Swarthmore's Externship Program**

Swarthmore's Externship Program enables students to spend a week immersed in the activities and work life in a career of their interest by providing shadowing opportunities with college alumni. Currently, programs are available in New York, Philadelphia, Washington, D.C., San Francisco and Boston.

FAST FACTS

STUDENT PROFILE

# of degree-seeking undergraduates	1,525
% male/female	48/52
% African American	10
% American Indian or Alaska Native	1
% Asian or Pacific Islander	16
% Hispanic	11
% White	45
% International	7
% Pell grant recipients	15

ACADEMICS

full-time faculty	175
full-time minority faculty	29
student-faculty ratio	8:1
average class size	15
% first-year retention rate	97
% graduation rate (6 years)	93

Popular majors Biology, Engineering, Political Science, English, Economics

CAMPUS LIFE

% live on campus (% freshmen)	87 (100)

Multicultural student clubs and organizations ENLACE (Latino Student Organization), MULTI (Multicultural Student Organization), Students of Caribbean Ancestry, Swarthmore African Student Association, Native American Student Association, COLORS, Deshi (South Asian Student Organization), Han (Korean Student Organization), Swarthmore Asian Organization, Swarthmore African American Student Society, Intercultural Center, Black Cultural Center

Athletics NCAA Division III, Centennial Conference, Eastern College Athletic Conference

ADMISSIONS

# of applicants (class of 2014)	6,041
% accepted	16
# of first-year students enrolled	388
SAT Critical Reading (middle 50%)	670-760
SAT Math (middle 50%)	670-770
SAT Writing (middle 50%)	680-770
ACT (middle 50%)	29-33
average HS GPA	n/a

Deadlines

early decision	11/15
regular decision	1/1
application fee (online)	\$60 (\$60)
fee waiver for applicants with financial need	yes

COST & AID

tuition	\$40,816
room & board	\$12,100
total need-based institutional scholarships/grants	\$29,000,000
% of students apply for need-based aid	75
% of students receive aid	52
% receiving need-based scholarship or grant aid	100
% receiving aid whose need was fully met	100
average aid package	\$36,540
average student loan debt upon graduation	\$0

Temple University

Temple University
1801 North Broad St.
Philadelphia, PA 19122
Ph: (888) 340-2222 / (215) 204-7200
tuadm@temple.edu
www.temple.edu

Temple University attracts the nation's brightest and most motivated minds from all 50 states and 130 foreign countries. Offering a combination of large-school resources and a small-school feel, Temple has something for every kind of student. Students choose between suburban and city campuses. Temple University instills a sense of global perspective in their students and offers the ability to study at their campuses in Rome, Italy and Tokyo, Japan. With an average class-size of just 27, students have the access they need to thrive within the classroom. Temple is renowned in areas such as Business, Communications, Education, Art, Music, Science, and the Health Professions. With a campus that is home to 25,000 students, activities are as diverse as the student body. In addition to cultural, athletic, and social events on campus, students always have the nation's 5th largest city at their fingertips.

OPPORTUNITY Philadelphia Diamond Scholars Program (PhDS)

The Temple University Philadelphia Diamond Scholars program, or PhDS for short, is a mentoring program administered by the Center for Social Justice and Multicultural Education of the Office of Multicultural Affairs to improve the retention and graduation rates of Temple University students from Philadelphia. Scholars receive support from a wide array of student leaders, as well as administrators and alumni who participate in various program activities. The program is open to any incoming new or first year transfer student who is committed to being academically successful at Temple by participating in a variety of academic, social and professional development activities.

SUCCESS First Year Seminar I and II

First Year Seminar I is a 1-credit academic course that introduces first-year students to the opportunities and rigors of higher education, as well as to the skills needed to use academic resources successfully in college. The topics covered in the seminar help first year students articulate and reach their academic goals. Seminar II is a 1-credit course that introduces first-year students discovering major interests through applied learning and other career-oriented experiences. The course exposes students to career paths and encourages major exploration through discussions with faculty, informational interviews, reading, and opportunities to practice skills needed to be a more efficient student.

SUCCESS Academic Resource Center

The Academic Resource Center offers University Studies students a place to explore majors and career options. They can find information on Temple majors ("checksheets"), reference their career library, or pick up a test that can help you learn about your career interests.

SUCCESS University Writing Center

The Writing Center offers a variety of services designed to support Temple students in their writing. The most important of these services is one-on-one tutoring, and it is available to undergraduate and graduate students across the curriculum. Tutoring is available on a drop-in basis or by appointment, and e-mail tutoring is available through the Web site. In addition, the Writing Center offers in-class writing workshops.

FAST FACTS

STUDENT PROFILE	
# of degree-seeking undergraduates	27,075
% male/female	48/52
% African American	14.9
% American Indian or Alaska Native	0.4
% Asian or Pacific Islander	10.3
% Hispanic	4.0
% White	59.4
% International	2.5
% Pell grant recipients	33
ACADEMICS	
full-time faculty	1,462
full-time minority faculty	268
student-faculty ratio	19:1
average class size	27
% first-year retention rate	89
% graduation rate (6 years)	65

Popular majors Biology, Psychology, Elementary Education, Accounting, Marketing

CAMPUS LIFE	
% live on campus (% freshmen)	18 (77)

Multicultural student clubs and organizations Asian Student Association, Asociacion de Estudiantes Latinos, Black Public Relations Society, Black Student Union, Esencia Latina, National Association of Black Accountants, National Society of Black Engineers, Organization of African Students, Society of Emerging African Leaders, Student Organization for Caribbean Awareness

Athletics NCAA Division I, Atlantic-10 Conference

ADMISSIONS	
# of freshman applicants	17,051
% accepted	63
# of first-year students enrolled	4,329
SAT Critical Reading (middle 50%)	500-600
SAT Math (middle 50%)	510-610
SAT Writing (middle 50%)	500-600
ACT (middle 50%)	20-26
average HS GPA	3.42
Deadlines	
regular decision	3/1
application fee (online)	$50 ($50)
fee waiver for applicants with financial need	yes
COST & AID	
tuition	in-state: $11,834; out-of-state: $21,662
room & board	$9,550
total need-based institutional scholarships/grants	$32,720,489
% of students apply for need-based aid	94
% of students receive aid	74
% receiving need-based scholarship or grant aid	69
% receiving aid whose need was fully met	32
average aid package	$15,802
average student loan debt upon graduation	$31,123

University of Pennsylvania

Founded by Benjamin Franklin in 1740, the University of Pennsylvania is the nation's oldest university and a member of the Ivy League. The university offers undergraduate programs in the College of Arts & Sciences, the School of Engineering & Applied Science, the School of Nursing, and the Wharton School (Business). Penn's beautiful Philadelphia campus combines the best elements of a traditional collegiate experience with the excitement and energy of city living. The University of Pennsylvania is a popular choice among high achieving students who are the first in their families to attend college. Family income is not considered in the admissions process — the university is "need-blind" and committed to meeting 100 percent of demonstrated financial need. More than 260 years after its founding, it remains faithful to Franklin's philosophy of clear-headed practicality and limitless intellectual inquiry.

OPPORTUNITY QuestBridge College Prep Scholarship

QuestBridge has partnered with the University of Pennsylvania to offer students a unique opportunity to take college-level courses on a top-tier university campus while residing in a dormitory with peers from across the country and the world. These scholarships offer outstanding low-income students a special chance to experience life beyond high school and to see first-hand what to expect from attending a selective university.

OPPORTUNITY Loan-Free Aid for Qualifying Students

All undergraduate students eligible for financial aid receive loan-free aid packages, regardless of family income level, making it possible for students from a broad range of economic backgrounds to graduate debt-free. This initiative will ensure that talented, high-achieving students can chart their educational path without regard to financial resources. Typical students from families with income less than $40,000 will pay no tuition, fees, room or board (receiving aid of approximately $53,000). Students from typical families with incomes less than $90,000 will pay no tuition and fees (receiving aid of approximately $38,000).

"Coming from a family of Penn alums, I grew up not too far from Philadelphia, but it wasn't until I came to Penn that I really had the chance to explore everything that Philly has to offer. One of the things that I love about Penn is that it really feels like Philadelphia is an extension of the campus. You can walk right off the campus and experience everything that Philadelphia has to offer. I'll go downtown and look at the architecture, or to the art museum to see a new exhibit. As a student, there's just something about Philadelphia that just draws you in makes you want to stay."

– Bryce S., '10
Bristol, PA
Chemical and Biomolecular Engineering (concentration: Pharmaceutics and Biotechnology)

SUCCESS Pre-Freshman Program (PFP) and Pennsylvania College Achievement Program (PENNCAP)

The Pre-Freshman Program, a four-week summer academic experience, helps students become acclimated to the university. Through PENNCAP, academically talented students, many from low-income or educationally disadvantaged backgrounds, receive coaching, counseling, academic support and assistance in identifying personal priorities, clarifying career objectives and developing a financial plan.

SUCCESS Cultural Resource Centers

Cultural resource centers are important parts of the Penn community. Student leaders and staff mentors inspire involvement and facilitate communication among groups across campus, creating a network of personal and academic support communities. Centers serve as meeting places for many cultural groups, and include the Greenfield Intercultural Center, La Casa Latina, the Lesbian Gay Bisexual Transgender Center, Makuu: The Black Student Cultural Center, and the Pan Asian American Community House.

University of Pennsylvania
Office of Undergraduate Admissions
1 College Hall, Room 1
Philadelphia, PA 19104-6376
Ph: (215) 898-7507
info@admissions.upenn.edu
www.admissions.upenn.edu

FAST FACTS

STUDENT PROFILE

# of degree-seeking undergraduates	9,865
% male/female	49.3/50.7
% African American	7.3
% American Indian or Alaska Native	0.4
% Asian or Pacific Islander	18.6
% Hispanic	6.5
% White	46.1
% International	10.8
% Race/ethnicity unknown	8.6

First-generation and minority alumni Harold Ford Jr., former U.S. Representative from Tennessee, current chairman of the Democratic Leadership Council; John Legend, five-time Grammy Award-winning recording artist; William Thaddeus Coleman Jr., first African-American Supreme Court law clerk and co-author of NAACP brief on Brown v. Board of Education; Sadie Tanner Mossell Alexander, first African-American woman to earn a Ph.D. (economics)

ACADEMICS

full-time faculty	2,161
student-faculty ratio	6:1
average class size	<25
% first-year retention rate	99
% graduation rate (6 years)	96

Popular majors Business, Bioengineering, History, Economics, Nursing

CAMPUS LIFE

% live on campus (% freshmen)	62 (100)

Multicultural student clubs and organizations United Minorities Council Alliance and Understanding, Asian Pacific Student Coalition, Black Student League, Brazilian Club, Canadians at Penn, Caribbean-American Student Association, Chinese Students and Scholars, Chinese Students Association, Club Singapore, Dessalines Haitian Students Association, Hellenic Association, Hong Kong Student Association, Japan Student Association, Korean Student Association, Lambda Alliance, Mexico@Penn, Muslim Students Association, Onda Latina, Program for Awareness in Cultural Education, Penn African Students Association, Pakistan Society, Penn Arab Students Society, Penn Philippine Association, Penn Polish Society

Athletics NCAA Division I, Ivy League

ADMISSIONS (ENTERING FALL 2009)

# of applicants	26,941
% accepted	14.2
# of first-year students enrolled	2,410
SAT Critical Reading (middle 50%)	660-750
SAT Math (middle 50%)	690-780
SAT Writing (middle 50%)	680-770
ACT (middle 50%)	30-35
Deadlines	
early decision	11/1
regular admission	1/1
application fee (online)	$75 ($75)
fee waiver for applicants with financial need	yes

COST & AID

tuition	$37,620
room & board	$11,878
total need-based institutional scholarships/grants	$130,000,000+
% of students receive aid	60
% receiving need-based grant aid	40
% receiving aid whose need was fully met	100
average aid package	$34,435
average student loan debt upon graduation	$19,085

Brown University

Brown University is a leading Ivy League institution located in Providence, Rhode Island — three hours northeast of New York City and one hour south of Boston. Brown is proud of its distinctive undergraduate program, world-class faculty, and tradition of innovative and multi-disciplinary study. Students at Brown are distinguished by their academic excellence, self-direction, and collaborative style of learning. As the architects of their own education, undergraduates work closely with advisors to design a curriculum that allows them to maximize their education goals. Brown faculty are preeminent in their fields, deeply committed to teaching undergraduates, and are leaders in advancing knowledge. With over 80 fields of concentration (majors), myriad research and individualized study opportunities, and numerous study abroad options, Brown University provides a wealth of resources to its students.

ACCESS **Outreach Efforts**

Through its own outreach efforts and partnerships with community based organizations and schools Brown University participates in a variety of programs designed to assist students of underrepresented groups in the college application process as well as fostering success for students once they attend college.

OPPORTUNITY **Fall Open House**

A day-long program is held each Fall on the Brown campus which is specifically tailored towards the interests of underrepresented minority students.

"As a Hmong student, my involvement in Southeast Asian Heritage Week gave me a comfortable space to explore my identity and its politics. The experience was not only personally and culturally meaningful, but also academically enriching."

– Teng Y., '11
Milwaukee, WI

OPPORTUNITY **Admissions**

Brown University admissions is "need-blind," meaning that decisions regarding admission are made without consideration of the applicant's financial need. All admitted students will be awarded the financial aid necessary for them to attend Brown. The typical financial aid package allows students whose family income is less than $100,000 per year to graduate with no debt when they graduate from Brown.

SUCCESS **Multicultural Center**

Brown's Multicultural Center is the heart of the community for students of color. It is designed to serve their needs in particular, as well as to promote racial and ethnic pluralism on campus.

SUCCESS **Fall Pre-Orientation Programs**

An intensive, five-day writing program is offered to selected incoming students who would benefit from additional orientation to Brown's academic culture. The program includes five classes taught by distinguished Brown professors from a range of academic disciplines. Students complete reading and writing assignments and work with staff at Brown's Writing Center. Brown's Multicultural Center hosts a community-building event for entering students that promotes interracial understanding. The program helps all students identify and increase their awareness of issues encountered by minority students at Brown. During the weekend following the first several days of fall classes, students may participate in a program which helps students build community and leadership skills through dialogue, interaction, and outreach across cultural experiences and group identities, including race, ethnicity, class, gender, sexual identity, ability, and religious affiliation.

SUCCESS **A Variety of Academic Enhancement Programs**

The Dean of the College office provides a variety of academic support programs such as tutoring and study skills workshops. It also offers advising to students regarding research opportunities and the planning of independent study projects which encourage and facilitate the optimal use of the academic resources at Brown.

Brown University
45 Prospect Street
PO Box 1876
Providence, RI 02912
Ph: (401) 863-2378
admission_undergraduate@brown.edu
www.brown.edu

FAST FACTS

STUDENT PROFILE

# of degree-seeking undergraduates	5,800
% male/female	52/48
% African American	7
% American Indian or Alaska Native	1
% Asian or Pacific Islander	16
% Hispanic	9
% White	40
% International	9
% Pell grant recipients	11

ACADEMICS

full-time faculty	700
full-time minority faculty	105
student-faculty ratio	9:1
average class size	<20
% first-year retention rate	97
% graduation rate (6 years)	95

Popular majors Biological Sciences, Economics, International Relations, History, Neuroscience

CAMPUS LIFE

% live on campus	79

Multicultural student clubs and organizations 40+

Athletics NCAA Division I, Ivy League

ADMISSIONS

# of applicants	31,000
% accepted	8.7
SAT Critical Reading (middle 50%)	670-770
SAT Math (middle 50%)	680-780
SAT Writing (middle 50%)	670-770
ACT (middle 50%)	26-32
average HS GPA	n/a
Deadlines	
early decision	11/1
regular decision	1/1
application fee	$75 ($75)
fee waiver for applicants with financial need	yes

COST & AID

tuition	$41,328
room & board	$10,906
total need-based institutional scholarships/grants	$79,606,270
% of students apply for need-based aid	49
% of students receive aid	43
% receiving need-based scholarship or grant aid	43
% receiving aid whose need was fully met	100
average aid package	$36,815
average student loan debt upon graduation	$21,280

Bryant University

Bryant is an internationally recognized, private university located on 428 acres just outside Providence, RI. Bryant's nearly 150-year tradition of innovation empowers students to collaborate with accomplished faculty who bring a global perspective and real-world experience into the classroom. Bryant's unique integration of business with the liberal arts and sciences is enhanced by multicultural events, travel-study opportunities, and co-curricular programs. With a distinct, competitive edge—and a 97 percent employment and graduate school placement rate—Bryant graduates are well prepared to meet the challenges of the 21st century.

"From the first time I came to campus junior year of high school to this day, I have never stopped feeling welcome at Bryant, in the classroom or in an organization. The Academic Center for Excellence has provided extra help while I balance school, sports, and clubs."

– Yeawoma J. '13
Franklin, MA
Business Administration: Marketing

ACCESS **The Linkages in International Business & Foreign Affairs Empowerment (L.I.F.E.) for Youth Program**

The L.I.F.E. summer program introduces Black/African American, Latino/a, Hispanic, Asian American, and Native American high school sophomores to career opportunities in international business.

ACCESS **PricewaterhouseCoopers Accounting Careers Leadership Institute (PwCACLI)**

PwCACLI is a week-long, hands-on opportunity for Latino/a and African American/Black rising high school seniors to learn more about the accounting profession and the role accountants play in society. Applications are available by mid-January.

OPPORTUNITY **Diversity 24/7 Open House Weekend**

Bryant's 24/7 Open House Weekend, held in October, welcomes diverse and academically successful students to campus to experience life as a Bryant student. Space in this program is limited, and students must submit an application and a copy of their transcript to be considered for participation. Bryant covers the cost of transportation to campus for those attending the program.

OPPORTUNITY **Trueheart Scholarship**

The William E. Trueheart Scholarship, named for Bryant's first African American president, is designated for students of color and is based on academic merit and financial need.

OPPORTUNITY **Fly-in Reimbursement Program**

Bryant reimburses students for half the cost of their plane ticket to visit Bryant's campus. Students who enroll full-time receive the remainder of their airfare, up to $300 total.

SUCCESS **The Academic Center for Excellence (ACE) and The Writing Center**

ACE and the Writing Center help Bryant students adopt study habits to achieve success and meet the University's rigorous academic standards. Services include: peer tutoring, individual learning and study assessments, learning disability specialists, student-athlete specialists, and writing workshops.

SUCCESS **Foundations for Learning (FFL)**

In the FFL course, every first-year Bryant student is taught to become an active participant in the learning process.

SUCCESS **4MILE@Bryant**

4MILE supports incoming multicultural and international students through a network of mentors and advisors. First year students take part in team building, leadership skills development, and self-exploration activities facilitated by team leaders. Throughout the semester, students are part of a cluster and are mentored by current Bryant students.

Bryant University
1150 Douglas Pike
Smithfield, RI 02917
Ph: (800) 622-7001 or (401) 232-6100
admission@bryant.edu
www.bryant.edu

FAST FACTS

STUDENT PROFILE

# of degree-seeking undergraduates	3,365
% male/female	58/42
% African American	4
% American Indian or Alaska Native	<1
% Asian or Pacific Islander	3
% Hispanic	4
% White	80
% International	6
% Pell Grant recipients	10

ACADEMICS

full-time faculty	161
full-time minority faculty	28
student-faculty ratio	16:1
average class size	22
% first-year retention rate	87
% graduation rate (6 years)	76

Popular majors Accounting, Communication, Environmental Science, International Business, Marketing

CAMPUS LIFE

% live on campus (% freshmen)	85 (96)

Multicultural student clubs and organizations Multicultural Student Union; International Student Organization; Alliance for Women's Awareness; Amnesty International; Bryant Christian Fellowship; Bryant University Spanish Culture Organization; Chinese Dragon Dance Team; Hillel; Bryant Pride; Francophones de Bryant University; Greek Life

Athletics NCAA Division I, Northeast Conference

ADMISSIONS

# of applicants	5,050
% accepted	69
# of first-year students enrolled	833
(Standardized test optional)	
SAT Critical Reading (middle 50%)	500-590
SAT Math (middle 50%)	540-630
SAT Writing (middle 50%)	510-590
ACT (middle 50%)	22-26
average HS GPA	3.34

Deadlines

early decision	11/15; 1/16
regular decision	2/1
application fee (online)	$50 ($50)
fee waiver for applicants with financial need	yes

COST & AID

tuition	$34,288
room & board	$12,579
total need-based institutional scholarships/grants	$20,304,279
% of students apply for need-based aid	76
% of students receiving aid	68
% receiving need-based scholarship or grant aid	57
% receiving aid whose need was fully met	50
average aid package	$21,206
average student loan debt upon graduation	$39,490

Roger Williams University

Roger Williams University is a 54-year-old independent, coeducational liberal arts university that has quickly established itself as a leader in higher education. A dynamic educational environment in which students live and learn to be global citizens, the university is committed to its mantra of learning to bridge the world. With 42 academic programs and a robust array of co-curricular activities available on its waterfront campus in historic Bristol, RI, the University looks to a set of core values in fulfilling its mission to prepare students for life as 21st century citizen-scholars. Following in the footsteps of the institution's namesake, it is dedicated to the principles Roger Williams advocated – education, freedom and tolerance. Roger Williams University places particular emphasis on the value of civil discourse and is home to an array of initiatives designed to bring to campus individuals from a tremendous variety of backgrounds and perspectives.

ACCESS **Discovery Series**

Each year, the University hosts a series of college discovery events for students from local school districts, many of whom are first-generation and from underrepresented communities. Annual events include 5th Grade Day, a program that brings local fifth-graders to campus for tours and student presentations; the FIRST LEGO League Robotics Competition, which brings young minds to campus to inspire their curiosity in technology and engineering; and GRRL Tech, a collaborative, interactive technology exposition for outstanding young women interested in science and technology education. RWU also hosts Junior Jumpstart, a program aimed at high school students and their parents who wish to learn how to navigate the college application process, annually.

"In high school, I did Bridge to Success for four years. Every Wednesday I came to campus and just absolutely fell in love with RWU. I applied to all of the schools in the area, but I definitely knew this was my first choice. When I got the Intercultural Leadership Award, it sealed the deal."

– Melisa C., '11
Newport, RI
Anthropology, Sociology

ACCESS **Bridge to Success**

The University's Bridge to Success Program (BTS), founded in 1993 through a grant from the Balfour Foundation, partners with select Newport and Providence high schools and service organizations to promote the development of academic, social and emotional support systems for high school students in under-resourced communities. BTS provides academic tutoring, student-to-student mentoring, intensive college prep, and parental outreach to hundreds of high school students throughout Rhode Island so that they may achieve academic success toward admission into RWU or any other four-year college/university.

OPPORTUNITY **The Intercultural Leadership Award (ILA)**

Established in 2007, the Intercultural Leadership Award program at Roger Williams provides financial and programmatic support to high-achieving students who are proven community leaders and who have overcome a significant life challenge while meeting at least one of the following three criteria: first-generation college student, ethnic diversity, or English as the second language spoken at home. In its initial 2007-08 cycle Roger Williams welcomed 13 ILA students, granting them $26,000 scholarships and organizing a structured series of co-curricular learning opportunities.

SUCCESS **The Intercultural Center**

A landing zone for international students, spiritual life, LGBT student advocacy, the Multicultural Student Union, and Bridge to Success, the university's Intercultural Center is a nexus of different social identities. At its essence, the center provides a welcoming environment for all students in which ideas concerning personal identity and diversity are discussed freely. The Intercultural Center sponsors a wide range of cultural programming at RWU, all of which encourage an open dialogue on diversity, social justice and global citizenship.

Roger Williams University
Office of Admission
1 Old Ferry Road
Bristol, RI 02809
Ph: (401) 254-3500
admit@rwu.edu
www.rwu.edu

FAST FACTS

STUDENT PROFILE	
# of degree-seeking undergraduates	4,310
% male/female	52/48
% African American	2
% American Indian or Alaska Native	<1
% Asian or Pacific Islander	1
% Hispanic	4
% White	87
% International	2
% Pell grant recipients	11
ACADEMICS	
full-time faculty	219
full-time minority faculty	30
student-faculty ratio	12:1
average class size	19
% first-year retention rate	78
% graduation rate (6 years)	61
Popular majors Architecture, Business/Commerce, Psychology	
CAMPUS LIFE	
% live on campus	63
Multicultural student clubs and organizations Multicultural Student Union	
Athletics NCAA Division III, The Commonwealth Coast Conference (TCCC)	
ADMISSIONS	
# of applicants	8,220
% accepted	77
# of first-year students enrolled	954
SAT Critical Reading (middle 50%)	500-580
SAT Math (middle 50%)	510-600
SAT Writing (middle 50%)	480-580
ACT (middle 50%)	21-25
average HS GPA	3.17
Deadlines	
early action	11/1
regular decision	2/1
application fee (online)	$50 ($50)
fee waiver for applicants with financial need	yes
COST & AID	
tuition	$28,968
room & board	$13,220
total need-based institutional scholarships/grants	$23,792,788
% of students apply for need-based aid	72
% of students receive aid	88
% receiving need-based scholarship or grant aid	35
% receiving aid whose need was fully met	4
average aid package	$20,807
average student loan debt upon graduation	$35,000

The University of Rhode Island

The University of Rhode Island
Newman Hall, 14 Upper College Road
Kingston, RI 02881
Ph: (401) 874-7100
admission@uri.edu
www.uri.edu/admissions

Founded in 1888 as an agricultural school, today The University of Rhode Island is the state's flagship institution that advances "Think Big - We Do" ideals in research, teaching, and service. From its very beginning under Roger Williams, Rhode Islanders were different: independent in thought and action and tolerant of the beliefs of others. The University of Rhode Island carries on that tradition with investments of time and energy toward creating a multicultural community of students, faculty and staff. Each year the University of Rhode Island reaches out in more imaginative ways to help diverse populations with opportunities to be a part of their research, teaching, and outreach work.

OPPORTUNITY Talent Development

In response to the assassination of Dr. Martin Luther King Jr. in 1968 and in recognition of the value of his work towards equality, the University of Rhode Island established a special admissions program, Talent Development (TD). TD's mission is to recruit, admit, support, and retain in-state students of color and students from disadvantaged backgrounds who, without the support of TD, could not expect to be admitted to URI. TD aids students in the admissions process, prepares them for full-time study at the college level, provides academic advisement and key support services through an assigned academic advisor, and assists with financial aid through the need-based Hardge/Forleo Grant. From a class of 13 students in 1968, TD has grown to more than 1,300 current students and 1,600 graduates.

"As a TD student, I have had the opportunity to receive an early college experience and get a feel of what will come in my freshmen year. This experience gave me the chance to explore the campus, classrooms, and tutoring centers, and complete three classes and receive credits. I have made many new friendships that will last forever.""

– Precious D., '15
Newport, RI
Biology

SUCCESS TD Spring Preparatory Program

Held in the spring before students enter the TD Summer Program, this mandatory event prepares students for a successful transition to URI. During the Preparatory Program (PREP), students review and select Summer Program courses, receive information about New Student Orientation, learn about housing contracts and meal plan options, and review financial aid. TD also offers a special Parent PREP breakout session for parents and guardians.

SUCCESS TD Summer Program

The Summer Program is a six-week residential program at the University of Rhode Island's Kingston campus. Students take one week of coursework in writing, computing and library services, and career development followed by a five-week session in which students take three University-credited courses (eight college credits). Content- and skills-based tutoring is provided. In addition to other requirements, students must pass all classes with a minimum C (2.00) GPA to successfully complete the Summer Program and enter URI as a member of the TD Nation. TD finances the cost of tuition, fees, housing, meals, and books during the Summer Program.

SUCCESS Academic Enhancement Center

The Academic Enhancement Center is a tutoring program which seeks to allow all students at URI to succeed academically. Students can receive help in specific subject areas at the AEC's Writing Center and Math, Physics, Biology and Chemistry Walk-In Centers (tutoring in other courses is also offered) as well as training in study skills and time management. The AEC additionally provides Supplemental Instruction sessions to help students on a weekly basis.

FAST FACTS

STUDENT PROFILE

# of degree-seeking undergraduates	13,094
% male/female	45/55
% African American	5
% American Indian or Alaska Native	<1
% Asian or Pacific Islander	3
% Hispanic	6
% White	72
% International	<1
% Pell grant recipients	23

ACADEMICS

full-time faculty	665
full-time minority faculty	104
student-faculty ratio	16:1
average class size	57% of classes have fewer than 30 students
% first-year retention rate	80
% graduation rate (6 years)	60.1

Popular majors Business, Management, and Marketing, Health Professions, Communication, Journalism, Family and Consumer Sciences/Human Sciences, Education

CAMPUS LIFE

% live on campus (% freshmen)	45 (94)

Multicultural student clubs and organizations Asian Student Association, Cape Verdean Students Association, Chinese Students Scholars Association, Classy Leaders Achieving Student Services (C.L.A.S.S), Latin American Student Association (LASA), Leadership & Mentor Program for Women of Color, Minority Association for Premedical/Prehealth Students-MAPS, National Association of the Advancement of Colored People (NAACP), National Society of Black Engineers, Native American Student Organization (NASO), Society of Hispanic Engineering (SHPE)

Athletics NCAA Division I, Atlantic Ten Conference

ADMISSIONS

# of applicants	20,004
% accepted	76
# of first-year students enrolled	3,150
SAT Critical Reading (middle 50%)	470-600
SAT Math (middle 50%)	470-600
SAT Writing (middle 50%)	470-600
ACT (middle 50%)	21-25
average HS GPA	3.38

Deadlines

regular admission	2/1
application fee (online)	$65 ($65)
fee waiver for applicants with financial need	yes (TD Applicants)

COST & AID

tuition	in-state: $9,824; out-of-state: $25,912; regional: $17,192
room & board	$10,800
total need-based institutional scholarship/grants	$8,713,115
% of students apply for need-based aid	89.6
% receiving need-based scholarship or grant aid	62
% receiving aid whose need was fully met	86.6
average aid package	$12,470
average student loan debt upon graduation	$22,750

College of Charleston

Founded in 1770, the College of Charleston is a nationally recognized, public liberal arts and sciences university located in the heart of historic Charleston, S.C. Students from 50 states and territories and nearly 70 countries choose the College for its small-college feel blended with the advantages and diversity of an urban, mid-sized university. The College provides a creative and intellectually stimulating environment where students are challenged by a committed and caring faculty of distinguished teacher-scholars. The city of Charleston serves students as a learning laboratory for experiences in business, science, teaching, the humanities, languages and the arts. For multicultural and first-generation college students, the College of Charleston is a particularly strong match. The College is intimately involved with these populations and offers a number of programs catered to them.

"My involvement in the Bonner Leader Program, offered through the Center for Civic Engagement, has allowed me to serve local, national and international communities, and has provided me travel, leadership and professional-development opportunities – and a scholarship. I've been so fortunate to have the benefits and life-changing educational experiences Bonner has afforded me."

– Paul B. '13
Cross, S.C.
Political Science w/ minor in African American Studies

> ACCESS **Call Me MISTER Program**

In an effort to address the critical shortage of African American male teachers, particularly in South Carolina's lowest performing schools, the School of Education, Health, and Human Performance's Call Me MISTER program selects students from backgrounds that are underrepresented or underserved in the teaching profession and provides them with tuition assistance and academic, social and cultural support as they pursue an approved program of study in teacher education.

> OPPORTUNITY **Bonner Leaders Grant**

Bonner Leaders are outstanding students who commit themselves to leadership through service and making positive change across campus and in the Charleston community. This four-year, service-based scholarship program allows students to apply theory to practice through real-life work experience at area nonprofit organizations. The program also facilitates students' transition from being volunteers to becoming leaders in their community through powerful leadership-development training and education. Grant recipients receive a graduated scholarship for participation in the program.

> OPPORTUNITY **Avery Scholars**

The College's Avery Research Center for African American History and Culture collects, preserves and documents the history and culture of African American's in Charleston and the South Carolina Lowcountry. The Avery Research Scholarship helps underrepresented freshman and transfer students fund their college education while also gaining valuable skills through cultural events, volunteer opportunities, academic and career advising, and undergraduate research.

> SUCCESS **Speedy Consolidation and Transition Program (SPECTRA)**

Through the Office of Multicultural Student Programs and Services (MSPS), the College offers a challenging transitional summer academic program, SPECTRA, for first-generation students and students from underrepresented populations who will attend the College full-time in the fall. During a five-week, on-campus experience, students learn to develop successful academic and social networks; bridge the gap between traditional, stereotypical barriers that students of color face on predominantly white campuses; and understand the academic rigors of college life. Students are further supported throughout the school year, receiving academic advising, peer mentoring, workshops, financial aid advising and special seminars.

> SUCCESS **South Carolina Alliance for Minority Participation (SCAMP)**

SCAMP, which is funded by the National Science Foundation, is another program offered through MSPS. It provides mentoring and summer-research opportunities to African American, Hispanic and Native American students who want to pursue a degree in the sciences, engineering or mathematics. Qualified students may receive an annual $500-$1,000 scholarship.

College of Charleston
66 George Street
Charleston, SC 29424
Ph: (843) 953-5670
admissions@cofc.edu
www.cofc.edu

FAST FACTS

STUDENT PROFILE

# of degree-seeking undergraduates	9,771
% male/female	37/63
% African American	5.5
% American Indian or Alaska Native	4
% Asian or Pacific Islander	1.9
% Hispanic	3
% White	84.5
% International	6
% Pell grant recipients	20.3

First-generation and minority alumni Kevin Summers, CIO, Whirlpool; Jon Bryant, Secret Service agent, on president's detail; Michelle Cooper, president, Institute of Higher Education Policy; Anthony Johnson, NBA player

ACADEMICS

full-time faculty	529
full-time minority faculty	57
student-faculty ratio	16:1
average class size	26.4
% first-year retention rate	82.2
% graduation rate (6 years)	66.1

Popular majors Biology, Communication, Business Administration, Psychology, and Political Science

CAMPUS LIFE

% live on campus (% freshmen)	32.4 (93.1)

Multicultural student clubs and organizations Black Student Union, Student Union for Multicultural Affairs, Aya Hwe M', Alpha Phi Omega Business Service Fraternity, Student Government Association: Campus Diversity Committee, Global Citizens Council, Color of We: All Power to the People, South Carolina Diversity Council, Coalition of Minority Leaders In Higher Education, Asian Student Association, Association of Black Accountants

Athletics NCAA Division I, Southern Conference

ADMISSIONS

# of applicants	11,280
% accepted	70
# of first-year students enrolled	2,010
SAT Critical Reading (middle 50%)	570-650
SAT Math (middle 50%)	570-640
SAT Writing (middle 50%)	n/a
ACT (middle 50%)	23-27
average HS GPA	3.87

Deadlines

early action	11/1
regular decision	rolling to 4/01
application fee (online)	$50 ($50)
fee waiver for applicants with financial need	yes

COST & AID

tuition	in-state: $9,616; out-of-state:$24,330
room & board	$10,179
total need-based institutional scholarships/grants	$5,096,004
% of students apply for need-based aid	60.4
% receiving need-based scholarship or grant aid	31.4
% receiving aid whose need was fully met	13.9
average aid package	$12,933
average student loan debt upon graduation	$20,541

Furman University

Founded in 1826, Furman University is a private, coeducational institution providing engaged learning to students at the undergraduate and graduate levels. Grounded in the humanities, arts and sciences, the University has gained a national reputation for its innovative program of engaged learning, an experience-based approach to liberal arts that encourages students to actively participate in internships, service learning, study abroad and research. Furman's heritage is rooted in the Baptist tradition, and faculty and students are encouraged to foster a sense of social justice and civic responsibility. Furman is fully committed to sustainability.

ACCESS **Bridges to a Brighter Future**

Bridges to a Brighter Future is a three-year enrichment program for Greenville County high-achieving high school students who come from backgrounds with limiting factors to their academic growth. The program provides students with education opportunities, tools for graduating high school, and college guidance. Students begin the program the summer before the 10th grade, and if they successfully maintain a 3.0 GPA they may continue participation through senior year. Students attend an annual four-week summer college at Furman University where they take liberal-arts and scientific classes taught by Greenville County teachers. During the academic year, weekend services include tutoring, success workshops, and mentoring programs.

"Bridges placed a lens before my eyes, making the image of my prospective self clearer. Stepping back into my reality, I was well aware of the fact that my circumstances remained the same, but the lenses subsisted, and my vision was forever transformed and no longer conformed to those circumstances."

– Cierra R., '12
Greenville, SC
Law, Communication

SUCCESS **The Office of Multicultural Affairs**

The Office of Multicultural Affairs works to enhance the quality of life of minority students, to increase recruitment of minorities and to promote an inclusive environment for students of all backgrounds. The office sponsors several programs to promote understanding of different cultures. There is a one-day workshop available, where cultural stereotypes are dispelled and participants learn skills to break down barriers between groups. Black Awareness, International, Asian History, and Hispanic Heritage months are all celebrated through the Office of Multicultural Affairs.

SUCCESS **The Office of Academic Assistance**

The Office of Academic Assistance provides students with academic assistance and general support services. Tutoring services are offered to all students free of charge. Office staff is available to advise and inform students about academic tools and resources to improve their study skills. Resources include online resources on time management, test taking, scheduling assistance and contact information for all Furman University professors. The Office of Academic Assistance Staff is dedicated to retaining students.

Furman University
Office of Admissions
3300 Poinsett Highway
Greenville, SC 29613
Ph: (864) 294-2034
admissions@furman.edu
www.furman.edu

FAST FACTS

STUDENT PROFILE	
# of degree-seeking undergraduates	2,728
% male/female	42/58
% African American	6
% American Indian or Alaska Native	<1
% Asian or Pacific Islander	2
% Hispanic	3
% White	83
% International	1
% Race/Ethnicity Unknown	4
% Pell grant recipients	14
ACADEMICS	
full-time faculty	235
full-time minority faculty	29
student-faculty ratio	11:1
average class size	18
% first-year retention rate	92
% graduation rate (6 years)	84

Popular majors Political Science, Business Administration, History, Communication Studies

CAMPUS LIFE	
% live on campus (% freshmen)	96 (98)

Multicultural student clubs and organizations Asia Club, NAACP, International Students Association, Hispanic Organization of Learning and Awareness, Student League for Black Culture, Minority Association of Pre-Medical Students

Athletics NCAA Division I, Southern Conference

ADMISSIONS	
# of applicants	4,611
% accepted	70
# of first-year students enrolled	686
SAT Critical Reading (middle 50%)	580-690
SAT Math (middle 50%)	570-690
SAT Writing (middle 50%)	560-680
ACT (middle 50%)	25-30
average HS GPA	3.8
Deadlines	
early decision	11/15
regular decision	1/15
application fee (online)	$50 ($0)
fee waiver for applicants with financial need	yes
COST & AID	
tuition	$37,728
room & board	$9,170
total need-based institutional scholarships/ grants	$24,614,906
% of students apply for need-based aid	56
% of students receive aid	83
% receiving need based scholarship/grant aid	38
% receiving aid whose need was fully met	43
average aid package	$28,495
average student loan debt upon graduation	$27,373

University of South Carolina

The University of South Carolina is a comprehensive research institution serving the needs of more than 29,500 students. Undergraduate students benefit from a friendly campus atmosphere where faculty and students form communities that encourage successful learning and personal growth. The campus embraces diversity and offers many programs designed to increase multicultural awareness and foster respect for each member of the Carolina community. USC's Student Success Center provides outreach and academic support, while the nationally-acclaimed University 101 course for new students eases their transition to college. USC's Gamecock Guarantee program keeps the college dream alive for South Carolina's underprivileged and/or first generation students. This past year, USC awarded $6 million worth of need-based scholarships and grants to its undergraduate students.

ACCESS **TRIO Programs**

USC's access programs include TRIO Programs, Upward Bound, Talent Search, and the Bridge Program. Upward Bound provides comprehensive educational support to prepare high school students for college. Talent Search provides long-term guidance on the college search process to students from middle school, through high school graduation, and up until college placement. The Bridge Program is designed for recent high-school graduates who are SC residents and who plan to attend a South Carolina technical college before transferring to USC. It provides pre-college guidance to ease the complex transfer process.

> ***"I am thrilled that, because of the Gamecock Guarantee program, I do not have to add any financial or emotional burdens on my mother. I can continue my dream of being at USC and continue to make my mom proud by accomplishing all that she has always told me that I could."***
>
> *– Jordan A., '13*
> *Goose Creek, SC*
> *Elementary Education*

OPPORTUNITY **The University's Gamecock Guarantee Program**

The University's Gamecock Guarantee Program ensures that South Carolina residents who are admitted to USC, who are most in need financially, and who meet specific eligibility requirements do not have to pay out-of-pocket for their USC tuition or technology fees. Gamecock Guarantee recipients receive a minimum award of $2,500 each year for up to four years. If tuition and technology fees exceed the value of a student's total financial aid/scholarship package, the Gamecock Guarantee makes up the difference.

SUCCESS **The Opportunity Scholars Program**

The Opportunity Scholars Program assists first-generation college students who come from low-income families. The program is structured as a learning community and includes a curriculum of seven freshman-level courses, support services designed to help students adjust to the campus environment, and financial assistance through the University's Gamecock Guarantee.

SUCCESS **The Office of Multicultural Student Affairs**

The Office of Multicultural Student Affairs promotes appreciation for the University's culturally diverse populations. It sponsors annual Minority Welcome receptions, as well as the Minority Assistance Peer Program, which provides outreach to freshmen by trained peer counselors. The African American Male Institute motivates its student members to pursue academic and personal success through leadership training.

University of South Carolina
Undergraduate Admissions
Columbia, SC 29208
Ph: (803) 777-7700
admissions-ugrad@sc.edu
www.sc.edu/admissions

FAST FACTS

STUDENT PROFILE

# of degree-seeking undergraduates	21,383
% male/female	46/54
% African American	11
% American Indian or Alaska Native	<1
% Asian or Pacific Islander	3
% Hispanic	3
% White	78
% International	2
% Pell grant recipients	23

First-generation and minority alumni James Bennett, Sierra Carter, Dean Lemuel W. Watson, Attorney Tom Bellinger, Attorney Moses Boyd, Lonnie Randolph, Rev. Ronnie Brailsford

ACADEMICS

full-time faculty	1,563
full-time minority faculty	159
student-faculty ratio	19:1
average class size	29
% first-year retention rate	86
% graduation rate (6 years)	67

Popular majors Business, Biology, Nursing, Pharmacy, Sport and Entertainment Management, Exercise Science, Psychology

CAMPUS LIFE

% live on campus (% freshmen) 36 (94)

Multicultural student clubs and organizations Association of African American Students, Brothers of Nubian Descent, International Student Association, National Student Exchange Association, Students Associated for Latin America, SAVVY (multicultural organization for women), Study Abroad Returnee Association, Women for a Multicultural Tomorrow

Athletics NCAA Division I, Southeastern Conference

ADMISSIONS

# of applicants	18,485
% accepted	70
# of first-year students enrolled	4,468
SAT Critical Reading (middle 50%)	530-630
SAT Math (middle 50%)	550-650
SAT Writing (middle 50%)	n/a
ACT (middle 50%)	24-28
average HS GPA	3.75

Deadlines

regular decision	12/1
application fee (online)	$50 ($50)
fee waiver for applicants with financial need	yes

COST & AID

tuition	$9,386
room & board	$7,764
total need-based institutional scholarships/grants	$6,066,500
% of students apply for need-based aid	67
% receiving need-based scholarship or grant aid	24
% receiving aid whose need was fully met	11
average aid package	$12,570
average student loan debt upon graduation	$19,526

Winthrop University

Winthrop University
Office of Admissions
Rock Hill, SC, 29733
Ph: (803) 323-2191
admissions@winthrop.edu
www.winthrop.edu

At Winthrop, you are our primary focus. You'll be part of a community of learners who want you to succeed, both academically and personally. You'll meet new people who share your interests and viewpoints or kindly introduce you to their own. You'll join clubs and participate in sports; enjoy concerts and theater productions. Your studies will begin in the classroom, but hands-on research, real life work settings, perhaps even a trip abroad, won't be far behind. After graduation, you'll be ready to become a leader in the world beyond campus, and that world will be a better place for your having been a part of the Winthrop community.

ACCESS Learning Excellent Academic Practices (LEAP)

LEAP is an academic support program designed to identify, support, and evaluate students before and during their first year at Winthrop. The components of the program are based on national best practices and Winthrop's own successful history of academic support programs.

"TRiO really made my transition into Winthrop a lot easier. The academic counselors give you both academic and moral support to help keep you on the right track and the TRiO Leadership Council allowed me to participate in great community service projects while bonding with other TRiO members."

– Ashley L., '14
Irmo, SC
Biology

SUCCESS Orientation

All freshmen entering in the fall are required to attend one of four two-day Orientation sessions offered each June. Family members are encouraged to take advantage of Family Orientation, a program offered concurrently with the first day of each of the student sessions.

SUCCESS Office of Multicultural Student Life

The mission of the Office of Multicultural Student Life is to provide a "more than me" experience for students. Its objective is to make opportunities available to the student body for participation in activities and events that enhance their awareness of diversity, encouraging them to learn more about themselves and others.

SUCCESS Academic Success Center

The Academic Success Center focuses on helping students achieve academic excellence and earn their college degrees. By providing them with tutoring opportunities and tools to excel in their classes, the center motivates students to be the drive behind their own educations.

SUCCESS The McNair Scholars Program

The McNair Scholars Program is designed to prepare undergraduate students for doctoral studies through involvement in research and other scholarly activities. McNair participants are either first-generation college students with financial need, or members of a group that is traditionally underrepresented in graduate education that have demonstrated strong academic potential.

SUCCESS TRiO

TRiO is an academic support program designed to increase the academic performance, retention rates, and graduation rates of program members. The TRiO Program promotes academic excellence and gives members the tools necessary to make the most of their undergraduate education, to graduate, and to seek employment and/or attend graduate or professional school.

FAST FACTS

STUDENT PROFILE

# of degree-seeking undergraduates	4,642
% male/female	32/68
%African American	28
% American Indian or Alaska Native	<1
% Asian or Pacific Islander	2
% Hispanic	2
% White	63
% International	3
% Pell grant recipients	35

ACADEMICS

full-time faculty	294
full-time minority faculty	39
student-faculty ratio	15:1
average class size	22
% first-year retention rate	69
% graduation rate (6 years)	58

Popular majors Business Administration, Biology, Education, Art, Psychology

CAMPUS LIFE

% live on campus (% freshmen)	n/a (89)

Multicultural student clubs and organizations Association of Ebonites, Culture Club, Multicultural Student Council, National Alliance of Black School Educators, TRiO Leadership Council

Athletics NCAA Division I, Big South Conference

ADMISSIONS

# of applicants	4,850
% accepted	70
# of first-year students enrolled	1,076
SAT Critical Reading (middle 50%)	470-570
SAT Math (middle 50%)	470-570
SAT Writing (middle 50%)	n/a
ACT (middle 50%)	20-25
average HS GPA	3.68

Deadlines

regular decision	rolling
application fee (online)	$40 ($40)
fee waiver for applicants with financial need	yes

COST & AID

tuition	in-state: $12,656; out-of-state: $23,796
room & board	$7,004
total need-based institutional scholarships/grants	n/a
% of students apply for need-based aid	77
% of students receive aid	n/a
% receiving need-based scholarship or grant aid	70
% receiving aid whose need was fully met	6
average aid package	$12,423
average student loan debt upon graduation	$26,066

Augustana College

Augustana College is a private, residential, comprehensive college of the Evangelical Lutheran Church in America. Augustana strives to provide students with an education of enduring worth that challenges the intellect, fosters integrity and integrates faith with learning and service in a diverse world. As such, Augustana embraces and celebrates five shared core values: Christian, liberal arts, excellence, community and service.

Augustana College
Office of Admission
2001 S. Summit Avenue
Sioux Falls, SD 57197
Ph: (800) 727-2844 / (605) 274-5516
admission@augie.edu
www.augie.edu

FAST FACTS

STUDENT PROFILE	
# of degree-seeking undergraduates	2,512
% male/female	36/64
% African American	2
% American Indian or Alaska Native	<1
% Asian or Pacific Islander	2
% Hispanic	<1
% White	94
% Pell grant recipients	24
ACADEMICS	
full-time faculty	132
full-time minority faculty	44
student-faculty ratio	12:1
average class size	21
% first-year retention rate	90
% graduation rate (6 years)	68
Popular majors Business Administration, Nursing, Biology	
CAMPUS LIFE	
% live on campus (% freshmen)	71 (95)
Multicultural student clubs and organizations International Student Club	
Athletics NCAA Division III, College Conference of Illinois and Wisconsin	
ADMISSIONS	
# of applicants	3,413
% accepted	69
# of first-year students enrolled	639
SAT Critical Reading (middle 50%)	520-610
SAT Math (middle 50%)	500-620
SAT Writing (middle 50%)	n/a
ACT (middle 50%)	22-28
average HS GPA	3.6
Deadlines	
regular decision	rolling
application fee (online)	$35 ($35)
fee waiver for applicants with financial need	yes
COST & AID	
tuition	$26,250
room & board	$6,400
total need-based institutional scholarships/grants	$20,291,779
% of students apply for need-based aid	79
% of students receive aid	67
% receiving need-based scholarship or grant aid	67
% receiving aid whose need was fully met	41
average aid package	n/a
average student loan debt upon graduation	n/a

ACCESS School-Based Mentor Program

Augustana participates in the Lutheran Social Services School-Based Mentor Program, providing positive role models to local youth. Through the program, Augustana students are matched with an elementary or middle school student from the Sioux Falls Public School District. In addition to increased self-esteem, a heightened sense of character and more confidence, the program helps students to improve their academic skills and provides them with a greater awareness of the importance of education. Mentors and students enjoy a variety of activities, such as working in the computer lab, playing board games, reading, playing basketball or simply eating lunch together and talking.

ACCESS Augie Reads

Augustana Reads is an after-school literacy program for English Language Learners that maximizes student learning by increasing engagement in the reading and writing process. This Sioux Empire United Way funded program is a collaborative effort among Augustana, the Multicultural Center and the Sioux Falls School District.

OPPORTUNITY Admission Possible

Augustana has partnered with Admission Possible, a non-profit organization focused on providing low-income high school students from the Twin Cities with access to higher education. The college organizes several campus visits for these students throughout the year. These visits include a campus tour, panel presentation by Augustana students, campus dining experiences and opportunities for classroom observation. Some include an overnight in the residence halls.

OPPORTUNITY Upward Bound Visit Program

Augustana hosts a summer visit program for Upward Bound, a federally funded program that assists low-income and first-generation high school students. The visit events include a campus tour, panel presentation by Augustana students, a campus dining experience and the opportunity to meet college faculty and staff.

OPPORTUNITY Circle of Courage Scholarship

This renewable scholarship is awarded to full-time students who are members of a minority ethnic group. The amount varies and is contingent upon financial need.

SUCCESS The Writing Center

Staffed by nationally certified peer tutors, the Writing Center promotes writing across the curriculum by offering workshops, presentations and tutoring services. Tutors help students complete writing assignments (not just in English), develop ideas, organize and plan papers and suggest editing and proofreading strategies.

SUCCESS A.S.A.P.

The Academic Success Achievement Program (A.S.A.P.) resides in first-year residence halls, creating opportunities that support first-year students in their academic success and in gaining greater understanding of themselves as learners. The program includes evening workshops on time management, editing papers, test-taking skills, and career exploration. Tutoring is available four nights a week. In addition, Study Cafés are held prior to exams in popular first-year general education courses. These study groups help students identify main points, review the information and clarify any areas of confusion. Study Cafés also provide a quiet, relaxing environment for study or reading.

The University of South Dakota

The University of South Dakota is a comprehensive, co-educational, non-denominational, public liberal arts university offering undergraduate, graduate and professional programs within the South Dakota System of Higher Education. Founded in 1862, the university is the state's oldest and the only liberal arts university. The University of South Dakota is home to the state's only law and medical schools as well as the College of Fine Arts, School of Health Sciences and Beacom School of Business. The school provides opportunities for involvement in music, theatre and a wide range of additional recreational, cultural, social and professional activities and organizations. The university seeks to provide graduate and undergraduate programs in the liberal arts and sciences and in professional education, to promote excellence in teaching and learning, to support research, scholarly and creative activities and to provide service to South Dakota and the region.

ACCESS **Math and Science Initiative Program (MSIP)**

Funded by the U.S. Department of Education, MSIP at The University of South Dakota provides high school students with an enriched math and science curriculum beyond what most high schools are able to offer. Each year, MSIP provides 40 rural South Dakota high school students an opportunity to experience college life through an intensive six-week summer program under the instruction and supervision of summer staff. Three separate components — Summer, Academic Year, and Bridge — expose students to math and science-based topics, courses of study and careers.

OPPORTUNITY **The Ullyot Endowment**

The University of South Dakota's Ullyot Endowment provides a select number of American Indian student scholarships each year. The Ullyot Scholarships will encourage and support students to pursue their dreams at The University of South Dakota. Applicants must be members of a federally recognized American Indian tribe from within the United States and enrolled or accepted at the university as full-time students in good standing. Entering first-year, returning undergraduate and graduate students receive full in-state (South Dakota) tuition, fees and book allowance. Scholarships may be renewed based upon student performance.

SUCCESS **Student Support Services (SSS)**

Student Support Services offers academic services including tutoring, improvement of study skills, counseling and academic advising. Student Support Services is a grant-funded project supported by the U.S. Department of Education. The primary purpose of the program is to improve the retention and graduation rates of students from "disadvantaged" backgrounds.

SUCCESS **Tiospaye Council**

The University of South Dakota Tiospaye Council was established to assist Native American students in adjusting to the college environment and to encourage their pursuit of higher education. In addition, the council works to promote a better understanding of the Native American culture by the university community and the Vermillion community. These undertakings are reflected in the council's efforts to provide an environment of cultural development, spiritual growth and social interaction by developing an extended community of resource people. Council-sponsored activities include the Wawokiya Mentoring Program, poetry readings, book signings, traditional music (drum practice and singing) and the annual spring pow-wow.

The University of South Dakota
414 East Clark
Vermillion, SD 57069
Ph: (605) 677-5434
admissions@usd.edu
www.usd.edu

FAST FACTS

STUDENT PROFILE

# of degree-seeking undergraduates	6,103
% male/female	37/63
% African American	2
% American Indian or Alaska Native	1
% Asian or Pacific Islander	1
% Hispanic	2
% White	88
% International	1
% Pell grant recipients	33

ACADEMICS

full-time faculty	366
full-time minority faculty	47
student-faculty ratio	17:1
average class size	18
% first-year retention rate	76
% graduation rate (6 years)	45

Popular majors Psychology, Business Management, Pre-Medicine, Education, Criminal Justice, Fine Arts

CAMPUS LIFE

% live on campus (% freshmen)	29 (83)

Multicultural student clubs and organizations Black Student Union, Tiospaye U, American Indian Science & Engineering Society, American Indian Business Leaders, International Students Club, Manga Sei'iki, Spanish Club, Taiwanese Student Association

Athletics NCAA Division I, Great West Conference

ADMISSIONS

# of applicants	3,452
% accepted	84
# of first-year students enrolled	1,175
SAT Critical Reading (middle 50%)	440-630
SAT Math (middle 50%)	450-610
SAT Writing (middle 50%)	n/a
ACT (middle 50%)	20-25
average HS GPA	3.25

Deadlines

regular decision	rolling
application fee (online)	$20 ($20)
fee waiver for applicants with financial need	no

COST & AID

tuition	in-state $2,994; out-of-state $4,491
room & board	$6,123
total need-based institutional scholarships/grants	$9,886,431
% of students apply for need-based aid	74
% of students receive aid	61
% receiving need-based scholarship or grant aid	30
% receiving aid whose need was fully met	28
average aid package	$7,005
average student loan debt upon graduation	$22,781

Belmont University

Belmont University, a private, Christian, coeducational university in Nashville at the heart of Music Row, offers its students an atmosphere of warmth, acceptance, and possibility within a student-centered, Christian community. Founded in 1891, Belmont offers undergraduate degrees in more than 75 major areas of study and is a great choice for students who intend to pursue a career in the entertainment and/or music business. Belmont boasts the only College of Entertainment and Music Business in the world, and it sends hundreds of students each year to work in every facet of the music industry, from publicists, to industry record labels, to law firms. Belmont is the largest Christian university in Tennessee.

ACCESS Belmont Students in Free Enterprise (SIFE)

Belmont Students in Free Enterprise (SIFE) students devote six weeks each summer and every other Saturday during the school year to the 100 Kings program. Sponsored by 100 Black Men of Middle Tennessee, 150 African-American students in Metro Nashville Public Schools are involved. The seven year program provides these students with English and math tutoring, personal finance counseling, and vocational orientation in interests such as Business, Law, and Engineering. The program offers preparation for the SAT and ACT exams, college counseling, and familiarity with Belmont University.

OPPORTUNITY Merit Scholarships

Belmont offers several substantial merit scholarships in addition to generous need-based aid. The William Randolph Hearst Endowed Scholarship is offered annually to an incoming freshman from a diverse background with outstanding academic and leadership records. It covers full tuition, room, board, books, and fees. The Ingram Diversity Leadership Scholarship, offered to four incoming freshmen with diverse backgrounds from the Nashville area, covers the full amount of tuition and is awarded based on outstanding academic and leadership records.

> ***"Coming from a small town, Belmont was a place that felt like home to me. The faculty and staff and the helpfulness that they showed to students pleased me. I knew that I was going to need that; moving away from home and to a new place, and I wanted that guidance that you get from a student professor relationship. Belmont's small size helped with that."***
>
> *– Ameshia C., '09*
> *Political Science and Journalism*

SUCCESS Black Student Association (BSA)

Belmont's Black Student Association promotes cultural awareness through campus events and forums. Open to students of all races, BSA strives to reach out to the Belmont and Nashville community through its involvement in the university's Martin Luther King Week, and community service projects in the Metro Nashville area.

SUCCESS Towering Traditions New Student Orientation

The Towering Traditions Orientation Program, founded more than 20 years ago, is designed to welcome new students to Belmont University. The program includes Summer Orientation and Welcome Week. Summer Orientation includes academic orientation, institutional orientation and registration sessions. Students have the opportunity to meet administration, faculty, and fellow students in preparation for their first days on campus in August.

Belmont University
1900 Belmont Boulevard
Nashville, TN 37212-3757
Ph: (615) 460-6785
admissions@belmont.edu
www.belmont.edu

FAST FACTS

STUDENT PROFILE

# of degree-seeking undergraduates	4,603
% male/female	42/58
% African American	5
% American Indian or Alaska Native	<1
% Asian or Pacific Islander	3
% Hispanic	2
% White	84
% International	1
% Pell grant recipients	17

First-generation and minority alumni Melinda Doolittle, American Idol contestant; Kimberly Locke, American Idol contestant; Rachel Smith, Miss USA

ACADEMICS

full-time faculty	269
full-time minority faculty	30
student-faculty ratio	13:1
average class size	n/a
% first-year retention rate	82
% graduation rate (6 years)	68

Popular majors Music Business, Nursing, Business Administration, Music, Biology

CAMPUS LIFE

% live on campus (% freshmen)	60 (95)

Multicultural student clubs and organizations Black Student Association, International Student Association

Athletics NCAA Division I, Atlantic Sun Conference

ADMISSIONS

# of applicants	3,322
% accepted	81
# of first-year students enrolled	1,019
SAT Critical Reading (middle 50%)	530-640
SAT Math (middle 50%)	520-630
SAT Writing (middle 50%)	n/a
ACT (middle 50%)	24-29
average HS GPA	3.53

Deadlines

regular decision	rolling to 8/1
application fee (online)	$50 (50)
fee waiver for applicants with financial need	yes, if received ACT/SAT waiver

COST & AID

tuition	$23,770
room & board	$9,320
total need-based institutional scholarships/grants	$3,827,486
% of students apply for need-based aid	89
% of students receive aid	70
% receiving need-based scholarship or grant aid	62
% receiving aid whose need was fully met	21
average aid package	$6,471
average student loan debt upon graduation	$19,123

Lipscomb University

Lipscomb University is a friendly community where the faculty knows their students and takes a personal interest in their success. With about 2,600 undergraduates and 1,000 graduate students, Lipscomb is a small, private university that focuses on offering challenging academic programs in a Christian environment. All of Lipscomb's academic programs integrate a service learning component into the curriculum giving students many opportunities to serve local and global communities and gain valuable work experience in their field. Lipscomb has three full-time staff dedicated to serving the needs of minority and first generation students, and a number of campus organizations and scholarship opportunities that help to make Lipscomb accessible and welcoming for these groups.

ACCESS **Bridges**

Bridges is a four-day residential summer program at Lipscomb that introduces minority students who are juniors and seniors in high school to college life and leading businesses in Middle Tennessee. Students hone their academic skills, prepare for the ACT and receive career counseling while having fun with like-minded peers.

OPPORTUNITY **Scholarships**

Outstanding students from traditionally underserved demographics have an array of scholarship opportunities at Lipscomb such as the Vision Award, a four-year scholarship specifically for minority and first-generation college students. First-generation, minority and low-income students with high scores on the ACT or SAT are awarded Merit Scholarships. Opportunities for Hispanic students include the Hispanic Achievers four-year scholarship, awarded to outstanding Hispanic students in partnership with the YMCA; and the St. Thomas Nursing Advantage Scholarship, a four-year, full-tuition award given to five Hispanic students annually. All qualifying international students are awarded the International Student Grant scholarship which provides 50% tuition for each of the four years.

> ***"My family came to the States as refugees from Kurdistan with big dreams. I never thought I would go to college, but Lipscomb was eager to recognize my achievements in high school and invited me to visit campus. Everyone was friendly, helpful and encouraging and I realized that going to college was an exciting and real possibility."***
>
> *– Bejan M., '14*
> *Nashville, TN*
> *Pre-Pharmacy*

SUCCESS **The Transitions Program**

The Transitions Program is designed to help students make a successful transition from high school to college. Students identified to be in need of special help are paired with a mentor and provided additional advising and academic support services.

SUCCESS **ADVANCE**

ADVANCE is a three day orientation program that all new students are required to participate in. At ADVANCE, students form relationships with their classmates and are introduced to all the resources available to them at Lipscomb.

SUCCESS **The Lipscomb University Multicultural Association (LUMA)**

The Lipscomb University Multicultural Association (LUMA) is a student-run organization which celebrates unique individuals of all ethnic groups, encourages cultural exchange and promotes their common bond in God. Created in 1996, LUMA strives to build a feeling of belonging and unity for all Lipscomb students, with a primary focus on minority and international students. This is accomplished through discussing and addressing relevant issues concerning various cultural groups and by promoting cultural awareness to the student body, faculty and staff.

Lipscomb University
One University Park Dr.
Nashville, TN 37204
Ph: (877) LU-BISON (582-4766)
Admissions@Lipscomb.edu
www.lipscomb.edu

FAST FACTS

STUDENT PROFILE	
# of degree-seeking undergraduates	2,600
% male/female	42/58
% African American	7
% American Indian or Alaska Native	<1
% Asian or Pacific Islander	3
% Hispanic	4
% White	81
% International	1
% Pell grant recipients	20
ACADEMICS	
full-time faculty	143
full-time minority faculty	5
student-faculty ratio	16:1
average class size	20
% first-year retention rate	72.6
% graduation rate (6 years)	60

Popular majors Business, Engineering, Education, Pre-Med, Nursing

CAMPUS LIFE	
% live on campus (% freshmen)	Unknown(100)

Multicultural student clubs and organizations Lipscomb University Multicultural Association (LUMA)

Athletics NCAA Divison I, Atlantic Sun Conference

ADMISSIONS	
# of applicants	3,261
% accepted	60
# of first-year students enrolled	656
SAT Critical Reading (middle 50%)	500-599
SAT Math (middle 50%)	500-599
SAT Writing (middle 50%)	n/a
ACT (middle 50%)	24-29
average HS GPA	3.5
Deadlines	
regular decision	rolling until 8/1
application fee (online)	$50 ($50)
fee waiver for applicants with financial need	yes
COST & AID	
tuition	$21,896
room & board	$8,790
total need-based institutional scholarships/grants	$8,966,389
% of students apply for need-based aid	95
% receiving need-based scholarship or grant aid	35
% receiving aid whose need was fully met	25
average aid package	$18,174
average student loan debt upon graduation	$20,105

Rhodes College

Rhodes College
2000 N. Parkway
Memphis, TN 38112
Ph: (901) 843-3000
adminfo@rhodes.edu
www.rhodes.edu

With 17 of its buildings and gateways listed on the National Register of Historic Places, Rhodes College can certainly boast of its classic and historic architecture. Founded in 1848, Rhodes has much more than a pretty face, however — it has been recognized in numerous publications for offering one of the best educational deals and it was a *CosmoGIRL* "Best College" because of its prominent female student leaders and faculty members and strong women's sports programs. Rhodes students also benefit from its location in Memphis, commonly known as the home of soul and barbeque.

"Being in a city like Memphis makes my experience at Rhodes even more diverse. Lots of private, liberal arts schools are far away from any kind of urban center—but to be in the heart of a city with so much cultural history, from the Civil Rights movement to the start of rock & roll, it only makes being a student here that much more enlightening."

– Jarrett T., '11
Atlanta, GA
English

ACCESS Kinney Program

Approximately 100 service programs operate under the auspices of the Kinney program, an initiative of the school's chaplaincy. Through the program, in which over 80 percent of graduating students participate, students can either help with one-time service drives or make an ongoing commitment to a particular service project. Furthermore, Kinney sponsors voter-registration drives, educational events on social issues, service training and reflection opportunities, social activism and advocacy, and works with faculty to develop service-learning courses and community-based research projects.

SUCCESS ALANA Orientation Dinner / Mentoring and Support

This activity provides African American, Latino/a, Asian and Native American students with important information to help facilitate their transition to college life at Rhodes. First-year ALANA students are assigned upperclassmen mentors who can help them acclimate to the campus experience. The mentoring program also offers structured monthly group meetings and workshops/programs to supplement the needs of students. Additionally, students can participate in two optional support groups — Brothers With Purpose (BWP) and African-American Women Speaking Our Minds on Empowerment (AWSOME) — that exist to promote connections between students, faculty, staff and alumni.

SUCCESS Office of Multicultural Affairs / Multicultural Resource Center

The Office of Multicultural Affairs has a unique role in offering programs & services that enhance the overall quality of life for students of color. All of the cultural organizations reside under the Office of Multicultural Affairs. These organizations are open to all faculty, staff and students. Also under the direction of the Office of Multicultural Affairs is the Multicultural Resource Center where faculty, staff and students can facilitate dialogue in a small, intimate and safe place about diversity-related issues, and conduct tutoring or study groups.

FAST FACTS

STUDENT PROFILE

# of degree-seeking undergraduates	1,800
% male/female	42/58
% African American	7
% American Indian or Alaska Native	<1
% Asian or Pacific Islander	5
% Hispanic	2
% White	75
% Pell grant recipients	9

First-generation and minority alums Charles Holt, Broadway and film actor; Willie Hulon, executive assistant director, National Security Branch, Federal Bureau of Investigation; Vicki Gilmore Palmer, executive vice president, Coca-Cola Enterprises

ACADEMICS

full-time faculty	196
full-time minority faculty	17
student-faculty ratio	9:1
average class size	13
% first-year retention rate	88
% graduation rate (6 years)	82

Popular majors Biology, Business, English, History, Political Science, Psychology

CAMPUS LIFE

% live on campus	75

Multicultural student clubs and organizations ASIA (All Students Interested in Asia), Black Student Association, Gay Straight Alliance, HOLA (Hispanic Organization for Language and Activities), RICE (Rhodes Indian Cultural Exchange)

Athletics NCAA Division III, Southern Collegiate Athletic Conference

ADMISSIONS

# of applicants	5,359
% accepted	49
SAT Critical Reading (middle 50%)	570-680
SAT Math (middle 50%)	580-700
SAT Writing (middle 50%)	580-680
ACT (middle 50%)	26-31
average HS GPA	3.8
Deadlines	
early decision	11/1
early action	11/15
regular decision(for Fall enrollment)	1/15
regular decision(for Spring enrollment)	11/1
application fee (online)	$0 ($0)
fee waiver for applicants with financial need	yes

COST & AID

tuition	$36,154
room & board	$8,976
total need-based institutional scholarships/grants	$15,483,353
% of students receiving aid	85
% receiving need-based scholarship or grant aid	47
% freshmen receiving aid whose need was fully met	25
average aid package (scholarship and grants)	$16,967
average student loan debt upon graduation	$24,946

Union University

Founded in 1823, Union University is an academic community, affiliated with the Tennessee Baptist Convention, equipping persons to think Christianly and serve faithfully in ways consistent with its core values of being excellence-driven, Christ-centered, people-focused, and future-directed. These values shape its identity as an institution which prioritizes liberal arts based undergraduate education enhanced by professional and graduate programs. The academic community is composed of quality faculty, staff, and students working together in a caring, grace-filled environment conducive to the development of character, servant leadership, and cultural engagement.

ACCESS **Rising High School Senior Program**

Union University offers an available Rising High School Senior Program to high school students who have already completed their junior year. This program offers academic classes at a discounted rate. In addition, the student life team provides leadership, career counseling and service opportunities for students involved in this program. The Rising High School Senior program helps minority and first-generation students achieve early success in college.

OPPORTUNITY **Minority Student Scholarship**

Two specific scholarships are offered for minority students, the African American Scholarship and Minority Student Scholarship. Awards range from $1,000 to $2,000 annually and are in addition to other institutional assistance.

OPPORTUNITY **Preview Days**

Union regularly invites and hosts groups of minority students, coordinating a comprehensive campus visit experience tailored around their needs and schedule. Minority participation in regularly scheduled Preview Days is very strong.

SUCCESS **The Hundley Center for Academic Enrichment**

The Hundley Center for Academic Enrichment is one of Union's initiatives to provide academic help to students. Peer tutoring is offered in more than 13 disciplines at no charge to the student. The program's director is also on hand to meet one-on-one with students who struggle with courses or time management.

SUCCESS **The Keystone Program**

Union also sponsors The Keystone Program where specific students facing academic uncertainties receive specialized help. The program also provides a select number of incoming students who are at higher academic risk a special opportunity for success. These students work with the full-time director of The Keystone Program, meeting weekly and following guidelines that provide a strong springboard for academic achievement.

SUCCESS **Minority Student Resources**

In an effort to build community and social support, minority student social support programs are offered, including TGI Friday's, African American Women's Bible Study Group, Minority Men's Bible Study Group, Mosaic Student Group and Open Mic Night. Black History Month Programming and the orientation "Dinner and Dialogue" are offered to all students and create conversations among student cultures.

Union University
1050 Union University Drive
Jackson, TN 38305-3697
Ph: 800.33.UNION
info@uu.edu
www.uu.edu

FAST FACTS

STUDENT PROFILE

# of degree-seeking undergraduates	2,810
% male/female	41/59
% African American	11
% American Indian or Alaska Native	<1
% Asian or Pacific Islander	1
% Hispanic	1
% White	81
% Pell grant recipients	24

First-generation and minority alumni Luis Ortiz, professional baseball player

ACADEMICS

full-time faculty	229
full-time minority faculty	16
student-faculty ratio	12:1
average class size	17
% first-year retention rate	84
% graduation rate (6 years)	63.3

Popular majors Elementary Education, Nursing, Christian Studies, Communication Arts

CAMPUS LIFE

% live on campus (% freshmen)	42 (86)

Multicultural student clubs and organizations Mosaic Student Group, Mu Kappa, International Student Organization, Common Ground

Athletics NAIA, TranSouth Athletic Conference

ADMISSIONS

# of applicants	1,749
% accepted	78
# of first-year students enrolled	634
SAT Critical Reading (middle 50%)	540-680
SAT Math (middle 50%)	540-680
SAT Writing (middle 50%)	n/a
ACT (middle 50%)	21-29
average HS GPA	3.65

Deadlines

regular decision	rolling
application fee (online)	$35 ($35)
fee waiver for applicants with financial need	yes

COST & AID

tuition	$23,330
room & board	$8,110
total need-based institutional scholarships/grants	n/a
% of students apply for need-based aid	96
% of students receive aid	64
% receiving need-based scholarship or grant aid	73
% receiving aid whose need was fully met	25
average aid package	$15,036
average student loan debt upon graduation	$21,543

Vanderbilt University

Founded in 1873, Vanderbilt University is a private, nonsectarian, co-educational research university. Vanderbilt is a center for research, dedicated to service to the community and society at large. Cultivating an atmosphere that prizes scholarship, the dissemination of knowledge through teaching and outreach, and the creative experimentation of ideas, the University supports intellectual freedom, open inquiry, equality, compassion and excellence in all endeavors.

> ***"Plain and simple, without assistance, college would not be a possibility…at Vanderbilt, the expanded aid program has encouraged discovery and exploration into realms of academia and social life that I never thought possible."***
>
> *– Richard C., '14*
> *Richmond Hill, GA*
> *Human and Organizational Development*

ACCESS **YMCA Mentor Program**

Run by Vanderbilt's Black Cultural Center, the YMCA mentor program provides disadvantaged low-income and minority junior high and high school students from the Nashville area with free tutoring, mentoring and training in important life skills.

ACCESS **PAVE Program**

Vanderbilt University's PAVE Program is a six-week summer course designed to strengthen the academic skills of high school juniors and seniors who are planning to enter a college engineering, pre-medical, science or technology program. PAVE participants can improve their problem solving skills, technical writing skills, computer application skills and laboratory skills by performing experiments in the sciences, pre-med and engineering disciplines.

ACCESS **Vanderbilt Summer Academy (VSA)**

VSA invites highly talented students (grades 7-12) to a residential summer program on campus. Vanderbilt Summer Academy offers engaging and challenging curricula in math, science, and the humanities. The program integrates resources from the university's many research programs directly into the classroom experience.

OPPORTUNITY **Vandy Fan for a Day**

Vandy Fan for a Day provides high school sophomores and juniors of diverse socioeconomic backgrounds with information about the selective college admissions process and Vanderbilt's need-based aid, and a chance to enjoy an SEC football game. High school counselors nominate students for this program held in the fall each year.

OPPORTUNITY **Posse Foundation**

Vanderbilt University is the founding collegiate partner in the Posse Foundation. Each year since 1989, Vanderbilt has recruited ten students from New York City through the Posse program to join our campus community. Many of these students are first-generation college students who are supported through the admission and educational process by the Vanderbilt-Posse partnership.

OPPORTUNITY **Chancellor's Scholar Program**

The Chancellor's Scholars Program, established in 1985, selects students with outstanding leadership, strength of character, academic achievement, and a deep-seated commitment to diversity and social justice. Chancellor's Scholars receive full tuition plus a one-time stipend, and programmatic support.

OPPORTUNITY **MOSAIC Weekend**

Held in mid-March, Vanderbilt University's MOSAIC Weekend is designed to introduce admitted students from diverse backgrounds to Vanderbilt's vibrant campus life. Selected admitted students receive early notice of their admission and an invitation to MOSAIC. The weekend features academic sessions, student activities, and performances at a variety of student shows including the annual Vanderbilt Step Show.

Vanderbilt University
2305 West End Avenue
Nashville, TN 37203-1727
Ph: (800) 288-0432 or (615) 322-2561
admissions@vanderbilt.edu
admissions.vanderbilt.edu

FAST FACTS

STUDENT PROFILE

# of degree-seeking undergraduates	6,879
% male/female	49/51
% African American	8
% American Indian or Alaska Native	1
% Asian or Pacific Islander	7
% Hispanic	7
% White	64
% International	5
% Pell grant recipients	14.6

First-generation and minority alumni Jamie Duncan, Shelton Quarles, Jamie Winborn, Corey Chavous, Jimmy Williams, Perry Wallace, professional basketball players; Joey Cora, professional baseball player; Muhammad Yunus, Economist

ACADEMICS

full-time faculty	901
full-time minority faculty	148
student-faculty ratio	8:1
average class size	n/a
% first-year retention rate	97
% graduation rate (6 years)	91

Popular majors Human and Organizational Development, Economics, English, Biomedical Engineering, Political Science, and Interdisciplinary

CAMPUS LIFE

% live on campus (% freshmen)	85 (100)

Multicultural student clubs and organizations African Students Union, Asian American Students Association, Black Student Alliance, Vanderbilt Association of Hispanic Students, Multicultural Student Leadership Council, MOSAIC Executive Board, Caribbean Student Association, South Asian Cultural Exchange (Masala-SACE), 12 multicultural Greek chapters on campus

Athletics NCAA Division I, Southeastern Conference

ADMISSIONS

# of applicants	21,811
% accepted	17.9
# of first-year students enrolled	1,600
SAT Critical Reading (middle 50%)	670-760
SAT Math (middle 50%)	690-770
SAT Writing (middle 50%)	660-750
ACT (middle 50%)	30-34

Deadlines

early decision	11/1
regular decision	1/3
application fee (online)	$50 ($50)
fee waiver for applicants with financial need	yes

COST & AID

tuition	$40,320
room & board	$13,560
total need-based institutional scholarships/grants	$112,806,838
% of students apply for need-based aid	53
% receiving need-based scholarship/grant aid	48
% receiving aid whose need was fully met	100
average aid package	$42,397
average student loan debt upon graduation	$18,605

Abilene Christian University

Abilene Christian University
Office of Admissions
ACU Box 29000
Abilene, TX 79699-9000
Ph: (800) 460-6228
info@admissions.acu.edu
www.acu.edu

Founded in 1906, Abilene Christian University is a private, coeducational institution offering undergraduate and graduate degrees. ACU's outstanding faculty members are committed to high-quality teaching, scholarship and service. The university also offers state-of-the-art facilities and innovative uses of mobile technology. The mission of the university is to educate students for Christian service and leadership throughout the world. Education is grounded in core Christian values, but the Abilene community is an inclusive environment for students from a variety of religious, ethnic, social, cultural and geographical backgrounds.

ACCESS **ACU en Español**

Abilene Christian University is dedicated to diversity and inclusion of other cultures, especially Hispanic students. The university provides a Spanish version of its Web site to ensure that Spanish-speaking students get any information they might need about ACU.

OPPORTUNITY **First-Generation and Diversity Scholarships**

Recognizing the roadblocks many minority students face in succeeding at institutions of higher learning, Abilene Christian University provides scholarships designed to attract multicultural students. For example, the Hispanic Leadership Council/Abilene Christian University Partnership Scholarship provides full tuition for four years to admit students who qualify. The Cultures of ACU scholarships provide awards for students of any ethnicity whose experience and perspective can help promote diversity at ACU. Admissions counselors are dedicated to aiding students in making their educational goals a reality. They can provide information on scholarships from many private organizations offering assistance to multicultural students.

"ACU has given me so many experiences that have helped me grow, as well as the knowledge to teach children and become a master teacher. Community with other students and community with faculty and staff - this community is always there to help you in academics and in faith."

– Geraldine C., '10
Abilene, TX
Education

SUCCESS **Keystone**

Members of this student group at Abilene Christian University are student leaders selected by the director of the Office of Multicultural Enrichment to serve the greater Abilene community and provide advising, mentoring and on-campus support to their peers among the campus body.

SUCCESS **The Office of Multicultural Enrichment**

The Office of Multicultural Enrichment oversees student groups at Abilene Christian University that are focused on multicultural diversity. Many student-led groups, each with their own cultural focus, meet on a monthly or bi-monthly basis. Each year, the number of diversity groups on campus increases.

FAST FACTS

STUDENT PROFILE

# of degree-seeking undergraduates	4,728
% male/female	45/55
% African American	6
% American Indian or Alaska Native	1
% Asian or Pacific Islander	1
% Hispanic	7
% White	78
% International	4
% Pell grant recipients	25.8

First generation and minority alumni Dr. Billy Curl, '66, ACU trustee and minister, Crenshaw Church of Christ, Los Angeles, Calif.; Wilbert Montgomery, '77, former NFL all-pro running back, assistant coach, Baltimore Ravens Football Club, Baltimore, Md.; Hubert Pickett, '77, ACU trustee and director of personnel, Abilene Independent School District, Abilene, Texas; Marcela Gutierrez, '06, accounts analyst for PFSweb, Dallas, Texas; Fabiola Leon, '08, elementary school teacher in Plano Independent School District, Plano, Texas

ACADEMICS

full-time faculty	241
full-time minority faculty	n/a
student-faculty ratio	15:1
average class size	n/a
% first-year retention rate	75
% graduation rate (6 years)	61

Popular majors Business, Education, Psychology, Biology, Journalism and Mass Communication

CAMPUS LIFE

% live on campus (% freshmen)	41 (96)

Multicultural student clubs and organizations Essence of Ebony, Hispanos Unidos, International Students Association, Milonga (Latin), Shades Step Squad, Virtuous African Heritage Sisterhood

Athletics NCAA Division II, Lone Star Conference

ADMISSIONS

# of applicants	4,106
% accepted	53
# of first-year students enrolled	979
SAT Critical Reading (middle 50%)	500-610
SAT Math (middle 50%)	510-520
SAT Writing (middle 50%)	n/a
ACT (middle 50%)	21-27
average HS GPA	3.7
Deadlines	
early decision	11/1
regular decision	2/15
application fee (online)	$50 ($50)
fee waiver for applicants with financial need	n/a

COST & AID

tuition	$22,760
room & board	$7,884
total need-based institutional scholarships/grants	$57,000,000
% of students apply for need-based aid	n/a
% of students receive aid	92
% receiving need-based scholarship or grant aid	n/a
% receiving aid whose need was fully met	n/a
average aid package	$12,000
average student loan debt upon graduation	n/a

Hardin-Simmons University

Hardin-Simmons University
2200 Hickory, HSU Box 16050
Abilene, TX 79698
Ph: (877) GOHSUTX / (325) 670-1000
enroll@hsutx.edu
www.hsutx.edu

With liberal arts and sciences, music, nursing and education classes offered, Hardin-Simmons University provides a range of academic opportunities to undergraduates, all while affording them a true Texas experience in the Old West town of Abilene. In addition to these offerings, Hardin-Simmons hosts special programs, such as the Center for Missionary Education, which provides continuing education opportunities to missionaries. In the Southern spirit, Hardin-Simmons also takes its athletic program seriously, but not to the detriment of its academics — the school strives for its students to be strong academic and social leaders.

ACCESS **Baptist Student Ministries**

Through the Baptist Student Ministries, students can participate in a number of service opportunities, including Christmas break projects, 10-week summer missions, two-week impact teams and study-abroad missions, as well as semester positions. Students reach out to the campus and community through campus Bible studies, a nursing home ministry, prayer meetings, care groups and children's outreach.

ACCESS **Hardin-Simmons University Community Renewal Program**

Hardin-Simmons' community renewal program works to rebuild houses, literacy and hope in the neighborhood around campus. Students participate in the program through a recycling center, winterization program, Bible studies, after-school care and tutoring, a Habitat for Humanity chapter and GED obtainment and assistance.

OPPORTUNITY **Campus Visits**

Interested students have a variety of ways to visit the Hardin-Simmons campus, all of which offer their own features. During Cowboy Fridays, for example, students can attend classes, participate in tours and take residual ACT exams, which can only be used at Hardin-Simmons, but which can be scored within the week. During Spring Round-Up, students can stay on campus overnight, as well as register for fall classes. In addition to these special visit opportunities, students can also schedule a personalized campus visit any day of the week.

SUCCESS **Student Success Seminar / New Student Orientation**

Hardin-Simmons offers a nationally recognized Student Success Seminar, which helps students transition into college life. This three-credit, cooperatively taught (by a faculty member, staff member and student leader) course covers such diverse subjects as note-taking, relationship issues and diversity. The New Student Orientation, where new students are placed in upperclassmen-lead teams, also provides support for students.

SUCCESS **Free Tutoring and Counseling**

Students at Hardin-Simmons can take advantage of both free tutoring and counseling. Tutoring is offered through the Advising Center, which employs academically successful undergraduates as peer tutors, while counseling is offered through the Department of Psychology, which employs graduate interns in the field.

FAST FACTS

STUDENT PROFILE

# of degree-seeking undergraduates	1,854
% male/female	46/54
% African American	5
% American Indian or Alaska Native	1
% Asian or Pacific Islander	1
% Hispanic	11
% White	74
% Pell grant recipients	38

First-generation and minority alumni Stedman Graham, nationally known author, speaker and founder of Athletes Against Drugs; Victor Carrillo, Chairman of the Texas Railroad Commission; Harvey Catchings, former NBA star, Former President Harvey Catchings Promotions, former Director of Player Programs National Basketball Association, current Sr. Tax Consultant Tax Masters, Inc.; Alex Vasquez, associate general counsel in the Office of the General Counsel of Wal-Mart Stores, Inc.; Consuelo Castillo Kickbusch, Lieutenant Colonel, U.S. Army (retired), Founder & President of Educational Achievement Services, Inc., author, motivational speaker, educator

ACADEMICS

full-time faculty	135
full-time minority faculty	3
student-faculty ratio	13:1
average class size	17
% first-year retention rate	70
% graduation rate (6 years)	50

Popular majors Psychology, Business, Education, Physical Therapy, Life Sciences

CAMPUS LIFE

% live on campus (% freshmen)	92

Multicultural student clubs and organizations M.E.S.H., Unity Group, International Student Fellowship

Athletics NCAA Division III, American Southwest Conference

ADMISSIONS

# of applicants	2,354
% accepted	38.6
SAT Verbal average	510
SAT Math average	540
SAT composite average (excluding writing)	1050
ACT composite average	22.4
average HS GPA	3.56

Deadlines

regular admission	rolling
application fee (online)	$50 ($50)
fee waiver for applicants with financial need	yes

COST & AID

tuition	$21,450
room & board	$6,408
total need-based institutional scholarships/grants	$8,458,000
% of students apply for need-based aid	96
% of students receive aid	95
% receiving need-based scholarship or grant aid	49
% receiving aid whose need was fully met	69
average aid package	$16,930
average student loan debt upon graduation	$35,429

Southern Methodist University

Southern Methodist University, a private university of 11,000 students, is a caring academic community in the heart of the vibrant city of Dallas, Texas. Students come from all 50 states and nearly 90 foreign countries and represent diverse economic, ethnic, and religious backgrounds. SMU offers an academic experience that prepares students for success in and out of the classroom. Academic advisers give students the framework and guidance needed to make and execute a successful academic plan. Internship opportunities and career advising give SMU students the edge needed in today's competitive job market, and nearly 180 student organizations allow students to be involved and make a difference. SMU offers an environment that fosters a sense of belonging, promotes physical and emotional well-being, and supports intellectual, cultural, moral and spiritual growth. SMU is a great place for the education of your life.

ACCESS **Hispanic Youth Symposium**

The Hispanic Youth Symposium is a four day, three night summer program that will bring more than 200 local Hispanic high school students and 100 community volunteers to SMU. The program is a life-changing event that inspires Hispanic high school students to achieve a college education, pursue a professional career, and invest in their community. Following the summer symposium, students participate in a yearlong institute which consists of mentoring and tutoring by SMU students, as well as activities at local businesses and internships.

ACCESS **Upward Bound**

SMU participates in the federally funded Upward Bound program, which serves first generation, low income high school students in Dallas County. The program provides a yearlong college preparation program in addition to a six week residential summer program where students are exposed to the college experience, as well as take academic and test preparation courses.

OPPORTUNITY **Multicultural Recruitment Conference**

Each year the Department of Student Activities and Multicultural Student Affairs collaborates with the Undergraduate Admission Office to host a Multicultural Recruitment Conference. Hundreds of local high school students are invited to campus to learn about the college admission and financial aid process, hear inspirational speakers on the importance of attending college, and interact with current students from various backgrounds.

OPPORTUNITY **A Different View of SMU**

A Different View of SMU is a targeted multicultural student preview day held at SMU in the fall. The program features sessions on SMU's academic programs, a presentation on admission and financial aid, multicultural faculty and student panels, a campus tour, as well as an activities fair featuring our student organizations and academic resources.

SUCCESS **Department of Multicultural Student Affairs/Minority Student Resources**

The Department of Multicultural Student Affairs works to recognize, educate, and celebrate diversity on the SMU campus. Within the department there is an African American, Hispanic, and Asian American coordinator who assist' with providing leadership development in addition to academic and social support services for multicultural students. Some of the events sponsored by this office include the annual Multicultural Student Retreat, the Association of Black Students Fish Fry, MLK week, the Hispanic Issues Forum, the Asian Arts and Dance Festival, Hispanic Heritage Month, and the Soul Food Dinner.

SUCCESS **CONNECT Mentorship Program**

The CONNECT mentorship program is geared towards first year and transfer multicultural students to support their transition to SMU. Each new student is matched with an upper-class student who serves as a friend on campus, as well as a resource helping them to identify key resources for their academic and social success.

Southern Methodist University
P.O. Box 750181
Dallas, Texas 75275
Ph: (214) 768-2000
enroll_serv@smu.edu
www.smu.edu

FAST FACTS

STUDENT PROFILE

# of degree-seeking undergraduates	6,116
% male/female	47/53
% African American	5
% American Indian or Alaska Native	<1
% Asian or Pacific Islander	6
% Hispanic	10
% White	70
% International	7
% Pell grant recipients	15.7

First-generation and minority alumni Jerry LeVias, '69, College Football Hall of Fame, President of LeVias Enterprises, Inc.; John W. Nieto, '59, Internationally renowned artist; Regina Taylor, '81, Actress, playwright, director; Richie L. Butler, '93, Founding senior Pastor of Union Cathedral community and Partner with CityView; Tony Garza, '83, Ambassador to Mexico

ACADEMICS

full-time faculty	668
full-time minority faculty	119
student-faculty ratio	12:1
average class size	25
% first-year retention rate	89
% graduation rate (6 years)	74

Popular majors Finance, Political Science, Economics, Psychology, and Business

CAMPUS LIFE

% live on campus (% freshmen)	33 (95)

Multicultural student clubs and organizations AAssociation of Black Students, College Hispanic American Students, Asian Council, Black Men Emerging, Sisters Supporting Sisters, The League of United Latin American Citizens, Voices of Inspiration Gospel Choir, Multicultural Greek Council, Asian-American Leadership and Educational Conference, Student Initiative to Promote Unity, Education, Determination, Empowerment, and Spirituality

Athletics NCAA Division I, Conference USA

ADMISSIONS

# of applicants	8,239
% accepted	59
# of first-year students enrolled	1,479
SAT Critical Reading (middle 50%)	560-670
SAT Math (middle 50%)	580-680
SAT Writing (middle 50%)	560-660
ACT (middle 50%)	25-30
average HS GPA	3.36
Deadlines	
early decision	1/15
regular decision	3/15
application fee (online)	$60 ($60)
fee waver for applicants with financial need	no

COST & AID

tuition	$34,990
room & board	$13,215
total need-based institutional scholarships/grants	$54,710,353
% of students apply for need-based aid	45
% of students receive aid	38
% receiving need-based scholarship or grant aid	31
% receiving aid whose need was fully met	35
average aid package	$32,632
average student loan debt upon graduation	$20,883

Texas Christian University

Founded Founded in 1873 by Addison and Randolph Clark, Texas Christian University is a religiously-affiliated research university in Fort Worth, Texas. TCU's College Access programs have reached out to thousands of first-generation and low-income students and allowed them to realize their college dreams. Though affiliated with the Christian Church (Disciples of Christ), TCU students belong to more than 60 different religions. TCU is giving back to its community by helping build a new urban village on Berry Street to the south of campus.

ACCESS **Minority High School Conference**

This two-day college-student run program brings local high school sophomores and juniors to campus for sessions about college life, financial aid, and academics. Students participate in various workshops and activities, attend classes with their appointed TCU mentor, and spend the night on campus over the course of the two-day program.

ACCESS **College Initiatives**

Trained professionals assist college-bound, minority students with completing college applications, building top-notch resumes, brainstorming excellent admission essays, and discussing ways to realistically fund a college education. Participants learn how to make sound decisions through their college search and how to effectively maximize a visit to a college campus. As college costs are constantly rising, various types of ways to fund a student's education, such as scholarships and financial aid, are discussed in great detail.

OPPORTUNITY **Community Scholar Program**

The Community Scholar Program currently networks with eleven local urban high schools with a disproportionate number of first-generation, low-income students of color. We select 20 students per year. The scholarship covers TCU's cost of attendance.

OPPORTUNITY **Access Granted**

Access Granted is a program designed for underrepresented minority populations (in the context of TCU) to experience life at TCU. You will spend the night in the TCU residence halls, and spend your days learning how to make well-informed decisions about college, hanging out in a collegiate environment, attending college classes, and interacting with current students, faculty, and staff from all walks of life. This program is supported by the Office of Admission. However, the entire program is essentially facilitated by multicultural student organizations.

SUCCESS **Frog Camp**

Frog Camp is all about you finding your place at TCU; whether that place is line dancing in the Fort Worth Stock Yards, on top of the tallest climbing wall in Texas, rafting down Colorado's Taylor River, or building a house with Habitat for Humanity. Each camp is unique, but every camp you'll make friends, discuss college issues, and prepare for life at TCU. Scholarships are available to those who demonstrate financial need.

SUCCESS **College 101**

This program enhances student retention by equipping students who fail to thrive in their first academic semester with resources and tools that will enable them to reach their academic goals.

"Coming from a single parent home TCU has really helped my family financially. Regardless, I do still work over the summer and have work-study during the school year just to help my mother with any other expenses. Academically, it's helped me want more. I've become much more ambitious with my education and want everything that it's worth."

– Elizabeth R., '13
Forth Worth, TX
Psychology

Texas Christian University
Office of Admission
TCU Box 297013
Fort Worth, TX 76129
Ph: (800) 828-3764 / (817) 257-7490
frogmail@tcu.edu
www.tcu.edu

FAST FACTS

STUDENT PROFILE	
# of degree-seeking undergraduates	7,853
% male/female	41/59
% African American	5
% American Indian or Alaska Native	<1
% Asian or Pacific Islander	3
% Hispanic	9
% White	77
% International	5
% Pell grant recipients	11

First-generation and minority alumni LaDanian Tomlinson, James Cash, and Sandora Irvin

ACADEMICS	
full-time faculty	523
full-time minority faculty	62
student-faculty ratio	14:1
average class size	27
% first-year retention rate	85
% graduation rate (6 years)	70

Popular majors Biology, Business, Nursing, Journalism, Education

CAMPUS LIFE	
% live on campus (% freshmen)	50 (95)

Athletics NCAA Division I, Mountain West Conference (through 2011) and Big East Conference (beginning 2012)

ADMISSIONS	
# of applicants	>14,000
% accepted	52
# of first-year students enrolled	1,800
SAT Critical Reading (middle 50%)	520-630
SAT Math (middle 50%)	530-650
SAT Writing (middle 50%)	520-630
ACT (middle 50%)	23-29
average HS GPA	3.4
Deadlines	
early action	11/1
regular decision	2/15
application fee (online)	$40 ($40)
fee waiver for applicants with financial need	yes

COST & AID	
tuition	$32,400
room & board	$10,000
total need-based institutional scholarships/grants	$46,055,245
% of students apply for need-based aid	55
% receiving need-based scholarship or grant aid	31
% receiving aid whose need was fully met	12
average aid package	$19,800
average student loan debt upon graduation	$18,700

Texas State University

Texas State values diversity in its classrooms, residence halls, dining venues and recreational events. The university offers 97 undergraduate programs in a supportive, academically challenging environment. Bobcats hail from across Texas and across the United States, as well as from countries as far away as India, China and Israel. No matter where they come from, students find countless campus organizations that serve as enclaves of activity and support for those searching for familiar faces and customs — or wanting to discover new ones. Approximately one-third of the more than 27,000 undergraduates are ethnic minorities; of these, approximately 25 percent are Hispanic/Latino. This diversity contributes to the richness of the Bobcat experience. Texas State's investment in students results in freshman-to-sophomore retention and graduation rates that rank among the highest in the state.

"Texas State is rapidly becoming one of our nation's leading public universities. With a growing student body of over 32,000, a high caliber faculty focused on teaching as well as research, over $400 million in new building projects, and a competitive NCAA athletic program, Texas State is a great place to get an education."

– Dawson M., '11, Brownfield, TX, Finance

ACCESS **Bobcat Days**

Texas State holds Bobcat Days four times a year to bring prospective students to campus and allow them visit and explore the academic and cultural environment of Texas State University. During the tour students can speak with faculty and staff about majors and coursework, speak with students from a student panel about campus life, take a campus tour, and dine at the university's student food court. Representatives from Multicultural Student Affairs also are available to visit with first-generation students.

OPPORTUNITY **LBJ Achievement Scholarship**

This $2,000 scholarship is offered to incoming freshmen each year who are full-time students, ranked in the top quarter of their high school graduating classes, and are either first-generation college students or current/past participants in one of the following programs: College Assistance Migrant Program (CAMP), Educational Opportunity Center High School Equivalency Program (HEP), Ronald E. McNair Post Baccalaureate Achievement Program, Subsidized High School Lunch Program, Summer Enrichment Program (SEP), Student Support Services Program, Talent Search, or Upward Bound.

OPPORTUNITY **National Hispanic Scholarship**

The National Hispanic Scholarship is an $8,000 scholarship awarded over four years to eligible incoming freshmen. Scholarship applicants must be National Hispanic Scholars, score 1200 or more on a single SAT or 27 or more on the ACT, and be ranked in the top 15 percent of their high school class or receive an IB diploma.

SUCCESS **Student Support Services**

This program assists eligible first-generation college students, low-income students and students with disabilities from all racial and ethnic backgrounds who have a need for academic and other support services in order to successfully complete their college education.

SUCCESS **The Foster Care Alumni Program**

The Foster Care Alumni Program works with students who are alumni of the foster care system to build a support community and provide helpful resources. The mentorship program allows students to get help from trained faculty/staff or peer/student mentors with academic and social activities during their first year at Texas State University.

Texas State University
429 N. Guadalupe Street
San Marcos, TX 78666
Ph: (512) 245-2364
admissions@txstate.edu
www.txstate.edu

FAST FACTS

STUDENT PROFILE

# of degree-seeking undergraduates	27,448
% male/female	45/55
% African American	6
% American Indian or Alaska Native	1
% Asian or Pacific Islander	2
% Hispanic	26
% White	62
% International	1
% Pell grant recipients	38

First-generation and minority alumni Tomás Rivera, '58 and '64, former chancellor, University of California-Riverside; Jerry Fields, '69, chief executive officer, J.D. Fields & Co.; Eugene Lee, '74, actor and playwright; Thomas Carter, '74, Emmy-winning director, producer and actor; Charles Austin, '91, Olympic gold medalist, owner of So High Sports and Fitness; Nina Vaca-Humrichouse, '94, chief executive officer, Pinnacle Technical Resources

ACADEMICS

full-time faculty	1,086
full-time minority faculty	240
student-faculty ratio	19:1
average class size	27
% first-year retention rate	79
% graduation rate (6 years)	55

Popular majors Education, Business (Management and Accounting), Psychology, Criminal Justice, and Communication Studies

CAMPUS LIFE

% live on campus (% freshmen)	20 (88)

Multicultural student clubs and organizations African Student Organization, Latino Student Organization, South Asian Student Association, First Generation Student Organization, Indian Student Association, Japanese Language and Culture, League of United Latin American Citizens, Native American Student Association, International Student Association, Bobcat Equality Alliance

Athletics NCAA Division I, Southland Conference

ADMISSIONS

# of freshmen applicants	16,675
% accepted	76
# of first-year students enrolled	3,930
SAT Critical Reading (middle 50%)	470-570
SAT Math (middle 50%)	490-590
SAT Writing (middle 50%)	450-550
ACT (middle 50%)	21-25
Deadlines	
regular decision	5/1
application fee (online)	$60 ($60)
fee waiver for applicants with financial need	yes

COST & AID

tuition	in-state: $8,232; out-of-state: $17,622
room and board	$6,912
total need-based institutional scholarships/grants	$79,767,205
% of students apply for need-based aid	72
% receiving need-based scholarship or grant aid	44
% receiving aid whose need was fully met	6
average aid package	$14,124
average student loan debt upon graduation	$21,667

University of Houston

Students chose the University of Houston for the diversity of its student body and the unlimited opportunities offered by UH's dynamic campus life. In fact, the reasons to choose UH are as diverse as the individuals on campus. Students choose from more than 100 undergraduate majors, several of which rank among the nation's best. The University of Houston's faculty members win awards, earn international acclaim and work closely with students as individuals. Students can take on internships at the largest medical center in the world or learn about the energy industry first-hand: professional opportunities are around every corner in Houston, the nation's fourth-largest city and a hub of international business. The University of Houston's graduates are CEOs, astronauts, judges, educators, Olympic athletes, actors, artists, and more. Across the world, UH alumni are fulfilling their dreams and making things happen.

OPPORTUNITY **Urban Experience Program**

The multifaceted components of the Urban Experience Program promote scholarship, community service, and personal and professional development. Opportunities include internships, community service, tutoring, mentoring, cultural enrichment activities, on-campus housing, academic success workshops, career development activities, personal development workshops, and monitoring to insure academic success. Participants are selected on the basis of demonstrated or potential ability for campus leadership, community service, and academic achievement. The selection process includes an application, an essay, interviews with candidates and their parents, demonstrated financial need, and exceptional life challenges in pursuing higher education.

SUCCESS **Challenger Program**

The Challenger Program seeks to help students develop positive academic and personal goals through offering an array of educationally and intellectually enriching programs. Tutors are available to assist students in a wide variety of academic subjects, along with academic and personal counseling services to address specific needs on an individual or group basis. A reading, writing, and study skills college course is available to provide academic support toward strengthening basic learning skills. The Challenger Program staff help students meet their financial needs, enabling them to continue to pursue post-secondary education. Additionally, the program supports campus social gatherings and cultural events.

> ***"I chose the University of Houston because of its location to the Texas Med Center – I want to be a doctor. My sister was in the hospital at 9 months old and I felt like the doctors were really knowledgeable and able to give her reassurance. I want to give others that reassurance and go into pediatrics."***
>
> *– Ashley L., '14*
> *Pasadena, TX*
> *Biology - Pre Medicine*

SUCCESS **University of Houston Wellness**

University of Houston Wellness, a campus-wide education and prevention program, promotes healthier choices and a healthier, safer learning environment. Goals include outreach programs on wellness topics, peer involvement in promoting health and wellness, consultation to students, faculty, and staff, and providing a clearinghouse of information on health and wellness. UH Wellness offers outreach and educational programs for the campus and community, along with referral information and resources on a wide range of health related topics including stress management, alcohol, drugs, and sexual health. The department co-sponsors large-scale prevention campaigns including Alcohol Awareness Month, the Texans' War on Drugs, Red Ribbon Week, Safer Sex Awareness Week, Eating Disorders Awareness Day, the Great American Smokeout, and the Safe Spring Break Campaign.

University of Houston
Welcome Center
4400 University Drive
Houston, TX 77204-2023
Ph: (713) 743-1010
admissions@uh.edu
www.uh.edu

FAST FACTS

STUDENT PROFILE

# of degree-seeking undergraduates	28,056
% male/female	49/51
% African American	13
% American Indian or Alaska Native	<1
% Asian or Pacific Islander	20
% Hispanic	21
% White	35
% International	9
% Pell grant recipients	34.4

First-generation and minority alumni Clyde Drexler, former NBA player; Carl Lewis, track and field legend/US Olympian; Loretta Devine, actress; Master P, hip hop artist; Henry Cuellar, US/Texas State Representative; Raul Gonzales, former Texas Supreme Court Justice

ACADEMICS

full-time faculty	1,256
full-time minority faculty	288
student-faculty ratio	22:1
average class size	20-29
% first-year retention rate	79
% graduation rate (6 years)	41

Popular majors Liberal Arts and Social Sciences, Business, Natural Sciences and Mathematics

CAMPUS LIFE

% live on campus (% freshmen)	13 (34)

Multicultural student clubs and organizations Caribbean Student Organization, Chinese Student Association, Colombian Students Association, Houston Bridges, Indian Students Association, League of United Latin American Citizens, Nigerian Students Association, Pakistan Students Association, The Houston Suitcase Theater (THST), Vietnamese Students Association

Athletics NCAA Division I, Conference USA

ADMISSIONS

# of applicants	11,393
% accepted	70
# of first-year students enrolled	3,295
SAT Critical Reading (middle 50%)	470-570
SAT Math (middle 50%)	500-620
SAT Writing (middle 50%)	n/a
ACT (middle 50%)	20-25
average HS GPA	4.59

Deadlines

regular decision	4/1
application fee (online)	$50 ($50)
fee waiver for applicants with financial need	yes

COST & AID

tuition	$7,342 in-state; $14,782 out-of-state
room & board	$7,300
total need-based institutional scholarships/grants	$20,714,828
% of students apply for need-based aid	63
% of students receive aid	85
% receiving need-based scholarship or grant aid	62
% receiving aid whose need was fully met	25
average aid package	$11,660
average student loan debt upon graduation	$13,000

The University of Texas at Austin

A major co-educational, nondenominational, public research university, the University of Texas at Austin is the flagship institution of The University of Texas System. Since 1883, the University of Texas at Austin has been dedicated to improving the quality of life of the people of Texas and the United States. As an enduring symbol of the spirit of Texas — big, ambitious and bold — the university drives economic and social progress in Texas and serves the nation as a leading center of knowledge and creativity. The University of Texas at Austin strives to transform lives for the benefit of society by encouraging learning, discovery, freedom, leadership, individual opportunity and responsibility in all of its students.

ACCESS The Neighborhood Longhorns Program (NLP)

The University of Texas at Austin's Neighborhood Longhorns Program is an educational incentive program operated in partnership with local elementary and middle schools. The program helps disadvantaged youth in grades two through eight improve overall grade performance in reading, math, science and language arts skills. The program also provides scholarships for students to obtain a college education.

ACCESS University Outreach Centers

The University Outreach Centers provide a five-year college preparatory program for students in grades 8-12. Group and individual services are designed to enhance students' success academically and to ensure they are college admissible upon graduation from high school. Staff assist students with potential barriers and equip them with the tools they need to successfully negotiate the college admissions process.

OPPORTUNITY Longhorn Opportunity Scholarships/Longhorn Scholars Program

Longhorn Opportunity Scholarships are awarded to students in economically disadvantaged and historically underserved Texas communities. The scholarships provide $5,000 per year up to four years. Once on campus, all recipients become part of a four-year comprehensive academic community, the Longhorn Scholars Program. Students benefit from interaction with program advisors, support from peer mentors and opportunities to make connections across disciplines that integrate classroom, research and internship experiences.

OPPORTUNITY Gateway Scholars Program

The University of Texas at Austin's Gateway Scholars Program seeks to maximize the academic success and social connections of new first-generation and underrepresented students. The program includes UTransition, a learning community for first generation and underrepresented transfer students, the Achieving College Excellence (ACE) Program, a service for students who seek additional academic assistance, and the Welcome Program, a diversity education program for incoming first-year students. In addition, scholars attend small-size classes in many math and science courses, receive coursework in critical thinking and college life skills, professional academic advising, individual counseling, peer advising, registration assistance and priority registration and tutoring, and participate in a variety of social, cultural and recreational activities.

"Coming to The University of Texas is the accomplishment that I am most proud of. In high school, I could have never imagined the experiences and changes I would go through that led me to where I am today. The prestige, honor, and culture that this school entails allows me to believe that everyday I spend on campus will truly fulfill our motto of 'What starts here changes the world."

– Claudio A., '09
Cedar Hill, TX
Nursing

The University of Texas at Austin
Office of Admissions
P.O. Box 8058
Austin, TX 78713-8058
Ph: (512) 475-7440
askadmit@austin.utexas.edu
www.utexas.edu

FAST FACTS

STUDENT PROFILE

# of degree-seeking undergraduates	37,689
% male/female	48/52
% African American	5
% American Indian or Alaska Native	<1
% Asian or Pacific Islander	18
% Hispanic	19
% White	52
% International	4
% Pell grant recipients	22.1

First-generation and minority alumni Kevin Alejandro, actor; Rodney Ellis, Texas senator; Charles Gonzalez, U.S. Congressman; Juliet Villarreal Garcia, president, UT Brownsville; Billy Ray Hunter, Jr., Principal Trumpet NY Metropolitan Opera Orchestra; Ron Kirk, U.S. Trade Representative; Robert Rodriguez, filmmaker; Moushaumi Robinson, Sanya Richards, Olympic Gold Medalists; Cedric Benson, Earl Campbell, Michael Huff, Leonard Davis, Derrick Johnson, Mike Williams, Ricky Williams, Roy Williams, DeAndre De Wayne Lewis, Shaun Rogers, NFL players; Kevin Durant, Maurice Evans, Daniel Gibson, James Thomas, NBA players; Betty Nguyen, anchor, CNN; Ricardo Romo, President, UT San Antonio; Stephanie Wilson, NASA astronaut; Judith Zaffirini, Texas senator

ACADEMICS

full-time faculty	2,714
full-time minority faculty	550
student-faculty ratio	18:1
average class size	n/a
% first-year retention rate	92
% graduation rate (6 years)	81

Popular majors Biology/Biological Sciences, Liberal Arts, Business, Government

CAMPUS LIFE

% live on campus (% freshmen)	20 (65)

Multicultural student clubs and organizations Afrikan American Affairs, Asian/Desi/Pacific Islander American Collective, Black Student Alliance, Latino Leadership Council, Longhorn American Indian Council, Student African American Brotherhood, Students for Equity and Diversity, Umoja, Vietnamese Student Association

Athletics NCAA Division I (football I-A), Big 12 Conference

ADMISSIONS

# of applicants	31,022
% accepted	47
# of first-year students enrolled	7,275
SAT Critical Reading (middle 50%)	530-670
SAT Math (middle 50%)	580-700
SAT Writing (middle 50%)	530-670
ACT (middle 50%)	24-30
average HS GPA	n/a

Deadlines

regular decision	rolling from 10/15
application fee (online)	$60 ($60)
fee waiver for applicants with financial need	yes

COST & AID

tuition	in-state: $9,416; out-of-state: $31,266
room & board	$10,112
total need-based institutional scholarships/grants	$114,393,299
% of students apply for need-based aid	56
% of students receive aid	42
% receiving need-based scholarship or grant aid	34
% receiving aid whose need was fully met	23
average aid package	$12,825
average student loan debt upon graduation	$17,000

University of Texas at San Antonio

University of Texas at San Antonio
One UTSA Circle
San Antonio, TX 78249-0617
Ph: (210) 458-4599
prospects@utsa.edu
www.utsa.edu

Founded by the Texas Legislature in 1969 to become a "university of the first class", UTSA has exceeded those expectations by becoming one of the most diverse, dynamic, and largest public universities in the state. The second largest of the UT System, UTSA has remained true to its mission of being an institution of access and excellence, serving as a center for intellectual and creative resources as well as a catalyst for socioeconomic development for Texas, the nation, and the world. UTSA ranks third overall in the total number of undergraduate degrees awarded to Hispanics in the country. It represents the San Antonio community with all the benefits of a big city and hospitality, personal attention, and feel of a small town.

ACCESS After School All Stars Tutoring Program

UTSA employs UTSA students as tutors in the after school program, and staffing for the summer enrichment program. UTSA tutors provide mentoring, as well as basic tutoring services to all students enrolled in the After School All Stars Program.

OPPORTUNITY UTSAccess

To help make higher education affordable, accessible, and provide financial support to students and families of Texas, UTSA has established UTSAccess (Undergradaute Tuition, Support, Access.) UTSA students who are first-time Freshmen as well as Texas residents with a family income of $30,000 or less and reported assets of less than $50,000 can qualify for grants and/or scholarships to cover tuition and mandatory fess for Fall and Spring Semesters. To qualify, one must apply and be admitted by March 15th.

SUCCESS Tomas Rivera Center for Student Success

The Tomás Rivera Center (TRC) is a comprehensive academic support center for students. Services offered at the TRC include; tutoring in quantitative subjects, academic coaching and study strategies, Supplemental Instruction (SI) to accompany difficult courses, Math Assistance Program, Online Study Skills Resources, and Learning Communities.

SUCCESS Academic Advising

UTSA academic advisors offer academic advising and guidance to empower students to realize their full potential. There are dedicated advisors who work exclusively with first year students to help assure a successful transition into the core curriculum. Each of the colleges has an extensive Advising Center that continues with the students once they move into their major field.

SUCCESS Business Scholars Program

The Business Scholars Program is a mentoring program for first generation college students pursuing careers in business. Established by the College of Business in 2002, the program is designed to help students make a smooth transition from high school to college and on to graduation. It is open to College of Business freshmen, sophomores and transfer students at the Downtown Campus. Currently, there are 100 students enrolled in the program.

SUCCESS Center for Excellence in Engineering Education

The Center of Excellence for Engineering Education (CE^3) provides a holistic approach for improving the quality of engineering education at The University of Texas at San Antonio. The center strives to improve the preparedness and marketability of the students in the College of Engineering for challenging and rewarding careers.

FAST FACTS

STUDENT PROFILE

# of degree-seeking undergraduates	24,308
% male/female	49/51
% African American	8
% American Indian or Alaska Native	<1
% Asian or Pacific Islander	7
% Hispanic	43
% White	39
% International	2
% Pell grant recipients	42.8

First-generation and minority alumni Maria Berriozabal, first elected Latina on San Antonio City Council, and past president of the National League of Cities

ACADEMICS

full-time faculty	976
full-time minority faculty	344
student-faculty ratio	22:1
average class size	n/a
% first-year retention rate	59
% graduation rate (6 years)	28

Popular majors Business/marketing, Interdisciplinary Studies, Biological/life sciences, Psychology, Social Sciences, Engineering

CAMPUS LIFE

% live on campus (% freshmen)	43(12)

Multicultural student clubs and organizations African Student Association, Chinese Student and Scholar Association, Filipino Student Association, Hispanic Student Association, Indian Cultural Association, Mexican Americans Studies Student Organization, Association of Latino Professionals in Finance and Accounting, National Society of Black Engineers, Society of Mexican-American Engineers and Scientists

Athletics NCAA Division III, Southland Conference

ADMISSIONS

# of applicants	12,442
% accepted	83
# of first-year students enrolled	4,858
SAT Critical Reading (middle 50%)	450-560
SAT Math (middle 50%)	465-580
SAT Writing (middle 50%)	430-540
ACT (middle 50%)	19-24
average HS GPA	n/a

Deadlines

regular decision	6/1
application fee (online)	$40 ($40)
fee waiver for applicants with financial need	yes

COST & AID

tuition	in-state: $8,790; out-of-state: $17,672
room & board	$9,271
total need-based institutional scholarships/grants	n/a
% of students apply for need-based aid	82
% of students receive aid	96
% receiving need-based scholarship or grant aid	79
% receiving aid whose need was fully met	23
average aid package	$7,856
average student loan debt upon graduation	$18,790

Westminster College

Westminster College
Office of Admissions
1840 South 1300 East
Salt Lake City, UT 84105
Ph: (800) 748-4753
admission@westminstercollege.edu
www.westminstercollege.edu

Westminster is a nationally recognized, comprehensive liberal arts college. With a broad array of graduate and undergraduate programs, Westminster is distinguished by its unique environment for learning. Westminster prepares students for success through active and engaged learning, real world experiences, and its vibrant campus community. Westminster's unique location, adjacent to the Rocky Mountains and to the dynamic city of Salt Lake, further enriches the college experience.

"Westminster has given me many tools to succeed and grow as a student and as a person by giving me opportunities to be involved in many activities while feeding my thirst for knowledge. Through the Latino Club and Allies Coalition, I took an active role in shaping the programming and culture of Westminster. In the Diversity Center, I found mentors and friends. Through these and other experiences, I have learned to be open and appreciate different points of view."

*– Princess G., '10,
West Jordan, UT
Pre-Law/Justice Studies,*

ACCESS **Access to Success**

Westminster recently partnered with a local high school to provide English Language Learners (ELL) and/or members of underrepresented groups with weekly opportunities to play sports and practice English language skills with college-level athletes. The Access to Success program offered students from the same high school summer field trips to Westminster that included campus tours and small group discussions between high school and college students who shared their experiences of what college is like.

OPPORTUNITY **Exemplary Achievement Scholarship**

Annual scholarships of $20,000 are awarded to 10 students who have demonstrated ability to overcome significant personal hardships and achieve academic excellence. Applicants are evaluated based on a personal statement or essay; resume of activities, awards, and achievements; and at least two letters of recommendation. Also considered are achievements outside of the normal academic setting including athletics and community service. Selection of recipients is based on character, background, excellence in any field, and whether a student has overcome significant difficulties. Eligible applicants must have a minimum of a 3.0 GPA.

SUCCESS **The Diversity & International Center**

Through mentoring, programming, and collaboration with students, the Diversity Center strives to foster student learning, leadership and identity development; build genuine community among and within diverse groups; and advocate for and provide safe, inclusive learning environments for all students.

SUCCESS **First-Year Orientation, Mentoring and Learning Communities**

Westminster's first-year student orientation includes a session specifically focusing on first-generation college students, and all first-year students are assigned to a faculty or administrator mentor to guide and support them through their first and second years of college. In addition, all first-year students are enrolled in a learning community, to connect with each other, faculty and the college community once they arrive on campus.

FAST FACTS

STUDENT PROFILE

# of degree-seeking undergraduates	2,308
% male/female	43/57
% African American	1
% American Indian or Alaska Native	<1
% Asian or Pacific Islander	3
% Hispanic	9
% White	74
% International	n/a
% Pell grant recipients	28.9

First-generation and minority alumni Silvia Thomas, Utah Hispanic/Latino Affairs Director; Forrest Cuch, Executive Director, Utah Division of Indian Affairs; Rev. France Davis, Pastor, Calvary Baptist Church

ACADEMICS

full-time faculty	140
student-faculty ratio	11:1
average class size	n/a
% first-year retention rate	79
% graduation rate (6 years)	59

Popular majors Nursing, Psychology, Economics, Accounting, Communications

CAMPUS LIFE

% live on campus (% freshmen)	27 (67)

Multicultural student clubs and organizations International Student Association, Latin@ Westminster, African American Intellectual Union, Alphabet Soup, Students Promoting Pacific Islander and Asian Mentoring at Westminster, Spanish Club, Multicultural Club, French Club, Chinese Club

Athletics NAIA, Frontier Conference

ADMISSIONS

# of applicants	1,963
% accepted	78
SAT Critical Reading (middle 50%)	500-620
SAT Math (middle 50%)	510-630
SAT Writing (middle 50%)	n/a
ACT (middle 50%)	21-27
average HS GPA	3.5
Deadlines	
regular decision	rolling
application fee (online)	$35 ($0)

COST & AID

tuition	$26,712
room & board	$7,584
% of students receiving aid	56
% receiving need-based scholarship or grant aid	56
% receiving aid whose need was fully met	30
average aid package	$19,342
average student loan debt upon graduation	$16,200

Middlebury College

Middlebury College
Emma Willard House
Middlebury, VT 05753
Ph: (802) 443-3000
admissions@middlebury.edu
www.middlebury.edu

Students who attend Middlebury College receive an education at one of the United States' top liberal arts colleges. Founded in 1800, Middlebury's campus is located in Champlain Valley of Vermont, surrounded by forests and mountains. Middlebury's 2,350 undergraduate students enjoy a broad curriculum that embraces humanities, arts, literature, foreign languages and sciences in addition to a historic commitment to internationalism. Middlebury seeks to bring together a community of distinct individuals that will share their many talents and experiences. This richness of backgrounds and melding together of ideas challenges students daily and happens in an environment where respect and honest discourse dominate and personal growth and ample learning opportunities abound.

"The 21st Century Atlanta Scholars is a program that encourages students from Atlanta Public Schools to consider New England colleges. This program helped me find Middlebury, and Middlebury helped me find myself. Now, I truly see the world surrounding me--it's not black or white, it's a rainbow of colors."

– Conetrise H., '10
Atlanta, GA

ACCESS Discover Middlebury

Each year, Discover Middlebury brings more than 60 high school seniors from traditionally underrepresented groups to campus to spend two days living the life of a college student. Students sleep in residence halls, attend classes, and interact with current undergraduates. The program was developed to give students a taste of the academic and social rewards of college with the hope that they will seriously consider higher education.

OPPORTUNITY Community-Based Organizations

Middlebury works closely with a number of community-based organizations in order to reach out to a variety of students. These organizations include the Posse Foundation (New York), 21st Century Atlanta Scholars, Bright Prospect (Pomona, Calif.), College Match (Los Angeles), Harlem Educational Activities Fund (New York), Leadership Enterprise for a Diverse America (New York), National Hispanic Institute (Maxwell, Texas), One Voice (Santa Monica, Calif.) and Prep for Prep (New York).

SUCCESS Office for Institutional Planning and Diversity (OIPD)

By collaborating with many other departments on campus, the Office for Institutional Planning and Diversity develops events and programming throughout the year that strive to encourage dialogue and provide diverse programming that helps to enhance an appreciation for difference in the Middlebury College community. OIPD is responsible for, among many other things, the Cafecito Hour Lecture Series, dinner discussions at the PALANA Academic Interest House and support of the many cultural organizations on campus.

SUCCESS Center for Teaching, Learning and Research (CTLR)

The educational mission of Middlebury College is served by the Center for Teaching, Learning and Research, where students can use tools developed to enhance scholastic performance. Staff at CTLR work with other departments across campus to offer workshops, study groups and one-on-one educational sessions which focus on oral presentation skills, effective note-taking, reading skills enhancement, test-taking preparation and time and workload management to develop skills for success inside and outside the classroom. CTLR also prepares students for leadership roles as mentors via Students for Academic Excellence and Study Group Leader programs, and implements prevention and intervention initiatives for students who are at academic risk or who face challenges related to learning styles or disabilities.

FAST FACTS

STUDENT PROFILE

# of degree-seeking undergraduates	2,502
% male/female	49/51
% African American	2
% American Indian or Alaska Native	1
% Asian or Pacific Islander	6
% Hispanic	7
% White	67
% International	10
% Pell grant recipients	8.9

First-generation and minority alumni Julia Alvarez, Middlebury's writer-in-residence, author, acclaimed books *How the Garcia Girls Lost Their Accents, In the Time of Butterflies*; Ron Brown, former chairman, Democratic National Committee, Secretary of Commerce under first Clinton administration, first African-American head of a national political party, first African-American Secretary of Commerce; Alexander Twilight, first African-American to earn a degree at an American college or university, first African-American member of the Vermont General Assembly

ACADEMICS

full-time faculty	261
full-time minority faculty	27
student-faculty ratio	9:1
average class size	16
% first-year retention rate	96
% graduation rate (6 years)	91

Popular majors Economics, English Language and Literature, Psychology, International Studies, Environmental Studies

CAMPUS LIFE

% live on campus (% freshmen)	97(100)

Multicultural student clubs and organizations African American Alliance, African Issues Awareness Club, Alianza Latinoamericana y Caribeña, Arabesque, Distinguished Men of Color, International Students Organization, Korea Town, Mediterranean Society, Middlebury Asian Students Organization, MIX Club, Pan-Caribbean Student Organization, Russian and Eastern European Society, Scandinavian Society, South Asian Association, Umoja, Voices of Indigenous People
Athletics NCAA Division III, New England Small College Athletic Conference

ADMISSIONS

# of applicants	7,984
% accepted	17
# of first-year students enrolled	577
SAT Critical Reading (middle 50%)	640-740
SAT Math (middle 50%)	650-740
SAT Writing (middle 50%)	650-750
ACT (middle 50%)	29-33
average HS GPA	3.73
Deadlines	
early decision	11/1
regular decision	1/1
application fee (online)	$65 ($65)
fee waiver for applicants with financial need	yes

COST & AID

tuition (includes room and board)	$53,800
total need-based institutional scholarships/grants	$38,562,710
% of students apply for need-based aid	56
% of students receive aid	46
% receiving need-based scholarship or grant aid	46
% receiving aid whose need was fully met	100
average aid package	$35,470
average student loan debt upon graduation	$19,981

Saint Michael's College

Saint Michael's College, a vibrant, Catholic, liberal arts college, is located in Colchester, Vermont, just five minutes from Lake Champlain and three miles from Burlington, Vermont's largest city and a metropolitan college town. Saint Michael's offers an abundance of ways to explore the liberal arts, with 30 majors, and provides financial aid to nearly all admitted students. Founded by the Society of Saint Edmund over 100 years ago, Saint Michael's is the only Edmundite college in the world. The Edmundites are known for their commitment to social justice and remembered for their role in helping Dr. Martin Luther King Jr. lead desegregation efforts in Selma, Alabama. Saint Michael's honors the Edmundite tradition with a strong residential campus community, a commitment to the liberal arts and a passion for social justice.

ACCESS Mobilization of Volunteer Efforts (MOVE)

Mobilization of Volunteer Efforts meets local needs directly, helping to build strong connections between the college and the town. These are mainly geared toward youth, education and college mentoring. Programs include Woodside Tutoring program, where Saint Michael's students act as role models and serve as tutors for young adults at the Woodside Juvenile Rehabilitation Center; Middle School Mentor program, where Saint Michael's students mentor middle school girls in the neighboring Winooski school system; and America Reads, a nationwide program designed to improve literacy among children.

"The multicultural recruiter arranged a campus visit for me and my mother that convinced us: even if we had to borrow most of the cost to attend, it was a sacrifice my family was willing to make. Then a great financial package ended up covering most expenses."

– Manuel F., '13
Tucson, AZ
Political Science

SUCCESS Office of Multicultural Student Affairs (MSA)

The Office of Multicultural Student Affairs supports and assists students from diverse racial, linguistic and cultural backgrounds in their pursuit of academic success, community involvement, personal development and intellectual engagement. The office is active in recruiting and retaining students from diverse backgrounds, and also provides leadership opportunities and training to students around issues of diversity and multiculturalism. Programs include Peer Diversity Educators, First-Year Transition Program, Faculty Staff Mentors and Peer Mentors.

SUCCESS Diversity Coalition

The Diversity Coalition at Saint Michael's promotes awareness of issues such as gender, race, religion and ethnicity and hosts many events on issues of diversity and social justice. Diversity Coalition also invites well-known speakers to campus to address relevant campus and societal issues. The coalition, which meets regularly twice a month, organizes one of Saint Michael's most well-attended and successful events: the International Festival.

SUCCESS Martin Luther King, Jr. Society

The Martin Luther King, Jr. Society encourages students to examine the content of their own character, regardless of skin color, and to be honest about whether or not their actions are in accordance with their principles. The society organizes two of the largest events on campus, the MLK Talent Show and the MLK Convocation. In addition, the society invites at least four speakers a year to address issues affecting our society.

SUCCESS Alianza

The Alianza Society celebrates Latino culture and experience through programs, workshops and lectures that focus on Latino heritage, address socio-political issues that impact the Latino community and raises awareness about issues of tolerance.

Saint Michael's College
One Winooski Park
Colchester, VT 05439
Ph: (802) 654-3000
admission@smcvt.edu
www.smcvt.edu

FAST FACTS

STUDENT PROFILE

# of degree-seeking undergraduates	1,859
% male/female	48/52
% African American	1
% American Indian or Alaska Native	<1
% Asian or Pacific Islander	1
% Hispanic	3
% White	92
% International	2
% Pell grant recipients	14.5

First-generation and minority alumni Loung Ung, nationally acclaimed author, *First They Killed My Father: A Daughter of Cambodia Remembers*, spokesperson, Campaign for A Landmine-Free World; Alex Okosi, senior vice president and general manager, MTV Africa; Most Reverend Moses Anderson, auxiliary bishop, Archdiocese of Detroit; Jason Curry, president/director of operations, Big Apple Basketball, Inc.; Jamila Headly, Rhodes Scholar, Oxford University

ACADEMICS

full-time faculty	148
full-time minority faculty	12
student-faculty ratio	12:1
average class size	18-20
% first-year retention rate	89
% graduation rate (6 years)	80

Popular majors Business Administration/ Management, English Language and Literature, Psychology, Journalism and Mass Communication, and Education

CAMPUS LIFE

% live on campus (% freshmen)	98 (99)

Multicultural student clubs and organizations Alianza, Diversity Coalition, Martin Luther King, Jr. Society

Athletics NCAA Division II, Northeast-10 Conference and East Collegiate Athletic Conference

ADMISSIONS

# of applicants	3,228
% accepted	70
# of first-year students enrolled	475
SAT Critical Reading (middle 50%)	520-630
SAT Math (middle 50%)	510-630
SAT Writing (middle 50%)	510-620
ACT (middle 50%)	22-26
average HS GPA	3.4
Deadlines	
early action	11/1
regular decision	2/1
application fee (online)	$50 ($50)
fee waiver for applicants with financial need	yes

COST & AID

comprehensive fee	$43,530
total need-based institutional scholarships/grants	$22,279,117
% of students apply for need-based aid	83
% of students receive aid	68
% receiving need-based scholarship or grant aid	88
% receiving aid whose need was fully met	27
average aid package	$22,625
average student loan debt upon graduation	$27,000

Southern Vermont College

Southern Vermont College
982 Mansion Drive
Bennington, VT 05201
Ph: (802) 447-6300
admissions@svc.edu
www.svc.edu

Located on a mountainside campus overlooking Bennington, VT, Southern Vermont College is a model of an enlightened educational community: diverse, supportive, environmentally respectful and socially responsible. Through its career-enhancing liberal-arts curriculum, Southern Vermont College endeavors to transform students into engaged citizens with a broad perspective of an ever-changing society. Whether students find themselves drawn to Criminal Justice, Nursing, Business, Humanities or Social Services, the college seeks to immerse students in the concept of becoming life-long and dynamic learners. At the same time, Southern Vermont College encourages students to combine classroom learning with real-life, real-world experiences, through internships and learn-by-doing service projects. In short, Southern Vermont College may be small in size, but is most assuredly not small in the skills and self-confidence it strives to give its students.

"Southern Vermont College encourages students to stray from the normal and leave a trail. Students even have the option of designing a major that is tailored to meet their future career goals. It's a great place."

*– Zach G., '09
Natick, MA
Political Science*

SUCCESS **Build the Enterprise**

"Build the Enterprise" is an entrepreneurship program which provides an opportunity for students to research, create and run a real business over the course of their Southern Vermont College education. Businesses of all kinds can be created — in retail, computer software, healthcare or whatever most interests students. The most successful ideas are funded through a college-created Venture Fund with $100,000 in assets. The program has four phases: Teams of students research business opportunities, finalize a plan of operation, manage their own enterprise — learning first-hand what it takes to run a business — and, upon graduation, can take it as a first job or sell it, with funds used to repay the Venture Fund.

SUCCESS **Quest for Success**

A required course for incoming freshmen enrolled in a degree program, "Quest for Success" combines academics with service-learning to acclimate students to the expectations of college-level education. During the course, students plan, implement and assess a project in the community, and through that project gain skills in teamwork, organization, problem-solving, decision-making and budgeting. "Quest for Success" has earned national and state recognition as one of the most effective and successful programs for creatively addressing first-year students.

SUCCESS **Service-Learning Initiatives**

Service-learning and civic engagement are central to the college's curriculum and its sense of community and social responsibility. At any one time, 40 percent of Southern Vermont College students are engaged in service-learning activities.

SUCCESS **The Success Center**

The "Success Center" is a student support services center. Funded in part by a TRIO grant, it provides personalized academic planning and support. Its services include counseling and career-counseling, special courses in composition and math, the Learning Differences Support Program and the Learning Cooperative, a peer-tutoring program. The Success Center is open and available to all students free of charge.

FAST FACTS

STUDENT PROFILE	
# of degree-seeking undergraduates	500
% male/female	37/63
% African American	7.5
% American Indian or Alaska Native	0.2
% Asian or Pacific Islander	1.6
% Hispanic	3.2
% White	78.2
% International	1
% Unknown	7.5
% Pell grant recipients	46
ACADEMICS	
full-time faculty	26
full-time minority faculty	n/a
student-faculty ratio	17:1
average class size	16
% first-year retention rate	56
% graduation rate (6 years)	42

Popular majors Nursing, Radiologic Science, Criminal Justice, Business, Psychology, Creative Writing

CAMPUS LIFE	
% live on campus (% freshmen)	60 (75)

Multicultural student clubs and organizations PRIDE, Diversity Advisory Committee

Athletics NCAA Division III – 10 sports; New England Collegiate Conference

ADMISSIONS	
# of applicants	600
% accepted	90
# of first-year students enrolled	220
SAT Critical Reading (middle 50%)	400-500
SAT Math (middle 50%)	400-500
SAT Writing (middle 50%)	n/a
ACT (middle 50%)	15-20
average HS GPA	2.75
Deadlines	
regular decision	rolling
application fee (online)	$30 ($0)
fee waiver for applicants with financial need	yes
COST & AID	
tuition (2011 - 2012)	$20,200
room & board	$9,568
fees	$980
total need-based institutional scholarships/grants	$2,761,934
% of students apply for need-based aid	98
% of students receive aid	95
% receiving need-based scholarship or grant aid	90
% receiving aid whose need was fully met	0
average aid package	$15,500
average student loan debt upon graduation	$26,000

University of Vermont

University of Vermont
Undergraduate Admissions Office
194 South Prospect St.
Burlington, VT 05401
Ph: (802) 656-3370
admissions@uvm.edu
www.uvm.edu

FAST FACTS

STUDENT PROFILE

# of undergraduate enrollment	11,593
% male/female	43/57
% African American	1
% American Indian	<1
% Asian	2
% Hispanic	3
% White	86
% International	1
% Pell grant recipients	17

First-generation and minority alumni Pedro Albizu Campos, Puerto Rican political leader

ACADEMICS

full-time faculty	611
minority faculty	91
student-faculty ratio	17:1
average class size	24
% first-year retention rate	87
% graduation rate (6 years)	77

Popular majors Business Administration, English, Psychology

CAMPUS LIFE

% live on campus (% freshmen)	51 (97)

Multicultural student clubs and organizations Alianza Latina, Black Student Union, Asian-American Student Union, Council for Unity, Muslim Student Association

Athletics NCAA Division I, American East Conference, Hockey East Association

ADMISSIONS

# of applicants	22,317
% accepted	70
# enrolled	2,472
SAT Critical Reading (middle 50%)	540-640
SAT Math (middle 50%)	545-640
SAT Writing (middle 50%)	540-640
ACT (middle 50%)	24-29
average HS GPA	n/a
Deadlines	
early action	11/1
regular decision	1/15
application fee (online)	$55
	($55 regular decision, $0 early action)
fee waiver for applicants with financial need	yes

COST & AID

tuition	in-state: $12,888; out-of-state: $32,528
room & board	$9,708
total need-based institutional scholarships/grants	$82,722,887
% applying for aid	70
% of students receiving aid	56
% receiving need-based scholarship or grant aid	48
% receiving aid whose need was fully met	20
average aid package	$18,364
average student loan debt upon graduation	$25,599

The University of Vermont, founded in 1791, is the fifth-oldest university in New England (following Brown, Dartmouth, Harvard and Yale) and is one of the 20 oldest institutions of higher education in the United States. Also known as UVM, an abbreviation for its Latin name, Universitas Viridis Montis, the university is a public, co-educational, liberal arts university that offers the best of both worlds — a research university's intellectual resources and breadth of opportunity and the student attention that's typical of a smaller college. UVM prepares students to lead productive, responsible and creative lives. University of Vermont students succeed after graduation. A recent study shows that more than 88 percent were employed and 22 percent enrolled in graduate school within a year of receiving their UVM degree.

ACCESS **Summer Happening Program**

The University of Vermont partners with the Abenaki community to sponsor the Summer Happening Program, which brings Abenaki middle school students to the university for three days to experience on-campus life. The goal is to convince participants that a college education is feasible. Participants get assistance with course selection and financial aid and gain valuable exposure to university programs, faculty and cultural activities. Past highlights of the Summer Happening Program have included an orienteering workshop and a dinner featuring authentic native foods.

ACCESS **Columbus Campus-University of Vermont Partnership**

The Christopher Columbus Campus-University of Vermont Partnership encourages greater diversity at the university. Christopher Columbus Campus is an urban, multicultural setting for several high schools in the Bronx. The partnership seeks to "catch" students from Columbus High School, Pelham Prep Academy and Collegiate Institute for Math and Science during their freshman and sophomore years to provide them with an "early awareness" of the college process. Participants attend workshops, sponsored by the University of Vermont, on topics such as college admissions and financial aid. In addition, participants may also receive fully paid trips to UVM campus to experience college life first-hand.

SUCCESS **ALANA Peer Mentoring**

The University of Vermont's ALANA (African-American, Latino, Asian, Native American) Peer Mentoring program pairs incoming first-year ALANA students with outstanding upperclassmen. These upperclassmen act as mentors, both academically and socially. Mentors help ALANA freshmen strive for academic excellence, directing them to tutors and/or other learning aids. The program also fosters a sense of community by sponsoring a series of social events including intergalactic bowling, skiing, free tickets to sporting events and the theater, pizza parties and apple picking. In addition, the program offers funds for mentors and mentees to engage in fun activities on their own, such as a night out at the movies or coffee at a local café.

SUCCESS **Summer Enrichment Scholarship**

The Summer Enrichment Scholarship at the University of Vermont is a bridge program sponsored by and administered through the ALANA Student Center. The program introduces incoming first-year ALANA, first-generation and low-income students to university life before the challenges of the first year formally begin. Participants earn credit for two classes (at no cost), a paid campus job, free room and board and a $500 stipend at the successful completion of the program. More importantly, participants build relationships with other students, enjoy a variety of recreational activities in the Vermont area (such as camping and a ropes course) and develop valuable leadership skills.

George Mason University

George Mason University, located in northern Virginia near Washington, D.C., is nationally recognized for leadership in educational innovation, and for successfully enrolling and graduating students from all cultures and socio-economic backgrounds. U.S. News & World Report named George Mason the number one national university to watch on its list of "Up-and-Coming Schools." The professors at George Mason are widely renowned for conducting groundbreaking research in such fields as cancer, climate change, information technoogy, and the biosciences. They offer strong programs in engineering, information technology, biotechnology, and healthcare that prepare their students to be successful in their future careers.

ACCESS **Early Identification Program**

George Mason University's Early Identification Program (EIP) is a college preparatory program meant to encourage middle and high school students who would be first generation college students to consider going to college. EIP partners with seven public school systems in the area, and they focus on educating the whole student, with the goal of developing students academically, professionally, and socially. The program involves academic enrichment programs, mentoring, parental involvement, and leadership workshops, all of which are meant to provide students with the knowledge and skills to get into college and succeed once there.

"As a first generation college student I am a product of adversity, a student molded by challenges overcoming the obstacles faced as a low income student. I am the product of opportunities such as the Early Identification Program at George Mason that invested in my success story long before it was written, ensuring I was equipped with the tools needed to succeed academically, professionally and personally."

– Johnetta S., '13
Falls Church, VA
Neuroscience

OPPORTUNITY **Full Tuition Scholarships**

George Mason provides a variety of need-based and merit-based scholarship opportunities. The University Scholars program annually provides 25 students a full-tuition merit-based scholarship for their four years at Mason. In addition to the scholarship opportunities provided to all students, The Early Identification Program provides four outstanding students from their program a four year, full tuition scholarship.

OPPORTUNITY **Student Transition and Empowerment Program (STEP)**

The Student Transition and Empowerment Program at George Mason is an initiative run by the Office of Diversity of Programs and Services, with the goal of recruiting and retaining a diverse array of undergraduate students. The program runs during the five weeks leading up to the start of the school year and gives students a head start to prepare them for life at college.

SUCCESS **University Transition Courses**

George Mason University offers several university transition courses to their students to ensure that students are equipped to succeed in college. All students are encouraged to take advantage of Mason's university transition courses, focusing on transition to college, choosing a major, and preparing for the college to workplace transiton.

SUCCESS **Office of Diversity Programs and Services**

Academic, social and emotional support is available through the Office of Diversity and Programs and Services. The Office of Diversity Programs and Services was created to support the diverse student and faculty population at George Mason University. Throughout the school year, they sponsor various programs for both students and faculty such as lectures, concerts, seminars, and awards. The office works specifically with African-American, Hispanic, Asian/Pacific Islander, American Indian, and Lesbian, Gay, Bisexual, Transgender and Questioning populations, but are committed to the success of all members of the George Mason community.

George Mason University
4400 University Drive, MS 3A4
Fairfax, VA 22030
Ph: (703) 993-2400
admissions@gmu.edu
www.admissions.gmu.edu

FAST FACTS

STUDENT PROFILE

# of degree-seeking undergraduates	19,702
% male/female	47/53
% African American	8
% American Indian or Alaska Native	<1
% Asian or Pacific Islander	16
% Hispanic	9
% White	4
% International	3
% Pell grant recipients	20

ACADEMICS

full-time faculty	1,128
full-time minority faculty	192
student-faculty ratio	15.5:1
average class size	n/a
% first-year retention rate	85
% graduation rate (6 years)	63

Popular majors Business/marketing, Social sciences, English, Health professions and related sciences

CAMPUS LIFE

% live on campus (% freshmen)	26 (70)

Multicultural student clubs and organizations Mason has 27 different International/Multicultural Student Organizations along with a multicultural Greek Council that includes 8 groups including Chi Upsilon Sigma Latin Sorority, Ince, Sigma Beta Rho Fraternity, Inc. etc.

Athletics NCAA Division I, Colonial Athletic Association

ADMISSIONS

# of applicants	13,732
% accepted	63
# of first-year students enrolled	2,628
SAT Critical Reading (middle 50%)	510-620
SAT Math (middle 50%)	520-630
SAT Writing (middle 50%)	n/a
ACT (middle 50%)	23-27
average HS GPA	3.55

Deadlines

regular decision	1/15; 12/1 priority
application fee (online)	$100 ($60)
fee waiver for applicants with financial need	yes

COST & AID

tuition	in-state: $8,484; out-of state: $25,248
room & board	$7,700
total need-based institutional scholarships/grants	$39,546,906
% of students apply for need-based aid	62
% receiving need-based scholarship or grant aid	36
% receiving aid whose need was fully met	8
average aid package	$11,991
average student loan debt upon graduation	$19,528

Norfolk State University

Norfolk State University
700 Park Avenue
Norfolk, Virginia 23504
Ph: (800) 274-1821
admissions@nsu.edu
www.nsu.edu/admissions

Norfolk State University is one of the nation's largest historically black universities. The university has evolved from a modest teachers' college to a doctoral-granting institution with a solid track record of producing outstanding graduates in every field of human endeavor. Norfolk State University's mission is to provide an affordable high-quality education for an ethnically and culturally diverse student population, equipping its students with the capability to become productive citizens who continuously contribute to a global and rapidly changing society. Strategic imperatives involve high-quality academic instruction, efficient management and a solid fiscal foundation.

ACCESS **Techno-Scholars Program**

The Techno-Scholars Program is designed to aid targeted male students who live in Norfolk (ages 12 to 16) become goal-oriented and community-conscious. This intervention is provided to inspire and prepare students for college and/or career success, thereby reducing their likelihood of falling prey to risk factors that affect African-American males. Participants will meet on-site at least five hours a week and/or via webcam and be matched with three different mentors. Community Mentors will provide positive guidance, academic assistance, life skills and male development sessions, and join students in social, cultural and educational field trips. Additionally, Career Professional Mentors will expose participants to their respective careers via workplace shadowing, panel discussions, career fairs and technical periodicals. Collegiate Mentors will provide academic tutoring, homework assistance and exposure to their respective technology studies and campus environments via classroom visits, related student programs and activities.

OPPORTUNITY **Financial Aid Awareness Month**

February is Financial Aid Awareness Month. During this month, the Financial Aid Office at Norfolk State hosts a number of events designed to improve financial literacy, deliver financial aid and scholarship information and provide personalized assistance to both current and prospective students. Parents and student are encouraged to participate in these activities. Some of the events are as follows: FAFSA Workshop, Financial Literacy Workshop and Scholarship Essay Writing Workshop. These activities attract new and prospective students as well as currently enrolled students.

SUCCESS **UNI 101**

UNI 101 is a course designed to help first-year undergraduate students adjust to the university, develop a better understanding of the college environment and acquire essential academic success skills. Common themes include Norfolk State's mission and history, orientation to campus services, students' rights and responsibilities and an appreciation of service-learning civic engagement. Students gain an overview of their learning strengths and weaknesses, and understand their learning style to learn more effectively and accomplish their goals.

SUCCESS **The Academy for Collegiate Excellence and Student Success (ACCESS)**

Norfolk State University's Academy for Collegiate Excellence and Student Success has been designed to prepare admitted freshmen for study at the college-level. Participants normally demonstrate academic achievement in high school, but have lower college examination (SAT/ACT) scores than are required for regular admission. Through intensive course work in areas such as communication skills and mathematics and through a required University Orientation course that stresses study skills and adjustment to college, these students are successful by the end of the freshman year.

FAST FACTS

STUDENT PROFILE

# of degree-seeking undergraduates	5,194
% male/female	38/62
% African American	85
% American Indian or Alaska Native	<1
% Asian or Pacific Islander	1
% Hispanic	1.5
% White	5
% International	n/a
% Pell grant recipients	55

First-generation and minority alums Nathan McCall, best-selling author, former reporter, The *Washington Post*; Rear Admiral (retired) Evelyn J. Fields, former director NOAA Corps (first woman/African-American to hold this position); Derek Dingle, executive editor of *Black Enterprise Magazine*

ACADEMICS

full-time faculty	269
full-time minority faculty	n/a
student-faculty ratio	18:1
average class size	18
% first-year retention rate	70
% graduation rate (6 years)	31

Popular majors Business, Nursing, Interdisciplinary Studies, Psychology, Mass Communications

CAMPUS LIFE

% live on campus (% freshmen)	43 (75)

Multicultural student clubs and organizations Caribbean Students Association, Gospel Choir/Voices of Inspiration, NAACP, National Society of Black Engineers, National Society of Minorities in Hospitality, Spanish Club

Athletics NCAA Division I, Mid-Eastern Athletic Conference

ADMISSIONS

# of applicants	3,973
% accepted	64
# of first-year students enrolled	966
SAT Critical Reading (middle 50%)	390-470
SAT Math (middle 50%)	400-470
SAT Writing (middle 50%)	380-460
ACT (middle 50%)	17-19
average HS GPA	2.71

Deadlines

priority deadline	5/31
regular admission	rolling
application fee (online)	$35 ($25)
fee waiver for applicants with financial need	yes

COST & AID

tuition	in-state: $6,327; out-of-state: $19,380
room & board	$7,329
total need-based institutional scholarships/grants	n/a
% of students apply for need-based aid	92.5
% of students receive aid	98.7
% receiving need-based scholarship or grant aid	89.9
% receiving aid whose need was fully met	8.6
average aid package	$8,834
average student loan debt upon graduation	$15,467

Old Dominion University

Old Dominion University
108 Rollins Hall
5115 Hampton Boulevard
Norfolk, VA 23529
Ph: (757) 683- 3685
admissions@odu.edu
www.odu.edu

Old Dominion University expects its students to thrive in the modern world, seek possibility around every corner, and know that knowledge and experience lead to success. With more than 160 mind-expanding programs, including 69 undergraduate degrees, and internships in every imaginable field, students are able to bring their thoughts to life at ODU. Students are a part of a vibrant, diverse, learning community and are encouraged to take advantage of the campus environment to understand and develop an appreciation of the different cultures, traditions and lifestyles in which they will encounter during and after their undergraduate experience at ODU.

"I chose ODU because I wanted diversity and ODU made me feel at home and comfortable. Out of the many schools that I looked into ODU made me feel like I was getting the true college experience."
– Brittany S., '10
Goodview, VA
Communications

> ACCESS **Upward Bound**

Located on the campus of Old Dominion University, the Upward Bound Program has two phases, a summer residential phase and an academic year phase. During the summer, students reside on campus for six weeks and receive intensive classroom instructions to prepare them for the upcoming school year. During the academic year phase, students attend sessions on Saturdays and receive individualized tutorial instructions designed to enrich their performance in high school classes. The Program is offered to ninth through twelfth grade students who reside in Norfolk and Portsmouth. Selected students shall show potential for success in a two or four-year college, but because of inadequate educational preparation, admission to such an institute would be difficult without the benefit of Upward Bound.

> OPPORTUNITY **Career Advantage Program (CAP)**

Old Dominion University's partnership with employers, alumni, mentors, and the community provides a wealth of experience opportunities for students through student employment, internships, cooperative education, employer events and career fairs. The Career Advantage Program (CAP) incorporates a wide variety of career related activities and *guarantees* all undergraduate students a credit bearing, practical work experience related to their major. At last count, there were more than 4,665 internships and career-relevant experiences available to students.

> SUCCESS **Student Support Services (SSS)**

Student Support Services is a comprehensive program designed to promote retention and academic success in college. It provides participants with academic and support services in a caring environment that seeks to ensure their successful completion of a baccalaureate degree at ODU. Services are provided free of charge to participants, who must apply to join the program, and include tutoring, academic advising, counseling, mentoring workshops, financial advising and cultural enrichment. Student Support Services not only helps students succeed at the undergraduate level but also encourages them to pursue graduate studies.

FAST FACTS

STUDENT PROFILE

# of degree-seeking undergraduates	17,891
% male/female	45/55
% African American	24
% American Indian or Alaska Native	1
% Asian or Pacific Islander	5
% Hispanic	4
% White	61
% International	2
% Pell grant recipients	25.7

ACADEMICS

full-time faculty	697
full-time minority faculty	154
student-faculty ratio	17:1
average class size	25
% first-year retention rate	80
% graduation rate (6 years)	51

Popular majors Criminal Justice, Business Administration, Education, Nursing, Engineering

CAMPUS LIFE

% live on campus (% freshmen)	25 (72)

Multicultural student clubs and organizations Black Student Alliance, Global Student Friendship, Latino Student Alliance, Society of Hispanic Professional Engineers, The F.O.R.E.I.G.N.E.R's, T.R.U.S.T, Xeqtion, African Caribbean Association, 3D, D.E.S.T.I.N.E.D

Athletics NCAA Division I, Colonial Athletic Association

ADMISSIONS

# of applicants	9,878
% accepted	72
# of first-year students enrolled	2,755
SAT Critical Reading (middle 50%)	480-570
SAT Math (middle 50%)	490-590
SAT Writing (middle 50%)	470-570
ACT (middle 50%)	18-23
average HS GPA	3.3

Deadlines

early action	12/1
regular decision	2/1
application fee (online)	$50 ($50)
fee waiver for applicants with financial need	yes

COST & AID

tuition	in-state $7,890; out-of-state $22,230
room & board	$8,700
total need-based institutional scholarships/grants	$36,625,615
% of students apply for need-based aid	70
% of students receive aid	69
% receiving need-based scholarship or grant aid	34
% receiving aid whose need was fully met	33
average aid package	$7,701
average student loan debt upon graduation	$17,250

University of Mary Washington

The University of Mary Washington is a mid-sized, public college that combines rich history and tradition with academic achievement. Nationally ranked as one of the top liberal arts colleges in the country, Mary Washington's academic program is rigorous, focusing on preparing students for success after college. The university's focus on diversity outreach is noteworthy, especially with the introduction of the Rappahannock Scholars Program, a program aimed at college preparation and guaranteed admission for local high school students of underrepresented groups. The University of Mary Washington campus is located in the picturesque, culturally active city of Fredericksburg, Va., only a short drive from Washington, D.C. and Richmond, Va.

ACCESS Rappahannock Scholars Program

In participation with local high schools in the Northern Neck region of Virginia, the Rappahannock Scholars Program guarantees admission to the University of Mary Washington when program criteria are met. The Rappahannock Scholars Program also provides support, guidance and encouragement throughout high school for prospective students to prepare for success in college. Students who attend participating high schools and exhibit promising academic, economic and leadership characteristics may be nominated by guidance counselors for the Rappahannock Scholars Program. Preference is given to students of underrepresented groups who will add cultural diversity to the university campus, first-generation students and students from economically disadvantaged backgrounds.

SUCCESS Summer Orientation Program

Summer Orientation Program begins five days prior to the beginning of classes, new students arrive on-campus and partake in various programs and activities designed to help them get to know each other, and to prepare for a successful first year at the University.

SUCCESS James Farmer Multicultural Center

The University of Mary Washington's James Farmer Multicultural Center facilitates student learning and personal development, particularly that of underrepresented groups, by increasing students' awareness and knowledge of diversity issues. Of particular note is the Student Transition Program, a three-week summer enrichment program for accepted students from underrepresented groups.

SUCCESS Study Skills Workshop

Mary Washington's Office of Academic Services offers a series of workshops that provide important strategies for academic success. Study Skills Workshops are original because they are developed and presented by Mary Washington students themselves. Workshop topics include Time Management, Test Taking Strategies, How to Study: Strategies for Success In and Out of Class and more. Study Skills Tutorials are also available online.

"My career goal is to become a successful businessman. Being team leader for the Service Learning Project at UMW has made me cognizant of the critical components needed to become an effective leader."

– Charles R., '11
Jersey City, NJ
Business Administration

University of Mary Washington
1301 College Avenue
Fredericksburg, VA 22401
Ph: (540) 654-2000
admit@umw.edu
www.umw.edu

FAST FACTS

STUDENT PROFILE	
# of degree-seeking undergraduates	4,354
% male/female	36/64
% African American	5
% American Indian or Alaska Native	<1
% Asian or Pacific Islander	5
% Hispanic	4
% White	58
% International	<1
% Pell grant recipients	13
ACADEMICS	
full-time faculty	239
full-time minority faculty	34
student-faculty ratio	15:1
average class size	22
% first-year retention rate	83
% graduation rate (6 years)	77
Popular majors Business Administration, Psychology, Biology, Education	
CAMPUS LIFE	
% live on campus (% freshmen)	57 (93)
Multicultural student clubs and organizations Black Student Association, Brothers of a New Direction, Students Educating and Empowering for Diversity, Hispanic Group, Women of Color	
Athletics NCAA Division III, Capital Athletic Conference	
ADMISSIONS	
# of applicants	4,766
% accepted	77
# of first-year students enrolled	966
SAT Critical Reading (middle 50%)	540-630
SAT Math (middle 50%)	530-600
SAT Writing (middle 50%)	530-610
ACT (middle 50%)	24-26
average HS GPA	3.29-3.85
Deadlines	
early action	11/15
regular decision	2/1
application fee (online)	$50 ($50)
COST & AID	
tuition	in-state: $8,806; out-of-state: $20,534
room & board	$8,612
total need-based institutional scholarships/grants	n/a
% of students apply for need-based aid	53
% of students receive aid	28
% receiving need-based scholarship or grant aid	15
% receiving aid whose need was fully met	4
average aid package	$8,000
average student loan debt upon graduation	$14,500

University of Virginia

University of Virginia
Box 400160
Charlottesville, VA 22904-4160
Ph: (434) 924-3587
undergradadmission@virginia.edu
www.virginia.edu

Founded by Thomas Jefferson, the University of Virginia has three core standards when admitting students: accessibility, diversity and affordability. As a research university, the University of Virginia values the liberal arts and boasts strong undergraduate programs in engineering, nursing, architecture, leadership and public policy, commerce and education, as well as the liberal arts and sciences. The University is committed to meeting the financial needs of every single student who qualifies for admission, regardless of economic circumstances. Its 14,297 undergraduate students come from every state, more than 100 nations, and every imaginable background. At 88.9%, the University of Virginia holds the highest graduation rate among major public institutions in America for African Americans and as of 2010, has maintained this distinction for sixteen consecutive years. Students are encouraged to take ownership of the University community and to become leaders not just at the University of Virginia, but in the world.

OPPORTUNITY **Access UVA**

Access UVa is a comprehensive financial aid plan that includes a new commitment to eliminate need-based loans with grants that low-income students do not have to repay as part of their financial aid package. For other students, the University caps the amount of need-based loans offered so that no student is left with an excessive amount of debt upon graduation. University of Virginia has pledged to meet 100 percent of demonstrated financial need for all undergraduate students, and will provide comprehensive financial education to prospective and current students and their families.

"Education is the great equalizer, and at UVA, AccessUVA facilitates that pursuit. You've already got the talent, AccessUVA provides the opportunity."

– Doralicia A. (Allie), '11
Woodbridge, VA
Political Philosophy, Policy, and Law

OPPORTUNITY **The Outreach Office**

The Outreach Office is a unit within the Office of Admission created specifically to work with minority, first generation, and low income students. The office oversees multicultural weekends, assisting students and families with visitations to the University, offers college counseling, and works with the financial aid office and scholarships programs specifically to encourage diversity.

SUCCESS **Transition Programs**

The College of Arts and Sciences Transition Program assists students accepted into the College with the college transition through academic and social programs. The School of Engineering Bridge Program supports students entering in the field of Engineering through academic programs and research. The Rainey Scholars Program is specifically for entering low income students and offers them academic and social support.

SUCCESS **Peer and Faculty Mentor Programs**

There are Peer and Faculty Mentor Programs specifically for minorities and low income students coming to the University. The Office of African American Affairs has established a Parent Organization that works together on behalf of African American students' experiences at the University.

FAST FACTS

STUDENT PROFILE

# of degree-seeking undergraduates	14,297
% male/female	44/56
% African American	9
% American Indian or Alaska Native	<1
% Asian or Pacific Islander	13
% Hispanic	6
% White	63
% International	6
% Pell grant recipients	7.8

First-generation and minority alumni Sean Patrick Thomas, actor, "Save the Last. Dance", "Courage Under Fire", "Barbershop", "The District"; Thomas Jones, pro-football player for the New York Jets; Helen Elizabeth, Assistant Secretary for Tax Policy at the Department of Treasury in Obama Administration; Dawn Staley, professionally in the WNBA/ head basketball coach at Temple University/ won three Olympic gold medals as a member of U.S. women's basketball teams

ACADEMICS

full-time faculty	2,125
full-time minority faculty	472
student-faculty ratio	16:1
average class size	25
% first year retention rate	97
% graduation rate (6 years)	93

Popular majors Psychology, History, English, Biology, Government and International Affairs

CAMPUS LIFE

% live on campus (% freshmen)	43 (100)

Multicultural student clubs and organizations Black Student Alliance, Asian Pacific American Leadership Training Institute (APALTI), Latino Student Alliance, American Indian Student Union, Brothers United Celebrating Knowledge and Success (BUCKS), Association of African and Caribbean Cultures, National Society of Black Engineers (NSBE) and Hispanic Engineers (NSHE)

Athletics NCAA Division I, Atlantic Coast Conference (ACC)

ADMISSIONS

# of applicants	22,514
% accepted	32
# of first-year students enrolled	3,286
SAT Critical Reading (middle 50%)	600-710
SAT Math (middle 50%)	620-740
SAT Writing (middle 50%)	610-720
ACT (middle 50%)	29-33
average HS GPA	n/a

Deadlines

early action	11/1
regular decision	1/1
application fee (online)	$60 ($60)
fee waiver for students with financial need	yes

COST & AID

tuition	in-state: $11,794; out-of-state: $36,788
room & board	$9,036
total need-based institutional scholarships/grants	$50,003,425
% of students apply for need-based aid	61
% of students receive aid	44
% receiving need-based scholarship/grant aid	n/a
% receiving aid whose need was fully met	100
average aid package	VA: $12,000; Non-VA: $27,000
average student loan debt upon graduation	$19,016

Virginia Commonwealth University

Virginia Commonwealth University
821 West Franklin Street
Richmond, VA 23284
Ph: (804) 828-1222
ugrad@vcu.edu
www.vcu.edu

Situated in Richmond, Virginia's capital city since 1779, Virginia Commonwealth University (VCU) continues to grow in size, programs and students. With more than 32,000 undergraduate, graduate and professional students, the university offers prestigious programs that have developed the university into an institution with an international reputation. VCU is one of the nation's top research universities, ranking among the top universities in the country in sponsored research. The university enrolls students in 208 certificate and degree programs in the arts, sciences and humanities. Sixty-five of the programs are unique in Virginia, many of them crossing the disciplines of Virginia Commonwealth University's 15 schools and one college. Since its founding, the university has combined the traditional and nontraditional, creating diversity in our academic programs, campus events, students, faculty and staff.

ACCESS Primeros Pasos (First Steps)

This one-day program, designed to motivate and encourage Latino high school students to attend college, showcases all that the university has to offer. Virginia Commonwealth University students, parents, administrators, faculty and alumni participate throughout the day sharing their experiences. Activities include a bilingual workshop for parents regarding financial aid and scholarships, a panel discussion with university students from the Latino community, conversations with undergraduate admissions counselors, and campus tours.

"Adjusting to the academic demands and college life was made easier thanks to the advising provided through the University College. My advisors have always been helpful in regards to classes, financial aid and school. I always receive encouraging words and motivation from them that give me the boost I need to continue."

– Moises E., '11
Alexandria, VA
Clinical Exercise Science, Spanish

OPPORTUNITY Acceleration Program

Students admitted into this program begin college with an on-campus, four-week summer enrichment program where they are exposed to a pre-health-specific math and science curriculum. Students participate in internships in various clinical health service provider settings and receive a stipend. Students are expected to commit to 50 hours of volunteer work per year in community health provider settings and receive specialized, career-related academic advising and support services throughout the program.

SUCCESS University College (UC)

The VCU University College is a central home for university-wide programs and resources that help to enhance students' undergraduate academic experience. Through academic advising, tutoring, writing assistance, group study sessions, orientation programs and courses introducing students to the demands of a university education, the University College provides opportunities for students to achieve greater levels of academic success.

SUCCESS Office of Multicultural Student Affairs (OMSA)

A resource for students, faculty and staff, the primary mission of the VCU Office of Multicultural Student Affairs is to assist traditionally underserved and/or underrepresented student populations (i.e. race, ethnicity, sexual orientation, and gender) through advising, support, program development, retention, and mentoring, as well as by promoting an appreciation of diversity throughout the campus community.

FAST FACTS

STUDENT PROFILE

# of degree-seeking undergraduates	23,149
% male/female	43/57
% African American	17
% American Indian or Alaska Native	1
% Asian or Pacific Islander	10
% Hispanic	5
% White	58
% International	4
% Pell grant recipients	18

ACADEMICS

full-time faculty	1,990
full-time minority faculty	390
student-faculty ratio	18:1
average class size	28
% first-year retention rate	84
% graduation rate (6 years)	51

Popular majors Biology, Psychology, Mass Communications, Business, and Criminal Justice

CAMPUS LIFE

% live on campus (% freshmen)	22 (79)

Multicultural student clubs and organizations African Student Union, Black Caucus, Filipino Americans Coming Together (FACT), Indian Student Association, Latino Student Association, NAACP at VCU, Vietnamese Student Association, Persian American Students, Caribbean Student Organization, and many more

Athletics NCAA Division I, Colonial Athletic Association (CAA)

ADMISSIONS

# of applicants	16,915
% accepted	59
# of first-year students enrolled	3,665
For middle 50% of admitted students:	
SAT Critical Reading (middle 50%)	500-600
SAT Math (middle 50%)	500-610
SAT Writing (middle 50%)	490-600
ACT (middle 50%)	21-26
average HS GPA	3.17-3.81

Deadlines

scholarship consideration	12/1
recommended freshman deadline	1/15
application fee (online)	$50($40)
fee waiver for applicants with financial need	yes

COST & AID

tuition	in-state: $9,517; out-of-state: $22,948
room & board	$8,231
% of students apply for need-based aid	59
% of students receive aid	47
% receiving need-based scholarship or grant aid	35
% receiving aid whose need was fully met	16
average aid package	$8,381
average student loan debt upon graduation	$22,610

Washington and Lee University

Founded in 1749, Washington and Lee University is the nation's ninth-oldest institution of higher learning. The university was the first in the U.S. to offer courses in business and journalism, and continues as the only institution ranked in the nation's top 20 liberal arts schools to have accredited schools of both business and journalism. As a national institution with teacher-scholars committed to teaching in small classes, Washington and Lee's 40 undergraduate majors are augmented by numerous study abroad opportunities and interdisciplinary courses and programs. The student-run Honor System defines a community of trust in which exams are unproctored and facilities are open 24/7. The university's strengths include the Speaking Tradition and the widely regarded quadrennial Mock Presidential Convention. Washington and Lee's students routinely win prestigious fellowships, including the Fulbright, Luce and Goldwater.

OPPORTUNITY **Diversity Open Houses**

It is nearly impossible to know if a university is the right "fit" unless you visit campus. Through a series of three day, all-expenses-paid diversity open houses at Washington & Lee, multicultural, low-income and first-generation students come to campus to meet current students, sit in on classes, and experience historic Lexington, Virginia for themselves.

"As a first-generation college student and the oldest of seven children, I have been the first to experience 'college life.' I knew that I wanted to go to a small school where I could really get a feel for what the students and faculty stood for, and where no one could say that their voice would not be heard. "

– Regina M., '09
Warrenton, VA
English, Sociology, Anthropology

OPPORTUNITY **QuestBridge**

Washington and Lee University partners with QuestBridge, a national program that connects bright, motivated, low-income students to 30 of the top colleges in the country. By centralizing information for both applicants and universities, this program makes the distance between intelligent, disadvantaged students and higher education much shorter and smoother. QuestBridge not only prepares applicants for the transition to college, but for success throughout college and beyond.

OPPORTUNITY **Johnson Scholarship Program in Leadership and Integrity**

An unprecedented gift of $100 million is allowing Washington and Lee University to invest in students of exceptional academic and personal promise by giving them the opportunity to graduate free of debt. Two hundred finalists — selected for their academic achievements and leadership potential — are invited to interview on campus each year. Ultimately, 44 Johnson scholars are named for each enrolling class, and they all receive scholarships in the amount of at least tuition, room and board.

OPPORTUNITY **H.J. Heinz Scholarship**

The H.J. Heinz Scholarship provides full tuition, room and board, plus a stipend for books and personal expenses for disadvantaged students who are interested in pursuing a career in business. Award winners also benefit from paid summer internships with the Heinz Corporation.

SUCCESS **The Bonner Scholars and Shepherd Poverty Program**

These programs both engage students in service within the Lexington community and beyond. The Bonner Scholars program provides scholarship assistance to students who commit to 1,800 hours of community service over four years. The Shepherd Poverty Program integrates academics with community service through interdisciplinary academic courses and an eight-week summer internship program.

Washington and Lee University
204 West Washington Street
Lexington, VA 24450
Ph: (540) 458-8710
admissions@wlu.edu
www.wlu.edu

FAST FACTS

STUDENT PROFILE

# of degree-seeking undergraduates	1,757
% male/female	50/50
% African American	3
% American Indian or Alaska Native	<1
% Asian or Pacific Islander	3
% Hispanic	2
% White	85
% Multiracial	2
% Ethnicity unreported	2
% International	4
% Pell grant recipients	4.2

First-generation and minority alumni Dr. Kenneth P. Ruscio, president, Washington and Lee University; Dr. Theodore C. DeLaney, head, history department, Washington and Lee University; William Thornton, senior vice president, SunTrust Bank; William B. Hill, Jr., former associate judge, George State Supreme Court

ACADEMICS

full-time faculty	187
full-time minority faculty	22
student-faculty ratio	9:1
average class size	15
% first-year retention rate	94
% graduation rate (6 years)	89

Popular majors Business Administration, Economics, Journalism, History, English

CAMPUS LIFE

% live on campus (% freshmen)	60 (100)

Multicultural student clubs and organizations International House, International Relations Association, Multicultural Student Association, Pan Asian Association Cultural Exchange, SABU

Athletics NCAA Division III, Old Dominion Conference

ADMISSIONS

# of applicants	6,386
% accepted	19
# of first-year students enrolled	471
SAT Critical Reading (middle 50%)	650-730
SAT Math (middle 50%)	660-730
SAT Writing (middle 50%)	640-730
ACT (middle 50%)	29-32
average HS GPA	n/a
Deadlines	
early decision	11/15 and 1/2
regular decision	1/2
Johnson scholarship	12/1
application fee (online)	$50 ($50)
fee waiver for applicants with financial need	yes

COST & AID

tuition	$40,990
room & board	$10,688
total need-based institutional scholarships/grants	$22,364,879
% of students apply for need-based aid	43
% of students with need to receive aid	100
% receiving aid whose need was fully met	100
average aid package	$34,315
average student loan debt upon graduation	$23,807

The Evergreen State College

The Evergreen State College is particularly committed to issues of social justice; it houses several public service centers, two of which serve local Native American communities, and the college offers extensive counseling and support to veterans who enroll in the school. Evergreen approaches learning in a dynamic, unique way. Students enroll in interdisciplinary, theme-based 'programs,' rather than in individual courses. Also, they receive narrative evaluations from their professors, rather than letter grades.

ACCESS College Success Foundation/Achievers Programs

Evergreen State works with the College Success Foundation, a non-profit organization that provides college scholarships and mentoring to low-income, high-potential students. The college supports the Achievers College Experience, which provides Achievers Scholarship Candidates with a college-readiness experience.

ACCESS Boys & Girls Club Partnership

The Office of Admissions sustains relationships with the Boys & Girls Club at 11 sites in Washington State and four in Portland, Oregon. Mentoring, high school course advising, college search counseling, and scholarship/financial aid assistance is provided.

ACCESS Gaining Early Awareness and Readiness for Undergraduate Programs (GEAR UP)

Low-income middle and high school students are encouraged through this program to stay in school, study hard, have high expectations, and go to college. Evergreen works in partnership with a number of national, state and local organizations to provide services to 1,200 Washington state students at 3 schools.

ACCESS Upward Bound

Evergreen serves 90 low-income students needing academic support who live in Tacoma and the Reservation of the Puyallup (Indian) Nation. The students are provided with tutoring, counseling, mentoring, cultural enrichment, and work-study programs in their preparation for college entrance.

> ***"I love the education that I received at Evergreen! I felt out of place my first year, and there will be times you might feel lost and alone too. But since I got involved in the campus community, my experiences here at Evergreen have been amazing. When times are rough, there will be people around you that genuinely care about your success and are here to help you."***
>
> *– Natasha C., '09*
> *Portland, OR*
> *Interdisciplinary Studies, Sociology*

SUCCESS Multicultural Services

First Peoples' Advising Services provides students of color with comprehensive academic, social and personal advising, as well as referral services to campus and community resources. Evergreen also offers a First Peoples' Scholars program, which offers students of color a chance to get acclimated to Evergreen by visiting in small groups.

SUCCESS Gateways for Incarcerated Youth

This academic program is dedicated to helping incarcerated youth develop self-esteem, achieve academic success, and increase their cultural awareness. Evergreen students are given the opportunity to be peer learners with incarcerated young men, held in two maximum-security institutions. Both groups of students address issues of diversity, equality and critical thinking.

SUCCESS Keep Enhancing Yourself (KEY) Student Services

Evergreen State offers this federally-funded program to students who meet eligibility requirements. Participants benefit from a comprehensive support system designed to increase graduation rates, including the assistance of a personal mentor. The campus also hosts a number of workshops and social events for participating students.

SUCCESS Washington TRIO Expansion Program (WaTEP)

Program staff strive to increase the retention, academic achievement and graduation rates of students by providing comprehensive academic needs assessment, academic and career planning, tutoring services and financial aid guidance. Eligible students must be first generation, low income, or have a documented physical or learning disability.

The Evergreen State College
2700 Evergreen Parkway NW
Olympia, WA 98505
Ph: (360) 867-6170
admissions.evergreen.edu
www.evergreen.edu

FAST FACTS

STUDENT PROFILE

# of degree-seeking undergraduates	4,227
% male/female	46/54
% African American	4
% American Indian or Alaska Native	4
% Asian or Pacific Islander	6
% Hispanic	5
% White	81
% International	<1
% Pell grant recipients	44

First-generation and minority alumni Sharon Tomiko Santos, former Washington Representative

ACADEMICS

full-time faculty	234
full-time minority faculty	54
student-faculty ratio	23:1
average class size	40
% first-year retention rate	73
% graduation rate (6 years)	58

Popular areas of study Culture & Language, Social Sciences, Liberal Arts/Interdisciplinary Studies, Expressive Arts, Environmental Studies

CAMPUS LIFE

% live on campus (% freshmen)	21 (80)

Multicultural student clubs and organizations Black Student Union, Committee in Solidarity with the People of El Salvador (CISPES), Iraqi Solidarity Committee, MEChA, Women of Color Coalition

Athletics NAIA, Cascade Collegiate Conference (CCC)

ADMISSIONS

# of applicants	3,337
% accepted	94
# of first-year students enrolled	3,135
SAT Critical Reading (middle 50%)	510-640
SAT Math (middle 50%)	460-590
SAT Writing (middle 50%)	480-590
ACT (middle 50%)	21-27
average HS GPA	3.08

Deadlines

regular decision	rolling
application fee (online)	$50 ($50)
fee waiver for applicants with financial need	yes

COST & AID

tuition	in-state: $6,609; out-of-state: $18,069
room & board	$8,052
total need-based institutional scholarships/grants	$1,273,998
% of students apply for need-based aid	70
% of students receive aid	80
% receiving need-based scholarship or grant aid	80
% receiving aid whose need was fully met	8
average aid package	$9,100
average student loan debt upon graduation	$16,987

Gonzaga University

Gonzaga University
502 East Boone Avenue
Spokane, WA 99258
Ph: (509) 313-6572
admissions@gonzaga.edu
www.gonzaga.edu

Gonzaga University is a medium-sized, private, four-year university founded in the Jesuit Catholic tradition. Gonzaga's educational philosophy is based on the Ignation model and aims to educate the mind, body and spirit through an integration of science, art, faith, reason, action and contemplation. This focus on the individual is at the core of Gonzaga's emphasis on academic success, community service and student involvement. Gonzaga's ongoing outreach into its local community includes diversity education and the installation of a college-bound culture in neighboring Yakima Valley.

OPPORTUNITY Act Six

Act Six, open to Spokane-area high school seniors, provides four-year, full-tuition, full-need scholarships to attend Gonzaga University. Act Six trains and prepares a small group of students in the year prior to college, equipping them to support each other, succeed academically, and grow as service-minded leaders and agents of transformation. The rigorous selection process seeks to identify student leaders who are passionate about learning, eager to foster intercultural relationships, willing to step out of their comfort zones, committed to serving those around them, and ready to make a difference on campus and at home. The selection process also places high value on applicants' teamwork, critical thinking and communication skills, and academic potential. While ethnicity and family income are factors in selecting an intentionally diverse group of scholars, there are no income restrictions, and students from all ethnic backgrounds are encouraged to apply. The deadline to apply for this competitive program is November 1.

OPPORTUNITY Gonzaga University Community Scholarship

The Gonzaga University Community Scholarship is a $20,000 award over four years for outstanding students who are first-generation college bound, from an under-represented cultural background or whose unique life experiences would contribute to the diversity of the Gonzaga community. Scholarship recipients should demonstrate significant contributions to school or community in promoting cultural awareness and exhibit intercultural leadership qualities. Students are automatically considered for the award upon admission to the university.

SUCCESS Academic Cultural Excellence (ACE) Student Leadership Program

The ACE program prepares African American, Hispanic, Asian and Native American students to assume leadership roles in diversity education and training for the purpose of promoting cross-cultural understanding and improving race relations within the Gonzaga campus and Spokane community. Students gain an understanding of servant leadership, develop facilitation skills in diversity training and create opportunities to serve others in pursuit of multicultural competency. Applications for the program are available through the Office of Intercultural Relations.

SUCCESS Building Relationships in Diverse Gonzaga Environments

The Summer BRIDGE Program (Building Relationships in Diverse Gonzaga Environments) is a pre-orientation program designed to support students of color as they enter Gonzaga University in the fall. The program complements the university's general Student Orientation Program by introducing students to diverse Gonzaga faculty, staff and students. Personal relationships are built and stories are shared as new students bond with each other and the Gonzaga campus.

FAST FACTS

STUDENT PROFILE

# of degree-seeking undergraduates	4,735
% male/female	47/53
% African American	1
% American Indian or Alaska Native	<1
% Asian or Pacific Islander	4
% Hispanic	6
% White	76
% Pell grant recipients	15

First-generation and minority alumni Frank Burgess, U.S. federal magistrate; Carl Maxey (deceased), Spokane attorney and civil rights leader; Steven Meneses, president and founder, Continental Financial; Ed Taylor, vice provost, University of Washington

ACADEMICS

full-time faculty	372
full-time minority faculty	30
student-faculty ratio	11:1
average class size	17
% first-year retention rate	92
% graduation rate (6 years)	81

Popular majors Business Administration, Communications, Engineering, Biology, Psychology

CAMPUS LIFE

% live on campus (% freshmen)	57 (95)

Multicultural student clubs and organizations Black Student Union, Chinese Club, Filipino American Student Union, First Nations Student Association, Hawaii Pacific Islanders Club, International Student Union, Japanese Club, La Raza Latina, NAACP – GU Student Chapter, Taiwanese Student Association

Athletics NCAA Division I, West Coast Conference

ADMISSIONS

# of applicants	6,258
% accepted	64
# of first-year students enrolled	1,119
SAT Critical Reading (middle 50%)	530-640
SAT Math (middle 50%)	550-660
SAT Writing (middle 50%)	n/a
ACT (middle 50%)	25-29
average HS GPA	3.6

Deadlines

regular decision	2/1
application fee (online)	$50 ($50)
fee waiver for applicants with financial need	yes

COST & AID

tuition	$31,730
room & board	$8,340
total need-based institutional scholarships/grants	$39,977,193
% of students apply for need-based aid	70
% of students receive aid	54
% receiving need-based scholarship or grant aid	54
% receiving aid whose need was fully met	26
average aid package	$23,089
average student loan debt upon graduation	$24,094

University of Puget Sound

Located in the pristine Pacific Northwest, the University of Puget Sound offers students both the urban amenities of local Tacoma and nearby Seattle, as well as access to a variety of outdoor activities, such as kayaking and hiking. Puget Sound might further appeal to those interested in environmental activism, as it supports a campus-wide sustainability program. Within this dynamic context, the college provides its students a broad-based, liberal arts education that focuses on critical thinking and writing skills. Students also benefit from the School of Music and the School of Business. Puget Sound seeks to create a diverse and welcoming campus community that will cultivate "effective citizen-leaders for a pluralistic world." The mission of the University is to develop in its students the capacities for critical analysis, aesthetic appreciation, sound judgment, and apt expression that will sustain a lifetime of intellectual curiosity, active inquiry, and reasoned independence. A Puget Sound education, both academic and co-curricular, encourages a rich knowledge of self and others, an appreciation of commonality and difference, the full, open, and civil discussion of ideas, thoughtful moral discourse, and the integration of learning, preparing the University's graduates to meet the highest tests of democratic citizenship. The University of Puget Sound is an independent, four-year liberal arts college founded in 1888 and located in Tacoma, Washington.

ACCESS Access Programs

Access Programs, sponsored by Puget Sound, specifically focus on students traditionally underrepresented in higher education. Through a partnership with the Tacoma Public Schools, the program provides day-long sessions, mentoring, tutoring and other programs such as the "Summer Academic Challenge" to participating students. Students in the program are recruited from Tacoma Public middle and high schools and are accepted into the program based on several criteria, including test scores, classroom performance, study habits, attendance patterns and social behavior.

OPPORTUNITY Students of Color Open House

Annually prospective students are invited to participate in a campus event introducing them to the academic and co-curricular opportunities they will experience as enrolled students. Typically scheduled around events in the arts and athletics, the Students of Color Open House enables students to see Puget Sound in action through several settings.

SUCCESS Student Diversity Center

Seeking to support historically underrepresented groups on college campuses, the Student Diversity Center serves as a resource library, study space and meeting space for the many multicultural groups on campus, which range from the Community for Hispanic Awareness to Hui-O-Hawai'i, a group representing native Hawaiians or those seeking to learn more about this culture. The Student Diversity Center also sponsors student programming, maintains a monthly calendar of multicultural events, and fosters communication between campus and Tacoma community groups. The center works with the University to publish an annual Cultural Resource Guide, which apprises students of relevant organizations and services that address culture-specific needs both on campus and in the Tacoma area.

SUCCESS Diversity Theme Year

For 16 years running, the University of Puget Sound sponsors a Diversity Theme Year. The theme year program included lectures, art events and student activities that highlight issues of visibility and invisibility, economic inequality and justice, religious conviction and acceptance of differences. The theme year program has proven successful in highlighting issues of identity and cultural awareness, in strengthening student affinity groups and coalitions, and in giving visibility to many groups that are underrepresented on campus.

University of Puget Sound
1500 N. Warner St.
Tacoma WA 98416
Ph: (253) 879-3211
admission@pugetsound.edu
www.pugetsound.edu

FAST FACTS

STUDENT PROFILE

# of degree-seeking undergraduates	2,577
% male/female	41/59
% African American	2
% American Indian or Alaska Native	1
% Asian or Pacific Islander	9
% Hispanic	5
% White	73
% International	<1
% Pell grant recipients	14

First-generation and minority alumni Thomas Dixon '71, founder, Tacoma Urban League; Jill Nishi '89, program manager, U.S. Libraries Initiative, Bill and Melinda Gates Foundation; George Obiozor '69, Nigerian Ambassador to the United States; Seema Sueko '94, founder, Mo'olelo Performing Arts Company

ACADEMICS

full-time faculty	227
full-time minority faculty	18
student-faculty ratio	12:1
average class size	n/a
% first-year retention rate	86
% graduation rate (6 years)	80

Popular majors Business Administration/ Management, Psychology, English Language and Literature, Biology, International Political Economy

CAMPUS LIFE

% live on campus (% freshmen)	60 (98)

Multicultural student clubs and organizations Asian and Pacific American Student Union, B-GLAD, Black Student Union, Community for Hispanic Awareness, First Nations, Hui-O-Hawai'i, International Club, Jewish Students Organization, Muslim Student Alliance, Pagan Student Alliance, Religious Organizations Council, Vox

Athletics NCAA Division III, Northwest Conference

ADMISSIONS

# of applicants	6,586
% accepted	52
# of first-year students enrolled	625
SAT Critical Reading (middle 50%)	570-680
SAT Math (middle 50%)	560-660
SAT Writing (middle 50%)	560-670
ACT (middle 50%)	26-30
average HS GPA	3.52

Deadlines

early decision I	11/15
early decision II	1/2
regular decision	2/15
application fee (online)	$50
fee waiver for applicants with financial need	yes

COST & AID

tuition	$35,440
room & board	$9,190
total need-based institutional scholarships/grants	$37,174,189
% of students apply for need-based aid	70
% of students receive aid	64
% receiving need-based scholarship or grant aid	63
% receiving aid whose need was fully met	19
average aid package	$23,776
average student loan debt upon graduation	$27,648

Washington State University

Washington State University is a public, co-educational, land-grant research institution that offers a premier undergraduate experience. The university is known for world-class research, scholarship and arts; the exemplary working and learning environment fosters student engagement. The university works hard to embody a set of core values: inquiry and knowledge, engagement and application, leadership, diversity, character, stewardship and teamwork. Toward this end, the university fosters learning, inquiry and engagement. Washington State University enhances the intellectual, creative and practical abilities of individuals, institutions and communities.

> ACCESS GEAR UP Program / Educational Talent Search / Upward Bound

The GEAR UP Program prepares middle and high school students for success in higher education. Serving low-income, migrant and rural students, the program provides tutoring, an enriched curriculum, visits to the Washington State campus, motivational speakers, and a limited number of scholarships to the university. The Educational Talent Search is designed to assist middle school and high school students, along with high school dropouts, with the necessary understanding, knowledge, skills and self-esteem to continue in, and graduate from, high school. This program also helps students that have been traditionally underrepresented to explore training and educational options, and enroll in post-secondary institutions. Upward Bound prepares and motivates low-income, first-generation high school students to pursue a college education. The federally funded program offers tutorial services, monthly workshops, a summer residential program, local and extended college visitations, career advising and assistance in researching and applying for financial aid and college admission.

> ACCESS Imagine U at WSU

A number of presenters (professors, graduate students, deans) are brought into underrepresented high schools for hands-on classes and discussion on the various fields of research. Presenters teach an interactive class, demonstration or workshop for different classes in grades seven to 12. This interaction enlightens them to the kinds of careers available to them, inspires the students and gives them motivation to pursue higher education. In the evening, there is a dinner meeting for parents allowing Washington State to develop a relationship with the entire family.

> OPPORTUNITY Future Cougars of Color (FCOC)

Washington State University offers the FCOC scholarship and visitation program for high-achieving high school seniors of color from across the state of Washington. The campus visit gives them insight into the academic environment and student life at the university. Participants who enroll at Washington State are eligible for scholarships of $1,000 to $10,000.

> SUCCESS College Assistance Migrant Program (CAMP) / Student Support Services / Ronald E. McNair Achievement Program

CAMP is designed to support students from migrant and seasonal farm worker backgrounds during their freshman year in college. The program provides students with both financial and academic support. CAMP is specifically designed to identify, recruit and monitor the academic achievement and retention of migrant students. Student Support Services is a college academic assistance program (TRIO) that has been at Washington State since 2001. Its purpose is to assist 160 eligible students per year by providing the academic assistance each student needs to help meet their educational goals. The McNair Achievement Program prepares qualified undergraduates for their future doctoral studies. The goal of the program is to increase the number of underrepresented students in Ph.D programs and to provide undergraduates with opportunities to participate in research activities.

> SUCCESS Future Teachers and Leaders of Color (FTLOC)

Future Teachers and Leaders of Color offers faculty mentoring, career guidance, student support services and scholarship assistance to select undergraduate and graduate students providing opportunities in becoming teachers, principals and educational administrators.

Washington State University
PO Box 641067
Pullman, WA 99164-1067
Ph: (888) 468-6978
admiss2@wsu.edu
www.wsu.edu

FAST FACTS

STUDENT PROFILE

# of degree-seeking undergraduates	21,374
% male/female	49/51
% African American	2
% American Indian or Alaska Native	1
% Asian or Pacific Islander	6
% Hispanic	7
% White	71
% Pell grant recipients	26

First-generation and minority alumni Sherman J. Alexie Jr., award-winning poet, author, screenwriter, film director; Phyllis J. Campbell, president/CEO, Seattle Foundation; James E. Blackwell, sociologist, scholar in the areas of minorities in higher education, social movement in black communities; William Julius Wilson, sociologist, author; Matsuyo Omori Yamamoto, first chief of the Rural Home-Living Improvement section, Japan's agricultural extension

ACADEMICS

full-time faculty	1,200
full-time minority faculty	156
student-faculty ratio	15:1
average class size	17
% first-year retention rate	82
% graduation rate (6 years)	69

Popular majors Business/Marketing, Social Sciences, Communication, Education, Health Professions

CAMPUS LIFE

% live on campus (% freshmen)	36 (99)

Multicultural student clubs and organizations There are clubs that represent African-American, American Indian, Chicano/a, Chinese, Hawaiian/ Pacific Islander, Japanese, Muslim, Russian, Latino/a, Filipino, Indian, Korean, Middle Eastern, Indonesian, Persian, Sikh, Somalian, Taiwanese, Thai and Vietnamese cultures

Athletics NCAA Division I, Pacific-10 Conference

ADMISSIONS

# of applicants	12,427
% accepted	69
# of first-year students enrolled	3,288
SAT Critical Reading (middle 50%)	480-580
SAT Math (middle 50%)	500-610
SAT Writing (middle 50%)	470-570
ACT (middle 50%)	21-26
average HS GPA	3.44

Deadlines

regular decision	rolling
application fee (online)	$50 ($50)
fee waiver for applicants with financial need	yes

COST & AID

tuition	in-state: $9,374; out-of-state: $20,652
room & board	$9,662
total need-based institutional scholarships/grants	$62,578,892
% of students apply for need-based aid	59
% of students receive aid	46
% receiving need-based scholarship or grant aid	31
% receiving aid whose need was fully met	26
average aid package	$12,441
average student loan debt upon graduation	n/a

Western Washington University

With 13,700 students, an increasingly multicultural community, an esteemed Honors Program, and a commitment to the empowerment of undergrads, Western Washington University is a premier choice for driven scholars looking to thrive as young professionals. By offering small classes and faculty mentorship, Western offers the type of individual attention one might only expect from a small private school. Additionally, Western is nationally recognized for environmental leadership, as well as vehicle research and design. *U.S. News & World Report* has ranked Western No. 1 among public, master's-granting universities in the Pacific Northwest and No. 2 in the western United States. Students enjoy a first-rate education, direct access to faculty, a tight-knit community, and an empowering experience at a prominent institution. At Western Washington University, administrators are preparing tomorrow's leaders one student at a time. This is the Western tradition, and for many, a fast track to lifelong success.

ACCESS **Encounter Youth Conference**

The annual Encounter Youth Conference is organized and staffed by students of Western's Ethnic Student Center (ESC), and attended by high school students from around the state. This event is aimed at encouraging minority youth to pursue higher education while developing leadership skills and learning to feel comfortable in a university setting. Workshops topics include media awareness, leadership, and community activism. Academic advising, financial aid, and college admissions guidance is also provided. The most empowering and poignant highlight is always the student panel; current Western students share their experiences, trials, and triumphs with younger students working hard to follow in their footsteps.

ACCESS **Helping Admit New and Diverse Students (HANDS)**

Helping Admit New and Diverse Students (HANDS) recruits and retains today's top leaders from multicultural backgrounds. Based out of the Office of Admissions, HANDS is a taskforce of current students who provide personalized mentoring relationships with prospective students. The HANDS team uses their own student experiences to connect with first generation, low-income, and students of color while providing college admissions guidance. From community outreach to reviewing personal essays, HANDS team members provide access to resources that many underrepresented students may otherwise not have.

"My professors care about me as a person and that definitely has helped me be a much better student. It is amazing—the more confident I feel in my academics, the more I'm able to take on leadership roles that help me model the way for others."

– Abraham R., '10
Bellevue, WA
American Cultural Studies and Spanish

OPPORTUNITY **The Multicultural Achievement Program (MAP)**

Through the MAP program, incoming freshmen and transfer students who have demonstrated an ongoing commitment to multiculturalism and/or diversity in their community are eligible for scholarships ranging from $500 to $2,000. There are additional two-year, $1,000 awards available in the form of on-campus meal plans for incoming freshmen living in the residence halls.

SUCCESS **Student Outreach Services (SOS)**

SOS serves underrepresented, non-traditional, and multicultural students by offering personalized advising on class selection, registration, and major declaration. SOS especially advises Washington State Achievers, Governor's Scholars, and Western's Access program, and plans the Women of Color & Empowerment Dinner and Strategies for Success. SOS's main role is to facilitate a smooth transition to university life and increase retention rates for groups with less historical access and fewer generational ties to higher education.

Western Washington University
WWU Office of Admissions
516 High Street
Bellingham, WA 98225-9009
Ph: (360) 650-3440
admit@wwu.edu
www.wwu.edu

FAST FACTS

STUDENT PROFILE

# of degree-seeking undergraduates	13,653
% male/female	44/56
% African American	2
% American Indian or Alaska Native	2
% Asian or Pacific Islander	7
% Hispanic	5
% White	76

First-generation and minority alumni Joyce Taylor, '84, news anchor, Seattle King 5 News; Jesse Moore, '05, Special Assistant for Public Affairs to the Administration for Children and Families (Presidential appointment), U.S. Department of Health and Human Services; Bill Wright, '60, first African-American USGA Champion (1959)

ACADEMICS

full-time faculty	504
full-time minority faculty	69
student-faculty ratio	21:1
average class size	10-19
% first-year retention rate	85
% graduation rate (6 years)	69

Popular majors Business, Social Sciences, English, Psychology

CAMPUS LIFE

% live on campus	29 (92)

Multicultural student clubs and organizations African Caribbean Club, Black Student Union, Brown Pride, Calling All Colors, Filipino American Student Association, Hui 'O Hawaii, La Mesa Espanola, mEChA (Movimiento Estudiantil Chicano/a de Aztlan), Mixed Identity Student Organization (MISO), MOSAIC, Native American Mentoring Program (NAMP), Native American Student Union, Ritmo Latino, South Asian Student Association, Taiwanese Student Association, Vietnamese Student Association, Western Sister Cities Association

Athletics NCAA Division II, Great Northwest Athletic Conference

ADMISSIONS

# of applicants	9,335
% accepted	74
# of first-year students enrolled	2,748
SAT Critical Reading (middle 50%)	500-620
SAT Math (middle 50%)	510-610
SAT Writing (middle 50%)	490-590
ACT (middle 50%)	22-27
average HS GPA	3.48
Deadlines	
regular decision	3/1
application fee (online)	$50 ($50)
fee waiver for applicants with financial need	yes

COST & AID

tuition	in-state: $4,890; out-of-state: $15,921
room & board	$8,393
total need-based institutional scholarships/grants	$31,088,115
% of students apply for need-based aid	60
% of students receive aid	41
% receiving need-based scholarship or grant aid	31
% receiving aid whose need was fully met	29
average aid package	$11,730
average student loan debt upon graduation	$15,560

Whitman College

Whitman College
345 Boyer Avenue
Walla Walla, WA 99362
Ph: (509) 527-5176
admission@whitman.edu
www.whitman.edu

Founded in 1882, Whitman College is a private, co-educational liberal arts institution. Located in Walla Walla, Wash., four hours southeast of Seattle, Whitman offers an ideal setting for rigorous learning and scholarship and encourages creativity, character, and responsibility. Through the study of humanities, arts and social and natural sciences, Whitman's students develop capacities to analyze, interpret, criticize, communicate and engage. A concentration on basic disciplines, in combination with a supportive residential life program that encourages personal and social development, is intended to foster intellectual vitality, confidence, leadership and the flexibility to succeed in a changing technological, multicultural world.

> ***"The college has done a great job in their efforts to enhance multicultural diversity recruitment programs. With these types of programs, support is available to all students regardless of their cultural background or economic status. The Visit Scholarship Program in particular really gives students a sense for what it would be like to be a Whittie."***
>
> *– Thanh V., '11*
> *Kent, WA*
> *Biochemistry, Biophysics, and Molecular Biology*

ACCESS **Continuing Relationships**

Whitman works collaboratively with a variety of community-based organizations to provide access to more students. Admission officers meet with organization leaders, recruit and counsel students, help arrange campus visits, and assist in scholarship application reading for the organizations. Partners include: One Voice, Bright Prospects, Admission Possible, Summer Search, GEAR-UP, College Horizons, the Achievers Program, and more.

ACCESS **College Horizons**

Whitman College participates annually in College Horizons, a five day pre-college workshop for Native American, Native Hawaiian and Alaska Native high school juniors and seniors. Students work one on one with experienced college guidance counselors and admission officers to prepare for the college admission and financial aid process. Whitman College has hosted the College Horizons program three times in the past 10 years, the most of any participating institution.

ACCESS **Whitman Institute for Summer Enrichment (WISE)**

WISE is an all-expenses-paid, pre-college program for local middle school students who show academic promise and are from first-generation, minority, or low-income families.

OPPORTUNITY **Visit Scholarship Program (VSP)**

Approximately 85 high school seniors from underrepresented socioeconomic, racial, and cultural backgrounds are invited for an expenses-paid visit to Whitman during the fall or spring semester. Visiting students stay with an overnight host in a residence hall, eat in campus dining halls, visit up to two classes, meet with coaches, faculty, staff and student leaders, and interview with an admission officer. The Visit Scholarship Program was created in an effort to increase socioeconomic and multicultural diversity at Whitman College.

OPPORTUNITY **Lomen-Douglas Scholarships**

Students whose backgrounds and experiences demonstrate the ability to contribute to increasing socioeconomic, racial or ethnic diversity awareness at Whitman are chosen to receive these scholarships. Lomen-Douglas scholarships range from $2,000 to $43,000 and vary depending on achievement and financial need.

FAST FACTS

STUDENT PROFILE

# of degree-seeking undergraduates	1,500
% male/female	42/58
% African American	2
% American Indian or Alaska Native	1.5
% Asian or Pacific Islander	10.9
% Hispanic	5.8
% White	67.4
% International	3
% Pell grant recipients	14

First-generation and minority alumni Danielle Garbe, Woodrow Wilson fellow, State Department; Ana Hernandez, President, Luna Textiles; Sarah Wang, College Overseer, Partner in Marr, Jones, & Wang; Bishop Othal Lakey, Presiding Prelate of the Sixth Episcopal District of the Christian Methodist Episcopal (CME) Church

ACADEMICS

full-time faculty	134
full-time minority faculty	22
student-faculty ratio	10:1
average class size	18
% first-year retention rate	93
% graduation rate (6 years)	89

Popular majors Biology, English, History, Environmental Studies, Psychology

CAMPUS LIFE

% live on campus (% freshmen)	61(100)

Multicultural student clubs and organizations American Indian Association, Asian Cultural Association, Black Student Union, Club Latino, First-Generation/Working-Class Students, Hui Aloha, International Students and Friends Club, South Asian Students Association, Vietnamese Club

Athletics NCAA Division III, Northwest Conference

ADMISSIONS

# of applicants	3,220
% accepted	53
# of first-year students enrolled	419
SAT Critical Reading (middle 50%)	630-730
SAT Math (middle 50%)	620-710
SAT Writing (middle 50%)	630-710
ACT (middle 50%)	28-32
average HS GPA	3.85

Deadlines

early decision	11/15
regular decision	1/15
application fee (online)	$50 ($50)
fee waiver for applicants with financial need	yes

COST & AID

tuition	$40,180
room & board	$10,160
total need-based institutional scholarships/grants	$20,500,000
% of students apply for need-based aid	70
% of students receive aid	75
% receiving need-based scholarship or grant aid	47.5
% receiving aid whose need was fully met	80
average aid package	$29,700
average student loan debt upon graduation	$14,285

West Virginia Wesleyan College

With over 70 campus activities and access to state parks, ski resorts and other outdoor- adventure destinations, West Virginia Wesleyan College offers students a range of opportunities both on campus and off. Wesleyan also offers a number of programs designed to help students support and tailor their academic experience, including a variety of freshmen seminars. Wesleyan is affiliated with the United Methodist Church, and it offers both weekly chapel services — during which no classes are offered — and access to the Dean of the Chapel, who functions as a pastoral caregiver.

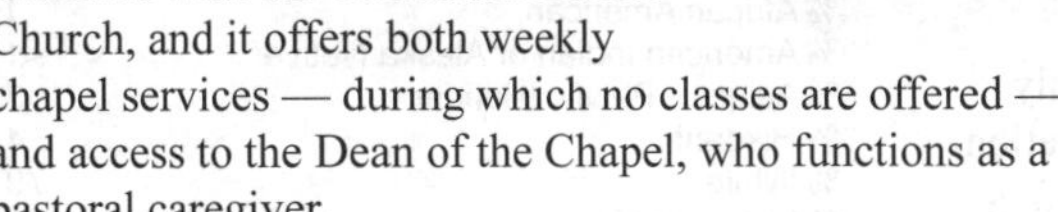

> *"Wesleyan strives to assist in the transition from high school to college, specifically through its housing department. As a Resident Assistant, I know the importance of "community building" and its contribution to a student's overall college experience. Wesleyan, as an institution, upholds this idea of community and it's undoubtedly evident when interacting with faculty, staff, and other students alike."*
>
> *– Keith B., '10*
> *Upshur County, WV*

ACCESS Leadership and Service

Students at Wesleyan are encouraged to participate in community service programming, whether through the Bonner Scholars program, newly formed service learning courses, work-study placements, or housing initiatives. Examples of service opportunities of which Wesleyan students take advantage include Project ISAAC (Increasing Student Achievement Advancing Communities), Upshur County Head Start, Big Brothers/ Big Sisters, Valley Green Learning Center, and many more. Additionally, a first-year seminar course titled Community Engagement: Recipes for Success introduces students to community service opportunities and leadership development.

SUCCESS Academic Advising

During the first semester of the freshman year, students are advised by their Freshman Seminar instructor. Following the first year of study, students are assigned to a faculty advisor in their particular field of study, or in a related field. If, after the first year, students are still undecided about their major, they are assigned to a faculty advisor who helps them to explore their personal and academic interests and work toward setting their educational goals. In addition to faculty advisors, members of the Academic & Career Office staff are available to assist students and provide guidance to those who are undeclared, in-between majors, or have unique advising needs.

SUCCESS The Office of Intercultural Relations

The Office of Intercultural Relations, an integral part of the Student Affairs division at Wesleyan, serves as a primary resource for multicultural education, information, and training. While serving the needs of underrepresented students continues to be at the core of its mission, the Office of Intercultural Relations is committed to initiatives designed to enhance Wesleyan student, faculty, and staff consciousness about issues of social justice and equality. Each year, the Office of Intercultural Relations sponsors an International Student Organization Banquet where students provide cuisine and entertainment from their native countries, and also provides numerous programs during Black History Month aimed at educating the campus on diversity issues. A daily trivia contest allows students the opportunity to conduct research on various cultural issues and win a variety of campus prizes.

SUCCESS Student Academic Support Services

Tutoring is available in all subjects through Student Academic Support Services, an office dedicated to supporting students with all aspects of their academic challenges. In addition to tutoring, the office will work with students to develop their study skills, time-management abilities, goal setting skills, and other productive habits. Students with specific disabilities are also supported through this office.

West Virginia Wesleyan College
59 College Avenue
Buckhannon, WV 26201-2998
Ph: (304) 473-8510
admission@wvwc.edu
www.wvwc.edu

FAST FACTS

STUDENT PROFILE

# of degree-seeking undergraduates	1,321
% male/female	46/54
% African American	3
% American Indian or Alaska Native	<1
% Asian or Pacific Islander	<1
% Hispanic	1
% Pell grant recipients	31

First-generation and minority alumni Sir John Swan, former premier of Bermuda, owner, John W. Swan Limited in Bermuda; Dr. Alfred Moye, independent consultant, former director of university relationships for Hewlett-Packard Company, worked in the Carter administration; William Stanley Norman, former president and CEO, Travel Industry Association of America

ACADEMICS

full-time faculty	75
full-time minority faculty	n/a
student-faculty ratio	13:1
average class size	18
% first-year retention rate	74
% graduation rate (6 years)	59

Popular majors Athletic Training, Biology, Business, Education, Nursing

CAMPUS LIFE

% live on campus (% freshmen)	76 (90)

Multicultural student clubs and organizations Black Business Student Association, Black Student Union, International Student Organization

Athetics NCAA Division II, West Virginia Intercollegiate Athletic Conference

ADMISSIONS

# of applicants	1,413
% accepted	78
# of first-year students enrolled	480
SAT Critical Reading (middle 50%)	425-530
SAT Math (middle 50%)	420-550
SAT Writing (middle 50%)	410-525
ACT (middle 50%)	20-25
average HS GPA	3.4

Deadlines

early decision	3/1
regular decision	rolling
application fee (online)	$35 ($0)
fee waiver for applicants with financial need	yes

COST & AID

tuition	$23,130
room & board	$7,140
total need-based institutional scholarships/grants	$1,280,000
% of students apply for need-based aid	84
% of students receive aid	75
% receiving need-based scholarship or grant aid	100
% receiving aid whose need was fully met	38
average aid package	$25,479
average student loan debt upon graduation	$19,750

Lawrence University

Lawrence University, one of the nation's first coeducational institutions, is the nation's only liberal arts college and conservatory of music both devoted exclusively to undergraduate education. Ranking among the nation's best, small private colleges, Lawrence is featured in the book *Colleges That Change Lives: 40 Schools That Will Change the Way You Think About College*. With a picturesque, residential campus nestled on the banks of the Fox River in Appleton, Wisconsin (metro pop. 225,000), Lawrence draws its 1,489 students from 47 states and more than 50 countries. One of the most internationally diverse campuses in the country, Lawrence attracts students from a wide variety of geographic, ethnic, socioeconomic and experiential backgrounds.

ACCESS College Readiness 21

Lawrence co-sponsors a northeast Wisconsin pre-college program called College Readiness 21. The initiative provides college visits, tutoring, personal and life-skills development, mentoring and college admissions coaching to low-income, minority and first-generation students. College Readiness 21 served 40 freshmen and sophomores from six northeast Wisconsin communities in its first year alone — all were the first in their families to aspire to go to college.

"Lawrence professors facilitate an environment of community. Their attitude is, 'We're here to learn from each other.'"

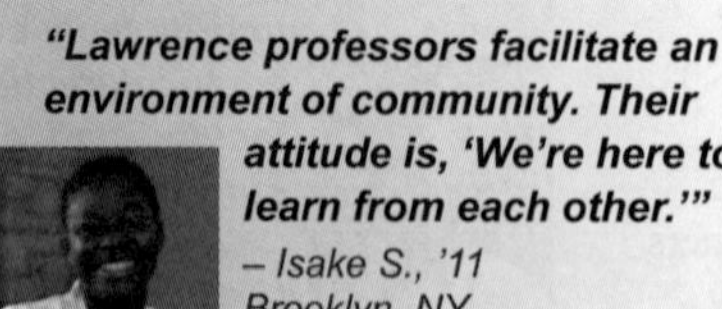

– Isake S., '11
Brooklyn, NY
Psychology

ACCESS The Partners Reaching Youth in Science and Math (PRYSM)

Through a one-to-one tutoring program between female Lawrence undergraduates who study math and science and seventh and eighth grade girls at Roosevelt Middle School in Appleton, Lawrence University's PRYSM program helps encourage girls to increase their skills and confidence in these fields. Lawrence has also hosted a GEMS (Girls Exploring Math and Science) Day on campus, where these students attended hands-on math and science workshops.

OPPORTUNITY Posse Foundation

Lawrence University participates in the Posse Foundation, a program that brings talented inner-city youth to campus to pursue their academics and to help promote cross-cultural communication. Posse students are nominated by their high school to the program and share a collaborative support system with a special mentor to adjust to campus and college life. Lawrence's Posse Scholars hail from New York City.

OPPORTUNITY Scholarships

Lawrence University strives to make it financially viable for all admitted students to enroll, including offering a variety of scholarships recognizing student achievement. For more information about scholarships and other financial aid, visit the Lawrence University admissions website.

SUCCESS Multicultural Affairs Office and Diversity Center

The staff of the Multicultural Affairs Office works to provide diversity resources through its various academic, social and cultural areas. By collaborating with university departments, student organizations and student services, the office aids various campus constituencies in developing large-scale events for the community inside and outside Lawrence University, such as the yearly Identity Forum, Women's Heritage Forum and many cultural celebrations. Nearby, the Diversity Center houses many multicultural groups, ranging from the Downer Feminist Council to the Latin American Students Organization.

Lawrence University
Office of Admissions
711 E. Boldt Way, SPC 29
Appleton, WI 54911
Ph: (920) 832-6500
excel@lawrence.edu
www.lawrence.edu

FAST FACTS

STUDENT PROFILE

# of degree-seeking undergraduates	1,489
% male/female	46/54
% African American	4
% American Indian or Alaska Native	<1
% Asian or Pacific Islander	3
% Hispanic	4
% White	79
% International	10
% Pell grant recipients	17.8

First-generation and minority alumni Cory L. Nettles, managing director at Generation Growth Capital Inc. and former secretary of the Wisconsin Department of Commerce; Dr. Crystal Cash, Family Practice Department Chair at Provident Hospital; Elijah Brewer III, Associate Professor of Finance at DePaul University; Michael Martino, vice president of Morgan Stanley

ACADEMICS

full-time faculty	169
full-time minority faculty	27
student-faculty ratio	9:1
average class size	15
% first-year retention rate	90
% graduation rate (6 years)	76

Popular majors Music Performance, Biology, Chemistry, Physics, Psychology, Geology

CAMPUS LIFE

% live on campus (% freshmen)	97 (99)

Multicultural Student Clubs and Organizations Amnesty International, Black Organization of Students, Latin American Students Organization, ¡Viva! (Spanish/Hispanic Student group), LUNA (Lawrence University Native Americans), Muslim Student Association, Hillel

Athletics NCAA Division III, Midwest Conference

ADMISSIONS

# of applicants	2,625
% accepted	66
# of first-year students enrolled	452
SAT Critical Reading (middle 50%)	580-710
SAT Math (middle 50%)	590-700
SAT Writing (middle 50%)	580-680
ACT (middle 50%)	27-31
average HS GPA	3.66
Deadlines	
early decision	11/15
early action	12/1
regular decision	1/15
application fee (online)	$40 ($40)
fee waiver for applicants with financial need	yes

COST & AID

tuition	$38,205
room & board	$7,890
total need-based institutional scholarships/grants	$19,005,671
% of students apply for need-based aid	71
% of students receive aid	93
% receiving need-based scholarship or grant aid	93
% receiving aid whose need was fully met	62
average aid package	$26,000
average student loan debt upon graduation	$23,433

Marquette University

Marquette University
P.O. Box 1881
Milwaukee, WI 53201-1881
Ph: (414) 288-7302
admissions@marquette.edu
www.marquette.edu/explore

Marquette University is a mid-sized, private, four-year, comprehensive university affiliated with the Society of Jesus (Jesuits) of the Catholic Church. Marquette is dedicated to fostering excellence, faith, leadership and service in all of its students and offers strong support to first-generation and underserved students. The university runs four unique programs under The Educational Opportunity Program (EOP) in addition to an institutionally funded college transition program. Marquette's Multicultural Center works hard to promote diversity awareness and cultural inclusiveness within the diverse student body and the Office of Student Services supports every individual student's educational goals. With an urban campus located in downtown Milwaukee, Marquette students take advantage of the many educational, cultural and social outlets the city has to offer.

FAST FACTS

STUDENT PROFILE

# of degree-seeking undergraduates	8,113
% male/female	48/52
% African American	6
% American Indian or Alaska Native	<1
% Asian or Pacific Islander	4
% Hispanic	6
% White	82
% International	1
% Pell grant recipients	21.7

ACADEMICS

full-time faculty	629
full-time minority faculty	88
student-faculty ratio	15:1
average class size	28
% first-year retention rate	91
% graduation rate (6 years)	83

Popular majors Nursing, Marketing, Engineering, Psychology, Business Administration

CAMPUS LIFE

% live on campus	95

Multicultural student clubs and organizations
African Students Association, Arab Student Association, Bayanihan Student Association, Black Student Council, Chinese Student Association, Cuban American Student Association, Global Village, Indian Student Association, Indonesian Student Association, Latin American Student Organization, Malaysian Student Organization, Pacific Islands Student Organization, Society of Caribbean Ambassadors.

Athletics NCAA Division I, Big East Conference

ADMISSIONS

# of applicants	22,500
% accepted	51
# of first-year students enrolled	1,950
SAT Critical Reading (middle 50%)	520-640
SAT Math (middle 50%)	540-650
SAT Writing (middle 50%)	530-630
ACT (middle 50%)	24-30
average HS GPA	3.5
Deadlines	
regular decision	12/1
application fee (online)	$0 ($0)
fee waiver for applicants with financial need	n/a

COST & AID

tuition	$31,400
room & board	$10,400
total need-based institutional scholarships/grants	$53,333,039
% of students apply for need-based aid	93
% of students receive aid	99
% receiving need-based scholarship or grant aid	99
% receiving aid whose need was fully met	27
average aid package	$22,000
average student loan debt upon graduation	$32,500

ACCESS **Upward Bound Math and Science**

Local high school students who come from low-income families in which neither parent holds a bachelor's degree can benefit from Marquette's Upward Bound Math and Science, a pre-college program that provides a group of students with the right tools to pursue their dreams of earning a college degree. This program is intended for students with a strong interest in math, science, computer technology, or engineering. Students benefit from weekly tutoring, field trips, workshops, and a six-week summer enrichment program.

OPPORTUNITY **Urban Scholars Scholarship Program**

Marquette's Urban Scholars Program provides 10 full-tuition awards to low-income students, including undocumented students, who show great academic promise. The award guarantees that a student's federal, state, and Marquette gift assistance cover tuition costs for a four-year undergraduate program, provided the student maintains a 2.0 GPA. Students are selected for this award based on academic merit, leadership and financial need. The 10 awards are granted to graduates from Milwaukee area high schools and the Cristo Rey High School network.

OPPORTUNITY **Goizueta Foundation Scholarship Award**

The Goizueta Foundation Scholarship Award is for Hispanic/Latino high school seniors who demonstrate financial need. The award covers one-half of the Marquette tuition.

OPPORTUNITY **Boys & Girls Club Scholarship**

Marquette University is proud to announce its new national partnership with the Boys & Girls Clubs of America (BGCA), targeting the Clubs' Youth of the Year (YOY) winners for three full-tuition scholarships to Marquette.

OPPORTUNITY **Opus Scholars Award**

The Opus Scholars Award (a full-tuition scholarship) recognizes a combination of outstanding academic achievement as well as financial need for two incoming engineering freshmen. Priority consideration is given to first-generation students who have participated in organizations that serve low-income youth, such as the Cristo Rey Network and the Boys & Girls Clubs.

"I have persevered through many obstacles in my life. My success can be attributed to the great people at Marquette University. The Educational Opportunity Program and Les Aspin Center for Government at Marquette University allowed me to grasp an education I once thought was impossible."

– Anthony G., '11
Milwaukee, WI
Political Science

St. Norbert College

With a liberal arts foundation that teaches students to think critically, solve problems and develop leadership skills, St. Norbert offers academic excellence, individual attention, and faculty members who make student success their top priority. St. Norbert is a private liberal arts college founded by the Norbertines, a Catholic order committed to community and service. Students have 40-plus programs to choose from, and a multitude of internship opportunities. Students can study abroad at 75 program sites on six continents and undergraduates regularly experience graduate-level collaborative research with faculty. Academic advisors guide students throughout their college careers, and an active alumni community provides valuable career networking.

ACCESS **Admission Possible**

St. Norbert partners with Admission Possible to help promising, low-income high school students prepare for and earn admission to college. Students receive ACT and SAT test preparation, guidance in preparing college applications and assistance in obtaining financial aid. St. Norbert sponsors campus visits and provides student hosts for Admission Possible students, who attend class, sleep in the res halls, eat on campus and really feel what it's like to be a college student.

"I didn't realize what an impact being a First Year Experience and Multicultural Student Services Mentor would have on my life. I was able to influence the first year students and they changed my perception of what a community is."

– Avery G., '11
Kewaunee, WI
International Studies, Spanish

ACCESS **Upward Bound**

Upward Bound is a pre-college program funded by the Department of Education to serve and assist low-income, first generation college and disabled students. The program provides the support and resources to help students develop the skills and motivation necessary to pursue and succeed in college, offering cultural and social activities, career and educational opportunities, and other hands-on experiences.

OPPORTUNITY **Diversity Leadership Award**

St. Norbert offers a Diversity Leadership Award that recognizes students who are committed to diversity and actively involved in bringing awareness to their community. This award is distributed on an annual basis in amounts ranging from $1,000 to $6,000. Recipients of the award are required to assist in at least two diversity-focused campus activities, thereby ensuring continued multicultural community involvement.

OPPORTUNITY **Red Carpet Program**

To increase minority enrollment, St. Norbert College instituted the Red Carpet Program. High school juniors and seniors visit the St. Norbert campus, meet with current students and faculty, and obtain information about financial aid and admission requirements.

SUCCESS **Students Taking Academic Responsibility Program (STAR)**

STAR is an early arrival program for first-year multicultural and first generation college students that helps them become familiar with the campus, establish supportive relationships with faculty and staff, develop valuable skills for academic success in college, foster leadership skills, and learn about financial aid and study tips.

SUCCESS **Academic Enhancement Program**

The Academic Enhancement Program is a one-semester program offering freshmen the opportunity to learn and practice academic habits associated with success in college. Support services include study skills, time management skills, note-taking skills and good academic habits.

St. Norbert College
Office of Admission
100 Grant Street
De Pere, WI 54115
Ph: (800) 236-4878 / (920) 403-3005
admit@snc.edu
www.snc.edu

FAST FACTS

STUDENT PROFILE

# of degree-seeking undergraduates	2,172
% male/female	41/59
% African American	<1
% American Indian or Alaska Native	<1
% Asian or Pacific Islander	1
% Hispanic	2
% White	88
% Multicultural	2
% International	6
% Pell grant recipients	25

First-generation and minority alums Tadashi Yamamoto, president, Japan Center for International Exchange; Nicole Bowman-Farrell, president, Bowman Performance Consulting

ACADEMICS

full-time faculty	135
full-time minority faculty	10
student-faculty ratio	15:1
average class size	22
% first-year retention rate	84
% graduation rate (6 yr)	76

Popular majors Business Administration, Elementary Education, Communication and Media Studies

CAMPUS LIFE

% live on campus (% freshmen)	77 (96)

Multicultural student clubs and organizations Discoveries International, Beyond Borders, Japan Club, Viva Espanol, La Alianza

Athletics NCAA Division III, Midwest Conference

ADMISSIONS

# of applicants	2,160
% accepted	81
# of first-year students enrolled	604
SAT Critical Reading (middle 50%)	n/a
SAT Math (middle 50%)	n/a
SAT Writing (middle 50%)	n/a
ACT (middle 50%)	22-27
average HS GPA	3.5

Deadlines

regular decision	rolling
application fee (online)	$25 ($10)
fee waiver for applicants with financial need	yes

COST & AID

tuition	$27,583
room & board	$7,349
total need-based institutional scholarships/grants	$27,133,330
% of students apply for need-based aid	80
% of students receive aid	100
% receiving need-based scholarship or grant aid	97
% receiving aid whose need was fully met	40
average aid package	$22,974
average student loan debt upon graduation	$20,559

University of Wisconsin – Parkside

The University of Wisconsin-Parkside is one of 13 four year campuses in the University of Wisconsin System. Founded in 1968, UW-Parkside brought together the University of Wisconsin campuses at Racine and Kenosha to form a unified institution. With just 5,300 students, UW-Parkside can offer students a small class environment that allows them to build strong relationships with their professors as well as with their classmates. The campus is located in Kenosha, Wisconsin on 700 acres of woodlands and prairie. The campus is 30 minutes south of Milwaukee and a hour north of Chicago. UW-Parkside offers the most diverse campus in the UW-System and is committed to cultural enrichment and the celebration throughout the year of cultural achievements and contributions.

ACCESS **Pre-College Program**

The transition from high school to college can be challenging for many students, the University of Wisconsin-Parkside's Pre-College Program provides resources and activities for students. The program seeks to enhance 6th-12th grade students in their preparation prior to entering the university setting. This includes preparation for the ACT, summer enrichment programs, yearly student support programs, and aided through the application process.

"My experience with getting involved at University of Wisconsin-Parkside has been the greatest thing to happen to me. I am able to learn more about organization [within organizations] and apply the principles to what I learn in the classroom; particularly Business."

– Cedric R., '12
Chicago, IL
Business Management-Marketing Concentration

ACCESS **Upward Bound Program**

During the school year, the Upward Bound Program offers weekly tutoring sessions where high-achieving UW-Parkside student tutors help with homework and teach academic skills that will help students in high school and college. The program also offers college visits, monthly events, special leadership workshops, test preparation and practice, and help with college, scholarship and financial aid applications. Additionally, UB offers a 6 week summer residential program for students to get a jump on college preparation and explore college and career options.

OPPORTUNITY **Bilingual Open House**

Bilingual Open House is an introduction to UW-Parkside in both English and Spanish. On-site admission is available with official high school transcripts and copies of ACT or SAT scores, with financial aid sessions as well as college preparation.

SUCCESS **Fresh Start Program**

The purpose of Fresh Start is to support the under-prepared first year student. Under-prepared students are defined as students whose ACT Scores place them into developmental skills courses by providing small, supportive learning communities.

SUCCESS **First Year Experience/Workshops**

FYE workshops are an opportunity for students to gain a better understanding of the skills necessary for college success. The workshops address college transitional challenges and provide tools to better navigate college. The workshops are offered each semester and are available to all students.

SUCCESS **Multicultural Professional Day**

Multicultural Professional Day is a mini-conference designed to prepare multicultural students for their career field. Its goal is to ensure that multicultural students are given the guidance, preparation, and opportunities to fully meet their career potential. Topics include how to write your resume and cover letter, interviewing do's and don'ts, transitional life topics, diversity in the workforce, and several others.

University of Wisconsin - Parkside
900 Wood Road
Kenosha, WI 53141
Ph: (262) 595-2355
admissions@uwp.edu
www.uwp.edu

FAST FACTS

STUDENT PROFILE

# of degree-seeking undergraduates	5,015
% male/female	46/54
% African American	10
% American Indian or Alaska Native	<1
% Asian or Pacific Islander	3
% Hispanic	9
% White	72
% International	1%
Pell grant recipients	58

First-generation and minority alumni Rita Thomas, 2005, Senior Associate producer, Harpo Radio Team; Dannie Moore, 2004, Director of African American Student Affairs, Northern Kentucky University; Jerome Garrett, 2005, Director of Operations, Mayo Clinic Health Systems; Andres Cerritos, 2003, Lawyer, Andres Cerritos Law Office; Ivan Ireland, 89, Surgeon, Hale Ireland Laser and Implant Center

ACADEMICS

full-time faculty	179
full-time minority faculty	49
student-faculty ratio	19:1
average class size	10-19
% first-year retention rate	65
% graduation rate (6 years)	27

Popular majors Applied Health, Business, Criminal Justice, Nursing, Sports Management

CAMPUS LIFE

% live on campus (% freshmen)	20 (50)

Multicultural student clubs and organizations Black Student Union, Latinos Unidos, Parkside Asian Organization, Sacred Circle

Athletics NCAA Division II, Great Lakes Valley Conference

ADMISSIONS

# of applicants	2,267
% accepted	65
# of first-year students enrolled	55
SAT Critical Reading (middle 50%)	n/a
SAT Math (middle 50%)	n/a
SAT Writing (middle 50%)	n/a
ACT (middle 50%)	18-23
average HS GPA	n/a

Deadlines

regular decision	rolling
application fee (online)	$44 ($44)
fee waiver for applicants with financial need	yes

COST & AID

tuition	in-state $5,659; out-of-state $13,232
room & board	$6,828
total need-based institutional scholarships/grants	$12,122,425
% of students apply for need-based aid	58
% receiving need-based scholarship or grant aid	43
% receiving aid whose need was fully met	n/a
average aid package	n/a
average student loan debt upon graduation	n/a

University of Wisconsin – Platteville

The University of Wisconsin-Platteville is a four-year comprehensive public institution, located 20 miles east of the Mississippi River. The University strives to demonstrate leadership, creativity and vision in supporting the continued development of creating a globally competitive and culturally sensitive student body and campus community. A few examples of these efforts are conferences such as The Midwest Culturally Inclusive Conference, unique cultural curriculum such as the Confucius Institute (part of an international network of over 525 Confucius Institutes), and programming at the Office of Multicultural Student Affairs whose primary purpose is assisting students of color towards degree completion. Faculty and staff are focused on student success and dedicate time not only for meetings with students during office hours but also for participating in special help sessions. There are a multitude of tutoring and mentoring opportunities available to UW Platteville students. Classes are taught by professors, not teaching assistants. UW Platteville curriculum often takes a hands on approach and course work includes practical demonstrations, group work, and field experience. There are numerous opportunities for students to participate in scholarly research projects with their professors. Additionally, students have the opportunity to practice the skills they learn in the classroom and develop leadership capacity through involvement in athletics, arts, study abroad and more than 220 student clubs and organizations.

ACCESS Pre-College Programs

The pre-college programs serve 6th-12th grade low-income underrepresented students through weekly and bi-weekly summer camps that are designed to provide exposure to higher education and create visible paths towards becoming a future UW Platteville Pioneer.

ACCESS Paths to Platteville

Paths to Platteville enables underrepresented high school students to visit campus and experience UW-Platteville. Students learn more about the admissions and financial aid process, take a campus tour and talk with current students about life at UW-Platteville.

"The Multicultural Educational Resource Center at UWP provides support systems for interested students on multiple levels. Study tables are set up in the center with tutors from a variety of majors available to assist. The staff motivates students to excel academically and socially."

– Brittany D., '11
Milwaukee, WI
Elementary Education

OPPORTUNITY Alliant Energy 5x5x5 Diversity Scholarship

The Alliant Energy 5x5x5 Diversity Scholarship is a $1,000 awarded to five students annually. To qualify, students must be entering their freshman year, have a high school GPA of a 3.0 or better, belong to a historically-underrepresented group and major in accounting, agricultural education, agri-business, business administration, communication technologies, comprehensive business, computer science, or engineering.

SUCCESS Office of Multicultural Student Affairs

The purpose of the Office of Multicultural Student Affairs is to assist students of color in the navigation of their undergraduate college career and engage them in high impact practices to enhance their collegiate experience and increase their marketability after degree completion. The Office of Multicultural Student Affairs houses Pre-College Programming focused on access for under-represented student populations. The DRIVEN Scholars Program which utilizes a comprehensive high touch advising model to monitor degree completion progress, provide leadership opportunities and assist students with advocacy in various social, cultural and academic advising needs. The Office of Multicultural Student Affairs also provides programming on campus to assist in the development of an inclusive campus environment and advising and support to student organizations. Student organizations frequently supported are: Asia Club, Black Student Union, Hmong Club, Inter Tribal Council and Students of Latinos.

University of Wisconsin – Platteville
1 University Plaza
Platteville, Wisconsin 53818
Ph: (877) UWPLATT (897-6288)
admit@uwplatt.edu
www.uwplatt.edu

FAST FACTS

STUDENT PROFILE

# of degree-seeking undergraduates	7,011
% male/female	60/40
% African American	2
% American Indian or Alaska Native	1
% Asian or Pacific Islander	1
% Hispanic	1
% White	92
% Pell grant recipients	25

First-generation and minority alumni Robert Jeter III, Head Men's Basketball Coach for UW-Milwaukee, 2005 Outstanding Alumni Recipient and 2006 Athletic Hall of Fame Recipient; Dr. Eduardo Manual, Senior Director, Development Chicago Region and Diversity, University of Wisconsin-Madison Foundation, CASE (council for Advancement and Support of Education) District V board of directors; Patricia Gomez, 2005 (MSED), Producer and Host for Milwaukee Public Television production, ¡Adelante!; Artanya M. Wesley, 2006 and 2008, Interim Dean of Students, University of Wisconsin-Platteville, 2009 Outstanding Woman of Color Award

ACADEMICS

full-time faculty	412
full-time minority faculty	50
student-faculty ratio	24:1
average class size	27
% first-year retention rate	76
% graduation rate (6 years)	57

Popular majors Agriculture, Biology, Business, Criminal Justice, Education, Engineering, Industrial Technology

CAMPUS LIFE

% live on campus (% freshmen)	40 (92)

Multicultural student clubs and organizations Black Student Union (BSU), Hmong Club, InterTribal Council, Student Organization of Latinos (SOL), Multicultural Educational Resource Center (MERC)

Athletics NCAA Division III, Wisconsin Intercollegiate Athletic Conference (WIAC)

ADMISSIONS

# of applicants	3,660
% accepted	80
# of first-year students enrolled	1,515
SAT Critical Reading (middle 50%)	450-550
SAT Math (middle 50%)	450-550
SAT Writing (middle 50%)	n/a
ACT (middle 50%)	20-25
average HS GPA	2.75

Deadlines

regular decision	rolling
application fee (online)	$44 ($44)
fee waiver for applicants with financial need	yes

COST & AID

tuition	in-state $6,774; MN resident $7,046; Tri-State Initiative $10,774; out-of-state $14,347
room & board	$5,806
total need-based institutional scholarships/grants	n/a
% of students apply for need-based aid	n/a
% of students receive aid	75
% receiving need-based scholarship or grant aid	36
% receiving aid whose need was fully met	n/a
average aid package	$9,100
average student loan debt upon graduation	$17,250

University of Wisconsin – Whitewater

The University of Wisconsin-Whitewater desires a reputation as an institution that truly values and nurtures diverse intellectual, cultural, creative, and service opportunities. To accomplish that, it must promote its image as a diverse, respected and empowering institution of higher learning. The university attracts and supports students from all parts of the region, nation and world, sustaining optimum enrollment, retention and graduation rates for all student populations. Wisconsin-Whitewater will create and maintain programs for intercultural or international study, research and service in every department along with developing, attracting, and retaining a diverse faculty and staff.

OPPORTUNITY King/Chavez Scholars

The King/Chavez Scholars program is designed to complement the array of multicultural/disadvantaged programs at UW-Whitewater that serve the interests and needs of first generation/low income TRIO students. The King Chavez Scholars program is designed to attract and retain scholars for the McNair Scholars Program, University Honors Program and Undergraduate Research. Students receive a scholarship during their freshman year.

SUCCESS Academic Network

Academic Network targets multicultural/disadvantaged students who are not designated users of Minority Business/Teacher Preparation Program, EOP, Latino Student Programs, the McNair Program, Native American Support Services, or Southeast Asian Support Services. Academic Network provides advising and referrals to academic services.

SUCCESS McNair Scholars Program

McNair Scholars Program prepares first-generation and multicultural students for doctoral study and eventually careers as college professors. The program matches each student with a faculty mentor in their major; provides resources for undergraduate research projects; enhances students' quantitative computer, test taking, research methods, and critical thinking skills; provides students with opportunities to present research findings at regional and national conferences; provides stipends for on-campus and external summer research internships.

"Attending the University of Wisconsin-Whitewater has been an incredible experience. I am a member of a few student organizations and I feel like I'm an important part of the campus community. My classes have been challenging, but the academic support resources have helped me perform at a high level."

– Shanika T., '12
Milwaukee, WI
Social Work

SUCCESS Minority Business/Teacher Preparation Program (MB/TPP)

Minority Business/Teacher Preparation Program provides support for targeted students majoring in business and education. The program is located in the College of Business & Economics and College of Education.

SUCCESS Minority Student Support Programs

Latino Student Programs, Native American Support Services (NASS), and Southeast Asian Student Services (SASS) foster the retention and graduation of Latino, Native American and Southeast Asian students through: academic advising, multicultural/ globalized programming, scholarships and study abroad experiences.

University of Wisconsin- Whitewater
Office of Admissions
800 West Main Street
Whitewater, WI 52190-1790
Ph: (262) 472-1440
uwwadmit@uww.edu
www.uww.edu

FAST FACTS

STUDENT PROFILE

# of degree-seeking undergraduates	10,114
% male/female	50/50
% African American	2
% American Indian or Alaska Native	<1
% Asian or Pacific Islander	2
% Hispanic	2
% White	89
% International	1
% Pell grant recipients	20

First-generation and minority alumni David Hill, Chief State Affairs Officer-Government Relations Legal Department, Assurant Health

ACADEMICS

full-time faculty	430
full-time minority faculty	76
student-faculty ratio	22:1
average class size	22
% first-year retention rate	76
% graduation rate (6 years)	56

Popular majors Accounting\Finance, Biology\Chemistry, Communications (Broadcast and Print Journalism), Education, Management Computer Systems

CAMPUS LIFE

% live on campus (% freshmen)	40 (90)

Multicultural student clubs and organizations Black Student Union, Latinos Unidos, Native Aboriginal Cultural Awareness Association, Southeast Asian Organization, National Association of Black Accountants, National Association of Black Journalists

Athletics NCAA Division III, Wisconsin Intercollegiate Athletic Conference (WIAC)

ADMISSIONS

# of applicants	5,501
% accepted	82
# of first-year students enrolled	2,420
SAT Critical Reading (middle 50%)	430-540
SAT Math (middle 50%)	460-600
SAT Writing (middle 50%)	430-540
ACT (middle 50%)	20-25
average HS GPA	3.20

Deadlines

regular decision	rolling to 8/1
application fee (online)	$44 ($44)
fee waiver for applicants with financial need	yes

COST & AID

tuition	in-state: $6,836; out-of-state: $14,409
room & board	$5,402
total need-based institutional scholarships/grants	$10,550,000
% of students apply for need-based aid	69
% of students receive aid	97
% receiving need-based scholarship or grant aid	45
% receiving aid whose need was fully met	64
average aid package	$7,280
average student loan debt upon graduation	$17,869

University of Wyoming

Wyoming's only four-year educational institution, the University of Wyoming is a co-educational, public university. Founded in 1887, the University of Wyoming combines big-university benefits and small-school advantages, offering students the opportunity to stand at the forefront in the exploration of emerging technologies and concepts, while at the same time, providing students with hands-on involvement and one-on-one attention.

ACCESS **I'm Going to College!**

This is a program designed to familiarize ethnic minority and first-generation elementary and middle-school students with a college campus. Providing students and their parents with a taste of college life, "I'm Going to College!" seeks to introduce a philosophy of expected attendance into the early school careers of underrepresented students. Academic stations on campus illustrate the avenues of study and potential career areas available to those individuals who obtain a college degree. Additionally, parents participate in sessions about motivating children and financing higher education.

ACCESS **Experimental Program to Stimulate Competitive Research**

This program provides a seven-week summer research apprentice program serving over 20 underrepresented high school students (grades 10 to 12) who are interested in pursuing a career in the sciences. Students are paired with research teams led by a Wyoming faculty member, and they present their research at a research symposium at the end of the summer program. Throughout the program, college preparation activities are held while the students live on the university campus. The university's program prides itself on its high rate of college attendees and graduation rates.

ACCESS **Shadows of Success**

This program provides an individualized opportunity for ethnic minority students to obtain a real-life college experience. Through the Shadows of Success program, high school students are paired up with current minority students on campus and have the opportunity to "shadow" that student through a day of college life. Students who participate can have their admission application fees waived.

OPPORTUNITY **American Indian Scholarships**

Given that Wyoming is home to two tribal governments, the Northern Arapaho Nation and the Eastern Shoshone Tribe, the university provides several scholarships for American Indian students. These include the Northern Arapaho Endowment, the Chief Washakie Scholarship, McCarthy Scholarship, Winner Scholarship, and Thorpe Scholarship. Additionally, the Office of Multicultural Affairs has received two bequests for American Indian students that will be offered in the future. These scholarships ensure the school's commitment to community involvement and multiculturalism.

SUCCESS **Student Success Services (SSS)**

The Student Success Services program provides a host of student-support services and information designed to increase the persistence, good academic standing, and graduation rates of first-generation, low-income students and students with disabilities. From study skill development to personal budgeting and money management assistance, these services are delivered individually through one-on-one structured advising or in small-group settings. Each participant meets regularly with her/his adviser to identify academic, financial, personal, social, career and major needs and to devise an individualized educational action plan to meet those needs.

University of Wyoming
1000 E. University Avenue
Laramie, WY 82070
Ph: (307) 766-5160
why-wyo@uwyo.edu
www.uwyo.edu

FAST FACTS

STUDENT PROFILE

# of degree-seeking undergraduates	8,352
% male/female	50/50
% African American	1
% American Indian or Alaska Native	<1
% Asian or Pacific Islander	1
% Hispanic	5
% White	80
% Pell grant recipients	24

First-generation and minority alumni Sol Trujillo '73, businessman; Gene Huey '71, NFL coach

ACADEMICS

full-time faculty	740
full-time minority faculty	70
student-faculty ratio	14:1
average class size	27
% first-year retention rate	73
% graduation rate (6 years)	55

Popular majors Elementary Education and Teaching, Nursing

CAMPUS LIFE

% live on campus (% freshmen)	28 (88)

Multicultural student clubs and organizations Asian American Pacific Islander Student Organization, MILAAP (Indian Students Organization), Students for Campus and Community Chicana Awareness, Turkish Student Organization, Wyoming African Students Association, American Indian Studies Alliance, Association of Black Student Leaders, Chinese Students & Scholars Association, Korean Student Association, Muslim Student Association

Athletics NCAA Division I (football I-A), Mountain West Conference

ADMISSIONS

# of applicants	3,713
% accepted	95
# of first-year students enrolled	1,458
SAT Critical Reading (middle 50%)	490-600
SAT Math (middle 50%)	490-610
SAT Writing (middle 50%)	n/a
ACT (middle 50%)	21-27
average HS GPA	3.43

Deadlines

regular decision	rolling
application fee (online)	$40($40)
fee waiver for applicants with financial need	yes

COST & AID

tuition	in-state: $3,120; out-of-state: $11,850
room & board	$8,759
total need-based institutional scholarships/grants	$613,131
% of students apply for need-based aid	63
% of students receive aid	44
% receiving need-based scholarship or grant aid	27
% receiving aid whose need was fully met	16
average aid package	$8,552
average student loan debt upon graduation	$12,500

Notes

Notes

Notes

Notes